UNDERSTANDING CORPORATE TAXATION
Second Edition

Leandra Lederman
William W. Oliver Professor of Tax Law
Indiana University School of Law—Bloomington

 LexisNexis

Library of Congress Cataloging-in-Publication Data	
Lederman, Leandra.	
Understanding corporate taxation / Leandra Lederman.--2nd ed.	
p. cm.	
Includes bibliographical references.	
ISBN 0-8205-6340-4 (softbound)	
1. Corporations--Taxation--Law and legislation--United States. 2. Income tax--Law and legislation--United States. I. Title.	
KF6464.L426 2006	
343.7305'267--dc22	2006007161

This publication is designed to provide accurate and authoritative information in regard to the subject matter covered. It is sold with the understanding that the publisher is not engaged in rendering legal, accounting, or other professional services. If legal advice or other expert assistance is required, the services of a competent professional should be sought.

ISBN#: 0-8205-6340-4

Editorial Offices
744 Broad Street, Newark, NJ 07102 (973) 820-2000
201 Mission St., San Francisco, CA 94105-1831 (415) 908-3200
701 East Water Street, Charlottesville, VA 22902-7587 (434) 972-7600
www.lexis.com

(Pub.03135)

DEDICATION

This book is dedicated to my husband, Mark Newton, with continuing thanks for his support of my efforts on this project.

ACKNOWLEDGMENTS

The author is very grateful to the following people who reviewed chapters in draft form and provided valuable comments: Linda Beale, Craig Boise, Danshera Cords, Charlotte Crane, Diane Fahey, Debby Geier, Brant Hellwig, Tony Infanti, Jeff Kahn, Jeff Kwall, Dan Lathrope, Roberta Mann, Stephen Mazza, Ajay Mehrotra, Gregg Polsky, Bill Popkin, and Robin Westbrook. Continuing thanks also go out to those who provided feedback on chapters for the first edition of this book: Bill Brown, Terry Chorvat, Diane Fahey, Bob Jacobs, Michael Kirsch, Jeff Kwall, Irene Vlissedes Levy, Joni Larson, Eric Lustig, Stephen Mazza, Dan Schneider, Filiz Serbes, and Suellen Wolfe. The author is also very grateful to Mark Newton for making the diagrams included in the book and to Danshera Cords, Ajay Mehrotra, Bill Popkin, and Robin Westbrook for their feedback on various diagrams. She would also like to thank the Indiana University School of Law—Bloomington, Dean Lauren Robel, and Associate Dean John Applegate for their support; the Indiana Law librarians for their assistance; Lara Gose, Sally Lederman, and Mark Newton for assistance with proofreading; and Indiana Law students Adam Christensen, David Ford, Brian Glazer, David Maijala, and Brian Schultz for research assistance.

Preface

Corporate taxation is a rich but complex area of law that students often find quite challenging. Understanding certain fundamental concepts that reappear throughout corporate taxation—such as nonrecognition and carryover basis rules, "double taxation" of corporate income, and characterization of income—can go a long way toward making sense of the details. This book is intended to facilitate such study of corporate taxation through step-by-step explanations, diagrams of transactions, discussion of important cases and rulings, and numerous examples. It is designed to supplement any corporate tax casebook.

The first chapter of the book provides an introduction to corporate taxation, including judicial doctrines such as economic substance and the step-transaction doctrine. It introduces the double taxation that is the hallmark of the classical corporate tax regime, compares that to pass-through taxation of electing small corporations under Subchapter S, and discusses choice of business entity and various ways to avoid double taxation. The next six chapters cover events in the life of a corporation from "cradle to grave," including transfers to a new or existing controlled corporation; capitalization of a corporation with debt or equity; dividend distributions; redemptions of stock; stock dividends; and corporate liquidations. Following this discussion of the tax treatment of events in the life of a corporation under Subchapter C, the next chapter turns to the study of corporations taxable under Subchapter S.

Four chapters discuss corporate reorganizations. The first of these chapters provides an introduction to and overview of reorganizations, including the requirements for a transaction to constitute a reorganization. The next chapter discusses acquisitive reorganizations. The following chapter focuses on divisive reorganizations, and the fourth of these chapters explores reorganizations involving one corporation. After this study of reorganizations, one chapter discusses carryover of tax attributes and a second chapter focuses on anti-abuse and special provisions, such as the corporate AMT.

The last two chapters of the book consider relevant policy issues. Chapter 15 discusses proposals to eliminate double taxation of corporate income, including the system proposed by President George W. Bush in 2003, as well as the current system of partial integration of corporate and shareholder-level taxes. The final chapter, new to this edition of the book, discusses corporate tax shelters.

TABLE OF CONTENTS

Page

Summary Table of Contents

Chapter 1. Introduction to Corporate Taxation 1

Chapter 2. Tax Consequences of Transferring Property to a New or Existing Controlled Corporation 23

Chapter 3. Capital Structure of a Corporation 69

Chapter 4. Non-Liquidating Distributions of Property to Shareholders (Dividends) 85

Chapter 5. Redemptions of Stock 121

Chapter 6. Stock Dividends 163

Chapter 7. Corporate Liquidations and Taxable Acquisitions 185

Chapter 8. The Pass-Through Regime of Subchapter S 211

Chapter 9. Reorganizations: Overview 237

Chapter 10. Acquisitive Reorganizations 273

Page

Chapter 11. Corporate Divisions 307

Chapter 12. Reorganizations Involving Only One
Corporation 335

Chapter 13. Carryover of Tax Attributes 347

Chapter 14. Anti-Abuse Measures and
Special Provisions 371

Chapter 15. Integration of Corporate and Shareholder
Taxes 397

Chapter 16. Corporate Tax Shelters 413

Table of Cases TC-1

Table of Statutes TS-1

Index I-1

Detailed Table of Contents

Chapter 1. Introduction to Corporate Taxation   1

§ 1.01   Introduction to the "Corporate Tax" and Resulting
          Double Taxation   1

§ 1.02   Avoiding Double Taxation   5

    [A] Avoiding the Corporate Form—Partnerships and
    Limited Liability Companies   5

        [1] A Very Brief Overview of the Partnership Tax
        Regime   6

        [2] LLCs and Other Unincorporated Entities . . .   6

            [a] A Brief History of the Taxation of Unincorpo-
            rated Entities   6

            [b] The "Check-the-Box" Rules   7

    [B] Avoiding Subchapter C—Introduction to
    Subchapter S   8

    [C] Avoiding Subchapter C—Corporation
    as Agent   11

    [D] Disguised Dividends   12

        [1] Introduction to Debt Versus Equity   13

        [2] Dividends Disguised as Salary   13

    [E] Introduction to the Integration of Corporate and
    Shareholder-Level Taxes   14

§ 1.03   The Relevance of Sale or Exchange Treatment to
          Corporate Taxation   14

§ 1.04   Introduction to the Judicial Doctrines Backstopping
          the Corporate Tax System   15

    [A] Substance Over Form   15

    [B] Sham Transaction Doctrine   16

    [C] Business Purpose   16

    [D] Economic Substance   17

    [E] The Step-Transaction Doctrine   18

        [1] In General   18

        [2] The Three Tests for a "Step Transaction" . . .   19

            [a] Binding Commitment Test   19

            [b] Mutual Interdependence Test   19

            [c] End Result Test   20

Page

§ 1.05   Conclusion   20

**Chapter 2. Tax Consequences of Transferring
             Property to a New or Existing Controlled
             Corporation** **23**

§ 2.01   Introduction   23
§ 2.02   Tax Consequences to Shareholders   25
         [A] Nonrecognition Treatment and Corresponding Basis
             Rules   25
             [1] General Nonrecognition Treatment Under Sec-
                 tion 351   26
                 [a] "Property"   26
                 [b] "Control"   27
                 [c] The "Transferor Group"   29
                     [i] In General   29
                     [ii] The "Accommodation Transferor" Prob-
                          lem   29
                 [d] The "Immediately After" Requirement . . .   32
                     [i] In General   32
                     [ii] Application of the Step-Transaction Doc-
                          trine   32
                 [e] Business Purpose   37
                 [f] The Effects of the Receipt of "Boot" . . .   37
                     [i] General Recognition Rules   37
                     [ii] Character of Gain Recognized   38
                          [I] Allocation of Boot   39
                          [II] Special Characterization
                               Issues   40
                     [iii] Dividend Treatment   41
             [2] Treatment of Liabilities   41
                 [a] General Non-Recognition Rule of Section
                     357(a)   41
                 [b] Exceptions to Section 357(a)   42
                     [i] Tax-Avoidance Motive:
                         Section 357(b)   42
                     [ii] Liabilities in Excess of Basis: Section
                          357(c)   43

Page

            [I]   Effect of a Shareholder Promissory
                  Note 44

            [II]   Excluded and Contingent
                  Liabilities 47

        [3] Basis Rules 49

           [a] Transferor Basis in the
              Absence of Boot 49

           [b] Transferor Basis in the
              Presence of Boot 49

           [c] Effect of Liabilities on Basis 51

        [4] Holding Period 53

     [B] Taxable Incorporations 53

     [C] Provisions that Override Section 351 54

§ 2.03   Tax Consequences to the Corporation 55

     [A] Nonrecognition on Issuance of Stock 55

     [B] Basis Rules 56

        [1] Corporate Basis if Section 351 Applies 56

           [a] Absence of Boot 56

           [b] Presence of Boot 59

           [c] Effect of Liabilities on
              Corporate Basis 60

        [2] Corporate Basis if Section 351
           Does Not Apply 61

     [C] Holding Period 61

        Chart 2.1: Checklist for Incorporations and
          Other Section 351 Transactions 62

        Chart 2.2: Comparison of Code Sections:
          Successful and Failed
          Section 351 Transactions 63

§ 2.04   Contributions to Capital 63

     [A] Tax Consequences to
        Shareholder Contributors 64

     [B] Tax Consequences to
        Non-Shareholder Contributors 65

     [C] Tax Consequences to the Corporation 65

        [1] In General 65

        [2] Transfers by Non-Shareholders 66

        [3] Corporation's Basis 66

Page

[a] In General   66

[b] Basis in Property Received from Non-
Shareholders   67

Chapter 3. Capital Structure of a Corporation **69**

§ 3.01   Overview of Debt and Equity   69

[A] Introduction to the Tax Consequences of Distributions with Respect to Debt and Equity   69

[B] Introduction to Types of Debt and Equity   71

[1] General Types of Equity   71

[2] General Types of Debt   71

§ 3.02   General Tax Consequences of Debt and Equity   72

[A] Investment   72

[B] Current Distributions   72

[C] Return of Investment   73

[D] Worthlessness   73

§ 3.03   Characterization: Distinguishing Debt from
Equity   75

[A] Section 385   75

[B] Case-Law Factors   76

[C] Possible Treatment of an Investment as in Part Debt
and in Part Equity   81

§ 3.04   Conclusion   82

**Chapter 4. Non-Liquidating Distributions of Property to
Shareholders (Dividends)** **85**

§ 4.01   Introduction   85

§ 4.02   Tax Consequences to the
Distributing Corporation   85

[A] Appreciated Property   86

[B] Treatment of Liabilities   88

§ 4.03   The Tax Treatment of Shareholders: 89

[A] General Rules under Section 301   89

Chart 4.1: Tax Consequences of Non-Liquidating
Distributions of Property   90

[B] Amount of the Distribution   90

Page

[C] Calculating the Dividend Amount 90

[1] Introduction to Earnings and Profits 91

[a] Current Versus Accumulated Earnings and Profits 91

[b] Calculating Earnings and Profits 92

[i] General Rules 92

[ii] Effects of Discharge of Indebtedness on Earnings and Profits 94

[iii] Effects of Distributions on Earnings and Profits 94

[2] Using Earnings and Profits to Calculate Dividends 95

[a] Single Distribution, Sole Shareholder 96

[b] Single Distribution, Multiple Shareholders 97

[c] Multiple Distributions, Sole Shareholder 99

[d] Multiple Distributions, Multiple Shareholders 100

[e] Special Rule for Calculating Dividend of Corporate 20-Percent Shareholder 102

[D] Tax Treatment of Individuals' Qualified Dividends 102

§ 4.04   Tax Consequences to Corporate Shareholders: Effect of the Dividends Received Deduction 103

[A] Dividends Received Deduction, in General 104

Chart 4.2: Amounts of Dividends Received Deduction 104

[B] Exceptions and Special Rules 105

[1] Debt-Financed Portfolio Stock 105

[2] Holding Period 106

[3] Extraordinary Dividends 107

Chart 4.3: Comparison of Limitations on Dividends Received Deduction 110

§ 4.05   "Bootstrap Acquisitions" 110

§ 4.06   Constructive Dividends 117

Chapter 5. Redemptions of Stock **121**

§ 5.01   Introduction   121
         [A] In General   121
         [B] Competing Analogies   121
§ 5.02   Constructive Ownership of Stock   122
         [A] Family Attribution   123
         [B] Attribution from Entities to Investors   123
         [C] Attribution to Entities from Investors   124
         [D] Options   125
         [E] Operating Rules   125
§ 5.03   Tax Consequences of Redemptions   126
         [A] Overview of Section 302   126
         [B] Redemptions Qualifying for Exchange
             Treatment   127
             [1] Complete Termination of Interest   127
                 [a] In General   127
                 [b] Attribution of Family-Owned Shares   127
                     [i] Waiver of Attribution of Family-Owned
                          Shares   128
                          [I]   No Interest in the Corporation Ex-
                                cept as a Creditor   129
                          [II] No Related-Party Transfers Within
                                the Previous Ten Years   129
                                [a] Pre-Redemption Receipt of
                                    Shares from
                                    Related Person   130
                                [b] Pre-Redemption Transfer of
                                    Shares to a
                                    Related Person   130
                          [III] No Acquisitions Within the Succeed-
                                ing Ten Years   131
                     [ii] Waiver of Family Attribution by
                          Entities   131
             [2] Substantially Disproportionate
                 Redemptions   132
                 [a] In General   132

Page

Chart 5.1: Computing 80% of the Percentage of Stock Owned Before a Redemption 135

[b] Series of Redemptions 135

[3] Redemptions "Not Essentially Equivalent to a Dividend" 136

[a] Majority Shareholder's Redemption 137

[b] Minority Shareholder's Redemption 138

[4] Partial Liquidations 139

Chart 5.2: Checklist for Corporate Redemptions of Stock 140

[C] Redemptions Treated as Distributions 140

[1] In General 140

[2] Basis-Shifting Redemptions 141

[3] The Seagram/DuPont Transaction 143

[D] Effects on Earnings and Profits 144

§ 5.04 Additional Issues Arising in Redemptions 145

[A] Form Versus Substance 145

[1] Sale or Redemption? 145

[2] Charitable Gift or Redemption? 146

[B] Combined Redemptions and Sales 147

[C] Redemptions Incident to Divorce 149

[D] Redemptions to Pay Death Taxes 152

§ 5.05 Redemptions Through Related Corporations 153

[A] Introduction 153

[B] The Control Requirement 155

[1] In General 155

[2] Application of Constructive Stock Ownership Rules, as Modified 155

[C] Types of Section 304 Transactions 156

[D] Application of Section 302 158

[1] In General 158

[2] Variations on Constructive Stock Ownership Rules 158

[3] Taxing Redemptions Treated as Section 301 Distributions 159

Page

Chart 5.3: Checklist for Redemptions Through
Related Corporations   160

[E] Overlap of Section 304 with Section 351   161

Chapter 6. Stock Dividends **163**

§ 6.01   Introduction   163
§ 6.02   Excludible Stock Dividends   165

[A] Section 305(a)   165

[B] Basis in the New Stock and in the Old Stock; Holding
Period   165

§ 6.03   Taxable Stock Dividends   166

[A] Section 305(b): Exceptions to Section 305(a)   166

[1] Choice of Stock or Property   166

[2] Disproportionate Distributions   167

[a] In General   167

[b] Series of Distributions   168

[3] Distributions of Common and Preferred Stock to
Common Stockholders   168

[4] Distributions to Preferred Stockholders   169

[5] Distributions of Convertible
Preferred Stock   170

[B] Deemed Distributions of Stock   170

Chart 6.1: Checklist to Apply Section 305 to
Stock Dividends   172

[C] Basis and Holding Period   172

§ 6.04   "Tainted Stock" (Section 306 Stock)   173

[A] History of the "Preferred Stock Bailout"   173

[B] Section 306 Stock   174

[1] Definition   174

[a] Preferred Stock Received Tax-Free Under
Section 305(a)   174

[b] Preferred Stock Received Tax-Free in a Reorganization   175

[c] Certain Preferred Stock Received in a Section
351 Transaction   177

[d] Stock with a Basis Obtained from Section 306
Stock   178

Page

Chart 6.2: Checklist for Ascertaining Whether
Stock is Section 306 Stock   179

[2] Disposition of Section 306 Stock by Gift or Bequest   179

[3] General Tax Consequences on Sale of Section 306
Stock   179

[a] Computing Amount of "Taint"   179

[b] Tax Treatment of Additional
Sales Proceeds   180

[4] General Tax Consequences on Redemption of
Section 306 Stock   181

[5] Exceptions to General Tax Treatment   181

[a] Complete Liquidation of Corporation   181

[b] Complete Termination of Shareholder Interest in Corporation   182

[c] Transactions not for Tax Avoidance   182

Chart 6.3: Checklist for Applying Section 306 to
"Tainted Stock"   183

**Chapter 7. Corporate Liquidations and Taxable
Acquisitions** **185**

§ 7.01   Introduction to Liquidations and
Taxable Acquisitions   185

§ 7.02   Partial Liquidations   186

§ 7.03   Tax Consequences of Complete Liquidations   186

[A] Taxable Liquidations   186

[1] Corporate-Level Tax Consesquences   187

[a] General Rule   187

[b] Historical Importance of Substance-Over-
Form Doctrine in Liquidations   188

[c] Distributions of Loss Property   189

[i] Distributions to Related Persons   189

[ii] Distributions of Property with Built-In
Losses   191

[2] Shareholders   193

[3] Basis Rules   194

[4] Earnings and Profits   195

Page

  [B] Non-Taxable Liquidation of
   Controlled Subsidiary 195

   [1] Subsidiary Corporation 195

   [2] Controlling Parent Corporation 196

    [a] In General 196

    [b] Avoiding the Application of
     Section 332 198

   [3] Minority Shareholders 200

   [4] Basis Rules 200

   [5] Earnings and Profits 200

   [6] Effects of Indebtedness 201

    Chart 7.1: Comparison of Taxable and Non-
     Taxable Complete Liquidations 201

   [7] Mirror Transactions 202

§ 7.04 Liquidation-Reincorporation Transactions 202

§ 7.05 Taxable Acquisitions 203

  [A] Introduction: History and Background 203

  [B] Section 338 Elections 204

   [1] "Qualified Stock Purchase" 204

   [2] Consistency Provisions 205

  [C] Tax Consequences to Target of a
   Section 338 Election 206

  [D] Calculation and Allocation of Target Corporation's
   New Asset Basis 206

  [E] The Section 338(h)(10) Election 208

**Chapter 8. The Pass-Through Regime of
     Subchapter S.** **211**

§ 8.01 Introduction 211

  [A] Overview of the Pass-Through Regime of Subchapter
   S 211

  [B] A Brief Comparison of Subchapter S with the
   Partnership Pass-Through Regime of
   Subchapter K 212

§ 8.02 Eligibility for S Corporation Status 213

  [A] Restriction on the Number of Shareholders 213

Page

[B] Types of Permitted Shareholders 214

[C] "One Class of Stock" Rule 215

[D] Ineligible Corporations 217

§ 8.03 Election, Revocation, and Termination of
S Status 217

[A] Election 217

[B] Termination 218

    [1] Termination by Revocation 218

    [2] Termination by Ceasing to Qualify as a Small
    Business Corporation 219

    [3] Termination Based on Excess Passive Investment
    Income 219

    [4] Inadvertent Terminations 220

§ 8.04 Tax Treatment of S Corporation Shareholders 221

[A] Calculation of Taxable Income 221

[B] Pass-Through of Items 221

    [1] General Rules 221

    [2] Election to Terminate Taxable Year 222

    [3] Limitation on Deductions 222

[C] Treatment of Distributions 225

    [1] S Corporations with no Earnings and
    Profits 225

    [2] S Corporations with Earnings and Profits . . . 225

    Chart 8.1: Tax Treatment of Distributions of a
    Subchapter S Corporation with Subchapter C
    Earnings and Profits 227

[D] Basis Adjustments 227

    [1] Increases in Basis 228

    [2] Decreases in Basis 229

[E] Application of Subchapter C Rules to
S Corporations 229

[F] Sale of S Corporation Shares 231

    Chart 8.2: Application of Subchapter S to
    Corporations Without Subchapter C Earnings
    and Profits 232

§ 8.05 Corporate-Level Taxes Imposed on
S Corporations 233

		Page
[A] Built-In Gains		233
[B] Excess Net Passive Investment Income		233

Chapter 9. Reorganizations: Overview **237**

§ 9.01 Introduction 237

[A] A Bit of History and Rationales for Nonrecognition in Corporate Reorganizations 237

[B] Statutory and Common Law Requirements of Valid Reorganizations 238

§ 9.02 Overview of Section 368 238

[A] Definition of "Reorganization" 239

[1] "A" Reorganizations: Statutory Mergers 239

[2] "B" Reorganizations: Stock-for-Stock Swaps 240

[3] "C" Reorganizations: "De Facto Mergers" . . . 241

[4] Acquisitive and Divisive "D" Reorganizations 242

[5] "E" Reorganizations: Recapitalizations 244

[6] "F" Reorganizations: Changes in Form 245

[7] "G" Reorganizations: Bankruptcy Reorganizations 245

[8] Triangular B and C Reorganizations 245

[9] Section 368(a)(2)(D) Reorganizations: Forward Triangular Mergers 246

[10] Section 368(a)(2)(E) Reorganizations: Reverse Triangular Mergers 247

[11] Ordering Rules 247

[B] Party to a Reorganization 248

[C] "Control" 248

§ 9.03 The "Plan of Reorganization" Requirement 249

§ 9.04 The "Business Purpose" Requirement 250

§ 9.05 The Continuity of Business Enterprise Requirement 251

[A] Acquisition of Target's Historic Business or Historic Business Assets 251

[B] Continuation of Target's Historic Business or Use of Target's Historic Business Assets 252

                                                            Page

§ 9.06   The Continuity of Proprietary
         Interest Requirement   253

         [A] Overview   253

         [B] Requisite Proprietary Interest   254

             [1] Qualitative Aspects   254

             [2] Quantitative Aspects   256

         [C] Requisite Continuity: Application of the Step-
             Transaction Doctrine   259

                 Chart 9.1: General Checklist for Valid
                 Reorganizations   263

§ 9.07   General Tax Consequences of Transactions Qualifying
         as Reorganizations   263

         [A] Target Shareholders   263

             [1] Calculating Gain Recognized   264

             [2] Character of Recognized Gain   265

             [3] Basis   267

                 [a] In General   267

                 [b] Basis with Respect to Securities or Multiple
                     Classes of Stock   268

             [4] Holding Period   269

         [B] Target Corporation   270

         [C] Acquiring Corporation's Shareholders   271

         [D] Acquiring Corporation   271

                 Chart 9.2: Principal Code Sections Applicable in
                 Reorganizations   271

         [E] Introduction to the Carryover of
             Tax Attributes   271

§ 9.08   Intersection of Section 351 and Section 368   272

Chapter 10. Acquisitive Reorganizations **273**

§ 10.01 Introduction   273

§ 10.02 Mergers Involving Two or Three Corporations   273

         [A] Statutory Mergers ("A" Reorganizations)   274

             [1] In General   274

             [2] "Divisive" Mergers and Mergers with Disre-
                 garded Entities   275

Page

[3] Tax Consequences and Basis Rules 276

[B] Triangular Mergers 277

[1] Background 277

[2] Forward Triangular Mergers 279

[a] Formalities 279

[b] Tax Consequences 280

[i] In General 280

[ii] Effect of Liabilities on Triangular Mergers 281

[3] Reverse Triangular Mergers 283

[4] Tax Consequences and Basis Rules 286

§ 10.03 Stock-for-Stock Acquisitions ("B" Reorganizations) 287

[A] The "Solely for Voting Stock" Requirement 288

[1] The "Solely" Requirement 288

[2] Definition of "Voting Stock" 289

[B] The "Control" Requirement 290

[C] Application of the Step-Transaction Doctrine: "Solely" in Creeping B Reorganizations 290

[D] Tax Consequences and Basis Rules 291

[E] Triangular B Reorganizations 292

§ 10.04 Stock-for-Assets Acquisitions ("C" Reorganizations) 292

[A] The "Solely for Voting Stock" Requirement 293

[1] Effect of Liabilities 293

[2] The "Boot Relaxation Rule" 294

[B] "Substantially All of the Properties" Requirement 294

[C] Application of the Step-Transaction Doctrine: "Creeping C" Reorganizations 296

[D] Tax Consequences and Basis Rules 298

[E] Triangular C Reorganizations 299

§ 10.05 Drop-Downs 300

§ 10.06 Transfer of Assets to Controlled Corporation (Acquisitive "D" Reorganizations) 301

[A] Introduction 301

                                                            Page

[B] "Substantially All of the Assets" Requirement . . . 302

[C] Distribution Requirement 303

[D] The "Control" Requirement 303

[E] Overlap with "C" Reorganizations 304

[F] Tax Consequences and Basis Rules 304

§ 10.07 Bankruptcy Reorganizations
("G" Reorganizations) 305

Chapter 11. Corporate Divisions **307**

§ 11.01 Introduction to Corporate Divisions 307
§ 11.02 Corporate Divisions Under Section 355 307

[A] Types of Section 355 Transactions 308

    [1] Spin-Offs 308

    [2] Split-Offs 309

    [3] Split-Ups 310

[B] "Stock or Securities" 311

[C] "Control" and "Distribution" Requirements 311

[D] "Business Purpose" Requirement 313

[E] The "Device" Prohibition 315

    [1] "Device" Factors 316

        [a] *Pro Rata* Distribution 316

        [b] Subsequent Sale or Exchange of the Stock Distributed 316

        [c] Presence of Nonbusiness or "Secondary Business" Assets 317

    [2] "Non-Device" Factors 318

        [a] Corporate Business Purpose 318

        [b] Publicly Traded, Widely Held Distributing Corporation 318

        [c] Distribution to Domestic Corporations . . . 318

    [3] "Non-Device" Transactions 318

[F] Active Trade or Business Requirements 319

    [1] Five-Year History 320

        [a] Same or Different Business? 321

        [b] Acquired Business 322

Page

       [2] "Immediately After" the Distribution 323

    [G] Continuity of Proprietary Interest 326

       Chart 11.1: Checklist for Section 355
          Transactions 327

    [H] Tax Consequences and Basis Rules 327

       [1] Shareholders 327

          [a] General Tax Consequences 327

          [b] Shareholder Basis 330

       [2] The Distributing Corporation 330

       [3] Allocation of Earnings and Profits 331

§ 11.03   Divisive "D" Reorganizations 332

    [A] In General 332

    [B] Qualification Under Section 355 332

    [C] Tax Consequences, Basis, and Earnings and Profits
       Rules 333

§ 11.04   Divisive "G" Reorganizations 334

**Chapter 12. Reorganizations Involving Only One
           Corporation** **335**

§ 12.01   Introduction 335

§ 12.02   Recapitalizations ("E" Reorganizations) 335

    [A] Introduction 335

    [B] Business Purpose Requirement 337

    [C] Types of Recapitalizations 337

       [1] Corporate Stock for Investors' Stock 337

       [2] Corporate Stock for Investors'
          Debt Securities 339

       [3] Corporate Debt Securities for
          Investors' Stock 340

       [4] Corporate Debt Securities for
          Investors' Debt Securities 341

       Chart 12.1: General Checklist for
          Recapitalizations 342

§ 12.03   Changes in Form ("F" Reorganizations) 343

    [A] In General 343

    [B] Carryback of Tax Attributes 344

Chapter 13. Carryover of Tax Attributes **347**

§ 13.01   Overview   347

          [A] Transactions Eligible for Carryover   347

          [B] Tax Attributes Subject to Carryover   347

          [C] Limitations in Section 381   348

§ 13.02   Limitations on Carryovers   349

          [A] History   350

          [B] Change-of-Ownership Limitations on Net Operating
              and Other Losses: Section 382   350

              [1] In General   350

              [2] Losses Subject to Section 382   351

              [3] Definitions   352

                  [a] "Stock"   352

                  [b] "Five-Percent Shareholder"   353

                  [c] "Ownership Change"   355

                  [d] "Testing Period"   356

              [4] Mechanics of the Section 382 Limitation   . . .   357

                  [a] General Rules   357

                  [b] The Long-Term Tax-Exempt Rate   358

                  [c] Reductions and Increases in the Section 382
                      Limitation   358

                      [i]   Continuity of Business Enterprise   . . .   358

                      [ii] Effect of Built-In Gains on the Section 382
                            Limitation   359

                      [iii] Effect of Unused Section 382
                            Limitation   360

                  [d] Valuation Issues   360

                      [i]   Anti-Stuffing Rule   360

                      [ii] Special Rule for Valuing Corporations
                            with Excess Nonbusiness Assets   360

                      [iii] Effect of Redemptions and Other Corpo-
                            rate Contractions   361

                  Chart 13.1: Checklist for Applying
                      Section 382   362

          [C] Change-of-Ownership Limitations on Other Tax At-
              tributes: Section 383   363

Page

[1] In General   363

[2] Mechanics of the Section 383
       Credit Limitation   363

       Chart 13.2: Checklist for Applying the Section
         383 Credit Limitation   365

[D] Limitation on Use of Pre-Acquisition Losses to Offset
      Built-In Gains: Section 384   365

       [1] In General   365

       [2] Mechanics   366

       Chart 13.3: Checklist for Applying
         Section 384   367

[E] Acquisitions with Tax-Avoidance Motive:
      Section 269   368

       [1] In General   368

       [2] Mechanics   368

       Chart 13.4: Checklist for Applying
         Section 269   369

**Chapter 14. Anti-Abuse Measures and
                Special Provisions** **371**

§ 14.01   Introduction   371

§ 14.02   The Accumulated Earnings Tax 371

          [A] In General   371

          [B] Tax-Avoidance Purpose   372

          [C] Reasonable Needs of the Business 373

          [D] Mechanics   376

§ 14.03   The Personal Holding Company Tax 377

          [A] In General   377

          [B] Definition of "Personal Holding Company" 378

          [C] Types of Personal Holding Company Income . . . 379

          [D] Mechanics of the Tax 380

          [E] Avoiding the Tax 382

§ 14.04   The Alternative Minimum Tax   382

          [A] In General   382

          [B] Mechanics   383

§ 14.05   "Controlled Group" Restrictions 385

Page

[A] Overview of the Definition of
"Controlled Group"   386

[B] Parent-Subsidiary Controlled Groups   386

[C] Brother-Sister Controlled Groups   386

[D] Combined Groups   388

§ 14.06   Income Splitting   388

[A] Income Splitting Between Corporation and Shareholder   389

[B] Income Splitting Between Corporations   389

[1] In General   389

[2] An Introduction to Reallocation of Income and
Deductions Under Section 482   390

[a] Overview   390

[b] Selected Case Law on Arm's-Length Standards   391

[c] Application of the Substantial Valuation Misstatement Penalty   394

[d] Advance Pricing Agreements   394

**Chapter 15. Integration of Corporate and Shareholder
Taxes** **397**

§ 15.01   Introduction   397

§ 15.02   The Current System of Partial Integration   399

§ 15.03   Major Integration Proposals   401

[A] Dividend Exclusion Methods   402

[1] Treasury's Dividend Exclusion Prototype . . .   402

[2] President George W. Bush's
2003 Proposal   403

[B] Treasury's Comprehensive Business Income Tax System   405

[C] Treasury's Shareholder Allocation Prototype   405

[D] Treasury's Imputation Credit Prototype   407

[E] The American Law Institute's Shareholder Credit
Proposal   409

§ 15.04   Additional Corporate Integration Possibilities   411

[A] Dividends-Paid Deduction System   411

Page

[B] Split-Rate Systems   412

Chapter 16. Corporate Tax Shelters **413**

§ 16.01   Introduction   413

§ 16.02   A Paradigmatic Corporate Tax Shelter: *ACM
          Partnership v. Commissioner*   417

§ 16.03   Subchapter C Shelters   422

          [A] Contingent Liability Shelters   423

          [B] Basis-Shifting Shelters   426

§ 16.04   Weapons in the War on Tax Shelters   429

          [A] Disclosure Requirements and Enforcement Penalties
              Applicable to Material Advisors   430

          [B] Disclosure Requirements and Certain Penalties Ap-
              plicable to Taxpayers Participating in Reportable
              Transactions   431

          [C] Opinion Practice Under Circular 230   431

Table of Cases **TC-1**

Table of Statutes **TS-1**

Index **I-1**

Chapter 1

INTRODUCTION TO CORPORATE TAXATION

§ 1.01 Introduction to the "Corporate Tax" and Double Taxation

A "corporation" is a legal entity created under a state or other statute that allows "incorporation" by persons who become the "shareholders" of the corporation. In general, the corporation's organizers complete appropriate forms and file them with the state or other jurisdiction in which the corporation will be incorporated. The owners of a corporation are its shareholders. JAMES D. COX & THOMAS LEE HAZEN, CORPORATIONS 2-3 (2d ed. 2003). Corporate shareholders may be individuals, other corporations, or other entities such as partnerships. In general, an entity recognized as a corporation under state law is also treated as a corporation for federal tax purposes. Treas. Reg. § 301.7701-2(b)(1).

For tax purposes, a corporation is a separate "taxpayer"[1] from its shareholders, meaning that the corporate entity is subject to taxation on corporate-level events. Section 11 of the Internal Revenue Code (Code) lists the progressive rates of tax on corporations, consisting of 15%, 25%, 34%, and 35% brackets.[2] I.R.C. § 11(b). However, section 11 also provides for additional taxation of corporations with taxable income over $100,000 (eliminating the benefit of the brackets below 34%), and for further additional taxation of corporations with taxable income over $15,000,000, effectively providing a 35% flat tax for corporations with the highest incomes.

The calculation of corporate tax liability is complicated by a deduction for income from "domestic production activities," enacted by the American Jobs Creation Act of 2004. *See* I.R.C. § 199. The deduction replaces the former extraterritorial income exclusion, which the World Trade Organization had found to be a prohibited export subsidy; it was repealed in the same Act. *See* H.R. Conf. Rep. No. 108-755. The domestic production deduction is phased in so that in 2005 and 2006, the taxpayer generally can deduct 3 percent of the "qualified production activities income of the taxpayer for the taxable year"[3] (or of taxable income computed without

---

[1] "The term 'taxpayer' means any person subject to any internal revenue tax." I.R.C. § 7701(a)(14).

[2] Throughout this book, a reference to a "section" without further elaboration is to a section of the Internal Revenue Code of 1986, as amended.

[3] "[Q]ualified production activities income" requires "domestic production gross receipts," which, subject to certain exceptions, derive from the "lease, rental, license, sale, exchange, or other disposition of . . . qualifying production property which was manufactured, produced, grown, or extracted by the taxpayer in whole or in significant part within the United States,

regard to section 199, if less); 6 percent in 2007, 2008, or 2009; and 9 percent after that. I.R.C. § 199(a). The provision is quite complicated and contains a number of limitations. For example, the amount of the deduction cannot exceed "50 percent of the W-2 wages of the employer for the taxable year." I.R.C. § 199(b). Although the deduction lowers the tax *base* by lowering taxable income, in effect, it lowers the rate of tax applicable to the activities it covers.

In addition to taxation at the corporate level,[4] shareholders must pay tax on dividends received, *see* I.R.C. § 61(a)(7), or if they sell their shares for a gain, *see* I.R.C. § 61(a)(3). In computing its federal income tax liability, a corporation may not deduct dividends paid although payment of the corporate tax reduces the amount the corporation has available to distribute to shareholders. "Double taxation" of profits—once at the corporate level and a second time to shareholders—is a hallmark of the "classical" corporate tax regime.

> *Example 1.1*: X Corporation is owned equally by Abby and Ben, unrelated individuals. They each have a basis of $250 in their X Corporation stock. In Year 1, the only tax-significant events are that X Corporation earns $10,000 of ordinary income and it distributes $100 to each shareholder. X Corporation will pay tax on the $10,000 under rates determined under section 11. In addition, Abby and Ben will each have $100 of dividend income.

Under current law however, shareholder-level taxation generally is reduced in some way. First, individuals currently are taxed at preferential capital gains rates on most dividends.[5] Similarly, individual shareholders' sales of shares held for more than one year will generally be taxed at preferential capital gains rates. *See* I.R.C. §§ 1(h)(1); 1222. In addition, a noncorporate taxpayer can exclude from gross income 50 percent of the "gain from the sale or exchange of qualified small business stock held for more than 5 years." I.R.C. § 1202(a)(1). The remaining gain is taxed at a 28 percent rate, *see* I.R.C. § 1(h)(4), resulting in an effective tax rate of 14 percent on the gain—just slightly less than the current general 15 percent rate applicable to individuals' net capital gain under section 1(h). Furthermore, as discussed in Chapter 4, corporate shareholders typically benefit

---

. . . any qualified film produced by the taxpayer, or . . . electricity, natural gas, or potable water produced by the taxpayer in the United States," I.R.C. § 199(c)(4)(i); "construction performed in the United States," I.R.C. § 199(c)(4)(ii); or "engineering or architectural services performed in the United States for construction projects in the United States," I.R.C. § 199(c)(4)(iii). The term "qualifying production property" includes tangible personal property and computer software. I.R.C. § 199(c)(5)(A), (B).

[4] It is not clear to what extent shareholders bear the "incidence" of the corporate tax, and to what extent it is borne by the employees or customers of the corporation. *See* Graeme S. Cooper, *The Return to Corporate Tax Evasion in the Presence of an Income Tax on Shareholders*, 12 AKRON TAX J. 1, 4 n.11 (1996).

[5] Individuals' "qualified dividend income" currently is treated as "adjusted net capital gain," which subjects it to tax at a maximum rate of 15 percent. *See* I.R.C. § 1(h)(3)(B), (11). This provision is scheduled to sunset on December 31, 2008.

from a dividends received deduction under section 243, so as to reduce or eliminate triple (or more) taxation. *See* I.R.C. §§ 61(a)(7), 1(h)(3)(B), (11), 243.

Double taxation is not the only paradigm of business taxation. Businesses conducted as sole proprietorships, partnerships, limited liability companies, or "S corporations" (electing small business corporations, *see* I.R.C. § 1361(a)(1)) generally are subject to only one level of federal income tax.[6]

> *Example 1.2*: Assume that in Example 1.1, X Corporation was a small business corporation that had elected to be taxed under Subchapter S. As in Example 1.1, in Year 1, the only tax-significant events are that X Corporation earns $10,000 of ordinary income and it distributes $100 to each shareholder. Abby and Ben will each have $5,000 of ordinary income (half of $10,000) but will not be taxed on receipt of the $100. Abby and Ben will each increase their stock basis by $5,000 to reflect the income they included and reduce their stock basis by $100 for the distribution.

Comparing Examples 1.1 and 1.2 indicates that, in the aggregate, Example 1.1, which involved a "C corporation," *see* I.R.C. § 1361(a)(2), resulted in $200 more gross income than Example 1.2, which involved an S corporation. That is, the dividend distributions were essentially taxed twice in Example 1.1. However, that is not the end of the story. Tax *rates* matter as much as the base to which the tax rates are applied. The $10,000 in Example 1.1, the C corporation example, will be taxed at corporate tax rates under section 11. The $10,000 in Example 1.2, the S corporation example, will be taxed at Abby and Ben's tax rates under section 1. Thus, the actual amount of tax paid on the $10,000 in each example may differ. In addition, the $100 that Abby and Ben are taxed on in Example 1.1 currently benefits from the same preferential tax treatment that individuals' capital gains do, in that it will be taxed at a maximum rate of 15%. *See* I.R.C. § 1(h)(1)(B), (C), (3)(B), (11). This preferential tax treatment is a form of partial "integration" of the corporate-level and shareholder-level taxes.[7]

There are a number of ways in which Subchapter C corporations traditionally have tried to minimize double taxation, such as treating distributions to shareholders as deductible interest on loans or as deductible payments of salary, or simply retaining earnings. However, as discussed in § 1.02, below, there are limits to the effectiveness of any of these devices. In addition, the application of preferential tax rates to most dividends received by individuals has changed the incentive structure somewhat.

Some businesses opt to avoid the corporate form entirely, operating through a non-corporate form, such as a partnership or limited liability company (LLC). Nonetheless, there are still a large number of businesses operating as corporations, many of which are C corporations. There are a number of reasons for that. First, some businesses may have chosen the

---

[6] Subchapter S is discussed in Chapter 8.

[7] Corporate integration is introduced in § 1.02[E] and discussed in further detail in Chapter 15.

corporate form for state law or other reasons. For example, *Lessinger v. Commissioner*, 872 F.2d 519 (2d Cir. 1989), discussed in Chapter 2, indicates that Mr. Lessinger contributed the assets of his sole proprietorship to a corporation because lenders required his use of the corporate form in order to charge a higher rate of interest without violating state usury laws.[8]

The corporate form also offers a number of advantages, though not all of the advantages are unique to corporations. Professors Cox and Hazen list the following non-tax advantages of the corporate form:

> (1) exemption of shareholders from personal liability; (2) continuity of the organization's existence despite changes in its members; (3) centralized management by a board of directors; (4) free transferability of a participant's interests; (5) access of the business to additional capital; (6) the organization's capacity to act as a legal unit in holding property, contracting, and bringing suit; and (7) standardized methods of organization, management, and finance prescribed by corporation statutes for the protection of shareholders and creditors, including a more or less standardized system of shareholder relations, rights, and remedies.

Cox & Hazen, *supra*, at 6.

As Example 1.2 illustrated, use of the corporate form does not necessarily have to entail taxation under Subchapter C; the Subchapter S pass-through regime is available to electing small business corporations. However, there are a number of restrictions on qualification for the simplified Subchapter S regime, as discussed below and in Chapter 8. Among them is a limit of one class of stock and restrictions on the number and types of shareholders. Accordingly, publicly traded corporations are taxed under Subchapter C.[9]

In addition, C corporations do not always face double taxation of profits. The second level of tax applies only to amounts taxed at the shareholder level. If the corporation retains most or all of its earnings, it may postpone double taxation; absent distributions, shareholders will not be taxed on the increase in value of the company until they sell their shares. Deferral of shareholder-level taxation may become exclusion for shareholders who hold on to stock until death, because section 1014 currently provides the heir with a step-up in basis to fair market value.[10] The corporation may then redeem the shares. If the redemption qualifies as an exchange under section 302, which is discussed in Chapter 5, there may be no tax on it, given the heir's fair market value basis in the shares.

This approach may not always be viable or successful. There is a penalty tax imposed on retention of earnings in excess of those for the reasonable

---

[8] *See* § 2.02[A][2][b][ii][I].

[9] Most publicly traded partnerships also are subject to corporate taxation. *See* I.R.C. § 7704.

[10] Section 1014 is scheduled to expire at the end of 2009. *See* I.R.C. § 1014(f). However section 1014(f) is scheduled to sunset at the end of 2010.

needs of the business.[11] *See* I.R.C. § 531. However, note that when it is successful, retaining earnings eliminates shareholder-level taxation of corporate profits but retains the corporate tax. Whether a single, corporate-level tax is lower than the single, investor-level tax that applies to a pass-through entity depends on whether the marginal tax rate applicable to the corporation is higher or lower than the marginal tax rates applicable to the investors (assuming the tax base is the same).

The incentive for a corporation to retain earnings to avoid shareholder-level taxation has declined, given that, under current law individuals' qualified dividends are taxed at preferential capital gains rates. That does not eliminate the incentive to reduce taxes, particularly at the corporate level. Corporations may reduce or eliminate corporate-level taxation through a variety of tax minimization techniques, including abusive corporate tax shelters, which are discussed in Chapter 16. "Indeed, if the corporate tax can be eliminated by self-help (by tax shelters or tax competition [for multi-national enterprises]), it is now possible for a corporate investment to be taxed at a total rate of 15%—significantly lower than non-corporate investment." Reuven S. Avi-Yonah, *Corporations, Society, and the State: A Defense of the Corporate Tax*, 90 VA. L. REV. 1193, 1253 (2004).

§ 1.02 Avoiding Double Taxation

As indicated above, in order to avoid the double taxation that typically accompanies the corporate form, corporations have sometimes sought to avoid Subchapter C; to retain earnings, thereby avoiding the shareholder-level tax on dividends; or to treat distributions as deductible payments, which reduces corporate-level taxation. In a closely held corporation, many shareholders may also be employees or creditors of the corporation. The shareholders may therefore cause the corporation to characterize distributions to shareholders who play other roles in the corporation as payments of interest deductible under section 163, payments of salary deductible under section 162, or rental payments deductible under section 162. The IRS generally has tried to combat perceived abuses in these areas. In addition, under current law, these approaches face a natural limitation because salaries, rent payments, and interest are all taxable at the rates applicable to ordinary income whereas most dividends received by individuals are taxed at the same rates applicable to long-term capital gains.[12]

[A] Avoiding the Corporate Form—Partnerships and Limited Liability Companies

Some businesses avoid Subchapter C by organizing as partnerships or other entities, such as LLCs. An LLC is an unincorporated organization organized under state law. The hallmark of the LLC is limited liability for

---

[11] The accumulated earnings tax is discussed in Chapter 14.

[12] Salaries are also subject to employment taxes.

its investors combined with pass-through taxation; as discussed in § 1.02[A][2][b], below, the "check-the-box" regulations under section 7701 generally permit partnership taxation for LLCs with two or more members.

[1] A Very Brief Overview of the Partnership Tax Regime

Partnership taxation is a "pass-through" paradigm under which the partnership is not a taxable entity; partnership-level tax consequences are "passed through" to investors. This pass-through approach results in a single layer of taxation at the partner level. In order to avoid systematic pass-through of items with particular tax aspects to the particular partners who are most able to use those items for advantageous tax treatment, partnership tax regulations require that the allocation of items among the partners have "substantial economic effect."[13] *See* Treas. Reg. § 1.704-1(b)(2). The partnership tax regime is more complex than the Subchapter S regime discussed below in § 1.02[B], primarily because the one-class-of-stock restriction of Subchapter S generally precludes taxation based on anything other than the percentage ownership of each shareholder.

[2] LLCs and Other Unincorporated Entities

There are two possible regimes of income taxation generally applicable to LLCs and other unincorporated entities: corporate taxation and partnership taxation.[14] Under current law, unincorporated entities generally have a choice of regime to adopt, with the default for domestic entities with more than one equity holder being the partnership tax regime. Those entities did not always have a purely elective choice, however.

[a] A Brief History of the Taxation of Unincorporated Entities

Under federal tax law, "associations" are taxed as corporations. *See* I.R.C. § 7701(a)(3). The test to distinguish an unincorporated entity taxable as a partnership from one treated as an association taxable as a corporation used to occur under the so-called "*Kintner* regulations." *See United States v. Kintner*, 216 F.2d 418 (9th Cir. 1954). These regulations were promulgated under section 7701 of the Code, which defines both "partnership" and "corporation." *See* I.R.C. § 7701(a)(2), (3).

---

[13] A detailed explanation of partnership taxation, which is extremely complex, is beyond the scope of this book. For further reading in this area, see JEROLD A. FRIEDLAND, UNDERSTANDING PARTNERSHIP AND LLC TAXATION (2d ed. 2003); LAURA E. CUNNINGHAM & NOEL B. CUNNINGHAM, THE LOGIC OF SUBCHAPTER K: A CONCEPTUAL GUIDE TO THE TAXATION OF PARTNERSHIPS (2d ed. 2000).

[14] Sole proprietorships are not entities separate from the individuals who own them, so they are not subject to separate taxation. Under the check-the-box rules, they cannot elect to be taxed as corporations. *See* IRS INFO 2005-0047, *available at* www.irs.gov/pub/irs-wd/05-0047.pdf.

The *Kintner* regulations adopted factors discussed in *Morrissey v. Commissioner*, 296 U.S. 344, 359 (1935). The six factors provided in the regulations were (1) associates, (2) an objective to carry on business and divide the gains therefrom, (3) continuity of life, (4) centralization of management, (5) liability for corporate debts limited to corporate property, and (6) free transferability of interests. Treas. Reg. § 1.7701-2(a)(1) (1996). Because the first two of these were common to both partnerships and associations taxable as corporations, the regulations focused on the other four factors, each of which are characteristic of corporations, not partnerships. For example, a corporation survives the death of a shareholder but a partnership does not survive the death of a partner. In *Larson v. Commissioner*, 66 T.C. 159 (1976), the Tax Court concluded that each of the four characteristics must be given "equal weight."

Under the *Kintner* regulations, an entity with more corporate characteristics than not was classified as an association taxable as a corporation. In other words, generally speaking, an entity needed three out of four corporate characteristics to be taxed as a corporation; if it lacked even two of the four corporate characteristics, it was taxed as a partnership. The anti-corporation bias reflected a history of desirability of classification as a corporation in order to receive certain tax benefits such as the opportunity to adopt a qualified pension plan, which at one time was available only to corporations. In addition, corporate tax rates used to be lower than rates applicable to individuals, which generally results in lower taxation of income earned by an entity taxed as a corporation than by an entity taxed as a partnership, if corporate earnings are not distributed.

In 1977, a Wyoming state statute authorized LLCs. In 1988, in Revenue Ruling 88-76, 1988-2 C.B. 360, the IRS ruled that entities formed under the Wyoming LLC statute would be treated as partnerships under the *Kintner* regulations. In Revenue Ruling 93-38, 1993 C.B. 38, the IRS considered the proper characterization of two LLCs organized under Delaware law. The IRS characterized one of the LLCs as a partnership because it lacked three of the four corporate characteristics. The IRS characterized the other LLC as an association taxable as a corporation because it had four corporate characteristics. This Revenue Ruling demonstrated that the proper tax classification of an entity organized under a flexible LLC statute depended on the specific provisions of the LLC agreement.

Following the IRS's approval of partnership tax treatment for properly structured LLCs, the LLC form began to flourish. Currently, every state allows the formation of LLCs. COX & HAZEN, *supra*, at 16.

[b] The "Check-the-Box" Rules

Effective January 1, 1997, the Treasury moved to an elective "check-the-box" system for classifying business entities for federal tax purposes. *See* Treas. Reg. §§ 301.7701-2, -3. Under the check-the-box regulations, a "business entity" is any entity recognized for federal tax purposes that is not properly classified as a trust or subject to other special treatment under the Code. A business entity with two or more "members" is classified as either a corporation or a partnership. A business entity with only one owner is either classified as a corporation or is "disregarded"; if an entity is disregarded, it is treated as a sole proprietorship, branch, or division of the owner. Treas. Reg. § 301.7701-2(a).

Under the check-the-box regulations, certain business entities are automatically taxable as corporations. In general, those entities are (1) those organized under a federal or state statute that refers to the entity as incorporated or as a corporation, body corporate, or body politic; (2) associations, as determined under Treasury Regulation 301.7701-3; (3) those organized as joint-stock companies or joint-stock associations under state law; (4) insurance companies; (5) state-chartered business entities conducting banking activities, if any of their deposits are insured under the Federal Deposit Insurance Act or a similar federal statute; (6) those wholly owned by a state or any political subdivision of a state; (7) those taxable as corporations under a provision of the Internal Revenue Code other than section 7701(a)(3); and (8) certain foreign entities. Treas. Reg. § 301.7701-2(b).

The check-the-box regulations allow a business entity that is not automatically classified as a corporation to elect its classification for federal tax purposes. An eligible entity with at least two members can elect to be classified as either an association or a partnership, and an eligible entity with a single owner can elect to be classified as an association or to be disregarded as an entity separate from its owner. Treas. Reg. § 301.7701-3. Unless the entity's members prefer a classification other than the default classification, the entity need not make an election. The default rules provide that any domestic unincorporated business organization with two or more owners is treated as a partnership for federal tax purposes unless it elects corporate tax treatment. *See id.* The default rule thus reflects the choice that many business owners would make if they made an election.

In sum, the check-the-box rules establish the presumptive classification of most domestic unincorporated entities as partnerships for federal purposes. They also allow a freely elective regime that avoids any test or analysis of the characteristics of the entity. Thus, for example, both of the LLCs discussed in Revenue Ruling 93-38 would presumptively be taxed as partnerships under the check-the-box rules even though one of the LLCs had four corporate characteristics. In addition, under the check-the-box rules, either or both LLCs could elect to be taxed as corporations.

[B]   Avoiding Subchapter C—Introduction to Subchapter S

Subchapter S of the Code, which was mentioned in § 1.01, generally allows qualifying small business corporations to elect to avoid taxation at the corporate level. Instead, income, gains, expenses, and losses are allocated to the S corporation's shareholders. Subchapter S is thus an elective regime with a fairly simple structure that generally results in only one level of tax. One cost of this election is the "one class of stock" restriction, discussed below, which precludes S corporations from making allocations based on anything other than the percentage of stock that each shareholder owns. Another cost consists of limitations on the number and types of shareholders, as discussed below. Subchapter S is discussed in detail in Chapter 8, and is outlined briefly in this section.

There are four requirements that an S corporation must meet in order to be eligible to make an S election. *See* I.R.C. § 1361(b). First, the corporation must have no more than a certain number of shareholders, 100 under current law. I.R.C. § 1361(b)(1)(A). Spouses (and their estates) are treated as one shareholder for this purpose. I.R.C. § 1361(c)(1)(A)(i). In addition, an election may be made by any member of a family to treat all the "members of the family," as defined in section 1361(c)(1)(B), as one shareholder. I.R.C. § 1361(c)(1)(A)(ii). Second, all shareholders must be individuals or certain eligible entities, which are certain trusts, certain exempt organizations, and estates. *See* I.R.C. § 1361(b)(1)(B).

The third restriction is that a nonresident alien cannot be a shareholder, I.R.C. § 1361(b)(1)(C), primarily because the income nonresident aliens receive from S corporations might not bear federal income tax. Subchapter S is intended to eliminate double taxation, but is not intended to allow corporate income to avoid taxation entirely. Fourth, as indicated above, an S corporation may not have more than one class of stock. I.R.C. § 1361(b)(1)(D). However, voting differences in stock may be disregarded, I.R.C. § 1361(c)(4), and there is a safe harbor to avoid debt being reclassified as equity and thus as a second class of stock, I.R.C. § 1361(c)(5).

An S election may be revoked if holders of more than half of the corporation's shares consent to revoke the election. I.R.C. § 1362(d)(1)(B). In addition, an S election terminates if the corporation ceases to qualify as a small business corporation. I.R.C. § 1362(d)(2). Thus, in general, issuance of a second class of stock will terminate an S election, as will transfer of shares in an S corporation to a prohibited type of shareholder.

Section 1366 governs the "pass-thru" of income and loss to the shareholders of an S corporation. In general, income and loss are passed through to shareholders on a current basis, and, in order to avoid double taxation of shareholders, the shareholder's basis in the S corporation's stock is increased to reflect income of the corporation that is included on the shareholder's return. *See* I.R.C. § 1367. That basis is decreased to reflect losses. *See id.* However, deduction of losses is capped at the shareholder's investment in the corporation (the sum of the shareholder's basis in the corporation's stock and in any indebtedness of the corporation to the shareholder).

Example 1.3: Close Corp. is owned equally by Diana and Edward, unrelated individuals. Assume that, at the end of Year 1, Diana has a basis of $50 in her stock and Edward has a basis of $75 in his stock. Assume that in Year 2, the only tax-significant event is that Close Corp.

earns $200 of ordinary income. Under section 1366, Diana and Edward will each have $100 of ordinary income. Note that they have this gross income despite the lack of any cash distribution that they could use to pay the tax. Diana's basis will increase to $150, and Edward's basis will increase to $175.

Because an S corporation's profits generally are taxed currently to shareholders, taxation of profits distributed would result in double taxation. Therefore, under section 1368, if an S corporation lacking "earnings and profits," such as an S corporation with no Subchapter C history, makes a distribution to shareholders of income that was previously taxed to the shareholders, the distribution is not included in income. Instead, under section 1367, the distribution serves to reduce the shareholder's basis in the S corporation shares. In other words, an S corporation shareholder's partial return of investment in the corporation through receipt of corporate assets reduces that shareholder's basis.

Example 1.4: Assume that Close Corp., discussed in Example 1.3, is an S corporation with no Subchapter C earnings and profits. The only event with tax significance in Year 3 is that Diana and Edward cause Close Corp. to distribute $40 to each of them with respect to their stock. There is no tax on the distribution. However, Diana and Edward must each reduce their basis by the amount received. *See* I.R.C. § 1367. Thus, Diana's basis at the end of Year 3 will be $110 ($150 – $40), and Edward's will be $135 ($175 – $40).

Those are the basic principles of the pass-through paradigm of Subchapter S.[15] Most other transactions involving an S corporation are subject to the same corporate tax treatment discussed throughout the remainder of this book because, under section 1371(a), when no special rule applies to an S corporation, the Subchapter C rules apply. Thus, for example, incorporation or liquidation of an S corporation is taxed the same way as incorporation or liquidation of a C corporation, with the proviso that, for the S corporation, corporate-level tax consequences pass through to the shareholders to be accounted for at the shareholder level.

S corporations are also subject to special rules designed to prevent C corporations from avoiding double taxation through opportunistic S elections. Therefore, under sections 1374 and 1375, an S corporation that previously was taxed as a C corporation may, in certain circumstances, have a corporate-level tax imposed on it. More specifically, under section 1374, an S corporation that held appreciated assets at the time it converted from C to S status will generally recognize a corporate-level tax at the time it sells those assets. Under section 1375, a corporate-level tax is imposed on an S corporation with accumulated earnings and profits (from its Subchapter C history) when the passive investment income of the corporation exceeds 25 percent of its gross receipts. This tax prevents a C corporation

---

15 The rules that apply to distributions by S corporations with accumulated earnings and profits are discussed in § 8.04[C][2].

from avoiding the personal holding company tax discussed in Chapter 14 by making an election under Subchapter S.[16]

[C] Avoiding Subchapter C—Corporation as Agent

Another way corporate tax treatment theoretically could be avoided would be if the corporation were disregarded as an entity separate from its shareholders. However, in *Moline Properties Corp. v. Commissioner*, 319 U.S. 436 (1943), the United States Supreme Court stated:

> The doctrine of corporate entity fills a useful purpose in business life. Whether the purpose be to gain an advantage under the law of the state of incorporation or to avoid or to comply with the demands of creditors or to serve the creator's personal or undisclosed convenience, *so long as that purpose is the equivalent of business activity or is followed by the carrying on of business by the corporation, the corporation remains a separate taxable entity.*

Id. at 438–39 (emphasis added).

Subsequently, in *National Carbide Corp. v. Commissioner*, 336 U.S. 422 (1949), the Supreme Court considered the possibility that an agency relationship might exist between a corporation and its shareholders so that tax treatment would be determined at the shareholder level, without corporate-level taxation, because the corporation would be acting as a mere agent on behalf of the shareholder-principals. The Court set forth a six-factor test for determining when an agency relationship exists, stating:

> (1) Whether the corporation operates in the name and for the account of the principal, (2) binds the principal by its actions, (3) transmits money received to the principal, and (4) whether receipt of income is attributable to the services of employees of the principal and to assets belonging to the principal are some of the relevant considerations in determining whether a true agency exists. . . . (5) [I]ts relations with its principal must not be dependent upon the fact that it is owned by the principal, if such is the case. (6) Its business purpose must be the carrying on of the normal duties of an agent.

Id. at 437 (footnote omitted). In *National Carbide*, the Court rejected the argument that an agency relationship existed. However, in *Commissioner v. Bollinger*, 485 U.S. 340 (1988), the Court revisited the issue on different facts.

In *Bollinger*, real estate developers formed a series of partnerships. Each partnership, in turn, entered into an agreement with a corporation wholly owned by Bollinger. The agreements with the corporations were necessary to secure loans under Kentucky's usury laws, which limited the annual interest rate for non-corporate borrowers. *Id.* at 341-42. Consequently, the agreements were entered into solely for the purpose of securing financing,

---

[16] *See* § 14.03.

and all parties who had contact with the apartment complexes (including lenders, contractors, managers, employees, and tenants) regarded the partnerships as the owners, and knew that the corporation was merely an agent of the partnership. *Id.* at 345. Bollinger personally indemnified and held the corporation harmless from any liability it might sustain as his agent and nominee. *Id.* at 342.

The developers reported their distributive shares of losses from the partnerships on their individual tax returns, even though title to the properties was held by the corporate nominees. The IRS disallowed the losses on the ground that they were attributable to the corporation as owner of the properties. The Tax Court disagreed, and held that the corporations were agents of the partnerships, and therefore should be disregarded for tax purposes. *Bollinger v. Commissioner*, T.C. Memo. 1984-560. The Court of Appeals for the Sixth Circuit affirmed, 807 F.2d 65 (6th Cir. 1986), and the Supreme Court of the United States affirmed the Sixth Circuit.

In *Bollinger*, the Supreme Court "decline[d] to parse the text of *National Carbide* as though that were itself the governing statute," 485 U.S. at 349, and seemed to replace the six-factor *National Carbide* test with a simplified three-factor test, stating:

> It seems to us that the genuineness of the agency relationship is adequately assured, and tax-avoiding manipulation adequately avoided, when the fact that the corporation is acting as agent for its shareholders with respect to a particular asset is set forth in a written agreement at the time the asset is acquired, the corporation functions as agent and not principal with respect to the asset for all purposes, and the corporation is held out as the agent and not principal in all dealings with third parties relating to the asset.

Id. at 349–50.

The Court held that the partnerships were the owners of the complexes for federal income tax purposes, even though Bollinger controlled the corporation, because it found that agency relationships existed between the corporation and the partnerships in both form and substance. First, each written agreement between a partnership and the corporation provided that the corporation "would hold such property as nominee and agent for" the respective partnership. *Id.* at 345. Second, the corporation functioned only as the partnerships' agent with respect to each apartment complex. The Court noted that "the corporation had no assets, liabilities, employees, or bank accounts." *Id.* at 343. Third, the corporation was represented to third parties to be a mere agent. *See id.* at 345. Thus, the *Bollinger* taxpayers avoided corporate taxation.

[D] Disguised Dividends

Corporations do not receive a deduction under the federal income tax for dividends distributed to shareholders. Dividends[17] therefore generally give

---

[17] As discussed in Chapter 4, "dividend" is a term of art, generally referring to distributions to stockholders out of a corporation's "earnings and profits." *See* I.R.C. § 316(a).

rise to two levels of taxation—corporate profits are first taxed at the corporate level and then again to the extent the remaining profits are distributed to shareholders.[18] Corporations are allowed to deduct certain other payments, notably interest and "reasonable" compensation for services, and shareholders may also serve as lenders to and/or employees of the corporation. Because corporations have a tax incentive to make deductible payments rather than nondeductible ones, there traditionally has been some tendency for corporations to treat payments to shareholder/creditors and shareholder/employees as interest or salary payments rather than as distributions in the nature of dividends. Of course, the playing field has changed now that most dividends received by individuals are taxed at reduced rates. See I.R.C. §§ 61, 1(h)(3)(B), (11). However, the IRS traditionally has recharacterized some purportedly deductible payments as nondeductible distributions to stockholders that may be taxed as dividends.

[1] Introduction to Debt Versus Equity

In general, a corporation can raise capital in two ways: debt (notes, bonds, debentures) and equity (stock). As indicated above, because interest on debt is deductible by the corporation, see I.R.C. § 163(a), whereas dividends paid on stock are not, there has traditionally been some incentive for a corporation to use debt rather than equity to raise capital. Chapter 3 explores the multi-factor tests used to distinguish debt from equity and to recharacterize purported debt as equity.

[2] Dividends Disguised as Salary

For publicly held corporations, section 162(m) generally limits deductibility of salary over $1 million paid to certain employees, subject to certain performance-based exceptions. There is no such restriction on closely held corporations. In closely held corporations where shareholders are also employees, shareholders have at times sought to have the corporation distribute its profits in the form of higher salaries rather than dividends, in order to allow a corporate-level deduction for amounts paid out. The IRS may respond by recharacterizing purported salary as dividend distributions. *See, e.g., Exacto Spring Corp. v. Commissioner*, 196 F.3d 833 (7th Cir. 1999).

Of course, salary is subject to employment taxes. In addition, as discussed above, under current law, the federal income tax rate applicable to an individual's dividends will generally be less than the federal income tax rate applicable to that individual's salary. The incentive to disguise dividends as salary is therefore much lower than it used to be.

---

[18] As indicated above, corporate shareholders benefit from a dividends received deduction, *see* I.R.C. § 243, so as to avoid triple taxation. The dividends received deduction and related issues are discussed in § 4.04 of Chapter 4.

[E] Introduction to the Integration of Corporate and Shareholder-Level Taxes

As the current reduced rate of tax on most dividends received by individuals may suggest, double taxation of corporate income is not a given. At first blush, it may seem that elimination of double taxation would merely require elimination of one of the two layers of corporate tax: the corporate-level tax or the shareholder-level tax. The reality is far more complicated, however. Exempting all dividends or all corporate earnings from taxation would provide ample opportunities for well-advised taxpayers to reduce a single-level tax to no tax at all, as you will see from the transactions discussed in this book.

Chapter 15 surveys the major proposals for corporate integration, including those discussed by the Treasury Department in its report entitled, *Report on Integration of the Individual and Corporate Tax Systems: Taxing Business Income Once* (1992) and the American Law Institute's *Reporter's Study of Corporate Integration* (1993) (Alvin C. Warren, Jr., Reporter). Chapter 15 also discusses President George W. Bush's 2003 proposal for a dividends exclusion method of integration. *See Treasury Releases Details of the President's Dividend Exclusion Proposal*, KD-3781 (Jan. 21, 2003), available at www.ustreas.gov/press/releases/kd3781.htm. President Bush's proposal was not adopted, but Congress provided for application of preferential capital gains rates to most dividends received by individuals, as indicated above. That reduction in the shareholder-level tax is effectively a form of partial integration, as Chapter 15 explains.

§ 1.03 The Relevance of Sale or Exchange Treatment to Corporate Taxation

As you will see in subsequent chapters of this book, a number of issues in corporate tax involve characterization of a transaction as either a distribution taxable as a "dividend" on the one hand or as a "sale or exchange of property" on the other hand. *See, e.g.,* I.R.C. § 302(a), (d). As you may have studied in an Income Tax course, realized "gain from the sale or other disposition of property" is the amount by which the amount realized exceeds the taxpayer's adjusted basis in the property, and realized loss is the amount by which the taxpayer's adjusted basis in the property exceeds the amount realized. I.R.C. § 1001(a). Sale or exchange treatment therefore typically lowers the amount subject to tax because return of capital (recovery of basis) occurs first.

> *Example 1.5*: Finite Corp. has two shareholders, Greta and Harold. Harold, who has a basis in his shares of $30, sells them for $100. Harold has taxable gain of $70 ($100 − $30).

Gain from the sale or exchange of a "capital asset" constitutes "capital gain." *See* I.R.C. § 1222. The term "capital asset" includes most stock. *See* I.R.C. § 1221(a). Thus, in Example 1.5, Harold's $70 gain is capital in character. Individuals benefit from preferential rates applicable to certain capital gains, typically those on assets held for more than one year.[19] *See* I.R.C. §§ 1(h)(1), 1222.

Dividends, which, as discussed in Chapter 4, essentially are distributions of corporate profits, are taxed without first allowing recovery of basis. Under prior law, they were taxed as ordinary income. Under current law, individuals' qualified dividends are included in "adjusted net capital gain," so they qualify for the same preferential capital gains rates that the profit on a sale of stock would, for example. Individuals thus currently have less incentive to prefer sale or exchange characterization to dividend characterization than they once did.

Corporate shareholders do not face a reduced rate of tax on dividends or capital gains, but, as discussed in Chapter 4, they benefit from a dividends received deduction that results in an exclusion from taxable income of all or part of each dividend received. Nonetheless, characterization of a transaction as a sale or exchange is beneficial even to corporate shareholders in some circumstances because of the basis offset that accompanies sale or exchange treatment. With a high enough basis, a sale or exchange, unlike a dividend, can even give rise to a loss for tax purposes.[20]

§ 1.04 Introduction to the Judicial Doctrines Backstopping the Corporate Tax System

Some transactions that apparently meet the letter of the law for favorable tax treatment at least arguably fail to comply with the intent of the law. As a result, courts have developed several doctrines that attempt to ferret out abusive transactions that do not qualify for the beneficial tax treatment sought. These doctrines arise in a wide variety of corporate tax cases, often overlap, and have become particularly important with respect to corporate tax shelters, which are discussed in Chapter 16.

[A] Substance Over Form

Compliance with the formalities of a corporate tax provision typically is required for favorable results allowed by that provision to apply. However, formal compliance with a provision is not necessarily sufficient. The substance of a transaction can triumph over its form, so that if a transaction complies with the letter of a statute but in substance violates it, the tax consequences of the transaction may be different than those that would result from a mechanical application of the statute. The IRS may raise the

---

[19] Under current law, there is no corporate capital gains preference. *See* I.R.C. §§ 11(b)(1), 1201.

[20] Note, however, that capital losses face limits on their deductibility. A corporation can only deduct capital losses to the extent of capital gains. I.R.C. § 1211(a). Individuals may offset their capital losses not only against capital gains but also against up to $3,000 of ordinary income. I.R.C. § 1211(b). Section 1211 disallows a current deduction of excess capital losses but section 1212 permits them to be applied to certain other taxable years.

substance-over-form doctrine in an effort to redetermine the tax consequences of a transaction engineered by the taxpayer. Courts generally are less sympathetic to taxpayers seeking to ignore the form of the transaction because, after all, it is the taxpayer that chose the form. Because substance-over-form often is a one-way sword, taxpayers are well advised to plan carefully, choosing the optimal form (consistent with the substance) up front, rather than attempting later to disavow the chosen form.

[B] Sham Transaction Doctrine

> Courts have recognized two basic types of sham transactions. Shams in fact are transactions that never occurred. In such shams, taxpayers claim deductions for transactions that have been created on paper but which never took place. Shams in substance are transactions that actually occurred but which lack the substance their form represents. *Gregory* [*v. Helvering*, 69 F.2d 809 (2d Cir. 1934), 293 U.S. 465 (1935)], for example, involved a substantive sham.

Kirchman v. Commissioner, 862 F.2d 1486, 1492 (11th Cir. 1989). "Shams in substance" often are transactions that do not pass muster under the related doctrine of economic substance, discussed below. For example, in *Winn-Dixie Stores, Inc. v. Commissioner*, 254 F.3d 1313 (11th Cir. 2001), *cert. denied*, 535 U.S. 986 (2002), the Court of Appeals for the Eleventh Circuit stated, "[the sham transaction] doctrine provides that a transaction is not entitled to tax respect if it lacks economic effects or substance other than the generation of tax benefits, or if the transaction serves no business purpose." *Id.* at 1316; *see also ACM Partnership v. Commissioner*, 157 F.3d 231, 248 n.31 (3d Cir. 1998); *Rice's Toyota World v. Commissioner*, 752 F.2d 89, 91 (4th Cir. 1985).

[C] Business Purpose

"Under the business purpose doctrine, if a transaction lacks a profit potential aside from its tax effects, courts disallow what the Code otherwise sanctions." Jay A. Soled, *Use of Judicial Doctrines in Resolving Transfer Tax Controversies*, 42 B.C. L. REV. 587, 593–94 (2001). The doctrine is widely understood to have originated in the landmark case of *Gregory v. Helvering*, 69 F.2d 809 (2d Cir. 1934), *aff'd*, 293 U.S. 465 (1935). In *Gregory*, the Supreme Court referred to the transaction at issue there as "an operation having no business or corporate purpose—a mere device which put on the form of a corporate reorganization as a disguise for concealing its real character, and the sole object and accomplishment of which was the consummation of a preconceived plan, not to reorganize a business or any part of a business, but to transfer a parcel of corporate shares to the petitioner." *Gregory*, 293 U.S. at 469. Business purpose has since become an express requirement for corporate reorganizations under the Treasury Regulations under section 368. *See* Treas. Reg. § 1.368-1(c) (last sentence).

In some cases, Congress has provided for favorable tax treatment only where a *bona fide* business purpose is present. Section 357, which is discussed in Chapter 2, provides an example. It generally exempts certain liability relief from being treated as the receipt of money or other property, but under section 357(b), the liability relief does not get that favorable treatment:

> [i]f, taking into consideration the nature of the liability and the circumstances in the light of which the arrangement for the assumption was made, it appears that the principal purpose of the taxpayer with respect to the assumption . . .
>
> (A) was a purpose to avoid Federal income tax on the exchange, or
>
> (B) if not such purpose, was not a bona fide business purpose . . . .

I.R.C. § 357(b)(1). Note that this section requires not only a *bona fide* business purpose as the principal purpose but also the absence of a tax avoidance purpose as the principal purpose. As this suggests, a tax avoidance purpose is not a "business" purpose.

[D]   Economic Substance

The "economic substance" doctrine has its origins in a number of classic cases, particularly *Gregory v. Helvering*, 293 U.S. 465 (1935), mentioned above, which is often cited by courts and commentators discussing or applying the doctrine.[21] It has taken on particular importance in recent tax shelter litigation, discussed in Chapter 16. Congress has considered codifying the economic substance doctrine, but, thus far, the doctrine remains uncodified.[22] *See* James M. Delaney, *Where Ethics Merge With Substantive Law—An Analysis of Tax Motivated Transactions*, 38 Ind. L. Rev. 295, 309 (2005).

Recent court decisions have described the economic substance doctrine as having both (1) an objective portion that focuses on the non-tax economic effects of the transaction and (2) a subjective portion that considers the taxpayer's "business purpose" for the transaction. *See, e.g., Long Term Capital Holdings v. United States*, 330 F. Supp. 2d 122, 171–72 (D. Conn. 2004); *ACM Partnership v. Commissioner*, 157 F.3d 231, 247–48 (3d Cir. 1998), *cert. denied*, 526 U.S. 1017 (1999); *see also* Joseph Bankman, *The Economic Substance Doctrine*, 74 S. Cal. L. Rev. 5, 9–10 (2000). The subjective portion necessarily will "look to objective indicia of intent:

---

[21] *Gregory v. Helvering*, which involved a transaction structured as a reorganization, is discussed in Chapter 11.

[22] For further reading on the issues involved in considering the codification of doctrines such as the economic substance doctrine, see, e.g., Ellen P. Aprill, *Tax Shelters, Tax Law, and Morality: Codifying Judicial Doctrines*, 54 SMU L. Rev. 9 (2001); Steven A. Bank, *Codifying Judicial Doctrines: No Cure for Rules But More Rules?*, 54 SMU L. Rev. 37 (2001).

contemporaneous documents, evidence of meetings, and the like." Bankman, *supra*, at 27. The business purpose requirement is also sometimes considered a separate doctrine.

> Courts have without exception insisted that the two legs [of the economic substance doctrine] are interrelated; however, courts have also stated that a transaction that has objective economic substance will be respected for tax purposes, regardless of the taxpayer's motivation. Courts are split as to whether a transaction that has subjective but not objective economic substance should be respected for tax purposes. In practical terms, then, the tests are interrelated in those cases in which evidence as to objective intent is inconclusive. In such cases, strong but not dispositive evidence of objective substance can offset weak evidence of subjective substance, and vice versa.

Id. at 26–27 (footnotes omitted).

Several scholars have argued that the government should make technical arguments before resorting to use of the economic substance doctrine. *See, e.g,* Karen Burke, *Deconstructing Black & Decker's Contingent Liability Shelter: A Statutory Analysis*, 108 TAX NOTES 211, 221 (2005); George K. Yin, *The Problem of Corporate Tax Shelters: Uncertain Dimensions, Unwise Approaches*, 55 TAX L. REV. 405, 407 (2002). Tax commentator Lee Sheppard explains:

> Throwing the economic substance doctrine at anything that moves is one of those instances [in which "what the litigators want is inimical to the sound development of the law"]. This tactic risks cheapening the economic substance doctrine, even if it does win cases. The economic substance doctrine is not a freestanding all-purpose answer to everything the IRS does not like. It is a doctrine of statutory interpretation that says the taxpayer is not entitled to the benefit of the statute that it seeks to abuse, even if it has a technical argument for the result. That is the way Judge Learned Hand decided *Gregory* [*v. Helvering*, 69 F.2d 809 (2d Cir. 1934), *aff'd*, 293 U.S. 465 (1935)].

Lee A. Sheppard, *Economic Substance Abuse*, 89 TAX NOTES 1095, 1099–1100 (2000).

[E] The Step-Transaction Doctrine

[1] In General

Because many corporate transactions involve multiple steps, determining where a transaction begins and ends may in turn determine the proper tax treatment. The step-transaction doctrine consists of three judicially developed tests to determine whether apparently or purportedly separate steps are in fact part of an integrated whole that forms "the transaction." More than one test may apply to the same set of facts.

[2] The Three Tests for a "Step Transaction"

[a] Binding Commitment Test

A binding contract or commitment to engage in step two (or three) that is in existence at the time of step one almost certainly will result in a collapsing of the steps into a single transaction.[23]

Example 1.6: Isaac, Janet, and Kevin plan to incorporate a corporation. Prior to doing so, they enter into a contract with Lisa to transfer 25 percent of the corporation's shares to her, once Lisa does all of the work necessary to organize the corporation and issue shares. Lisa will almost certainly be considered a member of the group organizing the corporation.

The binding commitment test has been referred to as "the most straight-forward and the least followed," Joshua D. Rosenberg, *Tax Avoidance and Income Measurement*, 87 MICH. L. REV. 365, 404 (1988); it "is invoked less frequently than the other two tests." Jeffrey L. Kwall & Kristina Maynard, *Dethroning King Enterprises*, 58 TAX LAW. 1, 13 (2004).

[b] Mutual-Interdependence Test

Absent an *ex ante* binding commitment to engage in step two or subsequent steps, those steps may still be amalgamated with step one to constitute a single transaction, if step one and the subsequent step (or steps) are so interdependent that the legal relationships created by the first step would have been pointless without completion of the series.

Example 1.7: Mary, Ned, and Oliver plan to incorporate a corporation for a new business venture. Mary and Ned both have appreciated property to contribute. Oliver only has services to contribute. In an attempt to achieve nonrecognition on the transfer of his property, Ned transfers cash to Oliver in a transaction structured as a loan, and a few weeks later, Oliver contributes the cash to the corporation, along with the services. Shortly after incorporation, the corporation buys back (redeems) the portion of Oliver's shares equal in value to the cash, and Oliver uses the cash to pay off the loan from Ned. The purported loan and redemption will likely be treated as components of the incorporation transaction rather than as separate transactions.

The mutual-interdependence test has been described as:

> essentially convert[ing] the business purpose doctrine into a test for application of the step transaction doctrine. . . . [T]his test incorporates the business purpose doctrine by segregating actions where each step was motivated by a business purpose existing independent of the other contemplated steps, and integrating steps where several "unnecessary" steps were taken only in contemplation of the others and without any independent business purpose.

---

[23] Examples 1.6 through 1.8 relate to the organization of a corporation, a topic that is a focus of Chapter 2. That chapter discusses in detail the requirements of section 351, which generally allows nonrecognition to transferors of property who control a corporation.

Rosenberg, *supra*, at 409 (footnotes omitted). It is "[t]he most widely used test." Kwall & Maynard, *supra*, at 13.

[c] End Result Test

The third test sometimes used under the step-transaction doctrine is the end result test. It provides that separate steps may be combined if they were prearranged components of a single transaction in which the parties intended from the outset to reach a particular result. "The end result test is the most flexible of the three alternative tests and allows the court to determine the substance of the transaction through the subjective intent of the parties." *Id.* at 14.

> *Example 1.8*: Pat, Quincy, and Rhonda plan to organize a corporation for a new business venture. They plan for the three of them to be equal shareholders in the corporation. In December, Pat and Quincy contribute appreciated property in return for 100 shares each of voting common stock in the newly organized corporation. In January, Rhonda performs services to establish and promote the business, and receives 100 shares of voting common stock in the corporation. Rhonda likely will be considered a member of the group organizing the corporation because the issuance of shares to make her an equal shareholder was intended from the beginning.

§ 1.05 Conclusion

This chapter has provided an overview of the corporation as a separate entity and the two levels of taxation that can result when profits taxed at the corporate level are also taxed to shareholders. The desire to avoid double taxation under Subchapter C has led some businesses to organize in non-corporate form or to organize as a corporation but make an election under Subchapter S. However, the corporate form remains popular, and large and publicly traded companies are hard-pressed to avoid Subchapter C.

Historically, some corporations experiencing double taxation, particularly small companies in which the shareholders also played other roles such as creditor or employee, tried to avoid the burden of double taxation through structuring payments in a non-dividend format, such as in the form of interest or salary. The current system, under which most dividends received by individuals are taxed at preferential capital gains rates, has reduced that incentive by reducing shareholder-level taxation. It has also reduced the importance of the capital gains/ordinary income distinction in corporate taxation. However, the marginal tax rates applicable to the corporation and the shareholders and their basis amounts are very important in determining how a transaction can be structured to achieve the most favorable tax result.

The application of preferential rates to individuals' dividends has not reduced the incentives for reduction of corporate-level taxes through means such as tax shelters or structuring corporate transactions so as to obtain the lowest possible tax cost. Judicial doctrines that require looking beyond the formalities of a transaction are as important to the determination of tax consequences as the technical provisions that may apply. They therefore reappear throughout the book in a variety of cases covering an array of corporate tax provisions.

Chapter 2

TAX CONSEQUENCES OF TRANSFERRING PROPERTY TO A NEW OR EXISTING CONTROLLED CORPORATION

§ 2.01 Introduction

The mere act of organizing a corporation and incorporating it under state law is not a taxable event. However, in order to capitalize a corporation, whether new or pre-existing, investors typically contribute money or other property in return for stock of the corporation.[1] The contribution of money in return for stock is a fairly straightforward stock purchase. The purchaser simply takes a cost basis in the stock under section 1012. However, a corporation recognizes no gain or loss on the exchange of its own stock for money or other property. *See* I.R.C. § 1032; *see also* Treas. Reg. § 1.1032-1(a).

Barter exchanges are slightly more complicated. An investor exchanging non-cash property for stock realizes gain or loss on that property measured by the difference between the amount realized and his or her basis in that property. That is, the investor's realized gain or loss will be the difference between the basis of the property he or she contributed to the corporation and the value of the stock received—which generally will equal the value of the property exchanged. *See Philadelphia Park Amusement Co. v. United States*, 130 Ct. Cl. 166 (1954). In the corporate tax context, barter exchanges include the exchange of assets for stock in a corporation. Such an exchange may occur, for example, if someone who previously operated a sole proprietorship decides to incorporate the business.

---

[1] Contributions to the capital of a corporation without the accompanying grant of shares of stock are discussed in § 2.04, *infra*.

Example 2.1: Abe organizes a new, solely owned corporation, ABC, Inc. He contributes land to the corporation in exchange for 100 percent of the corporation's stock. Abe's basis in the land was $100,000, and its value at the time Abe contributed the land to ABC, Inc. was $175,000. Abe realizes $75,000 of gain because the value of the stock he received, $175,000 (determined by reference to the value of the land received in exchange), exceeded Abe's basis of $100,000 by $75,000.[2]

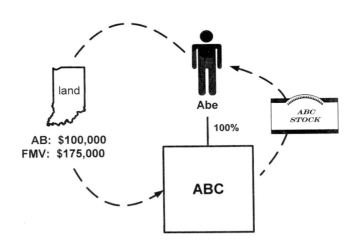

Absent a provision allowing exclusion of this $75,000 of realized gain (a "nonrecognition" provision), Abe would be required to *recognize* this realized gain, and thereby be taxed on the $75,000. This would discourage taxpayers from contributing appreciated property to corporations, which might impede businesses from adopting the corporate form. In addition, in the example above, Abe arguably has not truly divested himself of the land. His ownership of 100 percent of the shares of a corporation that owns only the land is equivalent to Abe's prior direct ownership of the land.[3]

In accordance with the notion of encouraging business formation and growth, section 351 allows investors to avoid taxation on the transfer of appreciated property to a corporation in return for stock—provided certain requirements are met. The basis rules applied in connection with section 351—section 358 for the transferors of property and section 362 for the

---

[2] This transaction is illustrated in the diagram on this page. Throughout this book, diagrams will use conventional illustrations, including boxes for corporations and lines to represent shareholders.

[3] Mere changes in form generally are not subject to taxation. *See* Treas. Reg. § 1.1001-1(a) (referring to recognition of "gain or loss realized from the conversion of property into cash, or from the exchange of property for other property differing materially either in kind or in extent"). However, this probably does not explain section 351. *See* Ronald H. Jensen, *Of Form and Substance: Tax-Free Incorporations and Other Transactions under Section 351*, 11 VA. TAX REV. 349, 375–96 (1991).

transferee corporation—are discussed below in §§ 2.02[A][3] and 2.03[B][1]. Note that section 1032, mentioned above, will always protect a corporation from tax consequences upon the issuance of its own stock in exchange for cash, other property, or even services, regardless of whether or not the investors recognize any gain or loss. *See* I.R.C. § 1032; Treas. Reg. § 1.1032-1(a).

§ 2.02   Tax Consequences to Shareholders

[A]   Nonrecognition Treatment and Corresponding Basis Rules

Section 351(a) provides: "No gain or loss shall be recognized if *property* is transferred to a corporation by *one or more persons* solely in exchange for stock in such corporation and *immediately after* the exchange such person or persons are in *control* (as defined in section 368(c)) of the corporation." I.R.C. § 351(a) (emphasis added). That is, if a transfer meets all of the requirements embodied in section 351(a), the transferors (who already are or become shareholders in the corporation) are entitled to nonrecognition of any gain or loss realized on the transfer.[4] Note, however, that section 351 does not apply to a transfer of property to an "investment company." *See* I.R.C. § 351(e).

As its language indicates, section 351 does not limit the requirements for nonrecognition to the narrow facts of Example 2.1, above. Rather, section 351 allows nonrecognition even when the property transfer involves a *group* of investors rather than a single investor, and, as discussed in § 2.02[A][1][b], even when the investors end up with a mere 80 percent of the corporation's stock, rather than 100 percent. Transfers by multiple transferors also need not be simultaneous in "a situation where the rights of the parties have been previously defined and the execution of the agreement proceeds with an expedition consistent with orderly procedure." Treas. Reg. § 1.351-1(a)(1).

In addition, as discussed below, section 351(b) addresses the situation of investors who receive from the corporation not only stock, but debt securities, money, or other property (that is, "boot"), as well. This leeway allows section 351 to accommodate the practical realities of transfers to controlled corporations.

---

[4] Regulations proposed in March of 2005 address transactions by insolvent companies, providing in part that "[s]tock will not be treated as issued for property" if it is has *no net value*—that is, if either "[t]he fair market value of the transferred property does not exceed the sum of the amount of liabilities of the transferor that are assumed by the transferee in connection with the transfer and the amount of any money and the fair market value of any other property . . . received by the transferor in connection with the transfer. . . ." or "[t]he fair market value of the assets of the transferee does not exceed the amount of its liabilities immediately after the transfer." Prop. Treas. Reg. § 1.351-1(a)(1)(iii). The proposed regulations would apply to "transfers occurring after the date these proposed regulations are published as final regulations in the Federal Register." Prop. Treas. Reg. § 1.351-1(a)(1)(iv).

[1]   General Nonrecognition Treatment Under Section 351

As the language of section 351 indicates, for investors to avoid recognition on the exchange of appreciated property for stock, section 351 requires that "immediately after" the transfer of "property" to the corporation, the investor group be in "control" of the corporation, which, generally speaking, requires ownership of 80 percent or more of the voting power and 80 percent of the total number of shares of nonvoting stock. *See* I.R.C. §§ 351, 368(c). The "property," "transferor group," "immediately after," and "control" requirements are discussed in turn below.

[a]   "Property"

"Property" is not defined in section 351 except by exclusion in subsection (d): "For purposes of this section, stock issued for— (1) services, (2) indebtedness of the transferee corporation which is not evidenced by a security, or (3) interest on indebtedness of the transferee corporation which accrued on or after the beginning of the transferor's holding period for the debt, shall not be considered as issued in return for property."[5] Cash, intangibles, personalty, and realty are all considered property for purposes of section 351. By contrast, under section 351(d), someone who performs services for the corporation, such as organizing it, has not transferred property within the meaning of section 351. Note that regardless of whether section 351 applies to the overall transaction, that service provider will have ordinary income in the amount of the stock received. *See* I.R.C. §§ 61(a)(1), 83.

Hempt Bros. v. United States, 490 F.2d 1172 (3d Cir.), *cert. denied*, 419 U.S. 826 (1974), interpreted the applicability of section 351(d) to accounts receivable and inventory. In that case, a partnership had transferred its assets to a newly organized corporation, Hempt Bros. (the taxpayer), solely in exchange for stock. The assets transferred from the partnership to the corporation included accounts receivable in the amount of $662,824.40. If section 351 applied to the transfer of accounts receivable to the corporation, then, under section 362 (discussed below), the corporation would take them at their basis in the hands of the partnership. That basis was zero because the partnership had used the cash method of accounting, so it had not yet taken the receivables into income. Therefore, upon collection of the receivables, the corporation would have gross income.

Hempt Bros. therefore argued that "property" under section 351 did not include accounts receivable. The Third Circuit disagreed. The court noted that "[r]eceivables possess the usual capabilities and attributes associated with jurisprudential concepts of property law. They may be identified, valued, and transferred." *Id.* at 1175. Furthermore, such receivables are

---

[5] Section 317(a), which provides a definition of the word "property," does not apply to section 351 transactions because the application of section 317(a) is limited to Part I of Subchapter C. *See* I.R.C. § 317(a). Section 351 is in Part III of Subchapter C.

"commonly thought of in the commercial world as a positive business asset."
Id. Hempt Bros. also argued that the assignment of income doctrine should
place the tax liability on the transferor of property (in this case, the
partnership), not the transferee (Hempt Bros.). Again, the court disagreed.
It found that the assignment of income doctrine did not override section
351, given "the broad Congressional interest in facilitating the incorporation of ongoing businesses." *Id.* at 1178.

[b] "Control"

The "control" requirement for purposes of section 351 is borrowed from
the corporate reorganization definitional provision, section 368. Section 368(c)
provides, in relevant part, "the term 'control' means the ownership of stock
possessing at least 80 percent of the total combined voting power of all
classes of stock entitled to vote and at least 80 percent of the total number
of shares of all other classes of stock of the corporation." Note that this
section contains two different 80-percent tests that must *both* be met to
constitute control: a voting power test and a numerical test that applies
to nonvoting shares. The IRS has ruled that *each* nonvoting class of stock
must meet the numerical 80-percent test. Rev. Rul. 59-259, 1959-2 C.B. 115.

Note also that although control is tested after the transaction, previously owned shares generally are counted (subject to the "accommodation transferor" exception, discussed below).

Example 2.2: Barbara owns 20 of the 30 outstanding shares of the only class of X, Inc. stock, which is voting common stock. Cathy owns the other 10 shares. Cathy and David agree to each contribute $100,000 worth of property to X, Inc. in return for 35 shares of stock each. Note that the issuance of these 70 shares will increase the number of outstanding shares to 100. After the transfers by Cathy and David, Cathy owns 45 shares and David owns 35 shares of the X, Inc. stock, with the remaining 20 shares still owned by Barbara. Thus, after the transfers, Cathy and David together own 80 percent of X, Inc.'s stock (80 out of 100 shares). Therefore, Cathy and David's transfers will qualify under section 351. The diagram below illustrates both the "before" picture (on the left) and the transfer itself, with the shareholders' "after" ownership reflected on the right.

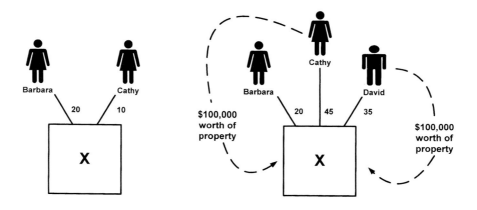

Note further that, although control was acquired in the transaction in Example 2.2, that is not a requirement for section 351 to apply.

Example 2.3: Ed owns 90 of the 95 outstanding shares of Y, Inc. stock. Fran owns the other five shares. Ed contributes appreciated real estate to Y, Inc. in return for five more shares of stock. The transfer is illustrated in the diagram below. After the transfer, Ed owns 95 of the 100 outstanding shares, which constitutes "control" of Y, Inc. Even though Ed already had control of Y, Inc. prior to the transfer of the real property, the transfer qualifies under section 351.

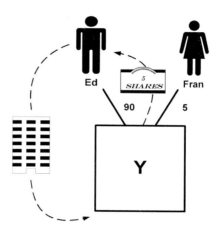

[c]   The "Transferor Group"

[i]   In General

As discussed above, section 351(a) provides that "no gain or loss shall be recognized if property is transferred to a corporation by *one or more persons*" and certain other requirements are met. Therefore, as Example 2.2 illustrated, the transferors of property may be a group rather than a single individual or entity. Section 351 also "does not necessarily require simultaneous exchanges by two or more persons, but comprehends a situation where the rights of the parties have been previously defined and the execution of the agreement proceeds with an expedition consistent with orderly procedure." Treas. Reg. § 1.351-1(a)(1).

The step-transaction doctrine, which was outlined in Chapter 1 and is discussed further below in § 2.02[A][1][d][ii], may be used to determine whether or not multiple transfers of property are all part of a single transaction. The primary relevance of this question is in ascertaining whether "control" exists immediately after the transaction.

[ii]   The "Accommodation Transferor" Problem

As Examples 2.2 and 2.3 indicate, pre-existing stock ownership is taken into account in determining control. In fact, in Example 2.2, Cathy's 10 previously owned shares were an essential part of the "control" Cathy and

David obtained after they each received 35 shares in return for property. Similarly, in Example 2.3, Ed's 90 previously owned shares were critical to the "control" he had after the transfer to Y, Inc.

What if, in Example 2.3, Fran, rather than Ed, were to have contributed the appreciated real estate in exchange for five more shares of Y, Inc. stock, as illustrated in the diagram below? In that case, Fran would have held only 10 shares out of 100, far short of "control" for purposes of section 351.

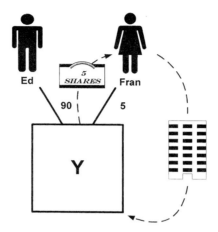

Unfortunately for Fran, she would have had to recognize any gain realized on the transfer of the real estate. It might occur to Fran that any property transfer Ed made in return for stock would qualify under section 351, as Example 2.3 implies. What if Ed were to contribute property—even a small amount—at the same time Fran made her contribution of the appreciated real estate? If Ed "accommodated" Fran in that way, perhaps contributing a small amount of money or other property in return for a single share of stock, while Fran contributed her appreciated property, would Fran be protected by section 351? It would *seem* that the two property transferors would together have "control" after the transaction: Ed would hold 91 of the 101 outstanding shares, and Fran would hold the other 10.

The Treasury Department was not pleased with the possibility that a *de minimis* transfer by a majority shareholder might bootstrap another party into obtaining nonrecognition. Consider the following regulation:

> Stock or securities issued for property which is of relatively small value in comparison to the value of the stock and securities already owned (or to be received for services) by the person who transferred such property, shall not be treated as having been issued in return for property if the primary purpose of the transfer is to qualify under this section the exchanges of property by other persons transferring property.

Treas. Reg. § 1.351-1(a)(1)(ii). Note that, although the regulation refers to "stock or securities," the Code has been amended since the regulation was promulgated so that only stock (not securities, which are debt instruments) may be received under section 351 without the recognition of gain.

Estate of Kamborian v. Commissioner, 469 F.2d 219 (1st Cir. 1972), provides a good illustration of how the regulation applies. In that case, four individuals owned 76 percent of the stock of X Corporation, and a trust held slightly over 13 percent of X Corporation stock. The same four individuals also owned 100 percent of stock in Y Corporation. For legitimate business reasons, X Corporation decided to acquire Y Corporation in exchange for shares in X Corporation. Thus, the four individuals contributed their Y shares (which constitute property under section 351) to X in return for X stock. Because, after the exchange, the individuals' stockholdings in X Corporation would constitute less than 80 percent in the aggregate, they entered into an agreement with the beneficiary of the trust whereby the trust would purchase a small amount of shares of X at the same time as the individuals' contribution of the Y shares to X. Accordingly, the four individuals contributed Y shares for X stock, while the trust contributed cash for X stock. After the transaction, the individuals' holdings in X aggregated 77.3 percent, but with the trust's holdings, the combined holdings exceeded 80 percent.

The IRS argued that the transaction did not qualify under section 351 because the transferors of property did not obtain at least 80 percent of the shares of X. That is, the IRS argued that the trust was not truly part of the transferor group. The IRS relied, in part, on regulation 1.351-1(a)(1)(ii), which was quoted above. The Court of Appeals for the First Circuit agreed with the IRS, and upheld the regulation as consistent with the statute.

The Court of Appeals noted that the term "property transferred" contemplates a single transaction, regardless of the number of participants. Accordingly, the court found that the transfers must have an economic connection, not be a mere "concatenation." *Id.* at 221. The court concluded that the four individuals, realizing that they were short of the "control" required immediately after the merger, "persuaded a shareholder of X, who was a complete stranger to Y, to make a token purchase of X shares." *Id.* at 222. The Court of Appeals further found that "[t]he trustees' desire to help the Y stockholders avoid taxes, warrantably found by the Tax Court to have been the primary motive for the trust's purchase, cannot be used to make a single transaction out of otherwise unrelated transfers." *Id.* (footnote omitted). Thus, the court held that the transaction did not constitute a tax-free exchange under section 351.

A Revenue Procedure provides that for IRS ruling purposes:

> When a person transfers property to a corporation in exchange for stock or securities of such corporation and the primary purpose of the transfer is to qualify under section 351 of the Code the exchanges of property by other persons transferring property, the property transferred will not be considered to be of relatively small

value, within the meaning of section 1.351-1(a)(1)(ii) of the regulations, if the fair market value of the property transferred is equal to, or in excess of, 10 percent of the fair market value of the stock and securities already owned (or to be received for services) by such person.

Rev. Proc. 77-37, 1977-2 C.B. 568, 570 § 3.07. Note that in Example 2.2 above, Cathy transferred $100,000 of property (in return for 35 shares of stock). One hundred thousand dollars ($100,000) is at least (here, much more than) 10 percent of the value of the 10 shares she already owned, so, under the Revenue Procedure, Cathy's transfer was not "of relatively small value."

[d] The "Immediately After" Requirement

[i] In General

The Tax Court has stated, "[t]he statutory words 'immediately after the exchange' require control for no longer period [than five days]; in fact, momentary control is sufficient." *American Bantam Car Co. v. Commissioner*, 11 T.C. 397, 404 (1948), *aff'd*, 177 F.2d 513 (3d Cir. 1949), *cert. denied*, 339 U.S. 920 (1950). However, that statement is subject to application of the step-transaction doctrine, which is discussed below.

[ii] Application of the Step-Transaction Doctrine

In *Intermountain Lumber Co. v. Commissioner*, 65 T.C. 1025, 1030 (1976), the taxpayer, Intermountain Lumber Co., was the parent company of S & W, Inc. S & W had been incorporated in 1964 by Shook, Wilson, and two other individuals. On the initial incorporation, the four individuals each received one share of S & W stock. Approximately eight days later, Shook deeded the sawmill site to S & W and received an additional 364 S & W shares. At the same time, Shook and Wilson entered a purchase agreement, under which Shook agreed to sell Wilson 182 shares of S & W stock at $500 per share, pursuant to a series of payments. As each payment was made, shares would be transferred from Shook to Wilson. The agreement gave Wilson the right to prepay and receive all 182 shares in advance. Wilson had the right to vote the 182 shares for the first year without purchasing them. *Id.* at 1026–28.

In *Intermountain Lumber Co.*, the usual positions of the taxpayer and the IRS were reversed because the taxpayer was not a shareholder who might be protected by section 351, but was Intermountain Lumber, the corporate parent of the transferee. If the transaction did not qualify under section 351, S & W would have a higher basis in the Sawmill properties—a fair market value basis determined in a taxable exchange, rather than a transferred basis determined under section 362. A higher asset basis would, in turn, support larger depreciation deductions. *See id.* at 1030. Therefore, Intermountain Lumber argued that the transaction incorporating S & W did not qualify under section 351, and the IRS argued that the transaction did qualify under section 351.

The applicability under section 351 turned on whether the property transferors had control of S & W "immediately after" the transaction. The Tax Court held that the transaction did not qualify under section 351 because Shook was the only property transferor, and Shook's preexisting contractual duty to transfer up to approximately 50 percent of the shares to a non-transferor of property (Wilson) eliminated 80-percent "control."

Although the Tax Court does not use step-transaction doctrine language, *Intermountain Lumber* provides an example of the "binding commitment" test, one of the tests used under the step-transaction doctrine to determine whether multiple steps are in fact part of a single transaction.[6] In *Intermountain Lumber*, the Tax Court considered Wilson's acquisition of shares from Shook part of the incorporation transaction because Shook had a preexisting contract to transfer certain shares in S & W corporation to Wilson. *See id.* at 1033. As a result, because Wilson was not a property transferor, the shares acquired by Wilson were not counted in determining "control" and Intermountain Lumber's argument that section 351 did not apply prevailed.

As discussed in Chapter 1, there are two other tests used to combine separate steps into a single transaction: the mutual-interdependence test and the end-result test.[7] The mutual-interdependence test asks: "Were the steps so interdependent that the legal relations created by one transaction would have been fruitless without a completion of the series?" *American Bantam Car Co.*, 11 T.C. at 405. The end-result test considers whether the ultimate result of the transaction was intended from the outset. *See King Enterprises, Inc. v. United States*, 189 Ct. Cl. 466, 475 (1969).

In *American Bantam Car Co.*, the taxpayer, American Bantam Car Company (ABC), was incorporated by a group of "associates" who had previously purchased the assets of American Austin Car Co. The incorporation of ABC essentially involved three principal transfers to ABC. *See American Bantam Car Co.*, 11 T.C. at 401–402.

---

[6] *See* § 1.04[E][2][a].

[7] *See* § 1.04[E][2][b], [c].

1. On June 3, 1936, the Associates transferred the American Austin Car assets and $500 in cash to ABC in return for 300,000 shares of common stock with one vote per share, as illustrated below. The non-cash assets had a value of $840,800 but a much lower basis. The 300,000 common shares were held in escrow.

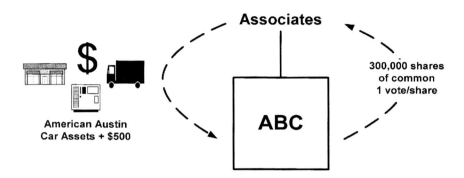

2. On June 8, 1936, the Associates entered into contracts with underwriters to sell convertible preferred stock with three votes per share, with payment to the underwriters in common stock when certain amounts of preferred stock had been sold. From October 1936 through October 1937, the underwriters sold to the public 83,618 shares of the preferred stock for a total amount of $866,410.

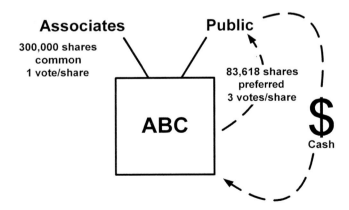

3. In October 1937, as compensation for underwriting services, the Associates transferred 87,900 shares of the common stock to an underwriter, Grant & Co.

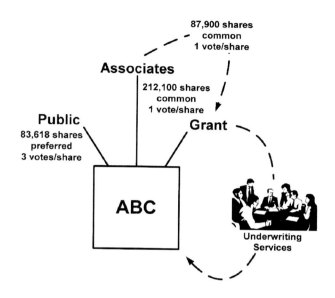

As in *Intermountain Lumber*, it was the corporate taxpayer, not the IRS, that argued that the transfer of property was not within section 351. ABC sought a cost basis in the assets contributed to it rather than the lower transferred basis it would receive under section 362; the higher basis would support larger depreciation deductions. ABC's argument was that the steps involved in issuing the corporation's stock should be considered part of a single, integrated transaction. *Id.* at 405. The IRS argued that each step should be viewed separately. The Associates owned 100 percent of the stock after the first step and were therefore "in control" of ABC after that step. Therefore, under the IRS's analysis, section 351 would apply.

The Tax Court agreed with the IRS, holding that the transfer of the stock to the underwriter, Grant, was not part of the same transaction as the transfer of property to ABC. It explained:

> First, there was no written contract prior to the exchange binding the associates to transfer stock to the underwriters. At the most, there was an informal oral understanding of a general plan contemplating the organization of a new corporation, the exchange of assets for stock, and marketing of preferred stock of the new corporation to the public. A written contract providing for the transfer of shares from the associates to the underwriters did not come until five days after the exchange. Secondly, when the transfer of shares to the underwriters was embodied specifically in a formal contract, the underwriters received no absolute right to ownership of the common

stock, but only when, as, and if, certain percentages of preferred stock were sold. How clearly contingent was the nature of their rights is illustrated by the fact that only one underwriter, Grant, met the terms of the agreement and became entitled to any shares. Thirdly, the necessity of placing the 300,000 shares in escrow with a bank is indicative of complete ownership of such stock by the associates following the exchange.

Id. at 406. Therefore, section 351 applied, and ABC did not obtain its larger depreciation deductions.

ABC's argument has an inherent problem, however. ABC's argument essentially was that the Associates transferred more than 20 percent of their stock to Grant, who was not a transferor of property. (Grant had contributed underwriting services.) Yet, ABC apparently did not consider all of the corporation's outstanding shares. Steps two and three above were intertwined because the transfer to Grant was contingent upon successful completion of sales to the public. After step three, Grant had 87,900 votes and the Associates were left with 212,100 votes. However, note that the public held the preferred stock, which had three votes per share, for a total of 250,854 votes in the 83,618 shares. Therefore, the Associates held approximately 38.5 percent of the votes, the public held 45.5 percent of the votes, and Grant had a mere 16 percent of the vote.

Did the public transfer property to ABC in return for stock? Yes—the public contributed cash in return for the preferred stock. Was the cash transfer by the public part of the same transaction as the Associates' transfer of the Austin Car assets? The Tax Court ruled that each step was separate. But, for ABC to argue that the transfer to Grant was part of the Associates' transaction with ABC, then surely the sale of shares to the public, upon which the transfer to Grant rested, was part of that transaction as well. *See* BORIS I. BITTKER & JAMES S. EUSTICE, FEDERAL INCOME TAXATION OF CORPORATIONS AND SHAREHOLDERS ¶ 3.09[2] n.188 (7th ed. 2000). Note that the presence or absence of intent to be part of the transferor group is irrelevant to section 351 analysis, so long as the transfers actually are part of a single transaction. Thus, on this analysis, even if ABC had convinced the Tax Court to consider all three steps a single transaction, it should still have lost the case.[8]

---

[8] Note that, "effective for qualified underwriting transactions occurring on or after May 1, 1996," Treas. Reg. § 1.351-1(a)(3)(ii):

> For the purpose of section 351, if a person acquires stock of a corporation from an underwriter in exchange for cash in a qualified underwriting transaction, the person who acquires stock from the underwriter is treated as transferring cash directly to the corporation in exchange for stock of the corporation and the underwriter is disregarded. A qualified underwriting transaction is a transaction in which a corporation issues stock for cash in an underwriting in which either the underwriter is an agent of the corporation or the underwriter's ownership of the stock is transitory.

Treas. Reg. § 1.351-1(a)(3)(i).

[e] Business Purpose

A section 351 transaction, like other transactions, must have a business purpose to be respected.[9] Thus, for example, one reason the IRS listed for denying the tax losses generated by a tax shelter known as the contingent liability shelter, which involves contribution to a corporation of property subject to contingent liabilities, is that "the purported § 351 exchange lacks sufficient business purpose to qualify as a § 351 exchange. . . ."[10] Notice 2001-17, 2001-1 C.B. 730, 731. Another situation in which the IRS might assert that a purported section 351 transaction lacks a sufficient business purpose is if an individual shareholder expecting a large dividend transfers the shares to a controlled corporation so that the dividend can be offset by the dividends received deduction available to corporations under section 243. See Rev. Rul. 60-331, 1960-2 C.B. 189; BITTKER & EUSTICE, *supra*, at ¶ 3.17[6].

[f] The Effects of the Receipt of "Boot"

[i] General Recognition Rules

Thus far, the section 351 transfers discussed have only involved receipt by the transferors of the type of property permitted to be received without recognition of gain or loss—stock. Although section 351 requires receipt of stock for a transaction to be covered by section 351, as indicated above, property transferors often receive additional property (such as securities, cash, or even realty or personalty) as well. Section 351(b) provides:

> If subsection (a) would apply to an exchange but for the fact that there is received, in addition to the stock permitted to be received under subsection (a), other property or money, then—
>
> (1) gain (if any) to such recipient shall be recognized, but not in excess of—
>
> (A) the amount of money received, plus
>
> (B) the fair market value of such other property received; and
>
> (2) no loss to such recipient shall be recognized.

In other words, section 351(b) relaxes the "solely in exchange for stock" restriction of section 351(a) and allows the receipt of "other property or money" but requires any gain realized by the property transferor to be recognized in the amount of the non-stock property ("boot") received. Anything received other than property permitted to be received without the recognition of gain or loss (under section 351, anything other than stock) is termed "boot" because the taxpayer has received not only permitted property but also something else "to boot."

---

[9] The business purpose doctrine is discussed in § 1.04[C] of Chapter 1.

[10] The contingent liability shelter is briefly described in § 2.02[A][2][b][ii][II] and is discussed in more detail in § 16.03[A] of Chapter 16.

Note that section 351 does not allow the recognition of loss, I.R.C. § 351(b)(2), and requires recognition of gain "if any" (subject to a cap, as explained below), I.R.C. § 351(b)(1). That means that only if gain is *realized* may it be recognized. Even then, realized gain is only recognized *to the extent of* "the amount of money received, plus . . . the fair market value of such other property received." I.R.C. § 351(b)(1).

Example 2.4: Glenda and Harold incorporate G & H, Inc. Glenda contributes land with a basis of $200,000 and a value of $300,000, and $50,000 cash. Harold contributes inventory with a basis of $250,000 and a value of $400,000. Glenda receives 50 shares for her $350,000 contribution. Harold receives 50 shares and $50,000 of cash for his $400,000 contribution.

Glenda realizes $100,000 of gain on the contribution of the land, but none of the gain realized is recognized because she received solely stock in return for her contribution, and section 351(a) therefore applies. Harold realizes $150,000 of gain on the transfer of the inventory. Section 351(b) applies to Harold because he not only received stock of G & H, Inc., but also received "boot" (here, cash). The $150,000 of gain realized is recognized only to the extent of the sum of money received ($50,000) and the fair market value of other property received (zero). Thus, Harold recognizes $50,000 of gain. (Because inventory is not a capital asset, the $50,000 of gain is ordinary income.)

For transfers occurring after June 8, 1997, section 351(g) provides that if a property transferor receives any "nonqualified preferred stock," section 351(a) (which applies to boot-free section 351 transactions) does not apply to that transferor, and only if that transferor also receives stock other than nonqualified preferred stock will 351(b) apply. The nonqualified preferred stock will then be treated as boot. Thus, nonqualified preferred stock is treated like notes or any other boot received by a property transferor.[11]

Nonqualified preferred stock is essentially debt-like preferred stock. In general, and subject to various exceptions, preferred stock constitutes nonqualified preferred stock if the stock is likely or required to be redeemed by the corporation or a related person, or if the dividend rate on the stock varies with "interest rates, commodity prices, or other similar indices." I.R.C. § 351(g)(2)(A).

[ii]   Character of Gain Recognized

As discussed in Chapter 1, Federal income tax law characterizes gains and losses as "ordinary" or "capital," with individuals' capital gains benefitting from preferential rates and capital losses of both corporations and individuals experiencing limitations on deductibility.[12] Therefore, the characterization of gain or loss can be very important.

---

[11] However, nonqualified preferred stock remains "stock" for purposes of determining "control" under section 368(c) in the absence of regulations providing otherwise.

[12] *See* § 1.03.

[I] Allocation of Boot

Example 2.4 considered a situation in which a property transferor who received boot transferred only one asset. What if that transferor contributed multiple assets to the corporation? How, then, would the boot be allocated among the various assets (including assets with built-in losses) to recognize the appropriate amount and character of gain?

In Revenue Ruling 68-55, 1968-1 C.B. 140, Corporation Y was organized by Corporation X and individual A. (A owned no stock in X.) A transferred $20 in cash in exchange for $20 worth of stock in Y, and X transferred three assets and received stock in Y worth $100, as well as $10 in cash. X's transfers are summarized in the table below.

ASSET	BASIS	FMV	REALIZED GAIN/LOSS, REFLECTING CHARACTER AND HOLDING PERIOD
1	$40	$22	$18 of long-term capital loss realized
2	$20	$33	$13 of short-term capital gain realized
3	$25	$55	$30 of ordinary income realized

The issue in the Revenue Ruling was the correct method for determining the amount and character of gain to be recognized by X under section 351(b). The IRS noted that "each asset transferred must be considered to have been separately exchanged." *Id.* at 141. The correct method for determining the amount and character of gain is thus the "asset-by-asset" approach. This approach requires that "the fair market value of each category of consideration received must be separately allocated to the transferred assets in proportion to the relative fair market values of the transferred assets." *Id.* Thus, the boot of $10 that X received had to be allocated to the three assets in proportion to their fair market values. That is as follows:

ASSET	FMV	PERCENT OF TOTAL VALUE	ALLOCATION OF BOOT
1	$22	20%	$2
2	$33	30%	$3
3	$55	50%	$5
	TOTAL: $110		TOTAL: $10

Comparing the gain or loss realized on each asset with the boot allocated to each asset provides the following results:

ASSET	REALIZED GAIN/LOSS AND CHARACTER	ALLOCATION OF BOOT	RECOGNIZED GAIN/LOSS AND CHARACTER
1	$18 of capital loss realized	$2	No gain (or loss) recognized
2	$13 of capital gain realized	$3	$3 of capital gain recognized (short-term capital gain)
3	$30 of ordinary income realized	$5	$5 of ordinary income recognized

Note that, as a result of the IRS's approach, only $8 of the $10 of realized gain is recognized because the loss asset "absorbed" $2 of the boot. Note also that the holding period (relevant for treatment of capital gain) was also determined asset by asset under the Revenue Ruling.[13]

[II] Special Characterization Issues

Specific Code provisions apply to recharacterize as ordinary income gains recognized on the transfer of depreciable property in section 351 transactions that would otherwise be capital in character. First, sections 1245 and 1250 provide for "recapture" as ordinary income of depreciation deductions on the disposition of depreciable property. These sections apply in section 351 transactions with respect to gain recognized on the transfer of depreciable property to the corporation (whether gain is recognized because of a property transferor's receipt of boot or because, as discussed below, section 357(c) applies because a transferred asset has liabilities that exceed basis).

> *Example 2.5*: Iris, Jason, and Kim incorporate IJK, Inc. Iris contributes inventory with a basis of $250,000 and a value of $300,000, and receives 100 shares. Jason contributes a building with a basis of $200,000 and a value of $350,000 that he had held as investment property. Jason had taken depreciation deductions of $30,000 with respect to the building. In the incorporation transaction, Jason receives 100 shares of IJK, Inc. and $50,000 of cash. Kim contributes cash of $300,000 and receives 100 shares.
>
> Section 351 applies to this transaction because the three property transferors together control IJK, Inc. Iris realizes $50,000 of gain on the contribution of the inventory, but none of her realized gain is recognized because section 351(a) applies to her. Jason realizes $150,000 of gain on the transfer of the building. Section 351(b) applies to Jason because he not only received stock but also boot. The $150,000 of gain realized is recognized only to the extent of the sum of the boot received ($50,000). That $50,000 of gain ordinarily would be capital because Jason exchanged a capital asset. However, under section 1250, $30,000 of the gain will be taxed as ordinary income, and only the remaining $20,000 is capital gain.

Section 1239 also applies to recharacterize as ordinary income gain recognized in certain section 351 transactions, namely those involving the transfer of property to a "related person" if the property will be depreciable by that person. Related persons include a shareholder and "a corporation more than 50 percent of the value of the outstanding stock of which is owned (directly or indirectly) by or for such person." I.R.C. § 1239(c)(1)(A); *see also* I.R.C. § 1239(b)(1); Treas. Reg. § 1.1239-1(c)(3)(ii).

> *Example 2.6*: Lyle incorporates Z Corporation, contributing a building with a basis of $200,000 and a value of $300,000. Lyle receives all of the corporation's shares plus $20,000 in cash. The building had not been

---

[13] *See* § 2.02[A][4], *infra*, for a discussion of holding period in section 351 transactions.

subject to depreciation in Lyle's hands because it had been used for personal purposes, but will be subject to depreciation by Z Corporation. In this section 351 transaction, Lyle realized $100,000 of gain, of which $20,000 is recognized. Although that gain ordinarily would be capital, under section 1239, because Lyle is "related" to Z Corporation, the $20,000 will be ordinary income to Lyle.

[iii] Dividend Treatment

Treasury Regulation 1.351-2(d) provides that section 301 applies to a section 351 transaction that has the effect of the distribution of a dividend. For example, in Revenue Ruling 80-239, 1980-2 C.B. 103, an individual taxpayer who owned all of the stock of X Corporation transferred all of that stock to a newly created corporation, Y Corporation, in exchange for all of the Y stock and $100,000 that Y borrowed from a bank. After the transfer, Y repaid the loan with funds received from X. Citing Treasury Regulation 1.351-2(d) among other authorities, the IRS held that the cash the individual taxpayer received constituted a dividend from X Corporation to the extent provided in section 301, which, as discussed in Chapter 4, would generally be to the extent of X's "earnings and profits." *See* I.R.C. §§ 301(c)(1), 316.

[2] Treatment of Liabilities

[a] General Non-Recognition Rule of Section 357(a)

Under current law, section 357 provides for the treatment of liabilities assumed by the corporation in connection with a transfer of property under section 351.[14] It provides a general rule of nonrecognition (subject to two exceptions), overruling *United States v. Hendler*, 303 U.S. 564 (1938), which had provided for recognition. Section 357(a) provides the following general rule:

> Except as provided in subsections (b) and (c), if—
>
> (1) the taxpayer receives property which would be permitted to be received under section 351 or 361 without the recognition of gain if it were the sole consideration, and
>
> (2) as part of the consideration, another party to the exchange assumes a liability of the taxpayer,
>
> then such assumption shall not be treated as money or other property, and shall not prevent the exchange from being within the provisions of section 351 or 361, as the case may be.

In short, subject to two very important exceptions discussed below, assumption of a transferor's liability by the corporation generally is not considered receipt of boot by the transferor.

---

[14] See I.R.C. § 357(d)(1) the discussion below regarding what constitutes an "assumed" liability for purposes of section 357.

Example 2.7: Mindy organizes M, Inc. Mindy contributes a building worth $500,000, subject to a longstanding $300,000 mortgage that M, Inc. assumes, in return for 200 shares of the new corporation. Mindy had a $400,000 basis in the building. She therefore realized a $100,000 gain on the transfer of the building, but absent facts suggesting the application of subsection (b) of section 357, will not recognize any of the $100,000 gain despite M, Inc.'s assumption of the liabilty.[15]

What is an assumed liability for purposes of section 357? The Code provides that "a recourse liability (or portion thereof) shall be treated as having been assumed if, as determined on the basis of all facts and circumstances, the transferee has agreed to, and is expected to, satisfy such liability (or portion), whether or not the transferor has been relieved of such liability . . . ." I.R.C. § 357(d)(1)(A). The Code further states that, subject to an exception, "a nonrecourse liability shall be treated as having been assumed by the transferee of any asset subject to such liability." I.R.C. § 357(d)(1)(B). The exception is that, if some assets subject to a nonrecourse liability are not transferred in the exchange, the amount of the liability treated as assumed by the transferee corporation is reduced by the lesser of (1) the amount of the liability the owner of the other assets has agreed to, and is expected to, satisfy, or (2) the fair market value of the other assets. I.R.C. § 357(d)(2).

[b] Exceptions to Section 357(a)

Subsections (b) and (c) contain two important exceptions to the general rule of section 357(a) that liabilities are not treated as money or other property. As discussed below, liabilities transferred without a *bona fide* business purpose may be treated as boot, *see* I.R.C. § 357(b), and aggregate liabilities transferred in excess of aggregate basis transferred are automatically recognized as gain, I.R.C. § 357(c).

[i] Tax-Avoidance Motive: Section 357(b)

Section 357(b) provides an important, intent-based exception to the anti-*Hendler* rule of section 357(a):

(1) In general. If, taking into consideration the nature of the liability and the circumstances in the light of which the arrangement for the assumption was made, it appears that *the principal purpose* of the taxpayer with respect to the assumption described in subsection (a)—

(A) was a purpose to avoid Federal income tax on the exchange, or

(B) if not such purpose, was not a bona fide business purpose,

---

[15] Section 357(c) does not apply to the facts of this example because the liabilities assumed by the corporation ($300,000) do not exceed the aggregate basis of the properties transferred ($400,000).

then such assumption (*in the total amount of the liability assumed pursuant to such exchange*) shall, for purposes of section 351 or 361 (as the case may be), be considered as money received by the taxpayer on the exchange.

I.R.C. § 357(b) (emphasis added).

Note that, under this exception, if the principal purpose of the taxpayer with respect to the assumption by the corporation of *any* liability was an impermissible one, then *all* liabilities assumed by the corporation will be treated as boot.

Example 2.8: Nan incorporates N Corporation, receiving 100 percent of its stock in return for a building worth $400,000 and inventory worth $200,000. Nan's basis in the building was $200,000, and her basis in the inventory was $250,000. The building was subject to a longstanding mortgage of $50,000 that was incurred for valid business reasons. Just prior to the incorporation transaction, to obtain some cash to use toward renovations on her personal residence, Nan borrowed $100,000 against the building, and transferred the building, subject to both liabilities, to the new corporation. Under section 357(b), N Corporation's assumption of the $150,000 of liabilities will be treated as $150,000 worth of boot received by Nan in the section 351 transaction.

[ii] Liabilities in Excess of Basis: Section 357(c)

Section 357(c) provides another exception to the general rule of nonrecognition for liabilities assumed by a transferee corporation. However, the tax consequences of applying this rule differ from those under section 357(b), and 357(b) overrides 357(c) if both would otherwise apply. I.R.C. § 357(c)(2)(A). Subsection (c) provides, in part:

(1) In general. In the case of an exchange—

(A) to which section 351 applies, or

(B) to which section 361 applies by reason of a plan of reorganization within the meaning of section 368(a)(1)(D),

. . . *if the sum of the amount of the liabilities assumed exceeds the total of the adjusted basis of the property transferred* pursuant to such exchange, then *such excess shall be considered as a gain* from the sale or exchange of a capital asset or of property which is not a capital asset, as the case may be.

I.R.C. § 357(c)(1) (emphasis added).

In other words, the amount by which the total liabilities assumed exceeds the total basis of assets transferred *automatically* is recognized as gain. Under section 357(c), there is no need to compute realized gain.

Example 2.9: Oscar organizes a new corporation, Ops, Inc. and contributes $100,000 of cash and a building worth $500,000, subject to a longstanding $400,000 mortgage, in return for 200 shares. Oscar had a

$200,000 basis in the building. Because the $400,000 liability assumption exceeds the aggregate $300,000 basis, Oscar will recognize $100,000 of gain, absent facts suggesting the application of subsection (b) of section 357.[16]

The IRS has ruled that if there are multiple transferors of property, section 357(c) is applied transferor by transferor. *See* Rev. Rul. 66-142, 1966-1 C.B. 66; *see also Smith v. Commissioner*, 84 T.C. 889, 902 (1985) (applying the Revenue Ruling).

As you will see below, in § 2.02[A][3][c], section 357(c) prevents what could otherwise be a "negative basis" problem for transferors of property.[17] That is, because liabilities assumed by a corporate transferee are subtracted from asset basis in determining the transferor's basis in the stock received, if liabilities exceed basis in the assets transferred, the transferor's basis would be less than zero. However, as discussed below, gain recognized by the transferor (including section 357(c) gain) is added in calculating the stock basis, thus bringing basis back up to zero.

[I] Effect of a Shareholder Promissory Note

The possibility that the transfer of the assets of a business with liabilities exceeding aggregate asset basis can cause gain recognition under section 357(c) can be a trap for the unwary. In *Lessinger v. Commissioner*, 872 F.2d 519 (2d Cir. 1989), Lessinger had owned and operated for 25 years a proprietorship engaged in the wholesale distribution of metal fasteners. In 1977, under pressure from lenders to incorporate so that they could charge higher interest rates, Lessinger transferred the proprietorship to a corporation he owned. Because Lessinger already owned all of the stock in the corporation, no new stock was issued. However, the IRS and Lessinger agreed that section 351 was applicable to the transfer, and that the transaction was not entered into for tax-avoidance purposes. *Id.* at 520.

As of December 31, 1976, the proprietorship had a negative net worth, with liabilities exceeding assets by $255,499.37.[18] This amount was debited to a corporate account as a loan receivable from Lessinger. Because section 351 applied to the transfer, section 357 was applicable to the liabilities. The

---

[16] If section 357(b) applied, all $400,000 would be treated as boot. Because, on the facts, realized gain is $300,000, Oscar would have recognized gain of $300,000 if section 357(b) applied.

[17] "[S]keptics say that negative basis, like Bigfoot, doesn't exist. *Compare Easson v. Commissioner*, 33 T.C. 963, 970 (1960) (there's no such thing as a negative basis), *with Easson v. Commissioner*, 294 F.2d 653, 657–58 (9th Cir. 1961) (yes, Virginia, there is a negative basis)." *Peracchi v. Commissioner*, 143 F.3d 487, 491 (9th Cir. 1998).

[18] In *Lessinger*, the proprietorship was on the accrual method, *see Lessinger v. Commissioner*, 85 T.C. 824, 825 (1985), so section 357(c)(3)(A) (which was enacted in 1978) would not have been helpful. That is, payment of the proprietorship's accounts payable would not have given rise to a deduction. *See Lessinger*, 872 F.2d at 528 n.8.

Note that once the proposed "no net value" regulations, mentioned in footnote 4, *supra*, become effective, they will apply to the transfer of assets and liabilities of an insolvent company in a section 351 transaction.

taxpayer argued that section 357 did not apply to create a taxable gain, because there was no actual gain from the transfer; rather the transfer "merely exchanged creditors from trade creditors to [the corporation]." *Id.* at 522. The taxpayer also argued that any gain in his situation was only "phantom" gain that Congress had not intended to tax.

The Tax Court agreed with the IRS and held that the taxpayer experienced a taxable gain under section 357(c) when he transferred the proprietorship's liabilities and assets to his corporation because the liabilities exceeded the taxpayer's adjusted basis in those assets. The Court of Appeals for the Second Circuit reversed. The Second Circuit noted that the payment of the taxpayer's liabilities by the corporation did "represent[] the type of relief from liability that section 357(c) was intended to tax." *Id.* at 523. However, the court also found that the taxpayer's obligation to repay the debt to the corporation was a binding one and would be enforced by a court to protect corporate creditors if the corporation failed. In determining the basis of the note, the Second Circuit held that the taxpayer had a zero basis in the note, but that the corporation took a basis equal to the face amount of the note. The court held that "in the situation presented here, where the transferor undertakes genuine personal liability to the transferee, 'adjusted basis' in section 357(c) refers to the *transferee's* basis in the obligation, which is its *face amount*." *Id.* at 526 (emphasis added).

The Second Circuit's decision in *Lessinger* has been criticized. *See, e.g.,* Ken Brewer, *Peracchi v. Lessinger: Two Circuits Divided by a Common Decision*, 79 TAX NOTES 1063 (1998); Michael M. Megaard & Susan L. Megaard, *Risky Business: Can a Shareholder's Own Note Truly Avoid Section 357(c) Gain?*, 89 J. TAX'N 69 (1998). It is not hard to see why. Section 357(c) treats as gain, on the transfer of property, liabilities in excess of basis. The relevant basis should be the *transferor's* basis. Lessinger had no basis in his own promise to pay. *See Alderman v. Commissioner*, 55 T.C. 662 (1971); Rev. Rul. 68-629, 1968-2 C.B. 154. In addition, even the Second Circuit's assertion that the *transferee corporation* had basis in the note is not very convincing. In a section 351 transaction, the corporation's basis in property transferred is the same as the transferor's basis (as adjusted under section 362). A zero basis asset retains its zero basis on transfer (unless the transferor has recognized gain on the transfer, and under the court's analysis, Lessinger recognized no gain).[19]

Despite criticism of *Lessinger*, the Ninth Circuit reached a similar result in *Peracchi v. Commissioner*, 143 F.3d 487 (9th Cir. 1998), though on a slightly different rationale. In *Peracchi*, the taxpayer contributed two parcels of real estate to his closely held corporation in order to comply with Nevada's minimum premium-to-asset ratio for insurance companies. The

---

[19] Note the circularity that would be necessary if the basis referred to were the corporation's, which is the transferor's basis plus gain recognized by the transferor, I.R.C. § 362(a)—but the gain recognized by the transferor depends on what his or her basis is. *See* John A. Bogdanski, *Corporations, Shareholder Debt, Corporate Debt: Lessons From Leavitt and Lessinger*, 16 J. CORP. TAX'N 348, 351–53 (1990).

parcels were encumbered with liabilities that exceeded the taxpayer's basis in them by more than $500,000. Aware that section 357(c) can result in the gain of excess liabilities over the transferor's adjusted basis, Peracchi also executed a promissory note to the corporation promising to pay $1,060,000 over a term of ten years at an interest rate of 11 percent. Peracchi argued that the note had a basis equal to its face value, which would make his total basis in the transferred property greater than the total liabilities. The IRS argued that the note did not constitute genuine indebtedness, but rather was an unenforceable gift, and that even if the note were valid, the basis in Peracchi's hands would be zero.

The Tax Court agreed with the IRS that the debt was a sham. It pointed out that "(1) NAC's decision whether to collect on the note is wholly controlled by Peracchi and (2) Peracchi missed the first two years of payments, yet NAC did not accelerate the debt." *Id.* at 495. Accordingly, the Tax Court found that the taxpayer recognized gain under section 357(c).

The Court of Appeals for the Ninth Circuit reversed, holding that the note had a basis equal to its face value in Peracchi's hands, so that the aggregate liabilities transferred to the corporation did not exceed the aggregate basis of the property transferred. The court found that Peracchi's obligation to repay was not "merely illusory," but rather that the note constituted a *bona fide* obligation:

> The IRS has stipulated that Peracchi is creditworthy and likely to have the funds to pay the note; the note bears a market rate of interest commensurate with his creditworthiness; the note has a fixed term. Second, the IRS does not argue that the value of the note is anything other than its face value; nothing in the record suggests NAC couldn't borrow against the note to raise cash. Lastly, the note is fully transferable and enforceable by third parties, such as hostile creditors.

Id. at 495. The court quickly dismissed the IRS's argument that the note was a "gift," stating that the "contribution of the note was no more a gift than the contribution of $1 million in cash to the corporation would have been; it does not reflect the 'detached and disinterested generosity' which characterizes a gift for purposes of federal income taxation." *Id.* at 496 (quoting *Commissioner v. Duberstein*, 363 U.S. 278 (1960)).

The Court of Appeals, unlike the Tax Court, reached the section 357(c) issue. It rejected the approach the Second Circuit had taken in *Lessinger* but found that Peracchi's basis in the note was its face value, so Peracchi had no gain under section 357(c). The court stated:

> It's true that all Peracchi did was make out a promise to pay on a piece of paper, mark it in the corporate minutes and enter it on the corporate books. It is also true that nothing will cause the corporation to enforce the note against Peracchi so long as Peracchi remains in control. But the IRS ignores the possibility that NAC may go bankrupt, an event that would suddenly make the note highly significant.

Id. at 492–93. Thus, the possibility that NAC would go bankrupt was the key to the court's holding. Because of the possibility of bankruptcy, the court found that "Peracchi's obligation on the note . . . . represents a new and substantial increase in Peracchi's investment in the corporation." *Id.* at 493. The court limited its holding to "a case such as this where the note is contributed to an operating business which is subject to a non-trivial risk of bankruptcy or receivership." *Id.* at 493 n.14. However, *Peracchi*, like *Lessinger*, has been criticized. *See, e.g.*, Brewer, *supra*, at 1063 & n.1; Stuart Lazar, *Lessinger, Peracchi, and the Emperor's New Clothes*, 58 TAX LAW. 41, 44 (2004).

One commentator argues that the transferor of a note in a situation like those in *Lessinger* and *Peracchi* should not recognize gain under section 357(c), not because the note takes a fair market value basis, but rather because the note reduces the amount of liabilities the transferee corporation assumes. Steven Quiring, *Section 357(c) and the Elusive Basis of the Issuer's Note*, 57 TAX LAW. 97, 97 (2003). Under his approach, the note would reduce the liabilities assumed only in situations in which the transferor actually retains liability. *Id.* He argues:

> Rather than looking to the note for basis in order to avoid section 357(c) gain, the note may be considered a means of allocating the liabilities between the shareholder and the corporation. If the note effectively allocates the liability to the shareholder, that liability ought not to be considered assumed by the corporation. If the transfer of a note is treated as reducing the transferor's liabilities assumed, gain recognition under section 357(c) can be avoided without attributing any basis to the note. In substance, there is no debt assumption if the piece of paper saying that the property is subject to a $100 liability is counterbalanced by another piece of paper saying that the transferor will pay that $100 liability.

Id. at 119 (footnote omitted).

[II] Excluded and Contingent Liabilities

For purposes of section 357(c), certain liabilities are excluded in calculating the amount of liabilities assumed by the corporation:

(A) In general. If a taxpayer transfers, in an exchange to which section 351 applies, a liability the payment of which either—

(i) would give rise to a deduction, or

(ii) would be described in section 736(a),[20] then, for purposes

---

[20] Section 357(c)(3)(A)(ii) provides that section 736(a) payments (those "made in liquidation of the interest of a retiring partner or a deceased partner") are not "liabilities" for purposes of section 357(c). Section 736(a) payments fall into two categories: payments for a partner's distributive share of partnership income, and "guaranteed payments," which are amounts computed without regard to the income of the partnership. Guaranteed payments are deductible by the partnership. Distributions of partnership income are not, but they are equivalent to deductions in that they reduce the taxable income of other partners. *See* JEROLD A. FRIEDLAND, UNDERSTANDING PARTNERSHIP AND LLC TAXATION 7 (2d ed. 2003).

of paragraph (1), the amount of such liability shall be excluded in determining the amount of liabilities assumed.

(B) Exception. Subparagraph (A) shall not apply to any liability to the extent that the incurrence of the liability resulted in the creation of, or an increase in, the basis of any property."

I.R.C. § 357(c)(3).[21]

Section 357(c)(3)(A)(i) coordinates the tax treatment of accounts payable and accounts receivable for a cash-method taxpayer because, absent section 357(c)(3), such a taxpayer would have a zero basis in receivables (thus not increasing aggregate basis of property transferred) yet be increasing the aggregate liabilities transferred. Liabilities might therefore exceed the basis of assets transferred even if the transferor transfers the same amount of payables and receivables. In addition, the transferor's benefit from having the liability assumed is offset by the transferor's relinquishment of the deduction that the transferor would have gotten had he or she paid the liability. However, those rationales do not hold for liabilities that, when incurred, gave rise to basis in property, so they are excluded from the exception.

The IRS has ruled that certain contingent environmental liabilities assumed by a transferee corporation in a section 351 transaction did not constitute liabilities for purposes of section 357 (and the basis rule of section 358(d), which is discussed below). See Rev. Rul. 95-74, 1995-2 C.B. 36. The IRS described the transaction as having been engaged in for valid business purposes. Environmental clean-up costs, if incurred by the transferor, would have constituted ordinary and necessary business expenses in part and capital expenditures in part. The IRS stated, "[w]hile § 357(c)(3) explicitly addresses liabilities that give rise to deductible items, the same principle applies to liabilities that give rise to capital expenditures as well." *Id.* at 37. In accordance with Revenue Ruling 80-198, 1980-2 C.B. 113, the IRS further held that the transferee corporation could deduct or capitalize (as appropriate) the contingent environmental liabilities, in accordance with the transferee's accounting method. Thus, Revenue Ruling 95-74 took a different approach to liabilities that, once paid, would give rise to basis (because they would constitute capital expenditures) from the approach section 357(c)(3)(B) takes to liabilities that gave rise to basis when they were incurred.

The IRS's approach in Revenue Ruling 95-74 has since been used in the "contingent liability tax shelter."[22] See *Black and Decker Corp. v. United States*, 340 F. Supp. 2d 621 (N.D. Md. 2004) *aff'd in part and rev'd in part*, 436 F.3d 431 (4th Cir 2006); Notice 2001-17, 2001-1 C.B. 730. However, Congress responded with section 358(h), discussed in § 2.02[A][3][c].

---

[21] The effect on a shareholder's basis of a liability excluded by section 357(c)(3) is discussed in § 2.02[A][3][c].

[22] The contingent liability shelter and other corporate tax shelters are discussed in Chapter 16.

[3] Basis rules

As is typical of nonrecognition transactions, the parties to a 351 exchange generally have substituted bases in the property received,[23] rather than fair market value bases. However, parties who performed services for the stock received will have fair market value (tax cost) bases in that stock.

Section 358 governs the transferors of property, and section 362, discussed below, governs the corporate transferee. With respect to transfers not involving boot, section 358 provides, in relevant part: "In the case of an exchange to which section 351 . . . applies . . . . [t]he basis of the property permitted to be received under such section without the recognition of gain or loss shall be the *same as that of the property exchanged* . . . ." I.R.C. § 358(a) (emphasis added). The "property permitted to be received . . . without the recognition of gain or loss" under section 351 is stock, so section 358 enables transferors to compute stock basis. In transfers involving boot, section 358 provides for a series of upward and downward adjustments to basis, as discussed below.

[a] Transferor Basis in the Absence of Boot

As the Code section excerpts above reveal, in any section 351 transaction in which the property transferors receive only stock, the transferors will retain in their newly received stock the basis they had in their transferred properties.

Example 2.10: Pam and Quincy organize PQ, Inc. In return for 200 shares, Pam contributes land worth $200,000 with a basis of $150,000. In return for 100 shares, Quincy contributes a machine worth $100,000 with a basis of $120,000. Section 351 applies to the exchange because the transferors of property, Pam and Quincy, received "control" of PQ, Inc., the transferee corporation. Pam's basis in her 200 shares will be $150,000, her basis in the land. I.R.C. § 358(a). Quincy's basis in his 100 shares will be $120,000, his basis in the machine. *Id.*

Note that if a transferor transfers multiple properties in return for the stock, the IRS's position, reflected in Field Service Advice, which cannot be relied on as precedent, is that the transferor has an aggregate basis in the stock, rather than different bases in each bundle of stock, determined with reference to each asset transferred. *See* FSA 199926003.

[b] Transferor Basis in the Presence of Boot

As indicated above, section 358 provides for basis adjustments to reflect boot received by property transferors. Section 358 provides, in relevant part:

---

[23] "Substituted basis property" is property that is "transferred basis property," or "exchanged basis property." I.R.C. § 7701(a)(42). "Transferred basis property" is property that has a basis determined in whole or in part by reference to the basis in the hands of the transferor of the property. I.R.C. § 7701(a)(43). "Exchanged basis property" is property that has a basis determined in whole or in part by reference to other property that is or was held by the same person holding the property in question. I.R.C. § 7701(a)(44).

(a) General rule. In the case of an exchange to which section 351 . . . applies—

(1) Nonrecognition property. The basis of the property permitted to be received under such section without the recognition of gain or loss shall be the *same as that of the property exchanged—*

(A) *decreased by—*

(i) the fair market value of any *other property* (except money) received by the taxpayer,

(ii) the amount of any *money* received by the taxpayer, and

. . . .

(B) *increased by—*

(i) the amount which was treated as a *dividend*, and

(ii) the amount of *gain* to the taxpayer which was recognized on such exchange (not including any portion of such gain which was treated as a dividend).

(2) Other property. The basis of any other property (except money) received by the taxpayer shall be its fair market value.

I.R.C. § 358(a) (emphasis added). Thus, in general, a property transferor takes as his basis in the stock received his basis in the property transferred, less any amount he or she "cashed out" by receiving boot, and increased by any amounts included in gross income. From a tax perspective, these adjustments make sense. Amounts divested through receipt of other property or money will have their own fair market value bases. Amounts included in gross income are entitled to basis on a "tax cost basis" analysis.[24]

Example 2.11: Renee, Sam, and Ted organize RST, Inc. Renee contributes cash of $30,000 and land worth $70,000 with a $30,000 basis, and receives 100 shares of stock. Sam contributes inventory worth $120,000 with a $150,000 basis, and receives 100 shares of stock and $20,000. Ted contributes a machine worth $110,000 with a basis of $95,000, and receives 100 shares of stock and $10,000.

The transaction qualifies under section 351 because Renee, Sam, and Ted collectively control RST, Inc. Renee realizes $40,000 of gain on the transfer of the land but does not recognize any of it under section 351(a) because she received no boot. Under section 358, Renee's stock basis will be $60,000, the combined total of the money she invested and the basis in the land she transferred.

Sam realized a $30,000 loss but will not recognize it under section 351 although he received boot. His basis in his stock will be $130,000, his

---

[24] *Cf.* Jasper L. Cummings, Jr., *Zero Basis Hoax or Contingent Debt and Failure of Proof? Sorting Out the Issues in the Lessinger Case*, 2 FLA. TAX REV. 283, 311 (1994) ("property received as compensation for services takes a basis equal to the gross income recognized on the property's receipt (often called a tax cost basis).").

$150,000 basis in the inventory, reduced by the $20,000 of money received. Note that the $30,000 of unrealized loss Sam had in the inventory is preserved in the 100 shares of stock he now holds (which, on the facts, is worth $100,000).

Ted realized a $15,000 gain on the transfer of the machine. Under section 351(b), $10,000 of that gain is recognized because a transferor's realized gain is only *recognized* under section 351 to the extent of the boot received. Ted's basis in his stock will be $95,000, that is, his $95,000 basis in the machine minus the $10,000 of boot he received plus the $10,000 of gain he recognized. That $95,000 basis preserves $5,000 of gain for recognition in a hypothetical future sale of the stock for its current value of $100,000. As $10,000 of the $15,000 gain built in to the machine was already recognized, the $95,000 basis is consistent with the deferral aspect of section 351.

[c] Effect of Liabilities on Basis

Section 358(d), which applies to transferors of property in section 351 transactions, provides, as a general rule, "[w]here, as part of the consideration to the taxpayer, another party to the exchange assumed a liability of the taxpayer, such assumption shall, for purposes of this section, be treated as money received by the taxpayer on the exchange." I.R.C. § 358(d). Thus, when the corporation assumes a liability of the property transferor, the assumption is treated as the payment of cash to the transferor (that is, as the receipt of boot). That approach is reasonable; assuming a liability of the transferor is economically similar to providing the transferor with the money to pay off the liability. Consider the facts of Example 2.11, with the change that Ted, instead of receiving $10,000 cash, transfers a $10,000 liability to the corporation:

Example 2.12: Renee, Sam, and Ted organize RST, Inc. Renee contributes cash of $30,000 and land worth $70,000 with a $30,000 basis, and receives 100 shares of stock. Sam contributes inventory worth $120,000 with a $150,000 basis, and receives 100 shares of stock and $20,000. Ted contributes a machine worth $110,000 with a basis of $95,000, subject to a $10,000 liability, and receives 100 shares of stock.

The transaction qualifies under section 351. Renee and Sam are treated as discussed in Example 2.11. Ted realized a $15,000 gain on the transfer of the machine. Under sections 351(a) and 357(a), Ted recognizes *none* of the gain (assuming the principal purpose for transferring the liability was a *bona fide* business purpose). However, under section 358(d), the $10,000 liability assumed by RST, Inc. is treated just like cash received by Ted (*i.e.*, boot). Ted's basis in his stock will be $85,000, that is, his $95,000 basis in the machine minus the $10,000 of boot he received.

Note that the effect of section 358(d) is to lower the transferor's stock basis by the amount of any liability assumed by the transferee corporation. As discussed above, section 357(c), providing for gain recognition when liabilities exceed basis, prevents a negative basis problem. Consider again the facts of Example 2.9:

> *Example 2.13*: Oscar organizes a new corporation, Ops, Inc., and contributes $100,000 of cash and a building worth $500,000, subject to a longstanding $400,000 mortgage, in return for 200 shares. Oscar had a $200,000 basis in the building. Because the $400,000 liability assumption exceeds the aggregate $300,000 basis, Oscar will recognize $100,000 of gain, absent facts suggesting the application of subsection (b) of section 357.

> Oscar's basis in the Ops, Inc. stock will be his $200,000 basis in the building plus $100,000 of cash contributed ($300,000 in the aggregate) less the $400,000 mortgage deflected to the corporation *plus $100,000 of gain recognized*, giving him a zero basis in the stock.

In fact, the practical effect of section 357(c) on stock basis is not simply to avoid negative basis, but to increase the otherwise negative basis to exactly zero.

Section 358(d)(2) provides an exception from treating as money received liabilities transferred for "the amount of any liability excluded under section 357(c)(3)." As discussed in § 2.02[A][2][b][ii][II], above, section 357(c)(3) lists those liabilities excluded from the definition of liability for purposes of section 357, namely those that would give rise to a deduction or would be described in section 736(a), unless the incurrence of the liability resulted in the creation of, or an increase in, the basis of any property. I.R.C. § 357(c)(3). In addition, certain contingent liabilities, such as environmental liabilities, are not considered "liabilities" for purposes of section 358(d) and 357(c). *See* Rev. Rul. 95-74, 1995-2 C.B. 36.

Liabilities, as defined in section 358(h)(3), that are not covered by section 358(d), are now subject to section 358(h), except that 358(h) does not apply if the entire trade or business with which the liability is associated is transferred in the exchange.[25] I.R.C. § 358(h)(2)(A). For purposes of section 358(h), the term liability is defined to "include any fixed or contingent obligation to make payment, without regard to whether the obligation is otherwise taken into account for purposes of [the Code]." Under section 358(h), if the basis of the transferor's stock would exceed its fair market value, then that basis is reduced (but not below its fair market value) by the amount of any liability to which section 358(d)(1) does not apply and that was assumed in the exchange. Section 358(h) provides a response to the contingent liability tax shelter mentioned above and discussed in Chapter 16. *See* Notice 2001-17, 2001-1 C.B. 730, 731.

---

[25] Temporary Treasury Regulations provide that the exception from section 358(h) for the transfer of "substantially all of the assets with which the liability is associated" in section 358(h)(2)(B) "does not apply to an exchange occurring on or after June 24, 2003." Temp. Treas. Reg. 1.358-5T(a).

[4] Holding Period

In general, the holding period of assets received in an exchange, such as the stock received in a section 351 transaction, includes the period during which the taxpayer held the property that he or she relinquished in the exchange, if the property received by the taxpayer has the same basis in whole or in part as the property relinquished and the property relinquished was a capital or quasi-capital asset. I.R.C. § 1223(1). Thus, a transferor of property in a section 351 transaction generally "tacks" the holding period of any capital or quasi-capital asset he or she transferred onto the holding period of the stock received. By contrast, the holding period of stock received in exchange for other assets begins on the day after the exchange. Rev. Rul. 85-164, 1985-2 C.B. 117.[26]

If the transferor transferred multiple properties, the stock received in a section 351 transaction will have split holding periods. Rev. Rul. 85-164, 1985-2 C.B. 117. That is, different shares of stock received will not have different holding periods that reflect the various assets transferred. Instead, each share will have a set of holding periods. The split in holding periods is determined with reference to the relative fair market value of the various assets transferred.

Revenue Ruling 85-164, which provides for split holding periods in this context, involved a taxpayer who transferred to a newly organized controlled corporation machinery with a fair market value of 10x dollars, real estate (land and building) with a fair market value of 30x dollars, and accounts receivable with a fair market value of 60x dollars. The taxpayer had held the real estate and machinery for more than one year, and both were quasi-capital assets under section 1231. In return for the assets transferred, the taxpayer received stock and securities; at the time, securities were permitted to be received without recognition of gain or loss under section 351. The IRS ruled:

> That fraction of each share of Y stock or security attributable to the real estate and machinery (40x/100x) is [treated] as including the period (over one year) for which A held the real estate and machinery . . . . The fraction of each share of Y stock or security attributable to the accounts receivable (60x/100x) has a holding period beginning on the day after the exchange . . . .

Id. at 118.

[B] Taxable Incorporations

The effect of failing the requirements of section 351 is that the transaction is treated as it would have been if the special rules of section 351 did not exist. As discussed above, when no nonrecognition provision such as section

---

[26] The corporation's holding period in property it receives in a section 351 transaction is discussed in § 2.03[C].

351 applies, the investors' gains or losses realized generally will be *recognized*. In addition, the investors will obtain cost bases in their stock.

Example 2.14: Uma and Violet organize a corporation, UV Company. Uma performs services worth $75,000 and receives 50 shares of stock. Violet contributes cash of $25,000 and land worth $50,000 with a basis of $30,000, and receives the other 50 shares of stock. Section 351 does not apply because the "control" requirement was not met; the only transferor of property, Violet, received only 50 percent of the shares. Violet, who realized $20,000 of gain on the transfer of the land, will therefore recognize that gain. (The corporation recognizes no gain under section 1032.) Uma and Violet will each take a cost basis ("tax cost" basis for Uma) of $75,000 in their 50 shares.

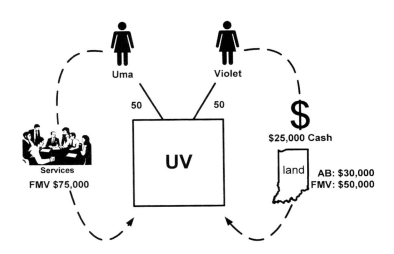

Note that section 1239 treats gain from the sale or exchange of depreciable property between related taxpayers as ordinary income if the property will be depreciable in the hands of the transferee. I.R.C. § 1239(a). Related taxpayers include a corporation and a shareholder that owns, directly or indirectly, more than 50 percent (by value) of the outstanding stock of the corporation. I.R.C. § 1239(b)(1), (c)(1)(A). In addition, on the loss side, section 267 generally precludes recognition of losses realized on sales between related parties—including between a corporation and a shareholder that owns, directly or indirectly, more than 50 percent (by value) of the corporation's stock. I.R.C. § 267(a)(1), (b)(2).

[C]   Provisions that Override Section 351

Certain provisions override section 351 where both apply. As discussed in Chapter 5, section 304 applies to transactions that qualify under both sections. By contrast, there is no unified scheme that determines the interaction of section 351 and the reorganization provisions. For example, in Revenue Ruling 77-11, 1977-1 C.B. 93, a transfer qualified both under section 351 and as a divisive D reorganization. The IRS stated, "in addition to the nonrecognition treatment X receives under section 351(a), it is also given nonrecognition treatment under section 361(a) and, in addition to the carryover basis Z receives under 362(a) for the property contributed by X, Z also is given a carryover basis for such property under section 362(b)." *Id.* at 94. The uncertainty over which provision governs in a transaction qualifying under both section 351 and the reorganization provisions means that it is unclear what the collateral consequences of the transaction are, such as whether section 381, providing for a carryover of corporate tax attributes, applies.[27] However, the IRS has ruled that failure to meet the reorganization requirements does not preclude application of section 351. *See* Rev. Rul. 84-71, 1984-1 C.B. 106.

Shareholder nonrecognition under section 351 may not result if a shareholder is shifting income to the corporation. For example, in *Brown v. Commissioner*, 115 F.2d 337 (2d Cir. 1940), an attorney transferred to his wholly owned corporation a claim for legal services. The court held that the transfer to the corporation had no purpose other than to avoid taxes and, that, under *Lucas v. Earl*, 281 U.S. 111 (1930), a seminal assignment of income case, the attorney was liable for the tax on the income that resulted from the legal services. However, in *Hempt Bros. v. United States*, 490 F.2d 1172 (3d Cir.), *cert. denied*, 419 U.S. 826 (1974), which is discussed above in § 2.02[A][1][a], the assignment of income doctrine did not override section 351. *See also* Rev. Rul. 80-198, 1980-2 C.B. 113.

§ 2.03 Tax Consequences to the Corporation

[A] Nonrecognition on Issuance of Stock

As indicated above, section 1032 prevents a corporation from recognition on issuance (sale) of its own stock. That provision applies regardless of whether the stock is newly issued or is Treasury stock, and regardless of whether the investors are protected by section 351. Consider again the facts of Example 2.14:

Example 2.15: Uma and Violet organize a corporation, UV Company. Uma performs services worth $75,000 and receives 50 shares of stock. Violet contributes cash of $25,000 and land worth $50,000 with a basis of $30,000, and receives the other 50 shares of stock. Although section 351 does not protect Violet from recognizing her $20,000 of realized gain, the corporation recognizes no gain under section 1032. The result would be the same even if Uma had contributed $75,000 of cash instead of

---

[27] *See* BITTKER & EUSTICE, *supra*, at ¶ 3.19. Section 381 and related provisions are discussed in Chapter 13.

services (and had thereby enabled Violet to avoid recognizing her realized gain under section 351).

However, note that section 1032 does not govern the corporation's transfer of property to the property transferors. If the corporation transfers non-cash property in a section 351 transaction, section 351(f) provides that section 311 applies to the corporation. (The property transferor who receives the property has received non-cash boot.) Section 311 is discussed in Chapter 4. In general, it provides for the recognition of gain to a corporation distributing appreciated property but allows no loss to be recognized on the distribution of property with basis in excess of value.

[B] Basis Rules

On any transfer of property to a corporation, it will be necessary to calculate the corporation's basis in that property. The basis rules differ depending on whether or not the transfer was part of a nonrecognition transaction for the investors (that is, a section 351 transaction), or was instead a taxable exchange.

[1] Corporate Basis if Section 351 Applies

If section 351 applies to the investors, then section 362(a) applies to determine the basis of the property received by the corporation. The general rule is less complex than the calculation under section 358 for the investors' bases. Section 362 provides:

> If property was acquired on or after June 22, 1954, by a corporation—
>
>   (1) in connection with a transaction to which section 351 (relating to transfer of property to corporation controlled by transferor) applies, or
>
>   (2) as paid-in surplus or as a contribution to capital,
>
> then the basis shall be the *same as it would be in the hands of the transferor, increased in the amount of gain recognized to the transferor* on such transfer.

I.R.C. § 362(a). However, the general rule is subject to exceptions under section 362(e), discussed below.

[a] Absence of Boot

With respect to transfers not involving boot, basis to the transferee corporation generally is "the same as it would be in the hands of the transferor," I.R.C. § 362(a), subject to important exceptions that are discussed below.

Example 2.16: Wanda and Xavier organize Y Corporation. In return for 200 shares, Wanda contributes equipment worth $200,000 with a basis of $150,000. In return for 100 shares, Xavier contributes land worth

$100,000 with a basis of $80,000. Section 351 applies to the exchange because the transferors of property, Wanda and Xavier, received "control" of Y Corporation, the transferee corporation. Wanda's basis in her 200 shares will be $150,000, her basis in the equipment. I.R.C. § 358(a). Xavier's basis in his 100 shares will be $80,000, his basis in the land. *Id.* Under section 362(a), Y Corporation's basis in the equipment will be $150,000, the same basis Wanda had in it. Y Corporation's basis in the land will be $80,000, the same basis Xavier had in it.

This example reveals that a section 351 transaction can double unrealized gains. That is, before the transaction, Wanda stood to realize (and recognize) $50,000 of gain if she sold her land. After the transaction, she will realize that gain if she sells her Y Corporation stock. In addition, Y Corporation will also realize $50,000 of gain if it sells the equipment it now holds. Similarly, Xavier stands to realize a $20,000 gain that could be duplicated by the corporation. The possible doubling of gains should be considered by taxpayers before engaging in a section 351 transaction.

Can losses also be doubled via the contribution of loss property to a corporation in a transaction governed by section 351? Congress has addressed that issue in part through certain disallowance rules that apply to liquidating sales or distributions of certain loss assets received in section 351 transactions. *See* § 336(d). Those rules are discussed in Chapter 7.

In addition, in 2004, Congress enacted section 362(e)(2), which limits the transfer of "built-in" losses in section 351 transactions and contributions to capital.[28] Section 362(e)(2) compares the *aggregate adjusted basis* of the properties transferred with the aggregate fair market value of the properties immediately after the transaction. If the aggregate basis of property transferred, in the hands of the transferee corporation, exceeds the aggregate fair market value of the transferred property,[29] its bases in the properties transferred generally must be reduced. *See* I.R.C. § 362(e)(2)(A). The reduction is allocated in proportion to each asset's relative built-in loss.[30] I.R.C. § 362(e)(2)(B).

Example 2.17: Zelda organizes Z Corporation and contributes land worth $200,000 with a basis of $150,000 and inventory worth $100,000 with a basis of $160,000, in return for all of the stock of Z Corporation. Section

---

[28] As discussed in § 7.03[A][1][c][ii] in Chapter 7, sections 362(e)(2) and 336(d) may overlap in some situations. Section 362(e)(1), which limits "importation" of built-in losses, is beyond the scope of this book. Note, however, that section 362(e)(2) does not apply if section 362(e)(1) applies. I.R.C. § 362(e)(2)(A)(1).

[29] This calculation appears to be done on a transferor-by-transferor basis. *See* I.R.C. § 362(a)(2)(A)(i) (referring to "property . . . transferred by *a transferor*") (emphasis added). However, the legislative history suggests otherwise. *See* Andrew M. Eisenberg, *Limitations on Importation and Transfer of Built-In Losses: Untangling the New Basis Adjustment Rules*, 107 TAX NOTES 869, 876 (2005).

[30] Thus, in Example 2.11, where Sam, who was part of a group of property transferors in a section 351 transaction, contributed only inventory worth $120,000 with a $150,000 basis, the corporation's basis in the inventory would be limited to $120,000 under section 362(e)(2), absent an election under section 362(e)(2)(C), discussed below.

351 applies to the exchange because Zelda received "control" of Z Corporation. Zelda did not receive any boot, so she does not recognize any gain on the exchange. She takes a $310,000 basis in the stock received, under section 358(a).

Ordinarily, under section 362(a), Z Corporation's basis in the land would be $150,000 and Z Corporation's basis in the inventory would be $160,000. However, the aggregate basis of the property Zelda transferred is $310,000, but the property's aggregate fair market value is only $300,000. Section 362(e)(2) therefore applies to the transfer and occasions a $10,000 reduction in basis. In this example, 100% of the built-in loss is in the inventory, so Z Corporation's basis in the inventory must be reduced. Z Corporation's basis in the inventory will therefore be $150,000. Its basis in the land will remain $150,000.

Note that Zelda could avoid the basis reduction by contributing additional property such that the aggregate basis of the property transferred did not exceed its fair market value. That is, if Zelda were to contribute an asset the fair market value of which exceeded its basis by $10,000 or more, section 362(e)(2) would not apply.

Section 362(e)(2) also allows the transferor and transferee of property in a situation in which section 362(e)(2) applies to elect to reduce the tranferor's stock basis rather than having the transferee's asset basis reduced. *See* I.R.C. § 362(e)(2)(C). Both the transferor and transferee corporation must make the election. Consider again the facts of Example 2.17:

> *Example 2.18*: Zelda organizes Z Corporation and contributes land worth $200,000 with a basis of $150,000 and inventory worth $100,000 with a basis of $160,000, in return for all of the stock of Z Corporation. Section 351 applies to the exchange because Zelda received "control" of Z Corporation. Zelda did not receive any boot, so she does not recognize any gain on the exchange. Ordinarily, she would take a $310,000 basis in the stock received, under section 358(a).

> Because the aggregate basis of the property Zelda transferred is $310,000 but the property's aggregate fair market value is only $300,000, section 362(e)(2) applies to the transfer and occasions a $10,000 reduction in basis. If Zelda and Z Corporation both elect to have Zelda's stock basis reduced, Z Corporation's basis will not be reduced and Zelda's stock basis will be reduced by $10,000, to $300,000.

This election does always lead to the best tax results, however. See Example 7.6 in § 7.03[A][1][c][ii] of Chapter 7 and Example 8.17 in § 8.04[E] of Chapter 8.

Although the application of the basis rules of sections 358 and 362 generally is reasonably straightforward in the absence of the receipt of boot by property transferors, complicated issues do sometimes arise. *Hempt Bros.*, 490 F.2d 1172, which was discussed above in connection with the definition of "property" for purposes of section 351(d), considered the application of section 362 to accounts receivable and inventory contributed to the taxpayer corporation by a cash-method partnership.

In *Hempt Bros.*, the partnership had contributed accounts receivable in the amount of $662,824.40. The partnership, on the cash method, had not taken the receivables into income, so it had a zero basis in the receivables. The partnership had also contributed inventory valued at $351,266.05, with respect to which the partnership had previously deducted costs in that amount. Hempt Bros. argued that the tax benefit rule required that the inventory have a basis of $351,266.05 rather a than zero basis. However, the court held that, because section 351 applied, basis was governed by section 362(a), which provides that "the basis shall be the same as it would be in the hands of the transferor" partnership. *Id.* at 1181. Accordingly, the court did not allow the inventory's basis to be stepped up from zero to its value of $351,266.05 merely because of the transfer to the corporation. The court similarly required Hempt Bros. to take a zero basis in the accounts receivable under section 362(a). *Id.* at 1178.

[b] Presence of Boot

As discussed above, section 362(a) provides that a corporation's basis in property received in a section 351 transaction "shall be the *same as it would be in the hands of the transferor, increased in the amount of gain recognized to the transferor* on such transfer." If the transferor transferred multiple assets and recognized gain because of boot received, the corporation should take as its basis in each asset the transferor's basis in that asset, increased by any gain recognized by the transferor on that asset. *See* BITTKER & EUSTICE, *supra*, at ¶ 3.11[2].

Example 2.19: Andy is the sole shareholder of X, Inc. Andy contributes land worth $50,000 with a $20,000 basis, and inventory worth $50,000 with a $50,000 basis, and receives in return 100 additional shares of X, Inc. stock and $10,000 in cash. The transaction qualifies under section 351 because Andy is in control of X, Inc. after the transaction.

Andy realized $30,000 of gain on the transfer of the land, and realized no gain on the transfer of the inventory because its basis equaled its value. Under Revenue Ruling 68-55, 1968-1 C.B. 140, discussed above in § 2.02[A][1][f][ii][I], the boot of $10,000 that Andy received is allocated to the two assets he contributed, in proportion to their relative fair market values. In this example, the land and inventory are each worth half of the aggregate $100,000 of value that Andy transferred to X, Inc. Therefore, $5,000 of the boot is allocated to each asset. Andy therefore recognizes $5,000 of his realized gain on the land.

Section 362(a) provides that the corporation's basis in each of these assets will be the transferor's basis, increased by any gain recognized by the transferor on the transfer. Accordingly, X, Inc.'s basis in the land will be $25,000 ($20,000 plus the $5,000 of gain recognized by Andy with respect to the land) and X, Inc.'s basis in the inventory will be $50,000.

Note that, in this example, X, Inc.'s basis in the assets Andy transferred did not exceed their fair market value, so section 362(e) did not apply. If the facts were instead such that section 362(e) were implicated, it appears that first, boot would be allocated as in the example above, and the 362(e) basis adjustment would be done after the upward adjustments for the transferor's recognized gain.

> *Example 2.20*: Bill is the sole shareholder of Y, Inc. Bill contributes land worth $50,000 with a $20,000 basis, and inventory worth $50,000 with an $80,000 basis, in return for 100 additional shares of Y, Inc. stock and $10,000 of cash. The transaction qualifies under section 351 because Bill is in control of Y, Inc. after the transaction.

> Bill realized $30,000 of gain on the transfer of the land, and realized a $30,000 loss on the transfer of the inventory. As in Example 2.19, the boot of $10,000 that Bill received is allocated to the two assets he contributed, in proportion to their relative fair market values. In this example, the land and inventory are each worth half of the aggregate $100,000 of value that Bill transferred to Y, Inc. Therefore, $5,000 of the boot is allocated to each asset. Bill therefore recognizes $5,000 of his realized gain on the land. He recognizes none of his loss on the inventory.

> Section 362(a) provides that the corporation's basis in each of these assets will be the transferor's basis, increased by any gain recognized by the transferor on the transfer. Accordingly, Y, Inc.'s basis in the land initially will be $25,000 ($20,000 plus the $5,000 of gain recognized by Bill with respect to the land) and Y, Inc.'s basis in the inventory initially will be $80,000. However, note that the aggregate basis of these two assets in Y, Inc.'s hands, $105,000, exceeds their aggregate value of $100,000. Accordingly, section 362(e)(2) applies, requiring a reduction of basis to fair market value. It allocates the basis reduction in accordance with the assets' built-in *losses* prior to the transfer. Only the inventory had built-in loss, so Y, Inc's basis in the inventory will be reduced. It is reduced by the $5,000 by which aggregate basis exceeds fair market value, so it is reduced to $75,000 (assuming that Bill and Y, Inc. do not elect to have him reduce his stock basis instead, under section 362(e)(2)(C)). Y, Inc.'s basis in the land remains $25,000.

Note that, in Example 2.20, the aggregate basis and value of the properties transferred by Bill both equaled $100,000 in his hands, so that basis did not exceed value. The excess of basis over value in Y, Inc.'s hands resulted from Bill's recognition of gain on the land because of his receipt of boot. The effect of section 362(e)(2), if applied in this manner, is to allow only one increase for the gain recognized by Bill.[31]

[c]   Effect of Liabilities on Corporate Basis

Under section 362, a corporation's basis in an asset contributed in a valid section 351 transaction is the transferor's basis plus any gain recognized by the transferor. There is no special adjustment for liabilities. That is,

---

[31] For an article reaching the result in Example 2.20 on similar facts, see *Eisenberg, supra* note 29, at 877.

liabilities assumed by the corporation on the transfer of an asset do not increase its basis in that asset. However, liabilities may have an indirect effect on basis, in that gain recognized to a transferor because of the application of section 357(b) or (c) increases the corporation's basis in an asset because of the upward adjustment in section 362 for gain recognized by the transferor. Under section 362(d)(1), the basis cannot be increased above the fair market value of such property by reason of any gain recognized to the transferor as a result of the assumption of a liability.

In addition, as indicated above, under section 357, if some assets subject to a nonrecourse liability are not transferred in the exchange, the amount of the liability is reduced by the lesser of (1) the amount of the liability the owner of the other assets has agreed to, and is expected to, satisfy; or (2) the fair market value of the other assets. I.R.C. § 357(d)(2). This prevents the abuse that would result if a transferor transferred part of a group of properties subject to a nonrecourse liability to one corporation and the remainder to another corporation, and both corporations increased basis by the full amount of the gain recognized to the transferor resulting from the liability assumption. *See* Ira B. Shepard & Martin J. McMahon, Jr., *Recent Developments in Federal Income Taxation: The Year 2000*, 5 FLA. TAX REV. 109, 181–82 (2001).

[2] Corporate Basis if Section 351 Does Not Apply

If section 351 does not apply to the transfer of property, it is a taxable exchange, as discussed above. Accordingly, the corporation will receive a tax cost basis in the property received (that is, a fair market value basis). This is the case even though the corporation itself is not taxed because of section 1032. *See* Treas. Reg. § 1.1032-1(d). Consider again the facts of Example 2.14:

> *Example 2.21*: Uma and Violet organize a corporation, UV Company. Uma performs services worth $75,000 and receives 50 shares of stock. Violet contributes cash of $25,000 and land worth $50,000 with a basis of $30,000, and receives the other 50 shares of stock. Section 351 does not apply. Violet, who realized $20,000 of gain on the transfer of the land, recognizes that gain. The corporation recognizes no gain under section 1032. Uma and Violet each take a basis of $75,000 in their 50 shares. UV Company takes the land with a basis of $50,000 (the amount it "paid" for the land in UV Company shares).

[C] Holding Period

To determine the period for which a taxpayer has held property, the period for which the property was held by any other person is included, if the property has the same basis in whole or in part in the hands of the transferee as it would have in the hands of the transferor. I.R.C. § 1223(2). Unlike section 1223(1), which applies to the shareholders, the tacking in section 1223(2) is not limited to capital and quasi-capital assets. The omission in section 1223(2) generally does not lend itself to abuse because holding period is irrelevant to property other than capital and quasi-capital assets, and the holding period is staying with the asset in question.[32] Thus, a corporate recipient of property in a section 351 transaction "tacks" onto each asset the holding period the property transferor had in that asset. In a failed section 351 transaction, holding periods are not tacked; they begin anew the day after the exchange.

CHART 2.1
Checklist for Incorporations
and Other Section 351 Transactions[33]

(1)   Find transferors of property (may be a group).

(2)   Check for requisite "control" by property transferors under I.R.C. § 368(c) (two 80% ownership tests).

   (A) Consider whether there is an "accommodation transferor" problem.

   (B) Make sure control exists "immediately after" the transaction; consider application of the step-transaction doctrine to transfers of stock to non-transferors of property.

(3)   Consider whether I.R.C. § 357(c) applies to create gain.

(4)   Compute gain/loss *realized* by each transferor of property under I.R.C. § 1001.

(5)   Compute gain/loss *recognized* by each transferor of property.

   (A)   If the transaction falls within I.R.C. § 351, realized gains are recognized to the extent of "boot." No loss is recognized.

   •   Consider whether liabilities constitute boot under I.R.C. § 357(b).

   (B)   If the transaction does not fall within I.R.C. § 351, realized gains and losses generally are recognized, under general tax principles.

(6)   Corporation: No gain or loss on the issuance of stock, under I.R.C. § 1032 and Treas. Reg. § 1.1032-1(a), regardless of whether or not the transaction is governed by section 351.

(7)   Bases of stock received by transferors and assets received by corporation:

   (A)   If the transaction falls within I.R.C. § 351, property transferors generally have exchanged bases in their stock, under

---

[32] In contrast to the transferee corporation, the property transferors in a section 351 transaction receive a capital asset (stock) in exchange for their property.

[33] This is a general checklist; it does not cover every issue that may arise on the individual facts of a particular transaction. For example, section 351 does not apply to transfers to an investment company. I.R.C. § 351(e)(1).

I.R.C. § 358; corporation takes transferred bases in the property, under I.R.C. § 362.

- Special basis rules apply if liabilities were transferred.

- If the corporation's aggregate basis of property transferred to it exceeds the property's aggregate fair market value, I.R.C. § 362(e)(2) requires a reduction in basis to fair market value. The reduction is at the corporate level, absent a special election.

(B)   If the transaction does not fall within I.R.C. § 351, bases will be fair market value (cost) bases.

(8)   Holding periods:

(A)   If the transaction falls within I.R.C. § 351, property transferors receive tacked holding periods with respect to capital and quasi-capital assets transferred. I.R.C. § 1223(1). Assets transferred to the corporation receive tacked holding periods. I.R.C. § 1223(2).

(B)   If the transaction does not fall within I.R.C. § 351, holding periods start anew.

CHART 2.2
Comparison of Code Sections: Successful and Failed Section 351 Transactions

PARTY	SUCCESSFUL SECTION 351 TRANSACTION	FAILED SECTION 351 TRANSACTION
Property Transferors (Shareholders)	I.R.C. § 351 applies; gains realized under § 1001 only recognized to the extent of boot received	Gains realized under § 1001 recognized under general tax principles
	I.R.C. § 358 for basis computation	Tax cost basis
Corporate Transferee	I.R.C. § 1032: no gain or loss on issuance of stock for property	I.R.C. § 1032: no gain or loss on issuance of stock for property
	I.R.C. § 362 for basis computation	Tax cost basis

§ 2.04   Contributions to Capital

Sometimes shareholders contribute money or other property to a corporation without receiving shares in return. The contributions are not "gifts" for tax purposes (they lack "detached and disinterested generosity"), but rather are contributions to the capital of a corporation, typically to improve its balance sheet or provide working capital. Similarly, a non-shareholder may contribute to the capital of a corporation, perhaps to induce the corporation to relocate its headquarters to the contributor's locale, for example.

[A] Tax Consequences to Shareholder Contributors

In general, a shareholder who makes a contribution to capital simply obtains an increase in the basis of his or her shares. *See* Treas. Reg. § 1.118-1. That is, the contribution is capitalized onto the basis the shareholder already has. The shareholder receives no deduction for the contribution. *See* I.R.C. § 263(a).

Example 2.22: Carol owns 100 shares of the 250 shares of XYZ, Inc., with a basis of $85,000. The corporation needs cash, so Carol contributes an additional $20,000. Carol's basis in her shares is now $105,000.

In *Commissioner v. Fink*, 483 U.S. 89 (1987), the United States Supreme Court considered whether the surrender of shares without consideration gave rise to an immediately deductible loss. In *Fink*, the principal (but not sole) shareholders of a financially troubled corporation voluntarily surrendered shares of stock in the corporation in an effort to "increase the attractiveness" of the corporation to outside investors. On their joint federal income tax return, they claimed an ordinary loss deduction for the full amount of their adjusted basis in the surrendered shares. The IRS disallowed the deduction, claiming that the surrendered stock was a contribution to the corporation's capital, and that the shareholders' basis in the surrendered shares should therefore be added to the basis in their remaining shares. *Id.* at 91. The Tax Court ruled in favor of the IRS but the Sixth Circuit reversed and upheld the deduction, except to the extent that the surrender increased the value of the remaining shares. *Id.* at 91, 93.

The Supreme Court considered the issue whether a controlling shareholder's *non pro rata* voluntary surrender of a portion of the shareholder's stock is treated as a contribution to capital.[34] The Finks argued that their surrender of shares, which reduced their interest in the corporation, resulted in an immediate economic and tax loss. The Supreme Court disagreed, finding that a shareholder who voluntarily surrenders stock is more analogous to "one who forgives or surrenders a debt owed to him by the corporation; the latter gives up interest, principal, and also potential voting power in the event of insolvency or bankruptcy. But . . . such forgiveness of corporate debt is treated as a contribution to capital rather than a current deduction." *Id.*, at 96. Accordingly, the Finks were required to reallocate their basis in the surrendered shares retained and wait to deduct any loss until they disposed of the remaining shares. *Id.* at 99.

The Court noted that the Finks remained in control of the corporation after the contribution of shares, and expressly declined to address a

---

[34] The Finks conceded that a *pro rata* stock surrender would not be a taxable event. *Id.* at 94–95 & n.6. A *pro rata* surrender of stock would not change the percentage ownership of any shareholder. *Cf. Eisner v. Macomber*, 252 U.S. 189 (1920).

situation in which a surrender of shares results in a loss of control by that shareholder. The Court pointed to provisions applicable to redemptions under section 302 that distinguish "between minimal reductions in a shareholder's ownership percentage and loss of corporate control." *Id.* at 100 n.15. However, Justice White, who concurred, found no "principled ground for distinguishing a loss-of-control case from this one." *Id.* at 100 (White, J., concurring).

Note that if a *sole* shareholder makes a contribution to capital of money or other property, it may be treated as a transfer of property under section 351, rather than a contribution to capital. *See Lessinger v. Commissioner*, 872 F.2d 519 (2d Cir. 1989). It may be analyzed under section 351 despite the lack of receipt of shares in return for the property transferred because issuance of additional shares to a sole shareholder is a meaningless gesture—the sole shareholder owns 100 percent of the shares regardless. The application of section 351 means, among other things, that section 357 will apply if the property transferred was subject to liabilities, as was the case in *Lessinger*.

[B]   Tax Consequences to Non-Shareholder Contributors

Non-shareholder contributors to a corporation are governed by general tax principles, rather than by Subchapter C. "Donations to organizations other than those described in section 170 (charitable contributions and gifts) which bear a *direct relationship* to the taxpayer's business and are made with a *reasonable expectation* of a financial return commensurate with the amount of the donation may constitute allowable deductions as business expenses . . . ." under section 162. Treas. Reg. § 1.162-15(b) (emphasis added). Accordingly, a non-shareholder contribution to a corporation to encourage it to relocate or enlarge its existing facility may be a deductible business expense under section 162 if the non-shareholder expects to receive a *direct* business benefit from this relocation or expansion of the corporation.

[C]   Tax Consequences to the Corporation

[1]   In General

With respect to a corporation that receives a contribution to its capital, section 118 governs both types of contributions, those of shareholders, and those of third parties. It provides, as a general rule, that "[i]n the case of a corporation, gross income does not include any contribution to the capital of the taxpayer." I.R.C. § 118(a). However, "the term 'contribution to the capital of the taxpayer' does not include any contribution in aid of construction or any other contribution as a customer or potential customer." I.R.C. § 118(b). The phrase "contribution in aid of construction" is defined in Treasury Regulations, see Treas. Reg. § 1.118-2, except that the Code expressly provides that the term does "not include amounts paid as service charges for starting or stopping services." I.R.C. § 118(c)(3)(A).

[2] Transfers by Non-Shareholders

If money or other property is "contributed to a corporation by a govern-ment unit or by a civic group for the purpose of inducing the corporation to locate its business in a particular community, or for the purpose of enabling the corporation to expand its operating facilities," then the contribution is excluded from the corporation's gross income as a "contribu-tion to its capital." Treas. Reg. § 1.118-1. On the other hand, property transferred in consideration for goods or services rendered, or subsidies paid to induce the corporation to restrict production, are not considered contribu-tions to capital, and, therefore, must be treated as gross income. Treas. Reg. § 1.118-1; *see also Detroit Edison Co. v. Commissioner*, 319 U.S. 98 (1943) (pre-section 118(a) case holding that a distributor of electricity could not treat the cost of extending services borne by its customers as a contribution to capital).

For a transfer by a non-shareholder to a corporation to be a tax-exempt contribution to the capital of the corporation, it must pass a five-factor test developed by the Supreme Court. *See United States v. Chicago, B. & Q. R.R.*, 412 U.S. 401 (1973); *accord* Rev. Rul. 93-16, 1993-1 C.B. 26. Under *Chicago, B. & Q.*, the contribution or asset transferred (1) had to become a permanent part of the transferee's working capital; (2) could "not be compensation, such as a direct payment for a specific, quantifiable service provided for the transferor by the transferee"; (3) had to be bargained for; (4) foreseeably had to "result in benefit to the transferee in an amount commensurate with its value"; and (5) ordinarily had to be "employed in or contribute to the production of additional income . . . ." *Chicago B. & Q.*, 412 U.S. at 413; *see also May Dept. Stores Co. v. Commissioner*, T.C. Memo. 1974-253 (holding that where the developer of a shopping center transferred to a department store company a parcel of land in consideration for building and operating a retail store on the developer's property, the transfer was a contribution to capital; the developer transferred the property in the hope of attracting customers to the other existing retail stores, an indirect and intangible benefit).

[3] Corporation's Basis

[a] In General

Section 118(e)(1) expressly cross-references section 362 for basis of property acquired by a corporation as a contribution to its capital. Under section 362(a), the same basis rules apply to contributions to capital as do to property acquired in a section 351 transaction:

> If property was acquired on or after June 22, 1954, by a corporation—
>
> (1) in connection with a transaction to which section 351 (relating to transfer of property to corporation controlled by transferor) ap-plies, or

(2) *as paid-in surplus or as a contribution to capital,*

then the basis shall be the same as it would be in the hands of the transferor, increased in the amount of gain recognized to the transferor on such transfer.

I.R.C. § 362(a)(emphasis added). These rules are discussed above in § 2.03[B][1]. In addition, it appears that the section 362(e) loss limitation rules also apply to contributions to capital (despite the reference in the heading of section 362(e)(2)), given that section 362(e) states that they apply to any transaction "described in subsection (a)" of section 362. I.R.C. § 362(e)(1)(A), (2)(A)(i). Section 362(e) is discussed in § 2.03[B][1].

[b]   Basis in Property Received from Non-Shareholders

Under subsection (c) of section 362, when a non-shareholder transfers non-monetary property as a contribution to capital on or after June 22, 1954, the basis in the transferred property is zero. *See* I.R.C. § 362(c)(1). With respect to monetary contributions to capital made on or after that date, if the transferee corporation uses the money acquired to purchase property within a 12-month period from the date of the contribution, then the basis in that property is reduced by the amount of the contribution. *See* I.R.C. § 362(c)(2); *but cf. John B. White, Inc. v. Commissioner*, 55 T.C. 729 (1971), *aff'd*, 458 F.2d 989 (3d Cir.), *cert. denied*, 409 U.S. 876 (1972) (holding that monetary payments by manufacturer to dealer to induce it to relocate was not a contribution to capital, and therefore, did not reduce the basis of leasehold improvements made by the dealer).

A regulation defines "[p]roperty deemed to be acquired with contributed money" as "that property, if any, the acquisition of which was the purpose motivating the contribution." Treas. Reg. § 1.362-2(a). If there is an excess of the amount of the contribution over the cost of the property, then the excess is applied as a proportional reduction of the basis of any other properties held by the corporation on the last day of the 12-month period. Treas. Reg. § 1.362-2(b). The basis of property subject to an allowance for depreciation is reduced first, followed by property with respect to which a deduction for amortization is allowable, then "[p]roperty with respect to which a deduction for depletion is allowable under section 611 but not under section 613," and finally, all other properties. *See* Treas. Reg. § 1.362-2(b)(1)–(4). Within each category, the reduction in basis is made in proportion to relative basis. Treas. Reg. § 1.362-2(b).

Chapter 3

CAPITAL STRUCTURE OF A CORPORATION

§ 3.01 Overview of Debt and Equity

The transactions discussed in Chapter 2 generally involved a transfer of property to a corporation in exchange for stock of the corporation—that is, in exchange for an equity interest in the corporation. Another method of financing the operations of the corporation is for investors[1] to lend funds to the corporation, accepting a debt interest in the corporation in exchange for the transfer of cash or other property. All corporations need to have some equity (stock). Most also have debt securities.

[A] Introduction to the Tax Consequences of Distributions with Respect to Debt and Equity

In economic terms, disregarding taxes, capital structure arguably is irrelevant. *See* Franco Modigliani & Merton H. Miller, *The Cost of Capital, Corporation Finance and the Theory of Investment*, 48 AM. ECON. REV. 261 (1958) (proving that, under certain assumptions, capital structure does not affect firm value); *but cf.* STEPHEN M. BAINBRIDGE, CORPORATION LAW AND ECONOMICS 73 (2002) ("Once we relax the assumptions made by Modigliani and Miller, it becomes clear that while there may not be a single optimal capital structure, there are nonoptimal capital structures."). Nonetheless, federal income tax law traditionally has favored debt over equity by providing corporations with a deduction under section 163 for interest paid but no deduction for dividend distributions. Chapter 1 explained that in order to avoid the double taxation of earnings, shareholders may prefer to capitalize a corporation with debt than with equity, where possible, because the corporate-level deduction for interest payments reduces the corporation's taxable income. As discussed in Chapter 1, the preferential tax treatment of individuals' qualified dividends under section 1(h) generally has reduced but not eliminated that incentive. The following example illustrates that with a comparison of two similarly situated corporations.

Example 3.1: X, Inc. and Y, Inc., which are domestic corporations, each have $100,000 of profits in Year 1. Each corporation has long been owned by two equal shareholders, Anne and Bob, who are both in the 28 percent tax bracket.

X, Inc. pays out its profits as dividends to Anne and Bob. X, Inc. cannot deduct those dividends. Assume, for simplicity, that no other deductions,

---

[1] As discussed below, these investors may be shareholders or third parties. Example 3.1, below, illustrates the tax advantages of debt for individual shareholders when compared to equity investment.

such as the domestic production deduction of section 199, apply. X, Inc. will have $100,000 of taxable income. X, Inc. will owe $22,250 in federal income tax under section 11. X, Inc. will therefore be able to distribute only $77,750 to Anne and Bob ($38,875 each). Anne and Bob will pay tax at a 15 percent rate on the amounts they received because they constitute qualified dividends under section 1(h). They will owe $5,831 each on the dividends they each received ($11,662 in total). Thus, Anne and Bob will each have kept $33,044 of X, Inc.'s profits, all of which it distributed to them.

Y, Inc. pays out its profits as interest to Anne and Bob on debt obligations they also hold. The $100,000 of interest paid generally will be deductible under section 163, so Y, Inc. will have no taxable income for Year 1 and will owe no federal income tax. It has $100,000 remaining after taxes, and distributes it all. Anne and Bob will each have $50,000 of interest income, taxed at a 28 percent rate. They will owe $14,000 each ($28,000 in total). Thus, Anne and Bob will each have kept $36,000 of the corporation's profits, all of which it distributed.

Note that, in Example 3.1, Anne and Bob had more after-tax return from the corporation when it distributed its profits with respect to debt, rather than equity. That was true even though Anne and Bob's dividends were taxed at a preferential rate and their interest was not eligible for any tax rate preference. As Example 3.1 suggests, it is the combination of shareholder and corporate taxes, which largely depend on tax rates, that is critical. In most situations involving noncorporate shareholders, as in Example 3.1, debt comes with less federal income tax cost than equity does.[2]

The IRS may question whether all of the purported "interest" payments paid by a closely held corporation in which shareholders are also creditors, as in Example 3.1, were in fact interest. The IRS may assert that some of the payments were actually disguised dividends. The same type of question can arise with respect to financial instruments that carry special privileges; they may be labeled debt but the IRS may question whether they are actually equity in substance. Over the years, courts have developed a multitude of factors that help distinguish "true debt" from equity, as discussed in § 3.03.

---

[2] As discussed in § 4.04 of Chapter 4, corporate shareholders benefit from a dividends received deduction. Corporate shareholders may therefore end up with more after tax if profits are paid out as dividends rather than interest. For example, in Example 3.1, if Bob were Bob, Inc., a corporation (instead of an individual), an 80 percent dividends received deduction would apply under section 243 to dividends it received. Assuming that Bob, Inc. were subject to taxation at a 34 percent marginal rate, it would pay only $2,643.50 in tax on the dividend of $38,875, resulting in retention of $36,231.50 of the $38,875 distributed to it. By contrast, in the interest scenario, Bob, Inc. would receive $50,000 from Y, Inc. but would bear federal income tax of $17,000, so Bob, Inc. would retain only $33,000 after tax.

[B] Introduction to Types of Debt and Equity

[1] General Types of Equity

Stock comes in a number of forms such as preferred, common, voting, and nonvoting. "Common stock" represents the residual ownership interest in a corporation. BAINBRIDGE, *supra*, at 66. Because an S corporation can only have one class of stock, common stock will be the *only* class of stock an S corporation has.[3] I.R.C. § 1361(b)(1)(D).

"Preferred stock" is called that because its holders receive a payment preference. That is, the preferred stock receives priority over the common stock for payment of dividend distributions and/or upon liquidation of the corporation. BAINBRIDGE, *supra*, at 66–67. Only creditors are paid before holders of preferred stock. Thus, preferred stock has lower downside risk than common stock. For that reason, it is usually ranked between debt and common stock in terms of its riskiness.

Preferred stock also has limited upside potential, however. A hallmark of preferred stock is its limited right to dividends and payments upon liquidation. That is, preferred stock generally has a contractual cap on the amount it receives. The common stock is entitled to the remainder of the corporation's assets. *See id.* Thus, common stock has the most upside potential, but it is also the riskiest because if the corporation lacks funds after paying off creditors and the preferred stockholders, it is the common stockholders who suffer.

Preferred stock typically is "cumulative," which means that accrued dividends that are unpaid for lack of funds cumulate so that the corporation is contractually obligated to pay the dividend arrearages before dividends can be paid on the common stock. Preferred stock may be convertible into common stock; such stock is called convertible preferred. *Id.* at 67.

Both preferred and common stock come in voting and nonvoting varieties. In an S corporation, differences in voting rights among classes of common stock are disregarded in determining whether the corporation has more than one class of stock. I.R.C. § 1361(c)(4). Preferred stock usually does not have voting rights, BAINBRIDGE, *supra*, at 67, but that is not always the case. In *American Bantam Car Co. v. Commissioner*, 11 T.C. 397 (1948), for example, which was discussed in Chapter 2, the company's preferred stock had three votes per share (and its common had one vote per share). In addition, voting rights may arise only on the occurrence of specific events or conditions. For example, *John A. Nelson Co. v. Helvering*, 296 U.S. 374, 376 (1935), involved preferred stock that had voting rights only if its dividends were in default.

[2] General Types of Debt

Debt securities involve loans to a corporation by investors. Generally, long-term loans are referred to as "bonds" or "securities" and short-term

---

[3] S corporations are discussed in Chapter 8.

loans are called "notes." Some debt instruments are convertible into stock. *See* BAINBRIDGE, *supra*, at 68, 70.

§ 3.02 General Tax Consequences of Debt and Equity

The characterization of an interest in a corporation as either debt or equity matters for many different events in the life-cycle of a corporation, beginning with the initial investment.

[A] Investment

Upon issuance of stock in return for money or other property, if section 351 applies, the receipt of the corporation's stock is counted towards qualifying the transaction under section 351.[4] By contrast, debt instruments received by the transferors of property constitute boot to them.[5] *See* I.R.C. § 351(a), (b). For the corporation, issuance of stock gives rise to no gain or loss under section 1032. Issuance of debt is tax-free to the corporation, just as borrowing money would be for any taxpayer. In other words, the issuance of $100,000 of bonds by a corporation is just as much a tax-free borrowing as obtaining a $100,000 loan from a bank would be.

[B] Current Distributions

Distributions to shareholders with respect to equity are tested under section 316 to determine the amount taxed as dividends, which, in general, is the amount of the distribution from the corporation's "earnings and profits," as discussed in Chapter 4. The corporation cannot deduct distributions with respect to equity.

At the shareholder level, if certain holding periods are met with respect to the underlying shares, individuals' dividends generally are taxed at preferential capital gains rates under section 1(h), while corporate shareholders benefit from a dividends received deduction under section 243, which is discussed in Chapter 4.

> *Example 3.2*: Z Corp., a highly profitable domestic corporation, has two long-time equal shareholders, Carol and D Corporation. Z Corp. distributes $100 to each of its shareholders as dividends. Z Corp. cannot deduct the dividends paid. Carol, the individual shareholder, will pay tax at a maximum rate of 15 percent on the $100. D Corporation will include the $100 in gross income but will be able to deduct 80 percent of it under section 243, so only $20 of the dividend will actually be taxed.

As indicated above, distributions with respect to debt are interest, includible in full in the gross income of the shareholder. Interest payments

---

[4] Section 351 transactions are discussed in detail in Chapter 2.

[5] "Boot" — property that is not permitted to be received without the recognition of realized gain — is discussed in § 2.02[A][1][f]. Note that "nonqualified preferred stock," which essentially is debt-like preferred stock, also constitutes boot. I.R.C. § 351(g).

are deductible by the corporation under section 163, subject to certain limited exceptions. *See* I.R.C. § 163(e), (f), (j)–(m).

> *Example 3.3*: XYZ, Inc. pays each of its bondholders, Ellen and F Corporation, $100 of interest. Ellen and F Corporation will each have $100 of interest income and, absent applicability of an exception, XYZ, Inc. will be able to deduct the interest.

[C] Return of Investment

Returning a particular shareholder's stock investment is done as a buy-back (or "redemption") of the stock.[6] The tax treatment of a redemption is discussed in Chapter 5. Generally speaking, under section 302, a redemption may be treated as either a sale of the stock to the corporation by the shareholder (and therefore generally subject to capital gains treatment) or as a distribution of property to the shareholder (and therefore tested to determine the amount taxed as a dividend). With respect to the corporation buying back its stock, the redemption is reflected in the corporation's "earnings and profits" account, as discussed in Chapter 5. The purchase is not deductible by the corporation.

A return of a shareholder's investment in a debt security is generally more straightforward for tax purposes. Return of proceeds lent is simply repayment of a loan. Repayment of loan principal is not subject to taxation. For the corporation, the repayment of principal is a similar non-event for tax purposes; no deduction is allowed.[7] Repayment of a loan also does not affect the corporation's earnings and profits.

[D] Worthlessness

The characterization of a security as debt or equity matters not only upon investment, distribution, and retirement of the security, but also for other tax purposes. For example, if the corporation's business fails, the investor's ability to recover some of the investment may depend on whether the investment was debt or equity. A loss on equity in a corporation that ceases operations may be deductible under section 165 as a capital loss. Unrecovered debt may be deductible as a bad debt loss under section 166. Business bad debts give rise to ordinary losses, while nonbusiness bad debts create only short-term capital losses. *See* I.R.C. § 166(a), (d)(1). The carryback of individuals' nonbusiness bad debt deductions is also restricted by section 172. *See* I.R.C. § 172(d)(2).

---

[6] The tax consequences of a "non-liquidating" distribution—one that is not made in connection with the liquidation of the corporation, see § 4.01—are discussed in § 3.02[B], *supra*.

[7] Note that if a corporation buys back its securities at less than the amount it lent (because the market value of the securities has decreased), the corporation generally will have income from the discharge of indebtedness. *See* I.R.C. §§ 61(a)(12), 108; *United States v. Kirby Lumber Co.*, 284 U.S. 1 (1931).

United States v. Generes, 405 U.S. 93 (1972), provides an example of the importance of the distinction between business bad debts and nonbusiness bad debts, in the context of a corporation that foundered. The taxpayer in that case, Allen H. Generes (Generes), was a 44-percent owner and president of the Kelly-Generes corporation, a family-owned corporation. The taxpayer occasionally lent the corporation money from his personal funds and guaranteed loans made to the corporation by banks. When the corporation seriously underbid two projects, he indemnified the corporation's underwriter for $162,104.57. That same year, he lent the corporation $158,814.49 to lessen financial difficulties. The corporation nonetheless went into receivership, and the taxpayer was not able to recover his funds. *Id.* at 97–99.

In *Generes*, there was no dispute over whether the funds advanced were loans. The issue was whether the bad debts arising from the loans were business bad debts or nonbusiness bad debts. Generes treated the loss on the direct loan as a nonbusiness bad debt, but he claimed the indemnification loss as a business bad debt and carried it back to prior years under the net operating loss provisions, giving rise to refund claims. At trial, the taxpayer argued that he made the loans solely to protect his $12,000-a-year employment with the corporation. *Id.* at 99.

In determining whether the indemnification loss was a business debt or a nonbusiness debt, the relevant consideration under the regulations was the relation the loss had to the taxpayer's business. The court explained:

> The fact responsible for the litigation is the taxpayer's dual status relative to the corporation. Generes was both a shareholder and an employee. These interests are not the same, and their differences occasion different tax consequences. In tax jargon, Generes' status as a shareholder was a nonbusiness interest. It was capital in nature and it was composed initially of tax-paid dollars. Its rewards were expectative and would flow, not from personal effort, but from investment earnings and appreciation. On the other hand, Generes' status as an employee was a business interest. Its nature centered in personal effort and labor, and salary for that endeavor would be received. The salary would consist of pre-tax dollars.

Id. at 100–101.

In *Generes*, the Court held that the taxpayer's *dominant* motivation is key; a "significant" business motivation is not enough. *Id.* at 103. The Court found unconvincing the taxpayer's argument that he sought solely to protect his $12,000 annual salary in light of his $38,900 initial investment in the corporation (a post-tax figure, unlike salary) and "his personal interest in the integrity of the corporation as a source of living for his son-in-law and as an investment for his son and his other son-in-law." *Id.* at 106. Thus, the Court held that the taxpayer's dominant motivation was not a business motivation, so the bad debt was not a business bad debt.

§ 3.03 Characterization: Distinguishing Debt from Equity

Characterizing securities, particularly hybrid securities, as either "debt" or "equity" is a highly fact-sensitive endeavor. Unlike the characterization of a business entity for tax purposes, with respect to which the Treasury has provided an elective "check-the-box" regime, the debt/equity distinction generally remains subject to the unpredictability of case law.[8] However, as discussed in Chapter 2, Congress has specifically provided that certain debt-like preferred stock (nonqualified preferred stock) is treated as boot for purposes of section 351.[9] *See* I.R.C. § 351(g); *cf.* I.R.C. § 356(e).

[A] Section 385

Section 385, "[t]reatment of certain interests in corporations as stock or indebtedness," provides the Secretary of the Treasury with authority to prescribe regulations: "The Secretary is authorized to prescribe such regulations as may be necessary or appropriate to determine whether an interest in a corporation is to be treated for purposes of this title as stock or indebtedness (or as in part stock and in part indebtedness)." I.R.C. § 385(a). Subsection (b) provides five factors that the regulations could include. Those factors are set forth below. However, there have never been regulations under section 385 that have become effective. *See* Anthony P. Polito, *Useful Fictions: Debt and Equity Classification in Corporate Tax Law*, 30 ARIZ. ST. L.J. 761, 786 n.68 (1998) (setting forth the history of the regulations, which were delayed in taking effect, amended, and then postponed indefinitely). In fact, it seems unlikely that the Treasury could design regulations that provide appropriate guidance without opening up avenues of abuse.

Section 385(b) provides the following with respect to factors to distinguish debt from equity:

> The regulations prescribed under this section shall set forth factors which are to be taken into account in determining with respect to a particular factual situation whether a debtor-creditor relationship exists or a corporation-shareholder relationship exists. The factors so set forth in the regulations may include among other factors:
>
> (1) whether there is a written unconditional promise to pay on demand or on a specified date a sum certain in money in return for an adequate consideration in money or money's worth, and to pay a fixed rate of interest,
>
> (2) whether there is subordination to or preference over any indebtedness of the corporation,
>
> (3) the ratio of debt to equity of the corporation,
>
> (4) whether there is convertibility into the stock of the corporation, and

---

[8] *See* § 1.02[A][2][b].

[9] *See* § 2.02[A][1][f][i].

(5) the relationship between holdings of stock in the corporation and holdings of the interest in question.

I.R.C. § 385(a), (b). In addition, under subsection (c), the issuing corporation's characterization of securities binds security-holders, except those who disclose the inconsistent treatment on their returns. I.R.C. § 385(c)(1), (2).

The factors listed in section 385(b) provide helpful guidance in distinguishing debt from equity. The first factor essentially reiterates a common definition of "straight debt." *Cf.* I.R.C. § 1361(c)(5)(B). The second factor reflects the hierarchical order of debt and equity (equity is subordinate to debt).

Factor three, the debt/equity ratio, refers to the capitalization of the corporation; in "thinly" capitalized corporations (those with disproportionate debt), some of the purported debt may actually be equity. The regulations proposed in 1982, which ultimately were withdrawn, provided for an "outside" (total) debt/equity ratio and an "inside" debt/equity ratio. Department of the Treasury, Internal Revenue Service, *Notice of Proposed Rulemaking, Treatment of Certain Interests in Corporations as Stock or Indebtedness*, 47 FR 164 (Jan. 5, 1982). Under the proposed regulations, the outside debt/equity ratio was the ratio of the corporation's liabilities (excluding such things as trade accounts payable) to stockholders' equity. The inside debt/equity ratio, was "determined in the same manner by excluding liabilities to independent creditors (except in computing stockholders' equity)." *Id.* Stockholders' equity is the difference between assets and liabilities. The proposed regulations used the adjusted basis of the corporation's assets, with an adjustment for depreciation, in this calculation. There was a safe harbor if the outside debt/equity ratio did not exceed 3:1 or if the inside debt/equity ratio did not exceed 3:1 and the outside debt/equity ratio did not exceed 10:1. *Id.*

The fourth factor in section 385 reflects the idea that some purported debt will inevitably be converted into stock, and should therefore be characterized as equity from the beginning. The fifth factor relates primarily to dual-role investors (stockholders/creditors), and particularly suggests that *pro rata* holdings of stock and the security in question indicate that the security is more likely an additional equity investment rather than true debt. That is, debt interests do not tend to be held proportionately to equity interests, whereas new equity may be issued *pro rata* so as to maintain the same ownership interests in the corporation.

[B] Case-Law Factors

Given the absence of regulations under section 385 and the fact-sensitive nature of the inquiry, the primary source of guidance for distinguishing debt from equity is case law. Courts have developed laundry lists of factors to be considered in determining whether a security is "true debt" or equity. As reflected in the cases discussed below, courts typically balance the factors they consider, often by discussing each factor individually. In wading through the case law, it may help to consider whether the context involves a dual-role investor or a hybrid instrument. *See* Polito, *supra*, at 779.

In *Estate of Mixon v. United States*, 464 F.2d 394 (5th Cir. 1972), the taxpayer, Travis Mixon, Jr., was the largest shareholder in a bank co-owned primarily by other members of his family. After the bank experienced embezzlements and losses on bad loans, the Deputy Commissioner of the Florida Commission of Banking (Deputy Commissioner) threatened to close the bank unless it raised an additional $200,000 in capital. A plan for a new issue of stock was abandoned because the bank had a large number of small shareholders with preemptive rights. Instead, the taxpayer and two other officers advanced a total of $200,000 to the bank. The funds were held in a separate account labeled "Reserve for Contingencies" controlled by the Deputy Commissioner. The bank was prohibited from distributing dividends without the consent of state and federal banking authorities. *Id.* at 399–401.

Once the bank began to recover its lost funds, the Deputy Commissioner allowed repayment to the three officers of a portion of the $200,000. The money was allocated in accordance with the needs of the individual officers at the time of disbursement. Eventually, the bank was permitted to repay the balance of the $200,000 and was also authorized to pay dividends not exceeding $10,000 per year. No interest was paid to the taxpayer or the other two officers. A request by the bank to pay interest was denied by the Deputy Commissioner. *Id.* at 401.

The IRS argued that the reimbursement by the corporation to the taxpayer was a dividend distribution. The taxpayer countered that the reimbursement was a tax-free repayment of a loan. Resolving that question required determination of whether the funds advanced obtained for the taxpayer a debt interest or an equity interest. The court listed thirteen factors that aid in the characterization of the advance as either debt or equity, but cautioned that "the various factors are not of equal significance and that no one factor is controlling." *Id.* at 402. The court then examined each of the thirteen factors, which are as follows.

1. *The name given to the certificate*: The trial court had found no evidence of a formal, unconditional promise to pay. However, the Court of Appeals found that the critical issue in this regard was that the parties had acted consistent with arm's-length standards.

2. *Presence or absence of a maturity date*: Although there was no fixed repayment date expressed, the court found that all of the surrounding factors pointed to an understanding between the parties involved that the advance would be repaid within two to three years.

3. *The source of the payments*: If the source of payments is earnings of the corporation, that points to equity, but if the source is not dependent on earnings, that suggests a *bona fide* loan. The court found that the payments were tied to the collection of outstanding loans—a source other than earnings.

4. *Right to enforce payment*: A definite obligation to repay suggests that the advance is a loan. The repayment here was dependent on the collection of loans, but this was an almost certain occurrence and not tied to the success of the corporation.

5. *Increased participation in management*: Because there was no increase in voting power or management after the advance, this factor indicated a loan.

6. *Subordination*: This factor focuses on whether the advance has equal footing for repayment with other corporate creditors or with other shareholders. The court found no support for the IRS's position that the advances were subordinated to other debt.

7. *The intent of the parties*: If the objective intent is inconclusive, as it was here, the court will look to the subjective intent of the parties. Taking all of the actions of the parties into account, the court found that the parties intended working capital instead of permanent financing and intended a debtor-creditor relationship.

8. *Thin or adequate capitalization*: The court found that the bank was not thinly capitalized but rather that the bank had simply faced a temporary shortage of cash.

9. *Identity of interest between creditor and stockholder*: As the advances in this case were disproportionate to the stockholders' equity interests in the corporation, the advances seemed to be more consistent with loans.

10. *Payment of interest only out of dividend money*: No interest at all was paid on the advance in this case. The court noted that typically, when investors do not insist on interest payments, it is because they intend an equity investment. However, because of the federal and state involvement in this case, the fact that the taxpayer did not insist on interest payments did not indicate an intent to make equity contributions.

11. *Ability to obtain loans from outside lending institutions*: This factor questions whether a reasonable creditor would have loaned money to the corporation at the time of the advance. The bank here did not seem to have exhausted all of its borrowing resources. Instead, the FDIC required the loan primarily to act as a bonding mechanism to ensure better management of the bank.

12. *The extent to which the advance was used to acquire capital assets*: The advance was used to maintain day-to-day operations, not to acquire capital assets (which would have tended to indicate an equity investment).

13. *The failure of the corporation to repay on the due date*: As soon as the bank was permitted to do so by outside regulators, it repaid the advance to the taxpayer.

Because almost all of the factors counseled a finding of a *bona fide* loan, the court affirmed the district court's characterization of the advance as a loan, stating:

The government would have us hold that a 15 percent shareholder, taxpayer here, advanced 80 percent of a capital contribution to his corporation with all its attendant risks and with no thought to acquiring interest, greater control over the corporation, a greater ownership percentage, a like contribution from other shareholders, or even an assurance that the advance would be returned. The facts, and our opinion that corporate directors are generally reasonably intelligent, dictate otherwise. Under such circumstances, we cannot say the district court erred in its judgment that the advance lacked the ingredients of high-risk capital investment.

Id. at 411.

In re Lane, 742 F.2d 1311 (11th Cir. 1984), applied the thirteen factors used in *Mixon* to purported loans and loan guarantees. In *Lane*, the taxpayer, James Lane (Lane), had made a very profitable investment in a hotel that netted approximately $1 million when he sold it in 1972. After that success, he purchased other hotels through wholly owned S corporations. To keep the hotels operating, Lane advanced several hundred thousand dollars of his own funds to the corporations and personally guaranteed various loans. In 1975, the corporations failed. Lane was unable to collect his outstanding cash advances and had to satisfy the loans he had guaranteed. He sought to have the amounts he was unable to recover from the corporations declared bad debts under section 166 and to allow him to carry back the bad debt losses to 1972 so that he could obtain a refund of the taxes paid on the profit from the sale of the first hotel. *Id.* at 1313.

The Court of Appeals for the Eleventh Circuit first considered whether Lane's advances of his own funds to the corporations were loans or contributions to capital (equity); the court noted that Treasury Regulation 1.166-1(c) provides that a contribution to capital is not a debt within the meaning of section 166. *Id.* at 1313–1314. In order to determine whether the amounts in issue constituted debt or equity, the court examined each *Mixon* factor in turn.

The court noted that the parties called the certificates "notes," connoting debt, but the real issue is what they were in substance. There was no fixed maturity date, and the fact that repayment was expected only when it was good for the corporation weighed heavily towards equity. Although the notes were enforceable, the taxpayer took no steps to ensure that they would be repaid if the corporation failed, again suggesting equity. The court also looked to the circumstances surrounding the transaction and found that none of the advances contained a provision for interest. The fact that the funds were placed at the risk of the business without interest suggested equity, not debt. In addition, there was nothing in the record that showed any meaningful attempt to repay the obligation or to seek a postponement. Thus, the court determined that taxpayer had advanced the funds as equity, not as debt, precluding deduction of a bad debt loss. *Id.* at 1315–1319.

Next, the court considered the amounts that Lane had paid out under the loan guarantees. The court determined that guaranteed debts, like loans, must be analyzed to determine whether they are debt or equity. Looking to the nature of the guarantees, the court determined "that it was Lane's intent at the time the guaranties were extended to use the guaranties as short-term substitutes for infusion of more capital stock," putting the funds "at the risk of the business." *Id.* at 1320. Therefore, the court treated the guarantees as equity and denied the claimed bad debt deduction.

In contrast to *Estate of Mixon* and *In re Lane, Fin Hay Realty Co. v. United States*, 398 F.2d 694 (3d Cir. 1968), applied a 16-factor test to distinguish debt from equity. In that case, the taxpayer corporation was originally established in 1934 with $30,000 transferred in return for notes bearing interest at six percent per year and $20,000 transferred in return for stock. The taxpayer corporation used its capital to purchase real estate. By 1949, the corporation essentially was wholly owned by two sisters who received payments characterized as "interest" by the corporation. The corporation deducted the payments to the sisters as interest under section 163. *Id.* at 695.

The court listed sixteen factors that courts use to help distinguish debt from equity:

> (1) the intent of the parties; (2) the identity between creditors and shareholders; (3) the extent of participation in management by the holder of the instrument; (4) the ability of the corporation to obtain funds from outside sources; (5) the "thinness" of the capital structure in relation to debt; (6) the risk involved; (7) the formal indicia of the arrangement; (8) the relative position of the obligees as to other creditors regarding the payment of interest and principal; (9) the voting power of the holder of the instrument; (10) the provision of a fixed rate of interest; (11) a contingency on the obligation to repay; (12) the source of the interest payments; (13) the presence or absence of a fixed maturity date; (14) a provision for redemption by the corporation; (15) a provision for redemption at the option of the holder; and (16) the timing of the advance with reference to the organization of the corporation.

Id. at 696. The court stated that no single criterion or set of criteria proves conclusive. The court further explained that, although the form of an investment in a public corporation generally reflects the actual character of the investments because of the arm's-length relationship between the corporation and its shareholders, for a closely held corporation, the true structure of the investments is not always discernable from the form. In the case of a closely held corporation, it helps to determine what the form would be for the same corporation if it were publicly held. *Id.* at 697.

The court found that although real estate values rose substantially during the period of the investment, "[i]t is difficult to escape the inference that a prudent outside businessman would not have risked his capital in six per cent unsecured demand notes in Fin Hay Realty Co. in 1934." *Id.* at 698. Thus, the court upheld the district court's disallowance of the interest deduction; in substance it was a dividend payment on equity investments.

[C] Possible Treatment of an Investment as in Part Debt and in Part Equity

Theoretically, a single investment could be partly debt and partly equity. In *Richmond, Fredericksburg & Potomac R.R. Co. v. Commissioner*, 33 B.T.A. 895 (1936), the Board of Tax Appeals [10] treated payments on certain "guaranteed stock" as partly interest and partly dividends. Section 385(a) provides Congressional support, stating that, "[t]he Secretary is authorized to prescribe such regulations as may be necessary or appropriate to determine whether an interest in a corporation is to be treated for purposes of this title as stock or indebtedness (*or as in part stock and in part indebtedness*)." I.R.C. § 385(a) (emphasis added). However, as the three cases discussed above reflect, most courts characterize any given security as either equity *or* debt, rather than a little of each. The primary exception is *Farley Realty Corp. v. Commissioner*, 279 F.2d 701 (2d Cir. 1960), a case involving a loan with an "equity kicker." [11]

In *Farley Realty*, an individual made a loan of $70,000 to a corporation, in return for a second mortgage on a building. The loan bore a fixed rate of interest of 15 percent for each of the first two years of the loan, and approximately 13 percent for each of the remaining eight years. In addition, the lender was given a right to 50 percent of the appreciation in value of the building. His share of the appreciation would be calculated as of the date that either he or the corporation proposed to buy out the interest of the other or sell the property to a third party; this agreement made it possible that the lender could share in appreciation occurring after the maturity of the loan. *Id.* at 703.

The Court of Appeals for the Second Circuit held that the lender's right to share in the appreciation of the building was severable from his right to repayment with interest of the $70,000 principal of the loan, and that it constituted an equity interest in the building. The court found that the fact that the lender could share in appreciation of the building occurring after the term of the loan was a critical factor in the debt/equity analysis, but also stated that even if the right to share in appreciation had terminated at the maturity of the loan, "it is unlikely that this could be considered interest on an indebtedness because of the indefiniteness of the amount." *Id.* at 704.

---

[10] The Board of Tax Appeals is the predecessor of what is now the United States Tax Court.

[11] "An 'equity kicker' is a term of art in the banking business and involves a loan arrangement under which a bank lends money at a lower rate of interest and makes up the difference by taking a share of the borrower's profits from the project for which the loan was made." Dennis Scholl & Ronald L. Weaver, *Loan Participations: Are They "Securities"?*, 10 FLA. ST. U. L. REV. 215, 216 n.6 (1982).

Thus, in *Farley Realty*, the potential for the lender to share in appreciation of the building occurring after the term of the loan was a factor that persuaded the court to separate the debt interest from the interest in the building that it characterized as equity. In addition, another important factor seems to have been "the indefiniteness of the amount" of the appreciation in which the lender could share. *Id.*

Increased use of bifurcation of an instrument into debt and equity components may be unlikely. One commentator notes:

> So long as the Treasury maintains a multi-factor view of the debt-equity problem, bifurcation may be an even more difficult task than that pursued by the Treasury's failed regulations. Without bifurcation, the Treasury must decide when the factors make a security enough like stock to treat it as equity. With bifurcation it must decide (1) if a security is equity-like enough to be bifurcated; (2) how much to treat as debt and how much as equity; and (3) if a security is so much like equity that it should be treated as entirely equity. Because every debt security has an equity component, a bifurcation approach would replace one fictional distinction with two fictional distinctions and a sliding-scale between them.

Polito, *supra*, at 790 n.85.

Professor Herwig Schlunk has argued that the government's either/or approach to debt and equity is not sensible. He explains:

> [T]here is no theoretical limit to the number of new instruments that can be created in an attempt to exploit the inconsistency in the tax treatment of corporate debt and equity. Indeed, recent years have seen a flood of new instruments that attempt to exploit the inconsistency. As financial engineers become more adept, and as financial markets become more sophisticated, there is no reason to believe anything but that this flood will accelerate. Faced with such a reality, legislators and tax administrators might want to consider what they have in the past felt unable to consider: whether, rather than trying to defend the line between debt and equity, they would simply be better served by abolishing it. Indeed, it is my belief that . . . as financial innovation becomes cheaper and cheaper (and in the limit becomes costless), the debt-equity distinction will be exploitable by taxpayers to such an extent that their choice of tax treatment will be effectively elective.

Herwig J. Schlunk, *Little Boxes: Can Optimal Commodity Tax Methodology Save the Debt-Equity Distinction?*, 80 TEX. L. REV. 859, 861–62 (2002); *cf.* David A. Weisbach, *Thinking Outside the Little Boxes: A Response to Professor Schlunk*, 80 TEX. L. REV. 893 (2002).

§ 3.04   Conclusion

All corporations are capitalized with some equity, and most corporations also have debt securities. Traditionally, debt has borne lower tax cost than equity investments. As Example 3.1 demonstrated, that may still be true in many cases for individual investors despite the preferential tax treatment afforded individuals' qualified dividends under section 1(h).

Because of the traditional tax advantages for debt characterization, courts have developed multi-factor tests to distinguish debt from equity in the context of hybrid instruments and purported "loans" made by shareholders in closely held corporations. If purported debt is recharacterized as equity, payments on the instrument that had been treated as interest will be recharacterized as distributions taxable under section 301, which, as discussed in Chapter 4, will be taxed as dividends to the extent of the corporation's "earnings and profits."

Chapter 4

NON-LIQUIDATING DISTRIBUTIONS OF PROPERTY TO SHAREHOLDERS (DIVIDENDS)

§ 4.01 Introduction

From time to time, a corporation may make distributions of cash or other property to its shareholders with respect to their stock. Distributions to shareholders with respect to their stock that are not made in connection with a liquidation of the corporation are known as "non-liquidating" distributions.[1] These distributions generally are paid in cash, but they may be made in non-cash property as well.

A corporate distribution to shareholders has consequences for both the corporation and the shareholders. As discussed below, distributions with respect to stock are not deductible to the paying corporation. Such distributions may or may not constitute gross income to the shareholders, depending primarily on whether the Code classifies them as "dividends."

§ 4.02 Tax Consequences to the Distributing Corporation

Not only must a corporation not deduct a distribution to a shareholder with respect to the shareholder's stock, a corporation does not recognize a loss on the distribution of property having a fair market value that is less than its basis (that is, property with built-in loss). *See* I.R.C. § 311(a)(2). Although the general rule under section 311(a) is that distributions to shareholders are tax-free to the corporation, as discussed below, that general rule is subject to an important exception for distributions of appreciated property. *See* I.R.C. § 311(b).

Distributions affect corporate "earnings and profits," as well. "Earnings and profits" is a mechanism used to track the amount of a distribution that is taxable to shareholders as dividends. Section 4.03 discusses the tax consequences of distributions to shareholders, including how to calculate the amount of a distribution that constitutes a dividend by reference to the corporation's earnings and profits.[2]

---

[1] Corporate liquidations are discussed in Chapter 7.

[2] The mechanism for calculating a corporation's earnings and profits is discussed in § 4.03[C][1][b].

[A] Appreciated Property

The Code currently provides that if a corporation distributes appreciated property, it recognizes gain on that property as if it had sold the property for its fair market value. I.R.C. § 311(b)(1). This provision overrules *General Utilities & Operating Co. v. Helvering*, 296 U.S. 200 (1935), which is probably the most famous corporate tax case although it is no longer good law.

In *General Utilities*, the taxpayer-corporation sought to sell low-basis stock in its subsidiary, Islands Edison. In an effort to avoid a considerable taxable gain, General Utilities arranged with the buyer that General Utilities would first distribute the stock to its shareholders, who, under a written agreement, would then sell the Islands Edison stock to the buyer. General Utilities did not report any gain on the distribution on the appreciated stock to its shareholders. However, the IRS asserted that the distribution did give rise to taxable gain. *Id.* at 201–03.

The Board of Tax Appeals (predecessor of what is now the United States Tax Court) held that General Utilities recognized no taxable gain from the distribution of the Islands Edison stock as a dividend because the law at the time was that "where the dividend resolution imposes only the obligation to distribute in kind and it is discharged in that way, no gain or loss results to the corporation" and the Board of Tax Appeals found that General Utilities intended to distribute to its shareholders dividends payable in Islands Edison stock, not in cash. *General Utilities & Operating Co. v. Commissioner*, 27 B.T.A. 1200, 1206 (1933). On appeal, the Court of Appeals for the Fourth Circuit agreed with the Board of Tax Appeals that the dividend was not in substance a cash dividend. However, it reversed on the ground that the sale to the buyer was in fact a sale by General Utilities, with its stockholders acting as agents. *See General Utilities*, 296 U.S. at 205–206.

The Supreme Court reversed the Court of Appeals. The Supreme Court found that both of the lower courts were correct in holding that General Utilities "derived no taxable gain from the distribution among its stockholders of the Islands Edison shares as a dividend." *Id.* at 206. It also held that the Court of Appeals should not have considered the issue of whether the seller of the shares was in substance General Utilities because that issue had not been presented to the Board of Tax Appeals. *Id.*

General Utilities therefore allowed appreciated property to leave corporate solution without gain being recognized to the corporation simply because the property was distributed to shareholders. The tax consequences would be markedly different if the appreciated stock (or other property) had been sold to a third party; General Utilities would have recognized gain on such a sale.

The *General Utilities* holding, which Congress later codified in section 311, therefore provided an incentive for corporate taxpayers to structure transactions involving appreciated property as distributions to shareholders. While *General Utilities* was still good law, many transactions took advantage of its holding to avoid or minimize tax in a variety of contexts, extending its reach. In *United States v. Cumberland Pub. Serv. Co.*, 338 U.S. 451 (1950), the Supreme Court respected the form of a transaction involving a liquidating distribution of appreciated property followed by a sale of the property by the shareholders. The Court therefore upheld the taxpayer's application of *General Utilities* principles to the distributing corporation. Congress also codified the holding of *Cumberland*. *See* I.R.C. § 337 (1954). Subsequently, in *Esmark, Inc. v. Commissioner*, 90 T.C. 171 (1988), *aff'd without opinion*, 886 F.2d 1318 (7th Cir. 1989), the courts upheld the taxpayer's tax treatment under *General Utilities* of a sale of a subsidiary to a purchaser (Mobil Oil Corp.) that first became a shareholder in the parent corporation.

In 1986, Congress reversed *General Utilities* with section 311(b), which provides, in part:

> If—
>
> (A) a corporation distributes property (other than an obligation of such corporation) to a shareholder in a distribution to which subpart A applies, and
>
> (B) the fair market value of such property exceeds its adjusted basis (in the hands of the distributing corporation),
>
> *then gain shall be recognized to the distributing corporation* as if such property were sold to the distributee at its fair market value.

I.R.C. § 311(b)(1) (emphasis added). This makes the tax treatment of a distribution of appreciated property consistent with that of sale of the property.

Example 4.1: X, Inc. distributes to its sole shareholder, Adam, with respect to his stock, land with a basis of $100,000 that is worth $125,000. X, Inc. realizes and recognizes $25,000 of gain. As discussed below, the distribution will also affect X, Inc.'s earnings and profits.

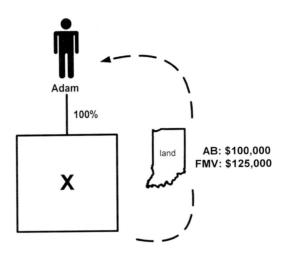

[B] Treatment of Liabilities

In computing the gain recognized by a corporation distributing appreciated property, liabilities that accompany the distribution must be considered. Under section 311(b), "rules similar to the rules of section 336(b) . . . apply . . . ." Section 336 provides tax consequences for a corporation distributing its assets in complete liquidation, and will be discussed in more detail in Chapter 7, but a brief introduction to the provision is appropriate here. Section 336(b) provides:

> If any property distributed in the liquidation is subject to a liability or the shareholder assumes a liability of the liquidating corporation in connection with the distribution, for purposes of subsection (a) and section 337, *the fair market value of such property shall be treated as not less than the amount of such liability.*

I.R.C. § 336(b) (emphasis added). Thus, for purposes of section 311, when a corporation distributes appreciated property to a shareholder, the fair market value of that property is treated as being no less than the amount of the liability, for purposes of computing the distributing corporation's gain.

Example 4.2: Y Corporation distributes to its sole shareholder, Barbara, a building with a basis of $100,000 and a fair market value of $125,000. The building is subject to a mortgage of $350,000, which Barbara assumes. Under section 311(b), the fair market value of the building is treated as $350,000 for purposes of computing Y Corporation's gain. Y Corporation therefore realizes and recognizes $250,000 of gain ($350,000 minus $100,000). As discussed below, the distribution will also affect Y Corporation's earnings and profits.

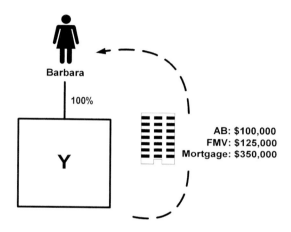

§ 4.03 The Tax Treatment of Shareholders

[A] General Rules under Section 301

Shareholders, whether individuals or corporations, generally are taxed on "dividends." *See* I.R.C. §§ 61(a)(7), 301(c)(1). However, as discussed in § 4.03[D], below, under current law, individuals' qualified dividends are taxed at preferential capital gains rates. *See* I.R.C. §§ 1(h)(3)(B), (11). In addition, as discussed in § 4.04, a corporate shareholder may be able to offset part or all of the gross income from a dividend with a "dividends received deduction."

Any amount distributed to a shareholder in excess of the amount treated by the Code as a dividend is treated as a tax-free return of capital, up to the amount of the shareholder's stock basis. *See* I.R.C. § 301(c)(2). Any remaining excess generally is taxed as gain from the sale or exchange of stock. *See* I.R.C. § 301(c)(3).[3]

Example 4.3: Z Corporation distributes $700 to its sole shareholder, Carol. Carol has a $100 basis in her shares. Assume that $400 of the $700 distribution constitutes a dividend. $100 will be a return of capital,

---

[3] Any portion of a distribution that is not a dividend and that exceeds the shareholder's stock basis, if it is drawn on pre-1913 earnings and profits, is exempt from tax. I.R.C. § 301(c)(3)(B).

reducing Carol's stock basis to zero. The remaining $200 will be treated as gain from the sale of her stock (generally capital gain).

The following chart summarizes the basics of distributions to shareholders under section 301:

CHART 4.1
Tax Consequences of Non-Liquidating Distributions of Property

TAX CONSEQUENCES	CODE SECTIONS
(1) Distribution is a "dividend" to the extent of E&P	I.R.C. §§ 301(c)(1), 316
(2) Remainder (if any) is return of capital to the extent of the stock's basis	I.R.C. § 301(c)(2)
(3) Remainder (if any) is gain from the sale or exchange of property (capital gain)	I.R.C. § 301(c)(3)

As this chart and Example 4.3 show, not every distribution of property to shareholders constitutes a "dividend" in full, or even in part. The rest of this section explores how to determine the amount, if any, of a distribution with respect to stock that is a dividend.

[B] Amount of the Distribution

Under section 301(a), a distribution of "property" (as defined in section 317) made by a corporation to a shareholder with respect to the shareholder's stock is treated in the manner set forth in section 301(c). Section 317 defines "property" as money, securities, and any other property, except that stock in the corporation making the distribution (or rights to acquire such stock) does not constitute "property." Thus, "stock dividends" (distributions of a corporation's own stock to shareholders) are treated differently; they are not subject to section 301, but rather are subject to section 305, which is discussed in Chapter 6.

The amount of a distribution to a shareholder is the fair market value of the property distributed to that shareholder, I.R.C. § 301(b), reduced by the amount of any liabilities to which the property is subject or that are assumed by the shareholder, I.R.C. § 301(b)(2). Thus, a distribution of $500 cash or of unencumbered property worth $500 each constitute distributions of $500 under section 301, but a distribution of property worth $500 and subject to a $200 liability would amount to a $300 distribution.

[C] Calculating the Dividend Amount

Determining the amount distributed to a shareholder by a corporation is only the first step in determining the amount of a dividend. Some or all of a distribution may not constitute a dividend, and, as indicated above, the non-dividend portion will be treated differently for tax purposes.[4] Section 301(c)(1) provides that the portion of the distribution that is a dividend under section 316 shall be included in gross income.

Under section 316, a dividend is any distribution of "property" made by a corporation to its shareholders (1) out of "earnings and profits" accumulated since February 28, 1913 or (2) out of its earnings and profits for the taxable year. "Property," which is defined in section 317, is discussed in § 4.03[B], above. The meaning of the term "earnings and profits" is more complicated, and is discussed below.

[1]   Introduction to Earnings and Profits

"Earnings and profits" (generally referred to as "E&P") is a tax concept used to determine the portion of a distribution that is a dividend. Unfortunately, the term earnings and profits is not defined in the Code, and it defies easy definition. Essentially, the objective of the construct of earnings and profits is to tax as a dividend only the portion of the distribution made from corporate profits. In other words, a distribution made by a corporation with no profits is not a true "dividend" but more likely a return of the investor's capital. Earnings and profits is the mechanism for calculating the amount of the corporation's funds that reflect corporate earnings rather than shareholder investment, loan proceeds, and the like. It bears some similarity to accounting profits, but, as a tax concept rather than an accounting concept, it is not identical to accounting profits.

[a]   Current Versus Accumulated Earnings and Profits

Section 316 refers to both earnings and profits accumulated since February 28, 1913 (generally referred to as "accumulated E&P"), and earnings and profits of the current year (generally referred to as "current E&P"). Current E&P and accumulated E&P must be calculated separately.

Current E&P reflects the effects on earnings and profits of events that occurred during the current year; section 316 requires current E&P to be calculated only at *year end. See* I.R.C. § 316(a)(2). Accumulated earnings and profits consist of the aggregate E&P of all prior years that the corporation operated, from February 28, 1913 until the end of the prior year. Thus, current E&P always reflects only a single year's worth of corporate profits; once the year is over, what was current E&P becomes part of the corporation's accumulated E&P.

Example 4.4: XY Corp. has been in existence for five years. It has accumulated E&P of $200,000. As of the end of this year, it has current E&P of $25,000. If XY Corp. did not make any distributions this year, at the beginning of next year, XY Corp.'s accumulated E&P will be $225,000.

---

[4] As discussed in § 4.03[A], the portion of a distribution that does not constitute a dividend is treated as a return of capital to the extent of the shareholder's basis and then as capital gain. I.R.C. § 301(c)(2), (3).

As discussed below, the fact that there are two types of E&P, current and accumulated, increases the possible amount taxable as a dividend. That is because, in general, a distribution will be taxed as a dividend if there is either current or accumulated E&P available to cover it. Even if one account is zero or negative (reflecting losses), some or all of a distribution may constitute a dividend if the other account is positive.

Example 4.5: ABC Corp. has one shareholder, Dan. ABC Corp. has been operating for two years but has no accumulated E&P. At year end, it has current E&P of $10,000. ABC Corp. makes a single distribution of $500 to Dan during the year. All $500 will be taxable to Dan as a dividend under section 301 because there is sufficient current E&P to cover the distribution.

[b] Calculating Earnings and Profits

[i] General Rules

Current earnings and profits are calculated each year at year end by starting with taxable income and adjusting that figure as described below. Although E&P could be calculated directly, typically it is easier to start with taxable income, which must be calculated for the corporation's federal income tax return, and then adjust it. In general, the adjustments account for items that are altered from their economic substance when computing taxable income. The adjustments to taxable income that must be made to arrive at E&P are the following:

(1)   Items that are receipts but that are excluded from gross income by statute are *added* to taxable income in arriving at earnings and profits. Examples include life insurance proceeds excluded from gross income by section 101 and municipal bond interest excluded under section 103.

(2)   Expenditures that are prohibited by statute from being deducted but that reduce earnings and profits are *subtracted* from taxable income in calculating earnings and profits. Examples include bribes that are non-deductible under section 162(c), as well as federal income tax payments.

(3)   Timing differences require appropriate adjustments to E&P. For example, if a deduction is front-loaded for purposes of calculating taxable income, some or all of that deduction will need to be added back to taxable income in computing the earnings and profits figure. Section 312(k) requires that the difference between accelerated depreciation and straight-line depreciation be added to taxable income in the earnings and profits calculation.

Note that some of these adjustments are varied when computing dividends of certain corporate shareholders. *See* I.R.C. § 301(e); § 4.03[C][2][e]. Also note that a corporation's "earnings and profits in any case will be dependent upon the method of accounting properly employed in computing taxable income . . . ." Tres. Reg. § 1.312-6(a).

Example 4.6: XYZ Corp., a cash method taxpayer, had the following events this year:

(1) Income from operations of $100,000;

(2) interest received on savings account of $5,000;

(3) tax-exempt income of $2,000 from municipal bonds;

(4) capital gain of $1,000;

(5) business expenses of $45,000;

(6) accelerated depreciation of $15,000 (the straight-line amount would be $10,000);

(7) capital loss of $1,500; and

(8) federal income taxes paid of $7,500.

XYZ Corp.'s gross income is therefore $106,000 ($100,000 + $5,000 + $1,000). Deductions total $61,000 ($45,000 + $15,000 + $1,000 of the capital loss because capital losses are only deductible to the extent of capital gains, I.R.C. § 1211(a)). XYZ Corp.'s taxable income is therefore $45,000 ($106,000 − $61,000).

Taxable income of $45,000 is the starting point for computing earnings and profits. Tax-exempt income of $2,000 is added to that figure so that it is included in E&P. The amount of depreciation for E&P purposes is limited to that determined under the straight-line method, so E&P is increased by the excess $5,000 depreciation that was claimed as a tax deduction. The *entire* capital loss reduces E&P, so an additional $500 must be subtracted from taxable income to arrive at E&P. Federal income taxes reduce E&P, even though they are not deductible, so $7,500 must be subtracted. Thus, to compute E&P, taxable income of $45,000 is increased by $2,000, increased by $5,000, reduced by $500, and reduced by $7,500. XYZ Corp.'s current E&P is therefore $44,000.

Example 4.6 began with taxable income and made appropriate adjustments to arrive at E&P. E&P could have been computed directly. However, as indicated above, that usually will entail duplicative work because taxable income will need to be calculated for the corporation's federal income tax return. Simply making appropriate adjustments to taxable income avoids doing the taxable income calculation twice.

Earnings and profits are also reduced to reflect distributions to shareholders of a corporation's own debt obligations (such as bonds). *See* I.R.C. § 312(a)(2). In general, E&P is reduced by the principal amount of the debt obligation. *Id.* However, if the debt instrument has "original issue discount," meaning that its issue price is less than its stated redemption price at maturity, E&P is reduced by the issue price. *Id.* The original issue discount will be taxed under the rules of section 1272.

[ii] Effects of Discharge of Indebtedness on Earnings and Profits

In general, discharge of indebtedness constitutes gross income, and accordingly increases E&P. *See* I.R.C. § 61(a)(12). However, section 108 protects insolvent debtors from taxation on discharge of indebtedness. To the extent of the section 108 exclusion, debtor tax attributes are reduced. *See* I.R.C. § 108(b). Section 312(*l*)(1) provides that E&P is not affected by discharge of corporate indebtedness to the extent that the reduction reduces the corporation's basis in some of its assets.

[iii] Effects of Distributions on Earnings and Profits

Dividend distributions are an example of non-deductible outlays that reduce E&P. In other words, E&P is not an endless well. When a dividend is distributed, the amount distributed reduces available E&P "to the extent thereof." I.R.C. § 312(a). Thus, a distribution cannot reduce E&P below zero. Note that, as discussed below, for purposes of determining the amount of a distribution that constitutes a dividend, current E&P is calculated at *year end*, without reduction for distributions made during the year.[5] I.R.C. § 316(a)(2). Otherwise, distributions could absorb E&P while escaping taxation as dividends.

If a distribution is made in cash, that is the amount of the distribution. For loss property (property worth less than its basis), the distribution amount is the adjusted basis of the property. I.R.C. § 312(a)(3).

The treatment of distributions of appreciated property is somewhat more complicated than the treatment of other distributions. As discussed below, a distribution of appreciated property gives rise to taxable gain to the corporation and, accordingly, increases E&P. Thus, a distribution of appreciated property produces E&P (in the amount of the gain) that is available for the distribution. After determining the tax consequences of the distribution to the shareholder who received it, E&P is reduced by the distribution (the fair market value of the property distributed). *See* I.R.C. § 312(b).

Example 4.7: Elff Corp. has only shareholder, Ellen. It has no accumulated E&P. Its only transaction this year is to distribute to Ellen, on the last day of the tax year, property with a basis of $1,000 and a value of $4,000.

The distribution generates $3,000 of taxable gain, which increases current E&P. Current E&P becomes $3,000. Ignoring any taxes on the $3,000 of gain, $3,000 of E&P is thus available for the distribution. The distribution amount is $4,000, so $3,000 will be taxed as a dividend. The $4,000 distribution decreases E&P *to the extent thereof*, so E&P is then reduced to zero.

---

[5] *See* § 4.03[C][2].

Adjustments to E&P must be made for liabilities to which the distributed property is subject or that are assumed by a shareholder in connection with the distribution. I.R.C. § 312(c). In such a case, the reduction in E&P occasioned by the distribution is less than it would otherwise be. In other words, after reducing E&P for the amount distributed, liabilities taken on by shareholders are *added back* in calculating E&P. *See* Treas. Reg. § 1.312-3.

Example 4.8: Francis, Inc. has only shareholder, Frank. In Year 1, it has no accumulated E&P and has current E&P of $10,000 from operations. Francis, Inc.'s only transaction this year is to distribute to Frank, on the last day of the tax year, property subject to a liability of $500 that has a basis to Francis, Inc. of $1,000 and a value of $4,000.

The distribution generates $3,000 of taxable gain, which increases E&P. Current E&P becomes $13,000. Therefore, ignoring taxes on the $3,000 of gain, $13,000 of E&P is available for the distribution. The distribution amount is $3,500 ($4,000 − $500), all of which constitutes a dividend to Frank, given Francis, Inc.'s ample current E&P. Current E&P is then reduced by $3,500 ($4,000 less $500) to $9,500, which becomes Francis, Inc.'s accumulated E&P at the beginning of Year 2.

[2] Using Earnings and Profits to Calculate Dividends

Once current and accumulated earnings and profits have been determined, and a distribution has been made, the next step is to determine the amount of the distribution that constitutes a dividend (and is thus includible in income by the shareholder). Examples 4.7 and 4.8 provided an introduction to this process. The Code and Treasury Regulations provide a series of rules for making that determination in a variety of contexts:

(1) Use current E&P before accumulated E&P. Treas. Reg. § 1.316-2(a).

(2) As indicated above, current E&P is determined at *year end*, regardless of when the distribution was made. I.R.C. § 316(a)(2).

(3) As indicated above, current E&P is not reduced for distributions made during the year until *after* dividends are calculated. I.R.C. § 316. That is, current E&P is computed at the end of the tax year, and without regard for any distributions made during the year.

(4) Current E&P is *not reduced by a deficit in accumulated E&P*. I.R.C. § 316. Thus, it is possible to have accumulated losses but a taxable dividend made in a profitable year. This is reminiscent of corporation statutes allowing "nimble dividends" (dividends that may be paid out of current earnings despite accumulated losses).

(5) A deficit in *current* E&P reduces accumulated E&P in a particular way. What is relevant is how much current E&P is available on the *distribution dates*. If the actual E&P on the date of distribution is known, that is used. Otherwise, the deficit in current

E&P is *pro-rated to the dates of distribution*, and the *pro-rated* amount is subtracted from accumulated E&P to see what portion of each distribution was a dividend. *See* Treas. Reg. § 1.316-2(b); Rev. Rul. 74-164, Situations 3 & 4.

(6)   If distributions are *only of money and exceed current E&P*, then that portion of each distribution which the total current E&P bears to the total distributions during the taxable year comes out of current E&P. That is, current E&P is allocated *pro rata* to each of the year's distributions. Treas. Reg. § 1.316-2(b). The easiest way to compute this is to allocate E&P proportionally to each of the distributions, so that, for example, if there are three *equal* distributions, current E&P is allocated one-third to each distribution. As another example, if the first distribution constitutes 25 percent of the total distributions, 25 percent of current E&P is allocated to the first distribution. The calculation is expressed in the following formula:

$$\text{Total current E\&P} \quad \times \quad \frac{\text{Distribution amount}}{\text{Total distributions}} \quad = \quad \text{Current E\&P allocated to that distribution}$$

Distributions of non-cash property generally are treated the same way except that distributions of appreciated property increase E&P, as explained above.

(7)   Unlike current E&P, accumulated E&P is used on a first-in-time basis. *See* Treas. Reg. § 1.316-2(b), (c). (Timing is most relevant if there is a shift in ownership of the corporation during the tax year.)

These principles are applied in the examples below.

[a]   Single Distribution, Sole Shareholder

A single distribution to one shareholder provides the most straightforward dividend calculation. In that situation, the distribution simply taps current E&P first and then accumulated E&P, subject to rule (5) above for reducing accumulated E&P for a deficit in current E&P.

Example 4.9: Green Corp., a calendar-year taxpayer, has one shareholder, Grace. Green Corp. has current E&P of $20,000 at year end and accumulated E&P of $10,000. On June 1, Green Corp. makes a single distribution of $24,000 to Grace. That $24,000 is taxable as a dividend. $20,000 of the dividend comes from current E&P and the remaining $4,000 comes from accumulated E&P. After the dividend amount is calculated, current E&P is reduced to zero by the distribution, and accumulated E&P is reduced to $6,000.

That example did not involve a deficit in either account. Consider the following example, which does:

Example 4.10: Half Corp., a calendar-year taxpayer, has one shareholder, Helen. Helen has a $7,000 basis in her stock. Half Corp. has a *deficit* of $10,000 in current E&P, and has accumulated E&P of $20,000. On July 1, Half Corp. makes a single distribution of $25,000 to Helen.

Because current E&P is negative, there is none available for the distribution. Accumulated E&P is positive, but it must be adjusted to reflect the deficit in current E&P. Unless the exact amount of the deficit as of July 1 is known, half of the deficit is deemed to have occurred by July 1 (as it is halfway through the tax year). That half, $5,000, reduces available accumulated E&P to $15,000. Accordingly, $15,000 of the $25,000 distribution is taxable to Helen as a dividend.[6]

At this point, the remaining $10,000 of the $25,000 distribution remains to be accounted for. Because Helen has a $7,000 basis in her stock, $7,000 of the distribution will be treated as a tax-free return of capital, reducing Helen's stock basis to zero. The remainder of the distribution, $3,000, will be taxed as gain from the sale or exchange of stock.

[b] Single Distribution, Multiple Shareholders

If a corporation with multiple shareholders makes a single distribution to its shareholders during the taxable year, the tax consequences are only slightly more complicated than those explained above. Consider the following example:

---

[6] At the beginning of next year, accumulated E&P will have a deficit of $5,000; the $15,000 dividend reduces accumulated E&P, and this year's current E&P deficit of $10,000 folds into the remaining $5,000 of accumulated E&P.

Example 4.11: Isle Corporation has two equal shareholders, Ian and Janet. Isle Corporation has $75,000 of current E&P and $200,000 of accumulated E&P, as shown in the diagram below. Isle distributes $50,000 to each shareholder. The total distribution is therefore $100,000. $75,000 comes out of current E&P, and the remaining $25,000 reduces accumulated E&P. Accordingly, Ian and Janet each have $50,000 of dividend income. At the beginning of the next year, accumulated E&P will be $175,000.

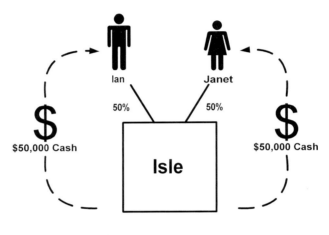

$75,000 current E&P
$200,000 accumulated E&P

Note that the distribution is first considered as an aggregate, and then the shareholders' tax consequences are determined by allocation proportionate to the shareholders' ownership interests in the corporation. Thus, if Ian had owned 60 percent of the shares and Janet had owned 40 percent, then, of the aggregate $100,000 distribution, Isle Corporation would have distributed $60,000 to Ian and $40,000 to Janet. Because all $100,000 was a dividend ($75,000 out of current E&P, and the remainder out of accumulated E&P), Ian would have had a $60,000 dividend, and Janet a $40,000 dividend.

Compare Example 4.11 to the following example:

Example 4.12: Kastle Corporation has two equal shareholders, Kathy and Lane. Kastle Corporation has $75,000 of current E&P and $200,000 of accumulated E&P. Kastle distributes $150,000 to each shareholder. The total distribution is therefore $300,000. $75,000 comes out of current E&P. The remaining $225,000 exceeds accumulated E&P, so $200,000 comes out of accumulated E&P, reducing it to zero. Thus, $275,000 of the aggregate distribution is taxable as dividends. Accordingly, Kathy and Lane each have $137,500 of dividend income.

There is $12,500 more that was distributed to each shareholder. Assume that Kathy had a $50,000 stock basis and Lane had a $10,000 stock basis. Kathy would treat the $12,500 as a return of capital, reducing her stock basis to $37,500. Lane would have a $10,000 return of capital, reducing his stock basis to zero. The remaining $2,500 of the distribution would be taxed to Lane as gain from the sale or exchange of stock.

In this example, the aggregate distribution exceeded aggregate current and accumulated E&P. Current E&P was tapped first, then accumulated. The excess distribution was considered separately as to each shareholder, with somewhat different tax results because of the two shareholders' different stock bases.

[c] Multiple Distributions, Sole Shareholder

In any situation in which a corporation makes multiple distributions to shareholders within the same taxable year, it is important to consider each distribution separately, in chronological order.

Example 4.13: Mint Corp., a calendar-year taxpayer, has one shareholder, Mason. Mason has a $6,000 basis in his stock. Mint Corp. has current E&P of $6,000 at year end and accumulated E&P of $15,000. On April 1, Mint Corp. distributes $10,000 in cash to Mason. On July 1, Mint Corp. distributes another $20,000 to Mason.

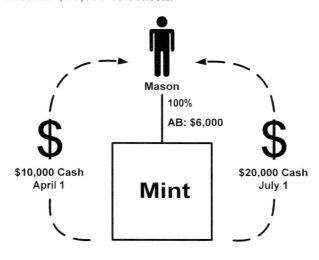

$6,000 current E&P
$15,000 accumulated E&P

In this example, distributions are only of money and exceed current E&P. Thus, current E&P is allocated *pro rata* to each of the year's distributions. The first distribution, $10,000, is one-third of the total distributions for the year ($10,000/($10,000 + $20,000)). Accordingly, one-third of current

E&P of $6,000 ($2,000) is available for the first distribution. The remaining two-thirds of current E&P, $4,000, is allocated to the second distribution (which is two-thirds of the total distribution amount for the year).

Accordingly, the April 1 distribution of $10,000 taps current E&P to the extent of $2,000. $8,000 of the distribution remains to draw on accumulated E&P. Accumulated E&P is tapped on a "first in time" basis, so the $8,000 is withdrawn from accumulated E&P, reducing it from $15,000 to $7,000. Thus, all $10,000 of the April 1 distribution is taxed as a dividend. The July 1 distribution of $20,000 first taps current E&P, taking the $4,000 that was allocated to the July 1 distribution. The remainder of the distribution is $16,000, but there is only $7,000 remaining in accumulated E&P. The July 1 distribution therefore constitutes a dividend only to the extent of $11,000, and reduces accumulated E&P to zero. The remaining $9,000 of the distribution first reduces Mason's stock basis to zero, leaving $3,000 to be taxed as gain from the sale of stock.

In Example 4.13, the order in which the distributions tapped each E&P account made no real difference because the total distributions to Mason of $30,000 could only constitute dividends to the extent of aggregate E&P, which was $21,000. However, if Mason had sold all of his shares to Margaret on June 1, the order would have been critical because the two distributions (which were treated differently) would have been received by two different shareholders. In that case, the $10,000 April 1 distribution, *all* taxed as a dividend, would be dividend income to Mason, the shareholder at that time, while the $20,000 July 1 distribution, $11,000 of which was taxed as a dividend, would be taxed to Margaret. In effect, because of the rules requiring apportionment of current E&P and first-in-time use of accumulated E&P, less E&P would be available for Margaret's distribution than for Mason's.

[d] Multiple Distributions, Multiple Shareholders

In Example 4.13, because there was only one shareholder receiving any given distribution, allocation among shareholders was not necessary. The second level of complication that multiple shareholders receiving multiple distributions occasions is considered in the following example.

Example 4.14: Nodd Corp. is owned 70 percent by Nancy and 30 percent by Oscar. Nancy's basis in her stock is $12,000 and Oscar's basis is $7,000. Nodd Corp. has $50,000 in accumulated E&P and current E&P of $30,000 at year end. During the year, Nodd Corp. distributes, *pro rata*, a total of $100,000 on April 1 (that is, $70,000 to Nancy and $30,000 to Oscar) and a total of $50,000 on July 1 ($35,000 to Nancy and $15,000 to Oscar).

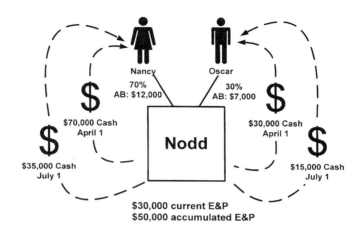

In this example, the distributions are solely of money and exceed current E&P, so current E&P is allocated ratably to the two distributions. The first distribution, $100,000, was two-thirds of the total of $150,000 for the year. Accordingly, two-thirds of current E&P of $30,000 (that is, $20,000) is available for the April 1 distribution. Of the $100,000 April 1 distribution, $20,000 is drawn from current E&P. The remaining $80,000 reduces accumulated E&P of $50,000 to zero. Thus, $70,000 of the April 1 distribution is taxable as a dividend. Seventy percent of that ($49,000) is taxable to Nancy and 30 percent ($21,000) is taxable to Oscar.

The July 1 distribution of $50,000 draws down the remaining $10,000 of current E&P, resulting in an additional $7,000 dividend to Nancy and a $3,000 dividend to Oscar.

Note that $30,000 of the April 1 distribution was not taxable as a dividend. Of that, $21,000 went to Nancy. Assuming that basis is reduced before year end (which would be most relevant if she sold her shares), her stock basis is reduced from $12,000 to zero, leaving her with $9,000 of capital gain. $9,000 of the non-dividend portion of the April 1 distribution went to Oscar. Oscar's $7,000 basis is reduced to zero, leaving him with $2,000 of capital gain.

With respect to the July 1 distribution, there is $40,000 left of the distribution but no remaining accumulated E&P. $28,000 of that went to Nancy. Her basis has already been reduced to zero, so she takes the $28,000 as additional gain. $12,000 of the remaining $40,000 went to Oscar. He too has no basis left in his stock; he takes the $12,000 as additional gain. Once again, the importance of these calculations would be magnified had any stock sales occurred between the dates of the two distributions.

[e] Special Rule for Calculating Dividend of Corporate 20-Percent Shareholder

Under section 301(e), the adjustments of section 312(k) (for depreciation) and all of section 312(n) (to reflect economic gain and loss) except for 312(n)(7) do not apply in determining the dividend amount to a corporation that owns at least 20 percent of the distributing corporation's stock (by vote or value, excluding preferred stock from the value calculation). *See* I.R.C. § 301(e). This provision effectively lowers the amount taxable as a dividend to corporations eligible for large dividends received deductions.[7] Accordingly, section 301(e) does not apply to dividends that would not be subject to a dividends received deduction under section 243, or to a deduction under the specialized provisions of sections 244 (dividends received on certain preferred stock of a public utility) or 245 (dividends received from certain foreign corporations). *See* I.R.C. § 301(e)(2)(B).

Note that section 301(e) does not affect the amount of earnings and profits of either the distributing corporation or the distributee corporation. Rather, it affects only the amount of earnings and profits deemed available for a distribution to a corporate 20 percent shareholder.

> *Example 4.15*: Par Corp. owns 100 percent of the stock of QuickCo. QuickCo. distributes cash of $7,000 to Par Corp. QuickCo. has no current earnings and profits, but it has accumulated earnings and profits of $6,000. However, that amount reflects an $800 adjustment under section 312(k) for depreciation in excess of straight line. Without that adjustment, earnings and profits would be $5,200. Under section 301(e), Par Corp.'s dividend amount is only $5,200, rather than $6,000. However, QuickCo.'s E&P is reduced by $6,000, and Par Corp.'s E&P is increased by $6,000.

[D] Tax Treatment of Individuals' Qualified Dividends

Under current law, individuals' "qualified dividend income" is treated as "adjusted net capital gain," which allows it to be taxed at a maximum rate of 15 percent without regard to the netting of capital gains and losses. *See* I.R.C. § 1(h)(3)(B), (11). That 15 percent rate is further reduced to 5 percent (and is scheduled to be reduced to zero percent for tax years beginning in 2008) if it would otherwise be taxed at a 10 or 15 percent rate. The rate reductions are scheduled to sunset on December 31, 2008.

Under section 1(h)(11), for dividends to constitute qualified dividend income, they must (1) constitute dividends within the meaning of section 316; (2) be received from eligible corporations, which are domestic corporations and qualified foreign corporations (subject to limited exceptions, such

---

[7] The dividends received deduction of section 243 is discussed in § 4.04.

as for tax-exempt corporations), *see* I.R.C. § 1(h)(11)(B)(i), (ii); (3) be received with respect to stock that the taxpayer has held for 60 days out of the 121-day period that begins on the date 60 days before the "ex-dividend date"[8] with respect to the dividend,[9] *see* I.R.C. § 1(h)(11)(B)(iii)(I); and (4) not be received on stock with respect to which "the taxpayer is under an obligation (whether pursuant to a short sale or otherwise) to make related payments with respect to positions in substantially similar or related property," I.R.C. § 1(h)(11)(B)(iii)(II). A dividend also does not constitute qualified dividend income if the taxpayer elects to treat it as investment income under section 163(d)(4)(B), I.R.C. § 1(h)(11)(D)(i); the taxpayer therefore *either* benefits from the preferential rate on the dividends or can treat the dividend income (which will then be taxed as ordinary income) as investment income for purposes of the limitation on the deductibility of investment interest.[10]

> *Example 4.16*: Rhonda receives a $300 distribution with respect to her stock in Righto Corp. She has held the Righto Corp. shares for the last six months and has a $150 basis in those shares. Righto Corp. is a domestic corporation with earnings and profits such that $100 of the distribution will be taxed as a dividend. Assume that the dividend constitutes a qualified dividend. Rhonda will pay tax on the $100 at a maximum rate of 15 percent. $150 of the distribution will be a return of capital, and the remaining $50 will be short-term capital gain.

§ 4.04   Tax Consequences to Corporate Shareholders: Effect of the Dividends Received Deduction

As discussed in Chapter 1, one of the hallmarks of the classical corporate tax regime is double taxation. That is, in general, taxation of a corporation on its earnings coupled with taxation of shareholders on earnings distributed as dividends amounts to two levels of tax on those amounts. What if the shareholder is itself a corporation? The $100 earned by the subsidiary corporation is taxed once. The amount of that $100 that remains is subject to taxation again on a distribution by the subsidiary corporation to its corporate shareholder (the parent corporation). The remaining amount would be taxed again if it were distributed to an individual shareholder of the parent corporation. To mitigate the effects of triple, quadruple, or even more layers of taxation, section 243 provides a dividends received deduction (DRD) for corporate shareholders.

Note that the DRD does not eliminate gross income to corporate shareholders. Instead, it provides a partial or total offsetting deduction. Unlike

---

[8] The ex-dividend date of stock is the first day on which a purchaser of the stock does not obtain the right to the dividend.

[9] Tacking under section 1223(4) does not apply. I.R.C. § 246(c)(3)(B).

[10] In addition, if a taxpayer's qualified dividends constitute "extraordinary dividends" within the meaning of section 1059(c), any loss on the sale or exchange of the stock with respect to which the qualified dividends were received will constitute long-term capital loss to the extent of the dividends. I.R.C. § 1(h)(11)(D)(ii). Section 1059 is discussed in § 4.04[B][3], below.

many deductions, the DRD is triggered by amounts *received* rather than expenditures or losses. In addition, the DRD does not apply to corporations taxed under the pass-through regime of Subchapter S ("S corporations"). Their income is computed in the same manner as income of individuals, *see* I.R.C. § 1363(b), and the pass-through regime of Subchapter S does not raise the specter of multiple levels of taxation on the same earnings.[11]

[A] Dividends Received Deduction, in General

There are three levels of deductions under section 243:

(1) The DRD starts at 70 percent under section 243(a)(1);

(2) under section 243(c), the DRD rises to 80 percent if the shareholder corporation owns 20 percent or more of the paying corporation's stock (by vote and value); and

(3) the DRD rises further to a 100-percent DRD under section 243(a)(3) and (b) in cases of certain dividends received by affiliated corporations— that is, corporations owning 80 percent or more of the payor's stock (by vote and by value).[12]

CHART 4.2
Amounts of Dividends Received Deduction

PERCENT OF STOCK OWNED IN PAYOR	PERCENT DEDUCTIBLE
less than 20%	70%
20% to less than 80% (by vote and by value)	80%
80% or more (by vote and by value)	100%

Example 4.16: Smith Corp is owned 80 percent by Topp Corp, 10 percent by Upper Corp, and 10 percent by Violet, an individual. Smith Corp distributes $100,000, which consists of $80,000 to Topp Corp, $10,000 to Upper Corp, and $10,000 to Violet. Assume that Smith Corp has $300,000 current E&P and $200,000 accumulated E&P. Because of the ample E&P, the entire distribution is taxed as a dividend. Each shareholder takes into gross income the amount of the dividend each received.

Topp Corp and Upper Corp, as corporate shareholders, are entitled to DRDs. Because Topp Corp owns 80 percent of Smith Corp, it may deduct the entire $80,000 dividend received. Upper Corp, which owns only 10 percent of Smith Corp, is entitled to the minimum DRD, 70 percent. Therefore, Upper Corp may deduct $7,000 from gross income. (Upper

[11] S corporations are the subject of Chapter 8.

[12] The 100-percent DRD also applies to small business investment companies, under I.R.C. § 243(a)(2).

Corp's *taxable income* from the $10,000 dividend distribution is therefore $3,000). Violet, as an individual, is not entitled to a DRD.

Corporations generally prefer to have their distributions characterized as dividends because, as a result of the large DRD, the net tax effect to corporate shareholders on receipt of a dividend is relatively small. Notice that this can create a strain between the interests of individual shareholders and corporate shareholders, though less so now that individuals' qualified dividends are taxed at capital gains rates. Individual shareholders generally will face better federal income tax consequences if the corporation's earnings accumulate at the corporate level, thereby deferring the second level of tax on the earnings. If the shareholder sells the shares, the sales price for the stock, and therefore the taxable gain, will be increased because of these accumulated earnings. However, the shareholder will benefit from deferral and basis offset, as well as paying tax on any gain at preferential capital gains rates. By contrast, a corporate shareholder generally would prefer to receive a dividend rather than leave earnings undistributed because stock sales do not receive the benefit of the DRD and there currently is no capital gains preference for corporate taxpayers.

[B] Exceptions and Special Rules

In addition to the limitation of section 301(e), discussed above,[13] there are three major limitations on the DRD, designed to prevent abuses: the debt-financed stock rule of section 246A, the holding period of section 246(c), and the extraordinary dividends rule of section 1059.

[1] Debt-Financed Portfolio Stock

Section 246A limits the DRD where a corporate shareholder borrows to finance a purchase of "portfolio stock" in another corporation. Under section 246A(c)(2), portfolio stock is any stock unless (1) the shareholder owns 50 percent or more (by vote and value) of the dividend-paying corporation *or* (2) the shareholder owns 20 percent or more (by vote and value) of the dividend-paying corporation, and five or fewer corporations own 50 percent or more of the stock of the dividend-paying corporation.

The basic purpose of section 246A is to prevent the taxpayer from obtaining a double tax benefit. That is, it prevents a corporate shareholder from obtaining the benefit of an interest expense deduction on the indebtedness used to acquire the stock and at same time getting a DRD on a dividend distribution with respect to the stock. For example, suppose X corporation borrows money in order to buy 10 percent of the stock of Y corporation. Then, Y corporation pays X corporation a $1,000 dividend. Assume that X corporation also incurs $1,000 of interest expense on the debt. The dividend income and the interest expense offset each other (gross income of $1,000 less $1,000 deductible interest equals zero taxable income). But, absent section 246A, X corporation would also be entitled to a DRD of $700. The

---

[13] *See* § 4.03[C][2][e].

result would be a net deduction of $700 available to X corporation to offset other income.

The $700 deduction in this example is what section 246A addresses. In general, the effect of section 246A is to *reduce the DRD percentage* to the extent that the stock paying the dividend is debt-financed. So, if X had borrowed half the cost of the stock, half the otherwise allowable DRD would be disallowed. If X borrowed the entire cost of the stock, it would receive no DRD. *See* I.R.C. 246A(a).

Thus, section 246A provides that, if there is indebtedness attributable to portfolio stock ("portfolio indebtedness"), the allowable DRD percentage will be 70 percent (or 80 percent in the case of a 20-percent owned corporation) multiplied by a percentage equal to *100 percent minus the "average indebtedness percentage."* The "average indebtedness percentage" under section 246A(d) is equal to (1) the average amount of indebtedness attributable to the stock divided by (2) the average adjusted basis of the stock.

Note that if section 246A applies, the total *dollar* reduction in the DRD cannot exceed the amount of the interest deduction allocable to that dividend. *See* I.R.C. § 246A(e). That is not surprising because the corporate shareholder already has a deduction that it can use to offset the dividend income—the interest deduction. The purpose of section 246A is to deprive the corporate shareholder of only the portion of the DRD that would give rise to a double deduction.

> *Example 4.17*: W Corp. purchases one percent of X Corp.'s common stock for $1,000, of which $200 is borrowed from a bank. Soon thereafter, W Corp. receives a fully taxable dividend of $100. W Corp. therefore has $100 of ordinary income. Section 246A applies to reduce W Corp.'s DRD by 20 percent because the dividend was received on portfolio stock that was 20-percent debt-financed. Accordingly, instead of a 70-percent DRD, W Corp. gets only 80 percent of that, or a 56-percent DRD. Therefore, $56 is deductible by W Corp., assuming that the $14 reduction in W Corp.'s DRD does not exceed the amount of W Corp.'s interest deduction allocable to the dividend. However, if W Corp.'s interest deduction with respect to the $200 W Corp. borrowed to purchase the stock were only $10, W Corp.'s DRD would only be reduced by $10, not $14, so its DRD would be $60.

As indicated above, section 246A only applies to debt-financed *portfolio stock*. In general, where the corporate shareholder owns at least 50 percent (or 20 percent in the case of a qualifying corporate joint venture), the cutback of section 246A will not apply. *See* I.R.C. § 246A(c)(2). Thus, section 246A will never reduce the amount of the 100 percent DRD for affiliated corporations.

[2] Holding Period

As a general rule, section 246(c) denies a DRD deduction *entirely* if a corporate shareholder holds stock for 45 days or fewer (90 days for preferred stock). The application of this rule is not limited to portfolio stock or debt-financed stock. Under section 246(c), to be eligible for a DRD, a corporate shareholder must hold the shares for the requisite number of days during the 91-day period beginning on the date which is 45 days before the ex-dividend date. (The period for preferred stock runs for 181 days, beginning on the date that is 90 days before the ex-dividend date.) As indicated above, a stock's ex-dividend date is the first day on which a purchaser of that stock does not obtain the right to the dividend. Tacking with respect to "substantially identical stock or securities" under section 1223(3) does not apply. I.R.C. § 246(c)(3)(B).

The purpose of section 246(c) is to avoid excessive tax benefits to a corporation that buys stock, receives a dividend and a corresponding DRD, and then immediately sells the stock at a lower price reflecting the decreased assets of the distributing corporation. For example, assume that a corporate shareholder buys 10 percent of another corporation's common stock on July 1 for $12,000. The corporate shareholder receives a dividend of $1,000 from the corporation on July 10, and then sells the stock on July 15 for $11,000. Economically, the corporation broke even. It paid $12,000 for the stock and received a total of $12,000 from the dividend and sales proceeds. Without section 246(c), however, the corporation would have $1,000 of dividend income, a $700 DRD and a $1,000 loss on the sale of the stock. That would amount to a net loss of $700 for tax purposes (ignoring character). Section 246(c) brings the tax result more in line with the economics by denying the DRD absent a 46-day or more holding period. In effect, section 246(c) requires a corporation to bear market risk for more than a minimal period in order to benefit from the DRD.

> *Example 4.18*: On July 1, Y Corp. purchases one percent of Z Corp.'s common stock for $1,000 cash. On July 10, Y Corp. receives a fully taxable dividend of $100; assume that July 7 was the ex-dividend date. On July 15, Y Corp. sells the stock. The purchase was not debt-financed. Section 246(c) applies because Y Corp. did not hold the stock for more than 45 days during the 91-day period beginning 45 days before the ex-dividend date of June 7. Thus, Y Corp. is *not entitled* to a DRD. Accordingly, Y Corp. cannot offset its $100 of ordinary income from the dividend with a dividends received deduction.

[3] Extraordinary Dividends

The holding period requirement of section 246(c) is fairly short, so it is generally not too difficult to avoid. Yet, the possibility of stripping a payor corporation of assets via a dividend, followed by a sale of that corporation's stock at an artificial loss may exist even if the holding period requirement of section 246(c) is met. Section 1059 provides another obstacle to this technique.

Section 1059 operates differently from section 246 in that, rather than disallowing the DRD, it triggers a reduction in stock basis. In general, under section 1059, if a corporate shareholder receives what is referred to as an "extraordinary dividend" and if the corporate shareholder has not held the stock for *more than two years* prior to the dividend announcement date, then the shareholder must reduce its basis in the stock by the untaxed portion of the dividend—that is, reduce the basis in an amount equal to the DRD. In addition, certain dividends are automatically subject to section 1059 without regard to the period that the stock was held and regardless of the amount of the dividend. *See* I.R.C. § 1059(e)(1).[14]

In general, the term "extraordinary dividend" is defined in section 1059(c) as a dividend that equals or exceeds *five percent of the taxpayer's basis in preferred stock*, if the dividend is paid with respect to preferred stock, or *ten percent of the taxpayer's basis in common stock*, if the dividend is paid with respect to common stock. Alternatively, under section 1059(c)(4), the taxpayer may elect to apply the percentages to the fair market value of the stock rather than its basis. A shareholder generally would make this election if the stock had appreciated in value in the hands of the shareholder prior to the dividend distribution.

There are some exceptions to the extraordinary dividend rules of section 1059. First, section 1059 generally does not apply if the "stock was held by the taxpayer during the entire period such corporation was in existence . . . ."[15] I.R.C. § 1059(d)(6). Second, "qualifying dividends" (which are subject to the 100 percent DRD of section 243(b)), generally do not constitute extraordinary dividends. *See* I.R.C. § 1059(e)(2). In addition, "qualified preferred dividends" do not constitute extraordinary dividends "if the taxpayer holds such stock for more than 5 years." *See* I.R.C. § 1059(e)(3). If the taxpayer holds for less than five years stock otherwise eligible for this exception, the Code provides for lesser relief. *See* I.R.C. § 1059(e)(3)(A)(ii).

> The term "qualified preferred dividend" means any fixed dividend payable with respect to any share of stock which—
>
> (I) provides for fixed preferred dividends payable not less frequently than annually, and
>
> (II) is not in arrears as to dividends at the time the taxpayer acquires the stock.
>
> Such term shall not include any dividend payable with respect to any share of stock if the actual rate of return on such stock exceeds 15 percent.

I.R.C. § 1059(e)(3)(C)(i). Section 1059(e)(3)(B) provides rules for calculating the stock's rate of return.

To prevent circumvention of section 1059 through the payment of several smaller dividends (so that no one particular dividend qualifies as an extraordinary dividend), there are aggregation rules in section 1059(c)(3). Under section 1059(c)(3)(A), the corporate shareholder must treat as one dividend all dividends on the same stock that occur within the same 85-day

---

[14] This rule is aimed at certain abusive transactions. *See* § 5.03[C].

[15] See section 1059(d)(6) for the limits to this exception.

period. In addition, under section 1059(c)(3)(B), all dividends that have ex-dividend dates within a one-year period must be aggregated if the total of these dividends exceeds 20 percent of the taxpayer's basis in its stock.[16] If that is the case, all of these dividends are treated as extraordinary dividends.

The stock basis reduction under section 1059 will affect the amount of gain or loss realized on a later sale. However, under 1059(a)(1), basis cannot be reduced below zero. The excess of the extraordinary dividend over the shareholder's basis is treated as *additional gain* from the sale or exchange of stock, at the time of the dividend. Basis is reduced as of the ex-dividend date of the extraordinary dividend. I.R.C. § 1059(d)(1).

> *Example 4.19*: Assume ABC Corp. buys two percent of DEF Corp.'s common stock for $1,000 cash and three months later receives a dividend of $200. The purchase was not debt-financed. One year later, ABC sells the stock for $800. Section 246A does not apply because the purchase was not debt-financed. In addition, section 246(c) does not apply because ABC Corp. held the stock for more than 45 days during the relevant time period. Thus, ABC Corp. is entitled to a 70-percent DRD. So, upon payment of the dividend, ABC has $200 of gross income and a $140 DRD, which results in net taxable income from the distribution of $60.
>
> However, section 1059 applies because ABC did not hold the stock for more than two years prior to the dividend announcement date, and the dividend is large enough to be extraordinary: $200 is 20 percent of ABC's basis in the stock, and the threshold percentage for common stock is 10 percent. Because section 1059 applies, ABC will have to reduce its stock basis by the "untaxed portion" of the dividend ($140). Thus, at the time of the sale of the stock one year later, ABC's basis is $860. As a result, ABC's loss on the sale of the stock for $800 is $60, not $200.

Thus, section 1059 operates on the back end of the dividend stripping transaction by reducing the loss on the disposition of the stock, rather than by disallowing the DRD up front.

---

[16] However, as suggested in the text above, "[i]f the taxpayer establishes to the satisfaction of the Secretary the fair market value of any share of stock as of the day before the ex-dividend date, the taxpayer may elect to apply paragraphs (1) and (3) by substituting such value for the taxpayer's adjusted basis." I.R.C. § 1059(c)(4).

CHART 4.3
Comparison of Limitations on
Dividends Received Deduction

CODE SECTION	CERTAIN HOLDING PERIOD PRECLUDES APPLICATION?	APPLIES TO	TAX CONSEQUENCES
I.R.C. § 246A	No	Debt-financed stock	Reduces DRD %
I.R.C. § 246(c)	Yes	Stock held briefly	Denies DRD
I.R.C. § 1059	Yes	Extraordinary dividends	Reduces stock basis

§ 4.05 "Bootstrap Acquisitions"

There is another limitation on corporations' use of the DRD, developed by courts. In general, it applies to transactions designed to obtain the benefit of the DRD incident to a sale of stock of the corporation paying the dividend. The transactions are "bootstrap acquisitions" because they use the target corporation's own assets to fund the purchase through distribution of a dividend to the selling shareholder. For example, assume that Parent Corporation owns 70 percent of Sub Corporation. The stock is worth $200,000 and Parent Corporation has a basis of $75,000 in the stock, which it has held for many years. Sub Corporation has ample E&P. Parent Corporation wants to sell its Sub stock, but also wants to minimize its taxable income from the disposition. If Parent simply sells its interest for $200,000, it will have $125,000 of gain.

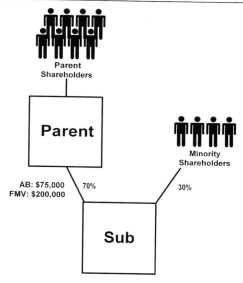

To avoid this treatment, Parent agrees with the potential buyer that, prior to the stock sale, Sub will distribute to Parent assets worth $100,000. (The minority shareholders of Sub also receive distributions, which are ignored in the interest of simplicity.)

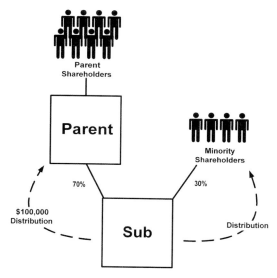

Parent will receive this distribution and offset the distributed amount with an 80-percent DRD, so its taxable income from the dividend will be $20,000. After the distribution, the 70-percent stock interest in Sub is worth somewhat less because Sub has fewer assets. Assume that the buyer will now only pay Parent $100,000 for its 70-percent interest in Sub. Thus, upon the sale of Sub stock to the buyer, Parent will have only $25,000 of additional income (amount realized of $100,000 less adjusted basis of $75,000).

Upon purchasing the Sub stock, the buyer may make a contribution to Sub to replenish the assets that were reduced because of the dividend to Parent. Assume the buyer makes a $100,000 cash contribution to Sub.

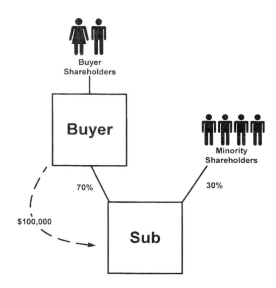

The net result of this is that Parent Corporation, the seller, has received $200,000 of total consideration. The buyer has expended $200,000 in total. But, if the form is respected, Parent only has $45,000 of taxable income ($20,000 of post-DRD taxable income from the dividend plus $25,000 of gain on the stock sale), instead of the $125,000 of income that Parent would have had if it had simply sold the stock with no pre-acquisition dividend.

Whether or not the form of a bootstrap acquisition is respected may depend on the timing of the various parts of the transaction, as well as other facts. There are several important cases, and they help illustrate the parameters of a successful bootstrap acquisition. *Waterman Steamship Corp. v. Commissioner*, 430 F.2d 1185 (5th Cir. 1970), *cert. denied*, 401 U.S. 939 (1971), is one of these cases. In that case, Waterman Steamship (Waterman) was the sole owner of two subsidiaries, Pan-Atlantic Steamship Corp. (Pan-Atlantic) and Gulf Florida Terminal Co. (Gulf Florida). Malcolm P. McLean (McLean) offered to purchase all of the stock of Pan-Atlantic and Gulf Florida from Waterman for $3,500,000. The management of Waterman determined that if they accepted the offer, they would realize $2,800,000 in capital gains because Waterman's basis in the two companies was approximately $700,000. For that reason, Waterman made a counter-proposal to sell the stock of the two subsidiaries for $700,000 payable in cash only after the directors of the subsidiaries "shall have declared and arranged for payments of dividends to the present stockholder, Waterman Steamship Corporation, amounting in the aggregate of $2,800,000." *Id.* at 1187. The $2,800,000 in dividends would be sheltered by what was then section 1052, and there would be no gain realized from the sale because the purchase price equaled Waterman's basis in the stock sold.

Within a 90-minute period, the parties agreed to the purchase and sale for $700,000; Pan-Atlantic declared a dividend of $2,799,820 in the form of a promissory note, and McLean paid $700,000 to Waterman for the subsidiaries' stock. The promissory note was then repaid with funds borrowed from McLean, who, at this point, owned the two subsidiaries. *Id.* at 1188–90.

The IRS determined a deficiency in the amount of the dividend as capital gain from the sale of stock, but the Tax Court ruled in favor of the taxpayer. On appeal from the Tax Court, the Fifth Circuit reversed, finding that the amount in question was part of the purchase price paid to Waterman. Holding that the dividend and the sale were one transaction, the court noted that the "distribution of funds was supplied by the buyer of the stock, with the corporation acting as a mere conduit for passing the payment through to the seller." *Id.* at 1191–92. The court agreed with the IRS that it must look to the substance of the transaction rather than the form to determine the proper tax treatment and found that it "is undisputed that Waterman intended to sell the two subsidiaries for the original offering price—with $2,800,000 of the amount disguised as a dividend which would be eliminated from income under Section 1502." *Id.* at 1194. The court also found no valid business purpose for the pre-sale dividend.

In *Waterman Steamship*, all of the steps occurred almost simultaneously, and the IRS was successful in its argument that the dividend was really a part of the sales proceeds to the seller. That is, the court in *Waterman Steamship* restructured the transaction and viewed the purported dividend as part of the sales price, because the money that supported the dividend really came from the buyer.

In *Basic, Inc. v. United States*, 549 F.2d 740 (Ct. Cl. 1977), the steps did not happen so close in time. In that case, Basic Incorporated (Basic) owned all of the outstanding stock in Falls Industries Incorporated (Falls). Falls owned all of the stock of Basic Carbon Corporation (Carbon). On November 24, 1964, Falls distributed all of the outstanding stock in Carbon to Basic, pursuant to a general plan of purchase entered into between Basic and a third party (Carborundum). *Id.* at 741–43. On December 29, 1964, Basic sold its stock in Falls and Carbon to Carborundum, pursuant to an outstanding offer for purchase. On Basic's 1964 tax return, it reported the transfer of Carbon stock from Falls as "dividend" income in the amount of $501,869.76, and claimed an 85-percent dividends received deduction.[17] Basic also claimed long-term capital gains of $2.3 million from the sale of Falls and Carbon stock to Carborundum. *Id.* at 743.

---

[17] Under current law, there is no 85-percent dividends received deduction—the percentages are 70, 80 and 100 percent. *See* I.R.C. § 243.

The IRS determined that the $501,869.76 was actually capital gain, not dividend income. *Id.* In reaching this conclusion, the court applied the substance-over-form doctrine.[18] Although the distribution did satisfy the literal "dividend" requirements of the Code, the court determined that treating it as a dividend would allow Basic to take a "cost-free" transferred basis in the Carbon stock equal to the basis held by Falls, while at the same time allowing Basic an 85-percent dividends received deduction, thereby reducing taxable gain. *Id.* at 744–45.

In its opinion, the court emphasized that the timing of the events did not support a valid business reason for the transfer of Carbon stock from Falls to Basic, noting that the transfer did not take place until after Basic received Carborundum's formal offer of sale. In addition, the corporate executives involved in negotiating the sale between Basic and Carborundum were the same individuals who were responsible for effectuating Falls' transfer of its Carbon stock to Basic. *Id.* at 746. These facts, combined with the fact that Basic did not present to the court any valid business reason for the distribution of Carbon stock from Falls to Basic, led the court to hold that the $501,869.76 "dividend" distribution was made purely for purposes of reducing taxation on the sale. *See id.*

In another case, *Coffey v. Commissioner*, 14 T.C. 1410 (1950), the usual positions of the government and the taxpayer were reversed because the taxpayers in *Coffey* were individual shareholders (who are not eligible for a DRD). That case involved negotiations for the sale of Smith Brothers Refinery to Hanlon-Buchanan, Inc. (Hanlon-Buchanan). Hanlon-Buchanan offered to pay $190,000 in exchange for all the issued and outstanding stock of Smith Brothers Refinery. However, the parties agreed that a payment owed to Smith Brothers from the Cabot Carbon Co. (Cabot) and certain other assets would be excluded from the purchase offer, primarily because the parties could not agree upon the valuation of those assets. *Id.* at 1413–14. Accordingly, an interest in the Cabot payment was distributed to each common stockholder based on each shareholder's *pro rata* ownership in Smith Brothers Refinery. The stockholders of Smith Brothers Refinery included, as part of the selling price of their stock, $200,000, the face value of the expected Cabot payment. *Id.* at 1416.

The Tax Court agreed with the IRS that the Cabot payment was a dividend distribution in the amount of its fair market value at the date of distribution. The court noted that the reserved $200,000 Cabot payment was not part of the sale of the stock because Hanlon-Buchanan specifically wanted it excluded from the assets of the corporation at the time Hanlon-Buchanan acquired the stock. The court thought "it quite significant that [the stockholders of Smith Brothers] did not transfer their stock to the purchaser until a resolution was passed by the board of directors assuring [the stockholders] of the receipt of the Cabot payment." *Id.* at 1417. In short, the Smith Brothers stockholders received $190,000 for their stock and "they did not sell or part with their interest in the Cabot contract." *Id.* at 1418.

---

[18] This doctrine is discussed in § 1.04[A] of Chapter 1.

Thus, the Tax Court held that the receipt of the Cabot payment was a dividend and the *pro rata* portion received by each Smith Brothers shareholder was taxable as ordinary income.

The IRS does not win every bootstrap acquisition case. *TSN Liquidating Corp., Inc. v. United States*, 624 F.2d 1328 (5th Cir. 1980) provides an example. The issue in *TSN Liquidating* was whether assets distributed to a corporation (TSN) by its subsidiary (CLIC) immediately prior to the sale by TSN of all of CLIC's stock to a third party (Union Mutual) should be treated as a dividend subject to an 85-percent dividends received deduction, or should instead be treated as consideration received from the sale of the stock.

In 1969, TSN owned 90 percent of the capital stock in CLIC and in the beginning of that year, CLIC began negotiations for the sale of all its capital stock to Union Mutual. On May 5, 1969, TSN and other CLIC stockholders entered into a stock purchase agreement with Union Mutual. The agreement required CLIC to dispose of stocks in its investment portfolio that Union Mutual disfavored. On May 14, 1969, the Board of Directors of CLIC declared a dividend to all CLIC stockholders, including TSN, consisting of the stocks held by CLIC that Union Mutual did not want to acquire. On May 20, 1969, Union Mutual purchased almost all of the stock of CLIC, including the stock owned by TSN. Union Mutual then contributed bonds to the capital of CLIC. TSN reported the receipt of the stock from CLIC as a dividend and claimed an 85-percent dividends received deduction. The IRS treated the distribution of assets from CLIC to TSN as "an integral part of the sale by TSN of capital stock of CLIC to Union Mutual" and added $1,677,082 (the value of the assets distributed) to the cash received by TSN on the sale of CLIC stock. *Id.* at 1329–30.

The Fifth Circuit reversed the district court, holding that the stock received by TSN from CLIC was a dividend distribution because Union Mutual did not want and would not pay for the undesired stocks that were in CLIC's investment portfolio prior to the sale. *Id.* at 1336. The court also emphasized that the stocks distributed prior to the sale to Union Mutual were retained by the selling CLIC stockholders. *Id.* at 1331. It found that the dividend distribution was also motivated by a valid business purpose— that of disposing of undesirable stocks prior to the sale of the CLIC stock to Union Mutual. The court concluded that the "fact that bonds and cash were reinfused into CLIC after the closing, in lieu of the unwanted capital stock of small, publicly held corporations, does not convert this case from a *Coffey* situation, in which admittedly unwanted assets were distributed by the corporation to its stockholders and retained by them, into a *Waterman* situation, in which the distribution of assets was clearly a sham, designed solely to achieve a tax-free distribution of assets ultimately funded by the purchaser." *Id.* at 1334–35.

The IRS also lost *Litton Industries, Inc. v. Commissioner*, 89 T.C. 1086 (1987). In that case, Litton Industries (Litton) acquired all the outstanding stock of Stouffer Corporation (Stouffer) in 1967. In early 1972, Litton discussed with the board of directors of each company the possibility of selling Stouffer. On August 23, 1972, Stouffer declared a $30 million dividend in the form of a promissory note to Litton. Two weeks later, Litton made a public announcement of its intent to sell its stock in Stouffer. After discussions with several corporations, business brokers, and underwriters, Litton accepted an offer of purchase from Nestle Corporation (Nestle) for $105 million. On March 5, 1973, Nestle paid Litton $74,962,518 in cash for all the outstanding stock of Stouffer, and $30 million in cash for the promissory note. *Id.* at 1088–89.

The issue in *Litton Industries* was whether the $30 million dividend declared by Stouffer on August 23, 1972, and paid after the sale of Stouffer to Nestle, was truly a dividend or whether that amount represented proceeds from the sale of stock. The Tax Court concluded that "[i]n this case, the form and substance of the transaction coincide," *id.* at 1100, and, therefore, the $30 million payable by promissory note prior to the sale of the subsidiary was a dividend, not part of the selling price.

In distinguishing the case from *Waterman Steamship*, the court noted that the timing of the dividend was a key factor in its decision. Although Litton had the intent to sell Stouffer at the time of the dividend, it had not yet taken formal action to initiate the sale of Stouffer. The declaration of the dividend was made two weeks prior to the public announcement that Stouffer was for sale, and six months prior to any sale negotiations. *Id.* at 1097–98.

The court further noted that if the sale had not occurred, the $30 million distribution would clearly have been a dividend since Stouffer had earnings and profits exceeding $30 million. "We are not persuaded that the subsequent sale of Stouffer to Nestle changes that result merely because it was more advantageous to Litton from a tax perspective." *Id.* at 1099. In addition, the court found two valid business reasons for the declaration of the dividend: (1) to avoid materially diminishing the market value of the Stouffer stock because payment of the dividend by promissory note would not substantially alter Stouffer's earnings, and (2) to avoid sharing the earnings with future additional shareholders while not diminishing the amount received for the stock. Under these facts, the Tax Court held that the $30 million distribution was not "entered into solely for tax reasons," but rather was structured by Litton as a dividend for legitimate business purposes. *Id.* at 1100.

Note that these "bootstrap acquisition" cases involved transactions that occurred when *General Utilities* was still good law. As discussed in § 4.02, under current law, a distribution of appreciated property by a corporation to a shareholder results in the recognition of gain by the corporation. *See* I.R.C. § 311(b). In addition, section 1059 will apply if the dividend is an "extraordinary dividend." *See* I.R.C. § 1059; § 4.04[B][3]. Futhermore, section 301(e) lowers the available earnings and profits for distributions to corporate shareholders that benefit from the dividends received deduction. *See* § 4.03[C][2][e].

§ 4.06　Constructive Dividends

Some transactions involving shareholders and a corporation may not be labeled distributions, but may nevertheless have hidden distribution-like effects. As a result, some recasting may be appropriate so that the substance of the transaction prevails. This may occur more commonly in closely held corporations, where a few shareholders control the corporation. Although these types of transactions are generally referred to as constructive dividends, they are properly treated as constructive *distributions* that will be subject to the rules of section 301. That is, the portion of the constructive distribution, if any, that will actually be taxable as a dividend will depend on the corporation's earnings and profits.[19]

Distributions may be camouflaged as such things as interest, rent, salary, or loans.[20] For example, a corporation might sell an asset to a shareholder at a bargain price (less than the asset's fair market value). Treasury Regulation 1.301-1(j) provides that in the case of such a transfer to a noncorporate shareholder, the shareholder is treated as having received a distribution to which section 301 applies in an amount equal to the difference between the fair market value of the property and the bargain purchase price. Whether or not the shareholder that made the bargain purchase was a corporation, the selling corporation's gain, if any, is computed under section 311. *See* Treas. Reg. § 1.301-1(k) Ex. 1.

> *Example 4.20*: Gina, an individual shareholder of GHI, Inc., purchased property from that corporation for $30. The fair market value of the property was $100, and its basis in the hands of GHI, Inc. was $35. The amount of the section 301 distribution is $70. The $70 will be taxed to Gina under section 301 just as if it were a cash distribution.[21]

If a bargain purchase is made by a *corporate* shareholder, there is less concern about the constructive distribution because corporate shareholders are entitled to dividends received deductions, as discussed above.[22] Accordingly, only if the sale to the corporate shareholder was for both less than fair market value and *less than the selling corporation's adjusted basis*, is the shareholder treated as having received a distribution to which section 301 applies. Treas. Reg. § 1.301-1(j). In that case, if "the fair market value

---

[19] *See* § 4.03[C].

[20] Section 7872(b) applies to "below-market loans." A below-market loan is a loan that is either a demand loan, interest on which is payable at a rate less than the applicable Federal rate, or a term loan where the amount loaned exceeds the present value of all payments due under the loan. If a below-market loan is made directly or indirectly between a corporation and any of its shareholders, the borrower will be taxed on the difference between the loan amount and the present value of all payments due under the loan. *See* I.R.C. § 7872(b)(1), (c)(1)(C). Present value is determined using a discount rate equal to the applicable Federal rate. *See* I.R.C. § 7872(f)(1). Thus, if the interest to be paid on a loan between a corporation and a shareholder is less than the applicable Federal rate, the present value of the difference will be treated as cash paid to the borrower, generally as of the date the loan was made. *See* I.R.C. § 7872(b)(1).

[21] Taxation of distributions under section 301 is discussed in § 4.03.

[22] *See* § 4.04.

of the property equals or exceeds its adjusted basis in the hands of the distributing corporation, the amount of the distribution shall be the excess of the adjusted basis (increased by the amount of gain recognized under section 311(b), (c), or (d), or under [certain other sections] to the distributing corporation) over the amount paid for the property . . . ." Treas. Reg. § 1.301-1(j)(1). If the fair market value of the property is *less* than its adjusted basis in the hands of the distributing corporation, the amount of the distribution under section 301 is the excess of the fair market value over the amount that the corporate shareholder paid for the property. Treas. Reg. § 1.301-1(j)(2). The shareholder corporation will take as its basis in the property the amount paid for the property increased by the amount of the section 301 distribution.

> *Example 4.21*: JKL, Inc., a corporate shareholder of MN, Inc., purchased property from the latter corporation for $30. The fair market value of the property was $100, and its basis in the hands of MN, Inc. was $35. The amount of the section 301 distribution is $5, assuming that sections 311(b) and (c), and other sections, such as 1245(a) and 1250(a), do not apply. The basis of the property to JKL, Inc. will be $35 ($30 + $5).

Green v. United States, 460 F.2d 412 (5th Cir. 1972), is a constructive dividend case that involved a bargain purchase. In *Green*, George Gardiner Green (Green) was both the director and president of Central Oil Co. (Central) and was entitled to purchase at a bargain price 7.90571 percent of the mineral interests offered by Central based on his *pro rata* portion of ownership in Central. However, Green did not purchase the interests himself, and instead allowed his adult son and two trusts for the benefit of his minor children to purchase the interests. The parties stipulated that a bargain sale of corporate property to a shareholder for less than fair market value results in a constructive dividend to the shareholder in the amount of the difference between the fair market value and the price paid, provided the corporation has sufficient earnings and profits for that amount to constitute a dividend. The parties, however, disputed whether or not the sale of the interests to Green's children constituted a constructive dividend to Green personally. *Id.* at 414.

Reversing the district court, the Court of Appeals for the Fifth Circuit held that Green had received a constructive dividend for tax purposes from Central's sale of the interests to his children because Green's position was one of "substantial influence" over the corporation's actions. The court noted "that a dividend does not escape taxation 'simply because it fails to pass through the hands of the particular taxpayer when . . . the dividend is diverted at the behest of the shareholder into the hands of others.'" *Id.* at 419 (quoting *Sammons v. United States*, 433 F.2d 728, 730 (5th Cir. 1970)). In explaining the "substantial influence" test to determine the shareholder's control over the disposition of corporate assets, the court emphasized five principal factors: (1) "the extent of the taxpayer's shareholdings in the corporation alleged to have diverted corporate resources at his behest;" (2) "the taxpayer's relation to the corporation, as officer or director;" (3) "the identity of the recipient of the corporate benefit, the recipient's own relation to the corporation (if any), and other circumstances tending to reveal the degree to which the taxpayer links corporation to recipient;" (4) "evidence of the origins of the transaction as may be available;" and (5) "that the corporation did in fact consummate a transaction with favorable consequences for the taxpayer personally or for his immediate family." *Id.* at 420–21.

Finding that less than absolute legal control was needed to satisfy this test, the court summarized its holding as follows:

> [W]e conclude that no reasonable inference is possible except that George Gardiner Green exercised significant influence over the sale of corporate assets to his children. Green was the President of Central, and when acting as a director, he presided over the other directors of the corporation. He was therefore in a key position to exercise great influence over the sale of corporate property simply by virtue of his corporate office and membership on the board. The recipients of the alleged bargain sale were Green's children, two of whom were minors at the time of the sale. Most important of all, Green's children were not shareholders of the Central Oil Company and they were strangers of the company save for their connection to it through their father and mother. . . . Green was a significant and intentional causative factor in Central's decision to sell its property to Green's children and the trusts created for them.

Id. at 421. Thus, *Green* involved both assignment of income and a constructive dividend. In effect, Green assigned the constructive dividend (the bargain purchase opportunity) to his children.

There are other types of constructive distributions, as well. For example, in Revenue Ruling 80-239, 1980-2 C.B. 103, A, an individual, owned all of the stock of X, a corporation. A transferred the X stock to a newly organized corporation, Y, in exchange for $100,000 (which Y borrowed from a bank) and the Y stock, making X a subsidiary of Y. Subsequently, Y repaid the loan with funds provided by X.

The transaction was designed to look like a section 351 transaction with $100,000 of boot, which would have resulted in having the gain realized on the exchange of the X shares recognized to A to the extent of the boot (allowing capital gains treatment and basis offset).[23] The IRS ruled that section 351 applied to the transfer of the X stock to Y. However, instead of applying section 351(b) to the cash, the IRS found that there was a disguised distribution because, in substance, it was as if X had distributed the $100,000 of cash to A (via Y). Thus, the $100,000 was treated as a section 301 distribution from X.

---

[23] Section 351 transactions are discussed in Chapter 2.

Chapter 5

REDEMPTIONS OF STOCK

§ 5.01 Introduction

[A] In General

A "redemption" of stock is a corporate buy-back of that stock. Thus, a corporation redeems stock from a shareholder by exchanging property for the stock. *See* I.R.C. § 317(b). Note that a redemption, unlike the purchase of stock by a third party, reduces the number of shares outstanding.

> *Example 5.1*: ABC Co. has three shareholders, Abby, Bob, and Cara, each of whom own 100 shares of ABC Co. stock. Abby decides to retire and ABC Co. agrees to redeem her stock. ABC Co. purchases Abby's 100 shares for their fair market value of $50,000. ABC Co. now has only 200 shares outstanding. As a result of the redemption of Abby's shares, Bob and Cara each own a 50-percent interest in ABC Co. The remaining 100 shares are no longer outstanding. The diagram below shows both the redemption transaction (on the left) and the "after" picture, in which the redeemed shares are shown as treasury stock.

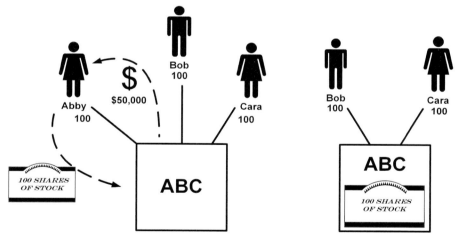

[B] Competing Analogies

As Example 5.1 illustrates, a redemption of stock involves both a *sale by a shareholder* and a *distribution of property* from the corporation to the shareholder. Should a redemption be taxed in the same way a sale to a third party would be or should it be treated instead as a distribution taxable as a dividend to the extent of the corporation's available earnings and profits?[1] Section 302 provides that some redemptions are treated as sales and some are treated as section 301 distributions. In fact, the principal function of section 302 is to distinguish the sale-type redemptions from distribution-type redemptions.

In general, redemptions taxable as sales (that is, those qualifying for "exchange" treatment under the general rule of section 302(a)) are those that leave the shareholder with a significantly reduced interest in the future earnings of the corporation. The reduction may be achieved through a complete redemption of all of the shareholder's shares; a "substantially disproportionate" redemption (leaving the shareholder with a small fraction of that shareholder's pre-redemption ownership); or a "meaningful reduction" in the shareholder's interest, a facts and circumstances test.[2] Thus, determining the tax consequences of a redemption requires comparing the relevant shareholder's pre-and post-redemption ownership interests. In effect, the Code requires a "before" and "after" snapshot of corporate stockholdings.

§ 5.02 Constructive Ownership of Stock

Particularly in a closely held corporation, a single shareholder's stock ownership may not tell the whole story. For example, if all of a taxpayer-husband's shares in a corporation are redeemed but the corporation remains in the control of that taxpayer's wife, the husband retains an ongoing (though indirect) interest in the welfare of the corporation despite the redemption. The same is true if the party who retains control of the corporation in question is the taxpayer's daughter, father, or a corporation that the taxpayer controls. Accordingly, in determining stock ownership for purposes of calculating the pre-and post-redemption ownership interests of a shareholder whose shares are redeemed, that shareholder is *deemed* to own the shares owned by related parties.

Section 318 sets forth rules for attribution of stock (also known as constructive ownership). In general, there is stock attribution between family members, from entities to investors, and from investors to entities. In addition, options to buy stock are deemed exercised, and section 318(a)(5) provides various procedural ("operating") rules. The constructive ownership rules of section 318 apply to redemptions because section 302(c)(1) explicitly provides that, in determining ownership for purposes of applying the tests of section 302(b), section 318(a) shall apply. Note that stock of a corporation taxed under Subchapter S may be attributed under section 318.[3] *See* I.R.C. § 318(a)(5)(E).

---

[1] Using earnings and profits to compute the portion of a distribution that is taxable as a dividend is discussed in Chapter 4.

[2] In addition, as discussed below, *see* § 5.03[B][4], a redemption from a noncorporate shareholder in partial liquidation of the corporation is also taxed as an exchange. *See* I.R.C. § 302(b)(4).

[3] Subchapter S is discussed in Chapter 8.

[A] Family Attribution

Under section 318(a)(1), an individual constructively owns stock owned (directly or indirectly) by his or her spouse, children, grandchildren, and parents. I.R.C. § 318(a)(1)(A). Note that the list does *not* include siblings, grandparents, aunts, uncles, cousins, and the like. Legally adopted children are treated like any other children for purposes of section 318(a). I.R.C. § 318(a)(1)(B).

> *Example 5.2*: Darren, Edna, Frank, Gertrude, and Hilda each own 20 percent of the shares of DEF, Inc. Darren is the son of Edna and Frank. Gertrude is Frank's sister, and Hilda is Gertrude's daughter. Darren is considering the possibility of having some of his shares redeemed by DEF, Inc. In counting the number of shares Darren owns actually and constructively, his shares are counted, as are those of Edna and Frank (his mother and father). Darren is *not* deemed to own the shares belonging to Gertrude (his aunt) and Hilda (his cousin) because aunts and cousins are not included in the definition of "family" under section 318(a)(1).

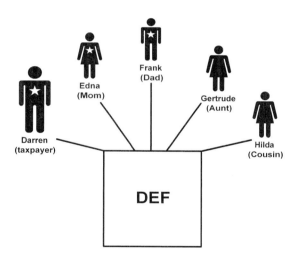

[B] Attribution from Entities to Investors

Under section 318(a)(2), stock owned by an entity is attributed to investors in that entity as follows:

> (1) Stock owned, directly or indirectly, by a partnership or estate is considered as owned *proportionately* by its partners or beneficiaries. I.R.C. § 318(a)(2)(A). For this purpose, an S corporation is treated as a partnership, and therefore is not subject to the 50 percent threshold discussed below with respect to corporations. *See* I.R.C. § 318(a)(5)(E).

> (2) If a *shareholder directly or indirectly owns 50 percent or more in value of the stock in a corporation*, stock owned, directly or indirectly, by that corporation is considered as owned *proportionately* by the shareholder

based on the ratio the value of the stock the shareholder owns bears to the value of all the stock in the corporation. I.R.C. § 318(a)(2)(C).

(3) Stock owned, directly or indirectly, by a tax-exempt trust (other than an employee-benefit trust) is considered as owned by its beneficiaries in *proportion* to their actuarial interest. I.R.C. § 318(a)(2)(B)(i).

(4) Stock owned, directly or indirectly, by a trust of which a person is considered the owner under the grantor trust rules is considered owned by the owner of the trust. I.R.C. § 318(a)(2)(B)(ii).

Note that attribution of stock ownership is proportionate for all but owners of grantor trusts, and that there is no attribution of stock owned by a corporation to shareholders that own less than 50 percent of the value of the stock in the corporation from which attribution is sought.

Example 5.3: IJK Co. is owned equally by Irene, Joint Venture Partnership, and Kapital Corporation (30 shares each). Irene is an equal partner in Joint Venture Partnership with John and Kyle. Under section 318, Irene is deemed to own (in addition to the 30 shares she actually owns), 10 shares in IJK Co. because of her one-third interest in Joint Venture Partnership.

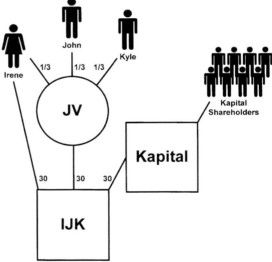

Note that if Irene also owned one-third of the stock of Kapital Corporation, none of the IJK shares owned by Kapital Corporation would be attributed to Irene because of her lack of a 50-percent or more stake in Kapital Corporation.

[C]   Attribution to Entities from Investors

Under section 318(a)(3), attribution of stock from investors to entities is done as follows:

(1) Stock owned, directly or indirectly, by or for a partner or beneficiary of an estate is considered as owned by the partnership or estate. I.R.C. § 318(a)(3)(A). For this purpose, an S corporation is treated as a partnership, and therefore is not subject to the 50-percent threshold discussed below. *See* I.R.C. § 318(a)(5)(E).

(2) *If 50 percent or more in value of the stock in a corporation is owned*, directly or indirectly, by or for any person, the corporation is considered as owning the stock owned by that person. I.R.C. § 318(a)(3)(C).

(3) Stock owned, directly or indirectly, by or for a beneficiary of an exempt trust (other than an employee-benefit trust) is considered as owned by the trust unless the beneficiary's interest in the trust is a remote, contingent interest. I.R.C. § 318(a)(3)(B)(i).

(4) Stock owned, directly or indirectly, by or for the owner of a grantor trust is considered as owned by the trust. I.R.C. § 318(a)(3)(B)(ii).

Note that attribution of stock ownership *to* entities is *not* proportionate. However, there is no attribution of stock to a corporation from a shareholder that owns less than 50 percent of the value of the stock in the corporation to which attribution is sought.

> *Example 5.4*: As in Example 5.3, IJK Co. is owned equally by Irene, Joint Venture Partnership, and Kapital Corporation (30 shares each). Irene is an equal partner in Joint Venture Partnership with John and Kyle. (See the diagram above.) In addition to the 30 shares Joint Venture Partnership actually owns in IJK Co., Joint Venture Partnership is deemed to own 30 additional shares of IJK Co. (for a total of 60 IJK Co. shares) because one of its partners, Irene, owns 30 shares in IJK Co. Note that the attribution is not proportionate (all 30 of Irene's IJK Co. shares are attributed to Joint Venture Partnership, rather than just 10).

[D]   Options

Under section 318(a)(4), if a person has an option to acquire stock, that stock is considered as owned by that person. In other words, for purposes of constructive stock ownership, options are *deemed exercised*.

> *Example 5.5*: Lauren and Marvin, who are unrelated, each own 50 shares of LaMar Corp. Lauren has an option to buy 10 of Marvin's shares. Under section 318(a)(4), Lauren constructively owns those 10 shares.

[E]   Operating Rules

Section 318(a)(5) provides a number of rules for applying section 318:

(1) Stock constructively owned is considered actually owned for purposes of the attribution rules. I.R.C. § 318(a)(5)(A).

Thus, reattribution of shares is permitted unless it is otherwise prohibited; there are several exceptions to reattribution in section 318(a)(5).

(2) There is no reattribution among family members. *See* I.R.C. § 318(a)(5)(B).

This is an exception to the general rule allowing reattribution. For example, stock owned by Husband may be attributed to Wife, but may not be reattributed from her to Wife's mother. (If it could be so reattributed, that would be equivalent to allowing attribution to Husband's mother-in-law, although an in-law is not defined as a family member in section 318(a)(1).)

(3) There is no attribution first *to* an entity and then *from* the entity for purposes of making another investor in the entity the constructive owner of the stock. *See* I.R.C. § 318(a)(5)(C).

This rule prevents attribution between investors via the entity in which they invest. For example, if Partner A owns stock in a corporation, that stock can be attributed to the partnership, but cannot be reattributed from the partnership to Partner B.

(4) The option rule overrides the family rule if both would apply. I.R.C. § 318(a)(5)(D).

For example, if Husband has an option on Wife's shares, the stock owned by Wife is attributed to Husband via the option rule and may then be reattributed to Husband's mother via the family attribution rules because this would not constitute double use of the family attribution rule.

(5) S corporations are treated as partnerships, and shareholders of S corporations are treated as partners, except "for purposes of determining whether stock in the S corporation is constructively owned by any person." I.R.C. § 318(a)(5)(E).

Note that partnerships, unlike corporations, do not have 50-percent ownership thresholds.

§ 5.03   Tax Consequences of Redemptions

[A]   Overview of Section 302

The general rule under section 302 is that a redemption is treated as an exchange (sale) of stock. I.R.C. § 302(a). A shareholder whose shares are redeemed would therefore realize capital gain on the difference between the redemption proceeds and the shareholder's basis in the stock redeemed. However, section 302(a) only applies if (1) the redemption is "not essentially equivalent to a dividend"; (2) the distribution is "substantially disproportionate" with respect to the shareholder; (3) there is a complete termination of the shareholder's interest in the corporation; or (4) there is a partial liquidation of the corporation and the shareholder is not a corporation. I.R.C. § 302(b). In addition, as discussed above, the "constructive ownership" rules of section 318 apply for purposes of determining stock ownership under section 302. I.R.C. § 302(c). If none of the four provisions of section 302(b) applies, the redemption is treated as a distribution under section

301, and is thus taxable as a dividend, in whole or in part, depending on the amount of the corporation's earnings and profits.[4] I.R.C. § 302(d).

[B] Redemptions Qualifying for Exchange Treatment

[1] Complete Termination of Interest

[a] In General

A complete termination of a shareholder's interest in a corporation is the clearest case for treating the redemption as an exchange because a complete termination of interest precludes the possibility of bail-out of corporate earnings and profits by a shareholder who preserves the opportunity to benefit from the corporation's future earnings.

Example 5.6: North Corp. is owned equally by Ned and Olga, who are otherwise unrelated. Upon Ned's retirement, North Corp. redeems all of his shares for their fair market value of $100,000. Ned had a basis of $20,000 in the shares. Under section 302(b)(3), the redemption constitutes a complete termination of Ned's interest in North Corp. Accordingly, the redemption is treated as an exchange under 302(a), and Ned has capital gain of $80,000 on the exchange.

Although, in Example 5.6, the complete redemption of Ned's shares constituted a complete termination of interest, it is extremely important to be aware that stock attribution (constructive ownership) may preclude a complete termination of interest, or make it possible only by following certain rules for "waiving" attribution of family-owned shares. The effects of the stock attribution rules and their exceptions are discussed below.

[b] Attribution of Family-Owned Shares

In a closely held corporation, the constructive ownership rules may make it impossible for a shareholder to effectuate a "complete termination of interest" in the corporation even if all of his or her shares are redeemed. Consider again the facts of Example 5.2.

Example 5.7: Darren, Edna, Frank, Gertrude, and Hilda each own 20 of the 100 outstanding shares in DEF, Inc. Darren is the son of Edna and Frank. Gertrude is Frank's sister, and Hilda is Gertrude's daughter. If Darren sells all 20 of his shares back to DEF, Inc., he will still be deemed to own 40 shares (those owned by his mother Edna and his father Frank) and he therefore will not have effectuated a complete termination of interest.

---

[4] The tax treatment of non-liquidating distributions in general, and of dividends in particular, is discussed in detail in Chapter 4.

[i] Waiver of Attribution of Family-Owned Shares

In order to allow an actual termination of all interest in a family-owned corporation to constitute an exchange, the Code provides for the possibility of "waiver" of the family attribution rules for purposes of determining complete termination of interest. *See* I.R.C. § 302(c)(2)(A). If the requirements of this provision are met, family attribution (that is, section 318(a)(1)) will not apply in determining whether there has been a complete termination of interest. Note that the availability of a waiver of family attribution means that, in some cases, a shareholder who cannot qualify under section 302(b) for a "substantially disproportionate" redemption[5] because of family attribution can accomplish a "complete termination of interest."

To qualify for the waiver of family attribution under section 302(c)(2)(A), three requirements must be met:

(1) Immediately after the redemption distribution, the shareholder in question (the distributee) retains no interest in the corporation other than as a creditor. The distributee cannot even remain an officer, director, or employee. I.R.C. § 302(c)(2)(A)(i).

(2) The distributee does not acquire any such interest (other than by bequest or inheritance) within ten years from the date of the distribution. If this provision is violated, the waiver will be invalidated retroactively. I.R.C. § 302(c)(2)(A)(ii). A special statute of limitations runs for one year from the date the shareholder notifies the IRS of the receipt of the stock. *See* I.R.C. § 302(c)(2)(A).

(3) The distributee files an agreement with the IRS to notify it of any prohibited acquisition described and to maintain necessary records. I.R.C. § 302(c)(2)(A)(iii).

In addition, under section 302(c)(2)(B), the waiver provision does not apply if (1) any portion of the stock redeemed was acquired directly or indirectly within the ten-year period ending on the date of the distribution from a person the ownership of whose stock would be attributable to the distributee *or* (2) any person who owns at the time of the distribution stock that is attributable to the distributee and such person acquired the stock in the corporation directly or indirectly from the distributee within the ten-year period ending on the date of distribution, unless the stock acquired from the distributee is redeemed in the same transaction. However, this restriction does not apply if the relevant acquisition or disposition did not have as one of its principal purposes the avoidance of Federal income tax. These requirements are discussed further below.

---

[5] Substantially disproportionate redemptions are discussed in § 5.03[B][2].

[I] No Interest in the Corporation Except as a Creditor

In order to be eligible for waiver of family attribution, the shareholder whose shares are redeemed must terminate any relationship with the corporation, such as officer, director, or employee. The Code allows the electing party to remain a creditor of the corporation, which allows the corporation to pay the redemption proceeds over time without precluding waiver of family attribution. The debtor-creditor relationship need not be connected to the redemption itself, however.

Example 5.8: Patty and Quincy are married to each other, and they each own 50 of the 100 outstanding shares of PQ, Inc., a corporation with substantial earnings and profits. Both Patty and Quincy are also employees of the corporation. Patty decides to retire, and tenders her 50 shares to PQ, Inc. for redemption. To qualify for waiver of attribution of her husband's shares to her, Patty must terminate her employment relationship with PQ, Inc. However, receipt of pension benefits from PQ, Inc. will not disqualify the waiver.

In a recent case, *Hurst v. Commissioner*, 124 T.C. 16, 23 (2005), the taxpayers remained creditors on notes providing for the payment for Mr. Hurst's stock and on a lease of the company's headquarters. In addition, Mrs. Hurst, who had not been a shareholder in the corporation, entered into a 10-year employment contract with the company. Each of the agreements also contained cross-default provisions. The court stated that:

> While acknowledging that each relationship between the Hursts and their old company—creditor under the notes, landlord under the lease, employment of a non-owning family member—passes muster, [the Commissioner] argues that the total number of related obligations resulting from the transaction gave the Hursts a prohibited interest in the corporation by giving Richard Hurst a financial stake in the company's continued success.

Id. The Tax Court ruled in favor of the taxpayers on this issue:

> The number of legal connections between Mr. Hurst and the buyers that continued after the deal was signed did not change their character as permissible security interests. Even looked at all together, they were in no way contingent upon the financial performance of the company except in the obvious sense that all creditors have in their debtors' solvency.

Id. at 28.

[II] No Related-Party Transfers Within the Previous Ten Years

There are two aspects to the restriction on related-party transfers: (1) a restriction on the *receipt* of shares from a related person, and (2) a restriction on the *transfer* of shares to a related person. Receipt of shares *from* a related person during the ten-year look-back period bars waiver of family attribution unless the transfer did not have a principal purpose of tax avoidance. *See* I.R.C. § 302(c)(2)(B)(i). Transfer of shares *to* a related person during the ten-year look-back period bars waiver of family attribution if the related person owns shares in the corporation at the time of the redemption, unless the transfer did not have a principal purpose of tax avoidance or the other shareholder has his or her shares redeemed in the same transaction. *See* I.R.C. § 302(c)(2)(B)(ii).

[a] Pre-Redemption Receipt of Shares from Related Person

Revenue Ruling 79-67, 1979-1 C.B. 128, provides an example of testing for tax-avoidance motive in the context of receipt of shares *from* a related person during the ten-year look-back period. In that ruling, the taxpayer-mother was the sole beneficiary of an estate holding stock in a corporation. The taxpayer's son owned the remaining stock. The executor of the estate transferred the stock to the taxpayer. Subsequently, the corporation redeemed the taxpayer's stock for fair market value. The redemption enabled the taxpayer's son, who was knowledgeable in the business and active in its management, to obtain sole ownership of the company.

If section 318(a)(1)(A) applied, the taxpayer would constructively own all of the corporation's stock (via her son), and the redemption would be taxed as a section 301 distribution instead of an exchange. By following the provisions of section 302(c)(2)(A), the taxpayer tried to avoid the application of section 318(a)(1)(A). However, the redeemed stock had been acquired by the taxpayer within ten years of the transfer from a related party, the estate.

The IRS held that the principal purpose of the transfer was not tax avoidance because the redemption of the mother's stock was intended to grant her son sole ownership of the business and because the taxpayer retained no control over the business after the transfer. Therefore, the redemption was considered a complete termination of interest under section 302(b)(3), and the IRS held that it would tax the redemption as an exchange so long as the taxpayer filed the agreement required by section 302(c)(2)(A)(iii).

[b] Pre-Redemption Transfer of Shares to a Related Person

Revenue Ruling 77-293, 1977-2 C.B. 91, provides an example of testing for a tax-avoidance motive in the context of a transfer of shares *to* a related person during the ten-year look-back period. In that ruling, the taxpayer-father transferred half of his stock in the family's business to his son, who had been working with him for some time to learn the skills necessary to run the business. Shortly thereafter, the taxpayer resigned and his son became president of the board of directors of the company. In addition, soon after the gift of the stock, the corporation redeemed the taxpayer's remaining shares, so that he was left with no interest in the corporation.

Because the taxpayer-father constructively owned all of the corporation's stock via his son (under section 318(a)(1)), the redemption would be taxed as a section 301 distribution instead of an exchange if family attribution rules applied. By following the provisions of section 302(c)(2)(A), the taxpayer tried to avoid the application of section 318(a)(1)(A). However, the taxpayer had transferred stock to his son, a related party, within ten years of the redemption, and the son still owned stock in the corporation at the time of the redemption. Therefore, only if the transfer to the son did not have a principal purpose of tax avoidance, would the taxpayer be eligible to elect waiver of the family attribution rules.

The IRS found that the purpose of section 302(c)(2)(B) is to prevent the bail-out of earnings and profits as capital gain while retaining control or economic interest in the corporation via a related person. To determine if the principal purpose of the transfer of the stock was tax avoidance, the IRS considered the facts. The IRS found that because the transfer was to a knowledgeable party who planned to manage the corporation, the transfer's main purpose was to allow the taxpayer-father to retire, not tax avoidance, although the transfer did reduce tax liability. Therefore, the IRS ruled that so long as the conditions of section 302(c)(2)(A) were met, the redemption of the stock would be considered a termination of interest under section 302(b)(3).

[III]   No Acquisitions Within the Succeeding Ten Years

A shareholder who elects to waive family attribution may not acquire any interest in the corporation (other than by bequest or inheritance) within ten years from the date of the distribution. I.R.C. § 302(c)(2)(A)(ii). If the shareholder does so, then the statutes of limitation on assessment and collection of tax are extended to one year following the date on which that person notifies the Secretary of the Treasury of the acquisition. See I.R.C. § 302(c)(2)(A). However, note that if a redemption qualifies under both the complete termination of interest paragraph as well as another paragraph of 302(b), this rule does not apply. See I.R.C. § 302(b)(5).

Example 5.9: In Example 5.8, if, after retiring and causing PQ, Inc. to redeem all of her shares, Patty acquires any interest in the corporation (other than by bequest or inheritance) within the ten years following the date of the distribution, the waiver will no longer be effective, and the statutes of limitation on assessment and collection of tax will be extended to one year following the date on which Patty notifies the IRS of the acquisition.

[ii]   Waiver of Family Attribution by Entities

Entities (partnerships, estates, trusts, and corporations) may waive application of family attribution rules if they meet certain requirements.

The waiver precludes application of *family attribution* to a related person where the shares so attributed would then be attributed from that person to the entity in question. For entity waiver, the requirements for waiver of family attribution must be met both by the entity and by any "related person," defined as "any person to whom ownership of stock in the corporation is (at the time of the distribution) attributable under section 318(a)(1) if such stock is further attributable to the entity under section 318(a)(3)." I.R.C. § 302(c)(2)(C)(ii)(II). The related persons must also agree to be jointly and severally liable for any deficiency resulting from a prohibited acquisition within the following ten years. *See* I.R.C. § 302(c)(2)(C)(i).

> *Example 5.10*: Ron and Sarah are husband and wife. Tom is their son. Ron, Sarah, Tom, and the estate of Tom's wife Ursula, of which Tom is the sole beneficiary, each own 25 percent of the shares of RST Corp. Ursula's estate seeks redemption of its 25 shares. Assume that the redemption does not qualify under section 303, discussed below.[6] For waiver of family attribution, Tom must join with the estate in the waiver because his parents' shares would be attributed through him to Ursula's estate. Tom also must agree to be jointly and severally liable with the estate for any deficiency resulting from a prohibited acquisition within the following ten years.

[2] Substantially Disproportionate Redemptions

[a] In General

Section 302(b)(2) provides that a reduction in ownership that falls short of a complete termination of interest may still qualify as an exchange. It allows for a "substantially disproportionate redemption," defined as a redemption in which the shareholder whose shares were redeemed is left with (1) less than 50 percent of the total combined voting power of all classes of stock entitled to vote, (2) less than 80 percent of the percentage of the voting stock that shareholder held immediately before the redemption, *and* (3) less than 80 percent of the percentage of the common stock (voting and non-voting) that shareholder held immediately before the redemption. I.R.C. § 302(b)(2)(B), (C). If there is more than one class of common stock, the determinations are made by reference to fair market value. I.R.C. § 302(b)(2)(C).

Thus, in analyzing whether a taxpayer's redemption that is not a complete termination of interest falls within section 302(b)(2), the first question is whether, after the redemption, the taxpayer holds *less than 50 percent of the total combined voting power in the corporation.* If not—that is, if the shareholder holds 50 percent or more of the votes—the redemption is not substantially disproportionate. Note that constructive ownership is taken into account in making this determination.

---

[6] *See* § 5.04[D].

Example 5.11: Veronica owns 80 shares of voting common stock in X, Inc., its only class of stock. William, who is not related to Veronica, owns the other 20 shares. In order to increase William's interest in the corporation, Veronica causes X, Inc. to redeem 60 of her shares for cash. After the redemption, Veronica owns 20 out of the 40 outstanding shares in the company. Because Veronica still holds 50 percent of the voting power, the redemption is not substantially disproportionate.

This example is illustrated in the diagram below; the redemption transaction is shown on the left and the "after" picture, in which the redeemed shares are shown as treasury stock, is on the right.

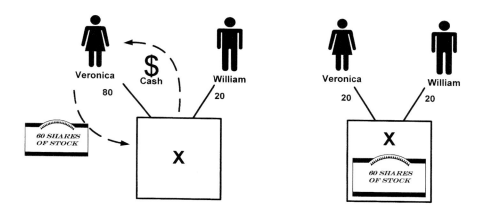

If the taxpayer whose shares were redeemed holds less than 50 percent of the votes after the redemption, the next step is to determine the ratio of the percent of votes that shareholder held before the redemption to the percent of votes he or she held after the redemption. The taxpayer must have less than 80 percent of the votes he or she had before the redemption for it to qualify as substantially disproportionate.

Example 5.12: Antonio owns 60 shares of voting common stock in Y, Inc., its only class of stock. Beth, who is not related to Antonio, owns the other 40 shares. Y, Inc. redeems 30 of Antonio's shares for cash. After the redemption, Antonio owns 30 out of 70 shares. That is less than 50 percent of the voting power. In addition, his interest in the voting stock has been reduced from 60 percent (60 out of 100) to 42.86 percent. Thus, his percentage interest in the voting stock of Y, Inc. after the redemption is less than 80 percent of his percentage interest in that stock before the redemption (48 percent would be exactly 80 percent of his pre-redemption interest).

This example is illustrated in the diagram below. The redemption transaction is pictured on the left. The "after" picture, in which the redeemed shares are shown as treasury stock, is on the right.

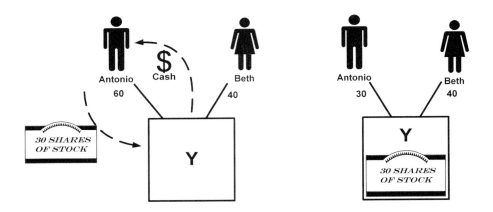

Note that the test must be applied again with respect to *common* stock. *See* I.R.C. § 302(b)(2). However, in the example above, as the only voting stock is also the only common stock, the figures are the same. Thus, in Example 5.12, the redemption is a substantially disproportionate redemption.

Applying the 80-percent test, though perhaps initially confusing, is actually rather straightforward. Taking a percentage of a percentage may not be intuitive at first, but it is just like computing a percentage of any other number. For example, 80 percent of 70 is 56, so 80 percent of 70 *percent* is 56 *percent*. The chart below contains the 80 percent calculation for various pre-redemption ownership levels.

CHART 5.1
Computing 80% of the Percentage of Stock Owned Before a Redemption

PERCENTAGE OWNERSHIP PRIOR TO REDEMPTION	80% OF OWNERSHIP PRIOR TO REDEMPTION
10%	8%
20%	16%
30%	24%
40%	32%
50%	40%
60%	48%
70%	**56%**
80%	**64%**
90%	**72%**
100%	**80%**

Note: The percentages in bold type exceed the post-redemption 50-percent voting stock threshold allowed for the redemption to qualify under section 302(b)(2) and therefore do not qualify as a substantially disproportionate redemption.

[b]   Series of Redemptions

A series of redemptions that in the aggregate is not a substantially disproportionate redemption precludes qualification under section 302(b)(2), if done pursuant to a plan. *See* I.R.C. § 302(b)(2)(D). Consider Revenue Ruling 85-14, 1985-1 C.B. 93. In that ruling, the sole class of stock of corporation X was owned by four shareholders: A, with 1,466 shares; B, with 210 shares; C, with 200 shares; and D, with 155 shares. According to the facts of the ruling, X had a repurchase agreement with every share-holder but A. The agreement provided that if a shareholder ceased to be actively connected with the business operations of X, the shareholder would promptly tender his X shares to X for an amount equal to the book value of the stock. X would then be required to purchase the shares at book value within six months. B informed A that B would be resigning. Two months later, and only one week before the date of B's resignation, A caused X to redeem 902 of A's shares, leaving A with less than 50 percent of X's shares. B subsequently tendered B's shares to X, and A regained majority owner-ship of X.

Taken separately from B's transaction, A's redemption would be treated as an exchange under section 302 because, as required by section 302(b)(2)(C), A reduced the ratio of his voting stock to the total voting stock by more than 20 percent, and, as required by section 302(b)(2)(B), A also owned less than 50 percent of the total voting power immediately after the redemption. However, if section 302(b)(2)(D) applied, A's transaction and B's transaction would be considered together, as a series of redemptions. If section 302(b)(2)(D) applied, A's redemption would not qualify to be taxed as an exchange because A's voting ratio was not decreased by more than 20 percent and because A owned a majority of the voting stock after the transaction as a whole. Section 302(b)(2)(D) would apply if a "plan" resulted in an aggregate series of transactions that were not substantially disproportionate to A.

In Revenue Ruling 85-14, the IRS found that the required plan can be the design of a single shareholder to use a series of transactions to regain majority voting control over a corporation after that control was apparently lost. Thus, although there was no actual agreement between A and B, the transactions of A and B qualified as a "plan." When the transactions were aggregated, A's redemption was not substantially disproportionate under section 302(b)(2).

[3] Redemptions "Not Essentially Equivalent to a Dividend"

A redemption that is neither a complete termination of interest nor substantially disproportionate may qualify as "not essentially equivalent to a dividend." *See* I.R.C. § 302(b)(1). Unlike the tests in section 302(b)(2) and (3), this test is not mechanical. Instead, it is a fact-sensitive last resort if the redemption does not qualify under other paragraphs of 302(b). *See* I.R.C. § 302(b)(5). *United States v. Davis*, 397 U.S. 301 (1970),[7] is a Supreme Court case interpreting 302(b)(1).

In *Davis*, Maclin P. Davis (Davis) and E.B. Bradley (Bradley) organized a corporation. Davis and his wife held 250 shares of common stock and Bradley held 500. In order for the corporation to be eligible for a loan, Davis purchased 1,000 shares of preferred stock at $25 per share with the understanding that the corporation would redeem the shares after the loan was repaid. Before the loan was repaid, Davis purchased Bradley's 500 shares and gave them to his son and daughter. Once the loan was repaid, the corporation redeemed Davis's 1,000 shares of preferred stock. Davis treated the $25,000 redemption proceeds as a sale of stock with no gain realized. The IRS believed that Davis should have treated the $25,000 as essentially equivalent to a dividend. *Id.* at 302–03.

Davis argued, in part, that the attribution rules of section 318(a) should not apply to redemptions considered under section 302(b)(1). The Court rejected this argument both under the language of section 302(c) and because accepting the argument would provide a loophole that would effectively end attribution under section 302(b)(2) and (3) as well. The Court then looked to the legislative history of section 302(b)(1) to determine the meaning of "not essentially equivalent to a dividend." The Court determined that Congress did not intend to allow a business motive for the transaction to weigh in, nor did it intend to look for a tax-avoidance plan. *Id.* at 305–08.

In *Davis*, the Court held that "to qualify for preferred treatment under that section [I.R.C. § 302(b)(1)], a redemption must result in a *meaningful*

---

[7] *Reh'g denied*, 397 U.S. 1071 (1970).

reduction of the shareholder's proportionate interest in the corporation." *Id.* at 313 (emphasis added). Applying the attribution rules, Davis owned 100 percent of the stock both before and after the redemption, so there was no reduction of his interest and the transaction was "essentially equivalent to a dividend" under section 302(b)(1). *See id.*

Thus, *Davis* teaches that where a sole shareholder (actually or constructively) has part of his or her stock redeemed, that will always be taxed as a section 301 distribution rather than as an exchange. In contrast to *Davis*, if a shareholder owns *only nonvoting preferred stock* of a corporation (even after application of constructive ownership rules), and the stock is not section 306 stock, the redemption of a part of that stock generally will qualify under section 302(b)(1), although it does not otherwise qualify under section 302(b).[8] *See* Treas. Reg. § 1.302-2(a).

[a]   Majority Shareholder's Redemption

The IRS's holdings in several Revenue Rulings provide further guidance regarding which redemptions are not essentially equivalent to a dividend. With respect to a majority shareholder, in Revenue Ruling 78-401, 1978-2 C.B. 127, the IRS ruled that a reduction from 90-percent interest to 60-percent was not a meaningful reduction because the shareholder whose shares were redeemed still controlled the company (although some corporate decisions required a two-thirds majority).

By contrast, in Revenue Ruling 75-502, 1975-2 C.B. 111, Corporation X was owned by three shareholders: an individual, B, with 750 shares; an estate with 250 shares; and an individual, A, related to the estate and the sole beneficiary of the estate, with 750 shares. Corporation X redeemed all of the estate's stock and the estate questioned the tax consequences of that redemption. Because of the attribution rules of section 318(a), the estate was deemed to also own A's stock. After the redemption, the estate's ownership in X decreased from approximately 57 percent to 50 percent.

Because the transfer did not result in the estate owning less than 50 percent of the stock, and it was not a complete termination of the estate's interest, neither section 302(b)(2) nor (b)(3) applied. As discussed above, *Davis* provided that for section 302(b)(1) to apply, the redemption must result in a "meaningful reduction" of the shareholder's interest, but it did not quantify what reduction qualifies as meaningful under this rule. In *Himmel v. Commissioner*, 338 F.2d 815 (2d Cir. 1964), the Court of Appeals for the Second Circuit had found that a shareholder's interest includes the right to vote and thereby exercise control; the right to participate in current earnings and accumulated surplus; and the right to share in net assets on liquidation. In the Revenue Ruling, the estate's proportionate interest decreased from 57 percent before the transaction to 50 percent after the transaction, a reduction in all three of the estate's rights, and the other 50 percent of the vote was held by a single unrelated shareholder. The IRS

---

[8] Section 306 stock is discussed in Chapter 6.

therefore found that the redemption therefore qualified as an exchange under section 302(a). The ruling also notes that if, after the redemption, the estate were left with more than 50 percent of the stock, the redemption would not qualify because the estate would still have "dominant voting rights."

[b] Minority Shareholder's Redemption

In Revenue Ruling 75-512, 1975-2 C.B. 112, a trust directly owning 7.5 percent of the shares of corporation X, and deemed under the attribution rules of section 318(a)(3)(B) to own a total of 30 percent of the shares, sold back to X corporation all of the shares it directly owned. Under the attribution rules of section 318, the trust was deemed to own 24.3 percent of the stock of X after the redemption. The redemption therefore did not qualify as a complete termination of interest, and it just missed qualification as a substantially disproportionate redemption under section 302(b)(2). The IRS therefore looked to section 302(b)(1), and, in particular, the factors set out in Revenue Ruling 75-502, discussed above, to determine if the redemption was a meaningful reduction in the trust's proportionate interest in X.

The IRS noted that the trust was a minority shareholder both before and after the redemption. As a result of the redemption, the trust experienced a reduction in voting power, a reduction in its right to participate in current earnings and accumulated surplus, and a reduction in its right to share in the net assets of X on liquidation. The IRS therefore found that the trust experienced a meaningful reduction in its proportionate interest in X, and determined that the redemption would be taxed as an exchange under section 302(a).

In Revenue Ruling 76-364, 1976-2 C.B. 91, a reduction from 27 percent to 22.27 percent also was meaningful because before the redemption the taxpayer had control with the agreement of any one of the three other shareholders and afterwards, he could not exercise control with the agreement of one other shareholder. Similarly, in Revenue Ruling 76-385, 1976-2 C.B. 92, where Y's ownership in Z, applying constructive ownership rules, was reduced from .0001118 percent to .0001081 percent, although that was 96 percent of its prior ownership, the transaction was not essentially equivalent to a dividend because Y's stock ownership of Z was minimal; Y exercised no control over Z; and Y experienced a reduction in its voting power, its right to share in current earnings and accumulated surplus, and in its right to a portion of the assets of Z on liquidation.

In Revenue Ruling 81-289, 1981-2 C.B. 82, by contrast, where A surrendered 2 percent of A's .02 percent of the shares of X corporation and afterwards A still owned exactly .02 percent because of redemptions of other shareholders' shares, the IRS found that the transaction did not qualify as an exchange because there was no reduction of A's ownership interest in X. Thus, as these rulings reflect, section 302(b)(1) requires an examination of all the facts relevant to the redemption. In general, minority shareholders that reduce their ownership interests fare well under the rulings.

[4] Partial Liquidations

Section 302 provides that a redemption of stock of *a non-corporate shareholder* in partial liquidation of a corporation is treated as an exchange under section 302(b)(4). *See* I.R.C. § 302(e)(4). For purposes of determining whether stock is held by a shareholder who is not a corporation, any stock held by a partnership, estate, or trust is treated as if it were actually held proportionately by its partners or beneficiaries. *See* I.R.C. § 302(e)(5). The exclusion of corporate shareholders from section 302(b)(4) was designed to correct abusive use of partial liquidations to step up basis while *General Utilities* was still good law.[9] *See* Boris I. Bittker & James S. Eustice, Federal Income Taxation of Corporations and Shareholders 9-55 – 9-66 n.188 (7th ed. 2000).

For purposes of section 302(b)(4), a distribution is treated as being in partial liquidation of a corporation if the distribution is not essentially equivalent to a dividend, determined at the *corporate level*, and the distribution is pursuant to a plan of partial liquidation. *See* I.R.C. § 302(e)(1).[10] The distribution must also occur in the taxable year in which the plan is adopted or in the following taxable year. Dividend equivalence at the corporate level means that shareholder-level facts (such as whether the distribution is *pro rata*) are irrelevant. Rather, the focus is on the extent to which the corporation has contracted its business—typically by distributing operating assets. *See, e.g.*, Rev. Rul. 74-296, 1974-1 C.B. 80 (change in business operation from department store to discount apparel store constituted genuine and sufficient contraction of corporation's business).

A safe harbor applies to distributions "attributable to the distributing corporation's ceasing to conduct, or consist[ing] of the assets of, a qualified trade or business" if, "[i]mmediately after the distribution, the distributing corporation is actively engaged in the conduct of a qualified trade or business." I.R.C. § 302(e)(2)(A), (B). A qualified trade or business is one that was actively conducted during the five-year period before the redemption, and was not acquired by the corporation within that period in a non-recognition transaction. *See* I.R.C. § 302(e)(3).

---

[9] *General Utilities & Operating Co. v. Helvering*, 296 U.S. 200 (1935), is discussed in § 4.02[A].

[10] Partial liquidations are also discussed briefly in § 7.02 of Chapter 7.

CHART 5.2
Checklist for Corporate Redemptions of Stock

(1)   Did a corporation buy back its own stock from a shareholder? (If no, section 302 does not apply.)

(2)   If yes, compute the shareholder's percentage interest *before* the redemption and *after* the redemption.

> (A) Section 318 attribution rules apply.

> (B) The number of shares outstanding after the redemption will be less than before the redemption because the shares redeemed are no longer outstanding.

(3)   Was this a redemption from a non-corporate shareholder in partial liquidation of the corporation?

(4)   If no, was this a complete termination of the shareholder's interest in the corporation?

(5)   If no, was this a "substantially disproportionate" redemption?

> (A)   After the redemption, the shareholder must have less than 50 percent of the vote.

> (B)   After the redemption, the voting power the shareholder has must be less than 80 percent of the voting power the shareholder had before the redemption.

> (C)   After the redemption, the common stock the shareholder has must be less than 80 percent of the common stock the shareholder had before the redemption.

(6)   If no, was this "not essentially equivalent to a dividend," a fact-sensitive test?

(7)   If the answer to any of questions (3) through (6) is yes, then the redemption is taxed as an exchange. The shareholder will have capital gain in the amount of the difference between the amount distributed and the shareholder's basis in those shares.

(8)   If the answer to *all* of questions (3) through (6) is no, then the transaction is taxed as a section 301 distribution. Apply section 301 to determine the dividend amount.

[C]   Redemptions Treated as Distributions

[1]   In General

Redemption transactions that do not qualify under section 302(b)(1), (2), (3), or (4) are taxed as distributions governed by section 301. *See* I.R.C. § 302(d). That means, as discussed in Chapter 4, that the distribution proceeds are a dividend to the extent of earnings and profits. Any excess of the distribution is a return of capital until basis is reduced to zero, and any further excess is taxed as capital gain.

Example 5.13: Cathy owns 70 shares of voting common stock in Z Corp., its only class of stock. Dennis, who is not related to Cathy, owns the other 30 shares. Assume that, in its only distribution for the year, Z Corp. redeems 10 of Cathy's shares for their fair market value of $6,000. Z Corp. has accumulated earnings and profits of $4,000 and current earnings and profits of $3,000 for the year of the redemption.

Before the redemption, Cathy owned 70% of the stock. After the redemption, Cathy owns 60 out of 90 shares, or 66.67% of the stock. Cathy has not completely terminated her interest in Z Corp. The redemption is not substantially disproportionate (she still holds 50% or more of the voting power in Z Corp.). The redemption also is not "not essentially equivalent to a dividend" because Cathy still holds the majority (in fact, a super-majority) of the votes. The redemption also is not in partial liquidation of the corporation. Therefore, the distribution proceeds of $6,000 are treated as a distribution governed by section 301. Because there are ample earnings and profits, the entire $6,000 is a dividend.

[2]   Basis-Shifting Redemptions

If a redemption is treated as a section 301 distribution, the shareholder's basis in his or her remaining stock generally is increased by the basis of the redeemed stock. *See* Treas. Reg. 1.302-2(c). Thus, the shareholder does not "lose" basis. If a shareholder sells *all* of his or her shares to the corporation but the redemption is treated as a section 301 distribution because of the constructive ownership rules of section 318, a basis problem arises. That is, because the selling shareholder is taxed under section 301, the shareholder does not recover basis, but the shareholder holds no more shares to which to allocate basis. A Treasury regulation traditionally addressed this dilemma without great precision, stating, "[i]n any case in which an amount received in redemption of stock is treated as a distribution of a dividend, *proper adjustment* of the basis of the remaining stock will be made with respect to the stock redeemed." *Id.* (emphasis added). The regulations also provide the following example:

> H and W, husband and wife, each own half of the stock of Corporation X. All of the stock was purchased by H for $100,000 cash. In 1950 H gave one-half of the stock to W, the stock transferred having a value in excess of $50,000. In 1955 all of the stock of H is redeemed for $150,000, and it is determined that the distribution to H in redemption of his shares constitutes the distribution of a dividend. *Immediately after the transaction, W holds the remaining stock of Corporation X with a basis of $100,000.*

Id. Ex. 2 (emphasis added). Thus, what the example generally provides is that, when the husband's stock in a corporation owned equally by husband and wife is redeemed, the wife's shares, which she had received from her husband, and which caused the redemption to be taxed under section 301, are allocated the $50,000 of basis that previously belonged to the shares of the husband.

Professor Glenn Coven has commented that "the example contains no guidance regarding the principle that might be applied to determine the identity of the remaining stock in a more complex case." Glenn E. Coven, *Basis Shifting—A Radical Approach to an Intractable Problem*, 105 TAX NOTES 1541, 1542 (2004). As discussed in Chapter 16, the ambiguity in the regulations has been exploited in "basis-shifting" tax shelters, to which the IRS responded with Notice 2001-45, 2001-2 C.B. 129.[11]

The Treasury Department also responded to basis-shifting shelters, proposing regulations under which, in any redemption treated as a section 301 distribution (not just a redemption of *all* of a taxpayer's actually-owned shares), the taxpayer's unrecovered basis in the redeemed stock would be treated as a loss to that taxpayer on the disposition of the stock. *See* Prop. Treas. Reg. § 1.302-5(a). The loss would be deemed to arise on the date of the redemption, so that "the attributes (e.g., character and source) of such loss" are determined on that date, *id.*, but the loss generally would not actually be deductible on that date, *see* Prop. Treas. Reg. § 1.302-5(b)(3)–(4), (c). Instead, the loss would be taken into account on the "final inclusion date" to the extent it was not taken into account on an "accelerated loss inclusion date." Prop. Treas. Reg. § 1.302-5(c)(1).

Under the proposed regulations:

> [T]he final inclusion date is the first date on which the redeemed shareholder would satisfy the criteria of section 302(b)(1), (2), or (3) if the facts and circumstances that exist at the end of such day had existed immediately after the redemption. In addition, a date is the final inclusion date if there is no later date on which the redeemed shareholder could take the loss into account. . . . For example, if the redeemed shareholder is an individual, the final inclusion date includes the date of death of such individual.

Prop. Treas. Reg. § 1.302-5(b)(3). "An accelerated loss inclusion date is a date other than the final inclusion date on which the redeemed shareholder must take into account gain from an actual or deemed sale or exchange of stock of the redeeming corporation." Prop. Treas. Reg. § 1.302-5(b)(4).

The proposed regulations provide the following example, among others, applying its provisions:

> (i) Facts. A and B, husband and wife, each own 100 shares (50 percent) of the stock of corporation X and hold the corporation X stock as a capital asset. A purchased his corporation X shares on February 1, Year 1, for $200. On December 31, Year 1, corporation X redeems all of A's 100 shares of its stock for $300. At the end of Year 1, corporation X has current and accumulated earnings and profits of $200. In connection with the redemption transaction, A does not file an agreement described in section 302(c)(2) waiving the application of the family attribution rules. The redemption

---

[11] *See* § 16.03[B].

proceeds, therefore, are treated under section 301(c)(1) as a dividend to the extent of corporation X's earnings and profits of $200, and under section 301(c)(2) as a recovery of basis in the amount of $100. On July 1, Year 2, B sells all of her shares of corporation X stock to G, her mother.

(ii) Analysis. Under this section, an amount equal to A's basis in the corporation X stock ($100 after application of section 301(c)(2)) is treated as a loss recognized on a disposition of the redeemed stock on December 31, Year 1, the date of the redemption. When B sells her shares to G, A no longer owns, actually or constructively, any shares of corporation X stock. Thus, if the facts that existed at the end of July 1, Year 2, had existed immediately after the redemption, A would have been treated as having received a distribution in part or full payment in exchange for the redeemed stock pursuant to section 302(a). Under this section, therefore, July 1, Year 2, is the final inclusion date and, on that date, A is permitted to take into account the loss of $100 attributable to his basis in the redeemed stock. Because that loss is treated as having been recognized on a disposition of the redeemed stock on the date of the redemption, December 31 of Year 1, such loss is treated as a short-term capital loss.

Prop. Treas. Reg. § 1.302-5(f) Ex. 1. Thus, the proposed regulations would eliminate shifting of basis in any redemption that was not taxed as an exchange. In the example above, the husband's unrecovered basis of $100 became deductible by him as a short-term capital loss, but not until seven months after the redemption, when his wife sold her shares to a third party so that the husband no longer actually or constructively owned any shares in the corporation. The same regime would apply to a redemption in which the husband had only part of his shares redeemed. See Prop. Treas. Reg. § 1.302-5(f) Ex. 3. The proposed regulations will not be effective until they become final. Prop. Treas. Reg. § 1.302-5(g).

[3] The Seagram/DuPont Transaction

Note that a corporate shareholder may prefer that a redemption be taxed as a dividend because of the availability of the dividends received deduction, discussed in Chapter 4. The notorious Seagram/DuPont transaction is an example of a redemption structured to be taxed as a dividend distribution. In that mid-1990s transaction, Seagram, which owned a sizeable block of DuPont stock, tendered 156 million DuPont shares to DuPont (retaining 8.2 million shares—1.2 percent of DuPont) in exchange for $8.3 billion in cash and notes and roughly $500 million in warrants (essentially options) to purchase DuPont shares. Seagram received one warrant for each share redeemed. Arguably, the warrants served to maintain Seagram's position as a shareholder of DuPont under section 318(a)(4). See Rev. Rul. 89-64, 1989-1 C.B. 91. If Seagram's position were unchanged, the distribution would be taxed as a dividend, and accordingly subject to an 80-percent dividends received deduction.

The tax that Seagram paid on the $8.8 billion redemption that it received was approximately $616 million. If instead the redemption were considered an exchange, Seagram would have been subject to tax on the difference between its amount realized and its basis in the shares redeemed. Seagram's amount realized would have been $8.8 billion. Its basis in the redeemed DuPont shares was reportedly $2.83 billion. Accordingly, Seagram would have recognized a taxable gain of $5.97 billion. This would have subjected Seagram to $2.08 billion in federal taxes, rather than the $616 million tax on the dividend after application of the dividends received deduction. DuPont and Seagram essentially shared Seagram's anticipated $1.5 billion tax savings; DuPont paid approximately $56 per share for shares that were trading at $63 each. *See* Lee A. Sheppard, *Can Seagram Bail out of DuPont Without Capital Gain Tax?*, 67 TAX NOTES 325 (1995).

Arguably, if this were a dividend to Seagram, it should have been treated as an extraordinary dividend under section 1059 because it was a *non pro rata* redemption.[12] *See* I.R.C. § 1059(e)(1)(A)(ii); Sheppard, *supra*, at 328. Under then-current law, Seagram would be required to reduce its basis in its remaining 8.2 million shares to zero and then track the excess so that it would have a potential gain on disposition of the shares equal to the amount by which the dividends received deduction exceeded Seagram's basis in those shares.

Section 1059 was subsequently amended so that, as discussed in Chapter 4, nontaxed amounts in excess of basis result in immediate gain recognition. *See* I.R.C. § 1059(a)(2). In addition, with respect to amounts treated as dividends as a result of constructive stock ownership under section 318(a)(4) (the "option rule") or as a result of section 304, only the basis of the *stock redeemed* is taken into account. I.R.C. § 1059(e)(1)(A).

[D] Effects on Earnings and Profits

A redemption taxed as a distribution has the same effect on earnings and profits as any other section 301 distribution. That is, earnings and profits are reduced by the amount taxed as a dividend.[13] A redemption taxed as an *exchange*, on the other hand, results in only a proportionate reduction of accumulated earnings and profits. *See* I.R.C. § 312(n)(7). For example, if a corporation redeems 25 percent of its shares, and the redemption is taxed as an exchange, accumulated earnings and profits cannot be reduced more than 25 percent.

---

[12] Section 1059 is discussed in § 4.04[B][3].

[13] The effect of a distribution on earnings and profits is discussed in § 4.03[C][1][b][iii].

§ 5.04 Additional Issues Arising in Redemptions

[A] Form Versus Substance

[1] Sale or Redemption?

Sometimes a purported sale may actually be a redemption in substance. In *Estate of Schneider v. Commissioner*, 855 F.2d 435 (7th Cir. 1988), Al J. Schneider (Schneider) was the primary shareholder of American National Corporation (ANC), which wholly owned Schneider Transport, Inc. (Transport). Transport adopted an employee bonus plan that would give employees the option of receiving stock or cash or both. If a Transport employee opted for stock as the bonus, Transport gave that employee new unissued stock based on the book value of the stock equivalent to the bonus amount. The stock the employees received carried a restriction (the ANC Restriction) that would allow the employee to recover the full book value of the stock only after ten years of continuous employment with Transport. *Id.* at 436–37.

ANC later adopted a slightly different plan for all of its subsidiaries and affiliated corporations. Under the new plan, stock given to the employees by ANC could be previously issued nonvoting shares. As of January 1, 1974, Schneider and his family owned 99.6 percent of ANC's nonvoting stock, as well as 100 percent of the voting stock. *Id.* at 437.

Under the plan, Transport employees were required to elect whether or not to receive at least 25 percent of their bonus in ANC stock before they knew how much they were receiving. If they elected the stock bonus, they would next be informed of the amount of bonus they would receive and then would specify an exact percentage of the bonus to receive in stock. The bonus would then be given to them in two checks, one for the bonus percentage as cash, and one already made out to Schneider in the amount of the bonus they had allocated to stock. When they endorsed the checks and turned them in, Schneider deposited the money into his account and ANC issued the employees their stock and deducted the same quantity of stock from Schneider's holdings. *Id.* at 437-38.

Schneider treated these stock transfers as sales that gave rise to capital gains, arguing that the employees received bonuses in cash and decided to purchase the shares from him. Accordingly, Schneider reported the gain from these sales as capital gains. However, the IRS viewed these transactions as redemptions followed by distribution of the stock to the employees. Using the step-transaction doctrine, the Tax Court determined that the real compensation for the employees was the stock, not the cash, and that the cash flowed from the company to Schneider, using the employees as mere conduits. *See id.* at 438 & n.4.

The Court of Appeals similarly found that the transaction was ultimately a redemption followed by a distribution. Schneider first argued that he did not need cash and that the plan was motivated by *bona fide* business purposes. The court did not find Schneider's motives dispositive. Schneider also argued that the bonus given to the employees by ANC was cash and that they decided to purchase the stock directly from him once ANC brought them together to make a sale. However, because the stock that the employees received carried a restriction that Schneider's stock did not carry, it followed that the stock did not move directly from Schneider to the employees. Finally, Schneider argued that the ANC Restriction was a restriction that Schneider imposed as a term of the sale. The court found that this would make ANC a third party beneficiary that would be unable to modify the contract between Schneider and the employees without their written consent. However, ANC had modified that contract in later years without consent from either party. Therefore, the court held that Schneider was not entitled to treat the stock transfers as sales of capital assets. Instead, in substance, Schneider's stock was redeemed by ANC and the stock was then transferred from ANC to the employees. *Id.* at 440–42.

[2] Charitable Gift or Redemption?

Sometimes a charitable gift may resemble a redemption. *Grove v. Commissioner*, 490 F.2d 241 (2d Cir. 1973), involved Philip Grove (Grove), a successful engineer, who began making yearly contributions to his *alma mater*, Rensselaer Polytechnic Institute (RPI), in 1954. *Id.* at 242. Grove was the majority shareholder in Grove Shepherd Wilson & Kurge, Inc. (the Corporation), a closely held corporation engaged in civil engineering projects both in the United States and abroad. Because these projects were capital intensive, the Corporation did not pay dividends, but rather reinvested its earnings. Under a plan created by RPI, Grove would donate stock to RPI (subject to a right of first refusal by the Corporation) on a yearly basis while retaining a life interest in the income from the gift. RPI would have the Corporation redeem the shares a year or two later. Following each redemption, RPI would invest the cash proceeds in an investment company suggested by Grove, the income from which would be given to Grove for life under the donation agreement. After Grove's life interest terminated, the corpus and income from the donation would belong wholly to RPI. *Id.* at 243–44.

While Grove argued that the donations were *bona fide* gifts and the money he received from RPI was interest from those gifts, the IRS claimed that the transaction was more accurately a redemption of shares followed by a cash payment from Grove to RPI. The court quoted *Commissioner v. Court Holding Co.*, 324 U.S. 331, 334 (1945) as stating, "the incidence of taxation depends upon the substance of a transaction," *Grove*, 490 F.2d at 245. The court ruled that even though Grove owned a majority of the Corporation's shares and was able to force redemptions, because the Corporation was not obligated to redeem RPI's shares, RPI was not merely a conduit to reduce Grove's taxes. Therefore, the transaction was not taxed as a redemption of Grove's shares. *Id.* at 247.

In dissent, Judge Oakes found sufficient evidence to hold that the transactions combined to create a taxable redemption to Grove. The gift of stock was from a closely held corporation that invariably redeemed the stock, and the proceeds from the donation were essentially controlled by and continued to benefit Grove. Judge Oakes therefore argued that "by virtue of retaining a life income from the reinvested proceeds and by retaining a measure of control over how those proceeds should be reinvested (by designating the investment advisor who was also the Groves' personal advisor), the Groves were able to achieve a bail-out from their non-dividend-paying closed corporation." *Id.* at 248 (Oakes, J., dissenting). He further stated that the conditions attached to the gift and the pattern of the parties' conduct "result[ed] in providing the equivalent of a safe pension fund for the donor stockholders . . . ." *Id.* at 250 (Oakes, J., dissenting). He would therefore have held the transaction taxable as a dividend to Grove.

[B]   Combined Redemptions and Sales

Bootstrap acquisitions, which were discussed in Chapter 4,[14] generally involve the use of a target's own assets to finance the purchase of the target. As discussed in Chapter 4, those transactions generally are designed to obtain for a corporate parent the benefit of the dividends received deduction incident to a sale of stock in a corporate subsidiary by causing the subsidiary to distribute a dividend to the parent corporation before the sale. In a paradigmatic bootstrap acquisition, the parent corporation benefits from a large dividends received deduction, sells the subsidiary's stock at a reduced price, and the buyer may then reinfuse cash into the subsidiary. As discussed in Chapter 4, whether the form of the transaction is respected will depend on its facts and circumstances.

A similar bootstrap acquisition may occur using a *redemption of stock* rather than a dividend distribution. In that case, the corporation redeems some shares, thereby decreasing the number of shares that need to be purchased. The following is an example of a bootstrap redemption:

> Individuals *S* and *B* are the two 50 percent shareholders of Corporation *T*, a "C" corporation. Each shareholder owns one hundred shares of stock with a value of $200,000 and a basis of $100,000. . . . *S* and *B* agree on a transaction that will result in *B* being the sole shareholder of the corporation, *S* having $200,000 cash, *B* paying $100,000 cash, and the corporation having $100,000 less cash. . . .
>
> *T* Corporation would redeem 50 of *S*'s shares for $100,000, with *B* purchasing the remaining 50 shares for $100,000 . . . .

Robert I. Keller, *Returning to Form: Untangling the Tax Jurisprudence of Bootstrap Acquisitions*, 16 VA. TAX REV. 557, 562–63 (1997).

Note that *S*'s interest in the corporation will be terminated as a result of the combined redemption and sale. Will the redemption thereby qualify as an exchange? The Court of Appeals for the Sixth Circuit addressed that issue in *Zenz v. Quinlivan*, 213 F.2d 914 (6th Cir. 1954). In that case, Mrs.

---

[14] *See* § 4.05.

Zenz, the sole shareholder of a corporation, sold some of her stock in the corporation, and then had the corporation redeem the remainder. Under then-current law, the redemption absorbed substantially all of the accumulated earnings and profits of the corporation. Zenz argued that the redemption was a complete termination of all of her interest in the corporation and should not be treated as a dividend for tax purposes. *Id.* at 916.

Even though Mrs. Zenz had structured the transaction to limit taxation, the Court of Appeals reversed the district court and found that because the redemption completely extinguished the taxpayer's interest in the corporation, it should not be taxed as a dividend. That is, because the taxpayer became "separated from all interest in the corporation," her redemption was not equivalent to a dividend. *Id.* at 917.

What if the redemption *precedes* the sale that terminates the shareholder's interest? In Revenue Ruling 77-226, 1977-2 C.B. 90, Corporation X made a tender offer of $250 per share for its common stock. An unrelated corporation, Y, purchased 4,000 shares of X stock in the market for $1,000,000, and immediately tendered 800 of those shares to X, receiving $200,000. Y treated the redemption as a section 301 distribution taxed as a dividend and claimed a dividends received deduction under section 243. Y sold the remaining 3,200 shares two weeks later for $800,000. As discussed above, Treasury Regulation section 1.302-2(c) provides that if a redemption is treated as a distribution, then the shareholder's basis in the remaining stock is increased by the basis of the redeemed stock. Y therefore claimed a short-term capital loss of $200,000 on the sale of the 3,200 shares.

The IRS stated that, under the reasoning of *Zenz v. Quinlivan* and Revenue Ruling 75-447, 1975-2 C.B. 113, it will treat a redemption and sale as one transaction if they are part of an integrated plan, regardless of which step occurs first. In Y's case, because the transactions were all part of an integrated plan and because the combined transactions completely terminated Y's interest in X, the transactions constituted a complete termination of interest under section 302(b)(3). Therefore, the redemption was taxed as an exchange under section 302(a) instead of as a dividend. As a result, Y was not entitled to a dividends received deduction, and did not receive a deduction for a loss on the final sale of the stock because the basis in the stock sold was $800,000, not $1,000,000.

Thus, under Revenue Ruling 77-226, even if a redemption precedes a sale that terminates the shareholder's interest in the corporation, the redemption will be taxed as an exchange so long as the redemption and sale of all remaining shares are part of a single transaction. Step-transaction doctrine analysis, discussed in Chapter 1, applies to determine whether separate steps constitute one transaction.[15]

In the scenarios discussed above, no non-redeeming shareholder had a primary and unconditional obligation to purchase the selling shareholder's stock. If a non-redeeming shareholder did have a primary and unconditional

---

[15] *See* § 1.04[E].

obligation to purchase that stock, which was instead satisfied by the redemption, then that non-redeeming shareholder would have constructively
received a distribution of property that is taxed under section 301. *See, e.g.,
Sullivan v. United States*, 363 F.2d 724 (8th Cir. 1966), *cert. denied*, 387
U.S. 905, *reh'g denied*, 388 U.S. 924 (1967); *Smith v. Commissioner*, 70 T.C.
651 (1978); Rev. Rul. 69-608, 1969-2 C.B. 43.

The principle of "primary and unconditional obligation" is well-illustrated
by Revenue Ruling 69-608, 1969-2 C.B. 43, in which the IRS ruled on the
following situation:

> *A* and *B* are unrelated individuals who own all of the outstanding
> stock of corporation *X*. *A* and *B* enter into an agreement that
> provides in the event *B* leaves the employ of *X*, he will sell his *X*
> stock to *A* at a price fixed by the agreement. The agreement provides
> that within a specified number of days of *B*'s offer to sell, *A* will
> purchase at the price fixed by the agreement all of the *X* stock
> owned by *B*. *B* terminates his employment and tenders the *X* stock
> to *A*. Instead of purchasing the stock himself in accordance with
> the terms of the agreement, *A* causes *X* to assume the contract and
> to redeem its stock held by *B*. . . .

Id. at 43. The IRS ruled, "In this case, *A* had a primary and unconditional
obligation to perform his contract with *B* at the time the contract was
assigned to *X*. Therefore, the redemption by *X* of its stock held by *B* will
result in a constructive distribution to *A*. . . ." *Id.*

[C] Redemptions Incident to Divorce

Redemptions of stock incident to the divorce of spouse-shareholders raise
a potential conflict between the regime generally applicable to transfers
between spouses and the stock redemption regime. Section 1041(a) provides, that "[n]o gain or loss shall be recognized on a transfer of property
from an individual to (or in trust for the benefit of)—(1) a spouse, or (2)
a former spouse, but only if the transfer is incident to the divorce." By
contrast, redemptions of stock generally are taxed (either as distributions
or as exchanges) under the regime of section 302 discussed above.

A number of cases have presented the issue of which spouse should be
taxed when a corporation redeems all the shares owned by one spouse
incident to the spouses' divorce. Part of the confusion was caused by a
Temporary Treasury Regulation that provided that certain transfers of
property by one spouse to a third party "on behalf of" the other spouse were
considered transfers to the spouse, and therefore were protected by section
1041. *See* Temp. Treas. Reg. § 1.1041-1T, Q&A 9 (2000). Is a redemption
of shares for cash a transfer "on behalf" of the remaining shareholder/
spouse? If so, does the remaining spouse have a constructive dividend? Or
does the sole non-redeeming shareholder have a constructive dividend only
if, as in the bootstrap redemption case law discussed above, that

shareholder's "primary and unconditional obligation" to purchase the stock was deflected to the corporation?

In the 1990s, a group of four cases addressed these issues. *See Arnes v. United States*, 981 F.2d 456 (9th Cir. 1992); *Arnes v. Commissioner*, 102 T.C. 522 (1994) (reviewed by the court); *Blatt v. Commissioner*, 102 T.C. 77 (1994) (reviewed by the court); *Hayes v. Commissioner*, 101 T.C. 593 (1993). In each of these cases, a husband and wife incorporated a corporation, together owning all of its stock. Later, the couple divorced and arranged for the wife's shares to be bought out. The buy-out was done by having the corporation redeem the wife's shares. In some cases, the husband guaranteed the payment, or had had an initial obligation to purchase the shares.

In the *Arnes* cases, the wife first paid tax on capital gains arising from the redemption, but then sought a refund. The District Court ruled in her favor under section 1041. *See Arnes v. United States*, 1991 U.S. Dist. LEXIS 15632 (W.D. Wash. 1991). The IRS appealed the case to the Court of Appeals for the Ninth Circuit, which affirmed, *see Arnes*, 981 F.2d 456 (9th Cir. 1992). While Mrs. Arnes's case was on appeal, the IRS sent Mr. Arnes a notice of deficiency, to protect its interests. Mr. Arnes petitioned the Tax Court. *See Arnes v. Commissioner*, 102 T.C. 522 (1994). The Tax Court ruled in favor of Mr. Arnes, holding that he did not receive a constructive dividend because he had not had a primary and unconditional obligation to acquire his wife's stock. The court avoided the application of *Arnes v. United States* because that case dealt solely with the consequences of the transfer to Mrs. Arnes and did not consider the possibility of a constructive dividend to Mr. Arnes on the same transaction. *Id.* at 526. Thus, in the *Arnes* cases, the IRS was whipsawed: neither of the Arneses paid tax on the $450,000 distribution from the corporation.

Blatt v. Commissioner, 102 T.C. 77 (1994) (reviewed by the court), presented the Tax Court with similar facts. *Blatt* was appealable to the Sixth Circuit, so *Arnes* was not binding precedent under *Golsen v. Commissioner*, 54 T.C. 742 (1970), *aff'd*, 445 F.2d 985 (10th Cir.), *cert. denied*, 404 U.S. 940 (1971). *See Blatt*, 102 T.C. at 82 n.12. However, in *Blatt*, the wife did not report the gain from this transaction. The IRS sent her a notice of deficiency in the amount of $39,184, her realized gain on the redemption. *Id.* at 78. Unlike the Court of Appeals for the Ninth Circuit, a majority of the Tax Court found that Temporary Treasury Regulation section 1.1041-1T, Q&A 9 did not apply. *Id.* at 81. The court distinguished *Arnes v. United States* on four grounds, including the fact that Mr. Blatt had not guaranteed the corporation's obligation to Mrs. Blatt. However, the court seemed also to reject the reasoning in that case. *See id.* at 83.

In *Hayes v. Commissioner*, 101 T.C. 593 (1993), neither of the Hayes spouses reported income from the redemption, and the IRS issued notices of deficiency to both of them. The IRS conceded that only one spouse should be liable for the tax on the transaction. The IRS argued that Mr. Hayes should be found to have received a constructive dividend and that Mrs.

Hayes should not have her gain recognized as a result of section 1041.[16] *Id.* at 597. The Tax Court consolidated the cases and ruled that Mr. Hayes had received a constructive dividend because the redemption satisfied Mr. Hayes's primary and unconditional purchase obligation. *Id.* at 605.

The cases discussed above were decided in the mid-1990s. More recently, the Tax Court decided *Read v. Commissioner*, 114 T.C. 14 (2000) (reviewed by the court). In *Read*, which involved the consolidated cases of husband, wife, and corporation, the Tax Court tried to reconcile the decisions in *Arnes*, *Blatt*, and *Hayes*. A majority of the Tax Court determined that the "primary and unconditional obligation" standard was not the same as the "on behalf of" requirement of the section 1041 regulations and, in addition, that it was not an appropriate standard for divorce-related situations. *Id.* at 33. The court further found that Mrs. Read's transfer of shares was "on behalf of" Mr. Read within the meaning of the Temporary Treasury Regulation. The court therefore ruled in favor of Mrs. Read and against Mr. Read. A few months later, the Court of Appeals for the Eleventh Circuit decided *Craven v. United States*, 215 F.3d 1201 (11th Cir. 2000) consistent with the Tax Court's majority opinion in *Read*.

Responding to the confusion in the case law, the Treasury Department promulgated new regulations. *See* Treas. Reg. § 1.1041-2. Under the regulations, application of section 1041 to the redeeming spouse is contingent on taxing the nontransferor (nonredeeming) spouse on a constructive distribution. More specifically, the regulations generally provide that if "under applicable tax law" a redemption is *not* treated as resulting in a constructive distribution to the nontransferor spouse, the transferor's redemption will be respected. Treas. Reg. § 1.1041-2(a)(1). The regulations' examples reference the "primary and unconditional obligation" standard in connection with applicable tax law. *See* Treas. Reg. § 1.1041-2(d) Ex. 1, 3.

If, under applicable law, the redemption *is* treated as resulting in a constructive distribution to the nontransferor spouse, the transaction will not be taxed as a redemption. *See* Treas. Reg. § 1.1041-2(a)(2). Instead, the stock is treated as having been transferred between the spouses in a transaction to which section 1041 applies, and then transferred by the *nontransferor spouse* to the corporation. *Id.* The property transferred by the corporation in the redemption is treated as having been transferred by the corporation to the nontransferor spouse in exchange for stock, and then transferred by that spouse to the other spouse in a transaction protected by section 1041. *Id.*

The regulations provide four examples, the first of which is the following:

> Example 1. Corporation X has 100 shares outstanding. A and B each own 50 shares. A and B divorce. The divorce instrument requires

---

[16] Note that, in a corporation with ample earnings and profits, there will be more tax on a distribution than on a redemption taxable as an exchange. The dividend portion of a distribution is included in full in income (and at the time, was taxed as ordinary income), while an exchange receives both basis offset and capital gains treatment. *See Arnes v. Commissioner*, 102 T.C. 522, 541 (1994) (Beghe, J., concurring).

B to purchase A's shares, and A to sell A's shares to B, in exchange for $100x. Corporation X redeems A's shares for $100x. Assume that, under applicable tax law, B has a primary and unconditional obligation to purchase A's stock, and therefore the stock redemption results in a constructive distribution to B. Also assume that the special rule of paragraph (c)(1) of this section does not apply. Accordingly, under paragraphs (a)(2) and (b)(2) of this section, A shall be treated as transferring A's stock of Corporation X to B in a transfer to which section 1041 applies (assuming the requirements of section 1041 are otherwise satisfied), B shall be treated as transferring the Corporation X stock B is deemed to have received from A to Corporation X in exchange for $100x in an exchange to which section 1041 does not apply and sections 302(d) and 301 apply, and B shall be treated as transferring the $100x to A in a transfer to which section 1041 applies.

Treas. Reg. § 1.1041-2(e) Ex. 1.

The regulations also provide an exception that allows the spouses to alter by agreement the tax consequences that would be obtained under applicable tax law: "if a divorce or separation instrument, or a valid written agreement between the transferor spouse and the nontransferor spouse" provides either that the transfer shall be treated as a stock redemption to the transferor spouse, or, alternatively, as a constructive distribution to the nontransferor spouse, the agreement will be respected if certain requirements are met. *See* Treas. Reg. § 1.1041-2(c). The requirements are that (1) the instrument or agreement supersedes any other instrument or agreement concerning the disposition of the stock in question and (2) the instrument or agreement is executed by both spouses prior to the date on which the transferor spouse (for a transfer treated as a redemption) or the nontransferor spouse (for a transfer treated as a constructive distribution) files a timely Federal income tax return for the tax year in question. This provides the spouses with the opportunity to reach an agreement that provides for the lowest aggregate tax cost.

[D]   Redemptions to Pay Death Taxes

Section 303(a) provides that a redemption of stock that is included in determining the gross estate of a decedent for federal estate tax purposes is treated as an exchange

> to the extent that the amount of such distribution does not exceed the sum of—
>
> (1) the estate, inheritance, legacy, and succession taxes (including any interest collected as a part of such taxes) imposed because of such decedent's death, and
>
> (2) the amount of funeral and administration expenses allowable as deductions to the estate under section 2053 (or under section

2106 in the case of the estate of a decedent nonresident, not a citizen of the United States) . . . .

I.R.C. § 303(a). Section 303(b) provides certain limitations on the general rule of section 303(a), including a time limitation. Under section 303(b)(1), section 303(a) applies only to amounts distributed after the death of the decedent but no later than 90 days after the expiration of the statute of limitations on assessment of the federal estate tax.

The intent of section 303 is to allow an estate to receive a corporate distribution for paying estate taxes without having to treat the distribution as ordinary income, alleviating some of the burden connected with seeking liquidity to pay estate taxes. Revenue Ruling 87-132, 1987-2 C.B. 82, illustrates how that intent affects application of the section. In that ruling, an estate and an individual with no interest in the estate, A, each owned 150 shares of corporation X's 300 outstanding shares. The estate needed to pay death taxes and sought a redemption of shares but did not want to change the relative voting power between the estate and A. To achieve this goal, X issued 10 shares of non-voting stock for every outstanding share (a total of 1,500 per shareholder) and then immediately redeemed 1,000 of those shares for cash.

The IRS found that the intent of section 303 did not conflict with the goal of corporation X to retain the relative voting power of its shareholders. It found that because section 303 provides a limited time period within which the redemption must take place, Congress intended "that section 303 be applicable to stock issued as part of the same plan as the redemption." *Id.* at 83. The IRS noted that section 303(c) provides that section 303 applies to "substituted basis stock" and that Treasury Regulations provide that stock received by an estate as a tax-free stock dividend under section 305(a) (discussed in Chapter 6) is entitled to section 303 treatment. Accordingly, the IRS found that for purposes of section 303, section 305 applied to the new issue of stock without regard to the subsequent redemption of 1,000 shares, and that that stock accordingly obtained a substituted basis under section 307(a) (also discussed in Chapter 6). Section 303 therefore applied to X's distribution of cash to the estate.

§ 5.05   Redemptions Through Related Corporations

[A]   Introduction

Imagine an individual taxpayer who owns 100 percent of the stock of two corporations, each of which is rich in earnings and profits. The taxpayer would like to obtain cash from the corporations, but doing so as a straightforward distribution would result in a dividend included in full in income because of the large earnings and profits accounts. *See* I.R.C. § 301. Similarly, if the taxpayer were to cause one or the other of the corporations to redeem some of his or her other shares for money or other property, the distribution would be taxed as a dividend. *See* I.R.C. §§ 301, 302. If the taxpayer were to sell shares in one of the corporations to a third party, the taxpayer would get capital gains treatment and basis offset, but at the price of a concomitant loss of ownership of the corporation. The taxpayer might therefore consider selling shares in one of the corporations to the other corporation. That sale would not result in any loss of control over the two corporations but would allow the taxpayer to pull cash out of one of the corporations.

Example 5.14: Ethan is the sole owner of both F Corp. and G Corp., each of which has tens of thousands of dollars of earnings and profits. Ethan sells ten percent of his F Corp. shares (10 shares) to G Corp. for their fair market value of $2,000. Ethan has a $500 basis in those shares. After the sale, Ethan still owns 100 percent of G Corp. He also owns 90 percent of F Corp. directly, and he controls the other ten percent through his 100 percent ownership of G Corp.

The transaction is illustrated below. The "before" picture, which also shows the sale, is on the left and the "after" picture is on the right.[17]

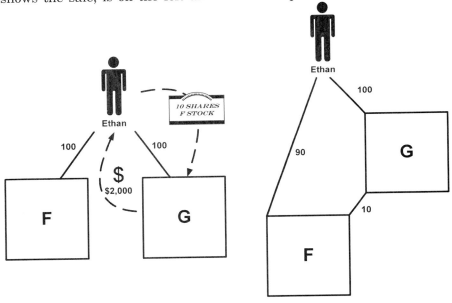

If this were taxed as a sale, Ethan would have to include only $1,500 in his gross income, taxed as capital gain, rather than including $2,000 as dividend income (which, under current law, would likely be taxed at the same preferential capital gains rate). Yet Ethan did not decrease his control of either corporation at all. This transaction is analogous to a redemption of shares from a 100-percent shareholder: property is distributed from the corporation without any decline in ownership. Such a redemption would

---

[17] This transaction also qualifies under section 351, discussed in Chapter 2. Resolution of this overlap issue is discussed in § 5.05[E], *infra*.

be taxed as a section 301 distribution. As explained below, section 304 assures the same treatment for Ethan's transaction by analyzing the transaction as a stock redemption under section 302.

[B] The Control Requirement

[1] In General

Section 304 applies if a person (or persons) who sells shares in one corporation to another corporation "controls" the two corporations or the selling shareholder controls a corporation that controls the purchasing corporation. *See* I.R.C. § 304(a)(1), (2). One hundred percent control is *not* required. In fact, control in this context requires less stock ownership than does control for purposes of section 351, which was discussed in Chapter 2. Under section 304(c), a taxpayer controls a corporation if that taxpayer holds either 50 percent or more of the voting power or 50 percent or more of the value of all of the shares in the corporation. In addition, "[i]f a person (or persons) is in control . . . of a corporation which in turn owns at least 50 percent of the total combined voting power of all stock entitled to vote of another corporation, or owns at least 50 percent of the total value of the shares of all classes of stock of another corporation, then such person (or persons) shall be treated as in control of such other corporation." I.R.C. § 304(c)(1). Furthermore, stock acquired in the transaction is considered in determining if the control requirements are met. I.R.C. § 304(c)(2).

Example 5.15: Harry owns 50 percent of the sole classes of stock of both I Corp. and J Corp. J Corp. owns 50 percent of the sole class of stock of K Corp. Under section 304(c), Harry controls I Corp., J Corp., and K Corp. In addition, J Corp. controls K Corp.

[2] Application of Constructive Stock Ownership Rules, as Modified

Section 304(c)(3) expressly makes applicable to section 304 the constructive ownership rules of section 318. This stands in stark contrast to the control rule of section 368(c), used both for section 351 transactions (discussed in Chapter 2) and certain reorganizations (discussed in Chapter 9). The application of constructive ownership rules to section 304 causes it to cast a wider net, sweeping more transactions into its scope.

Not only do the section 318 rules apply for purposes of determining control under section 304, they are modified so as to increase attribution from corporations to shareholders and from shareholders to corporations. For purposes of applying each of those rules to the control determination under section 304, the 50-percent threshold requirement for attribution is reduced to a mere five percent.

Example 5.16: Lanier owns 100 percent of all classes of stock of M Corp. and 40 percent of the stock of N Corp. O Corp., owned 30 percent by Lanier, owns the other 60 percent of N Corp. The other 70 percent of O

Corp. is owned by unrelated third parties. Lanier controls M Corp. directly. Lanier owns 40 percent of N Corp. directly. Through application of section 318(a)(2)(C), Lanier owns an additional 18 percent (30% * 60%) of N Corp. In total, therefore, Lanier is considered to own 58 percent of N Corp., which constitutes control of N Corp. under section 304(c).

Example 5.16 involved attribution from a corporation (O Corp.) to a shareholder (Lanier). The effect of the expansion of the attribution *from a shareholder to a corporation* (a context in which attribution is not otherwise proportionate under section 318(a)(3)(C)), is slightly mitigated under section 304(c). For that purpose, in any case in which attribution would not apply but for the lowering of the threshold from 50 percent to five percent, attribution *is* proportionate to the total value of all shares of the corporation. *See* I.R.C. § 304(c)(3)(B)(ii)(II).

> *Example 5.17*: P Corp. owns 30 percent of Q Corp. and 40 percent of R Corp. R Corp. owns 40 percent of Q Corp. and 100 percent of T Corp. R Corp. not only controls T Corp., but also controls Q Corp. within the meaning of section 304(c) because, although R Corp. only owns 40 percent of Q Corp. directly, the 30 percent of the Q Corp. shares that P Corp. owns are attributed proportionately to R Corp. via P's ownership of R Corp. Thus, R Corp. owns another 12 percent of the shares of Q Corp. indirectly.

Note that the attribution was proportionate because P Corp. does not own at least 50 percent of R Corp. (If it did, then *all* of the Q Corp. shares owned by P Corp. would be attributed to R Corp. for purposes of determining R Corp.'s control of Q Corp.)

[C] Types of Section 304 Transactions

There are two types of corporate relationships that can result in redemptions through related corporations under section 304: brother-sister corporations and parent-subsidiary corporations. The initial example above, Example 5.14, was a brother-sister redemption. A parent-subsidiary redemption would involve a shareholder selling parent stock to the parent's subsidiary. (The parent and subsidiary corporations would therefore end up with some overlapping ownership.)

Section 304(a)(1) applies to brother-sister redemptions. It provides that, "for purposes of sections 302 and 303, if . . . one or more persons are in control of each of two corporations, and . . . in return for property, one of the corporations acquires stock in the other corporation from the person (or persons) so in control, then (unless paragraph (2) applies) such property shall be treated as a distribution in redemption of the stock of the corporation acquiring such stock." Thus, technically, a brother-sister redemption is a redemption of the stock of the *acquiring corporation*.

There is a different rule for parent-subsidiary redemptions: "[f]or purposes of sections 302 and 303, if . . . in return for property, one corporation acquires from a shareholder of another corporation stock in such other

corporation, and . . . the issuing corporation controls the acquiring corporation, then such property shall be treated as a distribution in redemption
of the stock of the *issuing corporation*." I.R.C. § 304(a)(2) (emphasis added).
However, as discussed below, section 302 analysis is applied in either case
to the shares that were sold (that is, the shares of the issuing corporation).
See I.R.C. § 304(b)(1). In addition, if the transaction falls under section 304,
and is treated as a section 301 distribution under section 302, earnings and
profits from *both* corporations are available for the distribution. *See* I.R.C.
§ 304(b)(2). Nonetheless, note that if a section 304 redemption could be
analyzed either as a brother-sister redemption or a parent-subsidiary redemption, section 304(a)(1) provides that (a)(2) (parent-subsidiary redemption) applies. This type of overlap can occur through application of the
attribution rules discussed above.

Example 5.18: Ursula owns 50 percent of the sole class of stock of both
V Corp. and W Corp. V Corp. owns the other 50 percent of W Corp. Under
section 304(c), Ursula controls both V Corp. and W Corp. In addition,
Ursula controls V Corp., which controls W Corp. This ownership structure
is illustrated in Diagram 5.7. If Ursula sells some V Corp. shares to W
Corp., although this could be analyzed either as a brother-sister redemption or a parent-subsidiary redemption, it is in fact analyzed as a parent-
subsidiary redemption. Regardless, section 302 applies to the shares of
V Corp.

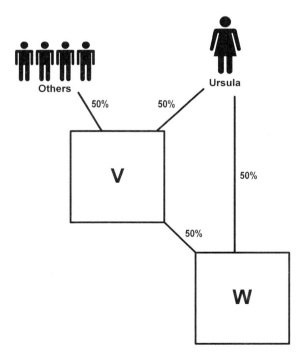

[D] Application of Section 302

[1] In General

If a transaction is governed by section 304 (it falls within 304(a)(1) and/or (a)(2)), section 302 is applied with respect to the stock of the *issuing corporation* regardless of whether the transaction was a brother-sister or parent-subsidiary redemption. *See* I.R.C. § 304(b)(1). In other words, the control person's (or persons') ownership of stock in the corporation whose stock was sold is tested under section 302 to determine whether it will be taxed as an exchange or as a section 301 distribution. Note that, unlike in a pure redemption, in a 304 transaction, the number of shares outstanding does not decline. In addition, recall that the section 318 rules apply for purposes of applying section 302.

> *Example 5.19*: Xavier owns 80 shares (80 percent) of the sole class of stock of Y Corp. and 50 shares (50 percent) of the sole class of stock of Z Corp. Unrelated third parties own the other Y Corp. and Z Corp. shares. Xavier sells 60 Y Corp. shares to Z Corp. Because Xavier controls both Y Corp. and Z Corp. under section 304(c), and sold Y Corp. shares to Z Corp., the transaction is governed by section 304. Section 302 therefore is applied to Xavier's ownership of the Y Corp. stock.

> Before the transaction, Xavier owned 80 percent of the Y Corp. stock. After the transaction, Xavier owns 20 Y Corp. shares directly and, through Z Corp., controls 50 percent of the 60 shares he sold, *i.e.*, 30 shares. Therefore, Xavier is deemed to own 50 shares out of 100, or 50 percent of Y Corp. The drop from 80 percent to 50 percent is neither a complete termination of interest nor a substantially disproportionate redemption, but it may be "not essentially equivalent to a dividend," as discussed in Chapter 4.

[2] Variations on Constructive Stock Ownership Rules

Not only do the section 318 constructive ownership rules apply for purposes of the section 302 test illustrated above, but the rules are slightly modified in this context. Note that the modifications to section 318 for purposes of testing a redemption through related corporations under section 302 are *not* the same as the modifications used in determining control under section 304(c). Instead, for applying section 302 to a section 304 transaction, the 50-percent thresholds that apply to attribution of shares from corporations to shareholders and from shareholders to corporations *are completely eliminated*. *See* I.R.C. § 304(b)(1).

> *Example 5.20*: Alex owns 80 shares (80 percent) of the sole class of stock of B Corp. and 50 shares (50 percent) of the sole class of stock of C Corp. D Corporation, owned 20 percent by Alex (and 80 percent by unrelated third parties), owns the other 20 B Corp. shares. Unrelated third parties own the other C Corp. shares. Alex sells 60 B Corp. shares to C Corp.

> Because Alex controls both B Corp. and C Corp. under section 304(c), and sold B Corp. shares to C Corp., the transaction is governed by section

304. Section 302 therefore is applied to Alex's ownership of the B Corp. stock. Before the transaction, Alex owned 80 percent of the B Corp. stock directly and four percent via D Corporation, given the absence of the 50-percent threshold for attribution on this context. After the transaction, Alex owns 20 B Corp. shares directly. In addition, Alex is proportionately attributed the B Corp. shares owned by C Corp. and D Corporation although Alex owns only 20 percent of D Corporation. Accordingly, Alex owns 34 percent of B Corp. indirectly, for a total of 54 percent.

[3] Taxing Redemptions Treated as Section 301 Distributions

As Example 5.20 may suggest, some transactions governed by section 304, after being tested under section 302, will be treated as section 301 distributions.

Example 5.21: Eileen owns 80 shares (80 percent) of the sole class of stock of FF, Inc. and 50 shares (50 percent) of the sole class of stock of GG, Inc. Unrelated third parties own the other FF, Inc. and GG, Inc. shares. Eileen sells 20 FF, Inc. shares to GG, Inc. for $5,000. Because Eileen controls both FF, Inc. and GG, Inc. under section 304(c), and sold FF, Inc. shares to GG, Inc., the transaction is governed by section 304. Section 302 therefore is applied to Eileen's ownership of the FF, Inc. stock.

Before the transaction, Eileen owned 80 percent of the FF, Inc. stock. After the transaction, Eileen owns 60 FF, Inc. shares directly and, through GG, Inc., controls 50 percent of the 20 shares she sold, *i.e.*, 10 shares. Therefore, Eileen is deemed to own 70 shares out of 100, or 70 percent of FF, Inc. The drop from 80 percent to 70 percent does not qualify under section 302(b) for exchange treatment. Therefore, the $5,000 will be taxed under section 301.

Under section 304(b)(2), in determining the amount constituting a dividend, first the earnings and profits of the acquiring corporation are used, then those of the issuing corporation. *See* I.R.C. § 304(a)(2)(A), (B). In Example 5.21, the $5,000 distribution would first tap the earnings and profits of GG, Inc. and then those of FF, Inc.

There is a special basis rule for a brother-sister redemption treated as a section 301 distribution, such as the redemption in Example 5.21: "the transferor and the acquiring corporation shall be treated in the same manner as if the transferor had transferred the stock so acquired to the acquiring corporation in exchange for stock of the acquiring corporation in a transaction to which section 351(a) applies, and then the acquiring corporation had redeemed the stock it was treated as issuing in such transaction."[18] I.R.C. § 304(a)(1). The deemed contribution of the acquired

[18] The language of this section, treating the parties as if they engaged in a section 351 transaction, raises a question as to whether section 362(e)(2), enacted in 2004, should apply. As discussed in Chapter 2, section 362(e)(2) provides for a basis reduction in section 351 transactions in certain contexts. *See* § 2.03[B][1][a].

stock is treated as having occurred before the deemed redemption. TAM 9748003. The transferor therefore increases his or her basis in the stock of the acquiring corporation by the basis of the stock sold. The deemed redemption distribution is treated as occurring next, and it is taxed under section 301.

Thus, in Example 5.21, Eileen and GG, Inc. are treated as if Eileen transferred the 20 shares of FF, Inc. stock to GG, Inc. in return for imaginary GG, Inc. shares in a section 351 transaction. Those FF, Inc. shares therefore take a transferred basis under section 362(a) and the GG, Inc. shares take an exchanged basis under section 358(a). The imaginary shares are then deemed redeemed, so they are no longer outstanding, and Eileen is taxed on the proceeds under section 301.[19] Note that if a redemption like this one involved a corporate shareholder rather than an individual shareholder (Eileen), the dividend would be treated as an extraordinary dividend under section 1059. See I.R.C. § 1059(e). This means that the corporate shareholder benefitting from a dividends received deduction under section 243 would likely recognize gain under section 1059. See §§ 4.04[A], [B][3].

Under section 304(b)(4), if the transaction involves two members of an affiliated group of corporations (as defined in section 1504(a)), the basis of stock owned in one corporation by another corporate member of the affiliated group ("intragroup stock") and earnings and profits of the corporations in the affiliated group may be adjusted as necessary to carry out the purposes of section 304.

CHART 5.3
Checklist for Redemptions Through Related Corporations

(1)   Are one or more persons in control of each of two corporations, or does one corporation control another?

      (A) "Control" is ownership of 50 percent of the stock (by vote *or* by value). I.R.C. § 304(c)(1).

      (B) Section 318 attribution rules apply in determining control, and the corporate attribution rules are modified by substituting five-percent thresholds for the 50-percent thresholds (attribution from shareholder to corporation is made proportionate between five and 50 percent). I.R.C. § 304(c)(3).

(2)   If yes, did the controlling person or group sell stock from one controlled corporation to another, or did a shareholder of the controlling corporation sell stock of that corporation to its controlled subsidiary?

(3)   If yes, section 302 applies to test whether the corporation whose stock was sold qualifies as an exchange.

---

19 Proposed regulations under section 304 would treat unrecovered basis in the stock deemed redeemed as a loss to be taken into account under proposed regulation section 1.302-5, discussed in § 5.03[C][2]. *See* Prop. Treas. Reg. § 1.304-2(a)(3), (c) Ex. 2.

  (A)   The same number of shares will remain outstanding.

  (B)   Section 318 attribution rules apply as they always do under
        section 302, except that the corporate attribution rules are
        modified by *removing* the 50-percent thresholds.

(4)   If the transaction fails to qualify as an exchange, it is a section
      301 distribution, and the dividend amount will be determined
      under that section.

      •   Earnings and profits of both corporations will be used to
          determine the dividend amount.

(5)   If the answer to question (1) and/or (2) is no, then the transaction
      is a sale, taxable under section 1001 and general tax principles.

[E]   Overlap of Section 304 with Section 351

Certain transactions seem to fall within both section 304 and section 351.
Consider again the facts of Example 5.14:

Example 5.22: Ethan is the sole owner of both F Corp. and G Corp., each
of which has tens of thousands of dollars of earnings and profits. Ethan
sells ten percent of his F Corp. shares (10 shares) to G Corp. for their
fair market value of $2,000. Ethan has a $500 basis in those shares. After
the sale, Ethan still owns 100 percent of G Corp. He also owns 90 percent
of F Corp. directly, and he controls the other ten percent through his 100-
percent ownership of G Corp.

As discussed above, in § 5.05[A], this is a section 304 transaction. However,
it is also a section 351 transaction: Ethan transferred property (F Corp.
stock) to a corporation (G Corp.), and, after the transaction, Ethan controlled G Corp. within the meaning of section 368(c). In fact, Ethan owns
100 percent of G Corp.

In general, the Code provides that in the case where both sections 304
and 351 could apply, section 304 trumps. *See* I.R.C. § 304(b)(3)(A). However, there are exceptions. In general, if the acquiring corporation in a 304
transaction assumes liabilities of the selling shareholder, the liability relief
constitutes property received by the shareholder. However, 304(a) does not
apply to a liability taken on by a corporation in a section 351 transaction
if the liability was incurred to acquire the stock transferred. *See* I.R.C.
§ 304(b)(3)(B)(i). In addition, "an extension, renewal, or refinancing" of the
liability is considered such a liability. I.R.C. § 304(b)(3)(B)(ii). The liability
exception does not apply to stock acquired from a person related under
section 318(a) (except section 318(a)(4), the option rule) unless that related
person's interests in both the acquiring corporation and the issuing corporation are terminated to the same extent as is required for waiver of the
family attribution rules. *See* I.R.C. § 304(b)(3)(B)(iii).

Chapter 6

STOCK DIVIDENDS

§ 6.01   Introduction

Corporations sometimes distribute shares of their own stock to their share-holders. These distributions are generally known as "stock dividends." A corporation that makes a stock dvidend recognizes no gain or loss under section 311(a)(1). The tax consequences of a distribution of stock to share-holders, like the consequences of the distribution of cash or other property to shareholders, may vary with the circumstances.

Eisner v. Macomber, 252 U.S. 189 (1920), an early United States Supreme Court case on the definition of gross income, considered the taxation of stock dividends. In that case, the Court held that a *pro rata* distribution of more common stock to common stockholders did not give rise to gross income, because the proportionate interests of the shareholders did not change. The *Macomber* result is the same today, under section 305(a).

Example 6.1: X Corp. has 100 shares of common stock outstanding and the stock is owned equally by 5 shareholders, A, B, C, D, and E. Therefore, each shareholder owns 20 shares and each has a 20% interest in the corporation. X Corp. then declares and pays a 10% stock dividend, so that for every 10 shares that the shareholders own, they receive one more share of common stock.

After the distribution, X Corp. has 110 shares outstanding. Each share-holder owns 22 shares, 20% of the outstanding shares. The diagram below shows the "before" and "after" pictures. Although the total number of shares has increased, the shareholders' percentage ownership interests in the corporation are unchanged. The shareholders do not have gross income from the stock distribution.

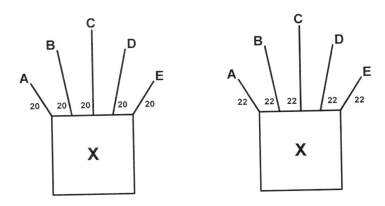

The *Macomber* case involved common stock distributed to common stockholders. As discussed in Chapter 3, there are two principal types of stock: common and preferred.[1] Either type of stock may be voting or non-voting. The main difference between preferred stock and common stock is that preferred stock generally has a defined, limited preference for both dividend distributions and distributions in liquidation. Common stock receives distributions (current or liquidating) only after the preferred stock is paid, but is entitled to the entire residual. Therefore, common stock has both more downside risk and more upside potential than preferred stock.

After *Macomber*, the Supreme Court held that if a stock distribution changes the shareholders' proportionate interests in the corporation, then it may be taxed. *See Koshland v. Helvering*, 298 U.S. 441 (1936). As discussed below, that result generally obtains today, under section 305(b), which provides that certain stock dividends will be treated as section 301 distributions. One way that shareholders' interests may be changed is if interests shift between common and preferred shareholders.

Example 6.2: Y Corp. has 100 shares of common stock outstanding, owned equally by Alex and Beth. It also has 50 shares of preferred stock outstanding, owned by Carol. Y Corp. declares and pays a stock dividend of common stock on preferred, so that Carol receives 50 shares of Y common stock. Under section 305(b)(4), the stock dividend will be treated as a section 301 distribution. Note that Carol's interest in Y's assets has increased at the expense of Alex and Beth because, unlike prior to the stock distribution, Carol will now share with Alex and Beth in the residual ownership of the corporation.

---

[1] *See* § 3.01[B][1].

§ 6.02 Excludible Stock Dividends

[A] Section 305(a)

Section 305(a) provides a general rule of exclusion for stock dividends. Note that rights to acquire stock are treated as stock for purposes of section 305. *See* I.R.C. § 305(d)(1). However, much of what section 305(a) gives, 305(b) takes away. As a result, in general, the types of stock dividends that are excludible under section 305(a) are primarily *pro rata* distributions of common stock to common stockholders, as in *Eisner v. Macomber*, and *pro rata* distributions of preferred stock to common stockholders, where common stock was the only outstanding class of stock prior to the distribution. However, preferred stock received tax-free under section 305(a) is "tainted" stock, subject to the rules of section 306, discussed below.[2]

A stock dividend that is tax-free under section 305(a) does not reduce the corporation's earnings and profits. *See* I.R.C. § 312(d)(1)(B). Thus, dividend potential is preserved for future distributions.

[B] Basis in the New Stock and in the Old Stock; Holding Period

If stock is received tax-free under section 305(a), basis in the old stock is generally allocated among the old stock and the stock newly received, in proportion to fair market value. *See* I.R.C. § 307(a); Treas. Reg. § 1.307-1(a). Also note that the holding period of the new stock will include the holding period of the old stock. *See* I.R.C. § 1223(4).

Example 6.3: Diane owns 10 shares of common stock in Z, Inc. She has a basis of $100 in her shares, which are currently worth $150. In a *pro rata* stock dividend, she receives 10 shares of preferred stock worth $50. The dividend is non-taxable under section 305(a). Accordingly, she must allocate her $100 stock basis between the old and new stock. The common stock is worth 75 percent of the total stock value ($150/$200) so it receives 75 percent of the total $100 basis, or $75. The preferred, which is worth 25 percent of the total stock value ($50/$200) receives the other 25 percent, or $25. The preferred stock also takes a holding period tacked from the common stock.

If stock "rights" are received, and the fair market value of the rights is less than 15 percent of the fair market value of the taxpayer's old stock at the time of receipt, then the rights take a zero basis unless the taxpayer elects to have section 307 apply. *See* I.R.C. § 307(b)(1).

Example 6.4: Earl owns 10 shares of common stock in Ell, Inc. He has a basis of $80 in his shares, which are currently worth $100. In a *pro rata* stock dividend, Earl receives 10 rights to acquire common stock, worth a total of $10. The dividend is non-taxable under section 305(a).

---

[2] *See* § 6.04.

The rights are worth less than 15 percent of the $100 fair market value of the common shares. Thus, the rights take a zero basis unless Earl elects under section 307 to allocate his $80 basis between his old stock and new rights.

§ 6.03   Taxable Stock Dividends

[A]   Section 305(b): Exceptions to Section 305(a)

Section 305(b) provides five exceptions to the general rule that stock dividends are tax-free. In general, the exceptions focus on stock distributions that cause a change in some shareholder's proportionate interest in the corporation. The determination of whether a stock dividend falls within section 305(b) is determined without regard to the presence of earnings and profits. Then, if any of the five exceptions applies, the stock distribution is treated as a section 301 distribution in an amount equal to the fair market value of the distributed stock. *See* Treas. Reg. § 1.305-1(b). This distribution will constitute a dividend to the extent of the distributing corporation's earnings and profits. *See* I.R.C. § 305(b). Earnings and profits will be reduced accordingly. *See* Treas. Reg. § 1.312-1(d).

[1]   Choice of Stock or Property

Section 305(b)(1) provides that if *any* shareholder has the right to elect to receive either stock or property, then any stock distributed will be a section 301 distribution. The definition of property in section 317 applies to section 305. Thus, "property" includes money but does not include stock (or stock rights) in the corporation making the distribution. *See* I.R.C. § 317(a).

Section 305(b)(1) reflects the notion that if some shareholders elect to receive stock and others elect to receive cash or other property, those shareholders receiving stock will have their proportionate interests in the corporation increased at the expense of the other shareholders. However, even if *all* shareholders elect to receive the stock, section 305(b)(1) still applies. In effect, constructive receipt principles spoil the possibility of a tax-free distribution once the property election is offered.

A standard method of offering a choice of stock or property distributions to shareholders is to provide a dividend reinvestment plan. Revenue Ruling 78-375, 1978-2 C.B. 130, explains why such a plan poses a problem under section 305(b)(1). In that ruling, Corporation X offered a plan that provided, in part, that a shareholder could elect to have all of the cash dividends otherwise payable to him automatically reinvested in shares of X common stock at a price equal to 95 percent of the fair market value of the stock on the dividend payment date (minus a quarterly service charge of $3).

The presence of the plan enabled shareholders to opt to receive stock dividends rather than the cash they would otherwise receive. Therefore, the stock dividends received under the plan fell within section 305(b)(1). Treasury Regulation 1.305-1(b) established the value of the stock as the fair market value of the X stock received on the distribution date increased under section 301 by the $3 amount paid as a service charge. The IRS noted that the basis of these "reinvested" shares was equal to the fair market value of X common stock on the date of distribution, and that a deduction would be allowed for the quarterly service charges (under section 212 or section 162, depending on whether the participant was an individual or corporation and on whether an individual participant paid the service charge in connection with a trade or business).

[2] Disproportionate Distributions

[a] In General

Section 305(b)(2), the second exception to the non-recognition rule of section 305(a), taxes a stock dividend as a section 301 distribution if the stock dividend involves the receipt of cash or property by some shareholders and an increase in the proportionate interests of *other* shareholders in the corporation's assets or earnings. However, there is an exception for cash issued in lieu of fractional shares. *See* Treas. Reg. § 1.305-3(c).

Example 6.5: F, Inc. has two classes of common stock, one of which is voting and one of which is non-voting. F, Inc. distributes cash to one class and a stock dividend to the other class. The cash dividend is directly analyzed under section 301. In addition, under section 305(b)(2), the stock dividend is taxable under section 301 because it serves to increase the recipient's proportionate interest in the corporation's assets and future earnings, while others receive property (here, cash).

Revenue Ruling 78-375, 1978-2 C.B. 130, discussed above with respect to dividend reinvestment plans, also discusses section 305(b)(2). In that ruling, Corporation X, in addition to offering its shareholders a dividend reinvestment plan, also offered participants in the plan the opportunity to purchase shares of X common stock at a price equal to 95 percent of the fair market value of the stock on the dividend payment date. Because such purchases increase the purchasing shareholders' interests in Corporation X, while shareholders not participating in the plan receive the regular cash dividends, section 305(b)(2) applied. The amount of the section 301 distribution was the difference between the fair market value on the dividend payment date of the shares purchased and the amount of the optional payment. The basis of the stock purchased under the optional purchase plan was (1) the optional payment plus (2) the excess of fair market value over the optional payment (which add up to the stock's fair market value).

A stock distribution that is taxed under section 305(b) qualifies as a distribution of property for purposes of section 305(b)(2)(A) because it is treated as a distribution of property to which section 301 applies. *See* Treas. Reg. § 1.305-5. In addition, shareholder receipt of property need not occur in the form of a distribution with respect to stock, so long as the property is received by shareholders in their capacity as shareholders and one of certain Code sections, including section 301, applies to the property. *See* Treas. Reg. § 1.305-3(b)(3). For example, if some shareholders receive stock, and, as part of the same transaction, other shareholders sell stock to a related corporation in a transaction governed by section 301 pursuant to section 304, section 305(b)(2) applies to the stock distribution. *Id.* However, an isolated redemption of stock will not occasion section 305(b)(2) treatment, even if the redemption distribution is taxed under section 301. *Id.*

[b] Series of Distributions

Section 305(b)(2) explicitly states that it applies to "a series of distributions of which [the distribution in question] is one" that has the result targeted by section 305(b)(2) (the receipt of property by some shareholders and an increase in the proportionate interests of other shareholders in the corporation's assets or earnings and profits). Treasury Regulations provide that, in general, a series of distributions need not be pursuant to a plan. *See* Treas. Reg. § 1.305-3(b)(2).

> For example, if a corporation pays quarterly stock dividends to one class of common shareholders and annual cash dividends to another class of common shareholders, the quarterly stock dividends constitute a series of distributions of stock having the result of the receipt of cash or property by some shareholders and an increase in the proportionate interests of other shareholders. *This is so whether or not the stock distributions and the cash distributions are steps in an overall plan or are independent and unrelated.*

Id. (emphasis added).

However, if the stock distribution and receipt of property occur *more than 36 months apart*, the "distribution or distributions will be presumed not to result in the receipt of cash or property by some shareholders and an increase in the proportionate interest of other shareholders, *unless the receipt of cash or property and the distribution or series of distributions of stock are made pursuant to a plan.*" Treas. Reg. § 1.305-3(b)(4). Thus, the regulations provide that when receipt of cash or other property by some shareholders, and stock distributions increasing other shareholders' proportionate interests, both occur within a 36-month period, the stock distribution will fall within section 305(b)(2). However, when the two events are separated in time by more than 36 months, the stock distribution will only fall within section 305(b)(2) if the two events occurred pursuant to a plan.

[3] Distributions of Common and Preferred Stock to Common Stockholders

Under section 305(b)(3), all shareholders who receive a distribution of stock will be treated as having a section 301 distribution if the distribution results in the receipt of *preferred* stock by *some common shareholders* and the receipt of *common* stock by *other common shareholders*. The distribution does not fall under section 305(b)(2) because, under section 317(a), no property was distributed, only stock was. Yet, changes in the shareholders' proportionate interests occur by virtue of the different distributions to previously similarly situated shareholders. In addition, if the preferred stock is sold, then those shareholders who received common stock would increase their proportionate interests and those who sold the preferred stock would get property. From that standpoint, 305(b)(3) serves as a backstop to 305(b)(2).

Example 6.6: G, Inc. has two classes of common stock, one of which is voting and one of which is non-voting. G, Inc. distributes preferred stock to one class and common stock to the other class. Under section 305(b)(3), both stock distributions are taxable under section 301.

[4]   Distributions to Preferred Stockholders

Section 305(b)(4) provides that any stock dividend *on* preferred stock (other than an increase in the conversion ratio of convertible preferred stock made solely to take account of a stock dividend or stock split with respect to the stock into which such convertible stock is convertible) is a section 301 distribution. The rationale is that any distribution of stock to preferred shareholders increases the preferred shareholders' proportionate interest in the corporation at the expense of the common shareholders. If preferred stock is distributed to preferred stockholders, that generally will increase the amount of those shareholders' preferred claim on earnings and profits as well as on liquidation proceeds. If common stock is distributed to preferred shareholders, that would add residual rights to the shareholders' preferred claims. By contrast, an increase in the conversion ratio of convertible preferred stock made to take account of a stock dividend or stock split with respect to the stock into which such convertible stock is convertible does not fall under section 305(b)(4) because rather than being disproportionate, the increase in the conversion ratio maintains the pre-existing proportions.

Example 6.7: H Corp. has two classes of stock, Class A, which is voting common stock, and Class B, which is non-voting preferred stock. It distributes a *pro rata* preferred stock dividend to the preferred stockholders. Under section 305(b)(4), the stock dividend is taxable under section 301.

As discussed above, a stock distribution that it is taxed under section 305(b) qualifies as a distribution of "property" under section 305(b)(2). Therefore, if shares of an existing class of preferred stock are distributed to common shareholders as well as to preferred shareholders, not only are the preferred shareholders who received more preferred stock taxed under section 305(b)(4), but in addition, the shareholders receiving preferred stock with respect to their common stock are taxed under section 305(b)(2), because the stock dividend gives them an increased residual interest in the corporation and the preferred shareholders are treated as having received property.[3] *See* Treas. Reg. § 1.305-3(e) Ex. 15.

> *Example 6.8*: As in Example 6.7, H Corp. has two classes of stock (both before and after the distribution), Class A voting common and Class B non-voting preferred. Assume that it distributes a *pro rata* Class B preferred stock dividend to the preferred stockholders as well as a *pro rata* Class B preferred stock dividend to the common stockholders. Under section 305(b)(4), the Class B preferred stock distributed to the preferred stockholders is taxable under section 301. In addition, under section 305(b)(2), the Class B preferred stock distributed to the common stockholders is taxable under section 301.

[5]   Distributions of Convertible Preferred Stock

Under section 305(b)(5), distributions of convertible preferred stock are taxable under circumstances in which there will likely be conversion of some, but not all, of the preferred stock by the shareholders. This would result in receipt of property by some shareholders and receipt of additional stock by others, echoing the concern behind section 305(b)(2). Where the conversion period is short, this is more likely to occur. However, if the conversion period is longer, it is more likely that *all* of the shareholders will convert, which would not be disproportionate. *See* Treas. Reg. § 1.305-6(a)(2). Factors, in addition to the length of the conversion period, that affect the likelihood of some but not all shareholders converting include the dividend rate on the preferred, its marketability, its conversion price, and its redemption provisions.

> *Example 6.9*: Isle, Inc. has one class of stock, common stock. With respect to each share of common, Isle, Inc. distributes one share of new preferred stock convertible into common stock for a period of six months from the date of issuance at a price slightly higher than the fair market value on the date of issuance. A third party has agreed to buy any shares from any shareholder that does not want to convert. Because it is likely that some shareholders will convert, receiving additional common shares, and others will sell, receiving cash, section 305(b)(5) renders the distribution of convertible preferred taxable under section 301.

[B]   Deemed Distributions of Stock

Section 305(c) provides the Secretary of the Treasury with authority to prescribe regulations under which certain events may be treated as constructive stock distributions to shareholders whose proportionate interests in assets or earnings increase as a result of those events. Examples of these

---

[3] If the preferred stock distributed to the common shareholders were a new class of preferred that is subordinate to the old class of preferred stock, the common stockholders' interest would not be increased at the expense of the interest of the preferred stockholders. Accordingly, the common stockholders would not be taxed under section 305(b)(2). *See* Treas. Reg. § 1.305-3(e) Ex. 3.

events include a redemption taxable under section 301, other than an isolated redemption; a change in conversion ratio; a change in redemption price; and a difference between the redemption price and the issue price of stock.[4] See I.R.C. § 305(c); Treas. Reg. § 1.305-7. In a sense, section 305(c) codifies substance-over-form doctrine with respect to certain transactions in stock. A transaction deemed a distribution under section 305(c) is then tested under section 305(b) to see if it is a section 301 distribution.

Revenue Ruling 83-119, 1983-2 C.B. 57, provides an example of this analysis. That ruling considered whether an excess "redemption premium" (the amount by which the redemption price exceeded the issue price) should be treated as a distribution of stock. In that ruling, X corporation had 100 shares of outstanding stock, owned by two related parties, A and B. At A's retirement, the corporation adopted a plan of recapitalization for the purpose of transferring control and ownership of the common stock to B. It authorized the exchange of a single class of non-voting, dividend-paying preferred stock for A's common stock. The preferred stock was only redeemable upon the death of A, and was payable by X corporation to A's estate at its par value of $1,000 per share. A exchanged 80 shares of his common stock for 80 shares of the preferred stock. The X common stock surrendered had a fair market value of $1,000 per share. The X preferred stock had a par value of $1,000 per share, but, at the time of the exchange, the fair market value of the preferred stock was only $600 per share, a difference of $400 per share at the time of the exchange.

The IRS found that, although the exchange of stock was a tax-free recapitalization under section 368(a)(1)(E), the difference between the fair market values at the time of the exchange must be treated as an additional distribution of stock under section 305(c). Regulation 1.305-5(b)(1) states that "[i]f a corporation issues preferred stock that may be redeemed under [certain] circumstances . . . at a price higher than the issue price, the difference (the redemption premium) is treated under section 305(c) as a constructive distribution . . . of additional stock on preferred stock . . . ." The IRS found, under then-applicable regulations, that a reasonable redemption premium was 10 percent of the stock's par value, or $60. The remainder of the redemption premium, $340, was excessive. It was therefore deemed, under section 305(c), to be an additional distribution of preferred shares.

Because the deemed distribution of shares was *with respect to preferred shares*, section 305(b)(4) applied to treat the deemed distribution as a section 301 distribution. Because the shareholders intended that A would not transfer the preferred stock, but that the stock would only be redeemed upon A's death, A was deemed to constructively receive additional stock

---

[4] In general, and as reflected in Revenue Ruling 83-119, issue price is the fair market value of the stock at the time of its issuance. *See* Richard L. Winston, *What Is Section 1504(a)(4) Preferred Stock?*, 76 TAX NOTES 111, 117 (1997). The redemption price is the amount to be paid upon redemption of the stock. If the redemption price exceeds the issue price, the stock has a redemption premium.

at $340 dollars per share ratably over A's life expectancy, which was 24 years at the time of the exchange, according to actuarial tables. The IRS also ruled that, if A should die earlier, any part of the dividends not yet constructively received would be deemed received at the time of A's death.

CHART 6.1
Checklist to Apply Section 305 to Stock Dividends

(1)   Was there an actual or constructive stock distribution with respect to stock? (If no, section 305 does not apply).

(2)   If yes, was the distribution *with respect to preferred stock*? If yes, it is taxable under section 301. I.R.C. § 305(b)(4).

(3)   If no, was any shareholder offered a *choice* to receive cash or other property instead? If yes, it is taxable under section 301. I.R.C. § 305(b)(1).

(4)   If no, did a shareholder of one class of stock receive cash or other property while a shareholder of another class of stock received the stock, increasing that shareholder's proportionate interest in the corporation? If yes, the stock distribution is taxable under section 301. I.R.C. § 305(b)(2).

(5)   If no, did any common stockholder receive *common stock* while any other common stockholder received *preferred stock*? If yes, the stock distribution is taxable under section 301. I.R.C. § 305(b)(3).

(6)   If no, is the distribution of *convertible preferred stock*? If yes, it is taxable under section 301, unless it is established to the satisfaction of the IRS that the distribution will not have the result of some shareholders obtaining cash or other property while other shareholders obtain stock. I.R.C. § 305(b)(5).

[C]   Basis and Holding Period

If stock distributed as a dividend falls within section 305(b), the shareholder takes a fair market value basis in the stock received, under section 301(d). The reason for providing the shareholder with a fair market value basis is that the shareholder has been taxed with respect to the value of the stock dividend. A fair market value basis ensures that the taxpayer is not taxed again on that tax-paid amount when the stock is sold. In addition, the holding period starts anew the day after the stock is received; section 1223 does not apply.

Example 6.10: In its sole distribution of the year, Jay Corp. distributes ten shares of preferred stock to each of its 100 preferred stockholders, each of whom own the same number of preferred shares. Ten shares of preferred stock are worth $1,000, so the entire distribution totals $100,000. The distribution is taxable to each recipient under section

305(b)(4). Jay Corp. has no current earnings and profits, and has $80,000 of accumulated earnings and profits. Each shareholder therefore includes $800 of the $1,000 as a dividend. The remaining $200 distributed to each shareholder reduces basis in his or her old preferred shares, and, if basis is reduced to zero, any remaining amount constitutes capital gain. Each shareholder takes a $1,000 basis in the new preferred under section 301(d). The new shares' holding period begins the following day.

§ 6.04   "Tainted" Stock (Section 306 Stock)

Section 306 was enacted in 1954 to deal with a "preferred stock bailout" that enabled shareholders to withdraw corporate profits as long-term capital gains, circumventing the dividend rules. Section 306 is logically linked to section 305 because, as discussed below, one way that "section 306 stock" is created is through the distribution of a tax-free preferred stock dividend.

Section 306 provides special rules for disposition of section 306 stock that traditionally sought to tax an appropriate amount of sales proceeds as ordinary income. Section 306 is less important for individuals now that individuals' qualified dividend income is taxed as net capital gain under section 1(h). That is, the application of preferential capital gains rates to qualified dividend income has reduced individual shareholders' incentive to try to convert dividends into capital gains. In addition, when Congress enacted the qualified dividend income provisions, it provided that, for purposes of section 1(h)(11), which applies to individual taxpayers, the ordinary income under section 306 is treated as a dividend. *See* I.R.C. § 306(a)(1)(D).[5]

However, section 306 does have continuing relevance. With respect to corporate taxpayers, the portion of the sales proceeds taxed as ordinary income by section 306 is *not* treated as a dividend, but rather as ordinary income. *See* I.R.C. § 306(a)(1). Thus, the dividends received deduction of section 243 does not apply. In addition, as discussed in § 6.04[B][3][a], when section 306 stock is sold, basis offset occurs *after* income inclusion, rather than up front as it would in a typical sale or exchange transaction. This income-first approach can result in greater tax liability even for an individual benefitting from the qualified dividend income rules.

[A]   History of the "Preferred Stock Bailout"

Chamberlin v. Commissioner, 207 F.2d 462 (6th Cir. 1953), *cert. denied*, 347 U.S. 918 (1954), is the leading case on preferred stock bailouts. In that case, Chamberlin and five other shareholders owned all of the outstanding common stock in Metal Moulding Corporation (Metal Moulding) from 1940 to 1946. In December 1946, Metal Moulding authorized 8,020 shares of

---

[5] This provision, which was included in Title III of the Jobs and Growth Tax Relief Reconciliation Act of 2003, is scheduled to sunset at the end of 2008.

preferred stock, and then distributed the preferred stock to Chamberlin and the other common stock shareholders on a *pro rata* basis. Two days later, the shareholders sold approximately half of Metal Moulding's preferred stock to two insurance companies pursuant to purchase agreements with specific redemption requirements. *Id.* at 464. Chamberlin and the other shareholders treated the transactions as exchanges, with the gain taxed at long-term capital gains rates. *Id.* at 466.

The IRS argued that while the preferred stock dividend distribution was non-taxable in form, the plan to sell the shares immediately following the dividend distribution made the sales proceeds, in substance, taxable as ordinary income. *Id.* at 467. The Court of Appeals for the Sixth Circuit, reversing the Tax Court held that the preferred stock dividend should not be taxed as ordinary income. It stated, "[a] non-taxable stock dividend does not become a taxable cash dividend upon its sale by the recipient" and "the legal effect of the dividend with respect to rights in the corporate assets is determined at the time of its distribution, not by what the stockholders do with it after its receipt." *Id.* at 468–69. The court also determined that the dividend distribution was a *bona fide* transaction in substance as well as in form because a large portion of the preferred stock remained "in the hands of the investing public." *Id.* at 471. The court found that the profits from the subsequent sale of the preferred stock to the insurance companies were taxable to Chamberlin and the shareholders as long-term capital gains.

Note that, in *Chamberlin*, Metal Moulding would likely redeem the stock held by the insurance companies, resulting in disbursement of corporate profits. Note also that not only did the scheme result in characterization of the income as capital gain, it also allowed basis offset because a *pro rata* stock dividend that is tax-free under section 305(a) will result in allocation of some of the stockholder's basis in the old stock to the new stock under section 307(a). Congress enacted section 306 to keep this situation from recurring. Section 306 left untouched the non-taxability of the *pro rata* distribution of preferred stock to common shareholders, but added rules that apply on the ultimate sale or redemption of the preferred stock.

[B] Section 306 Stock

[1] Definition

[a] Preferred Stock Received Tax-Free Under Section 305(a)

"Section 306 stock" is defined in part as "[s]tock (other than common stock issued with respect to common stock) which was distributed to the share-holder selling or otherwise disposing of such stock if, by reason of section 305(a), any part of such distribution was not includible in the gross income of the shareholder." I.R.C. § 306(c)(1)(A). As the *Chamberlin* case suggests, preferred stock is what may enable shareholders to bail out corporate profits without actually diminishing their interests in the corporation. As a result, section 306 focuses primarily on distribution of preferred stock (that is, of stock "other than common stock"). As discussed below, it is the *limitation* on preferred stock, not the preference, that distinguishes it from common stock for purposes of section 306.

Note that if a corporation lacks earnings and profits at the time the preferred stock is distributed, it will not constitute section 306 stock. I.R.C. § 306(c)(2). That is because there is no risk of bailout of corporate profits if the corporation has no profits to bail out. In other words, had the corporation distributed cash to the shareholders instead of preferred stock, the distribution would have constituted return of capital and capital gain, not dividend income. *See* I.R.C. § 301(c).

[b] Preferred Stock Received Tax-Free in a Reorganization

Preferred stock may be received in a reorganization, in circumstances that present the risk of a preferred stock bailout. Accordingly, section 306 further provides that stock that "is not common stock" and that was received in a reorganization or a section 355 transaction that was subject to nonrecognition in whole or in part constitutes section 306 stock *if* "the effect of the transaction was substantially the same as the receipt of a stock dividend, or the stock was received in exchange for section 306 stock." I.R.C. § 306(c)(1)(B)(ii).

> *Example 6.11*: In a corporate merger that qualified as a reorganization under section 368(a)(1)(A), Kara and other Target Corp. shareholders exchanged common stock in Target Corp. for *pro rata* amounts of common and preferred shares of Acquiring Corp. The preferred shares constitute section 306 stock. *See* Treas. Reg. § 1.306-3(d) Ex. 1.

In Revenue Ruling 81-91, 1981-1 C.B. 123, a corporation, pursuant to a plan of recapitalization undertaken for valid business reasons, issued shares of two new classes of stock, class A and class B. The recapitalization qualified as a reorganization under section 368(a)(1)(E), so the transaction was non-taxable under section 354(a)(1).[6] Each outstanding share of common stock was surrendered for one share of the new class A stock and one share of the new class B stock. The B stock had priority to the extent of an annual cumulative dividend of six percent of par value and repayment of up to par value upon liquidation. Once the class B stock preferences were met, each of the new classes of stock shared equally in dividends and liquidation proceeds, and each had equal voting rights and were non-redeemable.

The issue the IRS considered was whether the stock in question constituted section 306 stock. The IRS defined stock that is not "common stock" as stock that "because . . . [of its] preferred position is *limited* and the stock

---

[6] Section 368(a)(1)(E), which includes a recapitalization in the definition of reorganization, is discussed in § 12.02 of Chapter 12.

does not participate in corporate growth to any significant extent." *Id.* at 124 (emphasis added). The potential for a bailout occurs where shareholders receive a *pro rata* distribution of two new classes of stock under a plan of corporate recapitalization, and one class of stock can be disposed of without a surrender of the shareholder's interest in the corporation's future growth. In this situation, however, once the preferences of the class B stock were met, the two new classes of stock shared equally in voting rights, profits and dividends, and liquidation proceeds. Therefore, "a sale of the class B stock cannot occur without a loss of voting control and interest in the unrestricted growth of the corporation." *Id.* Due to the nature of the class B stock, there was no concern that a bailout abuse could occur with the sale of class B stock. Thus, the IRS determined that the stock was not section 306 stock.

Revenue Ruling 82-191, 1982-2 C.B. 78, also applied section 306(c)(1)(B). In that ruling, X corporation entered into a plan of recapitalization under which all X shareholders surrendered their voting common stock for newly created voting preferred stock. The recapitalization qualified under section 368(a)(1)(E) as a reorganization, so, under section 354, no gain or loss was recognized for the *pro rata* exchange of stock. The preferred stock was non-redeemable, limited and preferred as to dividends, and had a fixed liquidation preference.

A surrendered 20 shares of voting common stock for 15 shares of X voting preferred stock, while other shareholders exchanged 80 shares of common stock for 80 shares of the voting preferred stock. In addition, A purchased all of a new class of non-voting common stock at half of its fair market value, as part of the plan of recapitalization. This purchase gave A an unrestricted interest in the future equity growth of the corporation and enabled A to share in the unrestricted earnings and profits of X upon liquidation, after payment to the preferred stockholders.

The IRS found that A's preferred stock was "other than common stock" within the meaning of section 306(c)(1)(B) "because it was both limited and preferred as to dividends and had a fixed liquidation preference." *Id.* at 79. In order to determine whether the effect of the reorganization was "substantially the same as the receipt of a stock dividend," I.R.C. § 306(c)(1)(B)(ii), the IRS considered whether the voting preferred stock received by A would allow A to bail out earnings and profits of X without a loss of A's interest in the unrestricted growth of X through the continued ownership of the new non-voting common stock.

The IRS noted that the facts of the ruling differed from those of the classic bailout because the latter situation generally involves the issuance of preferred stock to shareholders who already own common stock of the corporation or who receive common stock "as part of a plan." *Id.* In the ruling, the recapitalization of X eliminated the old common stock. However, the IRS found that it would not be reasonable to assume that at the time of the recapitalization the intention was that no old shareholder would be entitled to participate in X beyond the preferred stock preferences. Therefore, the IRS determined that the new non-voting common stock would be treated as old common stock for the purposes of section 306. Thus, A was deemed to have exchanged 15 shares of common stock for 15 shares of preferred stock, and five shares of the old X common stock plus cash for five shares of new X common stock (treated as old common stock for purposes of section 306).

Under this analysis, sale of the preferred would bail out corporate profits without loss of A's interest in future growth of X. Therefore, the preferred stock constituted section 306 stock. Thus, in this ruling, the combination of the exchange of 20 common shares for only 15 preferred shares of apparently equal value per share, the bargain purchase of the new common shares, and the absence of any other common stockholders as a result of the transaction led the IRS to treat the transaction as a whole as substantially the same as the receipt of a preferred stock dividend by A.

[c] Certain Preferred Stock Received in a Section 351 Transaction

Preferred stock received in a section 351 transaction constitutes section 306 stock if receipt of money (instead of the stock) would have been treated as a dividend to any extent. I.R.C. § 306(c)(3). (Section 351 transactions are discussed in Chapter 2.) In effect, as illustrated in the example below, this provision addresses the scenario where, had cash been received, section 304 would have rendered the proceeds ordinary income.[7] It also rectifies the lack of parallelism with transactions structured as "B" reorganizations (stock-for-stock swaps); under 306(c)(1)(B), preferred stock received in a similar transaction structured as a "B" reorganization would be section 306 stock. B reorganizations are discussed in Chapter 10.

For purposes of section 306(c)(3), rules similar to the rules of section 304(b)(2) apply. I.R.C. § 306(c)(3)(A). Section 304(b)(2), which is discussed in Chapter 5, provides that earnings and profits of both the acquiring corporation and the issuing corporation are available for determining the amount that constitutes a dividend.

Example 6.12: Len owns 100 percent of the shares of L Corp., a corporation rich with earnings and profits. He organizes M Corp., and receives 100 percent of its newly issued common stock. In a transaction governed by section 351, Len contributes 20 percent of his L Corp. stock to M Corp., and receives in exchange newly issued voting preferred stock in M Corp.[8]

The transaction qualifies under section 351 because Len transferred property (L Corp. stock) to M Corp. and, after the transfer, was in control of M Corp. However, had cash been distributed to Len in lieu of the preferred stock, the transaction would have been governed by section 304. Once tested under section 302, the transaction would have been a section 301 distribution taxed as a dividend because of L Corp.'s ample earnings

---

[7] *See* § 5.05[D][3].

[8] Assume that the preferred stock is not "nonqualified preferred stock" under section 351(g). *See* § 2.02[A][1][f][i] for a discussion of section 351(g).

and profits. Accordingly, the M Corp. voting preferred stock constitutes section 306 stock.

Under section 306(c)(3), rules similar to the rules of section 304(b)(2) also apply for purposes of determining the application of section 306 to any subsequent disposition of section 306 stock acquired in a section 351 transaction. I.R.C. § 306(c)(3)(B). Thus, in Example 6.12, the amount of the "taint" on the section 306 stock is determined with reference both to the ample earnings and profits of L Corporation and the (probably non-existent) earnings and profits of M Corp.[9] In that example, therefore, it is likely that the preferred is tainted to the extent of its full fair market value. Were the earnings and profits of L Corporation disregarded for determining the amount of the taint, the taint would be much smaller or non-existent.

[d] Stock with a Basis Obtained from Section 306 Stock

What if section 306 stock is exchanged for *common* stock in a nonrecognition transaction? The taint infects the new stock: "Except as otherwise provided in subparagraph (B), stock the basis of which (in the hands of the shareholder selling or otherwise disposing of such stock) is determined by reference to the basis (in the hands of such shareholder or any other person) of section 306 stock." I.R.C. § 306(c)(1)(C). In addition, the exchange does not purge the taint on the old stock. Accordingly, exchanging section 306 stock for other stock in a tax-free transaction can result in a taint on *both* stocks. *See* Treas. Reg. § 1.306-3(e).

> *Example 6.13*: In a corporate merger that qualified as a reorganization under section 368(a)(1)(A), Noah exchanged section 306 stock in Target Corp. for common shares of Acquiring Corp. The common shares constitute section 306 stock. In addition, the old section 306 stock remains section 306 stock in the hands of the recipient.

There is an important exception to the definition of section 306 stock that applies to section 306 stock that was received with respect to common stock and is later exchanged for common stock in the same corporation. So long as the common stock is not convertible into preferred stock or property, it will not constitute section 306 stock. *See* I.R.C. § 306(e). This rule makes sense because if the section 306 stock is exchanged for non-convertible common stock of the same corporation, there is no risk of a bail-out of earnings and profits.

---

[9] The "taint" on section 306 stock is explained in § 6.04[B][3][a].

CHART 6.2
Checklist for Ascertaining Whether Stock is Section 306 Stock

(1)   Is the stock preferred ("other than common") stock that was received tax-free under section 305(a) in a distribution with respect to common stock? If yes, it is section 306 stock, assuming the distributing corporation had earnings and profits.

(2)   If not, is the stock preferred stock that was received tax-free in a reorganization or a section 355 transaction, if the effect was "substantially the same as the receipt of a stock dividend"? If yes, it is section 306 stock.

(3)   If not, is the stock preferred stock that was received in a section 351 transaction where receipt of money (instead of the stock) would have been treated as a dividend to any extent? If yes, it is section 306 stock.

(4)   If not, was the stock exchanged for section 306 stock in a nonrecognition transaction? If yes, it is section 306 stock, unless the original section 306 stock was received with respect to common stock and the exchange was for nonconvertible common stock in the same corporation.

[2]   Disposition of Section 306 Stock by Gift or Bequest

What if section 306 stock is disposed of by gift? Under section 306(c)(1)(C), "[e]xcept as otherwise provided in subparagraph (B), stock the basis of which (in the hands of the shareholder selling or otherwise disposing of such stock) is determined by reference to the basis (in the hands of such shareholder or any other person) of section 306 stock." Under section 1015(a), the donee's basis in a gift is generally the donor's basis. Thus, the section 306 stock remains tainted in the hands of the donee. By contrast, under current law, the basis to the recipient of a bequest is generally the fair market value of the property on the date of the decedent's death. *See* I.R.C. § 1014(a)(1); *but cf.* I.R.C. § 1014(f) (repealing section 1014 for decedents dying after December 31, 2009). Accordingly, under current law, death eliminates the taint on section 306 stock.

[3]   General Tax Consequences on Sale of Section 306 Stock

If stock constitutes section 306 stock, the "taint" on the stock comes home to roost when the shareholder sells the stock. If instead the section 306 stock is redeemed, the applicable rules are somewhat different. Those rules are discussed below, in § 6.04[B][4].

[a]   Computing Amount of "Taint"

When section 306 stock is sold, the amount of the "taint" on the stock will constitute ordinary income (though, under current law, that ordinary income will be taxed as a dividend if the seller is an individual, *see* I.R.C. § 306(a)(1)(D)). Under section 306(a)(1)(A)(ii), the taint amount is the "stock's ratable share of the amount which would have been a dividend at the time of distribution if (in lieu of section 306 stock) the corporation had distributed money in an amount equal to the fair market value of the stock at the time of distribution." In other words, the stock is tainted to the extent that the value of the 306 stock would have been a dividend if cash had been distributed instead. This test is sometimes called the "cash substitution test."

> *Example 6.14*: In its only distribution of the year, Oh, Inc. distributes 100 shares of preferred stock to each of two common stockholders, Pat and Quincy, each of whom owns half of the common shares. Each 100-share distribution is worth $5,000 ($50 per share), for a total distribution of $10,000. The corporation has no accumulated earnings and profits. It has current earnings and profits of $6,000. The preferred stock constitutes section 306 stock because it is not common stock, it was received tax-free under section 305(a), and Oh, Inc. had earnings and profits at the time of distribution. Had cash of $10,000 been distributed ($5,000 to each shareholder), $6,000 of it ($3,000 to each shareholder) would have constituted a dividend. I.R.C. §§ 301(c)(1), 316. Accordingly, each share in the blocks of preferred stock distributed has a taint of $30.

In Example 6.14, each share had a taint of $30. Its basis would have been determined upon receipt under section 307. Assume that Pat's basis in each share is $5. If Pat were to sell one share for $30, it would all constitute ordinary income. That is, upon sale, the proceeds constitute ordinary income to the extent of the taint.

The amount constituting ordinary income does not qualify as a dividend within the meaning of section 316, so it is not eligible for relief under the inter-corporate dividends received deduction, discussed in Chapter 4, and does not reduce corporate earning and profits. However, it *does* qualify as a dividend for purposes of the preferential tax rates applicable to individuals' qualified dividends. *See* I.R.C. § 306(a)(1)(D). Note also that any unrecovered basis ($5 in the hypothetical above) would revert to the common stock from which it came. Treas. Reg. § 1.306-1(b)(2) Ex. 2 & 3.

[b] Tax Treatment of Additional Sales Proceeds

"Any excess of the amount realized over the sum of . . . the amount treated under subparagraph (A) as ordinary income, plus . . . the adjusted basis of the stock, shall be treated as gain from the sale of such stock." I.R.C. § 306(a)(1)(B). Thus, after the taint precipitates out as ordinary income under 306(a)(1)(A), any remaining sales proceeds first reduce basis and then constitute gain from the sale of the stock (generally capital gain).

> *Example 6.15*: In Example 6.14, each share of preferred stock had a taint of $30. Assume that Quincy's basis in each share is $3. If Quincy were to sell one share for $35, $30 would constitute ordinary income, $3 would be return of capital, and $2 would be includible capital gain.

[4] General Tax Consequences on Redemption of Section 306 Stock

When section 306 stock is redeemed by the corporation that issued it, the tax treatment of the redemption proceeds differs from the procedure described above. Note that in a redemption, the issuing corporation actually distributes property in exchange for the stock. Therefore, there is no need to perform a historical "cash substitution test." In other words, *the taint amount is irrelevant in a redemption*. Instead, absent an applicable exception, the redemption proceeds constitute a section 301 distribution.

> *Example 6.16*: R Corp. distributes 100 shares of preferred stock *pro rata* to its two common stockholders, Sally and Ted, each of whom owns half of the common shares. Each 100-share distribution is worth $1,000 ($10 per share). The corporation has no accumulated earnings and profits. It has current earnings and profits of $6,000. The preferred stock constitutes section 306 stock because it is not common stock, it was received tax-free under section 305(a), and R Corp. had earnings and profits at the time of the distribution.
>
> Five years later, Sally tenders 1 preferred share in redemption. Sally receives $18, the stock's fair market value at that time. R Corp. has $10,000 of accumulated earnings and profits and $2,000 of current earnings and profits in the year of the redemption. Assume that R Corp. makes no other distributions that year. Given R Corp.'s ample earnings and profits, the entire $18 constitutes a dividend.

As this example reveals, redemption of section 306 stock differs in two key respects from the sale (or other non-redemption disposition) of section 306 stock. First, the corporation's earnings and profits for the time of redemption, not the year of issuance of the stock, is what matters. This provides an opportunity for a holder of section 306 stock to engage in some tax planning. Second, a redemption of section 306 stock is taxed as a section 301 distribution. Therefore, any ordinary income from the redemption constitutes a dividend, which both reduces earnings and profits and allows a corporate holder of section 306 stock a dividends received deduction. As discussed in § 6.04[B][3][a], this is not true of the ordinary income received upon sale of section 306 stock.

[5] Exceptions to General Tax Treatment

Section 306 does provide certain exceptions under which the disposition of section 306 stock is treated like the disposition of stock that is not tainted. These exceptions are discussed below.

[a] Complete Liquidation of Corporation

"If the section 306 stock is redeemed in a distribution in complete liquidation to which part II (sec. 331 and following) applies," the special rules of section 306 do not apply. I.R.C. § 306(b)(2). Liquidations are discussed in Chapter 7. In general, a complete liquidation to which section 331 applies is a taxable liquidation.

[b] Complete Termination of Shareholder Interest in Corporation

If a holder of section 306 stock disposes of it by sale or other disposition not in redemption, but *not* directly or indirectly to a person the ownership of whose stock would (under section 318(a)) be attributable to the selling shareholder, the sale will be treated as a regular sale if it *terminates the entire stock interest of the shareholder* in that corporation. I.R.C. § 306(b)(1)(A). Section 318 constructive ownership rules, which are discussed in Chapter 5, apply for determining whether there is a complete termination of the shareholder's interest. I.R.C. § 306(b)(1)(A)(ii).

If the disposal of the section 306 stock is by redemption, the rules of section 306 will not apply if section 302(b)(3) (complete termination of interest) or 302(b)(4) (redemption in partial liquidation) apply. I.R.C. § 306(b)(1)(B). Chapter 5 discusses those redemption provisions.

[c] Transactions not for Tax Avoidance

Section 306 also will not apply "[i]f it is established to the satisfaction of the Secretary . . . that the distribution, and the disposition or redemption . . . was not in pursuance of a plan having as one of its principal purposes the avoidance of Federal income tax." I.R.C. § 306(b)(4)(A). Note that both the distribution of the section 306 stock *and* the disposition must not be in pursuance of a plan with a principal purpose of tax avoidance. It is not easy to determine what constitutes "tax avoidance" for this purpose. Treasury regulation section 1.306-2(b)(3) provides that section 306(b)(4)(A) applies to "the case of dividends and isolated dispositions of section 306 stock by minority shareholders."

Section 306(b)(4) also applies "[i]f it is established to the satisfaction of the Secretary . . . in the case of a prior or simultaneous disposition (or redemption) of the stock with respect to which the section 306 stock disposed of (or redeemed) was issued, that the disposition (or redemption) of the section 306 stock was not in pursuance of a plan having as one of its principal purposes the avoidance of Federal income tax." I.R.C. § 306(b)(4)(B). This requires a prior or simultaneous disposition of the common stock with respect to which the preferred stock was issued, as well as the absence of an improper tax-avoidance purpose. Revenue Ruling 75-247, 1975-1 C.B. 104 held that "where only part of the common stock with respect to which the section 306 stock was issued is disposed of prior to or simultaneously with the section 306 stock, this circumstance alone does not establish that one of the principal purposes of the issuance and disposition of the section 306 stock was not in pursuance of a plan of tax avoidance." *Id.* at 104. *See also Fireoved v. United States*, 462 F.2d 1281, 1289 (3d Cir. 1972) ("when *only a portion* of the underlying common stock is sold, and the taxpayer retains essentially all the control he had previously, it would be unrealistic to conclude that Congress meant to give that taxpayer the advantage of section 306(b)(4)(B) when he ultimately sells his section 306 stock.").

By contrast, in Revenue Ruling 77-455, 1977-2 C.B. 93, the majority shareholder of the corporation, A, who owned both common stock and section 306 voting preferred stock that had been issued with respect to the preferred stock, decided to retire and terminate all of his interest in the corporation. A planned to sell a portion of A's stockholdings to two key employees, including his son, B, and have the corporation redeem the remainder of his stock. Id. at 93. The IRS stated:

> A's reasons for selling some of the preferred stock to B rather than having all of the preferred stock redeemed are to leave B with voting control of X [the corporation] for a smaller investment than would otherwise be necessary while giving the key employees other than B a greater participation in the growth of X than they would have if B owned more than half of the common stock. These goals will be accomplished because the preferred stock is worth only one-tenth as much per share as the common stock but entitles its holder to one vote per share, the same as the common stock.

Id. at 93–94. On these facts, the IRS ruled that "[t]he avoidance of Federal income tax within the meaning of section 306(b)(4) will not be considered to be one of the principal purposes of the sale by A of section 306 stock to B or of the redemption by X of A's remaining section 306 stock because it is inappropriate to impute to A an intention to remove corporate earnings at capital gains rates." Id. at 95.

CHART 6.3
Checklist for Applying Section 306 to "Tainted Stock"

(1) Confirm that the stock is section 306 stock. (See Chart 6.2.)

(2) Is the section 306 stock being disposed of by redemption?

> (A) If yes, if it is disposed of by an individual in a partial liquidation or constitutes a complete termination of the shareholder's entire interest in the corporation (direct and indirect), section 306 does not apply, and section 302 does. If it is a complete liquidation governed by section 331, section 306 does not apply, and the liquidation rules do.

> (B) If yes, and the transaction is *not* a partial liquidation, complete termination of the shareholder's interest in the corporation, or total liquidation, the distribution is taxed under section 301.

(3) If not, does the disposition result in a complete termination of the shareholder's entire interest in the corporation (direct or indirect)? If it does, section 306 does not apply, and the transaction is taxed as a sale or exchange.

(4)   If not, then compute the "taint" amount on the stock—the amount that *would have been a dividend* had cash been distributed instead of the stock (this requires considering earnings and profits amounts for the year in which the stock was distributed).

    (A)   The sales proceeds, up to the amount of the taint, are includible as ordinary income (though they are treated as dividend income for an individual shareholder).

    (B)   Any remaining sales proceeds reduce basis.

    (C)   Any remaining sales proceeds constitute gain from the sale of the stock (generally capital gain).

Chapter 7

CORPORATE LIQUIDATIONS AND TAXABLE ACQUISITIONS

§ 7.01 Introduction to Liquidations and Taxable Acquisitions

This chapter focuses on two related types of transactions: liquidation of a corporation and stock purchases treated as asset acquisitions. Corporate liquidations may be partial or complete. As discussed in Chapter 5, a partial liquidation of a corporation is generally analyzed as a redemption of stock with respect to noncorporate shareholders; it involves a distribution of corporate assets to shareholders in return for their stock.[1] Partial liquidations are briefly discussed in more detail below.

A complete liquidation of a corporation involves the distribution of all of its assets to its shareholders, with the shareholders assuming all of the corporation's liabilities. Before the repeal of the famous *General Utilities* case,[2] liquidations were tax-free to the liquidating corporation. Under current law, complete liquidations generally constitute taxable exchanges both to the shareholders and the liquidating corporation, except to the extent that they involve a parent corporation's liquidation of an 80-percent-or-more owned subsidiary (by vote and by value). Those parent-subsidiary liquidations are nonrecognition transactions. However, some liquidations are part of tax-free reorganizations. Those liquidations are governed by the reorganization provisions surveyed in Chapter 9, not by the liquidation provisions discussed in this chapter.

Section 338 permits certain purchases of a corporation's stock to be taxed as if the corporation's *assets* had been acquired directly. This so-called "taxable acquisition" provision, which is elective, was enacted in response to a case that allowed taxpayers to purchase stock in a target corporation, liquidate the target tax-free, and obtain what was essentially a cost basis in the target's assets. *See Kimbell-Diamond Milling Co. v. Commissioner*, 14 T.C. 74 (1950), *aff'd*, 187 F.2d 718 (5th Cir.), *cert. denied*, 342 U.S. 827 (1951). As discussed below, section 338 overruled *Kimbell-Diamond* and imposes a tax cost for the privilege of treating a stock purchase as an asset acquisition.[3]

---

[1] *See* § 5.03[B][4].

[2] *General Utilities & Operating Co. v. Helvering*, 296 U.S. 200 (1935), is discussed in § 4.02[A].

[3] *See* § 7.05[B].

§ 7.02 Partial Liquidations

As discussed in Chapter 5, *noncorporate shareholders* benefit from a special rule that provides exchange treatment for redemptions in partial liquidation.[4] I.R.C. § 302(b)(4). Section 302(e)(1) provides that a distribution is treated as being in partial liquidation if the distribution is not essentially equivalent to a dividend, determined at the *corporate level*, and the distribution is pursuant to a plan of partial liquidation. This provision is discussed in § 5.03[B][4] of Chapter 5.

At the level of the distributing corporation, section 311, discussed in Chapter 4, applies to determine gain or loss.[5] In addition, section 346(b), which is entitled "[t]ransactions which might reach same result as partial liquidations," provides that,

> [t]he Secretary shall prescribe such regulations as may be necessary to ensure that the purposes of subsections (a) and (b) of section 222 of the Tax Equity and Fiscal Responsibility Act of 1982 (which repeal the special tax treatment for partial liquidations) may not be circumvented through the use of section 355, 351, or any other provision of law or regulations (including the consolidated return regulations).

As yet, there are no regulations under this section.

§ 7.03 Tax Consequences of Complete Liquidations

As indicated above, there are two principal types of complete liquidations: taxable and non-taxable. This section discusses the two types, in that order.

[A] Taxable Liquidations

A complete liquidation involves one or a series of distributions to shareholders in redemption of all of the stock of the corporation.[6] *See* I.R.C. § 346(a). A formal plan of liquidation is not required but is helpful in avoiding the possibility of having early distributions treated as non-liquidating distributions that may be taxable as dividends. In general, a complete liquidation is a recognition event to both the liquidating corporation and its shareholders.

Example 7.1: X Corporation is owned by Aaron and Barbara. It has four assets, all of which are worth more than X Corporation's basis in that

---

[4] *See* § 5.03[B][4]. Prior to 1982, section 346 defined a "partial liquidation" as a distribution that either (1) was one of a series of distributions leading to a complete liquidation of a corporation; (2) was in redemption of part of the stock of the corporation, where the distribution was not essentially equivalent to a dividend; or (3) terminated one of two or more active trades or businesses engaged in by the distributing corporation. If a transaction met the definition, it was governed by sections 331 and 336 (which, under current law, tax *complete* liquidations).

[5] *See* § 4.02[A].

[6] Redemptions are corporate buy-backs of stock. They are discussed in detail in Chapter 5.

asset. Pursuant to a plan of complete liquidation, in January of this year, X distributes one asset each to Aaron and Barbara. In March, X distributes the other two assets. Under section 336, X will be taxed on the gains realized on the transfer of the four assets. Aaron and Barbara will also be taxed; each will realize gain or loss that reflects the difference between their stock bases and the value of the assets they received.

[1]   Corporate-Level Tax Consequences

[a]   General Rule

In general, a liquidation is taxed to the liquidating corporation as if the corporation sold its assets at fair market value to its shareholders. I.R.C. § 336(a).

Example 7.2: Y Corp. is owned equally by Cecil and Dina. Y Corp. has two assets, land worth $200,000 with a basis of $150,000, and a custom truck worth $200,000 with a basis of $120,000. Pursuant to a plan of complete liquidation, Y Corp. distributes the land to Cecil and the truck to Dina. Under section 336, Y Corp. will recognize $50,000 of taxable gain on the distribution of the land, and $80,000 of taxable gain on the distribution of the machine.

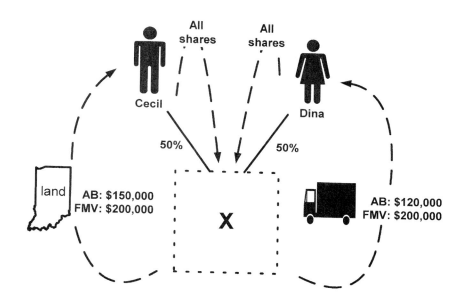

If an asset is distributed subject to a liability, the fair market value of that asset is deemed to be no less than the amount of the liability.

Example 7.3: Assume that in Example 7.2, the land distributed to Cecil is subject to a mortgage of $210,000, which Cecil assumes. (For simplicity, ignore the fact that this makes the distributions to Cecil and Dina unequal.) Under section 336, Y Corp. will recognize $60,000 of taxable gain on the distribution of the land because its amount realized on the distribution will be $210,000.

[b] Historical Importance of Substance-Over-Form Doctrine in Liquidations

Commissioner v. Court Holding Co., 324 U.S. 331 (1945), applied the substance-over-form doctrine to a purported liquidation. In that case, the taxpayer corporation was owned by the Millers. The sole asset of the corporation was an apartment building. In 1940, the corporation reached an oral agreement to sell the apartment building, but then withdrew from the sale because the income tax liability that would result from such a sale. Instead, the Millers caused the corporation to distribute the assets of the corporation in complete liquidation. *Id.* at 332–33. Under the applicable tax law, *General Utilities*[7] principles applied to a liquidating distribution of appreciated property to shareholders, so that, unlike a sale of that property, it would produce no corporate-level income.

The Supreme Court held that the transaction was *taxable to the corporation as a sale* because the "incidence of taxation depends upon the substance of a transaction." *Id.* at 334. The liquidating distribution occurred one day after the corporation withdrew from the original sale. The Millers had then entered into substantially the same agreement to sell the apartment building as the one the corporation had begun. The Supreme Court found sufficient evidence to support the findings of the Tax Court that "despite the declaration of a 'liquidating dividend' followed by the transfers of legal title, the corporation had not abandoned the sales negotiations; [and] that these were mere formalities designed 'to make the transaction appear to be other than what it was' in order to avoid tax liability." *Id.* at 333.

The outcome in the *Court Holding Co.* case contrasts with that of *United States v. Cumberland Public Service Co.*, 338 U.S. 451 (1950), which involved another application of the same tax regime. In *Cumberland Public Service Co.*, the taxpayer corporation was in the electric power business. When it realized it could not compete with a local cooperative, it offered to sell all of its stock to the cooperative. The cooperative refused the offer but offered to buy the corporation's transmission and distribution equipment. The corporation declined because of the tax liability that would have accompanied a sale. *Id.* at 452. The corporation's shareholders offered to obtain those assets and sell them to the cooperative; that offer was accepted. The corporation therefore distributed those assets to its shareholders in partial liquidation, sold the remaining assets, and dissolved. The sale by the shareholders then proceeded as planned.

---

[7] *See General Utilities & Operating Co. v. Helvering*, 296 U.S. 200 (1935), which is discussed in § 4.02[A].

The Court of Claims found that the method by which the stockholders disposed of the properties was avowedly chosen in order to reduce taxes, but that the liquidation and dissolution genuinely ended the corporation's activities and existence. *The court also found that at no time did the corporation plan to make the sale itself.* Accordingly it found as a fact that the sale was made by the shareholders rather than the corporation, and entered judgment for respondent.

Id. at 453 (emphasis added). In light of these findings, the Supreme Court ruled in favor of the taxpayer-corporation.

Thus, in both *Court Holding Co.* and *Cumberland Public Service Co.,* the Supreme Court ruled in accordance with the findings of the trial court. *See id.* at 455–56. Although the holding in each of these cases on the liquidation versus sale issue is largely of historical interest because, under current law, liquidating distributions of appreciated property are taxed to the corporation under section 336(a), the cases are interesting to consider in light of substance-over-form principles. In *Court Holding Co.,* the corporation had reached an agreement with the purchasers and the shareholders carried out the sale on virtually the same terms; in that case, the Supreme Court agreed with the trial court that, in substance, the corporation had sold the property. By contrast, in *Cumberland Public Service Co.,* the corporation never agreed to sell the property, and, although it declined to sell the property directly to the purchaser because of the tax liability such a sale would entail, the Supreme Court agreed with the trial court that the form of the transaction, a sale by the shareholders, had to be respected.

[c]   Distributions of Loss Property

As indicated above, section 336(a) provides a general rule that a liquidating corporation recognizes gain or loss on the distribution of property in complete liquidation. This general rule is subject to two important exceptions in section 336(d) that limit a liquidating corporation's recognition of losses.

[i]   Distributions to Related Persons

Section 336(d)(1) applies to preclude certain losses on distributions to *related persons* (within the meaning of section 267). Section 267 provides that an individual and a corporation are related if the individual owns (directly or indirectly) more than 50 percent in value of the outstanding stock of the corporation. I.R.C. § 267(b)(2). In addition, two corporations that are members of the same controlled group are considered related. I.R.C. § 267(b)(3). A controlled group may consist of parent and subsidiary corporations,[8] brother-sister corporations,[9] or a "combined group" of

---

[8] For purposes of section 267, a parent-subsidiary controlled group is *one or more chains of corporations connected through stock ownership with a common parent corporation if* (1)

corporations.[10] I.R.C. § 267(f).

On a liquidating distribution to such a related person, no loss will be recognized by the liquidating corporation if the distribution is not *pro rata* (proportionate to shareholder interest) or if the property distributed is "disqualified property." I.R.C. § 336(d)(1)(A). Disqualified property is property that was acquired by the liquidating corporation, during the preceding five years, in a transaction to which section 351 applied, or as a contribution to capital. I.R.C. § 336(d)(1)(B). In addition, disqualified property includes property the adjusted basis of which is determined in whole or in part by reference to the adjusted basis of disqualified property. *Id.*

> *Example 7.4*: Z Corp. is owned 40 percent by Ernest and 60 percent by Frank. As part of a plan of complete liquidation, Z Corp. distributes to Frank Blackacre, a plot of land worth $100,000 with a $120,000 basis. Z Corp. acquired the land from Ernest three years ago in a section 351 transaction. Section 336(d)(1) denies Z Corp. recognition of its $20,000 realized loss because the land is disqualified property and Frank is a "related person" with respect to Z Corp. under section 267(b)(2).[11]

Note that if the land distributed to Frank were Whiteacre, land that had been swapped for Blackacre in a like-kind exchange governed by section 1031, section 336(d)(1) would still apply because it applies to property the adjusted basis of which is determined in whole or in part by reference to the adjusted basis of disqualified property. *See* I.R.C. § 1031(d) (basis is calculated by reference to property for which it was exchanged).

---

one or more of the corporations other than the parent corporation owns stock possessing more than 50 percent of the total combined voting power of all classes of stock entitled to vote or more than 50 percent of the total value of shares of all classes of stock of each of the corporations, and (2) the common parent corporation owns stock possessing more than 50 percent of the total combined voting power of all classes of stock entitled to vote or more than 50 percent of the total value of shares of all classes of stock of at least one of the other corporations (excluding, in computing the voting power or value, stock owned directly by the other corporations). *See* I.R.C. §§ 267(f)(1); 1563(a)(1).

[9] A brother-sister controlled group consists of "[t]wo or more corporations if 5 or fewer persons who are individuals, estates, or trusts own . . . stock possessing more than 50 percent of the total combined voting power of all classes of stock entitled to vote or more than 50 percent of the total value of shares of all classes of stock of each corporation, taking into account the stock ownership of each such person only to the extent such stock ownership is identical with respect to each such corporation." I.R.C. § 1563(a)(2).

[10] A combined group consists of three or more corporations each of which is a member of a parent-subsidiary or brother-sister group of corporations, if one of the corporations is a common parent corporation included in a parent-subsidiary group of, and is also included in, a brother-sister group of corporations. *See* I.R.C. § 1563(a)(3).

[11] In addition, the distribution of Blackacre was not made *pro rata* to Ernest and Frank. It appears that, for a distribution of loss property to be *pro rata* within the meaning of section 336(d), each of the shareholders must acquire a proportionate interest in *that asset*, not merely in the set of distributions as a whole.

[ii] Distributions of Property with Built-In Losses

Section 336(d)(2) applies to preclude the recognition of losses built into property received in certain "carryover basis transactions," regardless of whether a related party receives the property. The property subject to section 336(d)(2) is property acquired by the liquidating corporation in a section 351 transaction or as a contribution to capital, if the acquisition of the property by the liquidating corporation was part of a plan a principal purpose of which was to recognize loss by the liquidating corporation with respect to such property in connection with the liquidation. An "unsafe harbor" provides that any such property acquired by the liquidating corporation within the preceding two years will (except as provided in regulations) be treated as acquired as part of such a plan. In addition, just as with section 336(d)(1), 336(d)(2) covers property the adjusted basis of which is determined (in whole or in part) by reference to the adjusted basis of the property in question.

Section 336(d)(2), unlike section 336(d)(1), applies not just to liquidating distributions but also to *sales or exchanges* by the liquidating corporation. *See* I.R.C. § 336(d)(2)(A). If section 336(d)(2) applies, it reduces the adjusted basis of the property to which it applies (but not below zero) by the excess (if any) of the adjusted basis of such property *immediately after its acquisition* by the liquidating corporation over the fair market value of the property *at that time*. In other words, the adjusted basis of the property, which is high compared to its fair market value, is reduced by the difference between its basis and its fair market value at the time it was acquired. That reduces the property's basis to fair market value as of the date the liquidating corporation acquired it, effectively disallowing recognition in the liquidation of any built-in loss.

Example 7.5: GH, Inc. is owned equally by Ginny and Harold. As part of a plan of complete liquidation, GH, Inc. distributes to Ginny a plot of land worth $100,000 with a $120,000 basis. Assume that GH, Inc. acquired the land from Ginny a year ago in a transaction to which section 351 applied. Assume that, at the time, the property was worth $105,000 and GH, Inc. took a basis in it of $120,000.

Because the property was acquired in a section 351 transaction within the preceding two years, section 336(d)(2) will adjust the land's basis from $120,000 to $105,000 (computed by subtracting from $120,000 the $15,000 by which the basis at the time of contribution exceeded its fair market value at that time). Accordingly, GH, Inc. will recognize only a $5,000 loss (the loss that arose subsequent to the contribution of the property).

Note that the Secretary of the Treasury may promulgate regulations "under which, in lieu of disallowing a loss under subparagraph (A) [of section 336(d)(2)] for a prior taxable year, the gross income of the liquidating corporation for the taxable year in which the plan of complete liquidation is adopted shall be increased by the amount of the disallowed loss." I.R.C. § 336(d)(2)(C). As yet, there are no such regulations.

Although the two limitations under section 336 on recognition of losses on liquidating distributions may appear unfavorable, section 336 as a whole presents a stark contrast to section 311, with respect to the treatment of realized losses on assets leaving corporate solution. As discussed in Chapter 4, section 311, which repealed the *General Utilities* doctrine, provides a general rule of nonrecognition of gain or loss on non-liquidating distributions of assets to shareholders.[12] The exception in section 311 is for appreciated property: realized gains are recognized, while realized losses are not. *See* I.R.C. § 311. By contrast, the general rule in section 336 allows recognition of corporate losses realized on liquidating distributions. Thus, viewed as a whole, Congress' approach is to disallow recognition of losses realized on the distribution of property to shareholders, unless the corporation completely liquidates in a taxable transaction and two narrow exceptions do not apply.

Section 336(d)(2) may present overlap issues with section 362(e)(2), which was enacted in 2004 and is discussed in Chapter 2, because section 362(e)(2) generally reduces a corporation's basis in assets contributed in a section 351 transaction where, in the aggregate, the basis of the assets transferred exceeds their fair market value. In Example 7.5, there would be no overlap if Ginny had contributed multiple properties in the same section 351 transaction, such that the aggregate fair market value of the assets exceeded their aggregate basis. In that case, section 362(e)(2) would not have applied to the section 351 transaction. If Ginny had contributed only the loss property, however, then section 362(e)(2) and section 336(d)(2) require some coordination, as the next example illustrates:

Example 7.6: Assume that, in Year 1, Ginny and Harold incorporate GH, Inc. and become equal owners. Ginny contributes a plot of land worth $105,000 with a $120,000 basis. Harold contributes $105,000 cash. In Year 2, as part of a plan of complete liquidation, GH, Inc. distributes to Ginny the land, which is now worth $100,000, and distributes its remaining asset, $100,000 of cash, to Harold.

Under section 362(e)(2), it appears that the corporation's basis in the land is reduced to $105,000.[13] In that case, on the distribution of the land to Ginny, section 336(d)(2) does not apply because there is no excess of "the adjusted basis of such property immediately after its acquisition by [the liquidating] corporation, over . . . the fair market value of such property as of such time. . . ." However, if Ginny had made an election under section 362(e)(2)(C) to reduce her stock basis instead, so that the corporation's asset basis remained $120,000, then, on the liquidating distribution, the corporation's basis in the land would be reduced to $105,000, as it was in Example 7.5. This would result in a double basis reduction; it is a potential trap for the unwary.

---

[12] *See* § 4.02[A].

[13] This assumes that section 362(e)(2) applies before section 336(d) because the section 351 transaction precedes the liquidation.

[2] Shareholders

Section 331(a) provides that amounts received by shareholders in a complete liquidation are treated as given in full payment in exchange for the stock, even if the shareholders do not physically surrender their shares. Thus, a shareholder computes realized gain or loss by subtracting basis in the stock from the amount realized, and reports the difference as capital gain or loss. Note that, as discussed below, the calculation must be adjusted for liabilities assumed by the shareholder, including any liability for corporate-level taxes.

Example 7.7: IJ, Inc. is owned equally by Irene and Jake. As part of a plan of complete liquidation, IJ, Inc. makes a single liquidating distribution. It distributes to Irene a plot of land worth $100,000, and to Jake inventory, cash, and equipment collectively worth $100,000. Irene has a $60,000 basis in her stock. Jake has a $110,000 basis in his stock. Ignoring any liability for corporate-level taxes, Irene recognizes $40,000 of capital gain, and Jake recognizes $10,000 of capital loss under section 331(a).

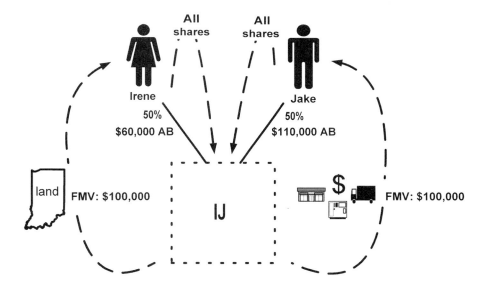

In *Robson v. Commissioner*, T.C. Memo. 2000-201, the Tax Court held that when a debt of a shareholder to the liquidating corporation was canceled in connection with the complete liquidation of the corporation, the shareholder did not have cancellation of indebtedness income, but rather, the amount of the canceled debt should be treated as an amount realized in exchange for the stock under section 331.

Regulations require the shareholder's gain or loss in a liquidation to be computed on a *per share* basis so that gain or loss is calculated separately for blocks of stock acquired at different prices and on different dates. *See* Treas. Reg. § 1.331-1(e) Ex.

> *Example 7.8*: Kristen owns 100 shares of stock of K Corporation, 50 shares of which she acquired in Year 1 at a cost of $1,200 and the other 50 shares of which she acquired in December of Year 4 at a cost of $3,000. In April of Year 5, she receives a distribution of $50 per share in complete liquidation, or $2,500 on each block of 50 shares. The gain of $1,300 on the shares acquired in Year 1 is a long-term capital gain. The loss of $500 on the shares acquired in Year 4 is a short-term capital loss.

When a shareholder receives multiple distributions, he or she recognizes *gain after all basis is recovered*, but does *not* recognize loss until the *final* distribution is received.

> *Example 7.9*: Lyle owns 100 shares of stock of L, Inc., with a cost basis of $1,500. In April, as part of a plan of complete liquidation, he receives a distribution of $1,000. In December of the same year, he receives a final liquidating distribution of $900. The April distribution results in no gross income to Lyle, but reduces his L stock basis to $500. The December distribution results in $400 of capital gain.

As indicated above, if, on complete liquidation, shareholders assume or take property subject to corporate liabilities, under section 1001, the amount realized is the *net* value of the distribution, thus reducing gain or increasing loss. *See* Rev. Rul. 59-228, 1959-2 C.B. 59.

> *Example 7.10*: Myra owns stock in M, Inc. As part of a plan of complete liquidation, M distributes to Myra a plot of land worth $100,000, but subject to a $20,000 mortgage. Myra's amount realized with respect to the land is $80,000.

For this purpose, corporate taxes are considered liabilities although they will be paid by the shareholders in their capacity as transferees, *see* I.R.C. § 6901.

By contrast, if an asset is distributed subject to a debt, even a nonrecourse one, exceeding its value, section 7701(g) probably does not apply to increase the deemed value of the asset, which is not surprising because shareholders are liable for corporate debts only up to the amount of the assets of the corporation. *See* BITTKER & EUSTICE, FEDERAL INCOME TAXATION OF CORPO-RATIONS AND SHAREHOLDERS ¶ 10.03[3] (7th ed. 2000). In addition, if the shareholder was *already liable* for the corporation's obligation, it does not reduce the amount realized. In that case, when the shareholder makes the payment, the shareholder may be entitled deduct the loss, *see Abdalla v. Commissioner*, 69 T.C. 697, 709 (1978), *aff'd*, 647 F.2d 487 (5th Cir. 1981); by contrast, the shareholder cannot deduct a loss if the liability did reduce the amount realized. *See* BITTKER & EUSTICE, *supra*, at ¶ 10.03[3].

[3] Basis Rules

As one might expect in a taxable transaction, basis of property received in a complete liquidation is the property's fair market value at the time of the distribution. I.R.C. § 334(a). More technically, if a shareholder recognized gain or loss on receipt of the property distributed (or if no gain or loss was recognized because fair market value equaled basis), then the basis of property received in a complete liquidation is the property's fair market value at the time of the distribution. *See id.*

> *Example 7.11*: Nelson owns stock in N, Inc. As part of a plan of complete liquidation, N, Inc. distributes to Nelson a plot of land worth $100,000. Because this transaction is taxable to Nelson under section 331, Nelson will take a $100,000 basis in the land under section 334(a).

If shareholders assume liabilities in the liquidation or take property subject to liabilities, their basis is the unencumbered fair market value of the assets. That amount is not further increased by the amount of the liability.

> *Example 7.12*: Assume that in Example 7.11, the plot of land worth $100,000 was subject to a $30,000 mortgage. Nelson will still take a $100,000 basis in the land under section 334(a).

Note that, in Example 7.12, Nelson's amount realized on receipt of the land will be only $70,000. His basis is the full fair market value of the land nonetheless; after all, Nelson now owes $30,000.

[4] Earnings and Profits

Following a taxable complete liquidation, the corporation's earnings and profits account is eliminated. This is the case although shareholder receipt of assets in exchange for stock is treated as an exchange rather than as a dividend distribution. By contrast, as discussed in Chapter 13, earnings and profits do carry over to the acquiring corporation in nonrecognition transactions, such as non-taxable liquidations and corporate reorganizations.[14] *See* I.R.C. § 381(a), (c).

[B] Non-Taxable Liquidation of Controlled Subsidiary

Special rules apply to liquidations involving a parent corporation that controls at least 80 percent of the stock of the subsidiary by vote and by value "on the date of the adoption of the plan of liquidation, and . . . at all times until the receipt of the property . . . ." I.R.C. § 332(b)(1); *see also* I.R.C. § 1504(a)(2). In general, that controlling parent corporation benefits from non-recognition, as does the subsidiary on its liquidating distributions to that parent. Not surprisingly, the parent takes the distributed property with the basis it had in the hands of the distributing subsidiary. The details are explored below.

[1] Subsidiary Corporation

Under section 337, a liquidating corporation does not recognize gain or loss on distributions to a parent corporation that meet the 80-percent control requirements of section 332.

---

[14] *See* § 13.01[B].

Example 7.13: Overlook, Inc. owns 90 percent of the stock (by vote and by value) of Petit Corp. As part of a plan of complete liquidation, Petit Corp. distributes to Overlook, Inc. a plot of land worth $90,000 with a basis of $60,000. Under section 337, Petit Corp. does not recognize its $30,000 gain realized on the liquidating distribution of the land.

Nonetheless, the subsidiary *does* recognize gain on distributions to minority shareholders; section 337 does not apply to protect those shareholders.

Example 7.14: Assume that in Example 7.13, Queens Corp. owns the remaining 10 percent of the stock of Petit Corp. As part of the plan of complete liquidation, Petit Corp. distributes to Queens Corp. equipment worth $10,000 with a basis of $8,000. Under section 336, Petit Corp. recognizes the $2,000 gain realized on the liquidating distribution of the equipment. (The resulting corporate tax liability will affect the gain or loss of the shareholder or shareholders who pay it.)

Losses realized on distributions to minority shareholders are not recognized, under section 336(d)(3): "In the case of any liquidation to which section 332 applies, no loss shall be recognized to the liquidating corporation on any distribution in such liquidation."

[2] Controlling Parent Corporation

[a] In General

The principle underlying the repeal of *General Utilities* is double taxation of corporate income.[15] But if a shareholder is itself a corporation, three or more levels of tax could result. Thus, when a parent corporation liquidates a subsidiary, the corporate parent generally will recognize no gain or loss under section 332.[16] The section 332 rules apply when the requirements of section 1504(a)(2) are met; that is, when the two corporations could file consolidated returns. Section 1504(a)(2) requires that the parent have 80 percent of the voting power and 80 percent of the value of the stock of the corporation. The control requirement must be met "on the date of the adoption of the plan of liquidation, and . . . at all times until the receipt of the property . . . ." I.R.C. § 332(b)(1).

---

[15] The *General Utilities* case and its repeal are discussed in § 4.02[A] of Chapter 4.

[16] Treasury Regulations provide, in part that "[s]ection 332 applies only to those cases in which the recipient corporation receives at least partial payment for the stock which it owns in the liquidating corporation." Treas. Reg. § 1.332-2(b).

Example 7.15: As in the prior two examples, Overlook, Inc. owns 90 percent of the stock (by vote and by value) of Petit Corp. As part of a plan of complete liquidation, Petit Corp. distributes to Overlook, Inc. a plot of land worth $90,000. (Assume that the other shareholder, Queens Corp., receives other assets.) Assume that Overlook, Inc. has a $70,000 basis in its stock. Overlook, Inc. does not recognize any of its $20,000 gain realized. This example is illustrated below.

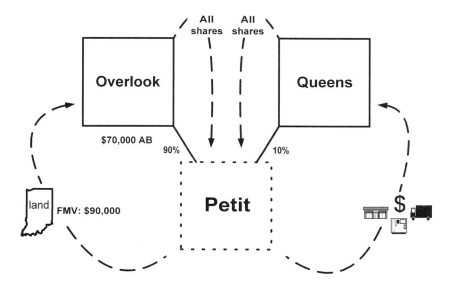

Note that section 332 does not apply to liquidation of an insolvent corporation because the worthless stock of an insolvent corporation does not constitute payment in exchange for the stock. *See* Treas. Reg. § 1.332-2(b). The Treasury Regulation directs the taxpayer to section 165(g), which applies to worthless securities.

The application of section 332 is highly favorable in most circumstances. Corporations may attempt to meet the 80-percent ownership requirements of section 332 in order to render a subsequent liquidation of a subsidiary tax-free. For example, in Revenue Ruling 75-521, 1975-2 C.B. 120, Corporation *X* was owned 50 percent by individuals and 50 percent by Corporation *Y*, but *Y* wanted to liquidate *X* in a non-taxable transaction under section 332(a). Corporation *Y* purchased all of the individuals' stock for cash so that *Y* held all of *X*'s shares. *Y* then completely liquidated *X* and received all of *X*'s property in complete cancellation of *Y*'s shares in *X*. The IRS held that *Y* met the 80-percent control requirement under section 332(b)(1), so that *Y* recognized no gain or loss on the distribution.

The ruling distinguished Revenue Ruling 70-106, 1970-1 C.B. 70, in which a 75-percent owner caused the corporation to redeem the minority shareholders' stock before liquidating the corporation. In that ruling, the corporation's redemption of the minority shares was found to be part of the plan of liquidation, so that the liquidation failed to meet the 80-percent control requirement of section 332(b)(1). By contrast, in Revenue Ruling 75-521, "the purchase of X stock by Y cannot be viewed as part of the distribution in liquidation of X because a mere sale of stock between shareholders does not constitute an adoption of a plan of liquidation." 1975-2 C.B. at 120–21.

[b]   Avoiding the Application of Section 332

A drawback of section 332 is that it renders the parent corporation's basis in the stock of the subsidiary irrelevant for tax purposes, which is unfortunate for corporations with a high basis in low value stock. Corporations in that situation may therefore try to *avoid* the application of section 332, raising the question of whether the step-transaction doctrine will apply. Two cases, one in which the taxpayer did not succeed and one in which it did, provide good illustrations of this point. *See Associated Wholesale Grocers, Inc. v. United States*, 927 F.2d 1517 (10th Cir. 1991), and *Granite Trust Co. v. United States*, 238 F.2d 670 (1st Cir. 1956).

In *Associated Wholesale Grocers*, the corporate taxpayer, Associated Wholesale Grocers, Inc., owned all of the stock of Super Market Developers, which in turn owned 99.97 percent of Weston Investment Co. (Weston). Weston owned and operated several grocery stores until 1980, when Associated Wholesale Grocers decided that it would be better for the company to have Super Market Developers own the grocery stores directly. Around that time, Thomas Elder, a manager of one of Weston's grocery stores, expressed an interest in owning the store he managed, Weston Market. *Associated Wholesale Grocers*, 927 F.2d at 1518.

Mr. Elder organized Elder Food Mart, Inc. (Elder) to purchase Weston Market from Associated. Associated and Elder then entered into two agreements that were signed (and later carried out) on the same day. Under the first agreement, Weston merged into Elder with Elder surviving and the Weston minority shareholders receiving cash from Elder for their stock. Under that agreement, Elder transferred $300,000 plus a non-interest bearing demand promissory note for $9,049,703. The second agreement was to take effect immediately after the merger and would allow Associated to repurchase all of Weston's assets except Weston Market for the amount of the promissory note plus the amount Elder paid to the minority Weston shareholders. *Id.* at 1518–19.

Associated treated the events as a taxable sale and declared a loss on the sale under section 1001(a). The IRS recharacterized the transaction as a liquidation and denied the loss under section 332. *Id.* at 1519. One of Associated's principal arguments was that although it did own 99.97 percent of Weston prior to the transaction, it did not own 80 percent continuously until the time it received Weston's assets as required under section 332(b)(1). The IRS suggested that if the court applied the step-transaction doctrine,[17] then the 80-percent ownership and value test would

---

[17] The step-transaction doctrine is discussed in § 1.04 of Chapter 4.

be continuously met. Applying the step-transaction doctrine would entail disregarding the sale to Elder and the subsequent repurchase. *Id.* at 1520–21.

Associated argued that the application of the step-transaction doctrine was barred by relevant case law, which the court rejected. Associated also cited business purposes for each step, but the court found that a business purpose did not bar the application of step-transaction analysis. The court considered the end-result test and the interdependence test (both of which are discussed in Chapter 1). *See Id.* at 1523–27.

The court found enough interdependence to apply step-transaction analysis, after looking at the termination clause and the purchase and sale clause, both in the merger agreement and the timing of the transactions. Under the termination clause, if Associated's contract to repurchase Weston's assets was terminated, then the sales contract to Elder was simultaneously terminated. The purchase and sale clause in the repurchase contract was so interdependent with the original sale contract to Elder that it referred to the assets valued at over nine million dollars solely through reference to that original sales contract. Finally, the schedule set out within the two contracts was designed so that the repurchase contract controlled the effective time of the sale to Elder and ensured that almost no time would separate the two transactions. Thus, the substance of the two transactions was found to be a sale of Weston Market to Elder for $300,000 cash and a liquidation of Weston to which section 332 applied to preclude recognition of gain or loss. *Id.* at 1527–29.

What if a corporation sells off stock to avoid the application of section 332? In *Granite Trust Co. v. United States*, 238 F.2d 670 (1st Cir. 1956), a pre-section 332 case discussed in *Associated Wholesale Grocers*, Granite Trust did just that. In that case, Granite Trust had a $1 million basis in the stock of Granite Trust Building Corporation, the sole asset of which was worth only $550,000. Granite Trust wanted to liquidate the corporation but, under section 112(b)(6) (now section 332), Granite Trust would not be able to deduct a loss because of its controlling stock interest in Granite Trust Building Corporation. *Id.* at 671.

Accordingly, Granite Trust sold some of its stock, so that, at the time Granite Trust Building Corporation was liquidated, Granite Trust owned only 79.5 percent of shares of common stock. *Id.* at 672. The IRS argued that the sales of stock should not be given effect for tax purposes for two reasons. First, the sale was "without legal or moral justification" and thus the court should consider the transaction as a complete liquidation of a subsidiary corporation, ignoring the intermediary steps. Second, it argued that there was no valid sale of stock because the stock was sold to friendly parties who knew that the corporation would be liquidated and they would get their money back within a few days. *Id.* at 674.

The court disagreed. The IRS's contention that the sales were "without legal or moral justification" was unavailing because taxpayers are free to construct transactions to minimize taxation. The court also found that "the very terms of § 112(b)(6) make it evident that it is not an 'end-result' provision, but rather one which prescribes specific conditions for the nonrecognition of realized gains or losses, conditions which, if not strictly met, make the section inapplicable." *Id.* at 675. The court also found that the fact that the sales were to friendly parties was inconsequential because legal title passed in the sale. *Id.* at 677.

[3] Minority Shareholders

Minority shareholders do not qualify for the protections of section 332. Therefore, they are governed by the rules of section 331, which were discussed above.[18]

> *Example 7.16*: Sub, Inc. is owned 85 percent by Topper, Inc., and 15 percent by Ursula. As part of a plan of complete liquidation, Sub, Inc. distributes to Ursula a plot of land worth $100,000. Ursula has a $90,000 basis in her stock. Under section 331(a), Ursula recognizes $10,000 of capital gain.

[4] Basis Rules

As is typical in nonrecognition transactions, the basis in the assets of the liquidating corporation transfers to the controlling parent corporation. Section 334(b) generally provides that "[i]f property is received by a corporate distributee in a distribution in a complete liquidation to which section 332 applies . . ., the basis of such property in the hands of such distributee shall be the same as it would be in the hands of the transferor . . . ." However, minority shareholders, because they received the property in a taxable transaction, take a fair market value basis in the property they receive. *See* I.R.C. § 334(a).

> *Example 7.17*: As in Examples 7.13 through 7.15, assume that Overlook, Inc. owns 90 percent of the stock (by vote and by value) of Petit Corp. Queens Corp. owns the remaining 10 percent of the stock of Petit Corp. As part of a plan of complete liquidation, Petit Corp. distributes to Overlook, Inc. a plot of land worth $90,000 with a basis of $60,000, and distributes to Queens Corp. equipment worth $10,000 with a basis of $8,000. Under section 337, Petit Corp. does not recognize its $30,000 gain realized on the liquidating distribution of the land. Overlook, Inc. takes a $60,000 basis in the land under section 334(b). Under section 336, Petit Corp. recognizes the $2,000 gain realized on the liquidating distribution of the equipment. Queens Corp. will take a $10,000 fair market value basis in the equipment under section 334(a).

[5] Earnings and Profits

When a corporation is liquidated, if section 332 applies, section 381 will govern the transfer of the earnings and profits to the parent corporation. Section 381 is discussed in more detail in Chapter 13.[19]

---

[18] *See* § 7.03[A][2].

[19] *See* § 13.01 of Chapter 13.

[6] Effects of Indebtedness

If a subsidiary corporation is indebted to the corporate parent that owns 80 percent or more of the subsidiary, any transfer of property to the "80-percent distributee" in satisfaction of the indebtedness is treated as a distribution to the corporate parent in the liquidation. I.R.C. § 337(b). This allows the distribution of appreciated property to avoid gain recognition under section 337(a).

If a parent corporation is indebted to its subsidiary, and the subsidiary distributes the debt instrument to the parent in liquidation, the question arises whether the unpaid debt will constitute discharge of indebtedness income for the parent. *See* I.R.C. § 61(a)(12). In general, it does not because the cancellation of indebtedness of a shareholder by a corporation is treated as a distribution of property to the shareholder. *See* Treas. Reg. § 1.301-1(m). So long as the distributing corporation is solvent, that property distribution will be tax-free under section 332. However, if the face amount of the indebtedness exceeds its adjusted basis in the hands of the subsidiary, then the IRS may require the parent to report cancellation of indebtedness income. *See* PLR 9102028. In addition, if the parent corporation had previously deducted accrued but unpaid interest that is now canceled, it might have to recognize income under the tax benefit rule. *See Hillsboro National Bank v. Commissioner*, 460 U.S. 370 (1983).

If the subsidiary is insolvent, section 332 does not apply to the liquidation because the worthless stock does not constitute "payment." *See* Treas. Reg. § 1.332-2(b). Instead, the parent may deduct its loss for the worthless stock of the subsidiary under section 165(g). However, the applicability of section 337 to the subsidiary hinges on applicability of section 332. *See* I.R.C. § 337(a). Accordingly, it appears that section 337 will not apply to the insolvent corporation.

CHART 7.1
Comparison of Taxable and Non-Taxable Complete Liquidations

Type of Liquidation	Liquidating Corporation's Tax Consequences	Shareholder's Tax Consequences	Basis Rules
Taxable	Gain realized is recognized; losses may or may not be recognized. *See* I.R.C. § 336.	Gain or loss realized is recognized. I.R.C. § 331.	Shareholders take FMV bases in assets. I.R.C. § 334(a).
Non-Taxable	Gain or loss realized on distributions to controlling parent corporation is not recognized. I.R.C. § 337.	Gain or loss realized by controlling parent corporation is not recognized. I.R.C. § 332.	Parent takes transferred bases in assets. I.R.C. § 334(b).

[7] Mirror Transactions

Treasury Regulations provide special aggregate stock ownership rules for various purposes, including section 332. *See* Treas. Reg. § 1.1502-34. That is, if two or more corporations owned by a common parent *together* own 80 percent or more of a subsidiary and file consolidated returns, they meet the ownership test of section 332.

> *Example 7.18*: V, Inc. wholly owns both W, Inc. and X, Inc. W, Inc. and X, Inc. incorporate Y Corp., with W, Inc. and X, Inc. each owning 50 percent of the stock of Y Corp. If they were subsequently to liquidate Y Corp., section 332 would apply.

This rule was used by corporations to effect, with a low tax cost, a corporate acquisition combined with a disposition of unwanted assets. The acquiring corporation would incorporate the "mirror" subsidiaries, infuse cash into them, and use them to purchase the stock of the target corporation. The acquiring subsidiaries would then liquidate the target under section 332, with the unwanted assets going to one of the subsidiaries. That subsidiary's stock would then be sold to a third party at little tax cost because the parent's stock basis would approximate the value of the assets acquired by that subsidiary.

> *Example 7.19*: Z, Inc. and ABC, Inc., which are wholly owned by DEF, Inc., use $500,000 cash furnished to each of them by DEF, Inc. to purchase all of the stock of GHI, Inc. They then liquidate GHI, Inc., with Z, Inc. taking the useful assets and ABC, Inc. taking the other assets. DEF, Inc. plans to sell the stock of ABC, Inc. for approximately $500,000, its basis in the ABC stock.

In reaction to this technique, Congress amended section 337 to provide, in part, that only distributions to a corporation that by itself owns 80 percent or more of the stock of the subsidiary escape tax. I.R.C. § 337(c). Thus, this particular technique works under current law only if the transaction is structured so that one of the subsidiaries acquires 80 percent or more of the target's stock. For instance, in Example 7.19, if Z, Inc. acquired 80 percent of GHI, Inc., and ABC, Inc. owned the remaining 20 percent, the liquidating distributions to Z, Inc. would be tax-free, but the liquidiating distributions to ABC, Inc. would be taxable to GHI, Inc. For additional variations on this type of transaction, see BITTKER & EUSTICE, *supra*, at ¶ 10.22[3].

§ 7.04 Liquidation-Reincorporation Transactions

Before *General Utilities* was overruled by statute,[20] liquidation of a corporation resulted in imposition of only one level of tax, the shareholder-level tax. Even after the repeal of *General Utilities*, however, the benefits of a taxable liquidation can be substantial. A taxable liquidation produces the following tax results: (1) capital gain or loss treatment of property

---

[20] *See* § 4.02[A] of Chapter 4.

received in return for stock, rather than section 301 distribution treatment; (2) elimination of the earnings and profits account of the liquidating corporation; (3) a fair market value basis in the property distributed, which is generally a stepped-up basis, and is particularly valuable for depreciable property; and (4) the elimination of the taint on section 306 stock. Those results make sense if the corporation in fact ceases existence. But what if the shareholders immediately incorporate a new corporation, transferring some or all of the assets of the old corporation to it in a purported section 351 transaction?

As you might imagine, the IRS has applied step-transaction doctrine analysis to determine whether a liquidation and subsequent incorporation are part of the same transaction.[21] If they are found to be part of the same transaction, the sought-after tax benefits generally disappear. Following a 1984 amendment to section 368(a)(2)(H), the IRS generally recharacterizes liquidation-reincorporations as non-divisive "D" reorganizations involving boot. Non-divisive D reorganizations are discussed in Chapter 10.

Previously, other analyses were used. For example, in Revenue Ruling 61-156, 1961-2 C.B. 62, the IRS ruled that a liquidation-reincorporation was in substance an "E" and "F" reorganization, with boot taxable as dividend income. (E and F reorganizations are discussed in Chapter 12.) In *Telephone Answering Serv. Co. v. Commissioner*, 63 T.C. 423 (1974), *aff'd per curiam*, 546 F.2d 423 (4th Cir. 1976), *cert. denied*, 431 U.S. 914 (1977), the court found that the corporation had failed to liquidate completely, resulting in gain recognition to the parent corporation on what was, in effect, the sale of a subsidiary.

§ 7.05   Taxable Acquisitions

[A]   Introduction: History and Background

There are three principal ways to acquire a company's assets: Acquire the assets directly, acquire the company's stock, or merge with the target company. But what if, following a stock acquisition, the new parent company liquidates the corporation it just acquired? In *Kimbell-Diamond Milling Co. v. Commissioner*, 14 T.C. 74 (1950), *aff'd per curiam*, 187 F.2d 718 (5th Cir.), *cert. denied*, 342 U.S. 827 (1951), Kimbell-Diamond Milling Co. (Kimbell) lost one of its mills to fire and received insurance reimbursement. Kimbell located comparable assets owned by Whaley Mill & Elevator Co. (Whaley) and purchased all of Whaley's outstanding stock for the sole purpose of acquiring its assets. Five days after the stock purchase, Kimbell caused a full liquidation of Whaley. *Id.* at 75–77.

Whaley had a higher basis in its assets than Kimbell had in the Whaley stock. Accordingly, Kimbell argued for a transferred basis from Whaley on the ground that the liquidation of Whaley qualified as a complete liquidation of a subsidiary. For Kimbell's argument to stand, the court would have

---

[21] The step-transaction doctrine is discussed in § 1.04[E] of Chapter 1.

to treat the purchase and liquidation of Whaley as two separate transactions. Instead, the court applied step-transaction analysis and determined that the two steps should be combined into one transaction whereby Kimbell purchased Whaley's *assets*. The result of combining the transactions in this way was that Kimbell obtained a cost basis in Whaley's assets, which was lower than the basis Whaley had had in the assets. *Id.* at 80.

The holding in *Kimbell-Diamond* was for the IRS but other taxpayers used it to their advantage by obtaining a high fair market value basis in assets acquired in a purchase followed by a liquidation despite the basis rules of section 334(b), which transfer basis from the liquidated corporation to the controlling parent corporation. Ultimately, Congress enacted section 338, which allows a purchasing corporation that acquires the requisite control of a target corporation to elect to treat the stock purchase as an asset acquisition, but at the price of a corporate-level tax. Although section 338 is elective, it displaces *Kimbell-Diamond* analysis.

[B] Section 338 Elections

Section 338 allows an eligible corporation to make an election to obtain what is essentially a cost basis in the assets of a purchased corporation. In return for what is generally a step-up in basis, the purchased corporation is treated as having sold the assets to itself, so that gain or loss is recognized.

[1] "Qualified Stock Purchase"

Eligibility to elect section 338 hinges on a "qualified stock purchase." A qualified stock purchase is "any transaction or series of transactions in which stock (meeting the requirements of section 1504(a)(2)) of 1 corporation is acquired by another corporation by purchase during the 12-month acquisition period." I.R.C. § 338(d)(3). Section 1504(a)(2) provides the same 80-percent control requirements that make a corporation eligible to liquidate a subsidiary tax-free. That 80-percent standard is a vote and value test. Given the background of section 338, which involved a stock acquisition followed by a tax-free liquidation in *Kimbell-Diamond*, it is not surprising that the same eligibility requirements applicable to a tax-free liquidation must be met for section 338 eligibility.

The 12-month acquisition period during which a corporation may acquire 80 percent of the stock of a target (by both vote and value) is "the 12-month period beginning with the date of the first acquisition *by purchase* of stock included in a qualified stock purchase . . . ." I.R.C. § 338(h)(1) (emphasis added). The term "purchase" is generally defined to refer to acquisitions that did not occur in a nonrecognition or transferred basis context. *See* I.R.C. § 338(h)(3).

Once the purchasing corporation has acquired the requisite 80-percent control within a 12-month period, the purchasing corporation is eligible to make a section 338 election no later than the 15th day of the ninth month beginning after the month containing the date on which 80-percent control was obtained (the "acquisition date"). *See* I.R.C. § 338(g)(1), (h)(2). Once made, the election is irrevocable. *See* I.R.C. § 338(g)(3).

In Revenue Ruling 90-95, 1990-2 C.B. 67, the IRS considered a situation in which a corporation made a qualified stock purchase of the target stock and immediately liquidated the target as part of a plan to acquire the assets of the target. The IRS treated this as a qualified stock purchase followed by a tax-free liquidation, rather than an asset acquisition under the *Kimbell-Diamond* doctrine, because section 338 replaced *Kimbell-Diamond* analysis.

More recently, in Revenue Ruling 2001-46, 2001-42 I.R.B. 321, the IRS ruled that if a newly formed, wholly owned subsidiary of an acquiring corporation merges into a target corporation, followed by a merger of the target corporation up into the acquiring corporation, pursuant to an integrated plan, the entire transaction will be treated as a reorganization under § 368(a)(1)(A) (assuming the other requirements of a reorganization are met) and will not be treated as a qualified stock purchase followed by a liquidation. Similarly, in Revenue Ruling 2004-83, 2004-32 I.R.B. 157, the IRS held that, "if, pursuant to an integrated plan, a parent corporation sells the stock of a wholly owned subsidiary for cash to another wholly owned subsidiary and the acquired subsidiary completely liquidates into the acquiring subsidiary, the transaction is treated as a reorganization under § 368(a)(1)(D)." *Id.* at 158. Reorganizations are discussed in more detail in Chapter 9 and subsequent chapters.

[2] Consistency Provisions

The Code provides that if a purchasing corporation is eligible to make a section 338 election but does not do so, it will nonetheless be deemed to make the election if it acquires any asset of the target corporation (or a target affiliate) during the "consistency period." I.R.C. § 338(e). The consistency period spans the 1-year period before the beginning of the 12-month acquisition period, the acquisition period, and the 1-year period beginning on the day after the acquisition date. *See* I.R.C. § 338(h)(4). The Code further provides for stock consistency rules where a corporation makes a section 338 election with respect to a target and also makes qualified stock purchases with respect to one or more target affiliates during the consistency period. I.R.C. § 338(f)

At the time Congress provided for the consistency rules of sections 338(e) and (f), *General Utilities* was still good law. *See* BITTKER & EUSTICE, *supra*, at ¶ 10.42[4]. When the *General Utilities* doctrine was repealed in 1986, the tax cost of a section 338 election increased. *Id.* Accordingly, Treasury regulations limit the asset consistency rules to acquisitions from subsidiaries in consolidated groups. *See* Treas. Reg. § 1.338-8(a)(2). The stock consistency rules have been "virtually abandoned, being relegated to a minor backstop role for the asset rules." BITTKER & EUSTICE, *supra*, at ¶ 10.42[4][b]; *see also* Treas. Reg. § 1.338-8(a)(2); (a)(6).

[C] Tax Consequences to Target of a Section 338 Election

If a purchasing corporation makes a section 338 election, its new subsidiary (the target corporation) is treated as having sold at fair market value all of its assets in a single transaction occurring at the close of the date on which the requisite 80-percent control was acquired (the "acquisition date"). *See* I.R.C. § 338(a)(1). This deemed sale is subject to complete recognition on the final tax return of the "old" target corporation. *See* H.R. Conf. Rep. No. 760, 97th Cong., 2d Sess. 539 (1982).

Because, in reality, the target did not sell its assets to a third party, but rather still owns them, the target is treated as a new corporation that purchased all of the assets as of the beginning of the following day.

Example 7.20: Purchasing Corp. completed a qualified stock purchase of Target Corp. on June 1, Year 1. On December 4, Year 1, it made a timely and proper section 338 election. Target Corp. is therefore deemed to have sold all of its assets at fair market value on June 1, Year 1. On that date, Target Corp. owned land worth $300,000 with a basis of $200,000, and equipment worth $50,000 with a basis of $60,000. Accordingly, Target Corp. recognizes $100,000 of gain on the land and $10,000 of loss on the equipment.

A section 338 election generally carries a fairly high tax cost; it results in immediate recognition of gains (and losses) by the subsidiary corporation. The benefit of the section 338 election is a higher asset basis, which will provide tax savings over a period of time, as assets are depreciated or sold. Tax savings over time are diluted by the time value of money. Why then would a purchasing corporation choose to make an election that results in immediate recognition of gains and losses by its new subsidiary? First, losses may exceed gains; as Example 7.20 indicates, losses are not disallowed. Second, net operating loss carryovers may be used to offset gains.

[D] Calculation and Allocation of Target Corporation's New Asset Basis

If a purchasing corporation makes a section 338 election, the *target corporation* (which still owns its old assets) will obtain an asset basis computed with reference to the amount the purchaser paid for the target stock. The aggregate asset basis will be "an amount equal to the sum of— (A) the grossed-up basis of the purchasing corporation's recently purchased stock, and (B) the basis of the purchasing corporation's nonrecently purchased stock." I.R.C. § 338(b)(1). Recently purchased stock is generally defined as stock that was purchased by the purchasing corporation during the 12-month acquisition period. Nonrecently purchased stock is all other stock in the target corporation held by the purchasing corporation on the acquisition date. Thus, the basis of previously acquired target stock is added to the grossed-up basis of stock acquired during the 12-month acquisition period.

The gross-up seeks to reflect the fact that less than 100 percent of the stock may have been acquired by the purchasing corporation in the 12-month acquisition period. Therefore, the basis of the corporation's "recently purchased stock" is "multiplied by a fraction . . . the numerator of which is 100 percent, minus the percentage of stock (by value) in the target corporation attributable to the purchasing corporation's nonrecently purchased stock, and . . . the denominator of which is the percentage of stock (by value) in the target corporation attributable to the purchasing corporation's recently purchased stock." I.R.C. § 338(b)(4). That is,

$$\text{Grossed-up basis} = \text{cost of stock} \times \frac{100\% - \% \text{ of nonrecently purchased stock}}{\% \text{ of recently purchased stock}}$$

The following example applies this formula:

Example 7.21: Purchasing Corp. completed a qualified stock purchase of Target Corp. on June 1, Year 1 by acquiring, for $900,000, 90 percent (90 shares) of Target Corp.'s stock in the 12-month acquisition period. It had not previously owned any of Target Corp.'s stock. Its grossed-up basis in the 90 shares will be $900,000 multiplied by 100/90 = $1,000,000.

In effect, the formula treats the stock held by others as having been acquired by Purchasing Corp. for the same average price as the shares that were actually purchased by Purchasing Corp. — $1,000 per share in Example 7.21.

The application of the formula is somewhat more complicated if the acquiring corporation also holds nonrecently purchased stock, as the next example illustrates:

Example 7.22: Purchasing Corp. completed a qualified stock purchase of Target, Inc. on June 1, Year 1 by acquiring, for $900,000, 90 percent (90 shares) of Target Corp.'s stock in the 12-month acquisition period. It had previously owned five percent of Target Corp.'s stock, in which it has a basis of $30,000. Its grossed-up basis *in the 90 shares* will be $900,000 multiplied by 95/90 = $950,000.

Recall that the grossed-up basis of the recently purchased stock is added to the basis of the nonrecently purchased stock. In Example 7.22, that increases the total basis to be allocated among target assets to $980,000.[22]

Alternatively, the purchasing corporation may step up its basis in the nonrecently purchased stock by making a "gain recognition election" under which it is treated as if it sold the nonrecently purchased stock on the acquisition date, recognizing gain but not loss. *See* Treas. Reg. § 1.338-5(d)(3). In general, the sale amount is deemed to be "the purchasing corporation's basis in recently purchased target stock at the beginning of the day after the acquisition date . . . multiplied by a fraction the numerator of

---

[22] In addition, under section 338(b)(2), basis is adjusted upwards for liabilities associated with the section 338 election, including tax liabilities. *See* Treas. Reg. § 1.338-5(e).

which is the percentage of target stock (by value, determined on the acquisition date) attributable to the purchasing corporation's nonrecently purchased target stock and the denominator of which is 100 percent minus the numerator amount." Treas. Reg. § 1.338-5(d)(3)(ii). The purchasing corporation's basis in the nonrecently purchased stock will then be stepped up to that amount. Treas. Reg. § 1.338-5(d)(3)(i)(B). In Example 7.22, such an election would result in a deemed sales price of $47,368 for the nonrecently purchased stock ($900,000 x 5/95). That would result in $17,368 of gain recognized but a corresponding step-up in basis.

The purchasing corporation's aggregate stock basis in the recently and nonrecently purchased stock, determined as described above (the "adjusted grossed-up basis") is then allocated among the target's assets in accordance with Treasury regulations. See I.R.C. § 338(b)(5). In general, the regulations require that the basis first be allocated to cash and cash equivalents (termed "class I assets" in the regulations). If the amount of those assets exceeds the adjusted grossed-up basis, the target immediately realizes ordinary income in an amount equal to the excess. See Treas. Reg. § 1.338-6. Next, adjusted grossed-up basis reduced for the cash and cash equivalents is allocated first by "class," and then within each class in proportion to the fair market value of the assets within that class. See id.

In general, Class II assets consist of (1) actively traded personal property, and (2) certificates of deposit and foreign currency, regardless of whether they are actively traded personal property. Class III assets generally are assets that the taxpayer marks to market at least annually for Federal income tax purposes and debt instruments (including accounts receivable), subject to certain exceptions. Class IV assets are stock in trade, inventory, and property held primarily for sale to customers in the ordinary course of the taxpayer's trade or business. Class V assets are all assets other than Class I, II, III, IV, VI, and VII assets, which would include plant and equipment. Class VI assets are all section 197 intangibles except goodwill and going concern value. Class VII assets are goodwill and going concern value. Treas. Reg. § 1.338-6(b)(2).

Example 7.23: In Example 7.22, the adjusted grossed-up basis totaled $980,000 ($950,000 + $30,000), ignoring liabilities. Assume that there were no liabilities. Assume further that Target Corp.'s assets consist of $500,000 of cash, land worth $300,000, inventory worth $100,000, and goodwill worth $100,000. The $980,000 will first be allocated to the cash (Class I). The remaining $480,000 will next be allocated the inventory (Class IV) in the amount of $100,000, giving the inventory a basis of $100,000. The remaining $380,000 will give the land (Class V) a $300,000 basis, and the goodwill (Class VII) an $80,000 basis.

[E]   The Section 338(h)(10) Election

Upon the sale of a corporate subsidiary (the target corporation), if the target corporation files a consolidated return with its selling parent corporation, or is a member of the same affiliated group, the seller group and the purchasing corporation may jointly make an election under section 338(h)(10). Under section 338(h)(10), no gain or loss is recognized by the selling group, but rather, the subsidiary is considered to have sold its assets and distributed the proceeds to its selling shareholders, in liquidation. The deemed liquidation generally will be protected by section 332. Treas. Reg. § 1.338(h)(10)-1(d)(4). The subsidiary will have an adjusted grossed-up basis in its assets determined as described above.[23] Treas. Reg. § 1.338(h)(10)-1(d)(2).

If the buyer and seller make a 338(h)(10) election, the resulting tax liability will be treated like any other liability. The seller often will agree to bear the liability. In that case, the election essentially allows the selling group to substitute gain on a deemed sale of the target's assets for the gain that would have been recognized on the sale of the target's stock. Unlike a sale of stock, the deemed asset sale results in a step-up in the basis of the target's assets. A basis step-up is valuable to the buyer, which should increase the purchase price. Thus, it may be more advantageous for the selling group to pay tax on the "inside" gain in the subsidiary's assets rather than to be taxed on "outside" gain (the gain selling shareholders would have on the sale of the subsidiary's stock).

A section 338(h)(10) election cannot be made without also making a section 338 election; a section 338(h)(10) election made by itself will deem a section 338 election made. *See* Treas. Reg. § 1.338(h)(10)-(1)(d)(3), (4). Also note that, although the 338(h)(10) election is valuable, the selling group could achieve virtually the same result by liquidating the subsidiary tax-free and then selling the target's assets. In that case, the acquiring company would obtain a cost basis in the assets it acquires, under section 1012.

---

[23] *See* § 7.05[D].

Chapter 8

THE PASS-THROUGH REGIME OF SUBCHAPTER S

§ 8.01 Introduction

Subchapter S provides a completely different tax regime from the Subchapter C regime that has been the focus of this book thus far. Unlike Subchapter C, which provides for double taxation of corporate profits, Subchapter S generally provides a single-tax, pass-through paradigm. In general, an S corporation does not routinely experience corporate-level tax.[1] *See* I.R.C. § 1363(a). Instead, taxation occurs at the shareholder level, and each tax-significant event is taxed only once.

A corporation for which an election under Subchapter S is in effect is called an "S corporation." I.R.C. § 1361(a)(1). All other corporations are termed "C corporations." I.R.C. § 1361(a)(2). Only certain corporations are eligible to elect to be taxed under Subchapter S. In particular, as discussed below, the corporation must have a limited number of shareholders, only certain types of shareholders, and may have only one class of stock. In general, an S corporation must have a calendar-year taxable year unless it establishes a business purpose for using a fiscal year.[2] I.R.C. § 1378(b).

[A] Overview of the Pass-Through Regime of Subchapter S

The general pass-through regime of Subchapter S, for an S corporation that has never been a C corporation, has three principal components. First, everything that occurs at the corporate level (income, gain, loss, deduction, or credit) passes through *pro rata* to the S corporation shareholders, even though the pass-throughs may not be accompanied by actual distributions to shareholders. Second, in general, each shareholder's stock basis is adjusted upwards for amounts included in gross income and adjusted downwards for losses. Third, distributions from the S corporation to its shareholders reduce shareholder basis. With respect to everything else, the provisions of Subchapter C apply. For example, as discussed in Chapter 7, a liquidating distribution of appreciated property to a shareholder of an S corporation will be treated as a deemed corporate sale or exchange for

---

[1] However, certain penalty taxes may be imposed on S corporations, at the corporate level, as discussed in § 8.05.

[2] As Treasury Regulation 1.1378-1(a) indicates, an S corporation may elect a different taxable year under section 444. Section 444(b) limits the taxable years that can be elected, so as to limit deferral of income. In addition, the election requires a payment under section 7519. *See* I.R.C. §§ 444(c); 7519.

fair market value, triggering the recognition of gain. *See* I.R.C. § 336(a); *see also* I.R.C. § 311(a) (taxation of gain realized on nonliquidating distributions by corporation).[3]

The principles discussed immediately above form the heart of Subchapter S with respect to S corporations that have no history as Subchapter C corporations. As discussed below, the taxation of an S corporation with a Subchapter C history is significantly more complicated.

[B] A Brief Comparison of Subchapter S with the Partnership Pass-Through Regime of Subchapter K

Subchapter S and Subchapter K of the Code (partnership taxation) both provide pass-through tax regimes. The pass-through tax regime of Subchapter S, however, is less flexible than that provided in Subchapter K. S corporations are permitted to have only one class of stock, so allocation of the corporation's tax items must be made in accordance with the shareholders' percentage ownership of the entity. Thus, there is little room for shareholders to manipulate tax consequences by funneling certain types of tax-significant items to certain shareholders. By contrast, partnerships and other entities subject to Subchapter K (such as limited liability companies) are not obligated to allocate their tax attributes on a *pro rata* basis. Rather, these entities may allocate their tax items in any manner to which they agree, provided those allocations have substantial economic effect. *See* I.R.C. § 704(b). Given the vast degree of flexibility afforded to taxpayers under Suchapter K, the Treasury Department promulgated detailed regulations designed to prevent taxpayers from making allocations that had no meaningful economic impact apart from reducing their tax liabilities. *See* Treas. Reg. § 1.704-1(b)(2). As a result, Subchapter K is significantly more complicated than Subchapter S.[4]

Another important difference between the Subchapter S and Subchapter K tax regimes is that, under Subchapter S, a shareholder generally can deduct losses only to the extent of the sum of the shareholder's adjusted basis in his or her stock in the S corporation and in any indebtedness of the S corporation to that shareholder, I.R.C. § 1366(d)(1). By contrast, although a partner in a partnership generally may only deduct losses to the extent of the partner's basis in the partnership interest, I.R.C. § 704(d), a partner receives basis in the partnership interest for that partner's share of partnership liabilities, I.R.C. §§ 722; 752(a). Thus, indebtedness of an S corporation only increases a shareholder's basis if the indebtedness is to that shareholder, while partnership indebtedness increases a partner's basis to the extent of the partner's share of that debt. "Because outside basis

---

[3] Section 311(a) is discussed in Chapter 4. *See* § 4.02[A].

[4] An explanation of Subchapter K is beyond the scope of this book. For further reading about Subchapter K, see JEROLD A. FRIEDLAND, UNDERSTANDING PARTNERSHIP AND LLC TAXATION (2d ed. 2003); LAURA E. CUNNINGHAM AND NÖEL B. CUNNINGHAM, THE LOGIC OF SUBCHAPTER K: A CONCEPTUAL GUIDE TO THE TAXATION OF PARTNERSHIPS (2d ed. 2000).

serves as a limit on the amount of the corporation's losses that a shareholder can take into account, the absence of a basis increase for firm liabilities under subchapter S is a factor that can influence participants in business ventures that rely on third-party financing, particularly those in startup ventures with initial losses, to select a form of business organization eligible for the regime of subchapter K." Bruce A. McGovern, *Liabilities of the Firm, Member Guaranties, and the At Risk Rules: Some Practical and Policy Considerations*, 7 J. SMALL & EMERGING BUS. L. 63, 75 (2003) (footnote omitted).

§ 8.02   Eligibility for S Corporation Status

To be eligible for taxation as an S corporation, a corporation must qualify as a "small business corporation," which means that it must be a domestic corporation; it can have no more than 100 shareholders; all of the shareholders must be individuals, estates, trusts, and/or certain exempt organizations; it cannot have a nonresident alien as a shareholder; the corporation may not have more than one class of stock; and it must not be an "ineligible corporation." I.R.C. §§ 1361(b)(1), 1362(a)(1). These restrictions are discussed further below.

[A]   Restrictions on the Number of Shareholders

Under current law, an S corporation can have no more than 100 shareholders. I.R.C. § 1361(b)(1)(A). For this purpose, a husband and wife (and their estates) are considered a single shareholder. I.R.C. § 1361(c)(1)(A)(i). In addition, an election may be made by any member of a family to treat all the "members of the family" as one shareholder. I.R.C. § 1361(c)(1)(A)(ii). The term "members of the family" generally is defined as "the common ancestor, lineal descendants of the common ancestor, and the spouses (or former spouses) of such lineal descendants or common ancestor."[5] I.R.C. § 1361(c)(1)(B)(i).

Example 8.1: The shares of X, Inc. are owned by Alice; Bob, who is Alice's husband; the Cone family (grandmother, son, and son's three children); and 98 unrelated individuals. Alice and Bob are treated as one shareholder for purposes of the 100-shareholder limitation applicable to small business corporations. The five members of the Cone family will be treated as separate shareholders unless any member of the Cone family elects to have the Cone family taxed as one shareholder. If any member of the Cone family makes such an election, X, Inc. will be considered to have a total of 100 shareholders for purposes of qualifying as a small business corporation.

---

[5] "[A]n individual shall not be considered a common ancestor if, as of the later of the effective date of this paragraph or the time the election under section 1362(a) is made, the individual is more than 6 generations removed from the youngest generation of shareholders who would (but for this clause) be members of the family." I.R.C. § 1361(c)(1)(B)(ii).

Also note that S corporations may form partnerships with other S corporations without terminating their Subchapter S elections. *See* Rev. Rul. 94-43, 1994-2 C.B. 198. Nonetheless, the cap on the number of allowable shareholders imposes a limitation on the use of the Subchapter S paradigm that provides administrative simplicity. *See id.* The permissible number of shareholders has increased over the years, which has reduced the importance of this limitation.

[B]   Types of Permitted Shareholders

An S corporation may only have certain types of shareholders: individuals, estates, certain trusts, and certain exempt organizations. *See* I.R.C. § 1361(b)(1)(B). An S corporation may not have a nonresident alien shareholder, I.R.C. § 1361(b)(1)(C); under the rules applicable to nonresident aliens, they may escape shareholder-level tax, which would eliminate federal income tax entirely, rather than reducing it to a single level.

In general, the trusts that may hold stock in an S corporation are (1) a "grantor trust" of an individual who is a citizen or resident of the United States; (2) such a trust two years after the death of that individual; (3) a trust holding the stock under the terms of a will, but only for two years after it receives the stock; (4) a voting trust; (5) a qualified Subchapter S trust; and (6) an electing small business trust. Foreign trusts do not qualify. I.R.C. § 1361(c)(2). Section 1361(c)(2) further provides how these trusts are treated for purposes of the limitation on the permitted number of shareholders. For example, in the case of a voting trust, each beneficiary of the trust is treated as a shareholder. I.R.C. § 1361(c)(2)(B)(iv).

A qualified Subchapter S trust is treated as a grantor trust, and therefore may hold stock in an S corporation. *See* I.R.C. § 1361(d)(1)(A). In order to constitute a qualified Subchapter S trust, the trust must contain terms requiring that: (1) all of the income from the trust will be distributed to the current income beneficiary; (2) during the current income beneficiary's lifetime, discretionary distributions of trust corpus will be made only to such beneficiary; (3) the income interest of the current income beneficiary will terminate on the beneficiary's death or the termination of the trust, whichever is earlier; (4) if the trust ends during the life of that beneficiary, the trust will distribute all of its assets to that beneficiary. *See* I.R.C. § 1361(d)(3).

An electing small business trust is a trust that is eligible to make a proper election, and the trustee of which has made the election. The following trusts are ineligible to make the election: (1) a qualified Subchapter S trust; (2) any trust exempt from tax under subtitle A of the Code; and (3) a charitable remainder annuity trust or a charitable remainder unitrust (defined in Code section 664(d)). I.R.C. § 1361(e). In general, an eligible trust may have as its only beneficiaries (1) individuals, estates, not-for-profit organizations described in section 170(c)(2)–(5), and (2) organizations described in section 170(c)(1) that hold only contingent interests in the trust and are not potential current beneficiaries. I.R.C. § 1361(e)(1)(A)(i). In addition, no interest in the trust can have been acquired by purchase. I.R.C. § 1361(e)(1)(A)(ii).

One of the primary benefits of an electing small business trust is its flexibility as an estate-planning vehicle. Whereas a qualified Subchapter S trust must have only one current income beneficiary to whom all of the trust income is distributed, an electing small business trust can authorize the trustee to distribute as much of the income of the trust as the trustee deems appropriate among a class of potential beneficiaries. In exchange for this added flexibility, the income of an electing small business trust is subject to tax at the highest marginal rate applicable to trusts. *See* I.R.C. § 641(c)(2)(A).

The exempt organizations that may hold stock in an S corporation are those exempt from taxation under section 501(a) and that are either (1) trusts described in section 401(a) (one that forms part of a pension, stock bonus or profit-sharing plan), or (2) not-for-profit organizations exempt from taxation under section 501(c)(3) of the Code. I.R.C. § 1361(c)(6).

[C] "One Class of Stock" Rule

An important limit on S corporations is that they may have only one class of stock. This means that the stock must have identical rights both to distributions and liquidation proceeds. Treas. Reg. § 1.1361-1(*l*)(1). The "one class of stock" limitation ensures both a simple tax regime and limited opportunities for manipulating tax consequences. The relevant factors in making the "one class of stock" determination all relate to the parties' economic rights to operating or liquidating distributions. Differences in voting rights, on the other hand, are disregarded in determining whether an S corporation has more than one class of stock. *See* I.R.C. § 1361(c)(4).

Example 8.2: All of the voting common stock of Y Corporation is owned by Father and Mother. They decide to make their children shareholders in the company. If Y Corporation were to issue non-voting common stock to the children, that would not preclude an election under Subchapter S. Alternatively, if the children were issued preferred stock in Y Corporation, Y Corporation would not qualify as a small business corporation and therefore would not be eligible to make an election under Subchapter S.

As discussed in Chapter 3, at times, purported debt of a corporation may be reclassified as equity by the IRS or a court. Any instrument, whether designated as debt or not, is treated as a second class of stock if it "constitutes equity or otherwise results in the holder being treated as the owner of stock under general principles of Federal tax law" and has a principal purpose of circumventing either (1) the rights to distribution or liquidation proceeds conferred by the outstanding shares of stock, or (2) the limitation on eligible shareholders. Treas. Reg. § 1.1361-1(*l*)(4)(ii). Convertible debt, call options, warrants, and similar instruments may also constitute a second class of stock. *See* I.R.C. § 1.1361-1(*l*)(4). The presence of such an instrument precludes an S election and terminates an existing S election, as discussed below.

Example 8.3: Z Corporation is seeking to make an election under Subchapter S. It has both common stock outstanding and "preferred payment notes." Recently, Z Corporation reached a settlement with the IRS that reflects that the preferred payment notes are actually equity, not debt, and that a principal purpose of issuing the preferred payment notes was to circumvent the limitation on eligible shareholders. Accordingly, Z corporation is not a small business corporation.

Code section 1361(c)(5) mitigates the risk that purported debt will be deemed equity with a safe harbor that prevents "straight debt" from being reclassified as equity and thus a second class of stock. Straight debt is defined as:

> any written unconditional promise to pay on demand or on a specified date a sum certain in money if—
>
>> (i) the interest rate (and interest payment dates) are not contingent on profits, the borrower's discretion, or similar factors,
>>
>> (ii) there is no convertibility (directly or indirectly) into stock, and
>>
>> (iii) the creditor is an individual (other than a nonresident alien), an estate, a trust described in paragraph (2), or a person which is actively and regularly engaged in the business of lending money.

I.R.C. § 1361(c)(5)(B).

In addition to the safe harbor in the Code, Treasury Regulations provide two additional safe harbors:

> (1) <u>Certain short-term unwritten advances</u>: "Unwritten advances from a shareholder that do not exceed $10,000 in the aggregate at any time during the taxable year of the corporation, are treated as debt by the parties, and are expected to be repaid within a reasonable time are not treated as a second class of stock for that taxable year, even if the advances are considered equity under general principles of Federal tax law."
>
> (2) <u>Proportionately held obligations</u>: "Obligations of the same class that are considered equity under general principles of Federal tax law, but are owned solely by the owners of, and in the same proportion as, the outstanding stock of the corporation, are not treated as a second class of stock. Furthermore, an obligation or obligations owned by the sole shareholder of a corporation are always held proportionately to the corporation's outstanding stock."

Treas. Reg. § 1.1361-1(*l*)(4)(B). These safe harbors reflect the practical reality that these types of debt do not pose significant potential for the abuse that could result if an S corporation had multiple classes of equity holders with different interests in the corporation.

[D] Ineligible Corporations

Certain corporations are ineligible to be taxed under Subchapter S. Those are financial institutions that use the reserve method of accounting for bad debts; insurance companies subject to tax under Subchapter L of the Code; corporations to which an election under section 936 applies; and Domestic International Sales Corporations (DISCs) and former DISCs.

§ 8.03   Election, Revocation, and Termination of S Status

[A] Election

A small business corporation—a corporation that meets all of the requirements listed above—is eligible to elect to be taxed under Subchapter S. *See* I.R.C. §§ 1361(b)(1), 1362(a)(1). The election requires the consent of all persons who are shareholders of the corporation on the day on which the election is made. I.R.C. § 1362(a)(2). The election may be made for any taxable year (1) at any time during the preceding taxable year, or (2) at any time during the taxable year and on or before the 15th day of the third month of the taxable year in question. I.R.C. § 1362(b)(1).

Example 8.4: Small, Inc. is a calendar-year small business corporation. It meets the requirements for eligibility under Subchapter S from January 1, Year 1, on. On February 5, Year 1, with the consent of all of its shareholders, Small, Inc. makes an election under section 1362. The Subchapter S election will be effective as of January 1, Year 1.

The Secretary of the Treasury has authority to treat untimely elections as timely if he determines that there was "reasonable cause" for the failure to make a timely election. I.R.C. § 1362(b)(5). In addition, if a corporation makes a Subchapter S election for a taxable year on or before the 15th day of the third month of that year, but either failed to qualify to make the election at the time it was made, or did not have the consent of all of its shareholders at the time, then the election will be treated as made for the following taxable year if the failure has been corrected by the time of the following year. *See* I.R.C. § 1362(b)(2).

Example 8.5: D Corp. is a calendar-year small business corporation. On February 5, Year 1, with the consent of all but one of its shareholders, it makes an election under section 1362. That shareholder consented to the election later in Year 1. The Subchapter S election will be treated as made for Year 2.

Note that a history as a Subchapter C corporation does not preclude an S election, so long as the C corporation meets the requirements necessary to constitute a small business corporation. However, because of the risk that C corporations with large earnings and profits accounts might make S elections to avoid Subchapter C treatment of earnings and profits, special rules, discussed below,[6] apply to S corporations with accumulated earnings and profits.[7]

Section 1362(f) allows the IRS to waive certain inadvertent defects in a Subchapter S election. Section 1362(f) addresses, in part, the situation in which a corporation's Subchapter S election was not effective for the taxable year for which it was made because of a failure to meet all of the eligibility requirements of section 1361(b) or to obtain the required shareholder consents. In that situation, if (1) the IRS determines that the circumstances that resulted in the ineffectiveness of the election were inadvertent; (2) within a reasonable period after the discovery of those circumstances, steps were taken to make the corporation a small business corporation; and (3) the corporation, as well as each person who was a shareholder of the corporation at any time during the relevant period, agrees to make appropriate adjustments specified by the IRS, then the corporation is treated as an S corporation during the period specified by the IRS. Section 1362(f) also applies to inadvertent *terminations* of a Subchapter S election, and is discussed in that regard below.[8]

[B] Termination

A Subchapter S election can terminate for several reasons: (1) the shareholders revoke the election; (2) the corporation ceases to qualify as a small business corporation; or (3) a corporation with accumulated earnings and profits (from a Subchapter C history or tax-free acquisition of a C corporation) has excess passive investment income. *See* I.R.C. § 1362(d).

[1] Termination by Revocation

A Subchapter S election may be revoked "if shareholders holding more than one-half of the shares of stock of the corporation on the day on which the revocation is made consent to the revocation." I.R.C. § 1362(d)(1). In general, a revocation made on or before the 15th day of the third month of a taxable year is effective retroactive to the first day of that taxable year. I.R.C. § 1362(d)(1)(C)(i). A revocation made after the 15th day of the third month of a year takes effect on the first day of the following taxable year. I.R.C. § 1362(d)(1)(C)(ii). However, if the revocation specifies a date for revocation on or after the day on which the revocation is made, the revocation becomes effective on the specified date. I.R.C. § 1362(d)(1)(D).

Example 8.6: Echo, Inc. is a calendar-year small business corporation. On March 1, Year 4, with the consent of holders of 60 percent of its shares, it revokes its Subchapter S election. The revocation takes effect as of January 1, Year 4, unless the revocation document specifies a revocation date after March 1, Year 4.

---

[6] *See* § 8.04[C][2].

[7] Earnings and profits and the tax treatment of distributions under Subchapter C are discussed in Chapter 4.

[8] *See* § 8.03[B][4].

[2] Termination by Ceasing to Qualify as a Small Business Corporation

In general, a Subchapter S election terminates immediately whenever a corporation ceases to be a small business corporation. I.R.C. § 1362(d)(2). This rule buttresses the requirements for election of Subchapter S by making those requirements mandatory even after election. In effect, this means that a single shareholder can terminate a Subchapter S election simply by transferring one share to an impermissible shareholder, such as a nonresident alien. *But cf. A.W. Chesterton Co. v. Chesterton*, 128 F.3d 1 (1st Cir. 1997) (affirming district court's grant of injunction enjoining minority shareholder from transferring S corporation stock to two shell corporations because that would have terminated the Subchapter S election, resulting in financial loss to the corporation, in violation of what court found to be fiduciary duty of shareholders in a closely held corporation). It is wise to provide with respect to S corporation stock transfer restrictions, such as a right of first refusal on the part of the corporation and a provision invalidating any transfer in violation of that right. *Cf.* Treas. Reg. § 1.1361-1(*l*)(2)(iii)(A). Such restrictions limit the risk that a transfer to an ineligible shareholder will terminate the S election. If the other shareholders act quickly after learning of the transfer, it might be treated as an inadvertent termination, which the IRS can waive, as discussed below.[9] *See* I.R.C. § 1362(f).

[3] Termination Based on Excess Passive Investment Income

A corporation will have its S election terminated if its passive investment income exceeds 25 percent of gross receipts for three consecutive taxable years during which it is an S corporation, and it has accumulated earnings and profits at the close of each of those three taxable years. I.R.C. § 1362(d)(3)(A)(i), (iii). (The presence of accumulated earnings and profits means that the S corporation has a Subchapter C history or acquired a C corporation in a transaction resulting in a carryover of earnings and profits under section 381.) The termination takes effect on the first day of the first taxable year beginning after the third consecutive taxable year. I.R.C. § 1362(d)(3)(A)(ii).

In general, passive investment income is "gross receipts derived from royalties, rents, dividends, interest, annuities, and sales or exchanges of stock or securities (gross receipts from such sales or exchanges being taken into account for purposes of this paragraph only to the extent of gains therefrom)." I.R.C. § 1362(d)(3)(C)(i). However, there is an exception for interest on notes from sales of inventory. *See* I.R.C. § 1362(d)(3)(C)(ii). In addition, for lending and finance companies that meet the requirements of section 542(c)(6) for the taxable year, passive investment income does not include gross receipts that are derived directly from the active and

---

[9] *See* § 8.03[B][4].

regular conduct of the lending or finance business. *See* I.R.C. § 1362(d)(3)(C)(iii). There are a number of other special rules, as well. *See generally* I.R.C. § 1362(d). Note also that, as discussed below, a corporate-level tax applies to S corporations with "excess net passive income."[10]

[4] Inadvertent Terminations

Code section 1362(f), which was discussed above in connection with inadvertent failures to meet the requirements of a Subchapter S election, also allows the IRS to waive certain inadvertent terminations of an S election. Section 1362(f) applies to terminations of Subchapter S status resulting from the corporation (1) ceasing to qualify as a small business corporation, or (2) exceeding the passive investment income limitation. *See* I.R.C. § 1362(f)(1). In those situations, if (1) the IRS determines that the circumstances resulting in termination were inadvertent; (2) within a reasonable period of time after discovery of the circumstances resulting in the termination, steps were taken so that the corporation is a small business corporation, and (3) each person who was a shareholder of the corporation at any time during the period in question, agrees to make the appropriate adjustments required by the IRS with respect to that period, then the corporation will be treated as continuing to be an S corporation during the period specified by the IRS.

As indicated above, the IRS may be willing to treat an intentional termination by a single shareholder as an inadvertent termination. For example, in PLR 9733002, Father and Son each held shares in an S corporation, X, but disagreed about continuing the business operated by X. Of his own accord, Son organized a wholly owned corporation, C Corp., and attempted to transfer all of his X stock to C Corp., in order to terminate X's Subchapter S election. Because Son had not offered the stock to X, the transfer violated an agreement that gave X a right of first refusal on transfers of its stock. The agreement provided, in part, that no transfer of stock "shall be effective" without first offering it to X.

Son notified the IRS of the transfer of shares. The IRS accordingly notified X that its S election had terminated. X's attorney and accountant then began negotiations with Son for Father to acquire Son's transferred shares. Ultimately, the parties entered into an agreement under which Son transferred all of his stock in X to Father. X then sought relief under section 1362(f). It represented that under applicable state law, Son's attempted transfer of X stock to C Corp. was void.

The IRS ruled that, because, under the terms of the agreement and applicable state law, Son's attempted transfer was void, X's Subchapter S election did not terminate with the transfer. In accordance with this ruling, the IRS required that X and all of its current and prior shareholders, including Son, treat X as having been an S corporation from the date of the attempted transfer through the date of the ruling. In addition, for the

---

[10] *See* § 8.05[B].

same period, they had to treat Son as the owner of the shares that he attempted to transfer to C Corp. That required that the parties amend within 60 days any prior tax returns that were inconsistent with that treatment.

§ 8.04   Tax Treatment of S Corporation Shareholders

[A]   Calculation of Taxable Income

The taxable income of an S corporation is computed in the same manner as in the case of an individual, with certain exceptions. *See* I.R.C. § 1363(b). First, certain items are separately stated, as discussed below. Second, deductions listed in section 703(a)(2) (such as personal exemptions, the deduction for taxes paid, and the charitable contribution deduction) are not allowed. Third, section 248 (regarding organizational expenditures) applies. Finally, section 291 (relating to corporate preference items) applies if the S corporation or any predecessor corporation was a C corporation for any of the three prior tax years. I.R.C. § 1363(b)(1)–(4). Note that because the income of an S corporation is computed like that of an individual, special corporate deductions, such as the dividends received deduction of section 243, do not apply. That protects the single layer of tax applicable to an S corporation and its shareholders.

[B]   Pass-Through of Items

[1]   General Rules

The pass-through of items from the S corporation to its shareholders is a key feature of Subchapter S. Section 1366 requires that a shareholder take into account the shareholder's *daily pro rata share* of the corporation's items of income, loss, deduction, or credit the separate treatment of which could affect the tax liability of any shareholder, and the remaining, nonseparately computed, income or loss. I.R.C. § 1366(a)(1). Character of all items passes directly through to shareholders. I.R.C. § 1366(b). The items are taken into account by the shareholder in the taxable year of the shareholder in which the taxable year of the S corporation ends. I.R.C. § 1366(a)(1).

Example 8.7: F, Inc., a calendar-year S corporation, has two equal shareholders, Gina and Harold. Gina has a $500 basis in her stock, and Harold has a $200 basis in his stock. In Year 1, F, Inc. has $100 of ordinary income and $80 of capital gain. Gina and Harold must each report $50 of ordinary income and $40 of capital gain on their Year 1 returns.

If stock in an S corporation becomes worthless, the items of loss and deduction will pass through and reduce shareholder basis in stock and debt before application of sections 165(g) (worthless stock deduction) or 166(d) (nonbusiness bad debts). I.R.C. § 1367(b)(3).

[2] Election to Terminate Taxable Year

As discussed above and illustrated in Example 8.7, section 1366 provides that each shareholder is taxed based on the shareholder's daily *pro rata* share of separately computed items and nonseparately computed income or loss. That means that if a shareholder owns 50 percent of the stock in an S corporation for half of the S corporation's tax year, the shareholder is taxed based on one quarter of each separately computed item and nonseparately computed income or loss.

> *Example 8.8*: At the beginning of the year, Ink, Inc., a calendar-year S corporation, has two equal shareholders, Julia and Ken. Halfway through Year 1, Ken sells all of his shares in Ink, Inc. to Lisa. In Year 1, Ink, Inc. has $100 of ordinary income and $80 of capital gain. Julia must report $50 of ordinary income and $40 of capital gain on her return. Ken and Lisa must each report $25 of ordinary income and $20 of capital gain on their Year 1 returns.

This general rule creates risks for departing shareholders because, if the corporation has a substantial gain after the shareholders sells the shares, the selling shareholder will be taxed on a share of the gain without having the opportunity for future distributions from the corporation. The purchasing shareholder may also face taxation with respect to events that occurred while he or she was not a shareholder—that is, based on past events. Accordingly, the Code provides an opportunity for the affected shareholders—the seller and all those who purchased shares from the seller—and the corporation to join in an election to bifurcate the taxable year with respect to the buying and selling shareholders on the date of sale. *See* I.R.C. § 1377(a)(2). The result of the election is that the buyer and seller are each taxed only on events that occurred while he or she actually held shares in the corporation. Consider again the facts of Example 8.8:

> *Example 8.9*: At the beginning of the year, Ink, Inc., an S corporation, has two equal shareholders, Julia and Ken. Halfway through Year 1, Ken sells all of his shares in Ink, Inc. to Lisa. In Year 1, Ink, Inc. has $100 of ordinary income and $80 of capital gain. Assume that all of the ordinary income and capital gain are earned in the second half of the year and that Ken, Lisa, and Ink, Inc. make an election under Code section 1377. Julia must report $50 of ordinary income and $40 of capital gain on her return. Ken will not have any income with respect to Ink, Inc. Lisa must report $50 of ordinary income and $40 of capital gain on her return.

[3] Limitation on Deductions

The deduction by shareholders of expenses and losses of the S corporation is limited to their investments in the corporation. That is, the Code precludes the deduction of amounts that exceed the sum of the shareholder's adjusted basis in his or her stock in the S corporation and his or her basis in any indebtedness of the S corporation to him or her, I.R.C. § 1366(d)(1), which, in general, is the amount lent to the corporation. Any deduction that is disallowed under this rule may be carried forward indefinitely. I.R.C. § 1366(d)(2).

Example 8.10: M, Inc., an S corporation, has two shareholders, Nancy and Oscar. Nancy has a $300 basis in her stock, and Oscar has a $200 basis in his stock. M, Inc. has no indebtedness to its shareholders. In Year 1, M, Inc. has a $600 ordinary loss. Nancy may deduct $300 of the loss. Oscar may deduct $200 of the loss and carry forward a $100 loss until he has basis to support a further deduction.

Does a guarantee of a debt of the corporation create shareholder basis in indebtedness? In *Selfe v. United States*, 778 F.2d 769 (11th Cir. 1985), Jane B. Selfe (Selfe) offered stock in Avondale Mills Corporation to a bank as consideration for a line of credit that she subsequently used to build her own incorporated retail business, Jane Simon, Inc. After the incorporation of Selfe's retail business as an S corporation, the bank requested that all loans made to the taxpayer be converted to corporate loans. The bank retained the pledged stock as collateral and retained its right to collect against Selfe as the guarantor of the loan if the corporation defaulted. Even though Jane Simon, Inc. never defaulted on its loan payments, it suffered operating losses from 1977 though 1980. In 1980, Selfe and her husband, the sole shareholders of the corporation, deducted the year's operating loss from their gross income on their joint income tax returns. The IRS disallowed a deduction in excess of Selfe's original basis in the stock and determined a tax deficiency. The issue was whether Selfe was able to increase the adjusted basis of her stock by the full amount of the debt. *Id.* at 770–71.

Selfe argued that the bank should be deemed to have made the loan directly to her and that she should be deemed, in turn, to have loaned the proceeds to Jane Simon, Inc. *Id.* at 771. The IRS countered that the form of the transaction should be respected. The Eleventh Circuit concluded that "a shareholder who has guaranteed a loan to a Subchapter S corporation may increase her basis where the facts demonstrate that, in substance, the shareholder has borrowed funds and subsequently advanced them to her corporation." *Id.* at 773. The court also found that a shareholder's guarantee of a loan to a corporation may be treated for tax purposes as an equity investment in situations "where the lender looks to the shareholder as the primary obligor." *Id.* at 774. The testimony of the loan officer supported this finding because he testified that the bank had "looked primarily to the taxpayer and not the corporation for repayment of the loan." In addition, the bank had initially loaned $120,000 to Selfe, secured by her personal stock in another corporation. *Id.* However, the court also noted that it was the bank that had requested that the line of credit be converted to a loan to the corporation. The Court of Appeals therefore found that summary judgment in favor of the IRS was not appropriate, and remanded to the district court for a determination of whether the bank primarily looked to Selfe for the repayment, which would allow an increase in her basis to the full amount of the debt, and then for the application of the multi-factor test of *In re Lane*, 742 F.2d 1311 (11th Cir. 1984),[11] to determine whether the loan guarantee actually amounted to an equity investment in the corporation. *Id.* at 775.

Compare *Selfe* to *Estate of Leavitt v. Commissioner*, 875 F.2d 420 (4th Cir.), *cert. denied*, 493 U.S. 958 (1989). In *Estate of Leavitt*, shareholders of VAFLA, an S corporation, claimed deductions that reflected the corporation's operating losses during 1979 through 1981. The IRS disallowed the deductions in excess of the shareholders' original basis in their shares, and determined a deficiency in that amount. The shareholders argued that because they had signed a guarantee agreement creating joint and several liability for the corporation's debt, they should be treated as having received a loan from the bank and subsequently loaned that amount personally to the corporation. To support their argument, they noted that VAFLA's liabilities exceeded its assets, and thus the corporation had no assets to use as collateral for the loan. *Id.* at 421–22.

The Fourth Circuit determined that the loan guarantee by the shareholders did not satisfy the requirement that there be an economic outlay, and thus the issue of whether any outlay should be characterized as debt or equity was irrelevant. *Id.* at 422. In distinguishing *Selfe*, the Fourth Circuit agreed with the Tax Court that " 'a shareholder's guarantee of a loan to a Subchapter S corporation may not be treated as an equity investment in the corporation absent an economic outlay by the shareholder.' " *Id.* at 426 (quoting the Tax Court's opinion below). The Fourth Circuit disagreed with the Eleventh Circuit's determination that "debt-equity principles must be applied to resolve the question of whether the bank actually lent the money to the taxpayer/shareholder or the corporation . . . ." *Id.* at 427. The court also noted that although the corporation's financial statements and records indicated that the loan was from the shareholders, there was no constructive income taxed to the shareholders when the corporation made such loan payments. Moreover, the court noted that if the corporation had had operating profits, rather than losses, the shareholders would be making the opposite argument so as to avoid income under the principles of *Old Colony Trust Co. v. Commissioner*, 279 U.S. 716 (1929). *Id.* at 424.

Thus, because the shareholders had not been called upon to repay any portion of the loan, they had not engaged in any economic outlay. If, however, the corporation had defaulted on the loan and the shareholders had made the loan payments, then the payments actually made would increase their bases, allowing for a higher deduction of operating losses under section 1374. *Id.* at 422–23.

---

[11] *In re Lane* and the thirteen-factor test it used to distinguish debt from equity are discussed in Chapter 3. *See* § 3.03[B].

[C] Treatment of Distributions

[1] S Corporations with no Earnings and Profits

An S corporation will only have earnings and profits if it has a Subchapter C history or acquired a C corporation in a non-taxable transaction. In the absence of earnings and profits, distributions to shareholders by an S corporation generally are tax-free. More specifically, distributions are first treated as a return of capital, to the extent of the shareholder's stock basis. I.R.C. § 1368(b)(1). Any excess over shareholder basis is treated as gain from the sale or exchange of the stock. *See* I.R.C. § 1368(b)(2).

Example 8.11: Pine Corp., an S corporation, has two equal shareholders, Quincy and Ron. Quincy has a $300 basis in his stock, and Ron has a $150 basis in his stock. In Year 1, Pine Corp. distributes $200 to each shareholder. Quincy has no gross income from the distribution. Ron has $50 of capital gain. In addition, as discussed below, each shareholder's basis is reduced by the amount treated as a return of capital.

As a general rule, basis adjustments to stock are made in the following order:[12]

(1) Any increase in basis attributable to income items, and excess depletion deductions;

(2) Any decrease in basis attributable to a distribution by the corporation;

(3) Any decrease in basis attributable to noncapital, nondeductible expenses, and the oil and gas depletion deduction; and

(4) Any decrease in basis attributable to items of loss or deduction.

See Treas. Reg. § 1.1367-1(f). Basis in debt is only reduced after stock basis is reduced to zero. I.R.C. § 1367(b)(2)(A). This reduces the instances in which a shareholder of an S corporation will realize gross income when the principal of a shareholder loan is repaid by the corporation.

[2] S Corporations with Earnings and Profits

An S corporation with accumulated earnings and profits must maintain an "accumulated adjustments account," as explained below, for the most recent continuous period during which the corporation has been an S corporation. *See* I.R.C. § 1368(c). A distribution to shareholders is analyzed in three parts:

(1) The portion of the distribution that does not exceed the accumulated adjustments account is treated first as a return of capital, and then, after all basis is recovered, the rest is taxed as a sale or exchange of property. *See* I.R.C. § 1368(c)(1).

---

[12] These rules apply to taxable years beginning on or after August 18, 1998. For ordering rules applicable to taxable years beginning before January 1, 1997, see Treas. Reg. § 1.1367-1(e), (g).

(2)   Any excess of the distribution over the amount in the accumulated adjustments account is taxed as a dividend to the extent it does not exceed the accumulated earnings and profits of the S corporation. *See* I.R.C. § 1368(c)(2).

(3)   The remainder of the distribution, if any, is treated first as a return of capital, and then, after all basis is recovered, is treated as a sale or exchange of property by the shareholder. *See* I.R.C. § 1368(c)(3).

Example 8.12: Small Corp., an S corporation that used to be a C corporation, has two equal shareholders, Tom and Ursula. Tom has a $60 basis in his stock, and Ursula has a $30 basis in her stock. Small Corp. has an accumulated adjustments account of $300 from its years as an S corporation and accumulated earnings and profits of $80 from its years as a C corporation. Small Corp. distributes $200 to each shareholder. $150 of each distribution is treated as coming out of the accumulated adjustments account, reducing it to zero. For Tom, the $150 is a $60 return of capital and $90 of capital gain. For Ursula, the $150 provides a $30 return of capital and $120 of capital gain. Each shareholder's basis is thereby reduced to zero. Of the remaining $50 distributed to each shareholder, $40 is a dividend for each shareholder, which reduces Small Corp.'s accumulated earnings and profits to zero. The remaining $10 received by each shareholder is taxed as capital gain.

An accumulated adjustments account is an account of the S corporation that begins with a zero balance. Treas. Reg. § 1.1368-2(a)(1). From the date the S election is effective, the account is adjusted upwards for items of gross income and downward for deductions and corporate expenses that are not deductible but are not capital expenditures. I.R.C. § 1368(e)(1)(A). However, no reduction is made for federal taxes attributable to any taxable year in which the corporation was taxed under Subchapter C. *Id.* Thus, the accumulated adjustments account generally reflects events that occurred while the corporation was an S corporation, rather than a C corporation. In the case of a redemption that is taxed as an exchange under section 302(a) or 303(a), the adjustment in the accumulated adjustments account is the proportion that equals the proportion of shares redeemed. *See* I.R.C. § 1368(e)(1)(B).

The accumulated adjustments account can be reduced below zero, I.R.C. § 1368(e)(1)(A), but not as a result of distributions, Treas. Reg. § 1.1368-2(a)(3)(D)(iii). In addition, "[e]xcept to the extent provided in regulations, if the distributions during the taxable year exceed the amount in the accumulated adjustments account at the close of the taxable year, for purposes of this subsection, the balance of such account shall be allocated among such distributions in proportion to their respective sizes." I.R.C. § 1368(c).

With respect to distributions made during a taxable year, the amount in the accumulated adjustments account as of the close of such taxable year is determined without regard to any net loss for the year. That is, if the reductions in the accumulated adjustments account for the taxable year (other than for distributions) exceed the increases in the account for such taxable year, the net negative amount is disregarded in determining the tax treatment of distributions for the year.

With the consent of all of the shareholders to whom a distribution is made by the S corporation during the year, an S corporation may elect not to have distributions taxed with respect to the accumulated adjustments account, but rather directly taxed based on accumulated earnings and profits. I.R.C. § 1363(e)(3). An S corporation might make such an election in order to use up the corporation's accumulated earnings and profits and thereby avoid the tax imposed under section 1375 on the net passive income of an S corporation with accumulated earnings and profits.[13]

CHART 8.1
Tax Treatment of Distributions of a Subchapter S Corporation with Subchapter C Earnings and Profits

(1) Determine the portion of the distribution that does not exceed the accumulated adjustments account.

> (A) This amount is treated first as a return of capital, to the extent of shareholder basis.

> (B) After all basis is recovered, the remainder of this amount is taxed as a sale or exchange of property. *See* I.R.C. § 1368(c)(1).

(2) Any remaining portion of the distribution is taxed as a dividend to the extent it does not exceed the accumulated earnings and profits of the S corporation. *See* I.R.C. § 1368(c)(2).

(3) The remainder of the distribution, if any, is treated as follows:

> (A) This amount is treated first as a return of capital, to the extent of any remaining shareholder basis.

> (B) After all basis is recovered, the remainder, if any, is treated as a sale or exchange of property by the shareholder. *See* I.R.C. § 1368(c)(3).

[D] Basis Adjustments

Because Subchapter S provides a pass-through paradigm, tax consequences pass through to shareholders, as discussed above. Consistent with general tax principles, shareholder deductions and distributions to shareholders (which, in effect, represent a return of amounts invested) each reduce shareholder basis. Conversely, shareholder gross income increases basis.

---

[13] Code section 1375 is discussed in § 8.05[B].

[1] Increases in Basis

Under Code section 1367, both separately computed items of income and nonseparately computed income (as well as the excess of depletion deductions over the basis of property subject to depletion) increase basis. I.R.C. § 1367(a)(1).

Example 8.13: As in Example 8.7, F, Inc., an S corporation, has two equal shareholders, Gina and Harold. Gina has a $500 basis in her stock, and Harold has a $200 basis in his stock. In Year 1, F, Inc. earns $100 of ordinary income. Gina and Harold must each report $50 of ordinary income on their returns. The $50 of ordinary income increases Gina's stock basis to $550, and Harold's to $250.

Note that tax-exempt items of income also serve to increase shareholder basis. *See* I.R.C. §§ 1366(a)(1)(A); 1367(a)(1)(A). Otherwise, the tax-exempt items would merely be tax-deferred. In *Gitlitz v. Commissioner*, 531 U.S. 206 (2001), the United States Supreme Court considered whether cancellation of indebtedness income of an insolvent S corporation increases the basis of the corporation's shareholders. Code section 108 allows an exclusion from gross the discharge of indebtedness of an insolvent taxpayer, to the extent of the taxpayer's insolvency. *See* I.R.C. § 108(a)(1)(B), (a)(3). The price for the exclusion is a reduction in favorable tax attributes, at the corporate level for an S corporation. *See* I.R.C. §§ 108(b), (d)(7)(A).

In *Gitlitz*, the taxpayers, David Gitlitz (Gitlitz) and Philip Winn (Winn) each owned 50 percent of the stock of P.D.W. & A., Inc. (PDWA), an S corporation that realized $2,021,096 of discharged indebtedness. At the time, PDWA was insolvent in the amount of $2,181,748. Because it was insolvent even after the discharge, PDWA excluded the discharge amount from gross income under Code section 108. Gitlitz and Winn then each increased their stock bases by their *pro rata* shares of the discharge, on the theory that the discharge of indebtedness was an "item of income" subject to pass-through under Code section 1366(a)(1)(A). *Id.* at 209–10. The Supreme Court, reversing the Court of Appeals for the Tenth Circuit, which had affirmed the Tax Court, agreed with the taxpayers. It also held that the pass-through occurs before the reduction of the S corporation's tax attributes under Code section 108(b). *Id.* at 219–20. That meant that Gitlitz and Winn could deduct losses previously suspended under Code section 1366(d) from the increased basis. In addition, "[b]ecause their basis increase is equal to their losses, [the taxpayers] have no suspended losses remaining. They, therefore, have no net operating losses to reduce." *Id.* at 218.

Gitlitz provided a windfall to the taxpayers by allowing a basis increase without an income inclusion. *See* Gregg D. Polsky, *Another* Gitlitz *Windfall: Double Basis Increases for S Corp. Shareholders?*, 92 TAX NOTES 314, 314 (2001). In 2002, Congress responded by amending Code section 108 to provide that any amount of discharge of indebtedness income excluded by an S corporation is not taken into account under Code section 1366(a). *See* I.R.C. § 108(d)(7)(A). As a result, excluded discharge of indebtedness income does not increase shareholder basis.

[2] Decreases in Basis

Separately computed items of loss and deduction and nonseparately computed loss all *reduce* shareholder basis, as do non-capital, nondeductible corporate expenses, and "the amount of the shareholder's deduction for depletion for any oil and gas property held by the S corporation to the extent such deduction does not exceed the proportionate share of the adjusted basis of such property allocated to such shareholder under section 613A(c)(11)(B)." I.R.C. § 1367(a)(2)(B)–(E).

Example 8.14: As in Example 8.10, M, Inc. has two equal shareholders, Nancy and Oscar. Nancy has a $300 basis in her stock, and Oscar has a $200 basis in his stock. M, Inc., an S corporation, has no indebtedness to its shareholders. In Year 1, M, Inc. has a $600 ordinary loss. Nancy may deduct $300 of the loss. Her stock basis is reduced to zero. Oscar may deduct $200 of the loss, reducing his stock basis to zero, and he may carry forward a $100 loss deduction until he has basis to support a further deduction.

Distributions from the corporation that were not includible in shareholder income under section 1368 also reduce shareholder basis. I.R.C. § 1367(a)(2)(A).

Example 8.15: As in Example 8.11, Pine Corp. has two equal shareholders, Quincy and Ron. Quincy has a $300 basis in his stock, and Ron has a $150 basis in his stock. In Year 1, Pine Corp. distributes $200 to each shareholder. Quincy has no gross income from the distribution, and his stock basis is reduced to $100. Ron's basis is reduced to zero, and the remaining $50 of the distribution results in $50 of capital gain for him.

[E] Application of Subchapter C Rules to S Corporations

The discussion above illustrates that Subchapter S provides special rules for pass-throughs, distributions, and adjustments to shareholder basis. What law applies more generally to S corporations? Code section 1371 generally provides that Subchapter C provides the rules applicable to S corporations and their shareholders in the absence of a conflict with Subchapter S. That means, for example, that section 351 applies to the organization of an S corporation, and sections 331 and 336 apply to its liquidation. Yet, corporate-level events are taxed to the shareholders.

Example 8.16: X, Inc., an S corporation, has two equal shareholders, Violet and Wendy. Violet has a $400 basis in her stock, and Wendy has a $200 basis in her stock. In Year 5, Violet and Wendy decide to terminate X, Inc.'s existence. They adopt a plan of liquidation, pursuant to which X, Inc. distributes one of its two assets to each shareholder. Violet receives land worth $1,000 with a basis of $700, and Wendy receives equipment worth $1,000 with a basis of $800.

Under section 336, the distribution of the two assets results in $300 of gain on the land ($1,000 − $700) and $200 of gain on the equipment

($1,000 – $800), for a total of $500 of gain that passes through to Violet and Wendy. Each shareholder therefore has $250 of gross income, and Violet's basis increases from $400 to $650, while Wendy's increases from $200 to $450. Under section 331, Violet and Wendy are also taxed on the exchange of their stock for $1,000 worth of corporate assets. Violet has $350 of additional gain ($1,000 – $650), and Wendy has $550 of gain ($1,000 – $450), in addition to the $250 of gain from the pass-throughs.

Note that because section 351 applies to S corporations, section 362(e)(2), which was discussed in § 2.03[B][1][a] of Chapter 2, can apply, as well. As discussed there, section 362(e)(2) allows a transferor and transferee of property to elect to reduce stock basis where otherwise a reduction in the corporation's asset basis would be required. However, although reduction of the shareholder's basis preserves possible loss recognition by the corporation on the transfer of the loss asset or assets, because corporate losses generally pass through to shareholders and reduce stock basis, but shareholder losses have no comparable effect on the corporation, the shareholder may end up worse off by making the election.

Example 8.17: In Year 1, Zelda incorporates XY, Inc. and, in a transaction governed by section 351, transfers to XY, Inc. land with a basis of $50,000 and a value of $40,000. Absent an election under section 362(e)(2), Zelda will take a $50,000 basis in her stock and XY, Inc. will take a $40,000 basis in the land. Although no loss is preserved in the land, the loss is preserved in Zelda's stock basis for possible future recognition on sale of the shares or liquidation of the corporation.

Alternatively, if Zelda and XY, Inc. were to make an election under section 362(e)(2) to reduce her stock basis, her basis in the XY, Inc. stock would be $40,000 and XY, Inc.'s basis in the land would be $50,000. The loss would thus be preserved in the land. If XY, Inc. were to sell the land for its fair market value of $40,000, the loss would pass through to Zelda under section 1366 and reduce her basis to $30,000 under section 1367. There would accordingly be a gain inherent in Zelda's XY, Inc. shares, so that if she were to sell her shares for their fair market value of $40,000, $10,000 of gain would be recognized, offsetting her prior loss. Thus, in this situation, as in Example 7.6 in § 7.03[A][1][c][ii] of Chapter 7, the election under section 362(e)(2) to reduce shareholder basis can be a trap for the unwary.

Note also that, for some provisions, S corporations are treated as partnerships. *See, e.g.,* I.R.C. §§ 1372 (partnership rules apply to S corporations for fringe benefit purposes), 1373 (referring to foreign income provisions). In addition, although the stock in an S corporation is subject to attribution, for purposes of attributing stock between an S corporation and its shareholders, S corporations are treated as partnerships. *See* I.R.C. § 318(a)(5)(E). Section 318 is discussed in detail in Chapter 5.[14]

---

[14] *See* § 5.02.

[F] Sale of S Corporation Shares

Shares of stock in an S corporation generally constitute a capital asset under section 1221. Thus, under section 1222, gain or loss on the sale or exchange of stock in an S corporation will generally be capital in character. However, an S corporation, unlike a C corporation, is a pass-through entity, and section 1(h)(9) authorizes regulations applying the section 1(h) capital gains preference to "sales and exchanges by pass-thru entities and of interests in such entities" including S corporations. *See* I.R.C. § 1(h)(9), (10). Treasury regulations provide "[w]hen stock in an S corporation held for more than one year is sold or exchanged, the transferor may recognize . . . collectibles gain, and residual long-term capital gain or loss."[15] Treas. Reg. § 1.1(h)-1(a). The regulations thus provide a "look through" for collectibles gain. *See* Treas. Reg. § 1.1(h)-1(a). In the case of an S corporation, "[l]ook-through capital gain is the share of collectibles gain allocable to an interest in . . . [the] S corporation . . . ." Treas. Reg. § 1.1(h)-1(b). Collectibles gain is taxed at a maximum rate of 28 percent, I.R.C. § 1(h)(4)(i), while residual long-term capital gain is taxed at a maximum rate of 15 percent, *see* I.R.C. § 1(h)(1)(C).

Under the regulations, when a taxpayer sells stock in an S corporation that was held for more than a year, the taxpayer recognizes as collectibles gain a proportionate share of the amount of net gain (but not net loss) that would have arisen had the S corporation sold all of its collectibles at their fair market value immediately before the sale of the shares. Treas. Reg. § 1.1(h)-1(b)(2)(ii) (hypothetical gain is allocated "to the extent attributable to the portion of the . . . S corporation stock . . . transferred that was held for more than one year"). The residual long-term capital gain or loss is the amount of long-term capital gain or loss that would the taxpayer would otherwise recognize on the sale (which the regulations term "pre-look-through long-term capital gain or loss") minus the look-through collectibles gain amount. Treas. Reg. § 1.1(h)-1(c). The regulations provide the following example:

> (i) A corporation (X) has always been an S corporation and is owned by individuals A, B, and C. In 1996, X invested in antiques. Subsequent to their purchase, the antiques appreciated in value by $300. A owns one-third of the shares of X stock and has held that stock for more than one year. A's adjusted basis in the X stock is $100. If A were to sell all of A's X stock to T for $150, A would realize $50 of pre-look-through long-term capital gain.
>
> (ii) If X were to sell its antiques in a fully taxable transaction for cash equal to the fair market value of the assets immediately before the transfer to T, A would be allocated $100 of gain on account of

---

[15] That regulation further provides that "the transferor may recognize ordinary income (e.g., under sections 304, 306 . . . 1254) . . . ." Treas. Reg. § 1.1(h)-1(a). That is not a look-through rule but rather reflects the reality that in some instances, such as transactions under section 304 or in section 306 stock, a sale or exchange can give rise to ordinary income. Section 304 is discussed in Chapter 5. Section 306 is discussed in Chapter 6.

the sale. Therefore, A will recognize $100 of collectibles gain (look-through capital gain) on account of the collectibles held by X.

(iii) The difference between the transferor's pre-look-through long-term capital gain or loss ($50) and the look-through capital gain determined under this section ($100) is the transferor's residual long-term capital gain or loss on the sale of the S corporation stock. Under these facts, A will recognize $100 of collectibles gain and a $50 residual long-term capital loss on account of the sale of A's interest in X.

Treas. Reg. § 1.1(h)-1(f) Ex.4. In this example, part (i) provides that A would realize $50 of pre-look-through long-term capital gain if A were to sell all of A's X stock for $150 because A has a $100 basis in the stock, all of which A has held for more than a year. Part (ii) provides that "[i]f X were to sell its antiques in a fully taxable transaction for cash equal to the fair market value of the assets immediately before the transfer to T, A would be allocated $100 of gain on account of the sale" because the appreciation on the antiques is $300 and A owns one-third of the shares. Part (iii) reflects the subtraction from the $50 pre-look-through long-term capital gain of the $100 of look-through collectibles gain, which yields negative $50, that is, a $50 residual long-term capital loss.

CHART 8.2
Application of Subchapter S to Corporations Without Subchapter C Earnings and Profits

(1) **Pass-through** under Code section 1366:

> (A) Each shareholder takes into account the shareholder's *pro rata* share of the corporation's items of income, loss, deduction, or credit the separate treatment of which could affect the tax liability of any shareholder; character of items therefore passes through.

> (B) Each shareholder takes into account the shareholder's *pro rata* share of the remaining, nonseparately computed, income or loss.

(2) **Distributions** under Code section 1368:

> (A) Distributions are first treated as a return of capital, to the extent of the shareholder's stock basis.

> (B) Any excess over shareholder basis is treated as gain from the sale or exchange of the stock (generally capital gain).

(3) **Basis adjustments** under Code section 1367:

> (A) Income items increase shareholder basis.

> (B) Losses, and deductions (including certain depletion deductions) reduce shareholder basis.

> (C) Distributions reduce shareholder basis.

(4)   <u>All other transactions</u> are subject to Subchapter C, under Code section 1371.

§ 8.05   Corporate-Level Taxes Imposed on S Corporations

[A]   Built-In Gains

A C corporation with highly appreciated assets might make an election under Subchapter S in an attempt to sell or distribute the assets with only one level of federal income tax. Code section 1374 prevents that result by imposing a corporate-level tax on certain dispositions of assets with built-in gains. The tax applies to dispositions of assets within ten years after the S election was made. *See* I.R.C. § 1374(a), (c)(2). The tax is computed by applying the highest rate of tax under section 11(b) to the "net recognized built-in gain" for the taxable year. I.R.C. § 1374(a), (b).

The tax base of "net recognized built-in gain" is defined through a series of highly technical definitions and is limited in several ways. First, the taxable income of the S corporation serves as a cap on net recognized built-in gain. Thus, net recognized built-in gain is the *lesser* of (1) the corporation's taxable income for the year determined under section 1375(b)(1)(B), or (2) the net of "recognized built-in gains" and "recognized built-in losses." I.R.C. § 1374(d)(2). In general, "recognized built-in gains"[16] and "recognized built-in losses"[17] are the gains and losses that were both (1) built into assets at the time of the S election, and (2) recognized during the 10-year period following the election. Note that netting recognized built-in losses with recognized built-in gains lowers the amount of net recognized built-in gain by the amount of any recognized built-in losses.

Section 1374(c) imposes yet another cap on the amount of net recognized built-in gain (the tax base): it cannot exceed "net unrealized built-in gain"— the amount by which the fair market value of the assets of the S corporation as of the beginning of its first taxable year exceeded the aggregate adjusted bases of such assets at such time. I.R.C. § 1374(d)(1). That is, if, for example, at the time of the S election, the value of the corporation's assets exceed the aggregate basis in its assets by $1,000, the S corporation will never have more than $1,000 subject to the tax under section 1374. The mechanics of this work as follows: as built-in gain is recognized over the course of the 10-year recognition period, the cap on net recognized built-in

---

[16] More technically, a "recognized built-in gain" is any gain recognized upon the disposition of an asset during the 10-year recognition period, except if the S corporation establishes that the asset was not held by the S corporation at the beginning of the taxable year in which it became an S corporation or the gain exceeds the gain that was built into the asset at the time of the S election. I.R.C. § 1374(d)(3).

[17] More technically, a "recognized built-in loss" is any loss recognized on the disposition of an asset during the 10-year recognition period if the S corporation establishes that the asset was held by the S corporation as of the beginning of the first taxable year for which it was an S corporation and the loss does not exceed the amount of loss that was built into the asset at the time of the S election. I.R.C. § 1374(d)(4).

gain is reduced so that no more will be taxed under section 1374, in the aggregate, than the net gain that was built in at the time of conversion to S status.[18] As a result, it is very helpful to have an appraisal of the assets at the time of the S election.

Example 8.18: After three years of operating as a C corporation, Y Corp. makes an S election in Year 4. At the relevant time, Y Corp. has three assets: land with a basis of $600 and a value of $1,000; equipment with a basis of $400 and a value of $200; and machinery with a basis of $100 and a value of $200. Y Corp.'s "net unrealized built-in gain" (the overall cap) is $300 ($1,400 − $1,100). Assume that Y Corp. has $2,000 of income each year in Years 5 through 7.

In Year 5, Y sells the machinery for $250. The corporate-level tax under section 1374 will be imposed on the $100 of net recognized built-in gain for the year. In Year 6, Y sells the equipment for $450. That was a loss asset, so there is no corporate-level tax in Year 6. In Year 7, Y sells the land for $1,200. The recognized built-in gain is $400 ($1,000 − $600). However, net recognized built-in gain cannot exceed net unrealized built-in gain of $300 less the $100 recognized in Year 5. Thus, only $200 is taxed at the corporate level under section 1374 in Year 7.

Note that the tax on built-in gains is treated as a loss for purposes of shareholder-level taxation. The character of the loss is determined by allocating it proportionately to the assets that gave rise to the built-in gains tax. I.R.C. § 1366(f)(2).

[B]   Excess Net Passive Investment Income

Under Code section 1375, a corporate-level tax is imposed on an S corporation that has accumulated earnings and profits at the close of the year, if its passive investment income exceeds 25 percent of its gross receipts. *See* I.R.C. § 1375(a). This tax backstops the personal holding company tax, *see* I.R.C. § 541, by limiting the possibility that a C corporation could avoid that tax by making an election under Subchapter S.[19] Just as with Code section 1374, discussed above, the tax is computed by applying the highest rate of tax specified in section 11(b) — in this case to the "excess net passive income." *See id.* In addition, "[n]o credit shall be allowed under part IV of subchapter A of this chapter (other than section 34) against the tax imposed by subsection (a)." I.R.C. § 1375(c). However, the amount passed through to shareholders is reduced by the tax imposed on the corporation under section 1375. *See* I.R.C. § 1366(f)(3).

Excess net passive income is defined as the amount that bears the same ratio to the net passive income for the taxable year as the amount by which

---

[18] More specifically, the amount of net recognized built-in gain taken into account for any taxable year cannot exceed the excess (if any) of the net unrealized built-in gain over the net recognized built-in gain for prior taxable years beginning in the ten-year recognition period. *See* I.R.C. § 1374(c)(2).

[19] The personal holding company tax is discussed in § 14.03 of Chapter 14.

the passive investment income for the taxable year exceeds 25 percent of the gross receipts for the taxable year, bears to the passive investment income for the taxable year. I.R.C. § 1375(b)(1)(A). A cap on the tax base provides that the amount of the excess net passive income for any taxable year cannot exceed the amount of the corporation's taxable income for the taxable year, determined under section 63(a) but with certain adjustments. See I.R.C. § 1375(b)(1)(B).

"Net passive income" is passive investment income reduced by "the deductions allowable under this chapter which are directly connected with the production of such income (other than deductions allowable under section 172 and part VIII of subchapter B)." I.R.C. § 1375(b)(2). As discussed in § 8.03[B][3], above, in connection with termination of S status, passive investment income generally includes royalties, rents, dividends, interest, annuities, and gains on sales or exchanges of stock or securities, subject to certain exceptions. See I.R.C. § 1362(d)(3)(C). However, under section 1375, the calculation of passive investment income does not take into account any recognized built-in gain or loss of the S corporation for any taxable year in the 10-year recognition period discussed above. I.R.C. § 1375(b)(4).

> *Example 8.19*: In Year 3 of its existence, Z Corp., an S Corporation with $800 of accumulated earnings and profits at the close of Year 3, earns $3,000 of income from royalties, rents, dividends and interest. Z Corp. has $10,000 of gross receipts for the year. Z Corp.'s passive investment income of $3,000 exceeds 25 percent of its gross receipts ($2,500) by $500. That $500 excess is one-sixth of the passive investment income of $3,000. Assuming that Z Corp. has no allowable deductions, Z Corp.'s net passive investment income is $3,000, one-sixth of which is $500. Accordingly, $500 constitutes the excess net passive income that is subject to the tax under section 1375. In addition, under Code section 1362(d)(3)(A)(i), discussed in § 8.03[B][3], if Z Corp.'s passive investment income exceeds 25 percent of gross receipts for three consecutive taxable years during which it is an S corporation, and it has accumulated earnings and profits at the close of each of those three taxable years, its S election will terminate.

The Secretary of the Treasury has the authority to waive application of the tax under section 1375 to an S corporation that establishes that it determined in good faith that it had no earnings and profits at the close of a taxable year, and during a reasonable period of time after it was determined that it did in fact have earnings and profits at that time, the corporation distributed the earnings and profits. I.R.C. § 1375(d).

Chapter 9

REORGANIZATIONS: OVERVIEW

§ 9.01 Introduction

This chapter provides an overview of the corporate reorganization provisions. Chapter 10 discusses acquisitive reorganizations in more detail; Chapter 11 focuses on corporate divisions; and Chapter 12 explores reorganizations involving a single corporation.

[A] A Bit of History and Rationales for Nonrecognition in Corporate Reorganizations

Before the current statutory regime governing corporate reorganizations, even reorganizations that simply changed a corporation's state of incorporation were taxable. For example, in *United States v. Phellis*, 257 U.S. 156 (1921), the United States Supreme Court held taxable a reorganization involving the change of E.I. du Pont de Nemours Powder Company from a New Jersey corporation to a Delaware corporation called E.I. du Pont de Nemours & Company. Similarly, in *Marr v. United States*, 268 U.S. 536 (1925), the Court held taxable the reincorporation of General Motors of New Jersey in Delaware.

In *Marr*, the taxpayer organized a Delaware corporation for the purpose of the reincorporation. That corporation exchanged five shares of its common stock for each share of common in the New Jersey corporation, and one and one-third shares of its preferred stock for each share of preferred in the New Jersey corporation. After the exchange, the Delaware corporation owned 100 percent of the New Jersey corporation. The New Jersey corporation was subsequently liquidated, and all of its assets and liabilities were transferred to the Delaware corporation. The Court found the exchange taxable because the corporations were organized in different states, and had different rights and powers.

These cases interpreted the Internal Revenue Code as it existed prior to 1919, when Congress first enacted a non-recognition regime for corporate reorganizations. *See* Daniel Q. Posin, *Taxing Corporate Reorganizations: Purging Penelope's Web*, 133 U. PA. L. REV. 1335, 1341 (1985). The 1919 Code did not define the term "reorganization," but the 1921 Act did. *See id.* at 1348. In 1924, 1934, and 1954, Congress reworked the statute. *See id.* at 1349–52.

Under current law, gains (and losses) realized in a transaction that qualifies as a reorganization and meets various judicial requirements benefit (or suffer) from general rules of nonrecognition. The tax consequences of a corporate reorganization are akin to those in a section 351 transaction, which was discussed in Chapter 2. In fact, some of the same Code sections apply to both section 351 transactions and reorganizations.

The traditional rationales for non-recognition of gains realized in corporate reorganizations have been described as follows: "the parties involved in a reorganization have maintained their ownership interests; that, in effect, the exchange of property as part of the reorganization is insufficient to constitute a realization event. . . . Buttressing this continuity-of-interest principle is the belief that valuation and liquidity concerns would make taxing corporate reorganizations impractical and unfair. . . ." Ajay K. Mehrotra, *The Story of the Corporate Reorganization Provisions; From "Purely Paper" to Corporate Welfare*, in BUSINESS TAX STORIES 29 (2005). However, given the array of transactions the corporate reorganizations apply to, including those in which a shareholder of a small, closely held corporation may receive publicly traded stock in a much larger corporation, "more recent critics have concluded that the ultimate effect of the corporate reorganization provisions . . . 'is . . . [a] hard-to-justify subsidy.' " *Id.* at 30 (*quoting* Yariv Brauner, *A Good Old Habit or Just an Old One? Preferential Treatment for Reorganizations*, 2004 B.Y.U. L. REV. 1, 4 (2004)) *but cf.* Steven A. Bank, *Mergers, Taxes, and Historical Realism*, 75 TUL. L. REV. 1, 6-7 (2000) (adoption of corporate reorganization provisions reflected a compromise between accretion and consumption models of taxation).

[B] Statutory and Common Law Requirements of Valid Reorganizations

For a transaction to constitute a valid reorganization, it must fit within the definition of reorganization in section 368(a), have a "plan of reorganization," as indicated by other Code sections that provide the tax results to transactions qualifying as reorganizations, and meet certain judicially developed requirements. As discussed below, section 368 provides for seven principal types of reorganizations, with three-party ("triangular") variations on some of them. The judicially developed requirements are business purpose, continuity of business enterprise, and continuity of proprietary interest. Each of these doctrines is discussed below.

§ 9.02   Overview of Section 368

Section 368 has three subsections. Subsection (a) defines "reorganization" and provides various rules relating to reorganizations. Subsection (b) defines the phrase "party to a reorganization." Subsection (c) defines control, a definition that was discussed in Chapter 2 with respect to section 351 transactions.[1] Each of these definitions is important for the various Code sections, outside section 368, that provide the tax consequences of reorganization transactions.

---

[1] *See* § 2.02[A][1][b].

[A] Definition of "Reorganization"

Under section 368(a)(1), there are seven principal types of reorganizations. In addition, section 368 contemplates variations on several of these. The principal reorganizations are discussed below.

[1] "A" Reorganizations: Statutory Mergers

Under section 368(a)(1)(A), a "statutory merger or consolidation," meets the definition of reorganization. This type of reorganization is called an A reorganization. Its formal requirements from the Code are limited to meeting applicable state law statutory requirements for a "merger" or "consolidation."[2] However, as discussed below, judicial doctrines impose further requirements. In particular, target shareholders must receive at least some stock consideration. *See* § 9.06 (discussing continuity of proprietary interest).

In general, in an A reorganization, the target shareholders exchange their shares for shares of the acquiring corporation. The diagram below illustrates the "before" and "after" pictures in a typical merger that constitutes an A reorganization.

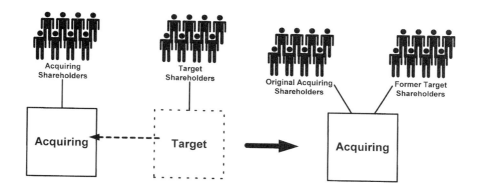

If the reorganization is a consolidation, the shareholders of the acquiring corporation also exchange their shares for shares in the new company.

There are no statutory restrictions on the consideration used in an "A" reorganization. Nonetheless, as discussed below, every reorganization must

---

[2] A Treasury Regulation specifies that "[f]or purposes of section 368(a)(1)(A), a statutory merger or consolidation is a transaction effected pursuant to the statute or statutes necessary to effect the merger or consolidation, in which transaction, as a result of the operation of such statute or statutes, [certain events listed in the regulations] occur simultaneously at the effective time of the transaction . . . ." Treas. Reg. § 1.368-2(b)(1)(ii). This regulation is generally effective for transactions occurring on or after January 23, 2006. Treas. Reg. § 1.368-2(b)(1)(v). A Temporary Regulation applied to transactions occurring before that date. *See id.*

also meet several common law requirements. In fact, because A reorganizations have so few statutory requirements, these common law limitations
provide the main restrictions on this type of reorganization. However, it
is important to note, as discussed in Chapter 10, that A reorganizations
are acquisitive, not divisive; a transaction that divides the assets of one
corporation between two or more corporations will not qualify as an A
reorganization. *See* Treas. Reg. § 1.368-2(b)(1)(ii), (iii) Ex. 1; Rev. Rul.
2000-5, 2000-1 C.B. 436.

[2] "B" Reorganizations: Stock-for-Stock Swaps

In general, a reorganization that qualifies under section 368(a)(1)(B) (a
B reorganization) is one that involves "the acquisition by one corporation,
in exchange solely for all or a part of its voting stock . . . of stock of another
corporation if, immediately after the acquisition, the acquiring corporation
has control of such other corporation (whether or not such acquiring
corporation had control immediately before the acquisition) . . . ." I.R.C.
§ 368(a)(1)(B). In other words, the acquiring corporation swaps its *voting
stock* with target shareholders for stock of the target corporation. The
acquiring corporation must acquire at least 80 percent of the stock of the
target corporation, so as to have "control" of it within the meaning of section
368(c). Thus, after the transaction, the target is at least an 80-percent
subsidiary of the acquiring corporation, and the former target shareholders
have become shareholders of the acquiring corporation (along with the pre-
existing acquiring corporation shareholders). The diagram below illustrates
the "before" and "after" pictures in a typical B reorganization, with the
"before" picture also showing the stock transfers.

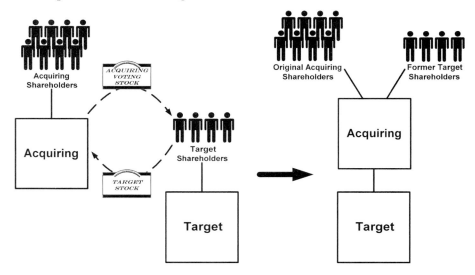

The acquiring corporation must use solely voting stock as the acquisitive
consideration; there can be no "boot" (property other than property

permitted to be received without the recognition of gain or loss) in a B reorganization. However, *triangular* B reorganizations (those using parent company stock as the acquisitive consideration) are permitted by statute, as discussed below.

[3] "C" Reorganizations: "De Facto Mergers"

Under section 368(a)(1)(C), a C reorganization is "the acquisition by one corporation, in exchange solely for all or a part of its voting stock . . . of substantially all of the properties of another corporation, but in determining whether the exchange is solely for stock the assumption by the acquiring corporation of a liability of the other shall be disregarded . . . ." I.R.C. § 368(a)(1)(C). The diagram below illustrates the "before," "during," and "after" pictures in a typical C reorganization.

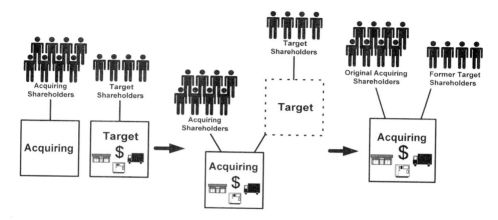

This type of reorganization involves an *asset* acquisition by the acquiring corporation. Because assets often are subject to liabilities, the statute facilitates C reorganizations by ignoring the liabilities in the context of the "solely for voting stock" requirement. This set of rules is further modified in section 368(a)(2)(B), which is discussed in Chapter 10.[3] In addition, the target corporation generally must be liquidated as part of the C reorganization. *See* I.R.C. § 368(a)(2)(G). Finally, as discussed below, triangular C reorganizations are permitted by statute.[4]

---

[3] *See* § 10.04[A][2].

[4] *See* § 9.02[A][8].

[4]   Acquisitive and Divisive "D" Reorganizations

Section 368(a)(1)(D) defines as a so-called D reorganization a transaction that involves "a transfer by a corporation of all or a part of its assets to another corporation if, immediately after the transfer, the transferor, or one or more of its shareholders (including persons who were shareholders immediately before the transfer), or any combination thereof, is in control of the corporation to which the assets are transferred; but only if, in pursuance of the plan, stock or securities of the corporation to which the assets are transferred are distributed in a transaction which qualifies under section 354, 355, or 356." In an acquisitive D reorganization, a corporation transfers substantially all of its assets to a corporation that it or its shareholders (or any combination) "controls" immediately after the transfer, in exchange for stock or securities of the transferee, followed by a liquidation of the transferor corporation and distribution to its shareholders of that stock or securities and any other assets it still has. The diagram below illustrates the "before," "during," and "after" pictures of an acquisitive D reorganization.

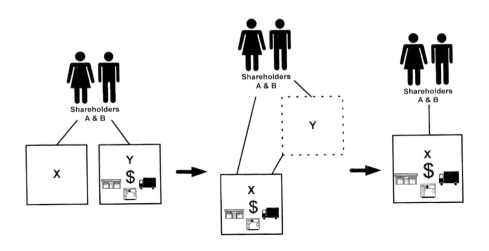

In a divisive D reorganization, the distribution qualifies under section 355 and therefore will accomplish a spin-off, split-off or split-up, as discussed in Chapter 11.[5] The diagram below illustrates the "before," "during," and "after" pictures of a typical divisive D reorganization.

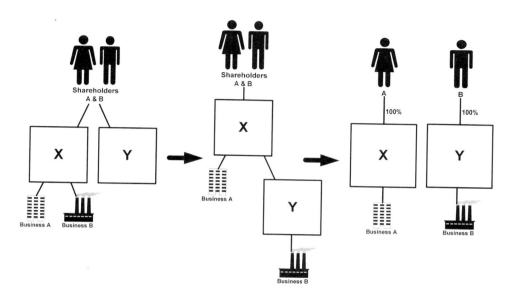

---

[5] *See* § 11.02.

[5] "E" Reorganizations: Recapitalizations

Section 368(a)(1)(E) defines the term "reorganization" to include a recapitalization. A recapitalization is a rearrangement of the capital structure of a corporation. It involves an exchange of some combination of stock and securities of a single corporation.[6] The diagram below illustrates the "before" and "after" pictures in a recapitalization involving a *pro rata* exchange of common stock for common stock and preferred stock. Note that the shareholders will have less common stock than they did before the recapitalization because they exchanged some common stock for the preferred stock. Note also that, in this particular example, the preferred stock will be section 306 stock. *See* I.R.C. § 306(c)(1)(B); §§ 6.04[B][1][b], 12.02[C][1].

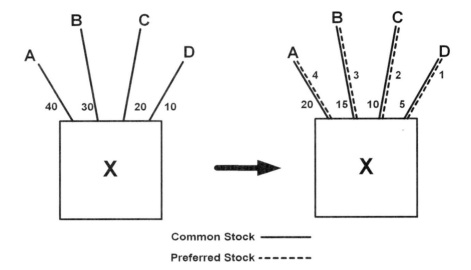

Common Stock ————
Preferred Stock --------

---

[6] Treasury regulations also provide that "for transactions occurring on or after February 25, 2005, a continuity of the business enterprise and a continuity of interest are not required for the transaction to qualify as a reorganization under section 368(a)(1)(E) . . . ." Treas. Reg. § 1.368-1(b).

[6] "F" Reorganizations: Changes in Form

An F reorganization also may involve a single corporation. Section 368(a)(1)(F) applies to "a mere change in identity, form, or place of organization of one corporation, however effected." Section 368(a)(1)(F) overrules the *Phellis* and *Marr* cases discussed above. The diagram below illustrates the "before" and "after" pictures in a typical F reorganization.[7]

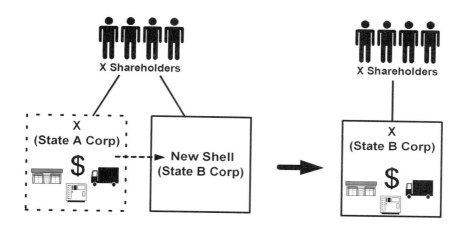

[7] "G" Reorganizations: Bankruptcy Reorganizations

A section 368(a)(1)(G) reorganization involves "a transfer by a corporation of all or part of its assets to another corporation in a title 11 or similar case; but only if, in pursuance of the plan, stock or securities of the corporation to which the assets are transferred are distributed in a transaction which qualifies under section 354, 355, or 356." It resembles a D reorganization, and similarly may be acquisitive or divisive.

[8] Triangular B and C Reorganizations

Both B reorganizations and C reorganizations permit the use of stock of a *controlling parent* of the acquiring corporation. In addition, as outlined below, sections 368(a)(2)(D) and 368(a)(2)(E) permit two different types of mergers using stock of a controlling parent company. The details of triangular reorganizations are discussed in Chapter 10.[8]

---

[7] As with "E" reorganizations, Treasury regulations provide that "for transactions occurring on or after February 25, 2005, a continuity of the business enterprise and a continuity of interest are not required for the transaction to qualify as a reorganization under section . . . [368(a)(1)(F)]." Treas. Reg. § 1.368-1(b).

[8] *See* §§ 10.02[B] (forward and reverse triangular mergers), 10.03[E] (triangular B reorganizations), 10.04[E] (triangular C reorganizations).

[9] Section 368(a)(2)(D) Reorganizations: Forward Triangular Mergers

Section 368(a)(2)(D) allows a merger of a target corporation into a subsidiary of the corporation in which the target shareholders receive stock. The target shareholders become shareholders of the parent corporation, and the parent's subsidiary, the acquiring corporation, receives the targets assets. The diagram below illustrates the "before" and "after" pictures in a typical forward triangular merger.

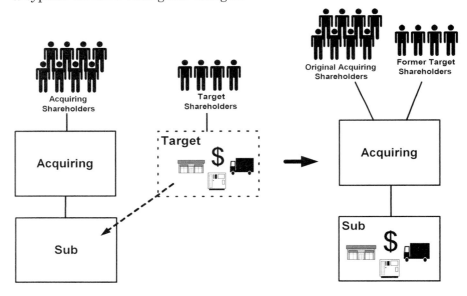

In form, this is an A reorganization that uses stock of the parent of the acquiring corporation. However, in substance, this is essentially a variety of C reorganization.

[10] Section 368(a)(2)(E) Reorganizations: Reverse Triangular Mergers

Section 368(a)(2)(E) contemplates a reverse triangular merger. Treasury Regulations provide that "[s]ection 368(a)(2)(E) does not apply to a consolidation." Treas. Reg. § 1.368-2(j)(2). In form, a reverse triangular merger is an A reorganization in which the acquiring subsidiary merges *into* the target corporation. The target corporation survives as the new subsidiary, and the target shareholders receive voting stock of the parent corporation. It is sometimes known as a "reverse B reorganization," although, unlike in a B reorganization, some boot is permitted in a reverse triangular merger. The diagram below illustrates the "before" and "after" pictures in a typical reverse triangular merger.

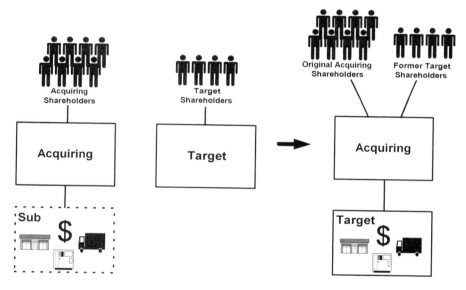

[11] Ordering Rules

Some transactions may meet the requirements of multiple Code sections, which, in some cases, could result in different tax consequences depending on which provision is deemed primary. The Code provides ordering rules for some of these overlap situations, and the IRS has ruled on others. The Code provides that a reorganization that is described in both section 368(a)(1)(C) and 368(a)(1)(D) is analyzed as a D reorganization. I.R.C. § 368(a)(2)(A). A reorganization that meets the requirements of both the A and C or D reorganization provisions probably should be treated as an A reorganization. BITTKER & EUSTICE, FEDERAL INCOME TAXATION OF CORPORATIONS & SHAREHOLDERS ¶ 12.22[7] (7th ed. 2000); *but see* Rev. Rul. 75-161, 1975-1 C.B. 114 (section 357(c)(1)(B), which applies to D reorganizations, applies to transaction that also qualifies as A reorganization).

A purported B reorganization followed by a planned liquidation of the newly acquired subsidiary will be tested as a C reorganization. *See* Rev. Rul. 67-274, 1967-2 C.B. 141. A reorganization that qualified as both a D reorganization and an F reorganization was treated as an F reorganization for purposes of section 357(c), so that section 357(c) did not apply to the transaction. Rev. Rul. 79-289, 1979-2 C.B. 145. If a reorganization could qualify as a G reorganization and another type of reorganization, it will be treated as a G reorganization. I.R.C. § 368(a)(3)(C).

A transaction that meets the requirements of section 351, which is discussed in Chapter 2, may also qualify as a reorganization. In general, if a transaction qualifies under both section 351 and section 368(a)(1), all of the provisions that apply to either type of transaction may apply.[9] Accordingly, the IRS has ruled that section 306(c)(1)(B), which is applicable to reorganizations, applies. *See* Rev. Rul. 79-274, 1979-2 C.B. 131. Similarly, sections 357(c) and 381 applied to a transaction that qualified both as a 351 transaction and a C reorganization. Rev. Rul. 76-188, 1976-1 C.B. 99. Failure to meet the reorganization requirements also does not preclude application of section 351. *See* Rev. Rul. 84-71, 1984-1 C.B. 106, 107 ("the fact that 'larger acquisitive transactions,' such as those described in Rev. Rul. 80-284 and Rev. Rul. 80-285, fail to meet the requirements for tax-free treatment under the reorganization provisions of the Code does not preclude the applicability of section 351(a) to transfers that may be described as part of such larger transactions, but also, either alone or in conjunction with other transfers, meet the requirements of section 351(a).").

[B] Party to a Reorganization

Under section 368(b), "the term 'a party to a reorganization' includes—(1) a corporation resulting from a reorganization, and (2) both corporations, in the case of a reorganization resulting from the acquisition by one corporation of stock or properties of another. . .," as well as controlling parent corporations in triangular reorganizations. *See* I.R.C. § 368(b).

[C] "Control"

As discussed in Chapter 2, in connection with section 351 transactions, control under section 368(c) means "the ownership of stock possessing at least 80 percent of the total combined voting power of all classes of stock entitled to vote and at least 80 percent of the total number of shares of all other classes of stock of the corporation."[10] I.R.C. § 368(c). The IRS has ruled that the second 80-percent rule in section 368(c) requires "ownership of at least 80 percent of the total number of shares of *each class* of

---

[9] This analysis suggests that section 362(e)(2), which, as discussed in § 2.03[B][1][a] of Chapter 2, eliminates the multiplication of built-in losses in section 351 transactions, will apply to a transaction qualifying both under section 351 and as a reorganization.

[10] *See* § 2.02[A][1][b].

outstanding non-voting stock." Rev. Rul. 59-259, 1959-2 C.B. 115, 116 (emphasis added).

§ 9.03 The "Plan of Reorganization" Requirement

Although section 368 does not itself require a plan of reorganization, sections 354 and 361 both refer to such a plan. Thus, in order to meet the requirements of section 354, 356 (which cross-references section 354), or 361, a plan of reorganization is necessary. Treasury Regulations require that "[t]he plan of reorganization must be adopted by each of the corporations parties thereto; and the adoption must be shown by the acts of its duly constituted responsible officers, and appear upon the official records of the corporation." Treas. Reg. § 1.368-3(a). Most reorganizations occur pursuant to formal agreements, but an informal arrangement may not necessarily disqualify the reorganization. BITTKER & EUSTICE, *supra*, at ¶ 12.21[10].

In *J.E. Seagram Corp. v. Commissioner*, 104 T.C. 75 (1995), J.E. Seagram Corp. (Seagram) argued that it had recognized a loss on the exchange of shares in Conoco, Inc. (Conoco), for shares in E.I. DuPont de Nemours & Co. (DuPont). Seagram had obtained approximately 32 percent of Conoco's shares for cash in a tender offer. *Id.* at 87–88. DuPont had acquired approximately 46 percent of Conoco's shares for cash pursuant to a tender offer under an agreement with Conoco whereby, following the tender offer, Conoco would be merged into DuPont Holdings, Inc. (DuPont Holdings), a wholly owned subsidiary of DuPont, pursuant to section 368(a)(2)(D). *Id.* at 79, 99. The public owned the remaining 22 percent of the shares of Conoco prior to the merger.

In accordance with the plan, Conoco merged into DuPont Holdings and the former Conoco shareholders received shares of DuPont. In the merger, Seagram obtained 20.2 percent of DuPont's shares. *Id.* at 89. The parties to the Tax Court case agreed that the merger was valid under state law, but Seagram argued that the merger did not qualify as a reorganization because it was not done pursuant to a "plan of reorganization" as required by section 354 and because there was insufficient continuity of proprietary interest, as discussed in § 9.06[C], below. Seagram's first argument was that DuPont's tender offer and the merger of Conoco into DuPont Holdings were separate transactions so that the Conoco stock DuPont acquired via tender offer was not in accordance with a plan of reorganization. *See id.* at 93.

The Tax Court disagreed, finding that the agreement between DuPont and Conoco "was the definitive vehicle spelling out the interrelated steps by which DuPont would acquire 100 percent of Conoco's stock." *Id.* at 96. The court added, "[t]he Agreement provides a discrete start and finish, and the record discloses no steps agreed to outside the agreement, or pre-Agreement activity by DuPont or its shareholders, that would invalidate the contemplated reorganization." *Id.* at 98. The court therefore held "that, because DuPont was contractually committed to undertake and complete the second step merger once it had undertaken and completed the first step tender offer, these carefully integrated transactions together constituted a plan of reorganization within the contemplation of section 354(a)." *Id.* at 99. Thus, the court applied the step-transaction doctrine to find that the separate steps constituted a single transaction undertaken pursuant to a "plan of reorganization."

§ 9.04 The "Business Purpose" Requirement

Reorganizations now require a business purpose. This concern emanates from the transaction involved in *Gregory v. Helvering*, 293 U.S. 465 (1935), *aff'g* 69 F.2d 809 (1934). In *Gregory*, the taxpayer, Evelyn F. Gregory (Mrs. Gregory), was the owner of all the stock of United Mortgage Corporation (UM). UM owned, among other assets, 1,000 shares of Monitor Securities Corporation (MS). Mrs. Gregory sought to obtain the MS shares to sell them at a profit. A direct transfer of the shares to her as a dividend would have been taxable as ordinary income. To reduce her tax liability, Mrs. Gregory planned a "reorganization." *Id.* at 467. Under the predecessor of section 368(a)(1)(D), the term "reorganization" included a transfer by a corporation of all or part of its assets to another corporation if immediately after the transfer, the transferor or the shareholders or both were in control of the corporation to which the assets are transferred.

For the purpose of the reorganization, Mrs. Gregory organized Averill Corporation (Averill). Three days later, UM transferred to Averill the 1,000 shares of MS stock, for which all the shares of Averill were issued to Mrs. Gregory. A few days later, Averill was liquidated and distributed all of its assets, namely the MS shares, to Mrs. Gregory. She immediately sold the MS shares. *Id.* Mrs. Gregory's theory, therefore, was that the transaction was a reorganization so that the distribution of the Averill stock was not taxable to her under what is now section 354(b). That is, UM had transferred to Averill the shares of MS stock and all the shares of Averill were issued to Mrs. Gregory so that the shareholder, Mrs. Gregory, was in control of Averill. Under this theory, Mrs. Gregory's basis in Averill would be an allocable portion of her basis in the UM stock, under what is now section 358(b)(2). When Averill was liquidated, she would have had gain under the predecessor of section 331, and accordingly would obtain a fair market value basis in the Monitor shares. Thus, she would have no further gain on the sale of the Monitor shares.

Judge Learned Hand wrote the opinion of the Court of Appeals for the Second Circuit. Reversing the Tax Court, he found that the steps in the transaction "were not what the statute means by a 'reorganization,' because the transactions were no part of the conduct of the business of either or both companies; so viewed they were a sham, though all the proceedings had their usual effect." *Gregory*, 69 F.2d at 811.

On appeal, the Supreme Court framed the question as whether what was done was what the statute intended, and held that it was not:

> Putting aside, then, the question of motive in respect of taxation altogether, and fixing the character of the proceeding by what actually occurred, what do we find? Simply an operation having no business or corporate purpose—a mere device which put on the form of a corporate reorganization as a disguise for concealing its real character, and the sole object and accomplishment of which was the consummation of a preconceived plan, not to reorganize a business or any part of a business, but to transfer a parcel of corporate shares to the petitioner. No doubt, a new and valid corporation was created. But that corporation was nothing more than a contrivance to the end last described. It was brought into existence for no other purpose; it performed, as it was intended from the beginning it should perform, no other function. When that limited function had been exercised, it immediately was put to death.

Gregory, 293 U.S. at 469–70. The "business purpose" concept apparent in both the Second Circuit and Supreme Court opinions is now embodied in the last sentence of Treasury Regulation 1.368-1(c):

> A scheme, which involves an abrupt departure from normal reorganization procedure in connection with a transaction on which the imposition of tax is imminent, such as a mere device that puts on the form of a corporate reorganization as a disguise for concealing its real character, and the object and accomplishment of which is the consummation of a preconceived plan having no business or corporate purpose, is not a plan of reorganization.

§ 9.05   The Continuity of Business Enterprise Requirement

The Court of Appeals for the Second Circuit was the first court to express the continuity of business enterprise requirement; in *Cortland Specialty Co. v. Commissioner*, 60 F.2d 937, 940 (2d Cir. 1932), the court stated: "Reorganization presupposes continuance of business under modified corporate forms." Currently, the continuity of business enterprise requirement is found in Treasury Regulation 1.368-1(d). Note that some portions of that regulation are effective only for transactions occurring after January 28, 1998. Regulations also provide that "for transactions occurring on or after February 25, 2005, a continuity of the business enterprise . . . [is] not required for the transaction to qualify as a reorganization under section 368(a)(1)(E) or (F)." Treas. Reg. § 1.368-1(b).

[A]   Acquisition of Target's Historic Business or Historic Business Assets

The transaction that brought the IRS's attention to the continuity of business enterprise requirement is reflected in Treasury Regulation 1.368-1(d)(5) Ex. 3:

T is a manufacturer of boys' and men's trousers. On January 1, 1978, as part of a plan of reorganization, T sold all of its assets to a third party for cash and purchased a highly diversified portfolio of stocks and bonds. As part of the plan, T operates an investment business until July 1, 1981. On that date, the plan of reorganization culminates in a transfer by T of all its assets to P, a regulated investment company, solely in exchange for P voting stock. The continuity of business enterprise requirement is not met. T's investment activity is not its historic business, and the stocks and bonds are not T's historic business assets.

Depending on how this transaction is structured, it may appear to qualify as an A or a C reorganization. However, in substance, T has sold its assets for the equivalent of cash: shares in a regulated investment company (a mutual fund).

The principal idea behind continuity of business enterprise is that, in distinguishing a reorganization from a sale, a reorganization must involve the acquiring corporation's use of the target's historic assets in some business-related way or continuation of the target's historic business. This is intended to ensure that "reorganizations are limited to readjustments of continuing interests in property under modified corporate form." Treas. Reg. § 1.368-1(d)(1). In the example quoted above, P did not acquire T's *historic* assets (or business) but instead acquired assets that had been recently acquired by T.

[B]   Continuation of Target's Historic Business or Use of Target's Historic Business Assets

Under Treasury Regulation 1.368-1(d), continuity of business enterprise requires that the acquiring corporation either continue the target corporation's historic business or use a significant portion of T's historic business assets in a business. Treas. Reg. § 1.368-1(d)(2). If the target has more than one line of business, the acquiring company need continue only a "significant" line of business—a facts and circumstances determination. Treas. Reg. § 1.368-1(d)(2)(ii).

Thus, mere *acquisition* of the target's historic assets is not enough; the acquiring corporation must also *use* them (or continue the target's historic business). However, Treasury Regulation 1.368-1(d) provides that a post-reorganization transfer of assets to a corporate or partnership member of a "qualified group" of the acquiring ("issuing") corporation will not violate the continuity of business enterprise requirement. *See* Treas. Reg.1.368-1(d)(4), (5) Ex. 6, 7. "A qualified group is one or more chains of corporations connected through stock ownership with the issuing corporation, but only if the issuing corporation owns directly stock meeting the requirements of section 368(c) in at least one other corporation, and stock meeting the requirements of section 368(c) in each of the corporations (except the issuing corporation) is owned directly by one of the other corporations." Treas. Reg.

1.368-1(d)(4)(ii). Section 368(c) provides an 80-percent ownership requirement (by vote and by value).

§ 9.06   The Continuity of Proprietary Interest
Requirement

[A]   Overview

"Continuity of proprietary interest" is another judicially developed doctrine that limits the transactions that can qualify as reorganizations.
However, Treasury regulations provide that "for transactions occurring on
or after February 25, 2005, . . . a continuity of interest [is] not required
for the transaction to qualify as a reorganization under section 368(a)(1)(E)
or (F)." Treas. Reg. § 1.368-1(b). Continuity of proprietary interest has both
qualitative and components. In other words, it asks both what type of
consideration qualifies quantitative and how much of that type of consideration is required, as discussed below.

Continuity of interest applies at the shareholder level, unlike business
purpose and continuity of business enterprise. The test is *what percent of
the consideration paid by the acquiring corporation to acquire the target is
equity*. At the extreme, a purchase of target stock solely for cash would not
have the requisite continuity to qualify as a reorganization. At the opposite
extreme, as the discussion below will make clear, an acquisition of target
stock solely for stock of the acquiring corporation would not raise a
continuity of proprietary interest issue. It is in the middle—acquisitions
partly for stock—that continuity of proprietary interest questions arise.

Consider *Pinellas Ice and Cold Storage Co. v. Commissioner*, 287 U.S.
462 (1933). In that case, the acquiring company acquired substantially all
of the taxpayer's properties in exchange for cash and short-term notes that
were promptly distributed to the stockholders of the taxpayer. *See id.* at
463. At the time, statutorily, an exchange of property for securities could
constitute a "reorganization." *See id.* at 466 (quoting then-section 203). The
taxpayer argued that such a reorganization had occurred, arguing that the
notes constituted "securities." However, the Court disagreed. It found that
the notes were not securities, *id.* at 468, and stated:

> [T]he mere purchase for money of the assets of one company by
> another is beyond the evident purpose of the provision, and has no
> real semblance to a merger or consolidation. Certainly, we think
> that to be within the exemption, the seller must acquire an interest
> in the affairs of the purchasing company more definite than that
> incident to ownership of its short-term purchase-money notes. . . .

Id. at 470. *See also Cortland Specialty Co. v. Commissioner*, 60 F.2d 937,
940 (2d Cir. 1932).

Statutorily, B reorganizations and C reorganizations generally require
that voting stock constitute 80 percent or more of the consideration (100

percent in the case of a B reorganization). Thus, generally speaking, the typical B or C reorganization will not face a continuity of proprietary interest problem. However, A reorganizations (statutory mergers) may run into continuity of proprietary interest problems because section 368(a)(1)(A) does not specify the proportion of consideration that must be stock.

[B] Requisite Proprietary Interest

Under current law, the primary aspects of continuity of proprietary interest are (1) the qualitative aspect of the type of interest that qualifies, and (2) the quantity necessary. In general, as indicated above, the type of interest that qualifies for continuity of proprietary interest purposes is equity (stock). This is discussed further immediately below. The quantity aspects are discussed in [B][2]. Retention of the interests used to be very important, as well, but, under current law, that is no longer the case.

[1] Qualitative Aspects

In general, stock is the type of consideration that provides continuity of proprietary interest. At the other extreme, cash consideration does not continue shareholder investment, but rather, resembles a sale. Other forms of consideration are neither obviously equity nor obviously cash-equivalents. Several cases illustrate the type of consideration that qualifies under the continuity of proprietary interest doctrine.

In *Helvering v. Minnesota Tea Co.*, 296 U.S. 378 (1935), Minnesota Tea Co. (Minnesota Tea), a corporation with only three shareholders, transferred all of its assets to the Grand Union Company (Grand Union) in exchange for voting trust certificates representing 18,000 Grand Union common shares and $426,842.53 cash. It distributed the cash to its shareholders. Minnesota Tea's shareholders also agreed to pay $106,471.73 of its outstanding debts. *Id.* at 379, 381. Although the IRS contended only that the debt assumption gave rise to taxable gain, the Board of Tax Appeals determined that the entire transfer to Grand Union should be treated as a sale rather than a reorganization, which would give rise to "taxable gain amounting to the difference between cost of the property transferred and the cash received plus the value of the 18,000 shares—$712,195.90." *Id.* at 382. The Court of Appeals reversed. *Id.*

The Supreme Court reiterated the position of *Pinellas Ice and Cold Storage Co. v. Commissioner*, 287 U.S. 462 (1933), discussed above,[11] that the mere purchase for money of the assets of one company by another is beyond the purpose of the merger provisions, and that the seller must acquire an interest in the affairs of the purchasing company that is more definite than short-term notes. The Court added that the transferring corporation acquire a "definite and material interest" in the acquiring corporation, "represent[ing] a substantial part of the value of the thing transferred." *Minnesota Tea*, at 385. In *Minnesota Tea*, the Court found that

---

[11] *See* § 9.06[A].

the transaction qualified as a reorganization. It held that Minnesota had received an interest in Grand Union that represented a "material part of the value of the transferred assets." *Id.* at 386.

In *John A. Nelson Co. v. Helvering*, 296 U.S. 374 (1935), John A. Nelson Co. (Nelson) and Elliot-Fisher Corp. (Elliot) developed a plan that would allow Elliot to gain control of almost all of Nelson's assets. Under the plan, Elliot organized a new corporation (New Corp.) with 12,500 shares of non-voting preferred stock and 30,000 shares of common stock. Elliot then purchased all of New Corp.'s common shares for $2,000,000, which New Corp. then transferred to Nelson along with all of the preferred shares in return for substantially all of Nelson's properties. Nelson used some of the cash to retire its own preferred shares and it distributed the remainder, along with the New preferred shares, to its stockholders. Nelson retained $100,000 in cash and continued to run its business franchise after the transfer. *Id.* at 376. Thus, the sole equity consideration used to acquire the Nelson assets was non-voting preferred stock.

Nelson claimed that the transfer qualified as a reorganization, but the IRS provided a number of reasons why this transfer did not qualify, including a lack of continuity of proprietary interest. The Court noted that the transfer would qualify as a reorganization if the seller obtained a "definite and substantial interest in the affairs of the purchasing corporation." *Id.* at 377. The Court held that preferred stock, even non-voting preferred stock, provides a substantial interest in the corporation; the Code does not require that the transferor participate in the management of the acquiring corporation. *Id.*

Paulsen v. Commissioner, 469 U.S. 131 (1985), involved a merger of two banks. Commerce Savings and Loan Association (Commerce), a state-chartered stock savings and loan association, merged into Citizens Federal Savings and Loan Association (Citizens), a federally chartered mutual savings and loan association. Pursuant to the merger, the taxpayers exchanged their "guaranty stock" in Commerce for passbook savings accounts and certificates of deposit in Citizens representing share interests in Citizens; Citizens had no other form of ownership interests. *Id.* at 132–34.

The Court noted that the Citizens shares (the passbook savings accounts and certificates of deposit) were "hybrid instruments having both equity and debt characteristics."[12] *Id.* at 138. They gave their owners the right to vote, owners received dividends rather than interest on their accounts, and owners would receive a *pro rata* distribution of assets in the event of a solvent dissolution. *Id.* at 134, 138. However, the shares were not subordinated to creditors' claims, the deposits were not considered permanent contributions to capital, and the shareholders had a right to withdraw the face amount of their deposits in cash. In addition, in practice, Citizens paid a fixed, pre-announced rate on all of its accounts. *Id.* at 139. Thus,

---

[12] The characterization of an ownership interest in a corporation as debt or equity is discussed in § 3.03 of Chapter 3.

the Supreme Court found that "the debt characteristics of Citizens' shares greatly outweigh the equity characteristics." *Id.* at 140.

The Court found that the debt value of the Citizens shares was the same as the face value. Accordingly, because no one would pay more than face value for the shares, the court found that the value attributable to equity features was zero. The Court therefore held "that petitioners' passbook accounts and certificates of deposit were cash equivalents." *Id.* Accordingly, the taxpayers were not entitled to treat the merger as a tax-free reorganization, and were taxable on the gain they realized.

Taken together, *Helvering v. Minnesota Tea Co., John A. Nelson Co.,* and *Paulsen* reflect the Supreme Court's position that stock consideration[13] is qualitatively sufficient under the continuity of proprietary interest doctrine, but cash, cash equivalents, and debt obligations are not.[14] *Paulsen* effectively precludes a tax-free merger of a stock savings and loan association into a mutual savings and loan association. However, it does not preclude a tax-free merger of a mutual savings and loan association into a stock savings and loan association. In the latter case, owners of the target would receive stock in exchange for their cash-equivalent ownership interests. The stock received should qualify as appropriate proprietary interest in the new company.

[2] Quantitative Aspects

In Revenue Ruling 66-224, 1966-2 C.B. 114, the IRS held that when one corporation merges into another, the continuity of interest requirement of Treasury Regulation 1.368-1(b) is satisfied if, in return for their shares of the acquired corporation, the shareholders of the acquired corporation receive at least 50 percent of their total individual or group consideration in stock of the acquiring corporation. This is true even if some shareholders in the group receive only cash. In other words, continuity of proprietary interest is considered for the transaction as a whole, *not* shareholder by shareholder.[15]

John A. Nelson Co. v. Helvering, 296 U.S. 374 (1935), discussed above, also provides information on quantitative sufficiency of continuity of proprietary interest. In that case, the Court held that John A. Nelson Co. (Nelson) received a substantial, and therefore adequate, interest in the new corporation, although the preferred stock Nelson received was also only slightly more than 38 percent of the consideration Nelson received for its assets. (The 12,500 shares of preferred stock carried a par value of $100

---

[13] Treasury Regulation 1.354-1(e) provides that stock rights are treated as securities without a principal amount. They will therefore be treated as securities but generally not constitute boot. *See* BITTKER & EUSTICE, *supra,* at ¶ 12.41[2]–[4].

[14] *See* Revenue Procedures 77-37, 1977-2 C.B. 568 and 84-42, 1984-1 C.B. 521 for the IRS's ruling guidelines on stock that will not be issued immediately. *See also* BITTKER & EUSTICE, *supra,* at ¶ 12.41[2].

[15] As discussed below, Treasury regulations promulgated in 2005 provide a lower threshold for sufficient continuity of proprietary interest.

making it only $1,250,000, or 38.46 percent, of the total $3,250,000 of value Nelson received in the transfer.)

Yoc Heating Corp. v. Commissioner, 61 T.C. 168 (1973), involved an even lower percentage of equity consideration. In that case, Reliance Fuel Oil Corp. (Reliance) purchased approximately 85 percent of the stock of Nassau Utilities Fuel Corp. (Nassau), in exchange for cash and notes. *Id.* at 171. Reliance then created a new corporation to acquire Nassau's assets, Yoc Heating Corp. (Yoc Heating). *See id.* at 170 n.2, 172. Over the objections of its minority shareholders, Nassau transferred all of its assets to Yoc Heating in return for cash and Yoc Heating shares. Nassau's minority shareholders chose to receive cash for their shares, so Reliance became Yoc Heating's sole shareholder. Shortly after transferring its assets, Nassau dissolved. *Id.* at 172.

The IRS argued that the transfer qualified as a reorganization either under section 368(a)(1)(F), or under section 368(a)(1)(D), providing Yoc Heating with a transferred basis in the assets it received from Nassau. The court held that, taken as a whole, the transfer did not qualify as a D reorganization. *Id.* at 177. In addition, the court held that there was no F reorganization, for lack of continuity of proprietary interest.[16] *Id.* at 178. The court found that "[t]he record . . . clearly reveals that each step that was taken by Reliance and New Nassau was an integral part of a plan whereby the assets of Old Nassau would be acquired by a new corporation in which Reliance would control more than 80 percent of the issued and outstanding stock and *the shareholders of Old Nassau would at most have no more than approximately a 15-percent interest in such stock.*" *Id.* at 177 (emphasis added). Therefore, the court held that the asset transfer should be characterized as a purchase. *Id.* at 178.

Note that the *Yoc Heating* transaction also constitutes a qualified stock purchase under section 338, raising potential overlap with taxable acquisitions, which were discussed in Chapter 7.[17] Treasury Regulations under section 338 provide that if an acquiring corporation makes a qualified stock purchase of target stock (generally the acquisition of 80 percent of a corporation's stock, by vote and by value), but does not make a section 338 election, "the purchasing corporation's target stock acquired in the qualified stock purchase *represents an interest on the part of a person who was an owner of the target's business enterprise prior to the transfer* that can be continued in a reorganization." Treas. Reg. § 1.338-3(d)(2) (emphasis added). This is the opposite approach of *Yoc Heating*, which treated Reliance's acquisition of approximately 85 percent of the target's stock for cash and notes as the introduction of a new party that was not a historic shareholder. Thus, under the regulations, the following scenario satisfies the continuity of interest requirement with respect to the former target shareholders:

---

[16] Note that Treasury regulations provide that "for transactions occurring on or after February 25, 2005, a continuity of the business enterprise and a continuity of interest are not required for the transaction to qualify as a reorganization under section . . . [368(a)(1)(F)]." Treas. Reg. § 1.368-1(b).

[17] *See* § 7.05.

> P, T, and X are domestic corporations. T and X each operate a trade or business. A and K, individuals unrelated to P, own 85 and 15 percent, respectively, of the stock of T. P owns all of the stock of X. . . . P purchases all of A's T stock for cash in a qualified stock purchase. P does not make an election under section 338(g) with respect to its acquisition of T stock. Shortly after the acquisition date, and as part of the same plan, T merges under applicable state law into X in a transaction that, but for the question of continuity of interest, satisfies all the requirements of section 368(a)(1)(A). In the merger, all of T's assets are transferred to X. P and K receive X stock in exchange for their T stock. P intends to retain the stock of X indefinitely.

Treas. Reg. § 1.338-3(d)(5) Ex.(i), (ii). Thus, the regulations provide that both T and P recognize no gain or loss and take substituted bases. Treas. Reg. § 1.338-3(d)(5) Ex.(iii), (iv).

However, the regulations further provide that the operative provisions of reorganizations do not apply to *minority shareholders*, such as K in the example, unless the transfer of the target's assets constitutes a reorganization *without regard to the regulations*. Treas. Reg. § 1.338-3(d)(1), (5) Ex.(v). The regulations thus bifurcate the transaction into component parts, and, in this example, find one part to be a nonrecognition transaction and the other to be taxable. Accordingly, the regulations provide:

> Under general principles of tax law applicable to reorganizations, the continuity of interest requirement is not satisfied because P's stock purchase and the merger of T into X are pursuant to an integrated transaction in which A, the owner of 85 percent of the stock of T, received solely cash in exchange for A's T stock. *See, e.g.,* § 1.368-1(e)(1)(I); *Yoc Heating v. Commissioner*, 61 T.C. 168 (1973); *Kass v. Commissioner*, 60 T.C. 218 (1973), *aff'd*, 491 F.2d 749 (3d Cir. 1974). *Thus, the requisite continuity of interest under § 1.368-1(b) is lacking and section 354 does not apply to K's exchange of T stock for X stock.* K recognizes gain or loss, if any, pursuant to section 1001(c) with respect to its T stock.

Treas. Reg. § 1.338-3(d)(5) Ex.(v) (emphasis added).

Thus, 15-percent continuity of equity interest, as in *Yoc Heating*, remains insufficient. Examples in Treasury Regulations promulgated in 2005 found 25-percent continuity insufficient. *See* Treas. Reg. § 1.368-1(e)(2)(v) Ex. 2(i) (acquisitive consideration consisting of $20 of stock and $60 of cash was insufficient); Treas. Reg. § 1.368-1(e)(2)(v) Ex. 4 (acquisitive consideration of $25 of stock and $75 of cash was insufficient).

By contrast, as discussed above, in 1935, *John A. Nelson Co.* held 38-percent continuity sufficient. The IRS's ruling that if 50 percent of the acquisitive consideration is equity, that is sufficient to provide continuity of proprietary interest, provides a safe harbor, but is less generous than the continuity requirements now contemplated in Treasury Regulations.

Examples in the Treasury Regulations promulgated in 2005 found 40-percent continuity sufficient. *See, e.g.,* Treas. Reg. § 1.368-1(e)(2)(v) Ex. 1 (acquisitive consideration of $40 of stock and $60 of cash was sufficient); Treas. Reg. § 1.368-1(e)(2)(v) Ex. 2(ii) (acquisitive consideration of $32 of stock and $48 of cash was sufficient).

[C]   Requisite Continuity: Application of the Step-Transaction Doctrine

In *J.E. Seagram Corp. v. Commissioner*, 104 T.C. 75 (1995), discussed above with respect to the requirement of a "plan of reorganization,"[18] Seagram also argued that the transaction lacked continuity of proprietary interest. (Failure to meet that requirement would render the transaction taxable, allowing Seagram to recognize the loss it realized on the exchange of its Conoco shares for DuPont shares.)

Seagram argued that because it had purchased about 32 percent of the Conoco shares for cash and DuPont had purchased 46 percent for cash, the combined cash purchases of Conoco shares left only 22 percent of Conoco's shareholders continuing their interest in DuPont. This analysis considered each step of the transaction separately.[19] However, when the merger transaction is considered as a whole, DuPont acquired 54 percent of the Conoco stock in exchange for DuPont stock—all but the 46 percent of the shares DuPont had acquired for cash via a tender offer. *Id.* at 100. In other words:

> In the "integrated" transaction . . . petitioner [Seagram], not DuPont, "stepped into the shoes" of 32 percent of the Conoco shareholders when petitioner acquired their stock for cash via . . . tender offer, held the 32 percent transitorily, and immediately tendered it in exchange for DuPont stock. For present purposes, there is no material distinction between petitioner's tender of the Conoco stock and a direct tender by the "old" Conoco shareholders themselves. Thus, the requirement of continuity of interest has been met.

Id. at 104.

As discussed above, the IRS guideline is that 50-percent continuity of interest will suffice for advance rulings, and the Supreme Court held that 38-percent equity continuity sufficed in *John A. Nelson Co.* Accordingly, the Tax Court found 54-percent continuity sufficient continuity of proprietary interest in the Seagram transaction.

Historically, maintenance of the proprietary interests for an appropriate period was an important component of continuity of proprietary interest. In general, the issue involved application of the step-transaction doctrine in order to determine whether subsequent dispositions of shares acquired

---

[18] *See* § 9.03.

[19] The step-transaction doctrine is discussed in § 1.04[E].

in the reorganization were part of the reorganization, or instead were separate transactions that did not spoil the tax consequences of the reorganization. Several cases on this point involved the acquisition by McDonald's Corporation of its corporate franchises. *See McDonald's Restaurants of Illinois, Inc. v. Commissioner*, 688 F.2d 520 (7th Cir. 1982); *Penrod v. Commissioner*, 88 T.C. 1415 (1987); *Estate of Christian v. Commissioner*, T.C. Memo. 1989-413.

In each of the these three cases, McDonald's desired to acquire the stock of certain corporate franchisees, while treating the acquisition as a "pooling of interests" for accounting purposes. A pooling of interests (as opposed to a "purchase") would allow McDonald's books to reflect target assets at their historic costs, rather than at their generally higher fair market value. That would increase book income by lowering depreciation and allowing higher gains on any eventual sale of the assets. In order to achieve pooling of interest accounting treatment, the acquisition of the target corporations would have to be made with McDonald's stock rather than cash. However, the stock would not be saleable unless it was registered.

In *McDonald's Restaurants of Illinois*, McDonald's and the franchisees, the Garb-Stern group, did not have a good business relationship. The Garb-Stern group wanted to sell their shares for cash, but agreed to the stock deal when McDonald's offered to include the stock in an upcoming registration so that the Garb-Stern group could promptly sell their McDonald's shares. Once the shares were registered, the Garb-Stern group sold almost all of the stock it had acquired in the transaction. *McDonald's Restaurants of Illinois*, 688 F.2d at 521–22. In that case, the Court of Appeals for the Seventh Circuit found no continuity of interest. It found that, under the step-transaction doctrine, the merger and subsequent sale of the shares were a single transaction. It found that the steps were so interdependent that the legal relations created by the merger would have been fruitless without the guarantees of saleability. It also found that the transaction satisfied the "spirit" of the binding commitment test. *Id.* at 524–25.

The *Penrod* case presented similar facts. However, in *Penrod*, there was no indication of any problems in the relationship between the taxpayers and McDonald's corporation. In addition, the taxpayers sought reorganization treatment. They did not request cash for their stock, but agreed to receive McDonald's stock. *Penrod*, 88 T.C. at 1418, 1420. Nonetheless, the taxpayers sold their stock approximately ten months after the merger. *See id.* at 1435–36. The court found "no binding commitment by the Penrods at the time of the acquisition to sell their stock" and further found "that, at the time of the acquisition, the Penrods did not intend to sell their McDonald's stock and that therefore the step-transaction doctrine is not applicable under either the interdependence test or the end-result test." *Id.* at 1434.

Estate of Christian also presented similar facts. In that case, the taxpayers, Messrs. Fein and Christian, also had a good relationship with McDonald's Corporation. The taxpayers never requested to receive cash. Their attorney, Mr. Baer, insisted that the transaction be structured as a tax-free reorganization. *Estate of Christian*, T.C. Memo. 1989-413. In addition, with respect to the "continuity of interest" requirement, Baer questioned the taxpayers about their plans for the stock they would receive. His notes reflected statements that Fein and Christian intended to keep the stock, rather than sell it. Nonetheless, Baer insisted that Fein and Christian receive guaranteed registration rights for the McDonald's stock they would receive. Shortly after the merger, Fein and Christian donated a few shares to charity, registered the remaining shares, and sold a number of them. *Id.*

The court found that Baer's insistence on guaranteed registration rights did not support an inference that the taxpayers had a preconceived intention to sell the McDonald's stock, but rather that Baer was acting of his own accord, in order to protect his clients. The court found the case factually distinguishable from *McDonald's Restaurants of Illinois*. It determined that the acquisition of the stock and the subsequent sale were not steps in a plan the end result of which was to cash out the taxpayers' interests in McDonald's corporation, were not interdependent steps, and were not linked by a binding commitment. Thus, the court held that the continuity of interest requirement was met. *Id.*

Subsequent to the McDonald's cases, Treasury Regulation 1.368-1(e) was amended to add the following sentence:

> For purposes of the continuity of interest requirement, a mere disposition of stock of the target corporation prior to a potential reorganization to persons not related (as defined in paragraph (e)(4) of this section determined without regard to paragraph (e)(4)(i)(A) of this section) to the target corporation or to persons not related (as defined in paragraph (e)(4) of this section) to the issuing corporation is disregarded and *a mere disposition of stock of the issuing corporation received in a potential reorganization to persons not related (as defined in paragraph (e)(4) of this section) to the issuing corporation is disregarded.*

Treas. Reg. § 1.368-1(e)(1)(i) (emphasis added). Under this regulation, step-transaction analysis is unnecessary, and all three McDonald's transactions, if they occurred today, would have the requisite continuity of proprietary interest. However, note that there is no such relief for section 351 transactions, which were discussed in Chapter 2—dispositions of stock of the controlled corporation in a section 351 transaction, if "stepped into" the exchange of property for stock, may cause the transaction to fail to qualify for nonrecognition.[20]

Are pre-reorganization redemptions of target stock or pre-reorganization distributions with respect to target stock integrated with the subsequent reorganization for continuity of interest purposes? Under regulation 1.368-1(e)(1)(ii), they are considered in the continuity of proprietary interest

---

[20] Application of the step transaction doctrine to section 351 transactions is discussed in § 2.02[A][1][d][ii].

calculation only to the extent that amounts received by target shareholders are treated as boot received in the exchange for purposes of section 356 (or would be treated as boot if target shareholders had also received stock of the acquiring corporation). In other words, amounts treated as boot in the reorganization are considered non-stock consideration to target shareholders.

> *Example 9.1*: Andrew owns all the stock of Target, which has a fair market value of $1,000. As part of a plan of reorganization, Target redeems stock worth $800 from Andrew. Target then merges into Acquiring, pursuant to which Andrew receives $200 of Acquiring stock, which constitutes 10 percent of the stock of Acquiring. If Andrew is treated under section 356 as having received $800 in boot, the continuity percentage for the merger would be only 20 percent ($200 worth of Acquiring stock divided by the pre-redemption $1,000 value of Target).

The determination of whether the redemption proceeds constitute boot is accomplished by applying section 356; that section generally treats as boot both money and non-stock property received in a reorganization, with special rules applying to securities.[21] Treating the amounts received as if they included stock of the acquiring corporation makes section 356 applicable rather than section 302. *See* Rev. Rul. 74-515, 1974-2 C.B. 118; Mark J. Silverman and Andrew J. Weinstein, *The New Prereorganization COI Regulations*, 91 TAX NOTES 805 (2001).

Treasury Regulations provide the following example, involving a B reorganization:

> T has two shareholders, A and B. P expresses an interest in acquiring the stock of T. A does not wish to own P stock. T redeems A's shares in T in exchange for cash. *No funds have been or will be provided by P for this purpose.* P subsequently acquires all the outstanding stock of T from B solely in exchange for voting stock of P. The cash received by A in the prereorganization redemption is not treated as other property or money under section 356, and would not be so treated even if A had received some stock of P in exchange for his T stock. The prereorganization redemption by T does not affect continuity of interest, because B's proprietary interest in T is unaffected, and the value of the proprietary interest in T is preserved.

Treas. Reg. § 1.368-1(e)(7) Ex. 9 (emphasis added). Commentators have disagreed as to whether the IRS would reach the same result in an A or C reorganization, and whether it depends on tracing the funds used for the redemption. *See* Michael L. Schultz, *Pre-Acquisition Distributions and COI: Another View*, 91 TAX NOTES 837 (2001).

Post-reorganization redemptions were not integrated with the reorganization in Revenue Ruling 99-58, 1999-2 C.B. 701, even though they were announced prior to the reorganization. In that Revenue Ruling, the target

---

[21] Section 356 is discussed in more detail in § 9.07.

merged into the acquiring corporation, a widely held, public company. In the merger, the target shareholders received 50 percent stock of the acquiring corporation and 50 percent cash. Prior to the merger, the acquiring company announced its intention to repurchase its shares on the open market, to prevent dilution resulting from the issuance of shares in the merger. The IRS did not integrate the repurchases with the merger because (1) the repurchase program was not negotiated with the target or its shareholders, (2) there was no understanding between the target shareholders and the acquiring corporation that the target shareholders' stock ownership would be transitory, and (3) the reality of an open market purchase is such that the identities of buyer and seller are not revealed, so the repurchase program did not favor participation by the former shareholders of the target corporation. *Id.* at 701.

CHART 9.1
General Checklist for Valid Reorganizations

(1)   The transaction must qualify as a reorganization under section 368.

(2)   There must be a "plan of reorganization."

(3)   There must be a business purpose for the transaction.

(4)   There must be continuity of business enterprise.[22]

(5)   There must be continuity of proprietary interest.[23]

§ 9.07   General Tax Consequences of Transactions Qualifying as Reorganizations

In general, qualification of a transaction as a reorganization means that those taxpayers receiving stock will recognize any realized gain only to the extent of boot received. In addition, old bases will generally carry over, with appropriate adjustments, such as for boot received and gain recognized.

[A]   Target Shareholders

In exchange for target stock, target shareholders generally receive stock in the acquiring corporation, as well as other possible consideration such as securities, cash, or other property. Note that some of the consideration received by target shareholders must be stock in order for continuity of proprietary interest to exist, but, as continuity of proprietary interest is considered for *the transaction as a whole*, not every shareholder necessarily will receive stock.

---

[22] Continuity of business enterprise is not required for E and F reorganizations occurring on or after February 25, 2005. Treas. Reg. § 1.368-1(b).

[23] Continuity of proprietary interest is not required for E and F reorganizations occurring on or after February 25, 2005. Treas. Reg. § 1.368-1(b).

[1] Calculating Gain Recognized

In general, because target shareholders relinquish target stock in exchange for other stock or property, their realized gain (or loss) is the difference between the value of the consideration received (their amount realized) and their basis in the target stock.[24] *See* I.R.C. § 1001. However, if the reorganization provisions apply, instead of recognizing *all* of the realized gain, sections 354 or 356 may apply to shelter some or all of each shareholder's realized gain.

Under section 354(a)(1), in general, no gain or loss is recognized if stock (or securities) in a corporate party to a reorganization is exchanged, in pursuance of the plan of reorganization, solely for stock (or securities) in that corporation or in another corporate party to the reorganization. Under section 356(a)(1), if a shareholder receives boot, the shareholder's gain realized is recognized to the extent of boot. Loss is not recognized in either instance. *See* I.R.C. §§ 354(a)(1), 356(c).

> *Example 9.2*: Bill and Carol are the sole shareholders of X, Inc. Y Corporation acquires it by statutory merger (X, Inc. merges into Y Corporation, with Y surviving). In return for their X, Inc. stock, Bill and Carol each receive a combination of stock and cash. For his 50 shares with basis of $200,000, Bill receives 100 Y shares worth $1,000,000, and $250,000 of cash. For her 50 shares with basis of $350,000, Carol receives 80 shares worth $800,000 and $450,000 of cash. Bill realizes $1,050,000 of gain, and recognizes $250,000 of it. Carol realizes $900,000 of gain and recognizes $450,000 of it.

Although the general rule of section 354(a)(1) applies to both stock and securities, section 354(a)(1) does not apply if "the principal amount of any such securities received exceeds the principal amount of any such securities surrendered, or . . . any such securities are received and no such securities are surrendered." I.R.C. § 354(a)(2)(A). If securities are received and the principal amount of such securities received exceeds the principal amount of any securities surrendered, *the fair market value of the excess principal amount constitutes boot.* I.R.C. § 356(d)(2)(B). Therefore, if no securities are surrendered, the excess is the entire principal amount of the securities received. *Id.* Thus, only if the principal amount of securities *surrendered* exceeds the principal amount of any securities received are the securities received *not* treated as boot at all.[25] *See* I.R.C. §§ 354(a)(1), (2)(A), 356(d)(2)(A).

> *Example 9.3*: David and Ellen are the sole shareholders of Z, Inc. Friendly Corporation acquires Z, Inc. by statutory merger. In return for their Z, Inc. stock and securities, David and Ellen each receive a combination of

---

[24] Note that under section 356(b), if section 355 would apply to a distribution (that is, a spin-off) but for the fact that boot was received, the boot is treated as a 301 distribution, without regard to realized gain.

[25] Note that original issue discount issues can arise when securities are exchanged. *See* BITTKER & EUSTICE, *supra*, at ¶ 12.44[1][c] n.756.

stock and securities. For his 50 shares with basis of $200,000, David receives 100 Friendly Corporation shares worth $1,000,000, and securities worth $250,000, with a principal amount of $250,000. For her 50 Z, Inc. shares with basis of $350,000, and Z, Inc. securities with principal amount and basis of $300,000 (worth $200,000), Ellen receives 80 shares worth $800,000 and $650,000 worth of Friendly Corporation securities. Assume that the Friendly securities have a fair market value equal to their principal amount.

David realizes $1,050,000 of gain, and recognizes $250,000 because David surrendered no securities; all $250,000 of securities received is treated as boot, in the amount of their fair market value. Ellen realizes $800,000 of gain. The excess principal amount ($350,000) of the securities received constitutes boot, so Ellen recognizes gain in the amount of the fair market value of that excess—here, $350,000.

Note that nonqualified preferred stock does not constitute stock or securities (it constitutes boot) unless it is received in exchange for nonqualified preferred stock. This "stock boot" is discussed in § 2.02[A][1][f][i].

[2] Character of Recognized Gain

The discussion and examples above demonstrate how to compute taxable gain. But how is that gain *characterized*—is it capital gain or dividend income?[26] In 1989, the United States Supreme Court provided an approach to the problem, in *Commissioner v. Clark*, 489 U.S. 726 (1989). In that case, the taxpayer exchanged his 100-percent stock interest in Basin Surveys, Inc. (Basin), the target corporation, for a 0.9-percent interest in NL Industries, Inc. (NL), the acquiring corporation, plus $3.25 million in cash. Before the transaction, Clark had not owned any interest in NL. The transaction qualified as a triangular merger under section 368(a)(2)(D). *Id.* at 731.

In determining that Clark's gain was capital in nature, the Court analyzed a hypothetical redemption. An important issue was whether to test the result of a hypothetical redemption *before* or *after* the reorganization. The IRS argued that "the boot payment is treated as though it were made in a hypothetical redemption by the acquired corporation (Basin) immediately *prior* to the reorganization. Under this test, the cash payment received by the taxpayer indisputably would have been treated as a dividend." *Id.* at 732–33. Instead, the Court agreed with the taxpayer, holding that "the effect of the exchange as a whole" needed to be considered, so it applied the hypothetical redemption to the *post-reorganization* facts. *Id.* at 737.

The Court applied the hypothetical-redemption test by comparing the stock Clark could have had if he had not received cash (a 1.3-percent interest in NL) with the stock Clark actually received (a 0.9-percent interest in NL). *Id.* at 733, 737–38. The difference of 0.4 percent of the NL stock

---

[26] *But cf.* I.R.C. § 356(b), discussed briefly in footnote 24, *supra.*

was treated as *redeemed* for the amount of boot the taxpayer received—
$3.25 million in cash. Under section 302(b)(2), such a redemption qualifies
as substantially disproportionate; 0.9 percent is less than 80 percent of 1.3
percent (it is only 69.23 percent of 1.3 percent) and 0.9 percent is also (far)
less than a 50-percent voting interest. Thus, the Court held that Clark's
gain was capital in nature. *Id.* at 745. Justice White dissented, arguing that
the transaction resembled *United States v. Davis*, 397 U.S. 301 (1970), a
redemption by a sole shareholder.[27]

The following example illustrates the *Clark* analysis:

Example 9.4: Glenda is the majority shareholder of G, Inc. HugeCo, Inc.
offers to acquire G, Inc., and Glenda agrees. Pursuant to a valid reorganization, she exchanges the 90-percent stake she has in G, Inc. for five
percent of the only class of stock of HugeCo, Inc. plus $400,000 of cash.
Assume that Glenda recognizes $300,000 of gain. Also assume that
$400,000 is the value of a two-percent stake in HugeCo, so Glenda could
have received seven percent of HugeCo instead. Rather than treating
Glenda as a 90-percent shareholder, under *Clark*, Glenda is treated as
if she redeemed two percent of the HugeCo stock for $400,000 cash.
Therefore, Glenda is deemed to have dropped from a seven-percent to a
five-percent interest in HugeCo. That deemed redemption is substantially
disproportionate because five percent is less than 80 percent of seven
percent, and is also less than a 50-percent voting interest. Accordingly,
Glenda's $300,000 gain is capital in character.

Note that, under the majority's holding in *Clark*, transactions taking
shareholders from sizeable holdings in a smaller corporation to smaller
holdings in a larger corporation, as in both *Clark* itself and Example 9.4,
are tested based upon the smaller stockholdings. It is easier for a shareholder with a small minority of the shares to obtain exchange treatment
under section 302 than it is for a large shareholder, because it is more likely
that a reduction in a minority interest will be substantial compared to the
prior ownership. At the extreme, a sole shareholder like Clark could never
obtain capital gains treatment through a pre-reorganization redemption,
under *United States v. Davis*, as Justice White pointed out in *Clark*.

The *Clark* holding has diminished in importance now that individuals'
qualified dividends are taxed at capital gains rates under section 1(h)(3)(B).
In fact, for individual shareholders, the distinction between qualified
dividend and exchange treatment has particularly little importance in this
context because *Clark* characterizes recognized gain after basis has already
been recovered. That is, in this context, unlike in most contexts, dividend
treatment does not lack the basis offset advantage that exchange treatment
provides. Also note that, as always, corporate shareholders may prefer dividend treatment to exchange treatment because of the availability of the
dividends received deduction of section 243. Dividend treatment will also
reduce the amount of earnings and profits the acquiring corporation
inherits under section 381, which is discussed in Chapter 13.

---

[27] *Davis* is discussed in § 5.03[B][3].

[3] Basis

[a] In General

The former target shareholders generally have exchanged at least some stock in a target corporation for some stock in the acquiring corporation, with gain recognition generally limited to the amount of boot received. In order to preserve any unrecognized gain or loss, each former target shareholder's basis in the newly received shares is computed with reference to the basis of his or her target shares, with appropriate upward and downward adjustments for gain (or loss) recognized, boot received, and the like. More specifically, section 358(a)(1) provides:

> The basis of the property permitted to be received under such section without the recognition of gain or loss [that is, stock in the acquiring corporation] shall be the same as that of the property exchanged—
>
> (A) decreased by—
>
> > (i) the fair market value of any other property (except money) received by the taxpayer,
> >
> > (ii) the amount of any money received by the taxpayer, and
> >
> > (iii) the amount of loss to the taxpayer which was recognized on such exchange, and
>
> (B) increased by—
>
> > (i) the amount which was treated as a dividend, and
> >
> > (ii) the amount of gain to the taxpayer which was recognized on such exchange (not including any portion of such gain which was treated as a dividend).

I.R.C. § 358(a)(1). "The basis of any other property (except money) received by the taxpayer shall be its fair market value." I.R.C. § 358(a)(2). Note that these provisions are the same ones that were applied under section 351 to transferors of property to a controlled corporation. [28]

Example 9.5: Inez is the sole shareholder of I, Inc. Jiant Corp. offers to acquire I, Inc., and Inez agrees. Pursuant to a valid reorganization, she exchanges all 100 shares of I, Inc. (worth $800,000, and having a $700,000 basis), and receives a five-percent interest in Jiant Corp. (worth $600,000) plus $200,000 of cash. Accordingly, Inez realizes $100,000 of gain and recognizes all $100,000 of it. Inez's basis in her five-percent stake in Jiant Corp. will be $600,000 ($700,000 – $200,000 cash, plus $100,000 of gain recognized).

---

[28] Section 351 transactions are discussed in Chapter 2. Section 358 is discussed in § 2.02[A][3].

[b] Basis with Respect to Securities or Multiple Classes of Stock

The same provisions generally apply if the reorganization includes an exchange of securities. If no boot is received in such an exchange, then the investor generally takes, as an aggregate basis in the stock and/or securities he now holds, the aggregate basis he had before the exchange.[29] Treas. Reg. § 1.358-1(a)(1). Allocation among the stock and securities is described below. If the investor receives boot, the investor's aggregate basis in the stock and/or securities he or she now holds is the aggregate basis the investor had before the exchange, minus the money and the fair market value of the non-cash boot received, and increased by the sum of the amount treated as a dividend (if any) and the amount of the gain recognized on the exchange. Treas. Reg. § 1.358-1(a)(1). The portion of a security that constitutes excess principal amount received (excess securities boot) is considered non-cash boot for this purpose. See Treas. Reg. § 1.358-2(a)(1). Any boot received takes a basis equal to its fair market value. I.R.C. § 358(a)(2).

Traditionally, the investor's allocation of the new basis among stock and securities, or among multiple classes of stock or securities, generally used an allocation method based on fair market value. See Treas. Reg. § 1.358-2. For example, if the investor owned only stock of one class before the transaction and owns stock of two or more classes after the transaction, then the aggregate basis would be allocated among the stock of all classes held after the transaction, in proportion to the fair market values of the stock of each class. Treas. Reg. § 1.358-2(a)(2). However, Treasury regulations proposed in May 2004 require basis "tracing" to the extent possible. The regulations state, in part:

> If more than one share of stock or security is received in exchange for one share of stock or one security, the basis of the share of stock or security surrendered shall be allocated to the shares of stock or securities received in the exchange in proportion to the fair market value of the shares of stock or securities received. If one share of stock or security is received in respect of more than one share of stock or security or a fraction of a share of stock or security is received, the basis of the shares of stock or securities surrendered must be allocated to the shares of stock or securities received in a manner that reflects, to the greatest extent possible, that a share of stock or security received is received in respect of shares of stock or securities acquired on the same date and at the same price.

---

[29] There is an exception for recapitalizations in which each holder of stock or securities of a particular class has an option to surrender some or none of such stock or securities in exchange for stock or securities. In that situation, if an investor "exchanges an identifiable part of his stock or securities, the basis of the part of the stock or securities retained shall remain unchanged and shall not be taken into account in determining the basis of the stock or securities received." Treas. Reg. § 1.358-2(a)(5).

Prop. Treas. Reg. § 1.358-2(a)(2)(i). The proposed regulations thus focus on *shares* rather than classes of stock.

The regulations also allow the taxpayer to designate which shares were received for which, in certain circumstances:

> If a shareholder or security holder that purchased or acquired shares of stock or securities in a corporation on *different dates or at different prices* exchanges such shares of stock or securities under the terms of section 354, 355, or 356, or receives a distribution of shares of stock or securities under the terms of section 355, and the shareholder or security holder is *not able to identify which particular share of stock or security* (or portion of a share of stock or security) *is received in exchange* for, or with respect to, a particular share of stock or security, *the shareholder or security holder may designate which share of stock or security is received in exchange for, or with respect to, a particular share of stock or security,* provided that such designation is consistent with the terms of the exchange or distribution.

Prop. Treas. Reg. § 1.358-2(a)(2)(iii) (emphasis added). The regulations provide the following example, among others:

> Example 1. (i) Facts. F, an individual, acquired 20 shares of Corporation N stock on Date 1 for $3 each and 10 shares of Corporation N stock on Date 2 for $6 each. On Date 3, Corporation O acquires the assets of Corporation N in a reorganization under section 368(a)(1)(A). Pursuant to the terms of the plan of reorganization, F receives 2 shares of Corporation O stock for each share of Corporation N stock. Therefore, F receives 60 shares of Corporation O stock. Pursuant to section 354, F recognizes no gain or loss on the exchange. *F is not able to identify which shares of Corporation O stock are received in exchange for each share of Corporation N stock.*
>
> (ii) Analysis. Under paragraph (a)(2) of this section, F has 40 shares of Corporation O each of which has a basis of $1.50 and is treated as having been acquired on Date 1 and 20 shares of Corporation O each of which has a basis of $3 and is treated as having been acquired on Date 2. On or before the date on which the basis of a share of Corporation O stock received becomes relevant, *F may designate which of the shares of Corporation O have a basis of $1.50 and which have a basis of $3.*

Prop. Treas. Reg. § 1.358-2(c) Ex. 1 (emphasis added).

[4] Holding Period

As discussed in Chapter 2 with respect to section 351 transactions, to determine the holding period for property received in an exchange, such as stock or securities, the taxpayer includes the period during which he held capital or quasi-capital assets relinquished in the exchange if the property received by the taxpayer has the same basis in whole or in part as the property he relinquished.[30] I.R.C. § 1223(1). Thus, a shareholder or security holder generally "tacks" the holding period of the capital and quasi-capital assets he transferred onto the holding period of the stock (or securities) he receives. If the transferor transferred multiple properties with different holding periods, the stock will have split holding periods for purposes of determining long-term or short-term capital gain or loss. *See* Rev. Rul. 85-164, 1985-2 C.B. 117 (discussed in Chapter 2).[31]

[B] Target Corporation

In some reorganizations (but not B or E reorganizations), the target corporation actually or constructively receives stock, securities, or other property from the acquiring corporation. The general rule of section 361 is that, so long as the target distributes to its shareholders anything it receives other than stock, it will not be taxed. However, if the target retains non-stock property, any gain realized by the target corporation generally will be recognized to the extent of the value of the retained property. Note that distribution to shareholders will necessarily occur if the target is deemed liquidated (as in an A reorganization) or actually liquidates as it generally must in a C reorganization, *see* I.R.C. § 368(a)(2)(G), and an acquisitive D reorganization, *see* I.R.C. § 368(a)(1)(D). *See* BITTKER & EUSTICE, *supra*, at ¶ 12.42[1][b].

> *Example 9.6*: Kyle is the sole shareholder of K, Inc. Large Corp. offers to acquire K, Inc., and Kyle agrees. The acquisition is structured as a C reorganization. Accordingly, Large Corp. issues to K, Inc. new shares representing a three-percent interest in Large Corp., plus $50,000 cash, in exchange for all of the assets of K, Inc. (worth $900,000, with a basis of $400,000). K, Inc. is then liquidated, so that Kyle receives the three-percent interest in Large Corp. and the $50,000 cash. Although K, Inc. realized $500,000 of gain on the receipt of the stock and cash in exchange for its assets, because K, Inc. distributed the cash to Kyle, K, Inc. recognizes none of the gain.

In general, if liabilities of the target are assumed by another party to the exchange, they are not treated as boot received by the target. I.R.C. § 357(a). However, the "tax-avoidance purpose" exception discussed in Chapter 2, in connection with the application of section 357 to 351 transactions, applies in this context as well.[32] *See* I.R.C. § 357(b). Furthermore, section 357(c), the exception where liabilities exceed asset basis, applies to divisive D reorganizations. *See* I.R.C. § 357(c)(1)(B).

---

[30] *See* § 2.02[A][4].

[31] *See id.*

[32] *See* § 2.02[A][2][b][i].

[C]   Acquiring Corporation's Shareholders

The existing shareholders of the acquiring corporation generally do not participate in any of the reorganization exchanges. Rather, in general, they hold onto their stock, which, after the reorganization, generally will reflect a smaller interest in a larger company.

[D]   Acquiring Corporation

The acquiring corporation generally exchanges some of its shares (sometimes treasury shares) with target shareholders for their shares in the target corporation or with the target for its assets. Under section 1032, stock issued in exchange for property is tax-free.[33] However, if it transfers boot, it can recognize gain or loss on that boot. *See* Rev. Rul. 72-327, 1972-2 C.B. 197.

The acquiring corporation takes as its basis in any property it acquires in the reorganization the transferor's basis increased by any gain recognized to the transferor on the transfer. I.R.C. § 362(b).

Example 9.7: In Example 9.6, Large Corp. acquired all of the assets of K, Inc. Its basis in those assets will be K's $400,000 basis, with no increase, because no gain was recognized by K, Inc.

The acquiring corporation will also tack the transferor's holding period in any property it acquires that has a basis computed under section 362. *See* I.R.C. § 1223(2).

CHART 9.2
Principal Code Sections Applicable in Reorganizations

Party Involved in the Reorganization	Applicable Code Sections
Target Shareholders	I.R.C. §§ 354, 356; § 358 for basis
Target Corporation	I.R.C. §§ 357, 361; § 358 for basis
Acquiring Corporation	I.R.C. § 1032; § 362(b) for basis
Parent of Acquiring Corp.	I.R.C. § 1032; Treas. Reg. § 1.358-6 for basis

[E]   Introduction to the Carryover of Tax Attributes

Section 381 provides for the carryover of numerous corporate "tax attributes" following the acquisition by one corporation of another, in a nonrecognition-type transaction. Section 381 applies both to liquidations governed by section 332 and to A, C, D, F, and G reorganizations governed by section 361. I.R.C. § 381(a). The attributes carried over to the other corporation generally include net operating loss carryovers, earnings and

---

[33] Regulations also provide that if a subsidiary exchanges its parent's stock for money or other property in a taxable transaction, the subsidiary is given a cost basis in its parent's stock by deeming the parent to have made a cash contribution to the subsidiary, which was used to purchase the shares for fair market value. *See* Treas. Reg. § 1.1032-3.

profits, capital loss carryovers, method of computing depreciation allowance, and charitable contributions in excess of prior years' limitations. *See* I.R.C. § 381(c). The details of section 381, as well as limitations on the carryover of certain favorable tax attributes, are discussed in Chapter 13.

§ 9.08   Intersection of Section 351 and Section 368

Some transactions that looked like failed reorganizations may qualify as nonrecognition transactions under section 351. The IRS has ruled that the fact that certain "larger acquisitive transactions," may fail to meet the requirements of a tax-free reorganization does not preclude the applicability of section 351(a) to transfers that may be part of such larger transactions, and that, either alone or in conjunction with other transfers, meet the requirements of section 351(a). Rev. Rul. 84-71, 1984-1 C.B. 106. The key to spotting section 351 transactions in this context is to remember that stock of one corporation constitutes "property" under section 351 when transferred to another corporation.

Example 9.8: Mark and Nan are the sole shareholders of MN, Inc. Mark owns 75 percent of the MN, Inc. shares, and Nan owns the other 25 percent. O, Inc. wishes to acquire majority control of MN, Inc. Mark agrees with O, Inc. to jointly form a new corporation for that purpose, P Corp. Mark contributes his MN, Inc. shares, and O, Inc. contributes cash, in return for which Mark and O, Inc. receive all of the stock of P Corp. The transaction qualifies under section 351 because Mark and O, Inc. transferred property to P Corp. solely in exchange for stock, and they control P Corp. immediately after the exchange.

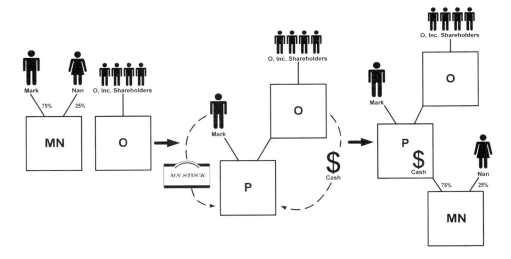

Note that qualification under section 351 typically renders applicable provisions that apply to section 351 transactions, such as sections 357 and 362(e)(2), both of which are discussed in Chapter 2.

Chapter 10

ACQUISITIVE REORGANIZATIONS

§ 10.01 Introduction

Acquisitive reorganizations involve an acquisition by an acquiring company of stock or assets of a target company. In order to qualify as a reorganization under section 368, the consideration paid to the target corporation or its shareholders will be at least partly stock. The acquiring company may use its own stock or stock of a parent corporation. When the acquiring corporation uses parent stock, the transaction is referred to as a "triangular" reorganization because of the three corporations involved.

This chapter discusses mergers, including triangular mergers; B reorganizations, including triangular B reorganizations; C reorganizations, including triangular ones; acquisitive D reorganizations; and acquisitive G reorganizations. It also briefly discusses "drop-downs" of assets acquired in a reorganization. Divisive reorganizations are discussed in Chapter 11, and reorganizations involving only one corporation are discussed in Chapter 12.

This chapter discusses the general tax consequences and basis rules that apply to each type of reorganization discussed in this chapter. Chapter 9 discusses the tax consequences of corporate reorganizations in general, as well as the application of basis provisions to corporate reorganizations generally.[1] The discussion there about allocation of basis among stock and securities of various classes is not repeated in this chapter.[2] The discussion of "tacked" holding periods also is not repeated in this chapter.[3]

§ 10.02 Mergers Involving Two or Three Corporations

Section 368(a)(1)(A) contemplates a statutory merger (or consolidation). In addition, two statutory types of triangular mergers qualify under section 368(a)(1)(A) if certain additional requirements are met. *See* I.R.C. §§ 368(a)(2)(D), (E). Each of these types of mergers is discussed below.

---

[1] *See* § 9.07.

[2] *See* § 9.07[A][3][b] for that discussion.

[3] *See* § 9.07[A][4] for that discussion.

[A] Statutory Mergers ("A" Reorganizations)

[1] In General

The Code's requirements for an A reorganization are noticeably limited. An "A" reorganization is "a statutory merger or consolidation," meaning that it meets applicable state law statutory requirements for a "merger" or "consolidation." *See* Treas. Reg. § 1.368-2(b)(1). In a merger, the acquiring corporation swallows the target corporation. In a consolidation, a new corporation is formed in the transaction. The diagram below illustrates the "before" and "after" pictures in a typical merger.

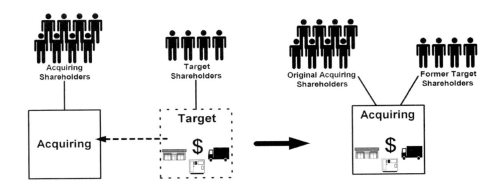

There are no statutory restrictions on the consideration used in an A reorganization. However, there are several common law requirements that must be met. In particular, A reorganizations, like most reorganizations,[4] must have a business purpose, continuity of proprietary interest, and continuity of business enterprise.[5] Because A reorganizations have so few statutory requirements, these common law limitations provide the main restrictions on this type of reorganization. In addition, sections 354, 356, and 361 require a "plan of reorganization."[6]

What if a purported A reorganization occurs in two steps? In *King Enterprises, Inc. v. United States*, 418 F.2d 511 (Ct. Cl. 1969), the acquiring company, Minute Maid Corporation (Minute Maid), first acquired more than half of the stock of Tenco, Inc. (Tenco), the target, for stock, cash and notes (the first step). It then obtained the remainder of Tenco's stock in a pre-planned upstream merger of Tenco into itself (the second step). *Id.*

---

[4] Treasury regulations provide that "for transactions occurring on or after February 25, 2005, a continuity of the business enterprise and a continuity of interest are not required for the transaction to qualify as a reorganization under section 368(a)(1)(E) or (F)." Treas. Reg. § 1.368-1(b).

[5] These common law requirements are discussed in §§ 9.04–9.06 of Chapter 9.

[6] *See* § 9.03 of Chapter 9.

at 513–14. If the two steps were considered separately, the Tenco stockholders, which included King Enterprises, would have had to report the gain recognized on the sale of Tenco stock for Minute Maid stock, cash, and notes. Instead, the Court of Claims agreed with King Enterprises that the transaction should be considered as an integrated whole. Thus, the step-transaction doctrine applied to combine the purchase and merger into a single transaction, a valid A reorganization,[7] *id.* at 515, although "[w]hen Minute Maid acquired the Tenco stock, none of the Tenco shareholders, including King Enterprises, could have known that [the] later merger would occur." Jeffrey L. Kwall & Kristina Maynard, *Dethroning King Enterprises*, 58 TAX LAW. 1, 4 (2004).

[2] "Divisive" Mergers and Mergers with Disregarded Entities

A valid A reorganization may not be divisive, even if it would meet the requirements of a state merger statute. *See* Treas. Reg. § 1.368-2(b)(1)(ii), (iii) Ex. 1; Rev. Rul. 2000-5, 2000-1 C.B. 436. Thus, the IRS ruled that each of the following situations failed to qualify as an A reorganization, despite the fact that each of them complied with the applicable state merger statute:

> *Situation (1).* A target corporation transfers some of its assets and liabilities to an acquiring corporation, retains the remainder of its assets and liabilities, and remains in existence following the transaction. The target corporation's shareholders receive stock in the acquiring corporation in exchange for part of their target corporation stock and they retain their remaining target corporation stock. . . .

> *Situation (2).* A target corporation transfers some of its assets and liabilities to each of two acquiring corporations. The target corporation liquidates and the target corporation's shareholders receive stock in each of the two acquiring corporations in exchange for their target corporation stock. . . .

Rev. Rul. 2000-5, 2000-1 C.B. 436, 436. The IRS explained, "Congress intended that § 355 be the sole means under which divisive transactions will be afforded tax-free status and, thus, specifically required the liquidation of the acquired corporation in reorganizations under both §§ 368(a)(1)(C) and 368(a)(1)(D) in order to prevent these reorganizations from being used in divisive transactions that did not satisfy § 355." *Id.* at 437 (citing Senate Reports); *see also* Steven A. Bank, *Taxing Divisive and Disregarded Mergers*, 34 GA. L. REV. 1523, 1531 (2000) ("Not only does the divisive merger potentially provide a more liberal tax-free spin-off provision, it may also

---

[7] *King Enterprises* is also discussed briefly in §§ 10.02[B][2][a] and 10.02[B][3] with respect to forward triangular mergers and reverse triangular mergers. The step-transaction doctrine is discussed in § 1.04[E] of Chapter 1.

allow parties to circumvent the restrictions in section 355(e) against combining spin-offs with mergers in a 'Morris Trust' transaction.").[8]

A related issue is the merger of a corporation with a "disregarded entity" with a corporate owner—an entity, such as a single-member LLC, that is treated as a division of its corporate owner under the "check-the-box" regulations that determine the federal income tax regime to which an entity is subject.[9] Under Treasury Regulations, where a disregarded entity merges into an acquiring corporation, that effectuates a divisive transaction under which the target corporation retains all of its assets but those of the disregarded entity. As a divisive transaction, it will not qualify as an A reorganization. *See* Treas. Reg. § 1.368-2(b)(1)(iii) Ex. 6. However, in the reverse situation—if a target corporation merges into a disregarded entity and the former target shareholders receive stock in the corporate owner of the disregarded entity—that is an acquisitive transaction that can qualify as an A reorganization if other applicable requirements, such as continuity of proprietary interest, are met. *See* Treas. Reg. § 1.368-2(b)(1)(iii) Ex. 2.

[3]   Tax Consequences and Basis Rules

In an A reorganization, target shareholders exchange their stock for stock of the acquiring corporation. Unless the target shareholders receive boot, section 354(a) applies to exclude from gross income gain realized on the exchange; loss is disallowed regardless of whether boot is received.

Section 356(a) applies to any target shareholder that received boot. Under section 356(a), gain realized by a target shareholder is recognized to that shareholder to the extent of the boot he received. Each target shareholder takes a basis in the new shares that, in general, is the old share basis, adjusted upward for gain recognized, and downward for boot received and for liabilities assumed by another party. *See* I.R.C. § 358(a).

Shareholders of the acquiring corporation do not exchange their shares in a merger, so they have no tax consequences. In a *consolidation*, by contrast, shareholders of the acquiring corporation receive shares in the new corporation. Their basis, under section 358, will be the basis in the shares they exchanged, assuming that they do not receive any boot. If they do receive boot, their basis will require adjustment under section 358, as explained above.

The target corporation does not recognize gain in an A reorganization because it does not retain assets. *See* I.R.C. § 361(b). In effect, it is deemed to receive stock of the acquiring corporation and then distribute that to its shareholders. The acquiring corporation takes an asset basis under section 362(b): target's asset basis plus gain recognized to the target on the transfer (none).

---

[8] Section 355(e) and *Commissioner v. Mary Archer W. Morris Trust*, 367 F.2d 794 (4th Cir. 1966), are discussed in § 11.02[F][2] of Chapter 11.

[9] The check-the-box regulations are discussed in Chapter 1. *See* § 1.02[A][2][b].

Example 10.1: P corporation is a publicly held company. For valid business reasons, it would like to acquire T corporation. T is held equally by Anita and Bob, each with a $100,000 stock basis. T has two assets, land worth $400,000 with a basis of $300,000, and machinery worth $200,000 with a basis of $280,000. Pursuant to a plan of reorganization, and in accordance with applicable state law, P corporation provides to each former T shareholder $270,000 worth of non-voting common stock (270 shares) and $30,000 of cash. In return, T merges into P, with P retaining the land and machinery for use in its business.

This is a valid A reorganization. It is a statutory merger, there is a business purpose, continuity of proprietary interest exists (90 percent of the consideration to the T shareholders was stock), there is continuity of business enterprise (P will use T's assets in its business), and there was a plan of reorganization.

Anita and Bob each realized gain of $200,000 ($300,000 minus $100,000) but recognize only $30,000 of gain each. I.R.C. § 356(a). Each takes a basis in the P stock of $100,000 under section 358 ($100,000 + $30,000 − $30,000). Finally, T realizes $100,000 of gain on the land and $80,000 of loss on the machinery. It recognizes neither under section 361. P corporation takes a $300,000 basis in the land and a $280,000 basis in the machinery, both under section 362(b).

[B]   Triangular Mergers

As indicated above, triangular mergers typically involve the use of stock of the parent of the acquiring corporation. Two types of triangular mergers are varieties of A reorganizations and are discussed in this section. Triangular B and C reorganizations are discussed in §§ 10.03[E] and 10.04[E].

[1]   Background

Prior to changes in the Code to accommodate triangular reorganizations, the presence of a third corporation could be problematic. Two historically important cases illustrate the background. First, in *Groman v. Commissioner*, 302 U.S. 82 (1937), Groman and other shareholders of an Indiana corporation (Indiana) entered into a merger agreement with Glidden Company (Glidden) and a new corporation that Glidden planned to organize (Ohio). Pursuant to the merger agreement, the Indiana shareholders transferred their shares to Ohio and received from Glidden shares of preferred stock in both Glidden and Ohio, as well as cash. After the transfer, Glidden caused Indiana to transfer all of its assets to Ohio and liquidate. On his income tax return, Groman did not report the value of the preferred stock in Glidden and Ohio. *Id.* at 83–84.

The IRS determined that Glidden was not "a party to a reorganization" and thus the exchange for Glidden stock was taxable to Groman. The Court noted that although Glidden was a party to the *agreement* for reorganization, it did not receive anything from the Indiana shareholders as a result of the merger; the exchange was solely between the Indiana shareholders and Ohio. *Id.* at 88. The purpose of the reorganization sections in the Code, according to the Court, was to exempt gain or loss from recognition "where, pursuant to a plan, the interest of the stockholders of a corporation continues to be definitely represented in substantial measure in a new or different one . . . ." *Id.* at 89.

In *Helvering v. Bashford*, 302 U.S. 454 (1938), the Atlas Powder Company (Atlas) organized a plan for consolidating three of its corporate competitors: Peerless Explosives, Union Explosives, and Black Diamond Powder. Under the plan of reorganization, Atlas was to receive a majority holding (57 percent) of the new, consolidated corporation. The shareholders in the three competitor companies agreed to Atlas' plan of consolidation, and in exchange for their stock in the competitors, they received stock in the new consolidated company, some stock in Atlas, and cash. *Id.* at 455–56. Bashford, a shareholder in one of the competitor companies, did not include in income any gain on the receipt of stock from the new corporation or Atlas. The IRS determined that gain should have been included because Atlas was not "a party to the reorganization." *Id.* at 456. Applying *Groman*, the Court agreed with the IRS. *See id.* at 458. Bashford tried to distinguish *Groman*, but the Court stated that "[a]ny direct ownership by Atlas of Peerless, Black Diamond, and Union was transitory and without real substance; it was part of a plan which contemplated the immediate transfer of the stock or the assets or both of the three reorganized companies to the new Atlas subsidiary." *Id.*

Thus, by 1938, the Supreme Court had twice ruled that receipt of stock in a third-party corporation was not protected by the corporate reorganization provisions. Congress ultimately responded by amending the Code.

[2] Forward Triangular Mergers

Section 368(a)(2)(D) recognizes a merger of a target corporation into a subsidiary of the corporation in which the target shareholders receive stock. In other words, the target shareholders become shareholders of the parent corporation, and the parent's subsidiary, the acquiring corporation, receives the target assets. No stock of the acquiring corporation itself (just the parent corporation's stock) can be used in such a reorganization. I.R.C. § 368(a)(2)(D)(i). In addition, it must be the case that the "transaction would have qualified under paragraph (1)(A) had the merger been into the controlling corporation." I.R.C. § 368(a)(2)(D)(ii). The diagram below illustrates the "before" and "after" pictures in a typical forward triangular merger.

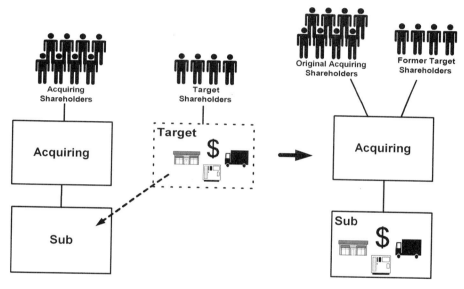

In form, this is an A reorganization that uses stock of the parent of the acquiring corporation. However, in substance, this is essentially a variety of C reorganization.[10]

[a] Formalities

To meet the formalities of section 368(a)(2)(D), the acquiring corporation must acquire "substantially all" of the target's properties, the same requirement as for a C reorganization. *See* Treas. Reg. § 1.368-2(b)(2). In general, Revenue Procedure 77-37, 1977-2 C.B. 568, provides that, for ruling purposes, 70 percent of the assets' gross fair market value before transfer

---

[10] This effect of this exchange is also similar to an A reorganization followed by a "drop down" of the acquired assets into a controlled subsidiary of the acquiring corporation. *See* § 10.05, below.

and 90 percent of the assets' net fair market value before transfer must be acquired. The substantially all requirement is discussed further below, in connection with C reorganizations.[11]

In addition, "no stock of the acquiring corporation [may be] used in the transaction . . . ." I.R.C. § 368(a)(2)(D)(i). Thus, the use of a mix of acquiring corporation and parent corporation stock will not qualify. Furthermore, the reorganization must have been able to qualify as an A reorganization, I.R.C. § 368(a)(2)(D)(ii), meaning that the requirements of business purpose, continuity of business enterprise, and continuity of interest must be met. It is *not* relevant whether an A reorganization with the controlling corporation could have been effected pursuant to state or federal corporation law. Treas. Reg. § 1.368-2(b)(2).

Can a forward triangular merger be accomplished in two steps? *King Enterprises, Inc. v. United States*, 418 F.2d 511 (Ct. Cl. 1969), discussed briefly above in section 10.02[A][1], combined a tender offer and pre-planned merger into a single valid A reorganization. In *J.E. Seagram Corp. v. Commissioner*, 104 T.C. 75 (1995), discussed in § 9.03, E.I. DuPont de Nemours & Co. (DuPont), made a tender offer for Conoco, Inc. (Conoco) stock, acquiring 94 percent of the Conoco shares that way. Under a pre-existing plan, DuPont then merged Conoco into its wholly owned subsidiary, DuPont Holdings, Inc. The remaining six percent of the Conoco shares was exchanged for DuPont stock in the merger. *Id.* at 89. As in *King Enterprises*, the Tax Court considered the tender offer and subsequent merger part of a single unified transaction. The transaction as a whole constituted a forward triangular merger under section 368(a)(2)(D).

[b] Tax Consequences

[i] In General

In a reorganization under section 368(a)(2)(D), the target corporation merges into a subsidiary of the corporation in which the target shareholders receive stock. Thus, the target shareholders exchange target stock for stock of the parent corporation, and the subsidiary receives the target assets. The target shareholders are taxed under sections 354 and 356; as discussed in Chapter 9, they do not recognize any of their gain realized on the exchange, except to the extent of boot received. Their stock bases will be their old stock bases, adjusted as required under section 358 for boot received, gain recognized, and the like.

The parent corporation has no tax on issuing stock. I.R.C. § 1032(a). The acquiring corporation takes target asset bases transferred under section 362(b). The parent's basis in the stock of its subsidiary is then adjusted up as if it had acquired the target's assets directly and transferred the assets to its subsidiary in a transaction covered by section 358. *See* Treas. Reg. § 1.358-6(c)(1). In other words, the parent's basis in its subsidiary

---

[11] *See* § 10.04[B].

stock is grossed up by the basis in the assets of target that were acquired in the transaction. For a discussion of how liabilities affect this process, see the next section.

Example 10.2: Carissa and Derek are the sole shareholders of a successful corporation, CD, Inc. Each shareholder has a $20,000 stock basis. Enorma Corporation proposes to acquire CD, Inc., using stock of its parent corporation, Fathco, Inc. In accordance with a plan of reorganization, Carissa and Derek each receive 100 shares of Fathco stock worth $900,000 plus $100,000 cash, in exchange for the 50 shares of CD stock they each owned. CD merges into Enorma, and Enorma acquires all of CD's assets (which have a combined basis of $40,000).

Carissa and Derek each realize $980,000 of gain under section 1001, and recognize $100,000 of it under section 356. Each will have a basis of $20,000 in their new shares ($20,000 + $100,000 − $100,000). The corporate asset bases do not change as they move from CD to Enorma. I.R.C. § 362(b). However, Fathco increases its basis in the Enorma stock by $40,000. Treas. Reg. § 1.358-6.

[ii]   Effect of Liabilities on Triangular Mergers

As in other reorganizations, section 357 applies with respect to the assumption of liabilities. Section 357(a) generally provides that if "another party to the exchange" assumes a liability of the taxpayer, the assumption shall not be treated as boot and will not prevent the application of section 361. Although the Code now provides that the parent of the acquiring corporation is a "party to the reorganization," it does not provide who qualifies as a party to the "exchange" discussed in section 357.[12] In Revenue Ruling 73-257, 1973-1 C.B. 189, which involved a reorganization under section 368(a)(2)(D), the IRS found that X was "a party to a reorganization" under section 368(a)(2)(D) and, therefore, should be considered a "party to the exchange" as used in section 357(a). *Id.* at 190. Treasury Regulations now address this issue: "the controlling corporation may assume liabilities of the acquired corporation without disqualifying the transaction under section 368(a)(2)(D), and for purposes of section 357(a) the controlling corporation is considered a party to the exchange." Treas. Reg. § 1.368-2(b)(2).

The presence of liabilities in a forward triangular merger also affects the parent corporation's basis. As discussed above, in general, the parent's basis in the stock of its subsidiary is adjusted up as if it had acquired the target's assets directly and transferred the assets to its subsidiary in a transaction covered by section 358. *See* Treas. Reg. § 1.358-6(c)(1). If liabilities are assumed (or property is taken subject to liabilities), the parent is treated as if it had directly acquired the target's assets and liabilities and then transferred both to its subsidiary in a transaction covered by section 358. *See id.* The regulations provide the following example:

---

[12] As discussed below, Treasury Regulations now resolve this issue. *See* Treas. Reg. § 1.368-2(b)(2).

T has assets with an aggregate basis of $60 and fair market value of $100 . . . . ["T's assets are subject to $50 of liabilities."] Pursuant to a plan, P forms S with $5 cash (which S retains), and T merges into S. In the merger, the T shareholders receive P stock worth $50 in exchange for their T stock. The transaction is a reorganization to which sections 368(a)(1)(A) and (a)(2)(D) apply.

Under Treasury Regulation 1.358-6(c)(1), P's $5 basis in its S stock is adjusted as if P acquired the T assets and liabilities acquired by S in the reorganization directly from T in a transaction in which P's basis in the T assets was determined under section 362(b). Under section 362(b), P would have an aggregate basis of $60 in the T assets. P is then treated as if it transferred the T assets to S in a transaction in which P's basis in the S stock was determined under section 358 . . . .

Under section 358, P's basis in its S stock is increased by the $60 basis in the T assets deemed transferred and decreased by the $50 of liabilities to which the T assets acquired by S are subject. Consequently, P has a net basis adjustment of $10, and a $15 basis in its S stock as a result of the reorganization.

Treas. Reg. 1.358-6(c)(4) Example 1(a), (b), (e).

Note that if the amount of target liabilities assumed by the subsidiary (or taken subject to) equals or exceeds the target's aggregate adjusted basis in its assets, the amount of the adjustment is zero—thus avoiding a potential "negative basis" problem. *See* Treas. Reg. § 1.358-6(c)(1)(ii). The regulations provide the following Example:

The facts are the same as [those of the example above], except that T's assets are subject to liabilities of $90, and the T shareholders therefore receive only $10 of P stock in exchange for their T stock in the reorganization. [Because the liabilities that S assumed exceed the aggregate adjusted basis of T's assets,] P has no adjustment in its S stock, and P therefore has a $5 basis in its S stock after the reorganization.

Treas. Reg. 1.358-6(c)(4) Example 1(f). The regulations further provide that the parent in a triangular reorganization does not recognize section 357(c) gain. Treas. Reg. § 1.358-6(c)(1)(ii).

[3] Reverse Triangular Mergers

Section 368(a)(2)(E) allows a reverse triangular merger, sometimes known as a "reverse B reorganization." In form, it is an A reorganization in which the acquiring subsidiary merges *into* the target corporation. The target corporation survives as the new subsidiary, and the target shareholders receive voting stock of the parent corporation. The diagram below illustrates the "before" and "after" pictures in a typical reverse triangular merger.

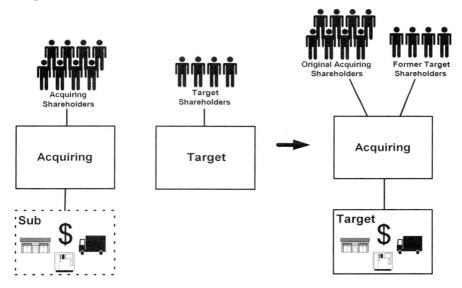

More technically, a section 368(a)(2)(E) reorganization is a merger in which stock of the parent of the merged corporation (the "controlling" corporation) may be used so long as (1) after the transaction the surviving corporation holds substantially all of both its properties and those of the merged corporation, and (2) in the transaction, the former shareholders of the surviving corporation exchanged, for an amount of voting stock of the controlling corporation, an amount of stock in the surviving corporation that constitutes "control" of that corporation. Recall that under section 368(c), control requires at least 80 percent of the total combined voting power *and* 80 percent of the total number of shares of all classes of non-voting stock. Thus, voting stock of the controlling parent corporation must be exchanged for at least 80 percent of the stock of the target corporation; the other 20 percent of the target stock may be acquired for other types of consideration.

Example 10.3: Frank and Grace are the sole shareholders of a successful corporation, FG, Inc. Merger Corporation proposes to acquire FG, Inc., using stock of its publicly held parent corporation, Parent, Inc. In accordance with a plan of reorganization, Merger merges into FG with FG surviving. Frank and Grace each receive 100 shares of Parent stock in exchange for the 50 shares of voting common FG stock they had each owned. In that manner, Parent has acquired 100 percent of the sole class of FG stock. FG retains all of its assets, as well as all of the assets previously held by Merger. Under section 368(a)(2)(E), the transaction qualifies as a reorganization.

The term "substantially all" in section 368(a)(2)(E) has the same meaning as in section 368(a)(1)(C), Treas. Reg. § 1.368-2(j)(3)(iii), and is discussed further below.[13] However, unlike in C reorganizations, discussed below, the "substantially all" requirement must be satisfied for *both* corporations involved in a reverse triangular merger. Each corporation must be tested separately. Treas. Reg. § 1.368-2(j)(3)(iii). In applying the "substantially all" test to the *merged* corporation, property transferred from the parent corporation "to the merged corporation in pursuance of the plan of reorganization is not taken into account."[14] *Id.*

If the target corporation redeems some of its stock prior to the merger, that stock is not considered outstanding for purposes of the *control* test, but the "substantially all" test is applied with respect to that corporation's *pre-redemption* assets. *See id.* ("In applying the 'substantially all' test to the surviving corporation, consideration furnished in the transaction by the surviving corporation in exchange for its stock is property of the surviving corporation which it does not hold after the transaction."). That can make the "substantially all" test harder to meet (that is, it requires acquisition of more of the remaining assets). The following example appears in the regulations:

> T has outstanding 1,000 shares of common stock, 100 shares of nonvoting preferred stock, and no shares of any other class. On January 1, 1981, S merges into T. Prior to the merger, as part of the transaction, T distributes its own cash in redemption of the 100 shares of preferred stock. In the transaction, T's remaining shareholders surrender their 1,000 shares of common stock in exchange for P voting stock. The requirements of section 368(a)(2)(E)(ii) are satisfied since, in the transaction, former shareholders of T surrender, in exchange for P voting stock, an amount of T stock (1,000/1,000 shares or 100 percent) which constitutes control of T. The preferred stock surrendered in exchange for consideration furnished by T is not considered outstanding for purposes of determining whether the amount of T stock surrendered by T shareholders for P stock constitutes control of T. *However, the consideration furnished by T for its stock is property of T which T does not hold after*

---

[13] *See* § 10.04[B].

[14] The regulations further specify that property so transferred that is to be used for the following purposes is not taken into account: (1) to pay additional consideration to shareholders of the surviving corporation; (2) to pay dissenting shareholders of the surviving corporation; (3) to pay creditors of the surviving corporation; (4) to pay reorganization expenses; or (5) to enable the merged corporation to satisfy state minimum capitalization requirements (where the money is returned to the controlling corporation as part of the transaction). Treas. Reg. § 1.368-2(j)(3)(iii).

the transaction for purposes of the substantially all test in paragraph (j)(3)(iii) of this section.

Treas. Reg. § 1.368-2(j)(6) Ex. 3 (emphasis added).

What if the acquisition of 80-percent control takes two steps? Recall that *King Enterprises, Inc. v. United States*, 418 F.2d 511 (Ct. Cl. 1969), discussed in § 10.02[A][1], combined a tender offer and pre-planned merger into a single valid A reorganization. Similarly, in *J.E. Seagram Corp. v. Commissioner*, 104 T.C. 75 (1995), discussed in § 9.03 and mentioned in § 10.02[B][2][a], the Tax Court treated a tender offer and pre-planned forward triangular merger as a single valid 368(a)(2)(D) reorganization.

In Revenue Ruling 2001-26, 2001-23 I.R.B. 1297, the IRS held that a tender offer followed by a reverse triangular merger would be taxed as a single transaction under section 368(a)(2)(E) where, overall, more than 80 percent of the consideration received by the target shareholders was parent stock. The situation approved in the Revenue Ruling is as follows:

> Corporation P and Corporation T are widely held, manufacturing corporations organized under the laws of state A. T has only voting common stock outstanding, none of which is owned by P. P seeks to acquire all of the outstanding stock of T. For valid business reasons, the acquisition will be effected by a tender offer for at least 51 percent of the stock of T, to be acquired solely for P voting stock, followed by a merger of a subsidiary of P into T. P initiates a tender offer for T stock, conditioned on the tender of at least 51 percent of the T shares. Pursuant to the tender offer, P acquires 51 percent of the T stock from T's shareholders for P voting stock. P forms S and S merges into T under the merger laws of state A. In the statutory merger, P's S stock is converted into T stock and each of the T shareholders holding the remaining 49 percent of the out-standing T stock exchanges its shares of T stock for a combination of consideration, two-thirds of which is P voting stock and one-third of which is cash. Assume that under general principles of tax law, including the step-transaction doctrine, the tender offer and the statutory merger are treated as an integrated acquisition by P of all of the T stock. Also assume that all nonstatutory requirements for a reorganization under §§ 368(a)(1)(A) and 368(a)(2)(E) and all statutory requirements of § 368(a)(2)(E), other than the require-ment under § 368(a)(2)(E)(ii) that P acquire control of T in exchange for its voting stock in the transaction, are satisfied.

Rev. Rul. 2001-26, Situation 1.[15]

---

[15] In the two situations analyzed in Revenue Ruling 2001-26, the initial step does not consti-tute a "qualified stock purchase" within the meaning of section 338. As discussed in Chapter 7, the IRS ruled in Revenue Ruling 90-95, 1990-2 C.B. 67, that a qualified stock purchase would not be integrated with a pre-planned upstream merger. *See* § 7.05[B][1]. For an excellent discussion of the two rulings and how they intersect, see Martin D. Ginsburg & Jack S. Levin, *Integrated Acquisitive Reorganizations*, 91 Tax Notes 1909 (2001).

Note that the "after" picture of a section 368(a)(2)(E) reorganization looks just like that of a B reorganization because the target survives as a subsidiary. However, there is a tax difference between a B reorganization and a 368(a)(2)(E) merger: in the latter type of transaction, the parent's basis in the target's stock is derived from target corporation's basis in its assets, while in a B reorganization, that basis is derived from the acquiror's basis in the stock of the target. *See* Treas. Reg. § 1.358-6. This is logical in that a B reorganization is a stock for *stock* swap, while a reverse triangular merger involves acquisition of the target's *assets*.

[4]   Tax Consequences and Basis Rules

In a reorganization under section 368(a)(2)(E), the target corporation is the survivor of a merger with the subsidiary of the corporation in which the target shareholders receive stock. Thus, the target shareholders exchange target stock for stock of the parent corporation, and the target receives the subsidiary's assets. The target shareholders are taxed under sections 354 and 356; they do not recognize any of their gain realized on the exchange, except to the extent of boot received. Their stock bases will be their old stock bases, adjusted as required under section 358. The parent corporation has no tax on issuance of stock. I.R.C. § 1032(a). The target takes the subsidiary's assets' bases carried over under section 362(b).

In general, the parent's basis in the stock of target is the basis it had in the stock of subsidiary, adjusted upward as if it had acquired the target's assets and then transferred them into a subsidiary in a transaction covered by section 358. *See* Treas. Reg. § 1.358-6(c)(2)(A).

Example 10.4: In Example 10.3, assume that Frank and Grace each have a $20,000 basis in their 50 shares of FG Inc. stock, and that the FG, Inc. assets have a combined basis of $40,000. As in that example, in accordance with the plan of reorganization, Merger Corporation, the subsidiary of the acquiring corporation (Parent), merges into FG, Inc. with FG, Inc. surviving. Frank and Grace each receive 100 shares of Parent stock worth $1,000,000 in exchange for their stock. FG, Inc. retains all of its assets, as well as all of the assets previously held by Merger. Assume that Parent had a $400,000 basis in its Merger stock.

This reverse triangular merger will be taxed as follows: Frank and Grace each realize $980,000 of gain under section 1001, and recognize none of it under section 354. Each will have a basis of $20,000 in their new shares under section 358. The corporate asset bases do not change as they move from Merger to FG, Inc. I.R.C. § 362(b). Parent's basis in the FG stock will be $440,000: the $400,000 basis it had in the Merger stock, increased by the $40,000 asset basis. Treas. Reg. § 1.358-6(c).

If the parent corporation acquires less than 100 percent of the target stock, the basis adjustment is reduced by the percentage of stock not acquired in the transaction. The percentage is determined by reference to the fair market value of all classes of target stock. Treas. Reg. § 1.358-6(c)(2)(B). Treasury regulations provide the following example:

T has assets with an aggregate basis of $60 and a fair market value of $100 and no liabilities. P has a $110 basis in its S stock. Pursuant to a plan, S merges into T with T surviving . . . .

X, a 10-percent shareholder of T, does not participate in the transaction. The remaining T shareholders receive $10 cash from P and P stock worth $80 for their Target stock. P owns 90 percent of the T stock after the transaction. . . .

P's basis in its T stock will be P's $110 basis in its S stock before the reorganization, adjusted as if T had merged into S in a forward triangular merger. In such a case, P's basis would have been adjusted by the $60 basis in the T assets deemed transferred . . . . [H]owever, the basis adjustment . . . is reduced in proportion to the percentage of T stock not acquired by P in the transaction. The percentage of T stock not acquired in the transaction is 10%. Therefore, P reduces its $60 basis adjustment by 10%, resulting in a net basis adjustment of $54. Consequently, P has a $164 basis in its T stock as a result of the transaction.

Treas. Reg. 1.358-6(c)(4) Example 2(a), (d).

§ 10.03   Stock-for-Stock Acquisitions ("B" Reorganizations)

A B reorganization is one that involves "the acquisition by one corpora-tion, in exchange *solely* for all or a part of its voting stock . . . of stock of another corporation if, immediately after the acquisition, the acquiring cor-poration has control of such other corporation (whether or not such acquir-ing corporation had control immediately before the acquisition) . . . ." I.R.C. § 368(a)(1)(B) (emphasis added). In other words, the acquiring corporation swaps its *voting stock* with target shareholders for enough stock of the target corporation as to have "control" of it after the transaction. Thus, after the reorganization is complete, the target is at least an 80-percent subsidiary of the acquiring corporation, and the former target shareholders are new shareholders of the acquiring corporation.

The diagram below illustrates the "before" and "after" pictures in a B reorganization in which Acquiring obtains 100 percent of Target. The "before" picture also shows the exchange of stock.

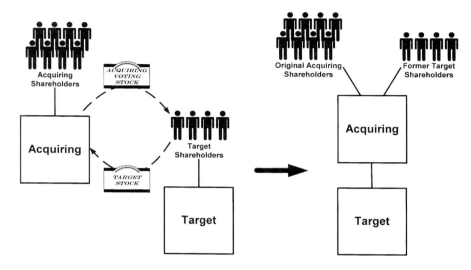

Note that if the newly acquired subsidiary is liquidated, the transaction may be tested as a C reorganization. *See* Rev. Rul. 67-274, 1967-2 C.B. 141.

[A]   The "Solely for Voting Stock" Requirement

As indicated above, section 368(a)(1)(B) requires that voting stock be the sole acquisitive consideration used to acquire the target stock in a B reorganization. As discussed below, there is extraordinarily little flexibility in this requirement.

[1]   The "Solely" Requirement

The use of any non-voting stock as consideration for the target stock will spoil a B reorganization: "If, for example, Corporation X in one transaction exchanges nonvoting preferred stock or bonds in addition to all or a part of its voting stock in the acquisition of stock of Corporation Y, the transaction is not a reorganization under section 368(a)(1)(B)." Treas. Reg. § 1.368-2(c). Similarly prohibited is the use of mix of acquiring and parent corporation stock, even if both types of stock have voting rights. *See id.*

There are certain exceptions, however. Cash or other property may be used in lieu of issuing fractional shares, without spoiling the B reorganization. Rev. Rul. 66-365, 1966-2 C.B. 116. The IRS has also ruled that a target corporation may make a dividend distribution to its shareholders without the cash being considered part of the reorganization proceeds and therefore boot. Rev. Rul. 56-184, 1956-1 C.B. 190.

The acquiring corporation may pay expenses incurred by the target that are "solely and directly related" to the acquisition. Rev. Rul. 73-54, 1973-1 C.B. 187. Revenue Ruling 73-54 provides the following example, involving a C reorganization:

> Pursuant to a plan of reorganization, X corporation proposes to transfer substantially all of its properties to Y corporation in exchange for shares of voting stock of Y followed by the distribution of the Y stock to the shareholders of X in the dissolution of X. As part of the plan of reorganization, Y agrees to pay or assume certain expenses. These expenses are legal and accounting expenses; appraisal fees; administrative costs of the acquired corporation directly related to the reorganization such as those incurred for printing, clerical work, telephone and telegraph; security underwriting and registration fees and expenses; transfer taxes, and transfer agents' fees and expenses. These expenses are solely and directly related to the reorganization.

Id. at 187. The ruling holds that the payments will not prevent the transaction from qualifying as a C reorganization. In addition, the Ruling states that its "principles . . . are equally applicable to such valid reorganization expenses that are paid or assumed by an acquiring corporation in a reorganization described in section 368(a)(1)(B) of the Code." *Id.* at 188.

The restriction on acquisitive consideration has no applicability to payments by the target corporation in redemption of its own stock—so long as the consideration was not supplied by the acquiring corporation. Treas. Reg. § 1.368-1(e)(7) Ex. 9; *see also* Rev. Rul. 68-285, 1968-1 C.B. 247; Rev. Rul. 55-440, 1955-2 C.B. 226. In addition, the redemption does not jeopardize continuity of proprietary interest if the consideration was not supplied by the acquiring corporation. Treas. Reg. § 1.368-1(e)(7) Ex. 9. Note also that *any* form of consideration may be used to acquire things *other* than target *stock*—such as target debt. BITTKER & EUSTICE, FEDERAL INCOME TAXATION OF CORPORATIONS AND SHAREHOLDERS ¶ 12.23[3] (7th ed. 2000).

> *Example 10.5*: Iris and Jon own all of the stock of IJ, Inc., and also own several IJ, Inc. bonds. As part of a stock-for-stock swap, K Corp. buys the bonds for cash. This acquisition will not violate section 368(a)(1)(B); it is the IJ, Inc. stock that must be acquired solely for K Corp. voting stock.

[2]   Definition of "Voting Stock"

Warrants are not "voting stock" for purposes of the "solely for voting stock requirement," *Helvering v. Southwest Consol. Corp.*, 315 U.S. 194, 200 (1942). In fact, even some forms of contingent consideration may constitute boot. Revenue Ruling 70-108, 1970-1 C.B. 78, found that the optional right to purchase additional shares was boot. On the other hand, Revenue Ruling 75-33, 1975-1 C.B. 115, held that a "dividend kicker" (an extra dividend based on the dividend of the rival acquiring corporation) did not constitute boot.

[B]   The "Control" Requirement

In a B reorganization, the acquiring corporation must finish the transaction with "control" of the target corporation within the meaning of section 368(c) (an 80-percent standard). However, control need not have been obtained *in* the transaction. That is, pre-existing control does not violate this requirement. As stated in the Treasury Regulations:

> The acquisition of stock of another corporation by the acquiring corporation solely for its voting stock (or solely for voting stock of a corporation which is in control of the acquiring corporation) is permitted tax-free *even though the acquiring corporation already owns some of the stock of the other corporation*. Such an acquisition is permitted tax-free in a single transaction or in a series of transactions taking place over a relatively short period of time such as 12 months.

Treas. Reg. § 1.368-2(c) (emphasis added).

However, note that some "creeping" B reorganizations (those in which control is acquired in a series of acquisitions) may present "solely" issues. That is, if the acquiring corporation's acquisition of some target shares for cash or other property is stepped into its subsequent acquisition of target shares for voting stock, an attempted B reorganization will be spoiled. As discussed below, the best approach to this problem is to let the shares acquired for consideration other than voting stock age until they are "old and cold."

[C]   Application of the Step-Transaction Doctrine: "Solely" in Creeping B Reorganizations

In *Chapman v. Commissioner*, 618 F.2d 856 (1st Cir.), *cert. dismissed*, 451 U.S. 1012 (1981), International Telephone and Telegraph Corporation (ITT) sought to acquire Hartford Fire Insurance Company (Hartford). ITT proposed that Hartford merge into an ITT subsidiary in a B reorganization. ITT had previously acquired eight percent of the Hartford shares for cash. The shares were not "old and cold," but the parties obtained a letter ruling from the IRS that the proposed merger would constitute a non-taxable reorganization if ITT unconditionally sold its eight-percent interest in Hartford to a third party before Hartford's shareholders voted on the proposal. The IRS ruled that a proposed sale of the stock to Mediobanca, an Italian bank, would satisfy this condition. *Id.* at 858.

ITT then sold the shares in question to Mediobanca before attempting a B reorganization. In the reorganization transaction, ITT obtained more than 95 percent of the stock of Hartford, in exchange for its voting stock. However, ITT reacquired the eight percent that it sold because Mediobanca tendered its shares in the stock-for-stock swap. The IRS subsequently retroactively revoked its ruling approving the sale of the Hartford stock to Mediobanca, on the basis that the ruling request had misrepresented the nature of the proposed sale. The IRS then determined that the taxpayers had deficiencies in the amount of the ITT stock they received, arguing that the 1968-1969 cash purchases and 1970 exchange offer shared a "common acquisitive purpose" and, therefore, should be considered as a single acquisition transaction. *Id.* at 858-59. Under the IRS's view, the reorganization failed the "solely for voting stock" requirement under section 368(a)(1)(B) because the initial transfer of the eight-percent interest was for cash.

The Court of Appeals for the First Circuit agreed with the IRS, and, reversing the Tax Court's grant of summary judgment for the taxpayers, held that related transactions must be considered together. The First Circuit further noted that the treatment of related transactions as one acquisition was supported by the statute's legislative history, Treasury regulations, and supporting case law. *Id.* at 862. The court held that the prior cash purchases by ITT must be considered part of the acquisition. Thus, the First Circuit essentially treated the sale to Mediobanca as a wash and the eight percent stock interest in question as purchased for cash.[16]

[D]   Tax Consequences and Basis Rules

In a B reorganization, the acquiring corporation acquires the stock of the target and the target remains in existence as a subsidiary of the acquiror. Thus, the target shareholders exchange their shares for shares of the acquiring corporation. As no boot may be paid to them, section 354 applies to shelter their realized gain from recognition. Each shareholder accordingly takes as his or her stock basis in the acquiror the basis he or she had in the stock of the target corporation, under section 358. The acquiring corporation takes a transferred basis in the stock of the target corporation. I.R.C. § 362(b); Treas. Reg. § 1.368-1(b).

---

[16] This circular effect is reminiscent of *Associated Wholesale Grocers*, which was discussed in Chapter 7. *See* § 7.03[B][2][b].

[E] Triangular B Reorganizations

In a triangular B reorganization, stock of a controlling parent of the acquiring company is used in lieu of stock of the acquiring company. The parenthetical in section 368(a)(1)(B) permits this type of transaction to qualify as a reorganization. Thus, the parent corporation exchanges *its* voting stock, in return for which the subsidiary acquires control of the target. (As the regulations state, "A triangular B reorganization is an acquisition by S of T stock in exchange for P stock in a transaction that qualifies as a reorganization under section 368(a)(1)(B)." Treas. Reg. § 1.358-6(b)(iv).) The acquiring corporation may *not* use a mix of its own stock and its parents' stock. *See* Treas. Reg. § 1.368-2(c). The diagram below illustrates the "before" and "after" pictures in a typical triangular B reorganization.

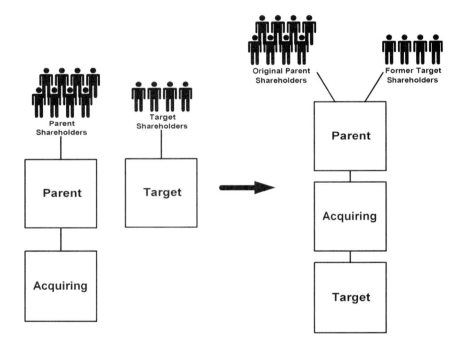

In a triangular B reorganization, the controlling parent's basis in the stock of its subsidiary is increased by the aggregate target shareholder basis in the shares acquired in the transaction (increased by any gain recognized by those shareholders). Treas. Reg. § 1.358-6(c)(3).

§ 10.04   Stock-for-Assets Acquisitions ("C" Reorganizations)

In a C reorganization, substantially all of target's assets are acquired solely for all or part of the voting stock of acquiror. The target generally does not remain in existence; it must liquidate as part of the plan of reorganization, unless the IRS waives this requirment, which is rare. *See* § 368(a)(2)(G). Thus, in a C reorganization, the target corporation transfers all of its assets to the acquiring corporation in return for temporary stockholdings in the acquiror. The target then liquidates, distributing the stock and any remaining assets to its shareholders (who accordingly become shareholders of the acquiror).

The diagram below illustrates the "before," "during," and "after" pictures in a typical C reorganization. The "after" picture of a C reorganization looks much like that of an A reorganization, and in fact, the two types of reorganizations are similar, although the C reorganization has many more *statutory* requirements than does the A reorganization.

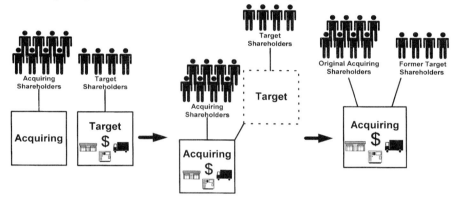

[A]   The "Solely for Voting Stock" Requirement

The "solely for voting stock" language of section 368(a)(1)(C) is reminiscent of the wording of section 368(a)(1)(B). One might therefore expect C reorganizations to be as strict as B reorganizations in limiting the acquisitive consideration. Fortunately for taxpayers, they are not. First, so long as solely voting stock is used as consideration, the assumption of liabilities is not regarded as the provision of boot. Second, boot *is* permitted so long as it does not exceed 20 percent of the acquisitive consideration. Each of these rules is discussed below.

[1]   Effect of Liabilities

Generally speaking, the assumption of a liability of another is comparable to the payment of cash or other consideration in that amount. However, with respect to C reorganizations, liabilities assumed by the acquiring corporation (or to which the acquired assets are subject) generally are *not* considered boot. *See* I.R.C. § 368(a)(1)(C); Treas. Reg. § 1.368-2(d)(1). This rule reflects the reality that many assets (unlike most stock) bear liabilities. If liabilities constituted boot, few asset-based acquisitions would qualify as C reorganizations.

Example 10.6: Nan and Olive are the sole shareholders of NO, Inc., a corporation with $500,000 of assets that are subject to $200,000 of liabilities. As part of an otherwise valid C reorganization, Acquiror, Inc. acquires all of the NO, Inc. assets for $300,000 worth of its voting stock plus the assumption of all $200,000 of liabilities. The transaction will constitute a C reorganization despite the liability assumption.

[2] The "Boot Relaxation Rule"

In section 368(a)(1)(C), the term "solely for voting stock" does not truly mean *solely* because a limited amount of other property may be used as consideration for the target's assets. Under the boot relaxation rule of section 368(a)(2)(B), only 80 percent of the gross fair market value of the property of the transferor corporation must be acquired for voting stock.

Example 10.7: Perry and Quincy are the sole shareholders of PQ Co., a corporation with $500,000 of assets (not subject to any liabilities). As part of a C reorganization, R, Inc. acquires all of the PQ Co. assets for $400,000 worth of its voting stock plus $100,000 cash. The transaction constitutes a valid C reorganization.

As the example above illustrates, the boot relaxation rule is extremely helpful in facilitating C reorganizations. However, when using this rule, liabilities to which the property is subject or that are assumed by the acquiror *are* treated as boot. *See* I.R.C. § 368(a)(2); Treas. Reg. § 1.368-2(d)(3).

Example 10.8: In Example 10.7 above, assume instead that the PQ Co. assets were subject to $50,000 of liabilities that were assumed by R, Inc. Thus, R, Inc. acquires all of the PQ Co. assets for $350,000 worth of its voting stock, $100,000 cash, plus $50,000 worth of assumption of liabilities. The transaction does *not* constitute a valid C reorganization because only 75 percent of the consideration ($350,000 of $500,000) consists of voting stock of R, Inc. However, if R, Inc. were to acquire all of the PQ Co. assets for $400,000 worth of its voting stock, $50,000 cash, plus $50,000 worth of assumption of liabilities, the transaction *would* meet the 80-percent limitation of the "boot relaxation rule."

[B] "Substantially All of the Properties" Requirement

The "substantially all the properties" requirement has both qualitative and quantitative aspects – *which* assets are counted, and *how much* of those must be acquired? Revenue Procedure 77-37, 1977-2 C.B. 568, did not mention the first issue, but states that, for ruling purposes, the "substantially all" requirement "is satisfied if there is a transfer of assets representing at least 90 percent of the fair market value of the net assets and at least 70 percent of the fair market value of the gross assets held by the corporation immediately prior to the transfer." *Id.* § 3.01. In addition, "[a]ll payments to dissenters and all redemptions and distributions (except for regular, normal distributions) made by the corporation immediately preceding the transfer and which are part of the plan of reorganization will be considered as assets held by the corporation immediately prior to the transfer." *Id.*

Case law on this point is also helpful. *Commissioner v. First Nat'l Bank of Altoona*, 104 F.2d 865, 870 (3d Cir. 1939), *cert. dismissed*, 309 U.S. 691 (1940), upheld a transaction in which "assets which the old company transferred to the new company constituted 86% of its total worth and included all of the assets essential to the operation of its business of distributing gasoline." However, in *Arctic Ice Machine Co. v. Commissioner*, 23 B.T.A. 1223, 1228 (1931), the court held that transfer of 68 percent of the assets of the target did not constitute "substantially all" of its properties.

Although the Revenue Procedure cited above is quantitatively specific, a Revenue Ruling provides more general guidelines, and is helpful on the qualitative issue. Revenue Ruling 57-518, 1957-2 C.B. 253, stated:

> The specific question presented is what constitutes "substantially all of the properties" as defined in the above section of the Code. The answer will depend upon the facts and circumstances in each case rather than upon any particular percentage. Among the elements of importance that are to be considered in arriving at the conclusion are the nature of the properties retained by the transferor, the purpose of the retention, and the amount thereof.

Id. at 254. In that ruling, which found that the "substantially all" test was met, the assets retained were of approximately equal value to the amount of the liabilities to be paid off, and were limited to cash, accounts receivable, notes, and three percent of its total inventory. *Id.* The implication was that the "substantially all" test focused on *operating* assets, an implication echoed in *First Nat'l Bank of Altoona*.

In Revenue Ruling 88-48, 1988-1 C.B. 117, X and Y were unrelated corporations. X operated two significant lines of business, a retail hardware business and another business. Y, which was also in the hardware business, wanted to acquire and continue to operate X's hardware business but did not want the other business. The parties developed a two-step plan. First, X sold its entire interest in the plumbing supply business, which constituted 50 percent of its total historic business assets, to third parties that were unrelated to either X or Y or their shareholders. Next, "X transferred all of its assets, including the cash proceeds from the sale, to Y solely for Y voting stock and the assumption of X's liabilities." *Id.* at 117. Finally, X distributed the Y stock, which at that point was its sole asset, to the X shareholders in complete liquidation of X. *Id.*

The transfer of assets from X to Y constituted a C reorganization, except that there was a question whether the "substantially all" requirement was met. Revenue Ruling 57-518, 1957-2 C.B. 253, had stated that what constitutes "substantially all" for purposes of section 368(a)(1)(C) depends on the facts and circumstances in each case. However, C reorganizations may not be divisive; divisive transactions must be tested as D reorganizations instead.

On the facts of the ruling, although Y had acquired substantially all the assets X held at the time of transfer, the prior cash sale prevented Y from acquiring substantially all of X's *historic business assets*. However, the IRS found that the transaction was not divisive because the sales proceeds were transferred to the acquiring corporation; they were not retained by the transferor corporation or its shareholders. In addition, the prior sale of X's historic business assets was to unrelated purchasers; the X shareholders retained no interest in those assets. Thus, the IRS held that "[t]he transfer of all of its assets by X to Y met the 'substantially all' requirement of section 368(a)(1)(C) of the Code, even though immediately prior to the transfer, X sold 50 percent of its historic business assets to unrelated parties for cash and transferred that cash to Y instead of the historic assets." Rev. Rul. 88-48, 1988-1 C.B. at 118.

Assets left behind raise more than one question. The first issue, the question of whether substantially all of the assets were acquired, was discussed above. A second issue is whether the assets may be distributed tax-free in the liquidation of the target corporation. Assets left behind in the target do not constitute "qualified property" as defined in section 361(c)(2)(B). Section 361(c)(2)(A) provides for corporate-level recognition of gains whenever such nonqualified property is distributed. With respect to the creditors or shareholders who receive those assets, creditors have a return of capital under section 1001(a). Shareholders, by contrast, would be taxable, under section 356(a). Another issue is whether continuity of business enterprise is met. *See* § 9.05 of Chapter 9.

[C] Application of the Step-Transaction Doctrine: "Creeping C" Reorganizations

Historically, creeping C reorganizations—those in which control was acquired over a period of time—presented a problem. In *Bausch & Lomb Optical Co. v. Commissioner*, 267 F.2d 75, 76 (2d Cir.), *cert. denied*, 361 U.S. 835 (1959), Bausch & Lomb Optical Company (B&L) owned 79.9488 percent of the 12,412 outstanding shares of its subsidiary Riggs Optical Company (Riggs). In March 1950, B&L desired to "amalgamate" Riggs with itself for valid business reasons. On April 22, 1950, B&L transferred 105,508 shares of its unissued stock in exchange for all of the Riggs' assets. Pursuant to a prearranged plan, Riggs then dissolved on May 2, 1950, and distributed its only asset (the B&L stock) to its shareholders *pro rata*. As a result, B&L received back 84,347 of its own shares previously distributed to Riggs. *Id.* at 76–77.

Based on this result, the IRS concluded that B&L had actually effected a taxable liquidation of Riggs, and determined a deficiency. The Commissioner argued that the acquisition of the Riggs assets and the subsequent dissolution must be viewed together, and as such, B&L's surrender of its Riggs stock *along with its own stock* furnished additional consideration outside the "solely for all or part of its voting stock" requirement of the C reorganization provisions. B&L countered that the amalgamation was a valid C reorganization, and should be viewed separately from the subsequent Riggs dissolution. Alternatively, B&L argued that even if the statutory requirements of the reorganization were not explicitly met, the exchange was, "in substance," one that satisfied the continuity of interest and "business purpose" requirements found in that section's legislative history. *Id.* at 77.

The Court of Appeals affirmed the Tax Court, holding that the two steps in the transaction had to be considered together. It stated that "while the amalgamation may have been for genuine business reasons, the division into two steps served only to facilitate the liquidation of Riggs." *Id.* at 77. Thus, the "business purpose" argument did not support B&L's characterization of the liquidation process as a C reorganization. The Second Circuit therefore found that B&L was attempting to "thwart taxation in this case by carrying out the liquidation process in two steps instead of one" and, thus, "fell short of meeting the requirements of a 'C' reorganization." *Id.* at 78.

Note that the recharacterized transaction was taxable because B&L did not own 80 percent or more of the stock of Riggs—it owned just short of 80 percent. If B&L had owned 80 percent of Riggs, a liquidation would have been tax-free under section 332. Note also that it is the quantity of the stock of Riggs that flowed back to B&L in the transaction that spoiled the reorganization. If less Riggs stock had been owned by B&L, it might have been possible for B&L to effectuate a C reorganization. That is, in that case, B&L might have been able to acquire 80 percent or more of the Riggs stock *in the transaction*.

Many years after the *Bausch & Lomb* decision, the Treasury Department promulgated regulations that allow such a transaction to constitute a valid C reorganization. *See* Treas. Reg. § 1.368-2(d)(4)(i) (". . . prior ownership of stock of the target corporation by an acquiring corporation will not by itself prevent the solely for voting stock requirement . . . from being satisfied."). Under the regulations, "in a transaction in which the acquiring corporation has prior ownership of stock of the target corporation, . . . *the sum of the money or other property* that is distributed in pursuance of the plan of reorganization to the shareholders of the target corporation other than the acquiring corporation and to the creditors of the target corporation pursuant to section 361(b)(3), *and all of the liabilities of the target corporation assumed by the acquiring corporation* (including liabilities to which the properties of the target corporation are subject), *[must] not exceed 20 percent of the value of all of the properties of the target corporation.*" *Id.* (emphasis added). Note that previously acquired target stock is not counted in computing the 20-percent limitation.

The regulations provide the following example:

> Corporation P (P) holds 60 percent of the Corporation T (T) stock
> that P purchased several years ago in an unrelated transaction. T
> has 100 shares of stock outstanding. The other 40 percent of the
> T stock is owned by Corporation X (X), an unrelated corporation.
> T has properties with a fair market value of $110 and liabilities
> of $10. T transfers all of its properties to P. In exchange, P assumes
> the $10 of liabilities, and transfers to T $30 of P voting stock and
> $10 of cash. T distributes the P voting stock and $10 of cash to X
> and liquidates. The transaction satisfies the solely for voting stock
> requirement of paragraph (d)(2)(ii) of this section because the sum
> of $10 of cash paid to X and the assumption by P of $10 of liabilities
> does not exceed 20 percent of the value of the properties of T.

Treas. Reg. § 1.368-2(d)(4)(ii) Ex. 1. Thus, contrary to *Bausch & Lomb*, the
regulations provide that the prior 60-percent ownership of the target did
spoil the reorganization.

[D] Tax Consequences and Basis Rules

In a C reorganization, the target corporation transfers all of its assets
to the acquiring corporation in return for temporary stockholdings in the
acquiror. The target then liquidates, distributing the stock and any remaining assets to its shareholders, who thereby become shareholders of the
acquiror. Section 354(a) applies to shelter realized gain or loss to target
shareholders on this exchange, except that section 356(a) applies to any
target shareholder that received boot. Under section 356(a), gain realized
by a target shareholder is recognized to that shareholder to the extent of
the boot he received. Each target shareholder takes a basis in the new
shares that, in general, is the old share basis, adjusted upward for gain
recognized, and downward for liability relief and boot received. *See* I.R.C.
§ 358(a)(1).

The target corporation does not recognize gain in a C reorganization
unless it has assets that the acquiring corporation does not acquire. *See*
I.R.C. § 361(b)(1). If it does have assets that are not transferred to the
acquiring corporation, taxation occurs upon the liquidating distribution under section 361(c)(2)(A) (those assets would also be boot to the shareholders,
and governed by section 356(a)). The acquiring corporation takes asset
bases determined under section 362(b).

Example 10.9: P corporation is a publicly held company. For valid business reasons, it would like to acquire T Corporation. T Corporation is held equally by Sally and Tom, each with a $100,000 stock basis. T has one asset, a building worth $600,000 with a basis of $420,000. Pursuant to a plan of reorganization, T transfers the building to P corporation, in return for which P corporation provides to T $540,000 worth of voting common stock (540 shares, 20 percent of the vote) and $60,000 of cash. T then liquidates, distributing half of the stock and half of the cash ($30,000) to each of its stockholders, Sally and Tom.

T exchanged its sole asset for stock of P. T realizes $180,000 of gain but none of that gain is recognized under § 361(a). Upon the distribution of the P stock and cash to Sally and Tom in liquidation of T, T realizes gain of $180,000 under § 336(a) but recognizes none of that gain under § 336(c) and 361(c). (T's basis in the stock acquired is $420,000 under § 358(a)(1)—an exchanged basis from the building).

Sally and Tom disposed of T stock and received P stock. They each realize gain of $200,000 ($300,000 amount realized less a $100,000 basis), and recognize $30,000 under § 356(a). They each take a basis of $100,000 in the P stock under § 358 ($100,000 − $30,000 + $30,000). P recognizes no gain on exchanging its shares for assets. I.R.C. § 1032. Under section 362(b), P's basis in the building will be a transferred basis of $420,000 (T's former basis).

[E] Triangular C Reorganizations

In a triangular C reorganization, stock of a controlling parent of the acquiring company is used in lieu of stock of the acquiring company. The parenthetical in section 368(a)(1)(C) permits this type of transaction to qualify as a reorganization. Thus, the parent corporation exchanges *its* voting stock, in return for which the subsidiary acquires substantially all of the target's properties. (As the regulations state, "A triangular C reorganization is an acquisition by S of substantially all of T's assets in exchange for P stock in a transaction that qualifies as a reorganization under section 368(a)(1)(C)." Treas. Reg. § 1.358-6(b)(2)(ii).) The diagram below illustrates the "before," "during," and "after" pictures in a typical triangular C reorganization.

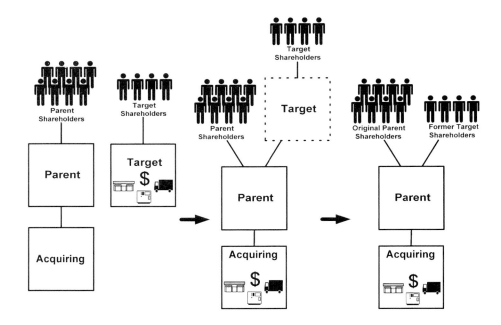

Note that the acquiring corporation may not use a mix of its own stock and its parent's stock. *See* Treas. Reg. § 1.368-2(d)(1). In a triangular C reorganization, the controlling parent's basis in the stock of its subsidiary is increased by the aggregate asset basis acquired in the transaction (increased by any gain recognized by those shareholders). Treas. Reg. § 1.358-6(c)(1).

§ 10.05   Drop-Downs

Following an A, B, C, triangular, or G reorganization, some or all of the assets can be "dropped down" into a controlled subsidiary. I.R.C. § 368(a)(2)(C). The statutory authorization of drop-downs means there is no loss of continuity of interest. In fact, an A, B, or C reorganization followed by a drop-down achieves the same end result as a triangular reorganization, also authorized by statute. The IRS extended the drop-down possibilty to aquisitive D reorganizations in Revenue Ruling 2002-85, 2002-2 C.B. 986. Regulations extend it to reorganizations qualifying under section 368(a)(2)(E), as well. *See* Treas. Reg. § 1.368-2(k)(2).[17]

Under Revenue Ruling 64–73, 1964-1 C.B. 142, direct control of the subsidiary into which the assets are dropped is apparently not required, so it is permissible for the acquiring corporation to drop the assets into a subsidiary several tiers below it. However, the subsidiary that acquires the

---

[17] Proposed regulations would apply this to all reorganizations. *See* Prop. Treas. Reg. § 1.368-2(k).

assets in a drop-down is not a "party to the reorganization." As a result, when liabilities are dropped along with assets, section 357(c) threatens gain recognition if liabilities exceed basis—even under Rev. Rul. 73-257, 1973-1 C.B. 189, discussed above in § 10.02[B][2][b][ii]. Also, note that a drop-down that introduces divisive features may cause it to be tested as a D reorganization.

§ 10.06   Transfer of Assets to Controlled Corporation (Acquisitive "D" Reorganizations)

[A]   Introduction

In an acquisitive D reorganization, a corporation transfers substantially all of its assets to a corporation it or its shareholders (or any combination) "controls" immediately after the transfer, in exchange for stock or securities of the transferee, followed by a liquidation of the transferor and distribution to its shareholders of that stock or securities and any other assets it still has. The diagram below illustrates the "before," "during," and "after" pictures in a typical acquisitive D reorganization.

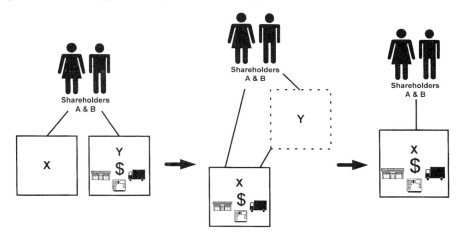

This reorganization resembles a C reorganization except that the corporation transferring its assets must obtain "control" of the transferee corporation. Control is defined under section 304(c), *see* I.R.C. § 368(a)(2)(H), so it is a low, 50-percent test, by vote or by value, and the attribution rules of section 318 apply, as modified by section 304(c)(3)(B) (discussed in Chapter 5).[18]

Example 10.10: P corporation is a publicly held company. For valid business reasons, it would like to acquire T corporation. T is held equally by Ursula and Vincent, each with a $100,000 stock basis. T has two

---

[18] *See* § 5.05[B][2].

assets, land worth $400,000 with a basis of $300,000, and machinery worth $200,000 with a basis of $120,000. Pursuant to a plan of reorganization, T transfers both of its assets to P corporation, in return for which P corporation provides to T $400,000 worth of voting common stock (400 shares, 60 percent of its voting stock) and $200,000 of cash. T then liquidates, distributing half of the stock and half of the cash to each of its stockholders, Ursula and Vincent. The transaction is not a C reorganization because only 66.6 percent of the acquisitive consideration is voting stock ($400,000 out of $600,000). However, it does constitute a D reorganization.[19]

As this example illustrates, an acquisitive D reorganization is essentially a type of merger: one corporation acquires the assets of another. However, it need not follow the state law strictures of a statutory merger (A reorganization). In addition, it has fewer restrictions on acquisitive consideration, particularly the quantity of boot permitted, than does a C reorganization. Similarly, because section 368(a)(1)(D) does not require that a D reorganization be "solely for voting stock," creeping D reorganizations do not present a problem.

[B] "Substantially All of the Assets" Requirement

Section 368(a)(1)(D) merely provides that the transferor (target) corporation transfer "all or a part of its assets" to a corporation it or its shareholders controls after the transfer. However, an acquisitive D reorganization must qualify under section 354, which requires that "the corporation to which the assets are transferred acquires substantially all of the assets of the transferor of such assets." I.R.C. § 354(b)(1)(A). Like "substantially all of the properties" in section 368(a)(1)(C), "substantially all of the assets" generally focuses on operating assets. At least that is true in cases in which the government has recharacterized an attempted liquidation-reincorporation transaction as a reorganization, with any distribution treated as a dividend under section 356(a)(2).[20] See, e.g., Smothers v. United States, 642 F.2d 894, 898-899 (5th Cir. 1981) (15 percent was sufficient where it included all operating assets); see also FSA 200117008 ("Courts generally have interpreted the 'substantially all the assets' requirement for D reorganizations to mean operating assets, rather than total assets."). The test under section 354(b) may be slightly looser than the analogous test under section 368(a)(1)(C). See BITTKER & EUSTICE, FEDERAL INCOME TAXATION OF CORPORATIONS AND SHAREHOLDERS ¶ 12.26[4] (7th ed. 2000) (citing cases). However, Revenue Procedure 77-37, 1977-2 C.B. 568, which interprets the "substantially all" test, and was discussed above with respect to C reorganizations, applies to section 354(b) as well.[21] The standard in the Revenue Procedure is 90 percent of net assets and 70 percent of gross assets.

---

[19] The tax consequences to the parties to a D reorganization are discussed in § 10.06[F], below.

[20] Liquidation-reincorporation transactions are discussed in Chapter 7. See § 7.04.

[21] See § 10.04[B].

[C]　Distribution Requirement

Under section 354(b)(1)(B), the stock, securities, and other properties received by the corporate transferor of properties (the target corporation), as well as the other properties of the transferor, must be distributed in pursuance of the plan of reorganization. Thus, the target generally is liquidated, as in a C reorganization.

[D]　The "Control" Requirement

The control standard in acquisitive D reorganizations is 50 percent by vote or value, by cross-reference to section 304(c). *See* I.R.C. § 368(a)(2)(H). In addition, under section 304(c), "[i]f a person (or persons) is in control . . . of a corporation which in turn owns at least 50 percent of the total combined voting power of all stock entitled to vote of another corporation, or owns at least 50 percent of the total value of the shares of all classes of stock of another corporation, then such person (or persons) shall be treated as in control of such other corporation." I.R.C. § 304(c)(1). Stock acquired in the transaction is considered in determining if the control requirements are met. *Id.*

Recall that, under section 304(c), attribution rules apply under section 304(c)(3)(A), as modified by 304(c)(3)(B).[22] Specifically, for purposes of applying corporate-shareholder attribution rules, the 50-percent threshold requirement for attribution is reduced to a mere five percent. However, section 304(c) mitigates somewhat the effect of the expansion of the attribution *from a shareholder to a corporation.* For that purpose, although attribution would not otherwise be proportionate under section 318(a)(3)(C), in any case in which attribution would not apply but for the lowering of the threshold from 50 percent to five percent, attribution *is* proportionate to the total value of all shares of the corporation. *See* I.R.C. § 304(c)(3)(B)(ii)(II).

Example 10.11: W Corp. owns 30 percent of X Corp. and 40 percent of Y Corp. Y Corp. owns 40 percent of X Corp. and 100 percent of Z Corp. Y Corp. not only controls Z Corp., but also controls X Corp. within the meaning of section 304(c) because although Y Corp. only owns 40 percent of X Corp. directly, the 30 percent of the X Corp. shares that W Corp. owns are attributed proportionately to Y Corp. via W Corp.'s ownership of Y Corp. Thus, Y Corp. owns another 12 percent of the shares of X Corp. indirectly. Note that the attribution was proportionate because W Corp. does not own at least 50 percent of Y Corp. (If it did, then *all* of the X Corp. shares owned by W Corp. would be attributed to Y Corp. for purposes of determining Y Corp.'s control of X Corp.)

---

[22] *See* § 5.05[B][2].

[E] Overlap with C Reorganizations

If a reorganization would qualify both as a C reorganization and as a D reorganization, it is generally treated as a D reorganization. *See* § 368(a)(2)(A).

[F] Tax Consequences and Basis Rules

In an acquisitive D reorganization, the target corporation transfers substantially all of its assets to a corporation it or its shareholders (or any combination) "controls" immediately after the transfer, in exchange for stock or securities of the corporate transferee. That is followed by a liquidation of the target corporation and distribution to its shareholders of that stock, securities, and any other assets it still has at that time. Section 354(a) applies to shelter realized gain or loss to target shareholders on this exchange, except that section 356(a) applies to any target shareholder that received boot.[23] Each target shareholder takes a basis in the new shares that, in general, is the old share basis, adjusted upwards for gain recognized, and downwards for boot received and liabilities transferred. *See* I.R.C. § 358(a)(1).

The target corporation does not recognize gain in an acquisitive D reorganization unless it retained assets. *See* I.R.C. § 361(b). If it did, those assets would be taxed upon the liquidating distribution under section 361(c)(2)(A) (those assets would also be boot to the shareholders, and governed by section 356(a)). The acquiring corporation takes an asset basis under section 362(b): target's asset basis plus gain recognized to the target on the transfer.

Example 10.12: P corporation acquires T corporation. T is owned equally by Armand and Bella, each with a $100,000 stock basis. T has one asset, a building worth $600,000 with a basis of $420,000. Pursuant to a plan of reorganization, T transferred its asset to P corporation, in return for which P provided to T $400,000 worth of voting common stock (400 shares, 60 percent of its voting stock) and $200,000 of cash. T then liquidated, distributing half of the stock and half of the cash to each of Armand and Bella. The transaction qualified as a D reorganization.

T exchanged its assets for stock of P. It realizes $180,000 of gain but nothing is recognized under section 361(a). Upon the distribution of the P stock and cash to Armand and Bella in liquidation of T, T realizes gain of $180,000 under section 336(a) but recognizes nothing under sections 336(c) and 361(c). (T's basis in the stock acquired is $420,000 under § 358(a)(1)—an exchanged basis from the building).

Armand and Bella disposed of T stock and received P stock. They each realize gain of $200,000 ($300,000 amount realized exceeds $100,000 basis) and recognize it under section 356(a) to the extent of the $100,000

---

[23] Section 357(c) applies to divisive but not to acquisitive D reorganizations. *See* I.R.C. § 357(c)(1)(B).

of boot that each received. They each take an exchanged basis of $100,000 in the P stock under section 358(a)(1). P recognizes no gain on exchanging its shares for assets. I.R.C. § 1032. P's basis in the building will be $420,000, transferred from T under section 362(b).

§ 10.07   Bankruptcy Reorganizations ("G" Reorganizations)

Section 368(a)(1)(G) applies to reorganizations that are part of a Title 11 bankruptcy proceeding or federal or state court receivership, foreclosure, or similar proceeding. *See* I.R.C. § 368(a)(1)(G), (a)(3)(A). The form of a G reorganization is a transfer to the acquiring corporation of "all or part of" the assets of the target, in exchange for stock or securities of the acquiring corporation, followed by distribution of the stock or securities of target. *See* I.R.C. § 368(a)(1)(G). In a G reorganization, the target corporation need not obtain "control" of the acquiring corporation. However, the distribution must satisfy either section 354, 355, or 356. *See id.* Because an acquisitive G reorganization must comply with section 354(b), the target must liquidate, just as it must for an acquisitive D reorganization. The diagram below illustrates the "before," "during," and "after" pictures in a typical G reorganization.

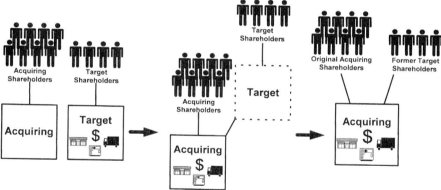

As the explanation and diagram reflect, there are substantial similarities between D and G reorganizations. In particular, both may be either acquisitive or divisive. Acquisitive reorganizations must satisfy section 354 or 356, and divisive reorganizations must satisfy section 355. Nonetheless, the "all or part of" the assets test is applied more liberally to G reorganizations than it is to D reorganizations in that consideration may be given to the target's need to pay off creditors with assets or with proceeds from selling those assets. *See* S. Rep. No. 1035, 9th Cong., 2d Sess.; BITTKER & EUSTICE, FEDERAL INCOME TAXATION OF CORPORATIONS AND SHAREHOLD-ERS ¶ 12.30[2][a] (7th ed. 2000). However, the transfer of assets in a G reorganization must be pursuant to a plan of reorganization approved by the federal or state court in which the bankruptcy or other proceeding is taking place. *See* I.R.C. § 368(a)(3)(B). In addition, a G reorganization must satisfy the continuity of proprietary interest doctrine, and, for this purpose, senior creditors' interests are counted, and if junior creditors receive consideration in the reorganization, they are counted as well. *See* S. Rep. No. 96-1035, 96th Cong. 2d Sess. (1980), 1980-2 C.B. 620, 638; *Helvering v. Alabama Asphaltic Limestone Co.*, 315 U.S. 179 (1942).[24]

In a valid G reorganization, the target is generally accorded nonrecognition treatment on the transfer of assets under section 361(a), and on the distribution of stock or securities to its shareholders under 361(c). However, if liabilities in excess of basis are not eliminated in the court proceeding and are assumed in the transaction (or, in general, property is taken subject to those liabilities, *see* I.R.C. § 357(d)(1), (2); Treas. Reg. § 1.357-2(a)), the target will recognize gain under section 357(c) if any former target shareholder receives consideration for his or her stock. *See* I.R.C. § 357(c)(2)(B). As with other reorganizations, the target shareholders are protected by sections 354, 355, or 356, and determine their bases under section 358. The acquiring corporation takes a basis in the target assets determined under section 362(b).

Triangular G reorganizations are permitted by section 368(a)(2)(D), which was discussed above. In addition, post-G reorganization drop-downs are authorized by section 368(a)(2)(C). Furthermore, section 368(a)(3)(E) permits a modified form of the reverse triangular merger of section 368(a)(2)(E). Under section 368(a)(3)(E), a reverse triangular merger is allowed to qualify as a G reorganization so long as no target shareholder receives consideration and the 80-percent test of section 368(a)(2)(E) is satisfied when treating creditors of the target as shareholders. *See* I.R.C. § 368(a)(3)(E).

---

[24] The proposed "no net value" regulations promulgated in March 2005:

[generally] provide that creditors will be treated as holding a proprietary interest in a target corporation for [continuity of interest] purposes under circumstances that satisfy the standard set forth by the Tax Court in *Atlas Oil* [*& Refining Corp. v. Commissioner*, 36 T.C. 675 (1961),] and reiterated by Congress in the legislative history of the Bankruptcy Tax Act of 1980. However, the proposed regulations go further than current law in several respects and generally make continuity easier to satisfy in transactions involving insolvent companies, both in terms of when creditors will be considered proprietors and in terms of counting continuity.

Unlike current law, the proposed regulations do not require the creditors to take any affirmative steps to enforce their claims against the target. Instead, the fact that they agree to take stock in the acquirer in exchange for their claims is sufficient for a creditor to be treated as holding a proprietary interest if the target is in a title 11 or similar case or is insolvent. Further, the shareholders of the target do not forfeit their proprietary interest by reason of the creditors' holding a proprietary interest.

Mark J. Silverman et al., *Assessing the Value of the Proposed No Net Value Regulations*, 108 TAX NOTES 1135, 1149 (2005) (footnotes omitted).

Chapter 11

CORPORATE DIVISIONS

§ 11.01 Introduction to Corporate Divisions

For any number of business reasons, taxpayers may seek to divide a business or businesses that were conducted through one corporation (or through a parent corporation and its subsidiary) into two or more corporations owned directly by the parent corporation's shareholders. Such a division may be accomplished as a nonrecognition transaction through the use of section 355, which allows corporate "spin-offs," "split-offs," and "split-ups," either alone, or as part of a divisive "D" reorganization. The nonrecognition aspect of corporate divisions prevents what might otherwise amount to a lock-in effect. That is, just as the corporate reorganization provisions facilitate acquisitive transactions, sections 355 and 368(a)(1)(D) facilitate divisive transactions.

"Spin-offs," "split-offs," and "split-ups" are transactions that would each be taxable under another provision but for section 355. A spin-off resembles a dividend-type distribution of property. It involves the *pro rata* distribution by a parent corporation to its shareholders of a controlling interest in its subsidiary. Absent section 355, it would be subject to taxation under section 301. A split-off resembles a redemption. It involves the distribution by a parent corporation to one or more of its shareholders of a controlling interest in its subsidiary in exchange for the surrender by the shareholders of some or all of their shares in the parent corporation. Absent section 355, it would be governed by section 302. A split-up resembles a liquidating distribution. It involves the liquidation of the parent corporation in which it distributes to its shareholders the stock of two or more subsidiary corporations. Absent section 355, it typically would be governed by section 331. Each of these transactions is diagramed below in connection with specific examples.

A spin-off, split-off, or split-up may also take place as part of a bankruptcy reorganization. That is, section 368(a)(1)(G) permits divisive "G" reorganizations as well as acquisitive ones. Acquisitive G reorganizations were discussed in Chapter 10, and divisive G reorganizations are discussed briefly in this chapter.

§ 11.02 Corporate Divisions Under Section 355

In general, section 355 allows nonrecognition treatment to transactions in which a corporate parent (termed the "distributing corporation") distributes to shareholders, with respect to stock, or to security holders, in exchange for securities, solely stock or securities of a subsidiary (termed the "controlled corporation") that it "controls" immediately before the distribution. I.R.C. § 355(a)(1)(A). As indicated above, section 355 allows three forms of qualifying transactions: spin-offs, split-offs, and split-ups. As discussed below, a section 355 transaction must also (1) have a business purpose, (2) not constitute a device for bailing out earnings and profits, (3) involve trades or businesses that have at least a five-year history and that remain active after the transaction, (4) reflect continuity of proprietary interest, and (5) effect distribution of "control." *See* I.R.C. § 355(a)(1)(B)-(D), (b).

Like section 351, which was discussed in Chapter 2, application of section 355 is mandatory if its requirements are met. Accordingly, as with section 351, taxpayers desiring a *taxable* transaction must structure it to fail one or more of the requirements of section 355.

[A] Types of Section 355 Transactions

[1] Spin-Offs

A spin-off resembles a dividend-type distribution of property. It involves the distribution by a parent corporation to one or more of its shareholders of a controlling interest in its subsidiary. A failed spin-off generally will be taxable under section 301, which is discussed in Chapter 4.[1]

---

[1] *See* § 4.03.

Example 11.1: Angela and Bud are equal shareholders of X, Inc. X, Inc. wholly owns Y, Inc. X, Inc. spins off Y, Inc. in a transaction in which Angela and Bud each receive half of the Y, Inc. stock. The diagram below illustrates the "before" and "after" pictures in this example.

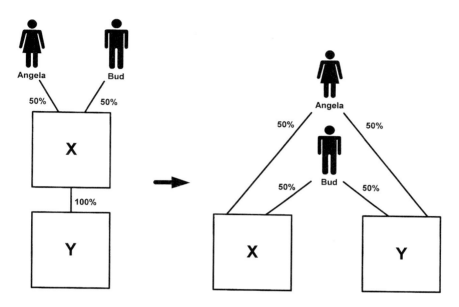

[2] Split-Offs

A split-off resembles a redemption. It involves the distribution by a parent corporation to one or more of its shareholders of a controlling interest in its subsidiary coupled with surrender by those shareholders of some or all of their shares in the parent corporation. The tax consequences of a failed split-off generally will be governed by section 302, which is discussed in Chapter 5.[2]

---

[2] *See* § 5.03.

Example 11.2: Conrad and Delia are the only shareholders of Y, Inc. Y, Inc. wholly owns SubCo, Inc. Y, Inc. distributes the stock of SubCo, Inc. to Delia in exchange for Delia's stock in Y, Inc. The diagram below illustrates the "before" and "after" pictures in this example.

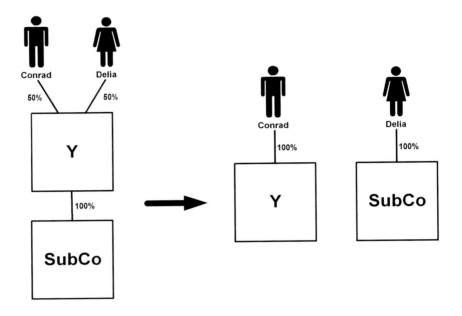

[3]   Split-Ups

A split-up resembles a liquidating distribution. It involves the liquidation of the parent corporation in which the parent distributes to its shareholders the stock of two or more subsidiary corporations. A failed split-up generally will be taxable under section 331, which is discussed in Chapter 7.[3]

---

[3] *See* § 7.03[A][2].

Example 11.3: Eileen and Frank are the sole shareholders of Z, Inc. Z, Inc. wholly owns Sub1, Inc. and Sub2, Inc. Z, Inc. distributes the Sub1, Inc. stock to Eileen, and the Sub2, Inc. stock to Frank, and then proceeds to liquidate. The diagram below illustrates the "before" and "after" pictures in this example.

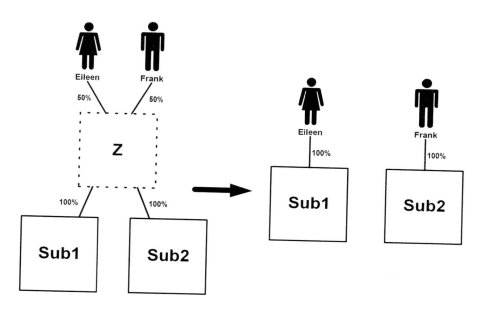

[B] "Stock or Securities"

In a section 355 transaction, the "distributing corporation" distributes to shareholders, with respect to their stock, or to security holders, in exchange for their securities, solely "stock or securities" of the "controlled corporation." Stock generally includes all forms of equity except for "nonqualified preferred stock," discussed in Chapter 2,[4] unless it is exchanged for nonqualified preferred stock. *See* I.R.C. § 355(a)(3)(D); Treas. Reg. § 1.356-6(a)(1). Stock rights generally qualify as securities (but have no principal amount). Treas. Reg. §§ 1.355-1(c), 1.356-3(b). However, rights to acquire nonqualified preferred stock do not qualify as securities unless they are received in exchange for nonqualified preferred stock or rights to acquire nonqualified preferred stock. Treas. Reg. § 1.356-6(a)(2).

[C] "Control" and "Distribution" Requirements

Section 355(a) requires that the distributing corporation distribute "solely stock or securities of a corporation . . . it controls immediately before the distribution . . . ." "Control" is defined in section 368(c). *See* I.R.C. § 355(a)(1)(D)(ii). Section 355(a) further requires that the distributing

---

[4] *See* § 2.02[A][1][f][i].

corporation distribute either (1) "all of the stock and securities in the controlled corporation held by it immediately before the distribution," or (2) "an amount of stock in the controlled corporation constituting control within the meaning of section 368(c), [if] it is established to the satisfaction of the Secretary that the retention by the distributing corporation of stock (or stock and securities) in the controlled corporation was not in pursuance of a plan having as one of its principal purposes the avoidance of Federal income tax." I.R.C. § 355(a)(1)(D).

As discussed in Chapter 2, "control" under section 368(c) is 80 percent of voting stock and 80 percent of all other classes of stock in the corporation.[5] *Commissioner v. Gordon*, 391 U.S. 83 (1968), considers the extent to which the step-transaction doctrine may apply to reach that 80-percent threshold. Note that in *Gordon*, it was the taxpayers who were trying to apply the doctrine to the transaction in which they participated.

In *Gordon*, Pacific Telephone & Telegraph Company ("Pacific"), a subsidiary of AT&T, transferred certain of its assets to a new company, Pacific Northwest Bell Telephone Company ("Northwest"), pursuant to a plan of reorganization. In 1961, Pacific distributed to its shareholders rights to purchase approximately 57 percent of the Northwest stock for less than fair market value. *Id.* at 86. Pacific also advised its shareholders that " '[i]t expected that within about three years . . . the Company by one or more offerings will offer for sale the balance of such stock.' " *Id.* at 97. Gordon and Baan, shareholders in Pacific, received rights and exercised them but did not report any income from these transactions. Three years later, the remaining stock was similarly offered to Pacific's shareholders. *Id.* at 87.

The IRS asserted a deficiency with respect to both shareholders for the difference between the purchase price and the fair market value of the Northwest stock, which the IRS characterized as ordinary income. *Id.* at 87-88. The principal issue in the subsequent litigation was whether the initial distribution of purchase rights to 57 percent of Northwest's stock should determine whether the "control" requirements of section 355(a)(1)(A) were satisfied. Although the initial offering was for only 57 percent of the Northwest stock, Pacific's shareholders argued that it was only an initial step in the complete distribution of Northwest, the remaining shares having been distributed three years later in accordance with a pre-arranged plan. Furthermore, Pacific's shareholders emphasized that there is no requirement in the Code requiring that a single distribution satisfy the "control" requirement. The Court refused to aggregate the distributions, however, and although it did not state that the Code required a single distribution, it determined that "if one transaction is to be characterized as a 'first step' there must be a binding commitment to take the later steps." *Id.* at 96.

Applying this test, the Court found that there was no binding commitment to make the subsequent distribution, and characterized the eventual distribution three years later as "little more than a fortuity." *Id.* at 97. The

---

[5] *See* §§ 2.02[A][1][b].

Court held that "if an initial transfer of less than a controlling interest in the controlled corporation is to be treated for tax purposes as a mere first step in the divestiture of control, it must at least be identifiable as such at the time it is made." *Id.* at 96. Pacific's shareholders, including Gordon and Baan, accordingly recognized ordinary income from their exercise of the rights to purchase shares in the amount of the difference between the purchase price and the fair market value of the Northwest stock on the date of purchase. [6]

Note that even if "control" is distributed, retained stock or securities raise the issue of whether they were retained in pursuance of a plan having as one of its principal purposes the avoidance of Federal income tax.

> Ordinarily, the corporate business purpose or purposes for the distribution will require the distribution of *all* of the stock and securities of the controlled corporation. If the distribution of all of the stock and securities of a controlled corporation would be treated to any extent as a distribution of "other property" under section 356, this fact tends to establish that the retention of stock or securities is in pursuance of a plan having as one of its principal purposes the avoidance of Federal income tax.

Treas. Reg. § 1.355-2(e)(2) (emphasis added). One possible valid reason for retention of some stock or securities is to serve as collateral for financing, in certain specialized scenarios. *See, e.g.,* Rev. Rul. 75-321, 1975-2 C.B. 123; Rev. Rul. 75-469, 1975-2 C.B. 126.

[D] "Business Purpose" Requirement

Recall that in *Gregory v. Helvering*, 293 U.S. 465 (1935), discussed in Chapter 9, the United States Supreme Court established a corporate "business purpose" requirement for tax-free reorganizations. [7] In *Gregory*, Mrs. Gregory caused her wholly owned corporation to spin off the shares of a new subsidiary, which she then liquidated, selling its assets, appreciated stock, at a gain. The Supreme Court referred to this as "an operation having no business or corporate purpose . . . ." *Id.* at 469.

Treasury regulations now provide that "[a] corporate business purpose is a real and substantial non-Federal tax purpose germane to the business of the distributing corporation, the controlled corporation, or the affiliated group . . . to which the distributing corporation belongs." Treas. Reg. § 1.355-2(b)(2). The IRS will not issue advance rulings on whether a section 355 transaction has a business purpose. *See* Rev. Proc. 2003-48 § 4.01(1), 2003-29 I.R.B. 86, 88. The regulations provide the following example of a business purpose:

> Corporation X is engaged in the production, transportation, and refining of petroleum products. In 1985, X acquires all of the

---

[6] For additional reading about this case and the role that the step-transaction doctrine played, see Robert A. Jacobs, *Supreme Court Further Restricts the Step Transaction Doctrine*, 29 J. TAX'N 2 (1968).

[7] *See* § 9.04.

properties of corporation Z, which is also engaged in the production, transportation, and refining of petroleum products. In 1991, as a result of antitrust litigation, X is ordered to divest itself of all of the properties acquired from Z. X transfers those properties to new corporation Y and distributes the stock of Y *pro rata* to X's shareholders. In view of the divestiture order, the distribution is carried out for a corporate business purpose. . . .

Treas. Reg. § 1.355-2(b)(5) Ex. 1.

Note that the regulations focus on a *corporate* business purpose. They explain:

A shareholder purpose (for example, the personal planning purposes of a shareholder) is not a corporate business purpose. Depending upon the facts of a particular case, however, a shareholder purpose for a transaction may be so nearly coextensive with a corporate business purpose as to preclude any distinction between them. In such a case, the transaction is carried out for one or more corporate business purposes.

Treas. Reg. § 1.355-2(b)(2). The regulations provide the following example of a scenario in which a shareholder purpose and corporate business purpose are coextensive:

Corporation X is engaged in two businesses: The manufacture and sale of furniture and the sale of jewelry. The businesses are of equal value. The outstanding stock of X is owned equally by unrelated individuals A and B. A is more interested in the furniture business, while B is more interested in the jewelry business. A and B decide to split up the businesses and go their separate ways. A and B anticipate that the operations of each business will be enhanced by the separation because each shareholder will be able to devote his undivided attention to the business in which he is more interested and more proficient. Accordingly, X transfers the jewelry business to new corporation Y and distributes the stock of Y to B in exchange for all of B's stock in X. The distribution is carried out for a corporate business purpose, notwithstanding that it is also carried out in part for shareholder purposes.

Treas. Reg. § 1.355-2(b)(5) Ex.2.

If the corporate business purpose may be met without a distribution, the distribution will not have a business purpose. The regulations provide the following example:

Corporation X is engaged in the manufacture and sale of toys and the manufacture and sale of candy. The shareholders of X wish to protect the candy business from the risks and vicissitudes of the toy business. Accordingly, X transfers the toy business to new corporation Y and distributes the stock of Y to X's shareholders. Under applicable law, the purpose of protecting the candy business from the risks and vicissitudes of the toy business is achieved as soon as X transfers the toy business to Y. Therefore, the distribution is not carried out for a corporate business purpose.

Treas. Reg. § 1.355-2(b)(5) Ex. 3.

As indicated below, the "business purpose" requirement and "device" prohibition are connected; in general, the more compelling the business purpose, the less likely the transaction is to be viewed as a device for bailing out earnings and profits, and *vice versa*. However, the business purpose is a separate, independent requirement that must be satisfied in addition to the device prohibition. *See* Treas. Reg. § 1.355-2(b)(1).

[E]   The "Device" Prohibition

The prohibition of a transaction that is a mere "device" to bail out corporate earnings and profits may be traced to *Gregory v. Helvering*, 293 U.S. 465 (1935), which was discussed briefly above. In *Gregory*, the Court stated:

> Putting aside, then, the question of motive in respect of taxation altogether, and fixing the character of the proceeding by what actually occurred, what do we find? *Simply an operation having no business or corporate purpose—a mere device which put on the form of a corporate reorganization as a disguise for concealing its real character*, and the sole object and accomplishment of which was the consummation of a preconceived plan, not to reorganize a business or any part of a business, but to transfer a parcel of corporate shares to the petitioner.

Id. at 469 (emphasis added).

Thus, transactions that principally constitute a device to bail earnings and profits out of the distributing corporation, controlling corporation, or both do not qualify under section 355. Treas. Reg. § 1.355-2(d)(1). "The purpose of the device restriction of section 355(a)(1)(B) of the Code is to prevent the use of section 355 to avoid the dividend provisions of the Code." Rev. Rul. 77-377, 1977-2 C.B. 111, 111.

The IRS will not issue advance rulings on whether a section 355 transaction is principally a device to bail out earnings and profits. *See* Rev. Proc. 2003-48 § 4.02, 2003-29 I.R.B. 86, 88. Treasury regulations provide that the "device" test is one of facts and circumstances, and that it focuses on situations in which shareholders are attempting to convert dividend income into sales proceeds (generally capital gain), with the accompanying recovery of basis. *Id.* The regulations also provide six helpful factors, three that are indicative of a device, and three that suggest the absence of a device. Treas. Reg. § 1.355-2(d)(2), (3). The "device" factors are: (1) a *pro rata* distribution, (2) subsequent sale or exchange of the stock, and (3) presence of substantial nonbusiness or secondary assets. Treas. Reg. § 1.355-2(d)(2). The "nondevice" factors are: (1) a corporate business purpose, (2) the distributing corporation is publicly traded and widely held, and (3) the distribution is to domestic corporations. *See* Treas. Reg. § 1.355-2(d)(3). These factors are discussed, in turn, below.

Note that, under current law, the "device" issue is less important than it once was, given that individuals' qualifying dividends are taxed at preferential capital gains rates. *See* I.R.C. § 1(h)(3)(B), (11) (scheduled to sunset December 31, 2008). That is, bailout of earnings and profits presents less of a concern when the same tax rate applies to dividends and capital gain. However, sale or exchange transactions allow basis recovery first, while dividends do not. Treasury regulations state, "[a] device can include a transaction that effects a recovery of basis." Treas. Reg. § 1.355-2(d)(1). Thus, one commentator argues:

> In light of the government's basis recovery concerns, there may still be justification for applying the device test to shareholders who hold some amount of basis in their Distributing shares, despite the unification of the rates. Conversely, the new tax rates make application of the device test unnecessary to a shareholder holding zero basis in his Distributing shares. . . .

Joshua D. Blank, *The Device Test in a Unified Rate Regime*, 102 TAX NOTES 513, 520 (2004).

[1]   "Device" Factors

Certain factors tend to suggest the presence of a device to bail out earnings and profits. These factors are discussed immediately below.

[a]   *Pro Rata* Distribution

The regulations suggest that a *pro rata* distribution of stock under section 355 has the greatest potential to reflect avoidance of the Code provisions taxing dividends. Treas. Reg. § 1.355-2(d)(4) Ex. 2. Thus, the presence of this factor is indicative of a device.

Example 11.4: In Example 11.1, Angela and Bud, 50-percent shareholders of X, Inc., each received half of the Y, Inc. stock. This distribution was *pro rata*, suggestive of a device to bail out earnings and profits.

[b]   Subsequent Sale or Exchange of the Stock Distributed

A pre-arranged sale of the stock (but not of securities) of the distributing corporation or the controlled corporation is "substantial evidence" of a device to bail out earnings and profits. Treas. Reg. § 1.355-2(d)(2)(iii)(B). Section 355 nonetheless provides that "the mere fact that subsequent to the distribution stock or securities in one or more of such corporations are sold or exchanged by all or some of the distributees (other than pursuant to an arrangement negotiated or agreed upon prior to such distribution) shall not be construed to mean that the transaction was used principally as such a device . . . ." I.R.C. § 355(a)(1)(B).[8] However, the regulations further provide that such a sale of stock, even in the absence of prearrangement, provides evidence of a device. Treas. Reg. § 1.355-2(d)(2)(iii)(A). "Generally, the greater the percentage of the stock sold or exchanged after the distribution, the stronger the evidence of device. In addition, the shorter the period of time between the distribution and the sale or exchange, the stronger the evidence of device." Treas. Reg. § 1.355-2(d)(2)(iii).

A recent example of a case involving a pre-arranged sale that the Tax Court found to be a device is *S. Tulsa Pathology Lab., Inc. v. Commissioner*, 118 T.C. 84 (2002). In that case, the taxpayer wanted to sell its clinical business to National Health Laboratories, Inc. (NHL). *Id.* at 87. The taxpayer "and NHL negotiated the sale of the clinical business and agreed to structure it as a sale of the stock of a yet-to-be-incorporated clinical laboratory company that would be capitalized with the clinical business and spun off . . . ." *Id.* The taxpayer then carried out the incorporation of the new corporation, Clinpath; a *pro rata* distribution of the Clinpath stock to its shareholders; and the prearranged sale by the shareholders to NHL. *Id.* at 88. The Tax Court found "that the facts and circumstances of this case present substantial evidence of device within the meaning of section 355(a)(1)(B)" and that the transaction therefore did not satisfy section 355. *Id.* at 94.

[c] Presence of Nonbusiness or "Secondary Business" Assets

As discussed below, section 355 contains an "active business" requirement. If either corporation participating in a section 355 transaction has substantial assets that are not part of the active business, that provides evidence of a device to distribute earnings and profits. *See* Treas. Reg. § 1.355-2(d)(2)(iv)(B). "For this purpose, assets that are not used in a trade or business that satisfies the requirements of section 355(b) include, but are not limited to, cash and other liquid assets that are not related to the reasonable needs of a business satisfying such section." *Id.* In addition:

> There is evidence of device if a business of either the distributing or controlled corporation (or a corporation controlled by it) is (1) a "secondary business" that continues as a secondary business for a significant period after the separation, and (2) can be sold without adversely affecting the business of the other corporation (or a corporation controlled by it). A secondary business is a business of either the distributing or controlled corporation, if its principal function

---

[8] As discussed below, section 355(e), enacted in 1997, generally provides that stock or securities in the controlled corporation will not be treated as "qualified property" for purposes of section 361(c)(2) when distributed as part of a plan (or series of related transactions), pursuant to which one or more persons acquire stock representing a 50-percent or greater interest in the distributing corporation or any controlled corporation. Accordingly, when section 355(e) applies, the distributing corporation (but not the shareholders) will recognize gain on the distribution. *See* § 11.02[F][2].

is to serve the business of the other corporation (or a corporation controlled by it). . . .

Treas. Reg. § 1.355-2(d)(2)(iv)(C).

[2] "Non-Device" Factors

Certain factors tend to suggest the *absence* of a device to bail out earnings and profits. These factors are discussed below.

[a] Corporate Business Purpose

As discussed above, the presence of a good business purpose for a section 355 transaction suggests that the distribution is not a mere device. The regulations specify that "[t]he stronger the evidence of device (such as the presence of . . . device factors . . .), the stronger the corporate business purpose required to prevent the determination that the transaction was used principally as a device." Treas. Reg. § 1.355-2(d)(3)(ii). The regulations further provide that the strength of the business purpose entails a "facts and circumstances" test, and lists three non-exclusive factors to consider:

> (A) The importance of achieving the purpose to the success of the business;

> (B) The extent to which the transaction is prompted by a person not having a proprietary interest in either corporation, or by other outside factors beyond the control of the distributing corporation; and

> (C) The immediacy of the conditions prompting the transaction.

Id.

[b] Publicly Traded, Widely Held Distributing Corporation

If ownership of the stock of the distributing corporation is widely dispersed, with no single shareholder owning (directly or indirectly) more than five percent of any class of stock, that fact suggests the absence of a device. Treas. Reg. § 1.355-2(d)(3)(iii).

[c] Distribution to Domestic Corporations

Domestic corporate shareholders are entitled to a dividends received deduction, as discussed in Chapter 4. Corporations meeting threshold ownership requirements are entitled to an 80-percent or 100-percent dividends received deduction. *See* I.R.C. § 243(a), (c). Accordingly, a distribution under section 355 to those corporations is unlikely to be a device for avoiding application of section 301. Treas. Reg. § 1.355-2(d)(3)(iv).

[3] "Non-Device" Transactions

Treasury Regulations set forth three types of transactions that ordinarily do not present the potential for a bail-out of earnings and profits. *See* Treas.

Reg. § 1.355-2(d)(5)(i). The first type of transaction is one in which neither the distributing corporation nor the controlled corporation have any earnings and profits, and "[n]o distribution of property by the distributing corporation immediately before the separation would require recognition of gain resulting in current earnings and profits for the taxable year of the distribution." Treas. Reg. § 1.355-2(d)(5)(ii). The logic of this provision is that a distribution would not have been taxable as a dividend even in the absence of section 355, because of the absence of earnings and profits. However, it is quite a restrictive exception; "[a] virgin S corporation (with no earnings and profits nor the potential to generate any current earnings and profits) would be the main beneficiary of this device-amnesty rule." BORIS I. BITTKER & JAMES S. EUSTICE, FEDERAL INCOME TAXATION OF CORPORATIONS AND SHAREHOLDERS ¶ 11.06[3] n.179 (7th ed. 2000).

The second type of transaction is a transaction in which, with respect to each shareholder receiving a distribution, the distribution would be a redemption to which section 303(a) applied. Treas. Reg. § 1.355-2(d)(5)(iii). Section 303, relating to redemptions to pay death taxes, is discussed in Chapter 5.[9] Section 303 redemptions constitute exchanges, so the distribution of the stock of the controlled corporation does not raise an issue of the conversion of ordinary income into capital gain. However, note that this type of transaction "is not protected . . . from a determination that it was used principally as a device if it involves the distribution of the stock of more than one controlled corporation and facilitates the avoidance of the dividend provisions of the Code through the subsequent sale or exchange of stock of one corporation and the retention of the stock of another corporation." Treas. Reg. § 1.355-2(d)(5)(i).

The third type is a transaction in which, with respect to each shareholder receiving a distribution, the distribution would be a redemption to which section 302(a) applied. In making this determination, sections 302(c)(2)(A)(ii) and (iii) do not apply. Treas. Reg. § 1.355-2(d)(5)(iv). Redemptions taxed under section 302(a) are taxed as exchanges, so the transaction does not present the possibility of converting what would otherwise be a dividend into capital gain. However, this type of transaction also "is not protected . . . if it involves the distribution of the stock of more than one controlled corporation and facilitates the avoidance of the dividend provisions of the Code through the subsequent sale or exchange of stock of one corporation and the retention of the stock of another corporation." Treas. Reg. § 1.355-2(d)(5)(i).

[F] Active Trade or Business Requirements

Under section 355(b)(1), various aspects of an "active trade or business" requirement must be met. First, either (1) "[t]he distributing and the controlled corporations are each engaged in the active conduct of a trade or business immediately after the distribution," Treas. Reg. § 1.355-3(a)(i),

[9] See § 5.04[D].

or (2) "[i]mmediately before the distribution, the distributing corporation had no assets other than stock or securities of the controlled corporations, and each of the controlled corporations is engaged in the active conduct of a trade or business immediately after the distribution," Treas. Reg. § 1.355-3(a)(ii).

Under the Treasury Regulations,

> A corporation shall be treated as engaged in a trade or business immediately after the distribution if a specific group of activities are being carried on by the corporation for the purpose of earning income or profit, and the activities included in such group include every operation that forms a part of, or a step in, the process of earning income or profit. Such group of activities ordinarily must include the collection of income and the payment of expenses.

Treas. Reg. § 1.355-3(b)(2)(ii).

The determination of whether business is "actively" conducted requires analysis of the facts and circumstances. Treas. Reg. § 1.355-3(b)(2)(iii). As a general rule, however, "the corporation is required itself to perform active and substantial management and operational functions." *Id.* Thus, although some activities may be performed by others, "[g]enerally, activities performed by the corporation itself do not include activities performed by persons outside the corporation, including independent contractors." *Id.* In addition, passive investment activity does not qualify as an active business. *See* Treas. Reg. § 1.355-3(b)(2)(iv) (excluding from the scope of "active conduct of a trade or business" the acts of "holding for investment purposes of stock, securities, land, or other property" and "ownership and operation (including leasing) of real or personal property used in a trade or business, unless the owner performs significant services with respect to the operation and management of the property.").

Rafferty v. Commissioner, 452 F.2d 767, 768 (1st Cir. 1971), *cert. denied*, 408 U.S. 922 (1972), provides an example of an investment-type activity that did not constitute the active conduct of a trade or business. In that case, the taxpayers were the sole owners of Rafferty Brown Steel Co. (RBS). In 1960, RBS organized another corporation, Teragram Realty Company (Teragram), and transferred real estate to Teragram in exchange for all of its stock. Teragram then leased the real estate back to RBS for a ten-year period. The Court of Appeals affirmed the Tax Court's holding that Teragram was not engaged in an "active business" under section 355(b). *Id.* at 771-72. Teragram's sole "business" was a lease-back of real estate transferred to it from RBS—a passive investment. In addition, the absence of "indicia of corporate operations," such as salaries or rent paid, indicated that Teragram was not engaged in an active trade or business. *Id.* at 773.

[1] Five-Year History

The trade or business must also have been actively conducted throughout the five-year period ending on the date of distribution. I.R.C. § 355(b)(2)(B). The regulations provide the following example, among others:

Corporation X owns, manages, and derives rental income from an office building and also owns vacant land. X transfers the land to new subsidiary Y and distributes the stock of Y to X's shareholders. Y will subdivide the land, install streets and utilities, and sell the developed lots to various homebuilders. Y does not satisfy the requirements of section 355(b) because no significant development activities were conducted with respect to the land during the five-year period ending on the date of the distribution. . . .

Treas. Reg. § 1.355-3(c) Ex. 2.

[a]   Same or Different Business?

As indicated above, under section, 355(b)(2)(B), the trade or business must have been actively conducted throughout the five-year period ending on the date of distribution. For purposes of that provision, the fact that a trade or business evolved or developed during the relevant five-year period is disregarded unless the changes are such that the business is a different business than the one previously conducted. *See* Treas. Reg. § 1.355-3(b)(3)(ii).

In *Estate of Lockwood v. Commissioner*, 350 F.2d 712, 713 (8th Cir. 1965), Mr. Lockwood and his wife had been the sole shareholders in Lockwood Graders (Lockwood), a Nebraska corporation. From 1946 to 1951, Lockwood manufactured and sold parts and supplies to potato suppliers, and opened branch offices that were separately incorporated, under a plan designed to take advantage of section 355. The nature of the Lockwood business changed in the early 1950s, such that the corporation began selling to individual farmers as well as potato suppliers, and began manufacturing certain field equipment for the potato industry. In addition to its Midwest business, Lockwood began conducting active business in Maine in 1953. *Id.* at 713-14.

In 1954, Lockwood organized a branch office in Maine (Maine). In 1956, the branch office was incorporated as a Maine corporation. Under the terms of a plan of reorganization, Lockwood transferred various assets to Maine in exchange for Maine's stock and then distributed its Maine stock to Mr. and Mrs. Lockwood in what was intended to be a tax-free distribution under section 355. *Id.* at 714. The IRS asserted a deficiency, determining that the organization of Maine did not qualify for tax-free treatment because the requirements of section 355(b)(2)(B) had not been met. That was the only issue before the Court of Appeals for the Eighth Circuit.

The Eighth Circuit determined that the IRS and the Tax Court had "erred in looking only at the business performed by Lockwood in Maine to determine if the five-year active business requirement had been met prior to the incorporation of Maine, Inc." *Id.* at 715. The court held that the proper focus was on the length of time Lockwood had been an active business in the entire market, not from the date that Lockwood began conducting business in Maine. "Nothing in the language of § 355 suggests that prior business activity is only to be measured by looking at the business performed in a geographical area where the controlled corporation is eventually formed." *Id.*

In reaching this holding, the court noted that the test for this requirement of section 355 is "whether the distributing corporation, for five years prior to distribution, had been actively conducting the type of business now performed by the controlled corporation without reference to the geographic area." *Id.* at 717. Furthermore, the court stated that a mere change in business such as "'the addition of new . . . products, changes in production capacity, and the like'" does not constitute a change that would result in a new or different business. *Id.* at 718 (*quoting* Conf. Rep. No. 2543, 3 U.S.C.C.A.N. 5298 (1954)). Thus, the court found that the record clearly reflected that Lockwood had been in active business for the requisite five-year period prior to the Maine incorporation and that Maine's business therefore possessed the requisite five-year history.

Treasury regulations reach a similar result. *See* Treas. Reg. § 1.355-3(c) Ex. 8. A 2003 Revenue Ruling involving expansion to the internet does, as well. *See* Rev. Rul. 2003-38, 2003-17 I.R.B. 11 ("The creation by a corporation engaged in the retail shoe store business of an Internet web site that sells shoes at retail constitutes an expansion of the retail shoe store business rather than the acquisition of a new or different business under § 1.355-3(b)(3)(ii)."). *Cf.* Rev. Rul. 2003-18, 2003-7 I.R.B. 467 ("The acquisition by D, a brand X automobile dealer, of the brand Y automobile dealership constitutes an expansion of the brand X business and does not constitute the acquisition of a new or different business under § 1.355-3(b)(3)(ii).").

[b] Acquired Business

Under section 355, a corporation generally is treated as engaged in the active conduct of a trade or business if substantially all of its assets consist of stock and securities of a corporation controlled by it which is so engaged. However, the trade or business cannot have been "acquired within the [5-year period ending on the date of the distribution] in a transaction in which gain or loss was recognized in whole or in part . . . ." I.R.C. § 355(b)(2)(C); *see also* Rev. Rul. 2002-49, 2002-2 C.B. 288. In addition, control of the corporation engaged in the active conduct of a trade or business must not have been acquired within that 5-year period, I.R.C. § 355(b)(2)(D)(i), or, if it was, it must have been acquired "only by reason of transactions in which gain or loss was not recognized in whole or in part, or only by reason of such transactions combined with acquisitions before the beginning of such period." I.R.C. § 355(b)(2)(D)(ii).

In *McLaulin v. Commissioner*, 115 T.C. 255, 257 (2000), Ridge Pallets, Inc. (Ridge), an S corporation, owned 50 percent of the stock of Sunbelt Forest Products, Inc., a C corporation. The remaining 50 percent of Sunbelt was owned by John L. Hutto (Hutto). In 1993, Sunbelt redeemed all of Hutto's stock, leaving Ridge as Sunbelt's sole shareholder. The redemption was financed in part by a loan from Ridge. The same day, Ridge distributed all of the stock of Sunbelt to Ridge's three equal shareholders, *pro rata*. *Id.* at 258.

The distribution was treated by the shareholders as a tax-free spin-off under section 355. However, the Tax Court agreed with the IRS's position that, because the distribution of the stock of Sunbelt occurred less than five years after Ridge acquired control of Sunbelt in a transaction in which gain or loss was recognized (the redemption of Hutto's stock), the transaction failed the active business requirement of section 355. The Tax Court relied in part on the fact that cash for the redemption came from Ridge, concluding that, on the facts, there was no difference between the actual transaction and a direct purchase of Sunbelt from Hutto by Ridge. *Id.* at 264-65.

[2] "Immediately After" the Distribution

Section 355 generally requires that the distributing and the controlled corporation each be "engaged immediately after the distribution in the active conduct of a trade or business."[10] I.R.C. § 355(b)(1)(A). Consider the following example:

> For the past nine years, corporation X, a bank, has owned a two-story building, the ground floor and one half of the second floor of which X has occupied in the conduct of its banking business. The other half of the second floor has been rented as storage space to a neighboring retail merchant. X transfers the building to new subsidiary Y and distributes the stock of Y to X's shareholders. After the distribution, X leases from Y the space in the building that it formerly occupied. Under the lease, X will repair and maintain its portion of the building and pay property taxes and insurance. Y does not satisfy the requirements of section 355(b) because it is not engaged in the active conduct of a trade or business immediately after the distribution. . . . This example does not address the question of whether the activities of X with respect to the building prior to the separation would constitute the active conduct of a trade or business.

Treas. Reg. § 1.355-3(c) Ex. 13.

Commissioner v. Mary Archer W. Morris Trust, 367 F.2d 794 (4th Cir. 1966), also interpreted section 355(b)(1)(A). It involved a merger agreement that was negotiated between American Commercial Bank ("American") and Security National Bank ("Security") in 1960. Prior to the merger, American had operated an insurance department. Under applicable national banking laws, American was required to divest itself of its insurance business before the merger could take place. Consequently, American organized a new corporation, American Commercial Agency, Inc. ("Agency"), and transferred

---

[10] This requirement is also met if "immediately before the distribution, the distributing corporation had no assets other than stock or securities in the controlled corporations and each of the controlled corporations is engaged immediately after the distribution in the active conduct of a trade or business." I.R.C. § 355(b)(1)(B).

its insurance business to Agency in exchange for all of Agency's stock. American immediately distributed the Agency stock to its shareholders, and then completed the merger with Security. *Id.* at 795-96.

The IRS determined that section 355(b)(1)(A) was not satisfied because American's banking business was not continued in an "unaltered corporate form," and thus, the distribution of Agency stock to American's shareholders was taxable as ordinary income. *Id.* at 796. The issue before the Fourth Circuit was whether American, as merged into a national bank now named North Carolina National Bank, was engaged in an active trade or business "immediately after" the distribution, as required by statute.

Looking to the history behind section 355, the court noted that the substantive concern with the "immediately after" requirement was that there be a continuity of the business without the "opportunity for the stockholders to sever their interest in the business except through a separable, taxable transaction." *Id.* at 798. The Fourth Circuit held that American satisfied the "immediately after" requirement of section 355(b) because it continued to engage in the active conduct of the banking business immediately after the distribution to its shareholders. The fact that American had merged with a national bank and assumed a different corporate name did not adversely affect satisfaction of this "immediately after" requirement. "American's merger with Security, in no sense, was a discontinuance of American's banking business, which opened the day after the merger with the same employees, the same depositors and customers." *Id.* at 799.

The court found that the Code imposed no control requirements that implied a "limitation upon subsequent reorganizations of the transferor." *Id.* at 800. Agency had been organized by American for a valid business purpose and there was a business purpose for both the spin-off and the merger. The merger did not affect the continuity of interest of American's stockholders, and the requisite control requirement was clearly met. Therefore, the distribution of Agency stock to American's shareholders was tax-free under section 355.

Morris Trust permitted a post-355-transaction merger of the distributing corporation into another corporation. Subsequently, the IRS ruled that a post-355-transaction merger of another corporation into the distributing corporation also did not spoil the section 355 transaction. *See* Rev. Rul. 72-530, 1972-2 C.B. 148.

In 1997, Congress enacted section 355(e), "the anti-*Morris Trust* provision." *See* George K. Yin, *Morris Trust, Sec. 355(e), and the Future Taxation of Corp. Acquisitions*, 80 TAX NOTES 375 (1998). Section 355(e) targeted primarily the following type of "leveraged spinoff transactions that were the economic equivalents of cash sales of assets, where the spinoff rules resulted in no taxable gain to the 'seller,'" Michael L. Schler, *Simplifying and Rationalizing the Spinoff Rules*, 56 SMU L. REV. 239, 244 (2003):

> Suppose P had two divisions (A and B), each with a basis of $0 and value of $100. If X wanted to buy B, P would borrow $65, contribute

> the cash and A to new S, and spin off S to its shareholders. X would then acquire P (holding B and having $65 of debt) for $35 of X stock. S (holding A and $65 in cash, and renamed P) is in the same position as the old P, as if old P had sold B for $100 and paid $35 in tax. Likewise, X is in the same position as if it paid $100 ($65 in cash and $35 in stock) for B. However, no tax has been paid and the B assets do not have a stepped-up tax basis. The $35 in tax savings has gone to the old P shareholders in the form of X stock.

Id. at 244 n.35.

Section 355(e) targets *Morris Trust*-type transactions by providing for corporate-level gain recognition under section 361(c)(2) when the stock or securities in the controlled corporation are distributed as part of a plan or series of related transactions pursuant to which one or more persons acquire stock representing a 50-percent or greater interest in the distributing corporation or any controlled corporation. Thus, the application of section 355(e)(2) is not limited to spin-offs involving debt.[11] *See* Schler, *supra*, at 244.

Regulations under section 355(e) provide that "[w]hether a distribution and an acquisition are part of a plan is determined based on all the facts and circumstances." Treas. Reg. § 1.355-7(b)(1). The regulations also contain non-exclusive lists of various "plan factors" and "non-plan factors." *See* Treas. Reg. § 1.355-7(b)(3), (4). The regulations further provide, with respect to *post-distribution acquisitions*:

> In the case of an acquisition (other than involving a public offering) after a distribution, the distribution and the acquisition can be part of a plan *only* if there was an agreement, understanding, arrangement, or substantial negotiations regarding the acquisition or a similar acquisition at some time during the two-year period ending on the date of the distribution. In the case of an acquisition (other than involving a public offering) after a distribution, the existence of an agreement, understanding, arrangement, or substantial negotiations regarding the acquisition or a similar acquisition at some time during the two-year period ending on the date of the distribution tends to show that the distribution and the acquisition are part of a plan. . . . However, all facts and circumstances must be considered to determine whether the distribution and the acquisition are part of a plan.

Treas. Reg. § 1.355-7(b)(2) (emphasis added). Thus, for post-distribution acquisitions, "an agreement, understanding, arrangement, or substantial

---

[11] Section 355(e)(2) did not actually overrule *Morris Trust* "because the actual shareholders of the distributing corporation in *Morris Trust* still maintained a majority interest in the merged entities." Karim H. Hanafy, *Section 355 Spin-Off + Section 368 Reorganization ≠ Section 355(e). It's Simple Math: The Anti-Morris Trust Bill Simply Does Not Add Up*, 1 HOUS. BUS. & TAX L.J. 119, 167 (2001); *see also* George K. Yin, *Taxing Corporate Divisions*, 56 SMU L. REV. 289, 299 n.50 (2003).

negotiations" within the relevant two-year period is a necessary but not sufficient condition for the finding of a plan.

In 1998, partly in response to section 355(e), the IRS ruled that it would not apply the step-transaction doctrine or *Court Holding* principles[12] to a post-355 "acquisition or restructuring of the distributed corporation" merger of the controlled corporation with another corporation so as to deny section 355 treatment. *See* Rev. Rul. 98-27, 1998-1 C.B. 1159. Thus, adverse tax consequences in this context appear to be limited to corporate-level gain recognition. Note also that section 355(e) does not apply to distributions to which section 355(d) applies. I.R.C. § 355(e)(2)(D). Section 355(d), another corporate-level gain recognition provision, is discussed below, in § 11.02[H][2].

[G] Continuity of Proprietary Interest

Acquisitive reorganizations, discussed in Chapters 9 and 10, require "continuity of proprietary interest"—adequate continuing equity ownership in the newly transformed corporation. The same is true of divisive transactions.

> Section 355 applies to a separation that effects only a readjustment of continuing interests in the property of the distributing and controlled corporations. In this regard, section 355 requires that one or more persons who, directly or indirectly, were the owners of the enterprise prior to the distribution or exchange own, in the aggregate, an amount of stock establishing a continuity of interest in *each* of the modified corporate forms in which the enterprise is conducted after the separation.

Treas. Reg. 1.355-2(c)(1) (emphasis added).

The regulations' requirement that the persons who were the owners of the enterprise prior to the distribution own, in the aggregate, an amount of stock establishing a continuity of interest in *each* of the corporations in which the enterprise is conducted after the distribution can make this standard difficult to meet. *See* Treas. Reg. 1.355-2(c)(2) Ex. 3. The IRS's ruling position with respect to the continuity of proprietary interest requirement of regulation 1.368-1(b) traditionally has been that at least 50 percent of the total consideration must be equity. *See* Rev. Rul. 66-224, 1966-2 C.B. 114. However, examples in Treasury Regulations promulgated under section 368 in 2005 find 40-percent continuity sufficient. *See, e.g.,* Treas. Reg. § 1.368-1(e)(2)(v) Ex. 1, Ex. 2(ii).

---

[12] *Commissioner v. Court Holding Co.*, 324 U.S. 331 (1945), is discussed in § 7.03[A][1][b].

CHART 11.1
Checklist for Section 355 Transactions

(1)   Is there a distribution of stock or securities?

(2)   Does the distribution meet the form of a spin-off, split-off, or split-up?

(3)   Have all of the stock or securities of a controlled corporation been distributed in the transaction?

- If not, has an amount constituting control under 368(c) been distributed, and does the retention of any stock or securities fail to suggest a tax-avoidance motive?

(4)   Does the transaction have a corporate-level business purpose?

(5)   Does the transaction constitute a device for bailing out earnings and profits?

(6)   Does the transaction involve trades or businesses that have at least a five-year history and that remain active businesses after the transaction?

(7)   Is there continuity of proprietary interest?

[H]   Tax Consequences and Basis Rules

In general, in a section 355 transaction, shareholders of the controlling parent corporation receive stock and/or securities, perhaps in exchange for stock and/or securities. Their gain or loss realized and recognized must be calculated, as well as their basis in the stock or securities received. The controlling parent (distributing) corporation is taxed in accordance with what it distributes. The subsidiary corporation has no tax consequences on the distribution of its shares. The tax consequences to the parties to a section 355 transaction are explained in more detail below.

[1]   Shareholders

[a]   General Tax Consequences

Shareholders in a qualifying section 355 transaction do not recognize gain or loss if no boot is received, and do not recognize loss even if boot is received. I.R.C. §§ 355(a)(1), (4), 356(c). In a spin-off, *the fair market value of the boot received is treated as a 301 distribution.* I.R.C. § 356(b).

Example 11.5: Gary and Helene are the sole shareholders of GH, Inc. GH, Inc. wholly owns Subs, Inc. GH, Inc. spins off Subs, Inc. in a qualifying section 355 transaction in which Gary and Helene each receive half of the Subs, Inc. stock plus $30,000 cash. Because the transaction otherwise qualifies under section 355, Gary and Helene each have received boot in the amount of $30,000 that will constitute dividend income to the extent of the earnings and profits of GH, Inc. Their receipt of Subs, Inc. stock, however, remains tax-free.

Shareholders that receive boot in a split-off or split-up recognize realized gain only to the extent of boot received. I.R.C. § 356(a).

Example 11.6: Ike and Jean are the sole shareholders of IJ, Inc. IJ, Inc. wholly owns SubCo, Inc. IJ, Inc. distributes half of the SubCo, Inc. stock each to Ike and Jean, plus $10,000 to each of them. In return, Ike and Jean each surrender IJ, Inc. shares with a basis of $20,000 and fair market value of $70,000. Assuming that this split-off qualifies as a tax-free reorganization, Ike and Jean each realize $50,000 of gain and recognize $10,000 of that gain. I.R.C. § 356(a)(1).

The character of the gain recognized in a split-off or split-up depends on whether the exchange has the effect of the distribution of a dividend. I.R.C. § 356(a)(2). Section 302 principles apply in making this determination.[13] *See* Rev. Rul. 93-62, 1993-2 C.B. 118. Section 318 constructive stock ownership rules apply. I.R.C. § 356(a)(2). Revenue Ruling 93-62 involved the following facts:

> Distributing is a corporation with 1,000 shares of a single class of stock outstanding. Each share has a fair market value of $1x. *A*, one of five unrelated individual shareholders, owns 400 shares of Distributing stock. Distributing owns all of the outstanding stock of a subsidiary corporation, Controlled. The Controlled stock has a fair market value of $200x.

> Distributing distributes all the stock of Controlled plus $200x cash to *A* in exchange for all of *A*'s Distributing stock. The exchange satisfies the requirements of section 355 but for the receipt of the cash.

Id. at 118-19. The Revenue Ruling held that the hypothetical redemption takes place *prior* to the exchange. "This determination is made by treating the recipient shareholder as if the shareholder had retained the distributing corporation stock actually exchanged for controlled corporation stock and received the boot in exchange for distributing corporation stock equal in value to the boot." *Id.* at 119-20.

Thus, in the Ruling,

> before the exchange, *A* owned 400 of the 1,000 shares, or 40 percent, of the outstanding Distributing stock. If *A* had surrendered only the 200 shares for which *A* received boot, *A* would still hold 200 of the 800 shares, or 25 percent, of the Distributing stock outstanding after the exchange. This 25 percent stock interest would represent 62.5 percent of *A*'s pre-exchange stock interest in Distributing. Therefore, the deemed redemption would be treated as an exchange because it qualifies as substantially disproportionate under section 302(b)(2) of the Code.

---

[13] *See* § 9.07[A][2] for a discussion of *Clark* and the application of section 302 principles to characterize gain recognized in acquisitive reorganizations.

Id. at 119. Note that, although the Revenue Ruling applies an analysis similar to that of *Commissioner v. Clark*, 489 U.S. 729 (1989), the Ruling's approach is nonetheless slightly different because *Clark* applied a hypothetical redemption to the taxpayer's ownership interest in the corporation *after* the reorganization, in the context of a forward triangular merger.[14]

If a shareholder relinquishes multiple blocks of stock, each block is considered separately. *See* Rev. Rul. 68-23, 1968-1. Thus, gain or loss realized is determined separately for each block of stock, and boot is allocated proportionately to each block. As with Revenue Ruling 68-55, 1968-1 C.B. 140, explained in Chapter 2,[15] this process will result in less gain recognition than if boot were allocated only to those blocks of stock with realized gain. However, allocation when the exchange involves securities can be particularly complex.

Note that the following items constitute boot:

(1) Distributed securities in excess of securities received. I.R.C. § 355(a)(3)(A). The determination of *whether* distributed securities exceed relinquished securities is made by comparing *principal amounts*. Once it is determined that excess securities were distributed, *the boot amount is the fair market value of the excess securities*. I.R.C. § 356(d)(2)(C).

Example 11.7: As part of a section 355 transaction, Distributing Corporation distributes securities to Kyle with an aggregate principal amount of $100,000. Kyle relinquishes securities with an aggregate principal amount of $80,000. The securities with an aggregate principal amount of $20,000 constitute boot. Assuming that those securities are fairly valued at $25,000, Kyle will have received $25,000 of boot with respect to the securities.

(2) "[S]tock of a controlled corporation acquired by the distributing corporation by reason of any transaction . . . which occurs within 5 years of the distribution of such stock, and . . . in which gain or loss was recognized in whole or in part . . . ." I.R.C. § 355(a)(3)(B).

(3) "[S]tock (including nonqualified preferred stock . . .), securities, or other property received [that] is attributable to interest which has accrued on securities on or after the beginning of the holder's holding period." I.R.C. § 355(a)(3)(C).

(4) Nonqualified preferred stock, unless it was received in exchange for other nonqualified preferred stock or rights to acquire nonqualified preferred stock. *See* I.R.C. § 355(a)(3)(D); Treas. Reg. § 1.356-6(a)(1).[16]

(5) Rights to acquire nonqualified preferred stock, unless they were received in exchange for nonqualified preferred stock or rights to acquire nonqualified preferred stock. Treas. Reg. § 1.356-6(a)(2).

---

[14] *See* § 9.07[A][2].

[15] *See* § 2.02[A][1][f][ii][I].

[16] The definition of "nonqualified preferred stock" is discussed in Chapter 2. *See* § 2.02[A][1][f][i].

[b] Shareholder Basis

Under section 358, calculation of each shareholder's basis in stock or securities received in a section 355 transaction requires the following steps:

(1) Aggregate the shareholder's adjusted basis in *all* stock or securities of the parent corporation that the shareholder held before the transaction (whether or not they were transferred to the parent in the transaction).

(2) Add to that any gain recognized by the shareholder or dividend income to the shareholder resulting from the transaction.

(3) Subtract the amount of cash received and the fair market value of other boot received.

(4) Allocate the resulting basis figure among all stock and/or securities of the parent corporation that the shareholder retained and that the shareholder received in the transaction in proportion to their relative fair market values. If, before the transaction, the shareholder owned *only one class of stock and no securities or only one class of securities and no stock*, and now owns stock of two or more classes after the transaction, the allocation is based on relative fair market values. Treas. Reg. § 1.358-2(a)(2), (3). If, instead, before the transaction, the shareholder owned *more than one class of stock or more than one class of securities or both stock and securities*, the allocation is done block-by-block, as discussed in § 9.07[A][3][b]. Treas. Reg. § 1.358-2(a)(4).

Example 11.8: In Example 11.6, Ike and Jean each surrendered IJ, Inc. shares with a basis of $20,000. Assume that they each retained shares, of the same class, with a basis of $13,000 and fair market value of $30,000. Each shareholder would have an aggregate basis in his or her new and retained shares of $33,000 ($33,000 + $10,000 gain recognized − $10,000 boot received). That basis will be allocated between the retained IJ, Inc. shares and the SubCo, Inc. shares in accordance with their respective fair market values. The SubCo, Inc. shares received apparently were worth $60,000. As the retained IJ, Inc. shares are worth only $30,000, 1/3 of the $33,000 basis, or $11,000, is allocated to them, and 2/3, or $22,000, is allocated to the SubCo, Inc. shares.

[2] The Distributing Corporation

The distributing corporation may not recognize any loss on the distribution. I.R.C. § 355(c)(1). The distributing corporation generally does not recognize gain on the distribution of stock or securities of its controlled subsidiaries. *See* I.R.C. § 355(c)(2). However, the distributing corporation can recognize gain if section 355(d) or (e) applies. Section 355(e), the anti-*Morris Trust* provision, was discussed above in § 11.02[F][2]. Section 355(d) is an older provision that also provides for the recognition of corporate-level gain in certain situations. It applies to "disqualified distributions." I.R.C. § 355(d)(1).

[Distributing corporation] D's distribution of stock is a disqualified distribution if, immediately after the distribution, any person holds "disqualified stock" in either D or [controlled subsidiary] C, and the stock constitutes a 50% or greater interest. A person holds disqualified stock if it was acquired by "purchase," after October 9, 1990, and within five years prior to the distribution period. Either voting power or stock value is used to determine if a particular person holds stock that constitutes 50% or greater stock interest. . . .

Karim H. Hanafy, *Section 355 Spin-Off + Section 368 Reorganization ≠ Section 355(e). It's Simple Math: The Anti-Morris Trust Bill Simply Does Not Add Up*, 1 HOUS. BUS. & TAX L.J. 119, 154-55 (2001) (footnotes omitted). Note that sections 355(d) and (e) each provide for corporate-level gain where they apply but leave shareholder nonrecognition unaffected.

The distributing corporation also recognizes realized gain on the distribution of property other than stock or securities in the controlled corporation. *See* I.R.C. § 355(c)(2)(A), (B). If the property distributed is subject to a liability, the property's fair market value is deemed to be no less than the amount of the liability. I.R.C. § 355(c)(2)(C). If the distributing corporation receives its own stock in the transaction, the stock will be cancelled or become treasury stock.

[3] Allocation of Earnings and Profits

In a section 355 transaction not involving a newly organized controlled corporation (that is, not part of a D reorganization), earnings and profits of the distributing (parent) corporation are *decreased* by the *lesser of*:

(1) The amount by which the earnings and profits of the distributing corporation would have been decreased if it had transferred the stock of the controlled corporation to a new corporation in a reorganization to which section 368(a)(1)(D) applied and immediately thereafter distributed the stock of such new corporation or,

(2) The net worth of the controlled corporation. (For this purpose, the term "net worth" means the sum of the basis of all of the properties plus cash minus all liabilities.)

Treas. Reg. § 1.312-10(b).

If the earnings and profits of the controlled corporation immediately before the transaction are less than the amount of the decrease in earnings and profits of the distributing corporation (including a case in which the controlled corporation has a deficit), the earnings and profits of the controlled corporation, after the transaction, shall be equal to the amount of such decrease. If the earnings and profits of the controlled corporation immediately before the transaction are more than the amount of the decrease in the earnings and profits of the distributing corporation, they shall remain unchanged.

Id.

§ 11.03   Divisive "D" Reorganizations

[A]   In General

A divisive D reorganization is one in which a corporation transfers substantially all of its assets to a corporation it or its shareholders (or any combination) "controls" immediately after the transfer, in exchange for stock or securities of the transferee, followed by a liquidation of transferor and distribution to its shareholders of that stock or securities and any other assets it still has, in a transaction that qualifies under section 355. Control for this purpose is determined under section 368(c), which requires "ownership of stock possessing at least 80 percent of the total combined voting power of all classes of stock entitled to vote and at least 80 percent of the total number of shares of all other classes of stock of the corporation." I.R.C. § 368(c); *cf.* I.R.C. § 368(a)(2)(H)(i) (applying section 304(c) to acquisitive D reorganizations). Also note that "the fact that the shareholders of the distributing corporation dispose of part or all of the distributed stock, or the fact that the corporation whose stock was distributed issues additional stock, shall not be taken into account." I.R.C. § 368(a)(2)(H)(ii).

Thus, in a transaction qualifying as a divisive D reorganization, the target's transfer of assets to the controlled corporation, which generally is protected from the recognition of gain or loss, is immediately followed by a spin-off, split-off, or split-up.[17] The diagram below illustrates the "before," "during," and "after" pictures of a typical divisive D reorganization.

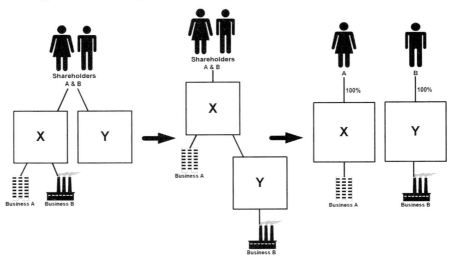

[B]   Qualification Under Section 355

As indicated above, a divisive D reorganization must contain a distribution that satisfies all of the requirements of section 355. This is the core

---

[17] However, note that section 357(c) can apply. *See* I.R.C. § 357(c)(1)(B).

difference between a divisive D and an acquisitive D;[18] in the divisive type of D reorganization, the distribution spins off, splits off, or splits up stockholdings, thereby dividing up businesses. Section 355 has a number of quite specific statutory and common law requirements that must be met, as discussed above.[19]

[C] Tax Consequences, Basis, and Earnings and Profits Rules

The tax consequences of a divisive D reorganization generally are the same as those for a corporate division under section 355, with certain exceptions. The tax treatment of the distributing (parent) corporation is primarily governed by section 361(c), rather than section 355(c). However, sections 355(d) and (e), which are discussed in §§ 11.02[H][2] and 11.02[F][2], respectively, can apply in either case. *See* I.R.C. §§ 355(d)(1), (e)(1).

The tax consequences of a divisive D reorganization are generally as follows:

(1) As would be expected, the distributing corporation may not recognize any loss on the distribution. I.R.C. § 361(c)(1).

(2) The distributing corporation generally does not recognize gain on the distribution of "qualified property." I.R.C. § 361(c)(1), (2). For this purpose, qualified property is defined as "any stock in (or right to acquire stock in) the distributing corporation or obligation of the distributing corporation, or any stock in (or right to acquire stock in) another corporation which is a party to the reorganization or obligation of another corporation which is such a party if such stock (or right) or obligation is received by the distributing corporation in the exchange." I.R.C. § 361(c)(2)(B).

(3) The distributing corporation does recognize realized gain on the distribution of other property. I.R.C. § 361(c)(2)(A), (B). If the property distributed is subject to a liability, its fair market value is deemed to be no less than the amount of the liability. I.R.C. § 361(c)(2)(C).

(4) The distributing corporation also generally can avoid gain recognition by distributing boot to "creditors in connection with the reorganization . . . ." I.R.C. § 361(b)(3). However, the relief in that provision is limited to the adjusted bases of the assets transferred. *Id.*

In a divisive D reorganization, earnings and profits generally are allocated between the distributing (parent) corporation and the controlled (subsidiary) corporation in proportion to the fair market values of the assets of each corporation immediately after the transaction. Treas. Reg. § 1.312-10(a). However, in appropriate cases, the allocation may be made in

---

[18] Acquisitive D reorganizations are discussed in § 10.06 of Chapter 10.

[19] *See* § 11.02 of Chapter 11.

proportion to aggregate asset basis net of liabilities. *Id.* The regulations do not specify what may constitute such a case. *But cf. Bennet v. United States,* 427 F.2d 1202 (Ct. Cl. 1970).

§ 11.04 Divisive "G" Reorganizations

As discussed in Chapter 10, section 368(a)(1)(G) authorizes divisive reorganizations that are part of a Title 11 bankruptcy proceeding or federal or state court receivership, foreclosure, or similar proceeding. *See* I.R.C. § 368(a)(1)(G), (a)(3)(A). In general, in a G reorganization, the target must distribute the stock or securities of the acquiring corporation in a transaction that may qualify under section 354, 355, or 356; the distribution in a divisive G must qualify under section 355. G reorganizations are discussed further in § 10.07 of Chapter 10.

Chapter 12

REORGANIZATIONS INVOLVING ONLY ONE CORPORATION

§ 12.01   Introduction

Some reorganizations involve a change in the corporate form of a single corporation. For example, a corporation may wish to alter its capital structure by retiring some of its debt in exchange for stock, or *vice versa*. A transaction of this type may qualify as a recapitalization, governed by the provisions of section 368(a)(1)(E). As another example, a corporation may wish to change its name or state of incorporation. Section 368(a)(1)(F) applies to this form of reorganization.

§ 12.02   Recapitalizations ("E" Reorganizations)

[A]   Introduction

As discussed in Chapter 3, a corporation's capital structure includes common stock, and may also include preferred stock, securities, and other debt instruments. The exchange between a corporation and its shareholders of the corporation's securities and equity instruments is a reorganization if it qualifies under section 368(a)(1)(E). Although a reorganization under section 368(a)(1)(E) is defined simply as a "recapitalization," a frequently quoted generalization describes such a reorganization as a "reshuffling of a capital structure within the framework of an existing corporation." *Helvering v. Southwest Consolidated Corp.*, 315 U.S. 194, 202 (1942).

The diagram below illustrates the "before" and "after" pictures of a type of stock-for-stock recapitalization. Afterwards, the X Corp. shareholders have less Class A common stock than they did before the recapitalization.

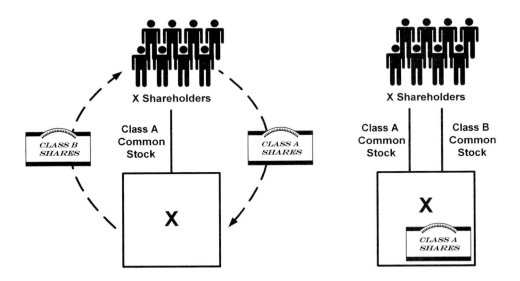

Treasury regulations provide the following examples, among others, of recapitalizations:

(1) "A corporation with $200,000 par value of bonds outstanding, instead of paying them off in cash, discharges them by issuing preferred shares to the bondholders," Treas. Reg. § 1.368-2(e)(1);

(2) A corporation cancels 25 percent of its preferred stock and issues no par value common stock in exchange, Treas. Reg. § 1.368-2(e)(2);

(3) "A corporation issues preferred stock, previously authorized but unissued, for outstanding common stock," Treas. Reg. § 1.368-2(e)(3); and

(4) A corporation issues new common stock in exchange for its "outstanding preferred stock, having certain priorities with reference to the amount and time of payment of dividends and the distribution of the corporate assets upon liquidation . . .," Treas. Reg. § 1.368-2(e)(4).

Note that even if an exchange qualifies as a recapitalization within the meaning of section 368(a)(1)(E), gain may still be recognized under the operative provisions applicable to corporate reorganizations.[1]

Note also that stock and "securities"—long-term debt instruments—are the only instruments that qualify under section 354. Short-term debt instruments (generally called "notes") constitute boot.

---

[1] *See* § 9.07 of Chapter 9.

[B]   Business Purpose Requirement

Although the continuity of proprietary interest doctrine and the continuity of business enterprise doctrine do not apply to recapitalizations, Treas. Reg. § 1.368-1(b), the business purpose doctrine does. However, the business purpose test may be easier to meet in this context than in the context of other reorganizations. *See Wolf Envelope Co. v. Commissioner*, 17 T.C. 471, 483 (1951) ("It is a sufficient and valid purpose if the exchange effects a shift in voting rights as between one group of stockholders and another"). Nonetheless, in *Bazley v. Commissioner*, 331 U.S. 737, 739 (1947), discussed below in § 12.02[C][3], in which the taxpayers exchanged stock for stock and bonds in a transaction resembling a dividend, the Supreme Court noted that the Tax Court concluded that "no legitimate corporate business purpose" existed for the so-called recapitalization. The Supreme Court, like the Tax Court and the Court of Appeals, concluded that the exchange constituted a disguised dividend. *See id.* at 743.

[C]   Types of Recapitalizations

Under Treasury Regulations, there are four general types of exchanges that may qualify as recapitalizations under section 368(a)(1)(E): stock for stock, stock for debt, debt for stock, and debt for debt. Each of these is considered in turn below. Note that for sections 354 and 356 to apply, the exchange must be pursuant to a plan of reorganization. *See* I.R.C. §§ 354(a)(1); 356(a)(1).

[1]   Corporate Stock for Investors' Stock

A stock-for-stock exchange can qualify as a recapitalization. In addition, a separate provision, section 1036, provides that no gain or loss is recognized if *common stock* in a corporation is exchanged solely for *common stock* in the same corporation, or if *preferred stock* in a corporation is exchanged solely for *preferred stock* in the same corporation. *See* I.R.C. § 1036; Treas. Reg. § 1.1036-1(a). Section 1036 therefore partially overlaps with section 368(a)(1)(E). *See* Treas. Reg. § 1.1036-1(a); Boris I. Bittker & James S. Eustice, Federal Income Taxation of Corporations and Shareholders ¶ 12.27[2][a] (7th ed. 2000). However, section 1036 applies to exchanges between shareholders (as well as to exchanges between a corporation and its shareholders), *see* Treas. Reg. § 1.1036-1(a), which the recapitalization provision does not. Also note that section 1036 does not apply to nonqualified preferred stock.[2] I.R.C. § 1036(b).

An exchange of common stock for preferred stock or preferred for common does not fall with section 1036. Treas. Reg. § 1.1036-1(a). However, this type of stock-for-stock exchange between a corporation and its shareholders can qualify as a recapitalization. *See* Treas. Reg. § 1.368-2(e)(2)-(4).

---

[2] Nonqualified preferred stock also is not treated as stock or securities for purposes of section 354 unless it is received in exchange for nonqualified preferred stock. *See* I.R.C. § 354(a)(2)(C). Nonqualified preferred stock is discussed in Chapter 2. *See* § 2.02[A][1][f][i].

Example 12.1: Aaron and Bartha are preferred shareholders of Y, Inc. Y, Inc. exchanges shares of its common stock for their preferred stock. Assuming that there is a business purpose for the exchange, this is a stock-for-stock recapitalization that should be protected by section 354.

If a shareholder receives boot in a stock-for-stock recapitalization, gain realized will be recognized to the extent of the boot received. I.R.C. § 356(a)(1). If the distribution has the effect of a dividend, it will be treated as such. I.R.C. § 356(a)(2). The shareholder's basis in the stock received will be the same as the basis of the stock exchanged, adjusted for any boot received and any gain recognized. *See* I.R.C. § 358(a)(1). Shareholders will also take tacked holding periods in the stock received. I.R.C. § 1223(1).

Example 12.2: In Example 12.1, Aaron and Bartha's bases in the common stock will be the same as their bases in the preferred stock, and they will each tack their holding period in the preferred stock onto the common stock they receive.

Although the exchange of stock for stock in a recapitalization generally does not have particularly adverse tax consequences, there are two situations to watch out for in particular. First, in certain circumstances, a recapitalization, "whether or not an isolated transaction," may constitute a stock dividend under section 305(c). Treas. Reg. §§ 1.305-7(c); *see also* 1.368-2(e)(5). Treasury Regulations provide that a recapitalization:

> will be deemed to result in a distribution to which section 305(c) and this section apply if—
>
> (i) It is *pursuant to a plan* to periodically increase a shareholder's proportionate interest in the assets or earnings and profits of the corporation, *or*
>
> (ii) A shareholder owning *preferred stock with dividends in arrears* exchanges his stock for other stock and, as a result, increases his proportionate interest in the assets or earnings and profits of the corporation. . . .

Treas. Reg. §§ 1.305-7(c)(1) (emphasis added). The regulations further provide that a preferred shareholder increases his or her proportionate interest "in any case where the fair market value or the liquidation preference, whichever is greater, of the stock received in the exchange (determined immediately following the recapitalization), exceeds the issue price of the preferred stock surrendered." *Id.* Thus, a recapitalization that is not done pursuant to a plan to increase a shareholder's proportionate interest in the corporation or with respect to preferred stock with dividends in arrears generally should not raise stock dividend issues under section 305(c).

The second major concern with respect to stock-for-stock recapitalizations is that preferred stock received by a shareholder in a recapitalization may constitute "section 306 stock." Section 306 is discussed in Chapter 6.[3] The

---

[3] *See* § 6.04.

preferred stock will be section 306 stock if, on its receipt, the shareholder is sheltered from gain recognition to any extent *and* the effect of the transaction is equivalent to payment of a stock dividend. *See* I.R.C. § 306(c)(1)(B). The dividend equivalence test generally requires considering whether had cash been received instead of the stock, it would have been treated as either a dividend under section 356(a)(2) or as a 301 distribution under section 356(b) or 302(d). Treas. Reg. § 1.306-3(d). However, an example in the regulations provides that where preferred stock received was "not substantially different from the preferred stock previously held" and the preferred stock previously held was not section 306 stock, the preferred stock received will not be section 306 stock. *See* Treas. Reg. § 1.306-3(d) Ex. 2.

[2] Corporate Stock for Investors' Debt Securities

If a corporation exchanges its stock for its bonds (securities) held by a bondholder, the bondholder generally does not recognize gain or loss. *See* Treas. Reg. § 1.368-2(e)(1); Rev. Rul. 59-98, 1959-1 C.B. 76. As indicated above, the debt exchanged by the investor must constitute "securities" (as opposed to short-term notes, for example), for section 354 to apply to protect the investor from the recognition of realized gain. *See* I.R.C. § 354(a)(1).

Example 12.3: Corinne and Daniel are bondholders of Z, Inc. Z, Inc. exchanges shares of its common stock for their long-term bonds. Assuming that there is a business purpose for the exchange, this exchange of stock for securities constitutes a recapitalization under section 368(a)(1)(E).

In general, each bondholder's basis in the stock received will be the same as the basis of the bonds exchanged, adjusted for any boot received and any gain recognized. *See* I.R.C. § 358. The bondholder will also be entitled to tack the bonds' holding period in the stock received. I.R.C. § 1223(1).

Under section 354(a)(2)(B), interest on the bonds that has accrued but remained unpaid until satisfied with a stock payment in the recapitalization will constitute gross income if the bondholder has not previously reported the accrued interest as income. The income will be ordinary in character.

Example 12.4: In Example 12.3, if Corinne's bonds had accrued but unpaid interest that was satisfied with a stock payment in the recapitalization, the amount of that interest would constitute ordinary income.

The corporation will not recognize gain on the issuance of stock in exchange for bonds, under section 1032(a). However, because the corporation also is retiring bonds, it is subject to the cancellation of indebtedness rules. That is, in general, if a corporation pays off its bonds for less than the face amount of the debt, the corporation will have cancellation of indebtedness income under section 61(a)(12) unless one of the exceptions in section 108 applies. *See* I.R.C. § 108(e)(8); *cf. United States v. Kirby Lumber Co.*, 284 U.S. 1 (1931). The exceptions in section 108 include bankruptcy under Title 11 and insolvency. *See* I.R.C. § 108(a)(1). As might be expected, when stock is used to pay off bonds, the payment amount is considered to be the fair market value of the stock. I.R.C. § 108(e)(8).

[3] Corporate Debt Securities for Investors' Stock

The exchange of corporate bonds for a stockholder's stock raises the concern that the transaction is a disguised dividend. The *pro rata* exchange of common stock for common stock and bonds payable on demand constituted the distribution of a dividend in *Bazley v. Commissioner*, 331 U.S. 737 (1947). *Bazley* was decided before excess principal amount of securities received constituted boot. In *Bazley*, debentures were distributed as part of a recapitalization of a family corporation in which Mr. and Mrs. Bazley owned all but one of the corporation's one thousand shares. Under the plan, the shareholders exchanged their old shares with a $100 par value for (1) five new shares of no par value but a stated value of $60 and (2) new debenture bonds with a face value of $400,000 payable in ten years but callable at any time. At the time of the exchange, the corporation had $855,783.82 in earned surplus. *Id.* at 739.

The Bazleys contended that the transaction was a tax-free reorganization. They also argued that the debentures did not result in any income, but instead were "securities in a corporation a party to a reorganization" that were "exchanged solely for stock or securities in another corporation" as part of a planned reorganization. The IRS disagreed, viewing the debentures as taxable to the full extent of their value. The Tax Court concluded that the recapitalization constituted a disguised dividend. The Third Circuit affirmed. *Id.*

The Supreme Court affirmed the decision of the Third Circuit. Emphasizing substance over form, the Court held that where a corporation has undistributed earnings, "the creation of new corporate obligations which are transferred to shareholders in relation to their former holdings, so as to produce, for all practical purposes, the same result as a distribution of cash earnings of equivalent value, cannot obtain tax immunity because cast in the form of a recapitalization-reorganization." *Id.* at 742. The fact that the debentures were callable at any time indicated that they were in essence a cash distribution. The Court stated, "[a] reorganization which is merely a vehicle, however elaborate or elegant, for conveying earnings from accumulations to the stockholders is not a reorganization . . . ." *Id.* at 743.

The *Bazley* holding is echoed in the Treasury Regulations:

> if a corporation having only common stock outstanding, exchanges one share of newly issued common stock and one bond in the principal amount of $10 for each share of outstanding common stock, the distribution of the bonds will be a distribution of property (to the extent of their fair market value) to which section 301 applies, even though the exchange of common stock for common stock may be pursuant to a plan of reorganization under the terms of section

368(a)(1)(E) (recapitalization) and even though the exchange of common stock for common stock may be tax-free by virtue of section 354.

Treas. Reg. § 1.301-1(*l*). Note that the regulation contemplates bifurcation of the exchange into its component parts.

If a corporation exchanges *only* debt securities for stock held by a shareholder, section 354 does not apply. Treas. Reg. § 1.354-1(d) Ex. 3 & 4. The regulations provide the following examples:

> Example 3. C, a shareholder in Corporation Z (which is not a railroad corporation), surrenders all his stock in Corporation Z in exchange for securities in Corporation Z. Whether or not this exchange is in connection with a recapitalization under section 368(a)(1)(E), section 354 does not apply. See, however, section 302.

> Example 4. The facts are the same as in Example 3 of this paragraph (d), except that C receives solely rights to acquire stock in Corporation Z. Section 354 does not apply.

Id. Note that, in these scenarios, which involve a corporate investor's surrender of his or her stock interest, the investor is terminating his or her status as a shareholder. Example 3 explicitly provides that the exchange is treated as a redemption of stock, which is what it resembles.[4] In addition, original issue discount may arise whenever debt is distributed. *See* Bittker & Eustice, *supra*, at ¶ 12.27[5][d].

[4] Corporate Debt Securities for Investors' Debt Securities

When bonds (securities) are exchanged for other securities, sections 354 and 356 applies to the bondholders. Note that a "significant modification" of a debt instrument can result in a deemed exchange of the old debt instrument for an instrument containing the new terms. *See* Treas. Reg. § 1.1001-3.

When securities are exchanged for securities, the *fair market value of the excess principal amount of securities received* constitutes boot under sections 354 and 356. Thus, a bondholder who receives securities with a greater principal amount than the principal amount of the securities he relinquished will recognize any gain realized *to the extent of the fair market value of the excess principal amount received.* I.R.C. §§ 354(a)(2), 356(a), (d)(2).

Example 12.5: Edna and Frank are bondholders of EF, Inc. They each have a basis of $110,000 in their bonds, which have a fair market value of $150,000, and a principal amount of $150,000. EF, Inc. exchanges its bonds worth $150,000 for their bonds. The new bonds have a principal amount of $200,000. Edna and Frank each realized gain of $40,000 ($150,000 − $110,000) and received $50,000 of excess principal amount ($200,000 − $150,000). Assuming that the excess principal amount is

---
[4] Stock redemptions are discussed in Chapter 5.

worth $37,500, that amount constitutes boot, and, on these facts, Edna and Frank will each recognize $37,500 of gain.

The same is true in the exchange by an investor of both stock and securities for securities with an excess principal amount; the fair market value of the excess principal amount of securities received constitutes boot. I.R.C. §§ 354(a)(2), 356(d)(2)(B).

As discussed above, under section 354(a)(2)(B), interest on the bonds that has accrued but remained unpaid until satisfied in the recapitalization will constitute ordinary income if the bondholder had not previously reported the accrued interest as income. In addition, as indicated above, original issue discount issues can arise on the distribution of debt instruments. *See* BITTKER & EUSTICE, *supra*, at ¶ 12.27[5][d]. Finally, if a corporation pays off its bonds for less than the amount owed, the corporation will have cancellation of indebtedness income under section 61(a)(12) unless one of the exceptions in section 108 applies.

A bondholder's basis in the bonds received will be the same as the basis of the bonds exchanged, adjusted for any boot received and any gain recognized. *See* I.R.C. § 358. The bondholder will also take tacked holding periods in the bonds received. I.R.C. § 1223(1).

Example 12.8: In Example 12.7, Edna and Frank each had a basis of $110,000 in their bonds. Edna and Frank each received boot of $37,500 and recognized $37,500 of gain. Therefore, under section 358, each of them will have a basis of $110,000 in the new bonds ($110,000 + $37,500 of gain − $37,500 of boot).

CHART 12.1
General Checklist for Recapitalizations

(1)   Is there a business purpose?

(2)   Is there an exchange of stock for stock, stock for debt, debt for stock, or debt for debt?

(3)   Check whether the distribution constitutes a dividend. *See* Treas. Reg. §§ 1.301-1(*l*); 1.305-7(c); 1.354-1(d) Ex. 3 & 4 (redemption that may be treated as a dividend); 1.368-2(e)(5).

(4)   If the distribution does not constitute a dividend, compute gain realized on the exchange.

(5)   If debt securities were received, does their principal amount exceed the principal amount of any securities surrendered? If yes, the fair market value of the excess constitutes boot.

(6)   Compute recognized gain, determine its character, and compute basis. Tack holding periods where applicable.

(7)   Check if any stock received constitutes section 306 stock. *See* I.R.C. § 306(c)(1)(B).

§ 12.03 Changes in Form ("F" Reorganizations)

[A] In General

F reorganizations involve a change in corporate name or place of incorporation. Section 368(a)(1)(F) was expanded over the years, until Congress amended it to limit its applicability to changes involving "one corporation." However, the legislative history refers to one "operating" company, so a corporate shell may be used to effect a name change or incorporation in another state. *See* BITTKER & EUSTICE, *supra*, at ¶ 12.28[4].

The F reorganization has no particular form of its own, so a transaction that resembles or qualifies as another type of reorganization may qualify as an F, see Rev. Rul. 57-276, 1957-1 C.B. 126, although there are fewer restrictions on the F form of reorganization. In Revenue Ruling 2003-19, 2003-7 I.R.B. 468, the IRS ruled that the conversion of a mutual insurance company to a stock company qualified under section 368(a)(1)(F) (as well as under section 368(a)(1)(E)). Similarly, in Revenue Ruling 2003-48, 2003-19 I.R.B. 863, the IRS ruled that the conversion of a mutual savings bank to a stock savings bank qualified under both sections 368(a)(1)(E) and (F).

The IRS has ruled that a transaction will not qualify as an F reorganization "unless there is no change in existing shareholders or in the assets of the corporation." Rev. Rul. 96-29, 1996-1 C.B. 50, 51. The ruling further provides that "a transaction will not fail to qualify as a reorganization under § 368(a)(1)(F) if dissenters owning fewer than 1 percent of the outstanding shares of the corporation fail to participate in the transaction." *Id.* Proposed Treasury Regulations provide further requirements for qualification as an F reorganization.[5] *See* Prop. Treas. Reg. § 1.368-2(m).

---

[5] The Proposed Regulations further provide that distributions to shareholders in connection with an F reorganization will not be governed by section 356(a). *See* Prop. Treas. Reg. § 1.368-2(m)(4).

The diagram below provides "before" and "after" pictures of an F reorganization in which the corporation changes its state of incorporation.

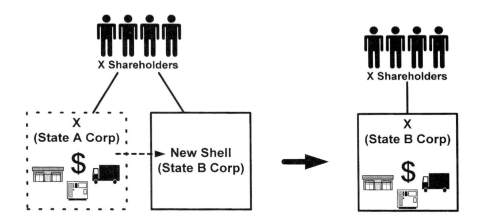

[B]   Carryback of Tax Attributes

Section 381(b)(3) bars carrying back to target corporation taxable years any net operating loss or net capital loss of an acquiring corporation, but the provision specifically states that it does not apply to F reorganizations.[6] *National Tea Co. v. Commissioner*, 793 F.2d 864 (7th Cir. 1986), which was decided before F reorganizations were limited to those involving a single operating corporation, addresses this issue. *National Tea* discusses *Libson Shops, Inc. v. Koehler*, 353 U.S. 382 (1957), a case in which the Supreme Court had prohibited netting pre-merger losses of some related entities against post-merger income of other related entities. *Libson Shops* is discussed in more detail in Chapter 13.[7]

National Tea involved National Tea Co. and Consolidated Subsidiaries (National Tea), an Illinois corporation that, along with its subsidiaries, operated a chain of retail food stores around the United States. In 1954, National Tea had acquired 98 percent of the outstanding stock in Supermarkets, a Louisiana corporation engaged in the same retail food store business. By December 26, 1974, National Tea owned almost 100 percent of Supermarkets' outstanding stock. From 1954 until that date, "Supermarkets operated as part of National Tea's single integrated retail marketing operation . . . ." *National Tea Co.*, 793 F.2d at 865. On December 26, 1974, Supermarkets merged into National Tea. *Id.* at 866.

---

[6] Section 381(b)(3) also does not apply to B or E reorganizations because they are not included in the list of transactions in section 381(a)(2), which 381(b)(3) cross references. *See Bercy Industries, Inc. v. Commissioner*, 640 F.2d 1058, 1061 n.4 (9th Cir. 1981).

[7] *See* § 13.02[A].

National Tea had net operating losses worth $3,304,858 (none of which was attributable to Supermarkets' business) for its 1974 taxable year. National Tea attempted to carry back the losses to Supermarkets' 1972 taxable year, which would have resulted in a $1,586,332 tax refund. *Id.* National Tea argued that the 1974 reorganization was an F reorganization, which would render inapplicable the section 381(b)(3) prohibition against carryback of post-reorganization losses incurred by the acquiring corporation to a pre-reorganization year of the transferor. The IRS conceded that the reorganization qualified as an F reorganization, but argued that the loss-tracing rule of *Libson Shops* and subsequently adopted by the IRS in Revenue Ruling 75-561 applied, and that National Tea failed to meet its requirements. The loss-tracing rule "limits the carryback of a post-reorganization net operating loss incurred by the acquiring corporation to a pre-reorganization year of the transferor corporation to those cases where the net operating loss was generated by 'a separate business unit or division of the acquiring corporation formerly operated by the transferor corporation.'" *Id.* (*quoting* Rev. Rul. 75-561, 1975-2 C.B. 129.).

The court found that the absence of a statutory scheme for carrybacks was evidence that "no one envisioned 'F' reorganizations as encompassing the merger of multiple operating corporations." *Id.* at 871. Because the IRS conceded that there was a valid F reorganization despite the involvement of multiple operating companies, the court applied the loss-tracing rule "as a necessary gap-filler to regulate the carryback of the acquiring corporation's net operating losses after an 'F' reorganization to the transferor corporation's income earned before the 'F' reorganization." *Id.* at 872. Thus, the Seventh Circuit adopted the loss-tracing rule for carrybacks and held that National Tea's attempt to carry back the net operating losses did not satisfy the limitations of the rule because the net operating loss that was carried back was not produced by substantially the same businesses that originally incurred the loss.[8]

---

[8] Carryovers of tax attributes are discussed in more detail in Chapter 13.

Chapter 13

CARRYOVER OF TAX ATTRIBUTES

§ 13.01 Overview

Under the Code, various nonrecognition transactions involving alterations in corporate form are eligible for the carryover of tax attributes, such as net operating losses (NOLs), which, under section 172(c), are the excess of the corporation's deductions over gross income, and may be carried back two years and forward twenty years, I.R.C. § 172(b)(2); capital losses, *see* I.R.C. § 1212(a); and earnings and profits. *See* I.R.C. § 381(a), (c). Because the carryover of certain attributes, such as NOLs, is highly desirable, various Code sections place restrictions on transactions that might be considered abusive, as discussed below. *See* I.R.C. §§ 269; 382–384.

[A] Transactions Eligible for Carryover

Section 381(a) lists the following transactions as eligible for carryover of tax attributes: Controlled subsidiary liquidations under section 332; A, C, and F reorganizations; and acquisitive D and G reorganizations that satisfy section 354(b)(1). B reorganizations are not listed because there is no need; in a B reorganization, the target stays in existence as a subsidiary of the acquiring corporation. E reorganizations do not require carryovers from another corporation because they involve only one corporation. Transactions that are not listed, including section 351 transactions, section 355 transactions, and divisive D reorganizations, may still be eligible for carryover of some tax attributes but are subject to cases applying pre-1954 law, such as *Libson Shops, Inc. v. Koehler*, 353 U.S. 382 (1957), which is discussed below in § 13.02[A]. *See* Boris I. Bittker & James S. Eustice, Federal Income Taxation of Corporations and Shareholders ¶¶ 14.20[3], 14.21[3][b], 14.24, 14.46[2] (7th ed. 2000).

[B] Tax Attributes Subject to Carryover

Section 381(c) lists over 20 tax items and attributes that are subject to carryover in at least certain circumstances.[1] They are:

(1) Net operating loss carryovers.

(2) Earnings and profits.

(3) Capital loss carryovers.

---

[1] The tax attributes are listed in section 381(c)(1)-(26), but some of the numbered items were repealed. *See* I.R.C. § 381(c)(7), (15), (20)-(21) (repealed paragraphs).

(4) Method of accounting.

(5) Inventories.

(6) Method of computing depreciation allowance.

(7) Installment method.

(8) Amortization of bond discount or premium.

(9) "Treatment of certain mining development and exploration expenses of distributor or transferor corporation," I.R.C. § 381(c)(10).

(10) "Contributions to pension plans, employees' annuity plans, and stock bonus and profit-sharing plans," I.R.C. § 381(c)(11).

(11) Recovery of tax benefit items.

(12) Involuntary conversions under section 1033.

(13) Dividend carryovers to personal holding companies.

(14) "Certain obligations of distributing or transferor corporation[s]," I.R.C. § 381(c)(16).

(15) Deficiency dividends of personal holding companies.

(16) "Percentage depletion on extraction of ores or minerals from the waste or residue of prior mining," I.R.C. § 381(c)(18).

(17) "Charitable contributions in excess of prior years' limitations," I.R.C. § 381(c)(19).

(18) The attributes listed in Subchapter L of the Code ("Insurance companies"), if the acquiring corporation is an insurance company.

(19) "Deficiency dividend of regulated investment company or real estate investment trust," I.R.C. § 381(c)(23).

(20) Credits under section 38.

(21) Credits under section 53.

(22) Items required to be taken into account for purposes of Subchapter U of the Code ("Designation and treatment of empowerment zones, enterprise communities, and rural development investment areas").

Tax attributes that are not on the list may nonetheless be subject to carryover. For example, section 362(b) generally provides for the transfer of asset basis in a corporate reorganization (subject to adjustment). In addition, tax attributes that are not the subject of statutory provisions may be held by the IRS or a court to be subject to carryover. For example, the IRS ruled in a private letter ruling that, in a parent-subsidiary liquidation, start-up expenses amortizable under section 195 were carried over and were amortizable by the parent company following the liquidation. *See* PLR 9828018.

[C] Limitations in Section 381

In addition to the anti-abuse rules discussed below, section 381 itself contains certain limitations on the carryover of certain tax attributes. For example, sections 381(c)(1) and (3) impose "conditions and limitations" on the carryover of NOLs and capital losses. Section 381(b)(3) generally limits the carryback of net operating losses and net capital losses by the acquiring corporation to a taxable year of the target corporation, except in F reorganizations.[2] However, section 381(b)(3) also does not apply to B or E reorganizations because they are not included in the list of transactions in section 381(a)(2) (as explained above in § 13.01[A]), which 381(b)(3) cross references. *See Bercy Industries, Inc. v. Commissioner*, 640 F.2d 1058, 1061 n.4 (9th Cir. 1981).

Section 381(b)(3) does not limit the carryback of target's own losses to a prior taxable year of target. Thus,

> [i]f, in a reverse triangular merger under § 368(a)(2)(E), [a wholly owned subsidiary of A] had merged into T, then T could carry its post-acquisition losses back to obtain a refund of taxes it paid on its own pre-acquisition income. In neither [a] forward nor [a] reverse acquisition, however, could T's excess losses be carried back to A's pre-acquisition income.

David W. LaRue, *A Case for Neutrality in the Design and Implementation of the Merger and Acquisition Statutes: the Post-Acquisition Net Operating Loss Carryback Limitations*, 43 TAX L. REV. 85, 110 (1987).

Furthermore, in *Bercy Industries*, 640 F.2d at 1062–63, the Court of Appeals for the Ninth Circuit, reversing the Tax Court, held that section 381(b)(3) did not apply in the context of a forward triangular merger involving only one operating company. In that case, Bercy Industries incorporated a shell subsidiary and then acquired it in the forward triangular merger. *Id.* at 1059. The court examined the legislative history of the provision and stated that it "strongly suggests that when a reorganization generates no complex problems of post-reorganization loss allocation, Congress intended that the surviving corporate taxpayer be able to carry back such losses without limitation." *Id.* at 1061.

§ 13.02   Limitations on Carryovers

Because favorable tax attributes are economically valuable, corporations might arrange to "sell" these attributes, absent limitations on such transactions. For example, a corporation with millions of dollars in net operating loss carryovers and little in the way of income stream or assets might be acquired by a profitable corporation at a price largely based on the economic value of the tax reduction the buyer would obtain upon using the net operating loss carryovers.

As indicated above, the Code currently imposes several restrictions on the carryover of favorable tax attributes, primarily to prevent what it considers "trafficking" in favorable tax attributes, particularly net operating losses. In general, sections 382 and 383 prescribe the extent to which

---

[2] Section 381(b)(3) is discussed further in § 12.03[B] of Chapter 12.

a target's favorable tax attributes survive an acquisition, and section 384 prescribes the extent to which an acquiror's favorable tax attributes survive an acquisition. Section 269 provides an intent-based test that applies to both target and acquiror.

[A] History

Prior to 1954, the Code did little to limit "trafficking" in tax attributes. *Libson Shops, Inc. v. Koehler*, 353 U.S. 382 (1957), which applies pre-1954 law and was discussed briefly in Chapter 12,[3] is an important case in the history of limitations on carryover of corporate tax attributes. In *Libson Shops*, seventeen separate corporations were merged into a single corporation, Libson Shops, Inc. *Id.* at 382. Prior to the merger, three of the corporations had net operating losses. Libson Shops carried over these net operating losses and deducted them from post-merger income. *Id.* at 383–84. The Supreme Court ruled in favor of the IRS, holding that to satisfy the carryover limitations, the taxpayer attempting to use pre-merger losses to offset post-merger income had to be "substantially the same businesses which incurred the losses." *Id.* at 390.

In 1954, Congress enacted sections 381 and 382, which together provide a fairly comprehensive regime for the carryover of net operating losses. This raised questions about the applicability of *Libson Shops* to post-1954 transactions. In 1976, Congress amended section 382, and made clear in the legislative history that *Libson Shops* would not apply to cases governed by the 1976 amendment. S. Rep. No. 938, 94th Cong., 2d Sess. 206 (1976). Congress amended section 382 again in 1986, and the Joint Committee's explanation of that Act similarly made clear that *Libson Shops* would not apply to cases governed by the 1986 amendment. Staff of Joint Comm. on Tax'n, 99th Cong., 1st Sess., General Explanation of the Tax Reform Act of 1986, at 324 (Joint Comm. Print 1987). Thus, *Libson Shops'* current importance is primarily historical. However, the disallowance rule of *Libson Shops*, which is more restrictive than section 382, may still apply to transactions that do not implicate section 382, as indicated above in § 13.01[A]. BITTKER & EUSTICE, *supra*, at ¶ 14.46[2].

[B] Change-of-Ownership Limitations on Net Operating and Other Losses: Section 382

[1] In General

Section 382 caps the annually deductible amount of net operating losses and certain built-in losses following an "ownership change"[4] of a

---

[3] *See* § 12.03[B].

[4] The meaning of "ownership change" under section 382 is discussed in § 13.02[B][3][c], below.

Section 382 does not apply in Title 11 or similar bankruptcy cases if the persons who were corporation (which may or may not occur in the context of a corporate reorganization).[5] *See* I.R.C. § 382(a), (g). This limits the extent to which new owners of the corporation can obtain the use of losses incurred while the corporation was owned by others. Section 382 also contains a continuity of business enterprise requirement; as discussed below in § 13.02[B][4][c][i], if this requirement is not met, the losses subject to section 382 will not survive the ownership change. *See* I.R.C. § 382(c).

In general, section 382 limits an acquiring corporation's use of a target corporation's net operating losses and built-in losses to the rate at which the *target corporation* could have used them had there been no ownership change and the aggregate net value of the target's assets (other than the losses addressed by section 382) were yielding an average market return. *See* I.R.C. § 382(b)(1). This hypothetical rate of loss utilization by the target corporation is determined by estimating the estimated income that would be produced each year if the target's equity value were invested in a safe investment vehicle. *See* I.R.C. § 382(b)(1)(B), (f). Section 382 allows the acquiring corporation to offset only that amount of income each year with target's losses.

The idea behind this limitation is economic neutrality. Absent the limitation, economically inefficient transactions might occur in order for profitable corporations to acquire net operating losses from other corporations (the "trafficking" in net operating losses that concerned Congress). The section 382 limitation essentially limits a profitable acquiring corporation's use of target losses to the rate that target would have used the losses, so as to discourage this trafficking.

[2] Losses Subject to Section 382

Section 382 applies to:

(1) Net operating losses, I.R.C. § 382(d)(1).

(2) Capital loss carryovers, Treas. Reg. § 1.382-2(a)(1)(A).

(3) Net unrealized built-in losses, I.R.C. § 382(h)(1)(B); Treas. Reg. § 1.382-2(a)(1)(C).[6]

(4) Carryovers of excess foreign taxes under section 904(c), of general business credits under section 39, and of minimum tax credits under section 53, Treas. Reg. § 1.382-2(a)(1)(A).

---

shareholders and creditors of the loss corporation immediately before the ownership change own, after the ownership change and as a result of being such shareholders or creditors, 50 percent of the "stock of the new loss corporation (or stock of a controlling corporation if it is also in bankruptcy)." I.R.C. § 382(*l*)(5)(A).

[5] Section 382 is extraordinarily complex; this chapter provides merely an overview of the basics of this complicated provision.

[6] A "net unrealized built-in loss" is the amount by which the fair market value of the assets of a corporation immediately before an ownership change is less than the aggregate adjusted basis of its assets at that time. I.R.C. § 382(h)(3)(A).

(5) To the extent provided in regulations, the alternative tax net operating loss deduction under section 56(d), I.R.C. § 382(*l*)(7).

[3] Definitions

[a] "Stock"

Section 382 is keyed to a change in stock ownership. For this purpose, the term "stock" does not include most non-voting, non-convertible preferred stock. *See* I.R.C. § 382(k)(6). Moreover, if preferred stock is allowed to vote only because of dividend arrearages, it is not treated as voting stock, and therefore will not constitute "stock" within the meaning of section 382. Treas. Reg. § 1.382-2(a)(3)(i). Temporary Regulations also provide that stock that, "[a]s of the time of its issuance or transfer to (or by) a five-percent shareholder, the likely participation of such interest in future corporate growth is disproportionately small when compared to the value of such stock as a proportion of the total value of the outstanding stock of the corporation" may not constitute stock if, among other requirements, "[t]reating the interest as not constituting stock would result in an owner-ship change." Temp. Treas. Reg. § 1.382-2T(f)(18)(ii). In addition, the Temporary Regulations provide that an interest that would not otherwise be treated as stock will be treated as stock if, among other requirements, "[a]s of the time of its issuance or transfer to (or by) a five-percent shareholder (or a person who would be a five-percent shareholder if the interest not constituting stock were treated as stock), such interest offers a potential significant participation in the growth of the corporation," and "[t]reating the interest as constituting stock would result in an ownership change." Temp. Reg. § 1.382-2T(f)(18)(iii).

In calculating stock ownership, the constructive ownership rules of section 318 apply, with certain modifications. *See* I.R.C. § 382(*l*)(3). (Section 318 is discussed in Chapter 5.)[7] The modifications are as follows:

(1) An individual and all members of his family, as defined by section 318(a)(1), are collectively treated as *one individual* for purposes of section 382.[8] Accordingly, section 318(a)(1) (family attribution) does not otherwise apply, and section 318(a)(5)(B), which prohibits reattribution of stock among family members, does not apply.[9] *See* I.R.C. § 382(*l*)(3)(A)(i); Temp. Reg. § 1.382-2T(h)(6).

---

[7] *See* § 5.02.

[8] An individual who may be treated as a member of more than one family that is or would be a five-percent shareholder if that individual were treated as a member of that family, is treated only as a member of the family that results in the smallest increase in the total percentage stock ownership of the five-percent shareholders on the testing date. Temp. Reg. § 1.382-2T(h)(6)(iv).

[9] The Court of Appeals for the Fifth Circuit has held that a transfer of shares between brothers gave rise to an ownership change because brothers are not "family" within the meaning of section 267, so their stockholdings are not aggregated. It also refused to allow aggregation through attribution of the shares between the brothers via a non-shareholder parent. *See Garber Indus., Inc. v. Commissioner*, 435 F.3d 555 (5th Cir. 2006). For critique of some of the court's reasoning in reaching its decision, see Robert Willens, *When Siblings Are Regarded As Strangers*, 110 TAX NOTES 1099 (2006).

Example 13.1: Alice, her husband Bob, and her mother Carol each own 25 percent of the sole class of stock of ABC Corp. Transfers from Alice to Bob and Carol therefore will not give rise to an ownership change for purposes of section 382.

(2) Section 318(a)(2) (attribution from entities to investors) is applied without regard to the 50-percent limitation with respect to attribution from corporations to shareholders, and, except as provided in regulations, by treating stock attributed thereunder as no longer being held by the entity from which it was attributed. I.R.C. § 382(*l*)(3)(A)(ii); *see* Temp. Reg. § 1.382-2T(h)(2).

Example 13.2: Doreen holds 30 percent of the sole class of stock of X, Inc., which holds 70 percent of the sole class of stock of Y, Inc. Doreen constructively owns 21 percent of the shares of Y, Inc. Those 21 Y shares are no longer treated as owned by X, Inc.

(3) Section 318(a)(3), attribution *to* entities, generally is not applied, except to the extent provided in regulations. I.R.C. § 382(*l*)(3)(A)(iii); *see* Temp. Reg. § 1.382-2T(h)(3).

(4) Except to the extent provided in regulations, an option to acquire stock is treated as exercised *if the exercise would result in an ownership change*. I.R.C. § 382(*l*)(3)(A)(iv); *see* Temp. Reg. § 1.382-2T(h)(4). A similar rule applies to contingent purchases, warrants, convertible debt, puts, stock subject to a risk of forfeiture, contracts to acquire stock, and similar interests. I.R.C. § 382(*l*)(3)(A).

(5) In attributing stock from an entity under section 318(a)(2), stock that is *not treated as stock* under section 382 in the case of attribution from a corporation (and, with respect to attribution from another entity, an interest in that entity similar to such stock) is not taken into account. I.R.C. § 382(*l*)(3)(A)(v).

In addition, if stock is acquired by reason of death (that is, it is subject to the current basis rule under section 1014), gift, or divorce (that is, its basis is determined under section 1041(b)(2)), the recipient is treated as owning the stock during the period the stock was owned by the person from whom it was acquired. I.R.C. § 382(*l*)(3)(B).

Example 13.3: In December, Ed received 30 shares of Z, Inc. stock from his mother as a gift. Ed's mother had purchased the stock six months before she gave the stock to Ed. For purposes of section 382, Ed is treated as having owned the Z, Inc. stock during that six-month period.

[b] "Five-Percent Shareholder"

A shift in the stock ownership of any five-percent shareholder is one component of a possible "ownership change" under section 382. In general, a five-percent shareholder is a person who held five percent or more of the stock of the "loss corporation" during the "testing period." *See* Bittker & Eustice, *supra*, at ¶ 14.43[2][b]. The loss corporation is the corporation with the loss subject to section 382. *See* I.R.C. § 382(k)(1). As discussed below, the testing period is the three-year period ending on the date the loss corporation is required to determine whether an ownership change occurred.[10] *See* I.R.C. § 382(i)(1). The determination of the percentage of stock held by a shareholder is made on the basis of *fair market value*, not vote. I.R.C. § 382(k)(5), (6)(C); Treas. Reg. § 1.382(a)(3)(i).

> *Example 13.4*: During the testing period under section 382, Fran owns seven percent of the stock of XYZ, Inc., determined by fair market value, and four percent of the voting power of XYZ, Inc. Fran is a "five-percent shareholder" of XYZ, Inc.

An unrelated group of shareholders, each of whom owns less than five percent of the loss corporation may also constitute a five-percent shareholder that is treated like one individual. *See* Treas. Reg. § 1.382-2T(f)(13), (j)(1)(ii). In general, each member of a particular public group is presumed not to be a member of any other public group and to be unrelated to all other shareholders of the loss corporation. *See* Treas. Reg. § 1.382-2T(j)(1)(iii). However, if the loss corporation has actual knowledge that either presumption is not true, the members of the public group may be aggregated into additional public groups. *Id.* Under the regulations, a loss corporation with knowledge of actual stock ownership on the testing date with respect to certain five-percent shareholders (or individuals who would be five-percent shareholders were it not for certain other provisions in the regulations) generally is required to take that stock ownership into account for purposes of determining whether an ownership change has occurred on the testing date. Treas. Reg. § 1.382-2T(k)(2).

The regulations provide the following example, among others:

> (i) All of the stock of P is owned by 1,000 unrelated shareholders, none of whom owns as much as five percent of P stock. L[1] is a wholly owned subsidiary of P. On January 2, 1988, P distributes all of the L[1] stock pro rata to its shareholders.

> (ii) Prior to the stock distribution, the public owners of P are members of a public group ("Public P") that is treated as a five-percent shareholder owning 100 percent of the stock of L[1]. . . . Following the stock distribution to the P shareholders, L[1] is owned by 1,000 public shareholders that are members of a public group ("Public L[1]") that is treated as a five-percent shareholder owning 100 percent of the stock of L[1]. . . .

> (iii) Public P and Public L[1] are treated as unrelated, individual five-percent shareholders . . . . Although the members of one public group are presumed not to be members of any other public group . . ., L[1] has actual knowledge that all of its public shareholders immediately following the distribution (Public L[1]) received L[1]

---

[10] As discussed below, *see* § 13.02[B][3][d], that date is either (1) the date an owner shift occurred, or (2) the date of the reorganization "in the case where the last component of an ownership change is an equity structure shift. . . ." I.R.C. § 382(j).

stock pro rata in respect to the outstanding P stock, and thus were also members of Public P. Applying paragraph (k)(2) of this section, the loss corporation may take into account the identity of ownership interests between Public L[1] and Public P to establish that Public L[1] did not increase its percentage ownership in L[1]. Accordingly, the transaction would not constitute an owner shift.

Treas. Reg. § 1.382-2T(j)(1)(vi) Ex. 2. As discussed below, an "owner shift" is one of two possible prerequisites for an "ownership change."

[c] "Ownership Change"

Under the Code, an "ownership change" has occurred if immediately after (1) an "equity structure shift" (in general, an acquisitive reorganization or a recapitalization) or (2) an "owner shift" (a shift in the stock ownership of any five-percent shareholder), the percentage of the stock of the loss corporation owned by one or more five-percent shareholders has increased by more than 50 percentage points. I.R.C. § 382(g). However, Temporary Treasury regulations provide that "any equity structure shift that is not also an owner shift, is not an event that requires the loss corporation to make a determination of whether an ownership change has occurred." Temp. Treas. Reg. § 1.382-2T(a)(2)(i)(B); *see also* BITTKER & EUSTICE, *supra*, at ¶ 14.43[4].

The reorganizations that constitute equity structure shifts are A, B, C, acquisitive D, E, acquisitive G reorganizations, and triangular reorganizations—but not divisive D or G reorganizations or F reorganizations, *see* I.R.C. § 382(g)(3)(A). In addition, certain taxable reorganization-type transactions, public offerings, and similar transactions will constitute equity structure shifts, to the extent the Treasury Department so provides in regulations. I.R.C. § 382(g)(3)(B).

Example 13.5: G Corporation was recently acquired by H Corp. in a "C" reorganization in which H Corp. issued solely voting stock to the former shareholders of G Corporation. G Corporation has undergone an equity structure shift within the meaning of section 382.

As indicated above, a shift in the stock ownership of any five-percent shareholder is termed an "owner shift." I.R.C. § 382(g)(2). The term "owner shift" is more technically defined as a change in the ownership of stock if the change affects the percentage of stock of the corporation owned by any person who is a five-percent shareholder *before or after* the change. *Id.*

Example 13.6: Until Irene sold one-third of her J Corporation shares to Kelly, Irene owned six percent of the stock (by value) of J Corporation. Irene now owns four percent of the stock (by value) of J Corporation. Kelly now owns two percent of J Corporation. An owner shift has occurred. However, this owner shift does not constitute an ownership change because it did not increase the percentage of the J Corporation shares owned by one or more five-percent shareholders by more than 50 percentage points.

As this example suggests, even though a corporation has experienced either an equity structure shift or an owner shift, there is no "ownership change" unless the percentage of the stock of the loss corporation owned by one or more five-percent shareholders has increased by *more than 50 percentage points* during the three-year testing period.[11] *See* I.R.C. § 382(g). This is determined by comparing (1) the percentage of the stock of the loss corporation owned by one or more five-percent shareholders to (2) the lowest percentage of stock of the loss corporation (or any predecessor corporation) owned by those shareholders (or, more precisely, shareholder groups) at *any time* during the testing period. If the percentage has increased more than 50 points following an equity structure shift or an owner shift, the corporation has experienced an ownership change.

> *Example 13.7*: During the testing period, Len owned 20 percent of the stock of M, Inc. (by value). After Len acquires an additional 60 percent of that stock from numerous small shareholders of M, Inc., the percentage of the shares owned by Len has increased to 80 percent. M, Inc. has sustained an ownership change. (If, instead, Len had acquired fewer shares, increasing his ownership interest from 20 percent to 55 percent, although the acquisitions would increase his ownership interest by more than half and would result in ownership of more than 50 percent of the corporation's stock, they would not constitute the increase required for an ownership change, which must be more than 50 percentage points.)

Note that "[e]xcept as provided in regulations, any change in proportionate ownership which is attributable solely to fluctuations in the relative fair market values of different classes of stock shall not be taken into account." I.R.C. § 382(*l*)(3)(C).

[d] "Testing Period"

As indicated above, the "testing period" generally "is the 3-year period ending on the day of any owner shift involving a five-percent shareholder or equity structure shift." I.R.C. § 382(i)(1). Temporary Treasury Regulations provide that "each date on which a loss corporation is required to make a determination of whether an ownership change has occurred is referred to as a testing date." Temp. Reg. § 1.382-2T(a)(2)(B). Thus, on a testing date, the loss corporation must look back three years "to see whether the sum of various ownership changes (whether or not related) exceeds the statutory 50-percent increase threshold." Bittker & Eustice, *supra*, at ¶ 14.43[7][c].

> *Example 13.8*: In Example 13.7, the date Len acquired the additional shares of M, Inc. stock is a testing date, given Len's pre-existing ownership of 20 percent of the shares of M, Inc.

The testing period generally is shortened (1) if there has already been an ownership change under section 382, and (2) in certain situations involving carryforwards of losses. *See* I.R.C. § 382(i)(2)-(3). In the case of

---

[11] The testing period is discussed in § 13.02[B][3][d], below.

a prior ownership change, the testing period for determining whether a second ownership change has occurred does not begin until the day after the change date for the first ownership change. I.R.C. § 382(i)(2). The "change date" of the first ownership change is defined as the date of the owner shift, if "the last component of an ownership change is an owner shift involving a five-percent shareholder," I.R.C. § 382(j)(1), and the date of the reorganization if "the last component of an ownership change is an equity structure shift," I.R.C. § 382(j)(2). Thus, where there are two ownership changes, the testing periods do not overlap. *See* Bittker & Eustice, *supra*, at ¶ 14.43[6][a].

In the second case (where losses are carried forward), the testing period does not begin until the earlier of (1) the first day of the first taxable year from which there is a carryforward of a loss or of an excess credit to the first post-change year, or (2) "the taxable year in which the transaction being tested occurs." I.R.C. § 382(i)(3). This provision does not apply to loss corporations with "net unrealized built-in losses" as defined in section 382(h)(3), except if "the loss corporation establishes the taxable year in which the net unrealized built-in loss first accrued." Temp. Treas. Reg. § 1.382-2T(d)(3)(B)(ii); *see also* I.R.C. § 382(i)(3).

[4]   Mechanics of the Section 382 Limitation

[a]   General Rules

If an ownership change has occurred, section 382(a) and (b) impose an *annual cap* on the amount of post-change-year income that may be offset by pre-change-year losses. *See* I.R.C. § 382(a). Recognition of built-in losses is also subject to the annual cap.[12] *See* I.R.C. § 382(h); Bittker & Eustice, *supra*, at ¶ 14.44[4][a]. In general, the annual cap, known as the "section 382 limitation," is the fair market value of the stock of the "old loss corporation," multiplied by the long-term tax-exempt rate. I.R.C. § 382(b)(1). Stock that is excluded for purposes of determining whether there was an ownership change is *not* excluded from this calculation. *See* I.R.C. § 382(e)(1). The "old loss corporation" is the corporation that had net operating losses or built-in losses and then experienced an ownership change. I.R.C. § 382(k)(1)-(2).

The annual Section 382 limitation is intended to approximate the amount of income that the loss company could have produced as a return on equity, absent the acquisition, had it invested its capital in tax-exempt securities. The limitation incorporates an implicit tax-avoidance restriction in that the limitation applies more stringently to cases where the amount of the carryovers is high when

---

[12] Notice 2003-65, 2003-40 I.R.B. 747 provides interim guidance with respect to recognized built-in gains and losses, including two safe harbor approaches to identifying them, the "1374 approach" and the "338 approach." Section 1374 is discussed in § 8.05[A] of chapter 8. Section 338 is discussed in § 7.05 of Chapter 7. The section 382 limitation on built-in losses is not discussed further in this book; for additional reading on this topic, see Bittker & Eustice, *supra*, at ¶ 14.44[4].

compared with the corporation's value; conversely, the lower the carryover in relation to value, the less significant will be the limitation on the ability to use those carryovers.

BITTKER & EUSTICE, *supra*, at ¶ 14.44[1][b].

[b] The Long-Term Tax-Exempt Rate

In general, the long-term tax-exempt rate referred to above is the highest Federal long-term rate in effect under section 1274(d) for any month in the three-month period ending with the month in which the change date occurs, adjusted to reflect the difference in rates on taxable and tax-exempt obligations. I.R.C. § 382(f). The IRS publishes monthly Revenue Rulings that state what the rates under section 1274(d) will be for that month. *See, e.g.,* Rev. Rul. 2005-71, 2005-45 I.R.B. 923, 924 (October 20, 2005) (Table 3 shows long-term tax-exempt rate for purposes of section 382 of 4.24 percent).

Example 13.9: N, Inc., a corporation with $200,000 of net operating losses, has experienced an ownership change. Its stock is worth $1,000,000. Assuming that the long-term tax-exempt rate is 4.60 percent, the section 382 limitation is $46,000. Thus, in general, N, Inc. or its successor will be able to deduct no more than $46,000 of the net operating losses each year.

Note that, as discussed immediately below, the amount of the section 382 limitation can be increased in certain circumstances.

[c] Reductions and Increases in the Section 382 Limitation

[i] Continuity of Business Enterprise

Section 382 imposes a "continuity of business enterprise" requirement; in general, the section 382 limitation generally is reduced to *zero* if the new loss corporation does not continue the business enterprise of the old loss corporation for the full two-year period beginning on the change date. I.R.C. § 382(c)(1). However, under no circumstances will the section 382 limitation for any post-ownership-change year be less than the sum of (1) recognized built-in gains for the year (calculated as discussed below) and gains recognized by reason of a 338 election plus (2) any increase in the section 382 limitation from such amounts that were carried forward from a prior year.[13] I.R.C. § 382(c)(2). Legislative history provides that the same standard applied under Treasury Regulation 1.368-1(d) for determining whether continuity of business enterprise exists in a corporate reorganization applies under section 382. *See* H. Conf. Rept. 99-841, at II-189 (1986). The continuity of business enterprise requirement for a corporate reorganization is discussed in § 9.05 of Chapter 9.

---

[13] The carryforward of the unused portion of a section 382 limitation is discussed in § 13.02[B][4][c][iii], below.

[ii] Effect of Built-In Gains on the Section 382 Limitation

For a loss corporation with "net unrealized built-in gain," the section 382 limitation is increased by "recognized built-in gains," up to a cap. I.R.C. § 382(h)(1)(A). In general, a recognized built-in gain is gain recognized on an asset that was owned by the old loss corporation before the change date, to the extent that the gain does not exceed the asset's built-in gain on the change date. *See* I.R.C. § 382(h)(2)(A). "Net unrealized built-in gain" is the amount by which the fair market value of the assets of a corporation immediately before an ownership change exceeds the aggregate adjusted basis of its assets at that time. I.R.C. § 382(h)(3)(A). The cap referred to above is the amount of the net unrealized built-in gain, reduced by recognized built-in gains for prior years ending in the recognition period. I.R.C. § 382(h)(1)(A)(ii). In other words, the overall amount by which the fair market value of the assets of a corporation immediately before an ownership change exceeds the aggregate adjusted basis of its assets at that time serves as a cap that is reduced each time built-in gains are recognized. The recognition period is the five-year period that begins on the change date. I.R.C. § 382(h)(7)(A).

Example 13.10: O, Inc. has net operating losses totaling $200,000. The fair market value of its assets immediately before an ownership change is $700,000, and that amount exceeds the adjusted basis in those assets by $300,000. O Inc.'s stock is worth $1,000,000. Assuming that the long-term tax-exempt rate is 5.20 percent, the section 382 limitation initially is $52,000. Recognized built-in gains will increase the section 382 limitation, but not above $352,000 ($300,000 + $52,000).

Under a *de minimis* rule, if the amount of the net unrealized built-in gain or loss is no greater than the lesser of (1) 15 percent of the fair market value of the assets of the loss corporation immediately before an ownership change, or (2) $10,000,000, it is deemed to be zero. I.R.C. § 382(h)(3)(B).

Example 13.11: P, Inc. has net operating losses totaling $200,000. The fair market value of its assets immediately before an ownership change is $700,000, which exceeds the adjusted basis in those assets by $50,000. Its stock is worth $1,000,000. Assuming that the long-term tax-exempt rate is 4.40 percent, the section 382 limitation is $44,000. Because the net unrealized built-in gain does not exceed $105,000 (15 percent of $700,000), the net unrealized built-in gain is treated as zero, so it does not affect the section 382 limitation.

Note that if a section 338 election is made in connection with an ownership change and net unrealized built-in gains are deemed to be zero (because they do not meet the amount in the *de minimis* described rule above), then the section 382 limitation for the year in which gain caused by the section 338 election is recognized is increased by the lesser of (1) the recognized built-in gains caused by the section 338 election, or (2) the actual amount of net unrealized built-in gains.[14] This "actual amount" is

---

[14] Section 338 is discussed in Chapter 7. *See* § 7.05.

the amount determined without regard to the threshold requirement discussed above. I.R.C. § 382(h)(1)(C). For example, in Example 13.11, the actual amount of built-in gains is $50,000.

[iii]   Effect of Unused Section 382 Limitation

If the section 382 limitation for any post-change year exceeds the taxable income of the new loss corporation that was offset by pre-change losses, that excess generally may increase the section 382 limitation in the following year.[15] I.R.C. § 382(b)(2).

Example 13.12: In Example 13.9, N, Inc.'s section 382 limitation was $46,000. Thus, in general, N, Inc. will be able to deduct no more than $46,000 of the net operating losses each year. Assume that in the first year after the ownership change, N, Inc. has only $40,000 of income, and therefore deducts only $40,000 of the net operating losses that were carried forward. The excess section 382 limitation is $6,000 ($46,000 − $40,000). Accordingly, in the second year after the ownership change, N, Inc.'s section 382 limitation will be $52,000 ($46,000 + $6,000).

[d]   Valuation Issues

[i]   Anti-Stuffing Rule

Section 382(*l*)(1)(A) provides that "[a]ny capital contribution received by an old loss corporation as part of a plan a principal purpose of which is to avoid or increase any limitation under this section shall not be taken into account for purposes of this section." This provision prevents "stuffing" the corporation with assets shortly before the ownership change so as to inflate its fair market value and thereby increase the amount of pre-change losses deductible under section 382. BITTKER & EUSTICE, *supra*, at ¶ 14.44[3][a]. It also prevents the use of such assets under the built-in gain rules of section 382(h), discussed above. *See id.* at ¶ 14.44[3][c].

Section 382(*l*) further provides that "any capital contribution made during the 2-year period ending on the change date shall, except as provided in regulations, be treated as part of a plan described in subparagraph (A)." I.R.C. § 382(*l*)(1)(B). The Conference Committee Report refers to specific types of contributions that Treasury regulations should exclude from the ambit of this provision. *See* H.R. Rep. No. 841, 99th Cong. 2d Sess. II-189.

[ii]   Special Rule for Valuing Corporations with Excess Nonbusiness Assets

If, immediately after an ownership change, *at least one-third* of the value of the total assets of a corporation that is not one of certain investment entities, I.R.C. § 382(*l*)(4)(B)(ii), consists of "nonbusiness assets" (that is,

---

[15] Section § 13.02[C][2], below, discusses a reduction of that amount as a result of the application of section 383.

investment assets, I.R.C. § 382(*l*)(4)(C)), the value of the corporation must be reduced by the excess, if any of (1) the fair market value of the nonbusiness assets of the old loss corporation, over (2) "the nonbusiness asset share of indebtedness for which such corporation is liable." I.R.C. § 382(*l*)(4). The nonbusiness asset share of the indebtedness of the corporation is the proportion of the indebtedness equal to the proportion of the nonbusiness assets of the corporation out of the total assets (determined by fair market value). I.R.C. § 382(*l*)(4)(D).

> *Example 13.13*: O Corp., which is not an investment entity, holds nonbusiness assets totaling $400,000 after an ownership change. At that time, O Corp. holds business assets of $600,000. O Corp. is liable for indebtedness of $100,000. Assume that the stock value of the corporation is $1,200,000. The value must be reduced by $360,000 (*i.e.*, $400,000 minus 40 percent of $100,000). Therefore, for purposes of determining the section 382 limitation, the value of the old loss corporation will be $840,000.

[iii]   Effect of Redemptions and Other Corporate Contractions on Valuation

Section 382(e)(2) provides that "[i]f a redemption or other corporate contraction occurs in connection with an ownership change, the value . . . shall be determined after taking such redemption or other corporate contraction into account." This provision thus lowers the value of the loss corporation for section 382 purposes, and thereby lowers the section 382 limitation. Accordingly, it "limit[s] bootstrap acquisitions of loss corporations' net operating loss carryovers . . . ."[16] *Berry Petroleum v. Commissioner*, 104 T.C. 584, 640 (1995).

In *Berry Petroleum*, later in the same year the target corporation (known as C.J. Co. after the acquisition) was acquired, it advanced its new corporate parent, Bush Oil Co. (Bush) a total of $3,625,946. *Id.* at 628. The following year, C.J. Co. cancelled the advances, which resulted in the formal distribution of a dividend from C.J. Co. to Bush. The court found that a distribution that would not have constituted a partial liquidation under the 1939 and 1954 Codes can constitute a corporate contraction within the meaning of section 382(e)(2). *Id.* at 641. The court also held that the events in *Berry Petroleum* constituted a corporate contraction:

> When Bush received the advances from C.J. Co., Bush executed unsecured demand notes providing a market rate of interest. Although interest was paid monthly, no principal payment was ever demanded or made, and the advances were discharged by cancellation less than 6 months after the first payment and less than 3 months after the second payment. The cancellation so soon after the advances were made is strong evidence that, when C.J. Co.

---

[16] Bootstrap acquisitions are discussed in § 4.05 of Chapter 4 and § 5.04[B] of Chapter 5.

made the advances to Bush, neither Bush nor C.J. Co. intended them to be repaid. . . .

Even if the advances standing alone did not amount to corporate contractions, C.J. Co.'s formal payment of a dividend by canceling the notes from Bush was a corporate contraction. C.J. Co.'s cancellation of the notes completed the process that the advances initiated, reimbursing Bush for a substantial portion of its investment in C.J. Co.

Id. at 642–43. The court further "conclude[d] that the canceled advances occurred in connection with the ownership change for the purpose of section 382(e)." *Id.* at 644. The court therefore held, in part, that the value of C.J. Co., which otherwise was $6.5 million, *id.* at 631, had "to be determined after taking into account the corporate contraction caused by the advances and their cancellation in the amount of $ 3,625,946." *Id.* at 644.

CHART 13.1
Checklist for Applying Section 382

(1)   Has there been a shift in the stock ownership of any five-percent shareholder of a "loss corporation" or an "equity structure shift" (a reorganization other than a divisive D, divisive G, or F reorganization) of a loss corporation? If yes, go to question 2.

(2)   Has the percentage of the stock of the loss corporation owned by one or more five-percent shareholders increased by more than 50 percentage points? If no, section 382 does not apply, but if yes, go to question 3.

(3)   What is the fair market value of the stock of the loss corporation on the ownership change date? Take into account special valuation rules.

(4)   Multiply the fair market value of the stock of the loss corporation (the answer to question 3) by the long-term federal tax-exempt rate, to determine the preliminary section 382 limitation.

(5)   If the loss corporation has net unrealized built-in gain, for each year in the five-year recognition period, add to the number computed in (4) the amount of *recognized built-in gain* for that year, if any, so long as total recognized built-in gain does not exceed net unrealized built-in gain.

(6)   If there was a section 338 election made in connection with the ownership change, and the net unrealized built-in gain was treated as zero because it did not exceed the statutory threshold, add to the number computed in (4) the lesser of the recognized built-in gains caused by the section 338 election or the actual net unrealized built-in gain (that is, the amount computed without regard to the threshold).

[C]   Change-of-Ownership Limitations on Other Tax Attributes: Section 383

[1]   In General

Under section 383, if a corporation undergoes an "ownership change," the carryover of certain tax attributes to post-ownership change years is limited as provided in Treasury regulations. The term "ownership change" has the same meaning in section 383 as it does for purposes of section 382. *See* I.R.C. § 383(e). In fact, much of section 383 is based on section 382, discussed above.[17]

After an ownership change, the following tax attributes are limited under section 383: net capital losses, I.R.C. § 383(b); foreign tax credits, I.R.C. § 383(c); and any unused general business credits and any unused minimum tax credits (so-called "excess credits"), I.R.C. § 383(a). The Code provides that the amount of any net capital loss for any taxable year prior to the first post-ownership change year that may be used in any year is limited under Treasury regulations based on section 382 principles. I.R.C. § 383(b). The Code further provides that the regulations shall provide that any net capital loss used in a post-change year reduces the section 382 limitation applicable to pre-change losses under section 382 for that year. *Id.* Similarly, the amount of any excess foreign taxes for any taxable year, prior to the first post-ownership change year, is to be limited under regulations that embody the purposes of both sections 382 and 383. *See* I.R.C. § 383(c).

The use of "excess credits" is limited to the amount of the corporation's tax liability attributable to the portion of its taxable income that does not exceed the section 382 limitation remaining available for the year, after the application of section 382 and sections 383(b) and (c). I.R.C. § 383(a). The mechanics of applying this provision is explained below.

[2]   Mechanics of the Section 383 Credit Limitation

In general, following an ownership change of a loss corporation, the "section 383 credit limitation" limits the amount of *regular tax liability* for a post-ownership change year that may be offset by pre-ownership change capital losses and credits. Treas. Reg. § 1.383-1(b). The term "loss corporation" has the same meaning as it does for purposes of section 382, discussed above. *See* I.R.C. § 383(e); Treas. Reg. § 1.383-1(c)(1).

The section 383 credit limitation "is an amount equal to the excess of . . . (A) The new loss corporation's[18] regular tax liability for the post-change year, over (B) The new loss corporation's regular tax liability for the post-change year," adjusted by allowing as an additional deduction the amount of section 382 limitation remaining after the application of certain other

---

[17] *See* § 13.02[B].

[18] As it is for purposes of section 382, the new loss corporation is the loss corporation, following the ownership change. *See* I.R.C. §§ 382(k)(3); 383(e).

paragraphs of the regulation. Treas. Reg. § 1.383-1(c)(6). In other words, the section 383 credit limitation is essentially the amount by which the loss corporation's regular tax liability exceeds the section 382 limitation. Note that, as explained below, other limitations on losses and credits may apply before application of either the section 382 limitation or the section 383 credit limitation. *See* Treas. Reg. § 1.383-1(d)(3)(i). The regulations provide the following example:

> L, a new loss corporation, is a calendar year taxpayer. L has an ownership change on December 31, 1987. For 1988, L has taxable income (prior to the use of any pre-change losses) of $100,000. In addition, L has a section 382 limitation of $25,000, a pre-change net operating loss carryover of $12,000, a pre-change minimum tax credit of $50,000, and no pre-change capital losses. L's section 383 credit limitation is the excess of its regular tax liability computed after allowing a $12,000 net operating loss deduction (taxable income of $88,000; regular tax liability of $18,170), over its regular tax liability computed after allowing an additional deduction in the amount of L's section 382 limitation remaining after the application of paragraphs (d)(2)(i) through (iv) of this section, or $13,000 (taxable income of $75,000; regular tax liability of $13,750). L's section 383 credit limitation is therefore $4,420 ($18,170 minus $13,750).

Treas. Reg. § 1.383-1(c)(6)(ii) Ex.

Thus, following an ownership change, other limitations on losses and credits apply first, the section 382 limitation next, and if taxable income remains, the section 383 credit limitation then applies to the otherwise available credits covered by section 383. The section 382 limitation is absorbed dollar-for-dollar by pre-change losses used to offset taxable income. Similarly, the section 383 credit limitation is absorbed dollar-for-dollar by pre-change credits used to offset regular tax liability. Treas. Reg. § 1.383-1(d)(2).

The Treasury regulations provide various ordering rules. First, pre-ownership change losses may offset taxable income in a post-change year "only to the extent that the section 382 limitation for that year has not been absorbed by pre-change losses described in any lower-numbered subdivisions." Treas. Reg. § 1.383-1(d)(2). A similar rule applies to pre-change credits. *See id.* In general, the section 382 limitation and the section 383 credit limitation are absorbed in the following order, as provided in Treasury Regulation § 1.383-1(d)(2):

1) Pre-ownership-change recognized built-in capital losses that are subject to the section 382 limitation for that year.

(2) Pre-ownership-change capital loss carryovers.

(3) Recognized pre-ownership-change losses (other than capital losses) that are described in section 1.382-2(a)(2) (certain net operating losses

and built-in losses) that are subject to the section 382 limitation for that year.

(4) All other pre-ownership-change losses.

(5) Pre-ownership-change foreign tax credits.

(6) Pre-ownership-change business credits.

(7) Pre-ownership-change minimum tax credits.

As discussed in § 13.02[B][4][c][iii], any unused section 382 limitation amount is carried forward to the following year under section 382(b)(2). However, the regulations under section 383 provide that the amount of the section 382 limitation that otherwise could be carried over is reduced by the "section 383 credit reduction amount." Treas. Reg. § 1.383-1(e)(1).

> The section 383 credit reduction amount for a post-change year is equal to the amount of taxable income attributable to the portion of the new loss corporation's regular tax liability for the year that is offset by pre-change credits. Each dollar of regular tax liability that is offset by a dollar of pre-change credit is divided by the effective marginal rate at which that dollar of tax was imposed to determine the amount of taxable income that resulted in that particular dollar of regular tax liability. The sum of these "grossed-up" amounts for the taxable year is the section 383 credit reduction amount.

Treas. Reg. § 1.383-1(e)(2). Examples in the regulations illustrate the application of this provision. *See* Treas. Reg. § 1.383-1(f) Ex. 2-4.

CHART 13.2
Checklist for Applying the Section 383 Credit Limitation

(1)   Has there been an ownership change of a loss corporation?

(2)   If yes, compute the section 382 limitation and the section 383 credit limitation.

(3)   Apply the section 382 limitation and the section 383 credit limitation, in that order, to disallow pre-ownership change losses realized and credits arising in a post-change year.

(4)   Reduce the excess section 382 limitation, if any, by the 383 credit reduction amount.

[D]   Limitation on Use of Pre-Acquisition Losses to Offset Built-In Gains: Section 384

[1]   In General

Section 384 generally restricts the use of pre-acquisition losses of one corporation to offset built-in gains of another corporation when the gains are realized within five years of the acquisition. The acquisition period begins whenever "control" of the target corporation is obtained, or via an A, C, or D reorganization. *See* I.R.C. § 384(a)(1). For this purpose, "control" is defined as ownership of 80 percent of the stock (by both vote and value). *See* I.R.C. §§ 384(c)(5); 1504(a)(2).

Several exceptions limit the scope of section 384. For instance, section 384 does not apply if both corporations were "members of the same controlled group at all times during the five-year period ending on the acquisition date." I.R.C. § 384(b)(1). Section 384 uses the definition of "controlled group" of section 1563(a) except that (1) the "at least 80 percent" threshold is reduced to "more than 50 percent;" (2) the ownership require-ments must be met by both vote *and* value; and (3) section 1563(a)(4), which relates to insurance companies, is disregarded. I.R.C. § 384(b)(2).

The corporation with pre-acquisition gains is termed the "gain corpora-tion," I.R.C. § 384(c)(4). The acquisition date is the date on which the acquiring corporation obtained control of the target corporation or the date of the reorganization, whichever is applicable. I.R.C. § 384(c)(2). The losses of the loss corporation subject to section 384 are net operating losses and certain built-in losses. *See* I.R.C. § 384(c)(3). The gains of the gain corpora-tion subject to section 384 are unrealized gains on assets held by the gain corporation on the acquisition date, and items of income attributable to the period prior to the acquisition date. I.R.C. § 384(c)(1). Although section 384(f) contemplates implementing regulations, at the present time, there are none.

Section 384 cross-references certain definitions in section 382(h). *See* I.R.C. § 384(c)(8). Because section 384 uses the definitions in section 382(h) for "net unrealized built-in gain" and "net unrealized built-in loss," section 384, like section 382, deems these amounts to be zero if they do not exceed the lesser of 15 percent of the value of the assets of the loss corporation immediately before the ownership change or $10,000,000.[19] *See* I.R.C. §§ 382(h)(3)(B); 384(c)(8); BITTKER & EUSTICE, *supra*, at ¶ 14.45[2].

[2] Mechanics

The primary prerequisite for application of section 384 is the acquisition by one corporation of control over another corporation or acquisition of assets of a corporation in an A, C, or D reorganization, where one of the corporations is a "gain corporation." I.R.C. § 384(a). Section 384 is triggered when a gain attributable to the gain corporation is realized within five years of the acquisition date. Those gains may not be offset by pre-acquisition losses of the loss corporation, to the extent that the gain was built in on the acquisition date. *See* I.R.C. § 384(c)(1).

Example 13.14: P Corp. has an unused net operating loss carryover of $50,000. It acquires control of Q Corp. on May 3, Year 1. At the time of the acquisition, Q Corp. has unrealized built-in gain of $40,000. On December 5, Year 2, Q Corp. sells one if its assets and realizes a $20,000

---

[19] This threshold requirement is discussed in § 13.02[B][4][c][ii].

gain. Of this $20,000 gain, $15,000 was built in at the time of the acquisition. Under section 384, P Corp. may not use any of its $50,000 net operating loss carryover to offset that $15,000 gain.

Unused pre-acquisition losses may be carried forward. I.R.C. § 384(e)(1). In addition, the five-year period is extended for installment sales. *See* Notice 90-27, 1990-1 C.B. 336.

Section 384 employs definitions and procedures similar to those of section 1374 (addressing built-in gains in certain S corporations), discussed in Chapter 8.[20] As with section 1374, section 384 places a cap on the amount of gains subject to section 384 for each year. The cap is the amount of the gain corporation's "net unrealized built-in gain," reduced by any gains that were subject to section 384 in prior years. I.R.C. § 384(c)(1)(C). "Net unrealized built-in gain" is defined, as it is for section 382, as any gain recognized during the relevant period on the disposition of any asset except to the extent that the asset was not held by the gain corporation on the acquisition date, or the recognized gain exceeds the amount of built-in gain on the acquisition date. *See* I.R.C. §§ 382(h)(3)(A), 384(c)(8).

Example 13.15: In Example 13.14, Q Corp. had a net unrealized built-in gain of $40,000. In Year 2, section 384 applied to a $15,000 gain of Q Corp. In subsequent years, no more than $25,000 ($40,000 − $15,000) of Q Corp.'s gains will be subject to section 384.

Section 384 applies in addition to section 382; presumably section 382 applies first. BITTKER & EUSTICE, *supra*, at ¶ 14.45[3]. In Examples 13.14 and 13.15, section 382 did not apply to P Corp., the corporation with the net operating loss carryover, because it experienced no ownership change. It did not apply to Q Corp. because Q Corp. was not a loss corporation.

CHART 13.3
Checklist for Applying Section 384

(1) Has a corporation either obtained control of a another corporation or acquired the assets of another corporation via an A, C, or D reorganization?

(2) If yes, is one of the corporations a gain corporation?

(3) If yes, has there been realization of a gain by the gain corporation within five years of the acquisition date?

(4) If yes, determine the net unrealized built-in gains of the gain corporation on the acquisition date. This amount serves as a cap on the gains subject to section 384.

(5) Also determine the amount of net operating losses and built-in losses of the loss corporation on the acquisition date.

(6) The losses calculated in (5) cannot be used to offset the gain realized in (3) except to the extent that the gains exceed the cap in (4).

---

[20] *See* § 8.05[A].

(7)   Unused pre-acquisition losses can be carried forward.

(8)   Repeat these steps for each taxable year for five years after the acquisition date.

[E] Acquisitions with Tax-Avoidance Motive: Section 269

[1] In General

Unlike the rules discussed above, section 269 is not a rule that automatically applies in specified circumstances. Instead, it focuses on *intent*. In general, under section 269, a transferred-basis type of corporate acquisition[21] or acquisition of "control" that has a principal purpose of tax avoidance will empower the Secretary of the Treasury to disallow favorable tax attributes, as well as to reallocate tax attributes. I.R.C. § 269(a), (c). Acquisition of assets or control may be direct or indirect. I.R.C. § 269(a). However, there is an exception from the asset-acquisition element of section 269 if the corporation from which the assets was acquired was "controlled, directly or indirectly, immediately before such acquisition, by such acquiring corporation or its stockholders . . . ." I.R.C. § 269(a)(2). For purposes of section 269, "control" is determined using a 50-percent ownership test, by vote *or* value. *Id.*

Section 269 also applies to certain liquidations following a qualified stock purchase within the meaning of section 338, discussed in Chapter 7.[22] If one corporation makes a qualified stock purchase of another but does not make a section 338 election, and liquidates the acquired corporation under a plan of liquidation adopted no more than two years after the acquisition date, and the principal purpose for the liquidation "is the evasion or avoidance of Federal income tax by securing the benefit of a deduction, credit, or other allowance which the acquiring corporation would not otherwise enjoy, then the Secretary may disallow such deduction, credit, or other allowance." I.R.C. § 269(b).

[2] Mechanics

The threshold requirement for application of section 269 is an acquisition of control of a corporation or of the assets of a corporation, as specified in section 269(a). If such an acquisition has occurred, section 269 is triggered if the principal purpose of the acquisition is avoidance of Federal income tax. For purposes of section 269, the proscribed avoidance is "evasion or avoidance of Federal income tax by securing the benefit of a deduction, credit, or other allowance which such . . . corporation, would not otherwise enjoy." Treas. Reg. § 1.269-3(a). "Principal purpose" is the purpose that exceeds any other purpose in importance. *Id.*

---

[21] That is, an acquisition in which "the basis of which property, in the hands of the acquiring corporation, is determined by reference to the basis in the hands of the transferor corporation . . . ." I.R.C. § 269(a)(2).

[22] *See* § 7.05[B][1].

The Treasury Regulations provide that the following transactions are among those which, in the absence of evidence to the contrary, reflect a principal purpose of tax avoidance, and therefore become subject to section 269:

(1) A corporation with substantial profits acquires control of a corporation with valuable tax attributes, and the acquisition is followed by the action necessary to connect the tax attributes with the profits. Treas. Reg. § 1.269-3(b)(1).

(2) Two or more corporations are organized in lieu of a single corporation, in order to obtain multiple surtax exemptions or minimum accumulated earnings credits. Treas. Reg. § 1.269-3(b)(2).

(3) "A person or persons with high earning assets transfer them to a newly organized controlled corporation retaining assets producing net operating losses which are utilized in an attempt to secure refunds." Treas. Reg. § 1.269-3(b)(3).

(4) A corporation acquires property with a "carryover basis" materially greater than its fair market value, "and utilizes the property to create tax-reducing losses or deductions." Treas. Reg. § 1.269-3(c)(1).

(5) A corporate subsidiary that has sustained large net operating losses and that has filed separate returns for the taxable years in which the losses occurred, acquires from its parent corporation high-earning assets comprising a different business. The acquisition occurs at a time when the parent would not inherit the net operating loss carryovers of the subsidiary if the subsidiary were liquidated, and the profits of the business the subsidiary acquired from its parent are sufficient to offset a substantial portion of the subsidiary's net operating loss carryovers. Treas. Reg. § 1.269-3(c)(2).

Note the broad sweep of section 269; it can apply to a wide range of transactions if the prohibited purpose exists.

In determining whether the principal purpose of a transaction was tax avoidance, the regulations consider whether the tax attributes have already been subject to section 382 and 383. Treas. Reg. § 1.269-7. That is, if favorable tax attributes have already been reduced substantially, that may indicate that the transaction was not principally motivated by acquiring them.

CHART 13.4
Checklist for Applying Section 269

(1)   Has there been a transferred-basis type of corporate acquisition, or an acquisition of "control" by one corporation of another? If yes, go to question 3.

(2)   Has there been a qualified stock purchase without a section 338 election, followed by liquidation of the acquired corporation under

a plan of liquidation adopted no more than two years after the acquisition date? If yes, go to question 3.

(3)   Did the transaction have a principal purpose of tax avoidance "by securing the benefit of a deduction, credit, or other allowance which such person, or persons, or corporation, would not otherwise enjoy"? If yes, go to question 4.

(4)   The Secretary may disallow the deduction, credit, or other allowance in question, or reallocate it among the corporations involved.

Chapter 14

ANTI-ABUSE MEASURES AND SPECIAL PROVISIONS

§ 14.01 Introduction

As discussed in Chapter 1, there are several ways in which corporations and their shareholders traditionally have tried to avoid the double taxation of corporate profits. Corporations may try to lower aggregate taxes in other ways, as well, such as shifting income from a higher bracket corporation to a lower bracket shareholder, or *vice versa*. This chapter provides a basic overview of several provisions directed at stopping such tax avoidance. The provisions discussed here are the accumulated earnings tax; the personal holding company tax; the alternative minimum tax; "controlled group" restrictions; and income splitting, including an introduction to the allocation of income and deductions under section 482. This chapter does not discuss the consolidated return rules, which allow an affiliated group of corporations to elect to file a single return, *see* I.R.C. §§ 1501–1504; they are beyond the scope of this book.

§ 14.02 The Accumulated Earnings Tax

[A] In General

As discussed in Chapter 1, the corporate "double tax" is occasioned by the combination of income taxation at the corporate level and the shareholder level.[1] Current law reduces but does not eliminate double taxation by providing for taxation of individuals' qualified dividends at preferential (capital gains) rates. *See* I.R.C. § 1(h)(3)(B), (11).

It might seem that an easy way for shareholders to avoid (or at least postpone) the second level of tax would be to cause the corporation to retain earnings. Congress determined that retention of earnings for the purposes of avoiding double taxation, rather than for the needs of a corporation's business, is abusive. Accordingly, Congress enacted an accumulated earnings tax as early as 1913. *See* Tariff Act of October 3, 1913, 38 Stat. 166 § II A, Subdiv. 2. Today, the provisions appear in sections 531 through 537. Note that the accumulated earnings tax does not apply to personal holding companies, corporations exempt from tax under subchapter F of the Code, and passive foreign investment companies. I.R.C. § 532(b). It also applies only to C corporations, not to S corporations. I.R.C. § 1363(a). Also, the

---

[1] *See* § 1.01.

accumulated earnings tax is not a self-assessed tax. BORIS I. BITTKER & JAMES S. EUSTICE, FEDERAL INCOME TAXATION OF CORPORATIONS AND SHAREHOLDERS ¶ 7.01 (7th ed. 2000).

The accumulated earnings tax is a tax penalizing the non-payment of dividends. Thus, until recently, the tax was imposed at the highest marginal tax rate applicable to unmarried individuals. However, under current law, until the Jobs and Growth Tax Relief Reconciliation Act of 2003 sunsets at the end of 2008, the tax rate is 15 percent. I.R.C. § 531. Not coincidentally, that is the same rate generally applicable to individuals' qualified dividends under current law. See I.R.C. § 1(h)(3)(B), (11).

The accumulated earnings tax is an annual tax imposed on the "accumulated taxable income" of a corporation "formed or availed of for the *purpose of avoiding the income tax* with respect to its shareholders or the shareholders of any other corporation, by permitting earnings and profits to accumulate . . . ." I.R.C. § 532(a) (emphasis added); see also I.R.C. § 531. "Accumulated taxable income" is the corporation's taxable income as adjusted as provided in section 535. See I.R.C. § 535(a). Thus, only *current earnings* affect the amount of accumulated earnings tax.

> *Example 14.1*: X Corporation, a closely held corporation that was availed of for the purpose of avoiding the income tax on dividends, has "accumulated taxable income" of $1,000,000 for taxable year 2006. Accordingly, the accumulated earnings tax imposed on X Corporation for the year 2006 is $150,000.

By statute, the accumulated earnings tax applies to both closely held and publicly traded corporations. See I.R.C. § 532(c). However, "closely held corporations are the most likely targets of this assessment since their shareholders often are perceived to be in a better position to influence dividend policy." John S. Ball and Beverly H. Furtick, *Defending the Accumulated Earnings Tax Case*, 72 FLA. BAR J. 28, 28 (Dec. 1998); see also BITTKER & EUSTICE, *supra*, at ¶ 7.02[2].

[B]   Tax-Avoidance Purpose

Section 532(a) provides that the accumulated earnings tax applies to corporations (other than those excluded by statute) "formed or availed of for the purpose of avoiding the income tax with respect to its shareholders or the shareholders of any other corporation, by permitting earnings and profits to accumulate instead of being divided or distributed." The United States Supreme Court has held that tax avoidance need only be *one* of the purposes for the excessive accumulation—it need not have been the principal or dominant reason for it. *United States v. Donruss Co.*, 393 U.S. 297, 301, *reh'g denied*, 393 U.S. 1112 (1969). If a corporation is a holding company or investment company, that is *prima facie* evidence of the tax-avoidance motive. I.R.C. § 533(b). Otherwise, section 533(a) provides that "the fact that the earnings and profits of a corporation are permitted to accumulate beyond the reasonable needs of the business shall be determinative of the purpose to avoid the income tax with respect to shareholders, unless the corporation by the preponderance of the evidence shall prove to the contrary."

In order to determine if a corporation's earnings and profits have accumulated "beyond the reasonable needs of the business," accumulated earnings is compared with the amount reasonably needed for use in the business. In general, if there is an excess accumulation, the corporation bears the burden of proof by the preponderance of the evidence, under section 533(a), quoted above. However, if, in a Tax Court proceeding, the IRS sent the taxpayer "by certified mail or registered mail a notification informing the taxpayer that the proposed notice of deficiency includes an amount with respect to the accumulated earnings tax," I.R.C. 534(b), and the taxpayer submitted a timely statement of the grounds on which it relies to establish that the earnings and profits, or part of them, have not accumulated beyond reasonable business needs, the IRS will bear the burden of proof on the grounds in the taxpayer's statement. I.R.C. § 534(a)(2). In addition, the IRS will bear the burden of proof if it sent no such notification. I.R.C. § 534(a)(1).

[C]   Reasonable Needs of the Business

What constitutes the reasonable needs of a business? In general, this is a facts and circumstances test. *See* Treas. Reg. § 1.537-2(a). The Code provides that the term includes "the reasonably anticipated needs of the business." I.R.C. § 537(a). Regulations provide "[a]n accumulation of the earnings and profits (including the undistributed earnings and profits of prior years) is in excess of the reasonable needs of the business if it exceeds the amount that a prudent businessman would consider appropriate for the present business purposes and for the reasonably anticipated future needs of the business." Treas. Reg. § 1.537-1(a). In addition, with respect to reasonably anticipated needs:

> In order for a corporation to justify an accumulation of earnings and profits for reasonably anticipated future needs, there must be an indication that the future needs of the business require such accumulation, and *the corporation must have specific, definite, and feasible plans for the use of such accumulation*. Such an accumulation need not be used immediately, nor must the plans for its use be consummated within a short period after the close of the taxable year, provided that such accumulation will be used within a reasonable time depending upon all the facts and circumstances relating to the future needs of the business. . . .

Treas. Reg. § 1.537-1(b)(1) (emphasis added).

The regulations also list the following as possible examples of business needs, if supported by the facts:

> (1) To provide for *bona fide* expansion of business or replacement of plant;

(2) To acquire a business enterprise through purchasing stock or assets;

(3) To provide for the retirement of *bona fide* indebtedness created in connection with the trade or business, such as the establishment of a sinking fund for the purpose of retiring bonds issued by the corporation in accordance with contract obligations incurred on issue;

(4) To provide necessary working capital for the business, such as, for the procurement of inventories;

(5) To provide for investments or loans to suppliers or customers if necessary in order to maintain the business of the corporation; or

(6) To provide for the payment of reasonably anticipated product liability losses, as defined in section 172(j), § 1.172-13(b)(1), and § 1.537-1(f).

Treas. Reg. § 1.537-2(b).

As another example, a district court found in a recent case, with respect to a provider of marine transportation:

> plaintiffs have met their burden of proving that *they had reasonable business needs to accumulate the amounts identified by their experts for fleet replacement, project funding, working capital, potential legal liabilities, and shareholder redemption.* Furthermore, the Court finds that the companies had specific, definite, and feasible plans for using the accumulations for those business needs. The Court heard the testimony of the Candies family members (i.e. the companies' management) and it finds that testimony to be credible. The Candies' testimony was corroborated in important respects by the testimony of disinterested third-party witnesses, by a considerable volume of documentary evidence, and even, in one important respect, by defendant's own expert, Captain Underhill, who acknowledged the companies' need to accumulate as much as $100,000,000 for fleet replacement.

Otto Candies, LLC v. United States, 288 F. Supp. 2d 730, 770 (E.D. La. 2003) (emphasis added).

On the other hand, accumulations of earnings for any of the purposes listed below may indicate an unreasonable accumulation of earnings:

(1) Loans to shareholders, or the expenditure of funds of the corporation for the personal benefit of the shareholders;

(2) Loans having no reasonable relation to the conduct of the business made to relatives or friends of shareholders, or to other persons;

(3) Loans to another corporation, the business of which is not that of the taxpayer corporation, if the capital stock of such other

corporation is owned, directly or indirectly, by the shareholder or shareholders of the taxpayer corporation and such shareholder or shareholders are in control of both corporations;

(4) Investments in properties, or securities which are unrelated to the activities of the business of the taxpayer corporation; or

(5) Retention of earnings and profits to provide against unrealistic hazards.

Treas. Reg. § 1.537-2(c). Note that many of the purposes on this list are suggestive of an intent to avoid paying out corporate profits as dividends.

In *Bardahl Mfg. Co. v. Commissioner*, T.C. Memo. 1965-200, the Tax Court found it unreasonable to have a cash reserve sufficient to cover an entire year's operating costs. Instead, it found that it was reasonable to have a cash reserve to cover one "operating cycle." In *Bardahl*, the operating cycle consisted of the "time required to convert cash into raw materials, raw materials into an inventory of marketable Bardahl products, the inventory into sales and accounts receivable, and the period required to collect its outstanding accounts . . . ." *Id.* The court found that that period averaged approximately 4.2 months. *Id.* Accordingly, the court found that cash accumulations that exceeded an amount necessary to cover a period of more than 4.2 months exceeded reasonable business needs. *See id.*

Myron's Enterprises v. United States, 548 F.2d 331 (9th Cir. 1977), also considered the amount of accumulation necessary for the reasonable needs of a business. In that case, the IRS determined that, during the years in question, the reasonable needs of the business were limited to working capital needs and never exceeded a small amount. The taxpayer-corporations argued that their much higher retained earnings for those years were due both to working capital requirements and to the planned purchase and remodeling of a ballroom they had been leasing and operating. *Id.* at 332. The court agreed with the taxpayers although the purchase never actually occurred, and although they might have been able to borrow some of the money necessary for the purchase and remodeling of the ballroom. The evidence suggested that the purchase might have happened at any time and would require quick payment. *Id.* at 335.

Ivan Allen Co. v. United States, 422 U.S. 617 (1975), the United States Supreme Court considered how to calculate the amount available to the corporation to cover its business needs. In that case, the Court held that, in determining the amount available to cover Ivan Allen's reasonable business needs, securities owned by Ivan Allen that were listed on a stock exchange and readily marketable had to be taken into account at their "net realizable value" (their fair market value less the expenses of selling them, including the resulting taxes), rather than at their historical cost to the corporation. *Id.* at 629. Note that this may force a corporation that wishes to avoid the accumulated earnings tax to sell appreciated securities that remain a valuable investment. The Court rejected the taxpayer's argument to that effect, finding it immaterial. It also found unimportant the fact that the valuation may conflict with standard accounting practice. *Id.* at 634–35.

[D] Mechanics

Although the accumulated earnings tax is a penalty tax, the base on which it is imposed is intended to reflect economic reality. Therefore, much like "earnings and profits," discussed in Chapter 4,[2] "accumulated taxable income" is the corporation's taxable income for the year, adjusted to reflect available economic profits that ordinarily are not included in taxable income.[3] The adjustments include a deduction for dividends paid. *See* I.R.C. §§ 535(a), 561. In addition, for purposes of the dividends-paid deduction, "a dividend paid after the close of any taxable year and on or before the 15th day of the third month following the close of such taxable year shall be considered as paid during such taxable year." I.R.C. § 563(a).

The dividends-paid deduction also includes "consent dividends," *see* I.R.C. § 565, which essentially are deemed distributions of dividends. More technically, consent dividends are amounts on "consent stock" that the shareholder agrees to treat as a dividend, in a consent filed with the corporation's tax return, I.R.C. § 565(a), and that would otherwise consti- tute a dividend under section 316,[4] I.R.C. § 565(b)(2). In general, consent stock is stock entitled to share in earnings and profits remaining after the payment of dividends on preferred stock. I.R.C. § 565(f)(1). Consent stock therefore includes common stock and "participating preferred" stock that has unlimited participation rights. Treas. Reg. § 1.565-6(a). The consent dividend procedure thus provides a mechanism for avoiding the corporate- level accumulated earnings tax without an actual distribution of earnings.

The adjustments to taxable income made to arrive at "accumulated taxable income" also include one for federal taxes, including income taxes, I.R.C. § 535(b)(1); like dividends paid, taxes paid reduce available resources without reducing taxable income. For the same reason, the dividends received deduction that reduces taxable income is disallowed in computing accumulated taxable income. I.R.C. § 535(b)(3). Other adjustments are (1) removal of the cap on the deduction for charitable contributions, I.R.C. § 535(b)(2); (2) disallowance of the net operating loss deduction, I.R.C. § 535(b)(4); and (3) adjustments for net capital gain and net capital loss, I.R.C. § 535(b)(5)-(7). There are also special rules for holding companies, investment companies, and foreign corporations. *See* I.R.C. § 535(b)(8)-(9).

Accumulated taxable income is also reduced by the "accumulated earn- ings credit." I.R.C. § 535(a). For corporations other than holding or invest- ment companies, the "accumulated earnings credit" is the amount of the

---

[2] *See* § 4.03[C][1].

[3] Foreign corporations that file returns use as accumulated taxable income their taxable income from sources within the United States with the adjustments prescribed by section 535(b) and Treasury Regulation 1.535-2 minus the sum of the dividends-paid deduction and the accumulated earnings credit. A foreign corporation that files no return uses as its accumulated taxable income its gross income from sources within the United States "without allowance of any deductions (including the accumulated earnings credit)." Treas. Reg. § 1.535- 1(b).

[4] The calculation of dividends under section 316 is discussed in § 4.03[C][2] of Chapter 4.

earnings and profits for the taxable year retained for reasonable business needs minus the deduction for net capital gains allowed by section 535(b)(6). I.R.C. § 535(c)(1). This allows the tax base to exclude any amount determined to be needed for the business in question. In addition, most corporations benefit from a minimum credit of $250,000 minus the corporation's accumulated earnings and profits at the close of the prior taxable year. I.R.C. § 535(c)(2).

In sum, in general, the following adjustments are made to taxable income to arrive at accumulated taxable income:

Subtract from Taxable Income:

(1)   The dividends-paid deduction of section 561.

(2)   The accumulated earnings credit of section 535.

(3)   Federal income and excess profits taxes accrued during the taxable year (no deduction is allowed for either the accumulated earnings tax itself or the personal holding company tax).

(4)   Certain non-deductible foreign taxes paid.

(5)   Charitable contributions that were disallowed because of the cap in section 170(b)(2).

(6)   The excess of the net long-term capital gain for the taxable year over the net short-term capital loss for such year (determined without regard to the capital loss carryover provided in section 1212) minus the taxes attributable to such excess.

Add Back to Taxable Income:

(1)   Any net operating loss deduction taken.

(2)   Any capital loss carryover deducted.

(3)   Any amounts deducted under sections 243 through 247.

Thus, in general, if a corporation was organized or availed of for the proscribed tax-avoidance purpose, a penalty tax can apply to a tax base consisting of taxable income adjusted to reflect the resources available to the corporation. A primary way of determining whether the prohibited tax-avoidance motive is present is to consider whether those resources are sufficient for the corporation's reasonable business needs. Reasonable business needs is a highly fact-sensitive determination. Much like valuation of an asset that is not publicly traded, the bottom line must be a precise number, yet experts may disagree on what that number should be.

§ 14.03   The Personal Holding Company Tax

[A]   In General

The personal holding company tax is designed to discourage assignment of income by an individual to a closely held corporation, in order to lower the rate of tax paid on that income through income splitting. The assignment of income typically would be accomplished by the transfer from shareholder to corporation of income-generating assets such as stock and securities ("incorporated pocketbooks," BITTKER & EUSTICE, *supra*, at ¶ 7.20); contracts for the performance of services by the shareholder ("incorporated talents," *id.*); or personal use property plus income-producing property, in an effort to deduct expenses related to the personal use property ("incorporated yachts, country estates, and so forth," *id.*).

The tax base of the personal holding company tax is "undistributed personal holding company income," I.R.C. § 541, which is defined in section 545 and discussed below. Just like the accumulated earnings tax, the tax rate traditionally was the highest rate under section 1(c) but, under current law, is 15 percent, the same as the maximum rate applicable to individuals' qualified dividends. *Id.*; *cf.* I.R.C. § 1(h)(3)(B), (11). The personal holding company tax, like the accumulated earnings tax, is applied in addition to the regular corporate tax. I.R.C. § 541.

[B] Definition of "Personal Holding Company"

The Code defines a "personal holding company" as a corporation other than one of the types listed below,[5] if (1) at least 60 percent of its "adjusted ordinary gross income" for the taxable year is "personal holding company income", and (2) at any time during the last half of the taxable year, more than 50 percent in value of its outstanding stock is owned, directly or indirectly, by or for not more than five individuals. I.R.C. § 542(a). For this purpose, certain pension funds, trusts forming part of a plan providing for the payment of supplemental unemployment compensation benefits, private foundations, and amounts in trust permanently set aside or to be used exclusively for certain charitable purposes, are considered individuals. *See* I.R.C. § 542(a)(2). In addition, certain stock attribution rules apply. *See* I.R.C. § 544.

In general, under section 543, "adjusted ordinary gross income" means a corporation's gross income determined by excluding gains from the sale or other disposition of capital assets and quasi-capital assets, I.R.C. § 543(b)(1), and adjusted as follows, I.R.C. § 543(b)(2):[6]

> (1) From the gross income from rents is subtracted the amount allowable as deductions for (a) "exhaustion, wear and tear, obsolescence, and amortization of property other than tangible personal property that is not customarily retained by any one lessee for more than three years," I.R.C. § 543(b)(2)(A)(i), (b) property taxes, (c) interest, and (d) rent, to

---

[5] An S corporation cannot be taxed as a personal holding company. *See* I.R.C. § 1363(a). However, S corporations with earnings and profits are subject to tax on excess passive investment income. *See* I.R.C. § 1375; § 8.05[B]. In addition, if the S corporation's passive investment income exceeds 25 percent of gross receipts for three consecutive taxable years and it has accumulated earnings and profits at the close of each of those three taxable years, the S election will terminate. *See* I.R.C. § 1362(d)(3)(A)(i), (iii); § 8.03[B][3].

[6] The definition of personal holding company income is discussed below. *See* § 14.03[C].

the extent that these items are allocable under regulations to gross income from rents. *See* I.R.C. § 543(b)(2)(A) (also imposing a limitation on the amount that can be subtracted).

(2) From the gross income from mineral, oil, and gas royalties, items similar to those listed in paragraph (1) immediately above (that is, depreciation deductions and the like), as well as severance taxes, are subtracted, to the extent they are allocable under regulations to gross income from mineral, oil, and gas royalties or gross income from working interests in oil or gas wells. *See* I.R.C. § 543(b)(2)(B) (also imposing a limitation on the amount that can be subtracted).

(3) From gross income consisting of "compensation, however designated, for the use of, or the right to use, any tangible personal property manufactured or produced by the taxpayer, if during the taxable year the taxpayer is engaged in substantial manufacturing or production of tangible personal property of the same type," I.R.C. § 543(b)(3)(D), similar items are subtracted, to the extent they are allocable under regulations to that gross income. *See* I.R.C. § 543(b)(2)(D) (also imposing a limitation on the amount that can be subtracted).

(4) The following interest is excluded: (a) "interest received on a direct obligation of the United States held for sale to customers in the ordinary course of trade or business by a regular dealer who is making a primary market in such obligations," and (b) "interest on a condemnation award, a judgment, and a tax refund." I.R.C. § 543(b)(2)(C).

The corporations that generally cannot constitute personal holding companies are (1) not-for-profit corporations, (2) banks and domestic building and loan associations, (3) life insurance companies, (4) surety companies, (5) certain lending or finance companies, (6) certain foreign corporations, (7) certain small business investment companies, (8) corporations undergoing bankruptcy reorganization, unless a major purpose of instituting or continuing such case is the avoidance of the personal holding company tax, and (9) passive foreign investment companies. I.R.C. § 542(c).

A former operating company that is liquidating and winding up its affairs can qualify as a personal holding company and become subject to the tax. *See, e.g., O'Sullivan Rubber Co. v. Commissioner*, 120 F.2d 845, 846 (2d Cir. 1941) (liquidating closely held corporation earned 80 percent of its income from interest in the year in question and met the definition of personal holding company). However, section 562(b)(2) provides some relief for liquidating corporations by providing that liquidating distributions to corporate distributees of their shares of undistributed personal holding company income made within 24 months of the adoption of a plan of liquidation constitute dividends for purposes of the dividends paid deduction if the personal holding company is completely liquidated.

[C]   Types of Personal Holding Company Income

In general, "'personal holding company income' means the portion of the [company's] adjusted ordinary gross income which consists of" (1) dividends;

(2) interest; (3) most royalties; (4) some rents; (5) annuities; (6) in some instances, amounts paid for the use of corporate property by a shareholder; (7) amounts received under a "personal service contract"; and (8) estate and trust income includible in the taxable income of a corporation under part I of Subchapter J of the Code. I.R.C. § 543. The various types of personal holding company income reflect the income-splitting concern behind the personal holding company tax. Thus, they include passive earnings such as dividends, interest, rents, and annuities, and income from personal service contracts.

A personal service contract is a contract under which the corporation is to furnish personal services, if the individual who will perform the services is designated in the contract or someone other than the corporation has the right to designate the individual who will perform the services, if at any point during the taxable year, 25 percent or more of the corporation's outstanding stock (by value) is owned, directly or indirectly, by or for the service-providing individual. *See* I.R.C. § 543(a)(7). In *Kenyatta Corp. v. Commissioner*, 86 T.C. 171 (1986), the issue was whether a corporation that contracted with third parties for the services of William Russell (Russell), a former professional basketball player and "highly regarded sports personality," *id.* at 173, received more than 60 percent of its adjusted ordinary gross income from "personal service contracts," and therefore constituted a personal holding company.

In *Kenyatta*, the corporation entered into a contract with the Seattle Supersonics for publicity and public relations services to be provided by Russell. *Id.* at 175. The corporation entered into other contracts that similarly designated Russell as the service provider. *See id.* at 177–179. One of the questions before the court was whether the stock ownership test of the personal holding company rules was satisfied. "Covey, the attorney responsible for organizing petitioner, testified that Russell was intended to be the majority stockholder in the corporation and that the majority of the equity in petitioner belonged to Russell in 'some unfocused way.'" *Id.* at 181–82. The Tax Court noted that the issuance of stock certificates is not determinative of stock ownership for purposes of section 542(a)(2). It found that the evidence showed that Russell was intended to be the majority stockholder in the corporation and nothing in the record showed that anyone other than Russell owned any of the corporation's outstanding stock at any time during the year in question. *Id.* Accordingly, the contracts constituted personal services contracts. The court further found that amounts from the contracts exceeded 60 percent of the corporation's adjusted ordinary gross income. Thus, the corporation constituted a personal holding company. *Id.* at 189.

[D] Mechanics of the Tax

As stated above, under current law, the tax rate of the personal holding company tax is 15 percent. I.R.C. § 541. For a domestic personal holding company, undistributed personal holding company income, the tax base, is the taxable income of the personal holding company, adjusted under section 545(b), minus a dividends-paid deduction.[7] See I.R.C. § 545(a).

In general, the adjustments under section 545(b) are (1) a deduction for otherwise nondeductible federal income and excess profits taxes and income, war profits and excess profits taxes of foreign countries and possessions of the United States (but not the accumulated earnings tax or the personal holding company tax); (2) a deduction for charitable contributions, subject to certain limitations; (3) disallowance of the dividends received deduction; (4) disallowance of a net operating loss deduction for the year in question, but a deduction for the amount of the net operating loss for the preceding taxable year computed without certain the deductions; (5) a deduction for the net capital gain for the taxable year, minus taxes attributable to the net capital gain (if the corporation is foreign, the gains and losses taken into account are only those that are effectively connected with the conduct of a trade or business within the United States and are not exempt from tax under treaty); and (6) the deduction for trade or business expenses and depreciation allocable to the operation and maintenance of property owned or operated by the corporation is generally limited to the amount of rent or other compensation received for the use of the property. I.R.C. § 545(b); see also BITTKER & EUSTICE, supra, at ¶ 7.24[1] & n.242 (also referencing "certain other minor technical adjustments").

The dividends-paid deduction effectuates the policy of the personal holding company tax because amounts distributed as dividends are taxed to the shareholders, thus reducing or eliminating the benefits of income-splitting. The deduction is allowed for (1) dividends paid during the taxable year, (2) dividends paid "on or before the 15th day of the third month following the close of such taxable year . . . to the extent the taxpayer elects in its return for the taxable year" but only to the extent of 20 percent of the dividends the corporation paid during the taxable year, and not in excess of the corporation's undistributed personal holding company income; (3) the "consent dividends" for the taxable year, and (4) a dividend carryover computed under section 564. I.R.C. § 561(a). The consent dividend procedure is the same as it is for the accumulated earnings tax. See I.R.C. §§ 545(a); 561(a)(2); 565; see also § 14.02[D], supra.

Section 547 provides for a similar deduction, after the fact. If the personal holding company tax would otherwise apply as a result of a court determination, for example, see I.R.C. § 547(a), (c), the taxpayer may take a deduction for "deficiency dividends" paid within 90 days of the determination in question, I.R.C. § 547(a), (d)(1), if the taxpayer files a claim within

---

[7] For a personal holding company that is a foreign corporation, and not more than 10 percent in value of the outstanding stock of which is owned during the last half of the taxable year by United States persons, undistributed personal holding company income means "the amount determined by multiplying the undistributed personal holding company income (determined without regard to this sentence) by the percentage in value of its outstanding stock which is the greatest percentage in value of its outstanding stock so owned by United States persons on any one day during such period." I.R.C. § 545(a).

120 days of the determination, I.R.C. § 547(e). Amounts distributed also do not constitute deficiency dividends unless they would have been eligible for the dividends paid deduction had they been distributed during the tax year to which the personal holding company tax applied. I.R.C. § 547(d)(1).

[E] Avoiding the Tax

Avoiding the personal holding company tax generally entails falling outside the personal holding company definition or the tax base of "undistributed personal holding company income." With respect to the latter, paying dividends or following the consent dividend procedures reduces the tax base. With regard to the former, the corporation could adjust its income mix so as to avoid having 60 percent or more of its income constitute personal holding company income, or could spread out stock ownership so that no more than 50 percent of its outstanding stock is owned by or for five or fewer individuals.

Making an election under Subchapter S also avoids the tax because an S corporation cannot be taxed as a personal holding company. *See* I.R.C. § 1363(a). However, S corporations with earnings and profits are subject to tax on excess passive investment income, *see* I.R.C. § 1375; § 8.05[B], and face termination of the S election if the S corporation's passive investment income exceeds 25 percent of gross receipts for three consecutive taxable years and it has accumulated earnings and profits at the close of each of those three taxable years.[8] I.R.C. § 1362(d)(3)(A)(i), (iii); § 8.03[B][3].

§ 14.04   The Alternative Minimum Tax

[A] In General

The Alternative Minimum Tax (AMT) reflects Congress' judgment that wealthy individuals and corporations should not be allowed to use tax preference items to such an extent that they pay little or no tax. *See* S. Rep. No. 99-313, at 518–9 (1986). The AMT addresses this issue by imposing a minimum tax on those taxpayers and disallowing many preference items that they could claim under the regular tax. In general, the AMT requires a corporate taxpayer to make two calculations: (1) its "regular tax" (based on taxable income),[9] and (2) its "tentative minimum tax" (based on alternative minimum taxable income, defined below).[10] *See* I.R.C. § 55(a).

---

[8] For further discussion of methods for avoiding the personal holding company tax, see BITTKER & EUSTICE, *supra*, at ¶ 7.24[4].

[9] Taxable income of a corporation is the corporation's gross income minus deductions allowed by the Code. I.R.C. § 63(a). Note that, unlike individuals, corporations do not have an intermediate figure comparable to "adjusted gross income." *See id.; cf.* I.R.C. § 62(a) (defining adjusted gross income, which applies to individuals).

[10] President George W. Bush has proposed repealing the corporate AMT. *See* "Congressional Leaders Continue Discussion on Stimulus, Tax Cuts," 2001 *TNT* 196-1 (October 9, 2001).

Regardless of the result of this calculation, the corporation must pay its regular tax liability. In addition, if its tentative minimum tax exceeds its regular tax liability, the corporation pays both the regular tax liability and the excess of the tentative minimum tax over its regular tax liability; the excess amount is what is termed the alternative minimum tax.[11] *See id.* In 2002, approximately 7,100 corporations reported AMT liability totaling $2.5 billion, the "second lowest [amount] in over a decade." Heather R. Duffy, *Corporation Income Tax Returns, 2002*, 72, Statistics of Income Bulletin (Summer 2005), *available at* www.irs.gov/pub/irs-soi/02corart.pdf.

> *Example 14.2*: Y Corporation has regular income tax liability of $100,000 for the tax year. Its tentative minimum tax is $120,000. Y Corporation must pay tax of $120,000, composed of $100,000 of regular income tax and $20,000 of AMT.

There are several exceptions to the application of the corporate AMT. First, the AMT does not apply to a corporation's first year of existence. I.R.C. § 55(e)(1)(C). Second, the AMT does not apply to "small" corporations; there is an exception for corporations that have average annual gross receipts not in excess of $7,500,000 for all three taxable-year periods ending before the taxable year in question. I.R.C. § 55(e)(1)(A). For this purpose, only taxable years beginning after December 31, 1993 are taken into account. *Id.* In addition, $5,000,000 is used instead of $7,500,000 for the first three-year period in question. I.R.C. § 55(e)(1)(B).

In addition, a corporation that has AMT liability in some taxable years may not have it in others. Section 53 provides a credit against regular tax liability for AMT imposed in prior taxable years. *See* I.R.C. § 53.[12] For this reason, it is important to remember that, as discussed above and illustrated in Example 14.2, the AMT is only the *excess amount* paid in addition to regular tax liability, not the entire tax payment. *See* I.R.C. § 55(a). The credit reflects the fact that AMT liability may have been caused by timing differences resulting from the different depreciation schedules used for regular tax purposes and AMT purposes, for example. The credit may have the effect that AMT paid in one year will be returned to the taxpayer in a later year, giving the government only the benefit of the time value of money.

[B] Mechanics

The tax base for the corporate AMT is alternative minimum taxable income (AMTI) less an exemption amount. *See* I.R.C. § 55(b)(1)(B). The tax rate is a flat 20 percent. *See* I.R.C. § 55(b)(1)(B)(i). The exemption amount is generally $40,000 for corporate taxpayers and is not indexed for inflation. *See* I.R.C. § 55(d)(2). Moreover, it is phased out for corporate taxpayers "by an amount equal to 25 percent of the amount by which the alternative

---

[11] The corporate AMT is reduced only by the alternative minimum tax foreign tax credit. *See* I.R.C. § 55(b)(1)(B).

[12] *See* I.R.C. § 53 for the mechanics of computing the credit and the limitations on it.

minimum taxable income of the taxpayer exceeds . . . $150,000 . . . ."
I.R.C. § 55(d)(3)(A). Thus, at AMTI of $310,000 ($160,000 in excess of
$150,000), the exemption phases out completely.

> *Example 14.3*: Z Corporation's AMTI is $250,000. Because AMTI of
> $250,000 exceeds $150,000 by $100,000, the exemption amount is reduced
> by $25,000 (25 percent of $100,000). The exemption amount is therefore
> reduced to $15,000 ($40,000 − $25,000). Z Corporation's tentative mini-
> mum tax will therefore be computed on a base of $235,000 ($250,000 −
> $15,000). The tax is computed at a 20 percent rate, so Z Corporation's
> tentative minimum tax will be $47,000.

A corporation's AMTI is its taxable income as adjusted by sections 56 and
58, and increased by the tax preference items listed in section 57. *See* I.R.C.
§§ 55(b)(1)(B), (b)(2); Bittker & Eustice, *supra*, at ¶ 5.08[1]. To reflect
the section 57 tax preference items, the corporation adds to its taxable
income such things as certain intangible drilling costs, tax-exempt private
activity bond interest, and accelerated depreciation of pre-1987 property.
See I.R.C. §§ 55(b)(2)(B), 57(a). The other adjustments to income are more
complicated.

The section 56 adjustments include adjustments for depreciation for
certain property; for mining exploration and development costs; income
from long-term contracts; and net operating losses, which must be recalcu-
lated to limit the deductible portion to 90 percent of AMTI. *See* I.R.C.
§ 56(a), (d). Section 58 restricts the allowance of farm losses for personal
service corporations and applies the passive activity loss rules with modifications specified in section 58(b). *See* I.R.C. § 58(a), (b). Because some of
these adjustments affect basis for the purposes of computing AMTI, even
a corporation that does not owe AMT for a particular year should compute
AMTI. Bittker & Eustice, *supra*, at ¶ 5.08[3].

Another major adjustment to corporate AMTI is based on the adjusted
current earnings (ACE) of the corporation, as required by section 56(g).
Under section 56(g), AMTI is increased by 75 percent of the amount by
which the corporation's ACE exceeds its AMTI determined without regard
to (1) the ACE adjustment of section 56(g) and (2) the alternative tax net
operating loss deduction. I.R.C. § 56(g)(1).

In general, the ACE adjustment increases the AMTI by including within
the AMTI many income items that, while not included in the corporation's
taxable income, are included in corporate earnings and profits. However,
the ACE adjustment can be *negative*, reducing AMTI. *See* I.R.C. § 56(g)(2)
(allowing a negative adjustment, subject to a limitation). ACE also denies
most deductions that are normally denied for earnings and profits purposes
but not for taxable income purposes, and also includes nondeductible expenses and dividends even though they reduce earnings and profits.
Bittker & Eustice, *supra*, at ¶ 5.08[5] (describing ACE as "a hybrid . . .
based on both earnings and profits and taxable income concepts.").

The issue the ACE adjustment addresses is that accounting ("book")
income, which is often reported to the public in some form, typically

includes items that are not included in taxable income. Including these items in AMTI reduces the perception that corporations are avoiding tax on profits that are not part of the regular taxable income of the corporation.[13]

§ 14.05 "Controlled Group" Restrictions

Incorporating multiple corporations in lieu of one corporation could facilitate tax avoidance through multiple use of the graduated rate brackets and repeated use of tax benefits such as the $40,000 alternative minimum tax exemption.[14] Section 1561 targets this potential abuse by imposing limitations on the multiple use of tax benefits by a controlled group of corporations.[15] Specifically, it limits each corporation that is a member of a controlled group of corporations to (1) no larger amount in each taxable income bracket than the maximum amount to which a single corporation is entitled; (2) one accumulated earnings credit; (3) one alternative minimum tax exemption; and (4) one environmental tax exemption. *See* I.R.C. § 1561(a). These amounts, except for the accumulated earnings credit "shall be divided equally among the component members of such group on December 31 unless all of such component members consent (at such time and in such manner as the Secretary shall by regulations prescribe) to an apportionment plan providing for an unequal allocation of such amounts." *Id.*[16]

---

[13] ACE requires its own adjustment to depreciation for property placed in service after 1989 through December 31, 1993, *see* I.R.C. § 56(g)(4)(A), so it requires that basis be tracked separately for purposes of the ACE adjustment. A corporation thus must keep four books for tax purposes: one for its regular tax liability, one for earnings and profits, one for AMTI, and one for the ACE adjustment. *See* BITTKER & EUSTICE, *supra*, at ¶ 5.08[5] n.336.

[14] *See* § 14.04[B].

[15] Section 1551 can also apply where:

> any corporation transfers, directly or indirectly, after June 12, 1963, all or part of its property (other than money) to a transferee corporation, or . . . five or fewer individuals who are in control of a corporation transfer, directly or indirectly, after June 12, 1963, property (other than money) to a transferee corporation and the transferee corporation was created for the purpose of acquiring such property or was not actively engaged in business at the time of such acquisition, and if after such transfer the transferor or transferors are in control of such transferee corporation during any part of the taxable year of such transferee corporation . . . .

I.R.C. § 1551(a)(2)-(3). Where it applies, the IRS can "disallow the benefits of the rates contained in section 11(b) which are lower than the highest rate specified in such section, or the accumulated earnings credit provided in paragraph (2) or (3) of section 535(c), unless such transferee corporation shall establish by the clear preponderance of the evidence that the securing of such benefits or credit was not a major purpose of such transfer." I.R.C. § 1551(a). "[A]lthough the enactment of § 1561 was not intended to supersede § 1551, the latter has fallen into desuetude. . . ." BITTKER & EUSTICE, *supra*, at ¶ 13.02[6]. It is not further discussed in this book.

[16] With respect to the accumulated earnings credit, *see* Treas. Reg. § 1.1561-2(c).

[A]   Overview of the Definition of "Controlled Group"

Section 1563(a) defines a "controlled group of corporations" as consisting of a "parent-subsidiary controlled group," a "brother-sister controlled group," or a "combined group." As discussed below, each of these terms hinges on stock ownership requirements. However, treasury stock and non-voting preferred stock is not counted for these purposes. I.R.C. § 1563(c)(1)(A), (B). As discussed below, certain other stock, termed "excluded stock" by section 1563(c), is not counted either. In general, it is disadvantageous to have stock fall into one of these categories because the more stock that it is outstanding, the higher the hurdle to achieve the disfavored "controlled group" status.

[B]   Parent-Subsidiary Controlled Groups

In general, a parent-subsidiary controlled group is a group of corporations owned by a common parent, if the parent owns 80 percent or more (by vote or by value) of all classes of stock of at least one corporation, and all other corporations in the group are connected by 80-percent or more stock ownership (by vote or by value). *See* I.R.C. § 1563(a)(1). However, certain stock is excluded from this calculation. *See* I.R.C. § 1563(c)(1)(C), (2)(A). Furthermore, certain constructive ownership rules apply. *See* I.R.C. § 1563(d)(1), (e)(1)-(3), (f)(3).

> *Example 14.4*: AB, Inc., CD, Inc., EF, Inc., and GH, Inc. each have one class of stock outstanding, voting common stock. AB, Inc. owns 90 percent of the stock of CD, Inc. and 85 percent of the stock of EF, Inc. EF, Inc., in turn, owns 80 percent of the stock of GH, Inc. AB, Inc., CD, Inc., EF, Inc., and GH, Inc. constitute a parent-subsidiary controlled group of corporations.

[C]   Brother-Sister Controlled Groups

For purposes of sections 1561 and 1563, a brother-sister controlled group consists of five or fewer individuals, estates, or trusts who own at least 50 percent of the stock (by vote or by value) of all classes of the stock of each corporation in the group, "taking into account the stock ownership of each such person only to the extent such stock ownership is identical with respect to each such corporation." I.R.C. § 1563(a)(2). However, as with parent-subsidiary controlled groups, certain stock is excluded from this calculation. *See* I.R.C. § 1563(c)(1)(C), (2)(B). Furthermore, certain constructive owner-ship rules apply. *See* I.R.C. § 1563(d)(2), (e), (f)(3).

Example 14.5: IJ, Inc., KL, Inc., MN, Inc., and OP, Inc. each have one class of stock outstanding, voting common stock. Quincy, Ron, and Susan each own 30 percent of the stock of IJ, Inc. They also each own 33 percent of the stock of KL, Inc. and MN, Inc. Quincy and Ron each own 40 percent of the stock of OP, Inc., and Susan owns 10 percent of the OP, Inc. stock. This ownership may be listed as follows:

	IJ	KL	MN	OP	IDENTICAL OWNERSHIP
Quincy	30	33	33	40	**30**
Ron	30	33	33	40	**30**
Susan	30	33	33	10	**10**
TOTAL					**70 percent**

IJ, Inc., KL, Inc., MN, Inc., and OP, Inc. constitute a brother-sister controlled group of corporations because, taking into account only the identical ownership of each corporation (shown in the right hand column of the chart), together, they own 70 percent of the sole class of stock of each corporation, which exceeds 50 percent.

Code sections other than sections 1561 and 1563 that impose "controlled group" restrictions (such as sections 179(d)(6)) use a different definition of brother-sister controlled group. *See* I.R.C. § 1563(f)(5). For purposes of those other sections, the Code contains an additional test: the five or fewer individuals, estates or trusts must own not only more than 50 percent of the stock (by vote or by value) of all classes of stock of each corporation, "taking into account the stock ownership of each such person only to the extent such stock ownership is identical with respect to each such corporation" but also must own at least 80 percent of the total voting power or at least 80 percent of the total value of all classes of the stock of each corporation in the group. *Id.* Consider how this test would apply to the facts of Example 14.5:

	IJ	KL	MN	OP	IDENTICAL OWNERSHIP
Quincy	30	33	33	40	**30**
Ron	30	33	33	40	**30**
Susan	30	33	33	10	**10**
TOTAL	**90**	**99**	**99**	**90**	**70 percent**

As this chart shows, IJ, Inc., KL, Inc., MN, Inc., and OP, Inc. constitute a brother-sister controlled group of corporations under this definition because not only do they meet the 50-percent test, taking into account only the identical ownership of each corporation (shown in the right hand column of the chart), as in Example 14.5, they also own more than 80 percent of the sole class of stock of each corporation (as shown in the bottom row of the chart).

As Example 14.5 shows, the ownership of a brother-sister controlled group of corporations may be somewhat dispersed. Does the statute require that each person in the group of five or fewer shareholders own stock in *every* corporation in the group in order for the group to constitute a brother-sister controlled group? *United States v. Vogel Fertilizer*, 455 U.S. 16 (1982) answered that question. In that case, Arthur Vogel (Vogel) owned 77.49 percent of Vogel Fertilizer Co. (Vogel Fertilizer). Richard Crain (Crain) owned the remaining 22.51 percent. In addition, Vogel held 87.5 percent of the voting power and between 90 and 94 percent of the value of the stock in Vogel Popcorn Co. (Vogel Popcorn). Crain owned no stock in Vogel Popcorn. *Id.* at 19–21.

For the tax years in question, the Code allowed an exemption of a certain amount from a surtax on corporate income. Vogel Fertilizer did not claim a full surtax exemption on its returns for the years in question because Treasury Regulation 1.1563-1(a)(3) interpreted the term "brother-sister controlled group" to include situations in which one or more persons in the group of five did not own stock in every corporation in the group, thereby barring such a claim. That is, the regulation provided that a brother-sister controlled group consisted of the same five or fewer persons that "singly or in combination" had the requisite stock ownership. However, in 1976, in an unrelated case, the Tax Court found that the regulation was invalid because the statute did not permit the Commissioner to take a person's stock ownership into account for purposes of the then-applicable 80-percent requirement unless that person owned stock in *every* corporation within the brother-sister controlled group. Accordingly, Vogel Fertilizer filed claims for refunds, asserting that Vogel Fertilizer and Vogel Popcorn were not members of a controlled group and that Vogel Fertilizer therefore was entitled to a full surtax exemption for each taxable year in issue. *Id.* at 21. Based on the text of the statute and its legislative history, the Court determined that the regulation was not a reasonable interpretation of the statute. *See id.* at 25–27. In addition, the technical explanation by the Treasury Department at the time of the adoption of the two-part percentage test in 1969 explicitly supported the taxpayer's position. *See id.* at 29. Thus, the Court affirmed the Court of Claims, invalidating the regulation and holding in favor of the taxpayer.

[D] Combined Groups

A combined group consists of three or more corporations each of which is a member of a parent-subsidiary controlled group or brother-sister controlled group and one of which is a common parent corporation in the parent-subsidiary controlled group and is also included in the brother-sister controlled group. I.R.C. § 1563(a)(2).

§ 14.06 Income Splitting

Income splitting refers to an action that divides between or among two or more taxpayers income that would otherwise belong to one taxpayer.

Taxpayers do that so as to lower aggregate taxation by taking advantage of the progressive rate structure. That is, deflecting part of one's income to someone in a lower tax bracket will lower the tax on that income. Income splitting may occur in a variety of contexts, including within families, between corporations and shareholders, and between and among corporations. This section focuses on income splitting that involves at least one corporation.

[A] Income Splitting Between Corporation and Shareholder

An individual shareholder may wish to assign income to his or her wholly owned corporation if corporate tax rates are lower than individual rates, or if, despite corporate tax rates that equal or exceed individual rates, the marginal rate applicable to the corporation's last dollar is higher than the marginal rate applicable to an individual's last dollar. Professor Isenbergh explains how this worked prior to 1986:

> The basic idea was for the shareholders of the corporation, if they were also directly engaged in its operations, to leave a substantial balance of its income in the corporation as retained earnings after the deduction of their salaries. The result was two separate trips through the rate brackets for the two separate components of the earnings in the year they arose. The gains left in the corporation as retained earnings would be exposed to additional taxation upon their subsequent distribution to the shareholders, but with the advantage of delay in taxation at the shareholder level.

Joseph Isenbergh, *The End of Income Taxation*, 45 TAX L. REV. 283, 300 (1995) (footnote omitted). Retaining earnings in corporate form is most advantageous if the stock in the corporation is held until death, providing a basis step-up to fair market value. *See* I.R.C. § 1014.

Under current law, where the top individual rate does not exceed the top corporate rate, there is much less occasion for this kind of income splitting. Nonetheless, because of progressive rates, successful shifting of income from an individual to a corporation can provide a second trip up the rate brackets that can result in tax savings if the corporation has very little income and thus is taxed at the lowest marginal rates.

[B] Income Splitting Between Corporations

[1] In General

Income splitting arises not only for corporations and shareholders, but also for commonly controlled corporations. One way commonly controlled corporations may manipulate income and deductions is by overcharging or undercharging for goods or services provided by one corporation to the other.

Example 14.6: ST Corporation is a highly profitable domestic corporation. UV, Inc. is a corporation with minimal profits, thus subject to lower tax rates. In order to take advantage of the lower rates applicable to UV, Inc., William, who controls both corporations, causes UV, Inc. to pay less than fair market value each time ST Corporation provides services to UV, Inc. This lowers ST's gross income. Although this also lowers UV's deductions, in the aggregate, the taxes borne by the two corporations are lower because of the shifting of taxable income from a higher-taxed corporation to a lower-taxed corporation.

The IRS may challenge this type of transaction under section 482. For example, in Revenue Ruling 69-630, 1969-2 C.B. 112, *A* controlled *X* and *Y* corporations and caused *X* to sell property to *Y* "for less than an arm's length price," for tax-avoidance purposes; the IRS ruled that *X*'s income was "increased under section 482 of the Code to reflect the arm's length price," *Y*'s basis in the property was similarly increased, and "the amount of such increase will be treated as a distribution to *A*, the controlling shareholder, with respect to his stock of *X* and as a capital contribution by *A* to *Y*." *Id.* at 112. Section 482 is discussed further below.

[2] An Introduction to Reallocation of Income and Deductions Under Section 482

[a] Overview

Section 482 allows the IRS to distribute, allocate, or apportion gross income, deductions, and other tax attributes between or among one or more businesses, whether or not they are in corporate form, and whether or not they are affiliated or commonly controlled, if the IRS "determines that such distribution, apportionment, or allocation is necessary in order to prevent evasion of taxes or clearly to reflect the income of any of such organizations, trades, or businesses." I.R.C. § 482. Section 482 may be applied to both foreign and domestic corporations. In both *B. Forman Company, Inc. v. Commissioner*, 453 F.2d 1144 (2d Cir. 1972), and *Achiro v. Commissioner*, 77 T.C. 881 (1981), both of which are discussed below, the corporations involved were domestic corporations. This chapter merely provides an introduction to section 482; a detailed discussion is beyond the scope of this book.

The primary focus of section 482 is "to ensure that taxpayers clearly reflect income attributable to controlled transactions, and to prevent the avoidance of taxes with respect to such transactions." Treas. Reg. § 1.482-1(a)(1). The regulations provide a detailed methodology. *See* Treas. Reg. §§ 1.482-1 *et. seq.* In general, the regulations embody the principle that the true taxable income of a transaction between two businesses controlled by the same interests is the income that would result from an arm's-length transaction with an unrelated party. *See* Treas. Reg. § 1.482-2. The main difficulty lies in reconstructing the hypothetical arm's-length transaction. The regulations address specific situations, including interest on loans,

Treas. Reg. § 1.482-2(a); the performance of services by one entity for another entity, Treas. Reg. § 1.482-2(b); use or transfers of tangible property, Treas. Reg. §§ 1.482-2(c), -3; and the transfer of intangible property, Treas. Reg. § 1.482-4.

[b] Selected Case Law on Arm's-Length Standards

B. Forman Company, Inc., provides an example of the application of section 482 to a loan arrangement. In that case, B. Forman Co., Inc. (Forman) and McCurdy & Co., Inc. (McCurdy) were competing, family-owned department store corporations in Rochester, New York. McCurdy and Forman had no shareholders, directors, or officers in common. In 1958, McCurdy and Forman incorporated Midtown Holdings Corp. (Midtown) to develop a shopping center that would adjoin the rear entrances of their existing stores. Each shareholder corporation received 50 percent of the Midtown shares. 453 F.2d at 1147–48.

In 1960, McCurdy and Forman each lent Midtown $1 million in return for three-year notes bearing annual interest of three and one-half percent. These notes were cancelled in 1961 and replaced with notes of $1 million bearing no interest. On their due date, these notes were in turn replaced with three-year non-interest-bearing notes of $1 million, and when the new notes came due, they too were replaced with three-year non-interest-bearing notes of $1 million. No interest or principal was ever paid on these notes. *Id.* at 1148, 1149.

The IRS imputed an annual interest rate of five percent and allocated to Forman and McCurdy the resulting imputed interest income under section 482. The Tax Court ruled for the taxpayers, finding that neither Forman nor McCurdy controlled Midtown, nor did Forman and McCurdy constitute a single entity that controlled Midtown. *Id.* at 1149–50. The Court of Appeals reversed. It stated, in part:

> If Midtown was the creature of only one of the taxpayers, and all of its stock were owned by that single parent . . . the most rigid, literal wooden interpretation of section 482 would bring Midtown within the ambit of that section. It is the contention of the taxpayers . . . that section 482 is not applicable because Midtown is the normal child of a father and a mother, the product of an earthy relationship between McCurdy and Forman, twentieth century parents exercising no control over their progeny.
>
> Midtown is the creation of a union of McCurdy and Forman—not in holy matrimony but in a legitimate business enterprise. Their interests in the existence and career of Midtown and the interests of Midtown are identical.
>
> To contend that these parents do not control their child is to fly in the face of reality.

Id. at 1153. Thus, the court found that section 482 could apply.

The court also found that Forman and McCurdy's waiver of interest reflected a lack of arm's-length dealing with Midtown. It further found that Forman and McCurdy could be charged with imputed interest income so long as Midtown was allowed a corresponding interest deduction. In addition, the court found the five-percent interest rate reasonable under the section 482 regulations. *Id.* at 1154–55. Thus, the Court of Appeals reversed the Tax Court and upheld the IRS's determination, finding five-percent interest "eminently reasonable." *Id.* at 1157.

In contrast to *B. Forman Company, Inc.*, *Achiro v. Commissioner*, 77 T.C. 881 (1981), provides an example of the limits on the application of section 482. That case involved several corporations owned by a group of individuals. Silvano Achiro (Achiro) and Peter Rossi (Rossi) each owned half the stock of Tahoe City Disposal Co. (Tahoe City), a company that managed landfills. In 1973, Achiro and Rossi joined Hubert Knoll (Knoll) in a waste collection business, Kings Beach Disposal Co. (Kings Beach). Achiro and Rossi each obtained a 25-percent interest in the business, and Knoll's son-in-law, Bud Schaffer, obtained the remaining 50-percent interest. *Id.* at 883. Achiro and Rossi each received salaries from both Kings Beach and Tahoe City. *Id.* at 884.

In 1974, Achiro, Rossi, Achiro's wife, and Achiro's brother organized A&R Enterprises, Inc. (A&R). Achiro's brother, Renato, received 52 percent of the stock and Achiro and Rossi each received 24 percent. One of A&R's purposes was to provide management, consulting, and advisory services. A&R entered into agreements for management services with Tahoe City and Kings Beach. In exchange for the management services, the disposal companies agreed to pay A&R a management fee and reimburse all direct costs and expenses incurred in the performance of the contracts. A&R executed employment contracts with Achiro and Rossi, and each received a salary and an annual bonus, and a death benefit plan and wage continuation plan. *Id.* at 884–86.

In 1974, A&R adopted a profit-sharing plan and an employees' pension plan. In 1975, Tahoe City and Kings Beach also adopted profit-sharing plans. The Tax Court found that Achiro and Rossi's principal purpose in forming A&R and distributing 52 percent of its stock to Renato was to obtain the benefits of larger contributions to A&R's pension and profit sharing plans. *Id.* at 886–88.

The IRS sent Achiro and Rossi notices of deficiency, adjusting the income of Tahoe City by disallowing as deductions the management fees paid to A&R. At trial, the IRS asserted that all of the income and deductions of A&R should be allocated to Tahoe City and Kings Beach under section 482, among other provisions. *Id.* at 888–89. The Tax Court recognized that the IRS can utilize section 482 to insure that the charges among the controlled entities represent arm's-length amounts. However, the court found that, instead of doing so, the IRS allocated all of A&R's income and deductions to Tahoe City and Kings Beach Disposal. The court found that the evidence presented showed that A&R received the arm's-length value of the services rendered under its contract with Tahoe City and Kings Beach. *Id.* at 897.

The court also found that the cases the IRS relied on did not support its position that without showing an arm's-length price for the services rendered, it may reallocate the entire price of such services from one corporation to another. *Id.* at 898. Accordingly, the court found that reallocating 100 percent of A&R's income was arbitrary and unreasonable. *Id.* at 900. In addition, the court disagreed with the IRS's position that incorporation for the principal purpose of taking advantage of corporate pension and profit-sharing plans amounts to an evasion or avoidance of income taxes, an unclear reflection of income, and/or an assignment of income. *See id.* at 895.

In a more recent case, *DHL Corp. v. Commissioner*, 285 F.3d 1210, 1213 (9th Cir. 2002), the tax years in issue were 1990-1992. One issue on appeal was the allocation under section 482 "to DHL of additional income arising from DHL's sale to Document Handling Limited, International ("DHLI") of the "DHL" trademark, which the tax court valued at $100 million . . . ." *Id.* at 1213.

Part of the background of the *DHL* case was that, in late 1989, a consortium consisting of Lufthansa; Japan Airlines Co., Ltd.; and Nissho Iwai Corp. (the Consortium) entered into an agreement with DHL Corporation (DHL), a domestic corporation, and Document Handling Limited, International (DHLI), a Hong Kong corporation, *id.*,

> under which the Consortium acquired (1) a 12.5% stock interest in DHLI/MNV, with an option to purchase an additional 45% interest based on a $450 million valuation of DHLI/MNV; (2) a 2.5% interest in DHL; and (3) an option to purchase the "DHL" trademark for $20 million, conditional upon the Consortium having first exercised its option to purchase the additional 45% interest. The trademark option provided that DHL could use the "DHL" trademark in the United States royalty-free for 15 years.

Id. at 1215. In 1992, the Consortium exercised the stock option, "reorganized the entity into DHL International Ltd., incorporated in Bermuda" and "caused this new entity to exercise its option to purchase the 'DHL' trademark rights for $20 million." *Id.*

The Court of Appeals agreed with the Tax Court "that the relevant time period for determining whether common control existed for purposes of § 482, given the particular business context here, is the period of negotiation and completion of the trademark option agreement between DHL, DHLI, and the Consortium. That is, the endpoint for the period over which there needed to be common control within the meaning of § 482 was the completion of the binding option agreement." *Id.* at 1217. It thus focused on a "transactional" approach rather than the point in time that the trademark option was actually exercised.

The Court of Appeals also found that the presence of a third-party such as the Consortium did not mean that the transaction necessarily was conducted at arm's-length. *Id.* The court further found that "the Consortium[] would be neither advantaged or disadvantaged by the income-shifting between DHL and DHLI, as long as the total price it paid for DHLI and the trademark rights remained the same." *Id.* at 1218. The court also noted that, "[w]ithout objection from the Consortium, the trademark price was reduced from $50 million in the initial agreement to $20 million in the final agreement." *Id.* at 1218. The Court of Appeals affirmed the Tax Court's determination that the arm's-length value of the DHL trademark was $100 million rather than the $20 million stated in the agreement. *Id.* However, the Court of Appeals reversed the Tax Court on the issue of its allocation to DHL of the portion of the $100 million attributable to foreign trademark rights, $50 million. *Id.* at 1220.

[c] Application of the Substantial Valuation Misstatement Penalty

Section 6662 provides a 20 percent penalty for a "substantial valuation misstatement," I.R.C. § 6662(a), (b)(3), defined, in part, as any situation in which:

> (i) the price for any property or services (or for the use of property) claimed on any such return in connection with any transaction between persons described in section 482 is 200 percent or more (or 50 percent or less) of the amount determined under section 482 to be the correct amount of such price, or

> (ii) the net section 482 transfer price adjustment for the taxable year exceeds the lesser of $5,000,000 or 10 percent of the taxpayer's gross receipts.

I.R.C. § 6662(e)(1)(B). The "net section 482 transfer price adjustment" is "the net increase in taxable income for the taxable year (determined without regard to any amount carried to such taxable year from another taxable year) resulting from adjustments under section 482 in the price for any property or services (or for the use of property)." I.R.C. § 6662(e)(3)(A). The penalty is increased to 40 percent for a "gross valuation misstatement." *See* I.R.C. § 6662(h).

An exception in section 6662 eliminates liability for the penalty if the portion of the underpayment attributable to substantial valuation misstatements is $10,000 or less ($5,000 or less for S corporations and personal holding companies). I.R.C. § 6662(e)(2). In addition, the "reasonable cause" exception of section 6664(c) is available, subject to a limitation. *See* I.R.C. § 6662(e)(3)(D).

[d] Advance Pricing Agreements

Given the fact-sensitive nature of 482 allocations, controversies over allocations can be lengthy and expensive. The taxpayer can face substantial penalties, as well, as discussed in § 14.06[B][2][c]. The IRS therefore has instituted a procedure for "advance pricing agreements" (APAs) in international transactions. *See* Rev. Proc. 2006-9, 2006-2 I.R.B. 278. "An APA is an agreement between a taxpayer and the [Internal Revenue] Service in which the parties set forth, in advance of controlled transactions, the best transfer pricing method ('TPM') within the meaning of § 482 of the Code and the regulations." *Id.* at § 2.04. "Under the APA request procedure, the taxpayer proposes a TPM and provides data intended to show that the TPM constitutes the appropriate application of the best method rule under the § 482 regulations. The Service, through an APA Team, evaluates the APA request by analyzing all relevant data and information submitted with the initial request and at any time thereafter." *Id.* at § 2.07.

As with a letter ruling request, payment of a user fee is required to obtain an APA. *See id.* at § 4.12 (providing a schedule of user fees ranging from $22,500 to $50,000). APAs themselves, applications for APAs, and background file information relating to APAs are defined as "return information" by section 6103(b)(2)(C) and therefore are subject to the confidentiality protections of section 6103.

Chapter 15

INTEGRATION OF CORPORATE AND SHAREHOLDER TAXES

§ 15.01   Introduction

The classical system for taxing corporations and their shareholders involves "double taxation" of corporate profits, once at the corporate level and again at the shareholder level, at least in theory. In practice,

> large amounts of economic income earned by corporations is not subject to any tax at the corporate level, due to corporate tax preferences, corporate tax sheltering activity, and defects in the corporate tax accounting provisions in the Code. And the supposed second, shareholder-level tax may be either nonexistent or minimal (in the case of stock held by tax-exempt charitable organizations or tax-deferred pension funds, or by foreign persons who pay a reduced tax on dividends under tax treaties and generally pay no tax on their capital gains from stock sales) . . . ."

Robert Peroni, *Tax Reform Interrupted: The Chaotic State of Tax Policy in 2003*, 35 McGEORGE L. REV. 277, 285–86 (2004).

There are other regimes that are expressly designed not to impose double taxation on businesses. Subchapter S, discussed in Chapter 8, generally provides one level of tax because it is a pass-through paradigm under which the corporation generally is not taxed. Partnerships and entities taxed as partnerships, which are not a focus of this book, also experience pass-through taxation. In recent years, more entities with limited liability have obtained pass-through taxation, most notably the LLC, which, as discussed in Chapter 1, is generally taxed as a partnership under the Treasury's "check-the-box" regulations.[1]

In contrast to these pass-through regimes, which "integrate" entity-level and investor-level taxation, double taxation of corporate profits may give rise to a number of economic distortions. The Treasury Department and tax scholars have identified the following principal possible distortions of the classical double tax system:[2]

---

[1] *See* § 1.02[A][2].

[2] *See, e.g., Eliminate the Double Taxation of Corporate Earnings* 1 (2003), *available at* www.ustreas.gov/press/releases/docs/bluebook.pdf; *Integration of the Individual and Corporate Tax Systems, Taxing Business Income Once* 3 (4 DTR G-2 Sp. Supp., 1/7/92), *available at* www.ustreas.gov/offices/tax-policy/library/integration-paper/; John Livingston, *Corporate Tax Integration in the United States: A Review of the Treasury's Integration Study*, 58 Mo. L. REV. 717, 720 (1993).

(1) It encourages investment in non-corporate form rather than the corporate form because investing in a form of business entity subject to pass-through taxation eliminates double taxation. Another way of looking at this is that the classical tax system decreases "horizontal equity" because, under the classical system, an individual who invests in stock will effectively be taxed at a higher rate (because of double taxation) than a similarly situated individual who invests in another asset.

(2) It may encourage corporations to retain earnings rather than distribute them.[3] Without a distribution to shareholders, the shareholder level of tax generally will not apply, except with respect to gains on sales or exchanges of shares, which typically will be taxed at capital gains rates.

(3) It encourages the financing of corporate investments with debt rather than equity. As discussed in Chapter 3, the income tax system generally favors debt financing over equity financing because interest is deductible and dividends are not. Similarly, it may provide an incentive for corporations to disguise distributions as deductible payments of salary or rent.[4]

(4) It may encourage corporations to distribute profits through share repurchases (redemptions of stock) because redemptions can be structured so as to qualify for "exchange" treatment under section 302, resulting in the taxation of gains at capital gains rates, as discussed in Chapter 5.

(5) "[D]ouble taxation increases incentives for corporations to engage in transactions for the sole purpose of minimizing their tax liability." *Eliminate the Double Taxation of Corporate Earnings* 1 (2003), *available at* www.ustreas.gov/press/releases/docs/bluebook.pdf (hereinafter, 2003 Treasury Release).

Some of these distortions have been questioned by scholars. For example, with respect to the incentive to retain earnings, the "new" view of dividends is that mature corporations pay the same amount as dividends that they would pay if the corporate-level and shareholder-tax were integrated. *Integration of the Individual and Corporate Tax Systems, Taxing Business Income Once* 116–17 (4 DTR G-2 Sp. Supp., 1/7/92), *available at* www.ustreas.gov/offices/tax-policy/library/integration-paper/ (hereinafter, 1992 Treasury Report). Under that view, there is no distortion reflected in a corporation's decision whether to retain earnings.

In addition, with respect to the fourth distortion listed above, there are limits on corporations' ability to replace dividend distributions with redemptions of stock.

> [I]f a share repurchase is structured in the proportionate manner characteristic of dividends it may be treated as "essentially equivalent to a dividend" for tax purposes. Thus, share repurchases have to be structured differently than dividends and empirical studies

---

[3] However, the accumulated earnings tax, discussed in § 14.02 of Chapter 14, can apply to accumulations beyond reasonable business needs.

[4] *See* § 1.02[D] of Chapter 1.

confirm that share repurchases are used differently than dividends. While dividends tend to be regular and flat, share repurchases tend to be large and transitory.

Steven A. Bank, *Is Double Taxation a Scapegoat for Declining Dividends? Evidence from History*, 56 TAX L. REV. 463, 520 (2003) (footnotes omitted). If corporations do not alter their distribution practices to conform to the section 302 provisions that generally treat substantially disproportionate redemptions as sales or exchanges of stock and dividend-equivalent redemptions as distributions, then the redemption possibility is not a source of economic distortion.

Finally, it may not be double taxation *per se* that encourages tax minimization by corporations. Many of the integration proposals discussed below, as well as the current system under which individuals' qualified dividends are taxed at preferential rates, provide shareholder-level relief from double taxation, rather than corporate-level relief. If corporate taxation is retained, corporations generally will continue to have an incentive to minimize their tax liabilities. However, the dividend exclusion proposals discussed in § 15.03[A] reduce that incentive by linking dividend exclusion to complete taxation at the corporate level.

§ 15.02   The Current System of Partial Integration

As discussed below, in 2003, President Bush proposed a dividend exclusion system for Subchapter C corporations, but it was not enacted. Instead, in the Jobs and Growth Tax and Reconciliation Act of 2003, the relevant part of which is scheduled to sunset on December 31, 2008, Congress opted to treat individuals' "qualified dividend income" as "adjusted net capital gain," which subjects it to tax at a maximum rate of 15 percent.[5] *See* I.R.C. § 1(h)(3)(B), (11). The 15 percent rate is reduced to 5 percent (0 percent for tax years after 2007, until the provision sunsets) for adjusted net capital gain that would not otherwise benefit from a rate reduction. *See* I.R.C. § 1(h)(1)(B).

In general, dividends from domestic corporations and "qualified foreign corporations," as defined in section 1(h)(11)(C) are qualified dividends. I.R.C. § 1(h)(11)(B)(i). However, certain dividends, such as those from organizations exempt from tax under section 501, do not qualify. *See* I.R.C. § 1(h)(11)(B)(ii). In addition, the taxpayer must have held the stock for 60 days during a 121-day period (90 days during a 181-day period for certain preferred stock dividends) for the dividend to qualify. Dividends also are not treated as qualified dividends "to the extent that the taxpayer is under an obligation (whether pursuant to a short sale or otherwise) to make related payments with respect to positions in substantially similar or related property." I.R.C. § 1(h)(11)(B)(iii)(II). Furthermore, amounts the

---

[5] Corporations do not benefit from this reduced rate on dividends, but they do benefit from a dividends received deduction. *See* I.R.C. § 243. The dividends received deduction and the limitations on it are discussed in § 4.04 of Chapter 4.

taxpayers treats as investment income for purposes of the section 163(d) limitation on investment interest are not treated as qualified dividends. I.R.C. § 1(h)(11)(D).

The current system is one of partial integration. *See* Reuven S. Avi-Yonah, *Corporations, Society, and the State: A Defense of the Corporate Tax*, 90 VA. L. REV. 1193, 1253 (2004). Another example of partial integration would be a system under which corporate income was taxed in full but only 50 percent of dividends received were taxed. Taxing individuals' dividends at a maximum rate of 15 percent is equivalent to taxing only a fraction of dividends but at the same rate as other income. For example, if a (hypothetical) tax rate of 30 percent were to apply to Taxpayer A's last dollars of income, applying a tax rate of 15 percent to her dividends received is the functional equivalent to taxing 50 percent of those dividends at a 30 percent rate.

The current system reduces some distortions of the classical system and alters some of the incentives of corporations and their shareholders. Consider a corporation owned entirely by individuals. Under prior law, the corporation would have an incentive to structure distributions as interest payments (or disguise them as other deductible payments) because, unlike dividends, they would be deductible at the corporate level, and distributions of either type would be taxed to individual shareholders as ordinary income. Under current law, with qualified dividends taxed to individuals at reduced rates, whether the aggregate tax due is less for a dividend or an interest payment depends on the marginal tax rates applicable to the corporation and its shareholders.

Example 15.1: X Corporation is taxed at a marginal rate of 35%. It transfers $1,000 to its sole shareholder, Alice. Assume that Alice's top marginal rate is 33%. In that case, if the $1,000 is an interest payment, X Corporation saves $350 in taxes and Alice owes $330, a net tax savings of $20. By contrast, if the $1,000 is a dividend, X Corporation gets no deduction and Alice owes $150 (15% of $1,000). On these facts, the dividend distribution bears more tax.

If, by contrast, X Corporation is taxed at a marginal rate of 15% and Alice's top marginal rate is 35%, if the $1,000 is an interest payment, X Corporation saves $150 in taxes and Alice owes $350, a net amount owed of $200. If the $1,000 is a dividend in this scenario, X Corporation gets no deduction and Alice owes $150. On these facts, the interest payment bears more tax.

The second scenario in Example 15.1 is an extreme case in that it uses the lowest marginal corporate rate and the highest marginal individual rate for 2005. Keep in mind, however, that, as under prior law, other scenarios exist that provide an incentive for the payment of dividends. For example, corporate shareholders benefit from a dividends received deduction that reduces or eliminates the tax they pay on dividends. *See* I.R.C. § 243. In addition, distributions to shareholders that exceed earnings and profits are not technically dividends. They are treated first as returns of capital, which are tax-free, and then as capital gain. *See* I.R.C. § 301(c)(2), (3).

Example 15.1 also suggests the changed dynamics individual investors have when considering whether to invest in corporate or non-corporate form; the corporate form bears less federal income tax cost than it did before the Jobs and Growth Tax and Reconciliation Act of 2003 was enacted. Similarly, dividend distributions are less costly for individual shareholders than they used to be. However, the reduced rate on individuals' dividends does not reduce *corporate-level* taxes, so it does not reduce the incentive to try to shelter corporate income. "Indeed, if the corporate tax can be eliminated by self-help (by tax shelters or tax competition [for multinational enterprises]), it is now possible for a corporate investment to be taxed at a total rate of 15%—significantly lower than non-corporate investment." Avi-Yonah, *supra*, at 1253.

§ 15.03   Major Integration Proposals

Over the years, a number of proposals have been made to integrate corporate and shareholder taxation. In its 1992 report, the Treasury Department identified and focused its discussion on four "prototypes" for integration of corporate-level and shareholder-level taxes: "dividend exclusion," "shareholder allocation," the Comprehensive Business Income Tax (CBIT), and "imputation credit." The Treasury Department's 1992 report also briefly discussed a "dividend deduction system." 1992 Treasury Report, *supra*, at 15.

In 1993, the American Law Institute (ALI) released a report, as well. *See Integration of the Individual and Corporate Income Taxes: Reporter's Study of Corporate Tax Integration* (ALI, 1993) (Alvin C. Warren, Jr., reporter) (hereinafter, ALI Study). More recently, in 2003, President George W. Bush advanced a proposal that is similar to one of the paradigms discussed in the Treasury's 1992 report. This section briefly surveys the principal integration paradigms reported on by the Treasury Department and the ALI in the early 1990s, as well as President Bush's 2003 proposal.[6]

---

[6] There have been a number of other proposals, as well. *See, e.g.*, Joseph M. Dodge, *A Combined Mark-to-Market and Pass-Through Corporate-Shareholder Integration Proposal*, 50 TAX L. REV. 265, 266–67 (1995) (proposing replacement of the tax on corporations with two-tier integration composed of (1) annual taxation of the increases in value (and deduction of declines in value) of publicly traded stock, and (2) pass-through taxation for holders of stock that is not publicly traded); Katherine Pratt, *The Debt-Equity Distinction in a Second-Best World*, 53 VAND. L. REV. 1055, 1158 (2000) (suggesting the possibility of combining a percentage limitation on the corporate interest deduction with a limited dividend exclusion for shareholders); *see also* Joseph Bankman, *A Market-Value Based Corporate Income Tax*, 68 TAX NOTES 1347 (1995) (proposing to replace the corporate tax on publicly traded corporations with a tax on the change in market value of the corporation's stock); Michael S. Knoll, *An Accretion Corporate Income Tax*, 49 STAN. L. REV. 1, 1 (1996) (similarly proposing to replace the corporate-level tax with a tax on the change in market value of the corporation's outstanding securities).

Although the pass-through paradigms mentioned above and the current system of partial integration may suggest that corporate integration is as simple as removing or reducing corporate-level or shareholder-level taxation, any such change would likely have a number of collateral consequences and could facilitate tax avoidance, possibly reducing a single-level tax to no tax at all. Therefore, each proposal discussed below is fairly complex. Only the major aspects of each proposal are discussed, with an emphasis on the basics of each system with respect to corporate and individual shareholders.[7]

[A] Dividend Exclusion Methods

Dividend exclusion methods provide shareholder-level relief from double taxation of distributed profits. The 1992 Treasury proposal and Bush's 2003 proposal are discussed, in turn, below.

[1] Treasury's Dividend Exclusion Prototype

Generally speaking, under the Treasury's dividend exclusion method, corporate taxes would be unchanged. However, shareholders who held stock for 45 days or more would exclude from their gross income dividends out of income that had been fully taxed at the corporate level, as discussed below. Dividend status would be determined as under current law, reflecting the amount of corporate earnings and profits. The taxation of all other distributions would be unchanged. Corporations would continue to pay income tax under applicable statutes, and the same tax rate would apply to both distributed and retained income. *See* 1992 Treasury Report, *supra*, at 17, 21; Livingston, *supra*, at 722.

To implement a dividend exclusion system, corporations would have to maintain an "Excludable Dividends Account" (EDA). The EDA would track corporate income on which corporate taxes have been paid. At a 35 percent corporate tax rate, for example, the corporation would convert the amount of tax shown on its return filed during the previous year into the amount of income that, if taxed at a 35 percent rate, would yield that amount of tax. The amount of federal income tax paid would then be subtracted to determine the EDA. 1992 Treasury Report, *supra*, at 19.

> *Example 15.2*: Y Corporation paid $350 of federal income taxable on its return filed in Year 1. Assuming no other relevant events occurred, its EDA for Year 2 is $650: $1,000 (the amount of income that would result in $350 of tax at a 35% rate) − $350 (federal income tax paid).

Thus, at a corporate tax rate of 35 percent, for each $35 of taxes paid by a corporation, $65 would be added to the EDA. A corporation's EDA would also increase when it received excludable dividends from other corporations. It would decrease when a corporation paid dividends or received a tax refund. 1992 Treasury Report, *supra*, at 20.

---

[7] Tax-exempt and foreign investors raise special issues under integration proposals, but those issues generally are not discussed here.

Dividends received by shareholders would only be excludible to the extent of the corporation's EDA. If the EDA were reduced to zero, subsequent dividends would become includable in the shareholder's gross income. This would ensure that dividends paid out of untaxed income, because of corporate tax preferences, for example, would not escape all levels of tax. 1992 Treasury Report, *supra*, at 20; Livingston, *supra*, at 722–23.

> *Example 15.3*: Z Corporation is wholly owned by Bob, who has held his shares for several years. Z Corporation has an EDA balance of $10. It distributes to Bob a $15 dividend. Bob would include $5 income ($15 minus the $10 excludible amount).

The dividend exclusion system would eliminate much of the tax bias against the corporate form by taxing distributed corporate income only once (though at corporate rates). Dividend exclusion would reduce the incentive for corporations to retain earnings because distributions of dividend up to the amount of the corporation's EDA would not be taxed to shareholders. *See* Livingston, *supra*, at 723–24. In fact, dividend exclusion might encourage corporations to distribute earnings up to the excludible limit. 1992 Treasury Report, *supra*, at 27.

The dividend exclusion system would also reduce the tax incentive for corporations to issue debt rather than equity because interest and dividends would each be taxed only once. It would not eliminate the different tax treatment of debt and equity, however, because interest payments would give rise to a corporate-level tax deduction and thus be taxed at the recipient's tax rate whereas dividend distributions out of previously taxed corporate income would be excluded by shareholders and thus bear taxation at corporate rates. *See id.* at 18.

The Treasury Department favored the dividend exclusion system for its "simplicity and relative ease of implementation." *Id.* at 17. In December of 1992, the Treasury Department made a specific proposal for a dividend exclusion method of integration. *See A Recommendation for Integration of the Individual and Corporate Tax Systems* (Dec. 1992), *available at* www.treas.gov/offices/tax-policy/library/integration-paper/recommendation-for-integration.pdf. The proposed system was similar to the dividend exclusion prototype discussed in the 1992 Treasury Report. *Id.* at 3–4.

[2]   President George W. Bush's 2003 Proposal

In 2003, President George W. Bush proposed a dividends exclusion method of integration. The Bush proposal, like the Treasury's dividend exclusion prototype discussed above, would require corporations to maintain an EDA (Excludible Dividends Account). Under the proposal, a corporation's EDA would reflect corporate income that was fully taxed at a rate of 35 percent, the maximum corporate tax rate in 2003. *See Treasury Releases Details of the President's Dividend Exclusion Proposal*, KD-3781 (Jan. 21, 2003), *available at* www.ustreas.gov/press/releases/kd3781.htm; 2003 Treasury

Release, *supra*, at 2. As under the Treasury's dividend exclusion prototype, that would mean that, at a corporate tax rate of 35 percent, for each $35 of taxes paid by a corporation, $65 would be added to the EDA. *Id.* at 2, 3.

Under President Bush's proposal, if the corporation's excludible dividend distributions did not exceed EDA, it could use EDA to increase common stockholders' stock bases. These "retained earnings basis adjustments" (REBAs) would not be taxable but would reduce both EDA and the corporation's earnings and profits. The proposal also included stock holding period requirements similar to the provisions applicable to the dividends received deduction under section 246(c) (which is discussed in Chapter 4). *Id.* at 4, 9.

Under the proposal, if a corporation's distributions exceeded EDA, they would be treated first as a return of capital and then as capital gain to the extent of the aggregate of all REBAs for prior years. Additional excess amounts would be taxed as dividends to the extent of the corporation's earnings and profits. Further excess amounts would be treated as a return of capital to the extent of any basis remaining in the shareholder's stock, and, finally, as capital gain.[8] *Id.* at 5.

Corporate shareholders would be eligible to receive excludible dividends. The 100 percent dividends received deduction of section 243 would be retained but the 70 and 80 percent dividends received deductions that exist for lower levels of stock ownership would be retained only for certain distributions and only until January 1, 2006. *Id.* at 10. Corporate shareholders that received excludible dividends would also have to make certain adjustments to EDA. First, the corporation would add to EDA excludible dividends received during the prior year so as to avoid more than one level of tax on corporate income. Second, it would add to EDA REBAs for the prior year with respect to the stock it owns. *Id.* at 3–4.

This system would mitigate the principal economic distortions of the classical system in the same way the Treasury's dividend's exclusion system would. That is, it would reduce the biases against the corporate form and in favor of debt financing and would eliminate the bias in favor of retaining earnings, replacing it with an incentive to distribute earnings up to the excludible limit. The Treasury Department also noted, in its 2003 Release, that this type of dividend exclusion system would reduce the incentive for corporate tax-minimization techniques because shareholders would only be able to exclude dividends paid out of income that was fully taxed at the corporate level. *Id.* at 1–2. Note that the current system, discussed in § 15.02, does not premise the reduced rate applicable to qualified dividends received by individuals on full (or any) taxation at the corporate level.

---

[8] For further reading on the Bush proposal, see Calvin H. Johnson, *The Bush 35 Percent Flat Tax on Distributions from Public Corporations*, 98 TAX NOTES 1881 (2003).

[B] Treasury's Comprehensive Business Income Tax System

Treasury's Comprehensive Business Income Tax (CBIT) prototype is a more complex version of the dividend exclusion prototype discussed above. CBIT would tax all businesses (except very small ones), regardless of form, at the entity level, but at a tax rate equal to the top individual rate. In other words, even partnerships and sole proprietorships would pay an entity-level tax under CBIT. In addition, because of entity-level taxation, CBIT would apply to amounts paid out as dividends or interest paid to tax-exempt entities and foreign investors not otherwise subject to federal income tax. 1992 Treasury Report, *supra*, at 39–41.

Under CBIT, no deduction would be allowed for interest or dividends paid. However, under CBIT, both dividends and interest paid out of earnings taxed at the level of the business would be exempt from investor-level taxation. Entity-level losses would not pass through to the equity holders. *Id.* at 39–40.

Example 15.4: Caramel Corporation earns $1,000 of taxable profits during Year 1. It distributes $200 to its shareholders that year and $300 of interest to its bondholders. Dana, one of the shareholders, receives a $10 dividend. Edgar, a bondholder, receives $20 in interest. Caramel Corporation would pay CBIT on the $1,000. (In fact, CBIT would be due even if Caramel were an unincorporated business.) Dana would exclude the $10 from gross income, and Edgar would exclude the $20 from gross income.

CBIT would tax corporate and non-corporate entities alike, so it would eliminate any federal income tax bias against the corporate form. It would also treat debt and equity alike, removing the favoritism for debt financing. CBIT would also eliminate any federal income tax incentive to retain earnings because dividends would be excludible by shareholders, unless an additional tax were imposed on distributions of amounts that had been preferentially taxed at the entity level. 1992 Treasury Report, *supra*, at 39, 40. Note that without such a tax on "preference income," CBIT would not reduce a corporation's incentive to shelter income.

CBIT would be a dramatic departure from the current system, particularly because, unlike most other forms of integration, it would apply to non-corporate entities. A shift to any form of corporate integration would likely occasion transition gains and losses by affecting the value of corporate stock, for example. CBIT would also change the tax treatment of debt and might therefore affect the value of debt securities. 1992 Treasury Report, *supra*, at 89, 91. The Treasury Report recommended further study of the CBIT regime and discussed the possibility of phasing in CBIT over a period of about ten years. *Id.* at 15, 39.

[C] Treasury's Shareholder Allocation Prototype

The Treasury Department's shareholder allocation prototype initially seems similar to the current system under Subchapter S because corporations would allocate their income among all of its shareholders as it is earned. However, losses would not flow through to shareholders, and the corporate-level tax would be retained. In addition, the corporation would still be treated as a separate entity for many reporting purposes. 1992 Treasury Report, *supra*, at 27; Livingston, *supra* at 724–25. This structure was designed to "enhance compliance and mitigate shareholder cash flow problems." 1992 Treasury Report, *supra*, at 27.

Under Treasury's shareholder allocation system, corporations would be required to report only aggregate income amounts, rather than reporting items separately. Shareholders would include allocated corporate income in their gross income and reduce their corresponding tax liability with credits derived from allocated portions of corporate taxes paid. The credits would be nonrefundable but they could be used against other federal income tax liability. *Id.* at 27–28. This would result in taxation at individual rates for "nonpreference, U.S. source income received by individuals," assuming that shareholders in lower brackets have other tax liabilities against which to offset the excess credits. *Id.* at 29.

Shareholders' stock bases would in turn be increased by the allocated income, less corporate taxes paid and corporate tax credits. Distributions to shareholders would be treated first as a return of capital up to their stock basis, and then as capital gain. *Id.* at 28.

Example 15.5: Fin Corp. earns $1,000 of taxable profits during Year 1. Fin Corp. would pay tax on the $1,000. Assuming that the rate of tax were 35%, Fin Corp. would pay $350 of tax. The $1,000 would also be included in shareholders' income. Assume that Gil is a five-percent shareholder of Fin Corp. As a five-percent shareholder, Gil would have $50 of gross income. If the tax rate applicable to Gil were 30%, the tax liability on that income would be $15. Gil would also be entitled to a $17.50 credit for corporate taxes paid (5% of $350). That would reduce his net tax on the dividend to zero and provide him with a $2.50 credit to use against other income tax liability, if any.

Assume that Gil has a $100 basis in his Fin Corp. stock. Also assume that he receives a $10 distribution during Year 2. Gil would have no gross income with respect to the $10 distribution. He would increase his $100 basis in his Fin Corp. shares by $32.50 (5% of $650) and decrease it by the $10 distribution. Thus, his stock basis would be $122.50.

Note that, in Example 15.5, if Gil is able to use the excess $2.50 credit to offset unrelated tax liabilities, the $50 of corporate profits allocated to him effectively would bear $15 of tax ($17.50 paid by the corporation, reduced by the $2.50 Gil used to reduce his other tax liabilities), which, not coincidentally, is Gil's 30 percent rate. On the other hand, if Gil were unable to use any of the $2.50, the $50 would bear tax at the corporation's 35 percent rate.

The shareholder allocation system would reduce the tax bias against the corporate form. In addition, under this system, retained earnings and

distributed earnings receive equal tax treatment. The shareholder allocation approach also reduces the incentive for corporations to prefer debt over
equity because dividend distributions would be taxed only once. *See id.*
However, the interest deduction would be retained, so amounts paid as
interest to tax-exempt and foreign investors would escape federal income
tax. *Id.* at 27 n.3.

The Treasury Department did not recommend adoption of the shareholder allocation system because of its administrative complexity and
certain policy problems. One important policy consideration is that, in order
for retained earnings and distributed earnings to receive equal tax treatment, the shareholder allocation system would require that the benefit of
preferential tax treatment at the corporate level pass through to shareholders. Extending corporate-level tax preferences to shareholders would raise
the cost of those preferences. *Id.* at 27, 30. In addition, the shareholder
allocation system would exempt from taxation foreign-source income, which
the Treasury Report found would more appropriately be addressed in
bilateral tax treaty negotiations. *Id.* at 27, 36.

[D]   Treasury's Imputation Credit Prototype

In a Part entitled "Roads not Taken," the 1992 Treasury Report included
a discussion of a shareholder imputation credit prototype that "closely
resembles the system that New Zealand adopted in 1988." 1992 Treasury
Report, *supra*, at 95. Imputation credit systems remain popular in other
countries, including many European countries. *See* HUGH J. AULT & BRIAN
J. ARNOLD, COMPARATIVE INCOME TAXATION 327 (2004).

Under the shareholder imputation credit system, corporations would
continue to pay tax at applicable rates. Every corporation would maintain
an account of its cumulative federal income taxes paid. Livingston, *supra*,
at 727–28. The Treasury Report terms this account a "Shareholder Credit
Account" (SCA). The SCA balance would serve as a limitation on the
amount that the corporation could use to "frank" dividends (attach a credit
to dividends). 1992 Treasury Report, *supra*, at 99.

Under this system, a shareholder that received a dividend would include
in gross income the amount of the dividend grossed up for an "imputation
credit" reflecting the tax paid by the corporation with respect to the
dividend. The shareholder would also receive a nonrefundable credit for the
tax paid by the corporation. This approach would eliminate the effect of
the corporate-level tax if the shareholder's tax rate is at least as high as
the corporate rate. However, the Treasury Report recommended allowing
the shareholder credit at the maximum individual rate of 31 percent, which
was lower than the maximum corporate rate at the time (which was 34
percent). Accordingly, a corporation's addition to its SCA for taxes paid
would not be the actual tax paid but the amount that would produce the
corporation's after-tax income at a tax rate of 31 percent. In addition, the
amount used to frank dividends would not be allowed to exceed the
grossed-up dividend amount, computed at a 31 percent rate. *Id.* at 95, 99.

Example 15.6:[9] High, Inc. earns $1,000 of taxable profits during Year 1 and pays tax on the $1,000. Assume that the tax rate was 34%, so the tax was $340. High, Inc. would have $660 after tax and would add $296.52 to its SCA—the amount of tax required to gross up $660 at a 31% rate ($660 + $296.52 = $956.52 x .31 = $296.52).

Assume that High, Inc. distributes a $33 dividend to its shareholder, Ian. The maximum credit High, Inc. could attach to that dividend is $14.83, the amount required to gross up the dividend at a 31% tax rate. Assume that it did so. That $14.83 credit would reduce High, Inc.'s SCA. Ian would include $47.83 in gross income ($33 + $14.83). Ian would receive a $14.83 credit for corporate-level tax paid. If Ian were in the 31% bracket, Ian would compute $14.83 of tax on the dividend, which he would offset with the $14.83 credit, reducing his net tax on the dividend to zero.

Note that, in Example 15.6, the corporation paid tax at a rate higher than that paid by the individual shareholder and the individual's rate was the 31 percent rate used to compute the gross-up. As a result, the amounts paid as dividends will effectively be taxed at the corporate rate (34 percent in the example). The same would be true for dividends paid to shareholders in lower brackets who are unable to use any excess credits to offset other tax liabilities. However, amounts paid as dividends to shareholders in brackets below 31 percent who are able to use excess credits to offset other tax liabilities will effectively reduce the rate applied to those dividends, though not as low as the individual rate, so long as the corporate rate exceeds the individual rate. *See id.* at 96.

For example, if the tax rate applicable to the $47.83 taxed to Ian in Example 15.6 were only 15 percent, Ian would compute $7.17 of tax on the dividend, which he would offset with the $14.83 credit, leaving him with a $7.66 credit to use against other tax, if any. If Ian were able to use some or all of the $7.66 credit against other tax liabilities, the effect would be to reduce the taxation of the $33 dividend paid to him, but it would not bring the rate on that dividend down to Ian's 15 percent tax rate or below.[10] *Id.* at 101.

Under the Treasury's imputation credit prototype, corporate shareholders would benefit from a 100 percent dividends received deduction on all dividends received. A corporation receiving a dividend would also add to its SCA the amount of any credit attached to the dividend. *Id.* at 95.

---

[9] This example is drawn from the 1992 Treasury Report at 99–100.

[10] If, unlike in Example 15.6, the corporation had paid tax at a rate lower than 34 percent (because it paid alternative minimum tax rather than regular tax, for example), the amount added to the SCA would be reduced to reflect the difference between corporate and shareholder tax rates. For example, if the corporation paid tax at a 20 percent rate, so that its tax on $1,000 were only $200, only $174.43 would be added to the SCA. *Id.* at 101 n.25. What that amount reflects is first, a calculation of how much income would yield $200 of tax at a 34 percent tax rate. That amount is $588.24. (This step was not necessary in Example 15.6 because the corporation had paid tax on its income at the full corporate rate of 34 percent.) In this scenario, taxes paid were $200, so the amount deemed available for distribution is $388.24 ($588.24 – $200). When that amount is grossed up at a 31 percent rate, the amount of the gross-up is $174.43 ($388.24 + $174.43 = $562.67 * .31 = $174.43).

By preserving corporate-level taxation, the imputation credit system would reduce but not eliminate the bias against the corporate form if corporate tax rates were higher than individual rates. Similarly, the imputation credit system would also reduce but not eliminate the tax bias against equity because interest and dividends would each be taxed only once but interest payments and not dividends would be deductible by the corporation. The system would eliminate the incentive for corporations to retain earnings. *Id.* at 96. The Treasury Department did not recommend the imputation credit approach in its 1992 Report, but the ALI Study, discussed immediately below, recommended a variation of this proposal.

[E] The American Law Institute's Shareholder Credit Proposal

Under the ALI's shareholder credit method proposal, every corporation would maintain a taxes-paid account (TPA). The initial balance of the TPA would be zero, and the account would increase for income taxes paid by the corporation, and decrease for refunds of corporate taxes. A dividend withholding tax (DWT) would be imposed on all dividends, possibly at a rate equal to the highest individual tax rate. If a corporation's TPA had a positive balance, a corporation would "pay" the DWT by simply reducing its TPA. After the TPA reached zero, additional dividends would require the DWT to be paid in cash to the government. Amounts actually paid by the corporation to the government as a DWT would be creditable against future corporate tax liability. This would create a carryforward, and would be subject to limits like those of section 382, discussed in Chapter 13, in the case of a corporate ownership change. ALI Study, *supra*, at 13.

In general, non-corporate shareholders would include in gross income the full amount of any dividend received (grossed up for the DWT) and would receive a refundable tax credit in the amount of the DWT. The proposal also included an Exempt Income Account to track tax-exempt income received by the corporation. That account could be drawn on for excludible dividends when a corporation's TPA reached zero. *Id.* at 13–14.

Example 15.7: Jaye, Inc. earns $1,000 of taxable profits during Year 1 and pays DWT on the $1,000. Assume that the corporate tax rate, which is also the highest individual tax rate, is 35%. That rate would be applied to Jaye, Inc., so the tax would be $350. The $350 tax payment would increase Jaye, Inc.'s TPA from zero to $350. During Year 1, Jaye, Inc. declares a gross dividend of $100. $35 of DWT would be due and could entirely be funded from Jaye, Inc.'s TPA, reducing the TPA to $315. The $35 of DWT also reduces the actual distributed amount to $65.

Assume that Kate, one of the shareholders, receives a $6.50 dividend from Jaye, Inc. Kate's dividend, grossed up for the 35-percent tax, is $10. She would compute the tax on $10 at the tax rate applicable to her and reduce that by a $3.50 credit ($10 − $6.50). If the rate applicable to her dividend were 20%, Kate's tax on the dividend (before application of the credit) would be $2, resulting in a remaining refundable tax credit of $1.50. If Kate's tax rate were 35%, her $3.50 tax on the dividend would be reduced to zero by the credit.

Note that, under this approach, the corporate tax becomes a withholding mechanism similar to the mechanism used for withholding tax from employees' wages. *Id.* at 50. Shareholder taxation is thus primary. *See* Michael L. Schler, *Taxing Corporate Income Once (or Hopefully Not at All): A Practitioner's Comparison of the Treasury and ALI Integration Models*, 47 TAX L. REV. 509, 519 (1992).

Under the ALI proposal, corporate shareholders generally would treat dividends the same way as non-corporate shareholders, and would increase their TPA accounts accordingly. However, an electing domestic corporation that owned more than 20 percent of the distributing corporation would exclude from gross income any dividend paid when the TPA balance of the distributing corporation is zero. Dividends paid between corporations filing consolidated returns would not be taxed. ALI Study, *supra*, at 17–18.

A corporation could elect to declare a constructive dividend of any amount. The constructive dividend would be subject to DWT just as an actual dividend would be. Because there would be no actual distribution, however, the amount of the constructive dividend, net of DWT, would, in turn, be treated as a reinvestment by shareholders in the corporation. If the TPA were later reduced to zero, any actual distributions that did not exceed these deemed contributions to the capital of the corporation would be treated as tax-free returns of shareholder capital (which would reduce shareholders' bases).[11] *Id.* at 15.

The proposal would tax shareholder gains from selling their stock at ordinary income rates. *Id.* at 16. Losses realized on the sale of stock would be recognized to the extent of the sum of (1) capital gains from stock sales, (2) dividend income, and (3) the amount by which the losses exceed net unrealized gains on stock. This would loosen the current restrictions on deductibility of capital losses, essentially allowing them in full except to the extent that the investor may be selectively recognizing losses but not gains. *Id.* at 132. That is why stock losses would be deductible to the extent they *exceed* net unrealized stock gains.

The ALI's proposal would reduce the bias against the corporate form by providing for one level of taxation. If the DWT rate imposed were the highest individual rate, that would eliminate the bias against the corporate form for earnings that were distributed because the refundable credit would allow shareholders taxed in lower brackets to be taxed at their applicable rates, not the highest rate. This would also eliminate the incentive to retain earnings but would create an incentive to distribute earnings, particularly

---

[11] Note the similarity between the constructive dividend aspect of the ALI proposal and the "retained earnings basis adjustments" of President Bush's integration proposal, discussed in § 15.03[A][2].

to lower-taxed shareholders.[12] The ALI proposal would also equalize the taxation of debt and equity by imposing a withholding tax on corporate interest payments and a refundable credit for recipients of corporate interest. *Id.* at 5.

§ 15.04 Additional Corporate Integration Possibilities

[A] Dividends-Paid Deduction System

Under a dividends-paid deduction system, corporations reduce their taxable profits by (or take a deduction for) amounts distributed to shareholders. *See* Graeme S. Cooper, *The Return to Corporate Tax Evasion in the Presence of an Income Tax on Shareholders*, 12 AKRON TAX J. 1, 34 (1996). Shareholders would include dividends in gross income. In effect, corporations would pay tax only on retained earnings, and generally at a penalty rate. Razeen Sappideen, *Imputation of the Corporate and Personal Income Tax: Is It Chasing One's Tail?*, 15 AM. J. TAX POL'Y 167, 199 (1998).

> *Example 15.8*: Link Corp. earns $1,000 of taxable profits during Year 1. It distributes $200 to its shareholders that year. Martin, one of the shareholders, receives a $10 dividend. Link Corp. would pay tax on only $800 ($1,000 less a deduction for the $200 distributed as dividends). In effect, the corporation would not have paid tax with respect to the $200 distributed as dividends. If the rate of tax applicable to the $10 received by Martin were 30%, he would pay $3 of tax on the dividend.

This system is effectively a dual tax rate system under which the corporate rate applicable to distributed earnings is zero.[13] Cooper, *supra*, at 34. It would increase corporations' cash flow, but dividends paid to shareholders would decrease that benefit. ALI Study, *supra*, at 52. This type of system was used by the United States between 1936 and 1938, when it was repealed because of the business community's extreme dissatisfaction with it. Scott A. Taylor, *Corporate Integration in the Federal Income Tax: Lessons from the Past and a Proposal for the Future*, 10 VA. TAX REV. 237, 283–84 (1990).

This system would eliminate the bias against the corporate form by taxing distributions at shareholder rates. It would also eliminate the bias against retained earnings but replace it with a bias for distributing earnings particularly if corporate rates exceed individual rates. 1992 Treasury Report, *supra*, at 107. In fact, a dividends-paid deduction would create a bias in favor of distributing earnings even when the corporation might need to retain earnings for business needs. *See* Taylor, *supra*, at 284–85. The deduction for dividends paid would increase parity between debt and equity for corporations. However, it would not eliminate the

---

[12] In order to maintain a single level of tax on the investment of tax-exempt investors in corporations, the ALI proposal would impose a tax on the corporate investment income of tax-exempt entities, with a refundable credit for DWT. ALI Study, *supra*, at 163–64.

[13] Dual tax rate systems are discussed in § 15.04[B].

disparity because the deduction for dividends paid would be in the year paid, whereas corporations generally deduct interest when it accrues. 1992 Treasury Report, *supra*, at 107.

In its 1992 Report, the Treasury Department did not recommend adopting this approach for several reasons. First, it would eliminate the corporate-level tax even on amounts distributed to tax-exempt entities and foreign investors, resulting in no tax at either the corporate or shareholder level on these amounts. Second, it would create a bias in favor of distributing earnings, particularly when shareholder-level rates are lower than corporate-level rates. Third, if the system did not limit deductible dividends to those on which corporate tax has been paid, it would allow a deduction for dividends paid out of tax preference or foreign source income on which no federal income tax has been imposed. *Id.*

[B] Split-Rate Systems

Under a dual tax or "split-rate" system of corporate integration, corporations pay tax on their profits at two different rates. In general, they would pay a lower rate of tax on earnings distributed to shareholders as dividends than on retained earnings.[14] Cooper, *supra*, at 34. Shareholders would continue to include dividends in gross income. A split rate system in which the rate applicable to distributions is greater than zero is equivalent to a dividends-paid deduction regime under which the deduction for dividends paid is less than 100 percent.

Example 15.9: Nota Corp. earns $1,000 of taxable profits during Year 1. It distributes $200 to its shareholders that year. Nota Corp. would pay two different rates of tax on the $800 it retained and the $200 it distributed. Assume that the rate of tax applicable to retained earnings is 30% and the rate of tax applicable to distributed earnings is 20%. Nota Corp. would therefore pay $280 in tax for Year 1 ($240 + $40).[15] Assume that Olga, one of the shareholders, receives a $10 dividend. Olga would pay tax at the applicable individual rate. If that were 25%, she would pay $2.50 in tax on the $10 she received.

---

[14] As discussed in the 1992 Treasury Report, at the time of that report, Germany applied a tax rate of 50 percent to retained income and a tax rate of 36 percent to distributed income. 1992 Treasury Report, *supra*, at 172.

[15] Note that a split rate system in which the tax rate applicable to dividends is one-third lower than the rate applicable to retained earnings is equivalent to a dividends-paid deduction system under which only one-third of the dividend paid is deductible. In other words, an equivalent system would apply a 30 percent tax rate with a one-third deduction for dividends paid. Nota Corp. would have $1,000 of gross income and a $66.66 deduction for the $200 of dividends paid. The resulting taxable income of $933.34, taxed at a 30 percent rate, would yield $280 in tax.

Chapter 16

CORPORATE TAX SHELTERS

§ 16.01 Introduction

"We now know that by 1988 promoters such as Merrill Lynch, outfitted with tax opinions from leading law firms and aided by national accounting firms such as PricewaterhouseCoopers, already were out peddling a new form of tax shelter to some of the largest, wealthiest corporations in the United States—companies like Colgate-Palmolive, Winn-Dixie Stores, and Compaq Computer Corp. to name but a few." Sheldon D. Pollack & Jay A. Soled, *Tax Professionals Behaving Badly*, 105 TAX NOTES 201, 202 (2004). The Chief Counsel of the IRS has explained, "the widespread use of computers and the exotica of modern corporate finance coupled with the desire of the Big 6 public accounting firms, investment bankers and some law firms to generate revenues, not based on the traditional billable hours, but instead based on contingency or premium fees, has led to a new phenomenon, commonly called Corporate Tax Shelters." Donald L. Korb, *Schemes, Shelters and Abusive Transactions*, 2005 TNT 29-61 (Feb. 11, 2005). In 1999, both the Treasury Department and the Joint Committee on Taxation released reports on the corporate tax shelter issue.[1]

The term "corporate tax shelter" is applied to a wide variety of transactions that share as a goal the reduction of corporate tax liabilities, but there is no consensus on a definition of that term. *See* Deborah H. Schenk, *Symposium on Corporate Tax Shelters, Part I: Foreword*, 55 TAX L. REV. 125, 127 (2002). One egregious example is the complex transaction in *Long Term Capital Holdings v. United States*, 330 F. Supp. 2d 122, 127 (D. Conn. 2004), which involved a claim that stock was sold "with a tax basis one hundred times in excess of its fair market value." As Professor Alvin Warren describes it:

> The intended result of the convoluted transaction in *Long Term Capital Holdings* was the creation of an artificial loss of $400 million that was cloned, sold twice, and deducted by two different groups of U.S. taxpayers. . . . [It involved] dubious behavior by public companies (taking millions in artificial deductions), Nobel Laureates (taking the same deductions a second time), prominent

---

[1] Department of the Treasury, White Paper: *The Problem of Corporate Tax Shelters* (*Discussion, Analysis and Legislative Proposals*) (July 1999); Joint Committee on Taxation, *Study of Present-Law Penalty and Interest Provisions as Required by Section 3801 of the Internal Revenue Service Restructuring and Reform Act of 1998* (*including Provisions Relating to Corporate Tax Shelters*) (JCS-3-99) (July 22, 1999); *see also* Joint Committee on Taxation, *Comparison of Recommendations Relating to Corporate Tax Shelters Made by the Department of Treasury and the Staff of the Joint Committee on Taxation* (JCX-25-00) (Mar. 7, 2000).

law firms (providing opinions that the court found superficial and devoid of legal analysis), and major accounting firms (counseling taxpayers to hide the deductions on the tax return).

Alvin C. Warren, Jr., *Understanding Long Term Capital*, 106 TAX NOTES 681, 681 (2005). The District Court sustained the government's claim of a 40-percent valuation misstatement penalty, and, in the alternative, a 20-percent substantial understatement penalty. *Long Term Capital Holdings*, 330 F. Supp. 2d at 196.

Tax attorney Peter Canellos has distinguished between tax shelters and "real transactions," pointing out the following differences, among others:

> Real transactions, most obviously, have as their origins and purpose making money in the short-run or the long-run by increasing revenues or reducing (non-tax) expenses. . . . Taxes of course play a role in analyzing financings and other business transactions, but they do not provide the primary motivation for undertaking the transaction. Tax shelters by contrast exist principally to reduce taxes by generating tax benefits usually derived from losses or credits that reflect outlays, expenses, and negative economic items. *The equity investment in a real transaction is aimed at generating a sufficient economic return* to exceed, on a risk-adjusted basis, the entity's cost of capital. *The investment in a tax shelter is a fee paid for tax benefits.* The investor either expects to lose it or expects a return with an economic yield that is below market on a risk-adjusted basis. The economic return, if present, is often a carefully calibrated item designed to satisfy a perceived talismanic business purpose standard. The economic risk is likewise circumscribed so that, while predictable small losses may exist, large unpredictable losses do not.

Peter C. Canellos, *A Tax Practitioner's Perspective on Substance, Form and Business Purpose in Structuring Business Transactions and in Tax Shelters*, 54 SMU L. REV. 47, 52–53 (2001) (emphasis added) (footnote omitted).

Tax attorney David Hariton has provided the following bright line to distinguish between tax shelters and tax-minimization transactions that do not constitute tax shelters: Tax shelters shelter unrelated income, while business transactions, however aggressively structured, do not. David Hariton, *Kafka and the Tax Shelter*, 57 TAX L. REV. 1, 11 (2003). Under his analysis, the tax minimization transaction in *United Parcel Service of America Inc. v. Commissioner*, 254 F.3d 1014 (11th Cir. 2001), was not a tax shelter because UPS structured an existing parcel insurance business to minimize taxes but the "transaction did not give rise to any 'tax benefit'— such as a loss, deduction or credit—that could be used to offset the tax on unrelated income." *Id.* at 12. By contrast, the "CINS" transaction in *ACM Partnership v. Commissioner*, 157 F.3d 231 (3d Cir. 1998), discussed below, which generated a large loss to shelter unrelated capital gains, was a tax shelter. Hariton, *supra*, at 11. As Professor Mark Gergen has stated, "you can pick up tax gold if you find it in the street while going about your business, but you cannot go hunting for it." Mark P. Gergen, *The Common Knowledge of Tax Abuse*, 54 SMU L. REV. 131, 140 (2001); *see also* Lee A. Sheppard, *Bury Your Tax Shelter in a Business*, 106 TAX NOTES 20, 22 (2005); Lee A. Sheppard, *Drafting Economic Substance*, 92 TAX NOTES 1258, 1258 (2001).

Transactions labeled tax shelters often consist of a series of steps that, when analyzed mechanically under the Code or an authority interpreting the Code, give rise to a loss or other large tax benefit without an actual economic loss or outlay of that magnitude. In *ACM Partnership*, for example, "ACM's transactions, at least in form, satisfied each requirement of the contingent installment sale provisions and ratable basis recovery rule . . . ." *ACM Partnership*, 157 F.3d at 246. Tax shelters typically are structured so as not to expose the parties to real economic risk, often through the use of derivative instruments. James S. Eustice, *Abusive Corporate Tax Shelters: Old "Brine" in New Bottles*, 55 TAX L. REV. 135, 145 (2002). Professor Eustice comments:

> Whatever the uses of derivatives in other commercial contexts, it is clear that they had little or no business-related purpose (save monkey business) when employed in the manner utilized by the *ACM Partnership* transactions. Virtual reality may be acceptable on the Internet, but a more tangible reality is required when analyzing the tax consequences of a purported business venture, especially one that is heavily freighted with tax reduction baggage. . . .

Id.

Tax shelters typically are expensive to develop but easy to replicate. Once a tax shelter has been developed, it often can be cloned and sold to a large number of unrelated corporations. Because of the large tax savings a tax shelter can generate, promoters and other participants in the transactions (such as a tax-indifferent accommodation party) can charge hefty fees for them, generally computed as a percentage of the tax avoided. *See Saba Partnership v. Commissioner*, 273 F.3d 1135, 1147 (D.C. Cir. 2001) (citing memorandum that Merrill Lynch would earn a fee equal to 5–10 percent of the "tax savings" from each "CINS" transaction); Canellos, *supra* at 48 ("revenues of [tax shelter products] departments are based directly or indirectly on the expected tax savings (generally representing a small sharing in the present value thereof")). The ability to earn substantial fees provides an incentive for the development of tax shelters. *See* Pollack & Soled, *supra*, at 205 ("accounting firms such as KPMG, shilling as promoters, can 'earn' an astounding $124 million in fees by establishing corporate tax shelters such as FLIP, BLIPS, OPIS, and SC2 . . . ."); *see also* Joseph Bankman, *The Economic Substance Doctrine*, 74 S. CAL. L. REV. 5, 19 (2000) ("Tax shelters have been a growth industry for financial intermediaries; these intermediaries have dramatically expanded shelter opportunities for corporate taxpayers; and while corporate tax revenues have risen with the booming economy, shelters have removed billions from government coffers.").

As indicated at the start of this Chapter, law firms may enable tax shelters by providing tax opinions; they, too, can earn large fees. As an extreme example, according to a 2005 Senate Report:

> Brown & Wood reported to the [Senate] Subcommittee that, in December 1999 alone, it issued 65 BLIPS [Bond Linked Issue Premium Structure] opinions totaling approximately $9,290,476. This data indicates that the law firm issued an average of two or more BLIPS opinions per day, at a cost of $142,000 per opinion— very quick and lucrative work. Brown & Wood also estimated that, altogether, [tax partner R.J.] Ruble spent about 2,500 hours preparing legal opinions for KPMG tax products, a pace that, in light of the firm's overall $23 million in fees, generated an average hourly rate of more than $9,000 per billable hour.

United States Senate, *The Role of Professional Firms in the U.S. Tax Shelter Industry, Report Prepared by the Permanent Subcommittee on Investigations of the Committee on Homeland Security and Governmental Affairs* (February 8, 2005), *available at* 2005 TNT 28-28 (footnotes omitted). "In October 2003, Sidley Austin Brown & Wood terminated R.J. Ruble for breaches of fiduciary duty and violations of its partnership agreements." *Id.* at n.436. Mr. Ruble has been indicted. *See* Sheryl Stratton, *Tax Professionals Indicted; KPMG Says Shelters Were Fraudulent*, 108 TAX NOTES 1085, 1086 (2005) (hereinafter, Stratton, Indictments).

Tax shelter promoters and investors may rely on at least four things to mitigate the risk that a tax shelter transaction will fail to deliver the intended tax benefits. First, promoters may solicit confidentiality agreements, purportedly to protect the shelters they have developed (which could potentially be duplicated by competitors), but also reducing the likelihood the IRS will discover them. *See* Korb, *supra*. Second, as the discussion below of *ACM Partnership* illustrates, these transactions often are extremely complex, which makes them harder to audit. Third, the transaction may be reported in a way that minimizes the risk of detection on audit (such as by netting certain gains and losses rather than reporting a large loss, *see* Notice 2000-44, 2000-2 C.B. 255). Fourth, the transaction often will be justified with a non-tax business purpose, so as to attempt to avoid a less favorable tax result through application of judicial doctrines.

If a tax shelter transaction is uncovered by the IRS, it will likely apply one or more of the judicial doctrines discussed in Chapter 1, such as economic substance or the sham transaction doctrine, to disallow the claimed tax benefits. The economic substance doctrine, in particular, which generally examines the non-tax economic effects of the transaction and the taxpayer's business purpose, is a doctrine commonly used by the IRS in tax shelter cases. The IRS also may attack a shelter on technical grounds, arguing that one or more of the authorities relied on for the claimed tax results should be interpreted differently. Some shelters rely on authorities with respect to which there is little interpretive guidance, leaving ample room for arguments that those authorities do not produce the tax results claimed by the taxpayer.

Several commentators have argued that the government should make technical arguments before resorting to reliance on judicial doctrines. For example, Professor Karen Burke argues, "[t]o avoid overworking the economic substance doctrine, it is essential that the government seek to resolve tax disputes based on technical arguments derived from the statutory language whenever possible." Karen Burke, *Deconstructing Black & Decker's Contingent Liability Shelter: A Statutory Analysis*, 108 Tax Notes 211, 221 (2005). *See also* George K. Yin, *The Problem of Corporate Tax Shelters: Uncertain Dimensions, Unwise Approaches*, 55 Tax L. Rev. 405, 407 (2002) ("My general conclusion is that tools such as 'economic substance' and 'business purpose' should be reserved to combat transactions that are more unambiguously objectionable than the ones involved in [the *Compaq Computer Corp., IES Indus.*, and *UPS*] cases."); Ethan Yale, *Reexamining Black & Decker's Contingent Liability Tax Shelter*, 108 Tax Notes 223, 225 (2005) ("the sentiment George Yin expressed [above] in response to similar arguments the government raised in earlier cases is equally relevant [to the *Black and Decker* case.]").

§ 16.02   A Paradigmatic Corporate Tax Shelter: *ACM Partnership v. Commissioner*

The transaction described in *ACM Partnership v. Commissioner*, T.C. Memo. 1997-115, *aff'd in part, rev'd in part, and remanded*, 157 F.3d 231 (3d Cir. 1998), *cert. denied*, 526 U.S. 1017 (1999), is an early and paradigmatic example of an abusive corporate tax shelter.[2] *ACM Partnership* involves Colgate-Palmolive Company (Colgate), which had reported a capital gain of approximately $105 million for tax year 1988, resulting from the sale of a subsidiary. *Id.* Merrill Lynch & Co., Inc. (Merrill Lynch) approached Colgate and "proposed an investment partnership that would generate capital losses which Colgate could use to offset some of its 1988 capital gains." *ACM Partnership*, 157 F.3d at 233.

The transaction Merrill proposed was termed the contingent installment sale (CINS) transaction and was designed to take advantage of Temporary Regulations under section 453, which required the seller of property receiving an uncertain amount over a fixed period to allocate basis over that period. The recovery of basis over multiple years reduces the amount of basis recovered each year. In *ACM Partnership*, this resulted in reporting of a capital gain for 1989 and a capital loss for 1991, as described below. *ACM Partnership*, T.C. Memo. 1997-115.

The transaction was structured such that the partnership interests changed between 1989 and 1991, resulting in allocation of most of the capital gain

---

[2] Professor James Eustice refers to the *ACM Partnership* case as "the modern reincarnation of *Gregory v. Helvering*." James S. Eustice, *Abusive Corporate Tax Shelters: Old "Brine" in New Bottles*, 55 Tax L. Rev. 135, 168 (2002).

to a partner exempt from U.S. tax and allocation of most of the capital loss to Colgate and a wholly owned subsidiary of Colgate.

The initial partners in ACM were Southampton, Colgate's wholly owned subsidiary, which had a 17.1% interest in the partnership; a Merrill Lynch subsidiary, MLCS, which had a .3% partnership interest; and Kannex Corp., N.V. (Kannex), a Netherlands Antilles corporation, which had an 82.6% interest. ACM was capitalized with a total of $205 million of contributions from the partners on November 2, 1989. The next day, ACM used the capital to purchase $205 million of highly illiquid floating rate Citicorp notes. *ACM Partnership*, 157 F.3d at 239. Three weeks later, ACM sold $175 million of the Citicorp notes (worth $175.5 million because of accrued interest) to Bank of Tokyo and Banque Francaise du Commerce Exterieure for $140 million in cash and notes issued by the banks worth approximately $35.5 million. The notes ACM received (the LIBOR Notes) had no stated principal amount but provided for 20 quarterly payments (spanning a six-year period) based on the London Interbank Offering Rate (LIBOR). *Id.* at 240. In early December of 1989, ACM used the cash received in the exchange to purchase three issues of long-term fixed rate Colgate debt that had been targeted for acquisition by ACM by July of that year. *ACM Partnership*, T.C. Memo. 1997-115.

Thus, in November 1989, ACM had exchanged recently purchased notes worth $175.5 million for LIBOR notes worth $35.5 million and $140 million in cash. ACM treated the exchange as an installment sale without a maximum selling price under the Temporary Regulations. It therefore subtracted from the $140 million it received in cash in 1989 one-sixth of its basis, approximately $29.3 million. That gave rise to $110.7 million of capital gain in 1989. The gain was allocated to the partners according to their partnership interests, so that approximately $91.5 million of the gain was allocated to Kannex, which was not subject to United States tax, and Southampton was allocated approximately $18.9 million. *ACM Partnership*, 157 F.3d at 242.

ACM had approximately $146.25 million of basis remaining to be recovered, with respect to notes that had cost $35.5 million. The amount by which basis exceeded the cost of the notes, not coincidentally, was *exactly the amount of gain that ACM reported for 1989* (approximately $110.7 million). The large difference between basis and cost effectively resulted from ACM's recovery of only one-sixth of its $175.5 million basis in 1989, when it received $140 million in cash, with the remaining five-sixths allocated to notes worth only approximately $35.5 million in the aggregate. *See id.* at 246 n.27.

The large difference between ACM's claimed basis in the LIBOR notes and the cost of those notes is the heart of the shelter. What remained was for the LIBOR notes to be disposed of in such a way that Colgate, or its subsidiary Southampton, was allocated the loss resulting from their sale. ACM distributed some of the notes to Southampton late in 1989 "as a partial return of capital." *ACM Partnership*, T.C. Memo. 1997-115. Southampton then sold them to a third party for approximately $9.4 million, recognizing a loss of $32.4 million in 1989.[3] *ACM Partnership*, 157 F.3d at 241. As a result of the $18.9 million capital gain discussed above and this $32.4 million capital loss, Southampton reported a net capital loss of $13.5 million for 1989 from these transactions. *Id.* at 243.

In June 1991, Colgate purchased an interest in ACM from Kannex, and in November 1991, Kannex's remaining interest in ACM was redeemed. *Id.* at 241–42. As a result, at that point, Colgate and Southampton together owned 99.7 percent of ACM. ACM then sold the remaining LIBOR notes for approximately $11 million, recognizing a capital loss of approximately $85 million. $84.5 million of the loss was allocated to Colgate and Southampton. Colgate carried the loss back to 1988, the year in which it had the large unrelated capital gain. *Id.* at 243–44.

Professor Eustice has commented:

> Few would deny that the artificial "loss generator" transaction exemplified by *ACM* and its progeny fit nearly everyone's definition of an objectionable abusive tax shelter (except possibly the person who gave the tax opinion). Prepackaged and marketed by an investment bank promoter, fully "wired" transactions, downside risk fully hedged by derivatives, no significant upside profit potential, participation of a tax-indifferent party to absorb the burden of taxable profits, generation of a temporary artificial loss by the challenged transaction itself, total lack of any credible business purpose, this deal had it all. The *ACM* transaction was not merely a tax shelter, it was a tax palace.

Eustice, *supra*, at 154–55 (footnotes omitted).

Colgate did purport to have a business reason for the transaction, however. It was looking to retire some of its outstanding long-term fixed rate debt to reduce its exposure to falling interest rates. As indicated above, the partnership used the $140 million cash from the sale of the Citicorp notes to acquire that debt. Because the acquisition was through the partnership, it could be kept off of Colgate's books. *ACM Partnership*, 157 F.3d at 234, 240 n.13. ACM further argued that its transactions presented a realistic prospect of a pre-tax profit, provided an interim investment until it acquired the Colgate debt, and reduced its interest rate risk. *Id.* at 254. Neither the Tax Court nor the Court of Appeals were convinced by these arguments, however.

The Tax Court referred to the idea of using the partnership as a vehicle to acquire Colgate debt as an "opportunity to design an elaborate superstructure of liability management functions around Merrill's original tax shelter transaction." *ACM Partnership*, T.C. Memo. 1997-115. The courts found that the acquisition of the Citicorp notes was not designed to give rise to a pre-tax profit because they were designed to be sold at exactly the amount for which they were purchased and the Citicorp notes paid an

---

[3] Southampton's tax basis in the notes was approximately $41.8 million. *See ACM Partnership*, 157 F.3d at 243 n.18.

interest rate that only slightly exceeded the interest rate ACM was already earning on its cash deposits.[4] The slightly higher interest rate "result[ed] in only a $3,500 difference in yield over the 24-day holding period, a difference which was obliterated by the transaction costs associated with marketing private placement notes to third parties."[5] *ACM Partnership*, 157 F.3d at 249.

ACM's "interim investment" argument therefore was not convincing, either. The Court of Appeals commented:

> Even if ACM had faced a delay before it could purchase Colgate debt and thus needed to locate a suitable interim investment, the Citicorp notes ill served the professed purpose of holding cash assets in anticipation of an impending purchase. The notes, which in order to qualify for treatment in a contingent installment sale could not be traded on an established market, see I.R.C. § 453(k)(2)(A), were highly illiquid and thus could not be converted back into the cash needed to purchase Colgate debt without significant transaction costs in the form of the bid-ask spread which Merrill Lynch deemed necessary to market the notes to third parties. These transaction costs rendered the illiquid Citicorp notes paying 8.78% significantly less advantageous as an interim investment than the fully liquid cash deposit account paying 8.75%.

Id. at 255.

With respect to the argument that the transactions reduced ACM's exposure to interest rate risk resulting from its acquisition of Colgate debt, the Third Circuit explained that Colgate's acquisition of its own debt via the partnership was itself designed to reduce Colgate's risk of "the increased burdens that Colgate effectively would sustain as the obligor on those instruments if market interest rates fell further below the fixed rate established on these obligations." *Id.* That is, the fixed-rate debt obligations in which Colgate would own an interest via the partnership would increase in value if interest rates fell. *Id.* The Third Circuit explained that ACM's acquisition of the LIBOR notes actually undermined the stated goal:

> While the acquisition of Colgate debt furthered [the] professed goal of decreasing the exposure associated with Colgate's fixed rate long term debt structure outside of the partnership, the acquisition of the LIBOR notes, whose value would decline as interest rates declined, conversely increased ACM's exposure to falling interest

---

[4] "ACM's exposure to any fluctuation in the rate of return on its Citicorp note investment was illusory, as the interest rates were scheduled to be reset only once per month and ACM had arranged to hold the notes for only 24 days, encompassing only one interest rate adjustment on November 15 that would affect the notes for only 12 days before their disposition." *Id.* at 250 n.35.

[5] When the purchase of the Citicorp notes was authorized, "Merrill informed Colgate that the section 453 investment strategy would result in transaction costs of between $2.3 and $3.1 million on a pretax present value basis, of which $1.3 to $2.0 million would be incurred in the contingent payment sale." *ACM Partnership*, T.C. Memo. 1997-115.

rates, offsetting the desired effect of the debt acquisition program which purportedly was a fundamental partnership objective. . . . Accordingly, *the LIBOR notes, by hedging against the Colgate debt issues acquired within the partnership, negated the potential benefit of ACM's acquisition of these issues as a hedge against Colgate's interest rate exposure outside the partnership.*

Id. at 255–56 (emphasis added).[6]

Although ACM "argue[d] that tax-independent considerations informed and justified each step of the strategy," the Tax Court found that tax considerations drove the transaction, which was "hard-wired" from the outset.

Each of the steps in the section 453 investment strategy was planned and arrangements commenced considerably in advance of execution. Before the negotiations to form ACM, Merrill had already begun negotiations to purchase the Citicorp Notes. Before their purchase, Merrill was negotiating for their disposition. By the time ACM acquired the LIBOR Notes, Merrill was arranging with [the buyer] the terms on which some of them would be sold. . . . The distribution and sale of [certain LIBOR] Notes was scheduled to occur before the end of Colgate's 1989 taxable year in order to offset Southampton's share of the contingent payment sale gain on Colgate's consolidated return. It was the understanding of the principals that Kannex would retire from the partnership by the fall of 1991 so that the LIBOR Notes could be sold in time for Colgate to carry back the taxable loss to its 1988 taxable year. *No supervening market forces or other nontax considerations disrupted the scheduled execution of these steps.*

ACM Partnership, T.C. Memo. 1997-115 (footnote omitted) (emphasis added).

Based on its analysis of the economics of the transaction, the Tax Court found that the CINS transaction lacked economic substance, concluding:

But for the $100 million of tax losses it generated for Colgate, the section 453 investment strategy would not have been consistent

---

[6] The Tax Court further explained:

The theory of the LIBOR Note hedge . . . forms the linchpin of petitioner's economic substance argument. It is, however, false. It is false even if we assume arguendo that there was as high a negative correlation between the interest rate sensitivity of the LIBOR Notes and that of the Colgate debt as petitioner asserts, a proposition that respondent and her experts vigorously contest. To recognize why the theory is false it is necessary to grasp this central insight: Neither ABN [the Dutch bank that effectively controlled Kannex] nor Colgate needed a hedge inside the partnership for the Colgate debt because both were effectively fully hedged outside the partnership—ABN through swaps and Colgate by virtue of being the issuer of the debt. Employing an additional hedging instrument within the partnership was not only redundant, but also flatly inconsistent with the manner in which both principals were otherwise managing their interests in the partnership.

ACM Partnership, T.C. Memo. 1997-115.

with rational economic behavior. The section 453 investment strategy lacked economic substance. It served no useful nontax purpose. Accordingly, the pertinent adjustments made by respondent to ACM's reported items of income and loss are sustained.

Id. The Court of Appeals affirmed the Tax Court on the economic substance issue but allowed the deduction of actual economic losses, approximately $6 million. *ACM Partnership*, 157 F.3d at 261.

ACM was apparently one of 11 similar partnerships formed in 1989 and 1990 by Merrill Lynch. *ACM Partnership*, T.C. Memo. 1997-115. A district court upheld a similar transaction in a case that was reversed by the Court of Appeals for the D.C. Circuit. *See Boca Investerings Partnership v. United States*, 314 F.3d 625 (D.C. Cir. 2003) (refusing to respect the partnership entity), *rev'g* 167 F. Supp. 2d 298 (D.D.C. 2001). The Court of Appeals for the D.C. Circuit ruled similarly in two other cases, as well.[7]

§ 16.03   Subchapter C Shelters

The CINS transaction Colgate entered into did not make use of provisions in Subchapter C. Instead, it exploited regulations under section 453. Some corporate tax shelters do take advantage of Subchapter C. Professor Eustice explains:

> despite the frequency of statutory changes, many parts of the Code have lingered undisturbed for decades, and these provisions have long provided opportunities for creative tax planning. Subchapter C examples include: Sections 358 and 362 permit the replication of built-in losses when depreciated assets are transferred down to controlled subsidiaries in a 351 transaction, which sets the table for various "loss generator" transactions. In contrast, intentionally "failed" stock redemptions (that result in dividend characterization) have a stock basis-shifting effect. Conversely, the subsidiary liquidation rules result in the total disappearance of outside stock basis, together with any built-in gain embedded in the subsidiary's stock. Finally, the liability assumption rules of 351 and 357 do not work well with "contingent liabilities," and can be exploited to create both outside built-in loss in the transferor's stock and a second deduction by the transferee corporation. These examples have played a featured role in several of the recent tax shelter transactions . . . .

Eustice, *supra*, at 141 (footnotes omitted).[8]

---

[7] *See Saba Partnership v. Commissioner*, 273 F.3d 1135 (D.C. Cir. 2001), *vacating and remanding* T.C. Memo. 1999-359; *ASA Investerings Partnerhip v. Commissioner*, 201 F.3d 505 (D.C. Cir. 2000), *aff'g* T.C. Memo. 1998-305, *cert. denied*, 531 U.S. 871 (2000).

[8] Section 362(e), enacted in 2004 and discussed in § 2.03[B][1][a] of Chapter 2, provides a new limitation on built-in losses.

[A] Contingent Liability Shelters

Two well-known types of tax shelters are contingent liability shelters and basis-shifting shelters. Contingent liability shelter transactions, which involve section 351 (discussed in Chapter 2):

> involve the transfer of a high basis asset (i.e., an asset with a basis that approximates its fair market value) to a corporation purportedly in exchange for stock of the transferee corporation, and the transferee corporation's assumption of a liability (such as a liability for deferred compensation or other deferred employee benefits or an obligation for environmental remediation) that the transferor has not yet taken into account for federal income tax purposes. The transferor typically remains liable on the underlying obligation. The basis and fair market value of the transferred asset, which may be a security of another member of the same affiliated group of corporations, are generally only marginally greater than the present value of the assumed liability. Therefore, the value of the stock of the transferee received by the transferor is minimal relative to the basis and fair market value of the asset transferred to the transferee corporation.

Notice 2001-17, 2001-1 C.B. at 730.

The parties treat the transaction as qualifying under section 351. *Id.* Accordingly, the party transferring the (high-basis) property to the corporation takes the same basis in the stock of the corporation that it had in the property. *Id.*; I.R.C. § 358(a). The key to the shelter is that the property transferor does not reduce the stock basis by the amount of the liability. *See id.* "The transferor typically sells the stock of the transferee corporation for its fair market value within a relatively short period of time after the purported § 351 exchange and claims a tax loss in an amount approximating the present value of the liability assumed by the transferee corporation. . . . In addition to the transferor's purported loss on the sale of the stock of the transferee corporation, the transferee corporation may claim a § 162 deduction with respect to payments on the liability." *Id.* at 730-31.

The transaction entered into by Black and Decker Corporation (B & D) is typical. After selling three businesses for amounts that gave rise to substantial capital gains,

> B & D created Black & Decker Healthcare Management Inc. ("BDHMI"). B & D transferred approximately $561 million dollars to BDHMI along with $560 million dollars in contingent employee healthcare claims in exchange for newly issued stock in BDHMI ("the BDHMI transaction"). B & D sold its stock in BDHMI to an independent third-party for $1 million dollars. In December 2001, because it believed that its basis in the BDHMI stock was $561 million dollars, the value of the property it had transferred to BDHMI, B & D claimed approximately $560 million dollars in capital loss on the stock sale, which it reported on its 1998 federal

tax return. B & D used a portion of the capital loss to offset its capital gains from selling the three businesses in 1998, and used the remaining loss to offset gains in prior and future tax years.

Black and Decker Corp. v. United States, 340 F. Supp. 2d 621, 622–23 (N.D. Md. 2004); *aff'd in part, rev'd in part, and remanded*, 436 F.3d 431 (4th Cir. 2006).[9]

As discussed in Chapter 2,[10] liabilities assumed by a transferee corporation in a section 351 transaction generally reduce the transferor's stock basis. I.R.C. § 358(d)(1). However, stock basis is not reduced for the amount of a liability governed by section 357(c)(3) (in general, liabilities the payment of which would give rise to a deduction). I.R.C. § 358(d)(2). It is Revenue Ruling 95-74, discussed in Chapter 2, that applied section 357(c)(3) to contingent environmental liabilities. *See* Rev. Rul. 95-74, 1995-2 C.B. 36. Revenue Ruling 95-74 also allowed the transferee corporation to deduct or capitalize (as appropriate) payments on those liabilities. *See id.* at 38. However, the Revenue Ruling stated in the facts that the transaction had *bona fide* business purposes. In addition, the Ruling stated, "The holdings described above are subject to § 482 and other applicable sections of the Code and principles of law, including the limitations discussed in Rev. Rul. 80-198, 1980-2 C.B. 113 (limiting the scope of the revenue ruling to transactions that do not have a tax avoidance purpose)." *Id.*

The IRS responded to contingent liability shelter transactions in Notice 2001-17 with a issued a Notice stating its intent to disallow losses claimed in these transactions. The Notice explained:

> Taxpayers assert several business purposes for these transactions. However, the Service and the Treasury are not aware of any case in which a taxpayer has shown a legitimate non-tax business reason to carry out the combination of steps described above. Moreover, the Service and the Treasury believe that any business purposes taxpayers may assert for certain aspects of these transactions are far outweighed by the purpose to generate deductible losses for federal income tax purposes.

Notice 2001-17, 2001-1 C.B. at 730.

Professor Christopher Hanna has argued that some transactions are "too perfect" in that they work so well to generate a tax benefit that that goal is transparent. With respect to the contingent liability shelter, he has commented,

> There are at least two aspects of the contingent liability tax shelter that can lead an observer to conclude that the transaction is too perfect. First, the closer the amount of the contingent liability is

---

[9] *Black and Decker* was a refund suit because B & D sought refunds for the 1995 through 2000 tax years, as a result of capital loss carrybacks and carryovers. *Black and Decker Corp.*, 340 F. Supp. 2d at 622.

[10] See § 2.02[A][2] of Chapter 2 for a discussion of the tax treatment of liabilities assumed by the transferee corporation in a transaction governed by section 351.

to the fair market value of the transferred asset, the more perfect the transaction becomes. Second, the more quickly the transferor sells the transferee stock, the more perfect the transaction becomes, because one of the main reasons for entering into a contingent liability tax shelter is for the transferor to accelerate a loss or deduction (as well as to duplicate a loss or deduction).

Christopher H. Hanna, *From Gregory to Enron: The Too Perfect Theory and Tax Law*, 24 VA. TAX REV. 737, 788 (2005).[11]

However, in *Black and Decker*, the District Court found that the BDHMI transaction was not a sham because it "had very real economic implications for every beneficiary of B & D's employee benefits program, as well as for the parties to the transaction." *Black and Decker*, 340 F. Supp. 2d at 624. The court therefore granted Black and Decker's summary judgment motion.[12] *Id.* at 622. On appeal, the Court of Appeals for the Fourth Circuit reversed the grant of summary judgment, finding that unresolved issues of material fact remained. It therefore remanded the case. *Black and Decker*, 436 F.3d at 431.

Congress responded to the contingent liability shelter in 2000, enacting section 358(h), which is discussed in Chapter 2.[13] In Notice 2001-17, mentioned above, the IRS stated that "[f]or transfers after October 18, 1999, the Service will assert that such losses are disallowed because the transferor's basis in the stock received is reduced under § 358(h) (reducing stock basis by the amount of certain liabilities)." *Id.* For transfers before that date, the IRS would rely on a variety of arguments, including insufficient business purpose to qualify under section 351 and that the transaction was "not, in substance, a transfer of property in exchange for stock within the meaning of § 351, but instead is either an agency arrangement for the transferor or simply a payment to the transferee for its assumption of a

---

[11] As the title of Professor Hanna's article may suggest, Enron was one of the taxpayers that entered into contingent liability shelter transactions. Christopher H. Hanna, *From Gregory to Enron: The Too Perfect Theory and Tax Law*, 24 VA. TAX REV. 737, 788 (2005).

[12] The district court also denied the IRS's summary judgment motion, which was based on the technicalities of the statute, and that denial was affirmed on appeal. *See Black and Decker Corp. v. United States*, 436 F.3d at 431, 437-38 (4th Cir. 2006).

The taxpayer prevailed in *Coltec Indus. v. United States*, 62 Fed. Cl. 716 (2004); in that case, the judge stated, "the court has determined that 'where a taxpayer has satisfied all statutory requirements established by Congress, as Coltec did in this case, the use of the 'economic substance' doctrine to trump 'mere compliance with the Code' would violate the separation of powers." *Id.* at 756. The government has appealed. Karen Burke, *Deconstructing Black & Decker's Contingent Liability Shelter: A Statutory Analysis*, 108 TAX NOTES 211, 212 n.10 (2005).

[13] Section 358(h) is discussed in § 2.02[A][3][c] of Chapter 2. Professor Glenn Coven has criticized this provision, arguing, "[o]ne of the most common mistakes in drafting corrective tax legislation is to focus narrowly on the specific result to be altered without understanding the underlying problem that is producing the result. In that regard, section 358(h) is a major offender. Because the section was focused on preventing an immediate, duplicate loss, it produces results that are arbitrary, unfair, and irrational." Glenn Coven, *What Corporate Tax Shelters Can Teach Us about the Structure of Subchapter C*, 105 TAX NOTES 831, 836 (2004).

liability . . . ." *Id.* Professor Burke has argued that section 357(c)(3) does not apply to the liabilities involved in Black and Decker's shelter. Burke, *supra*, at 214–15.

In 2002, the IRS announced a "global settlement initiative" of contingent liability shelters. *See* Rev. Proc. 2002-67, 2002-43 I.R.B. 733. In the Revenue Procedure, "the IRS offered taxpayers two options: a fixed taxpayer concession of 75 percent of the claimed capital loss, or a fast-track mediation (and, if necessary, a baseball arbitration) resulting in a concession by the taxpayer of between 50 percent and 90 percent of the loss. Under both options, future deductions would be reduced by the loss amount allowed to the taxpayer to avoid a double deduction." Sheryl Stratton, *Inside OTSA: A Bird's-Eye View of Shelter Central at the IRS*, 100 TAX NOTES 1246 (2003) (hereinafter, Stratton, OTSA). The IRS has stated that "while more than 50 percent of the eligible taxpayers had applied for the contingent liability settlement option, only 11 taxpayers had requested the fast-track option . . . ." Korb, *supra* (*citing* Stratton, OTSA, *supra*).

[B]   Basis-Shifting Shelters

The contingent liability tax shelter described above is just one example of a corporate tax shelter that exploits Subchapter C Code sections. IRS Notice 2001-45 describes a category of "basis-shifting" tax shelters that take advantage of redemptions under sections 302 and 318.[14] *See* Notice 2001-45, 2001-2 C.B. 129. The accounting firm KPMG marketed these shelters under the acronyms "FLIP" (Foreign Leveraged Investment Program) and "OPIS" (Offshore Portfolio Investment Strategy). Calvin H. Johnson, *Tales from the KPMG Skunk Works: The Basis-Shift or Defective-Redemption Shelter*, 108 TAX NOTES 431, 433 (2005). Professor Calvin Johnson explains, "FLIP is within a family of tax shelters that KPMG called a 'loss generator.' As UBS [Union Bank of Switzerland] candidly described the transaction, 'the losses are not real but only tax relevant. The [FLIP/ OPIS] uses provisions in the US Tax Code to create a synthetic loss.' " *Id.* at 434 (footnotes omitted).

The basic structure of such a shelter is as follows:

> a shell Cayman Islands corporation or partnership ["Cayman"] was set up that was related, within the constructive ownership rules of section 318, to the U.S. taxpayer who purchased the shelter. The Cayman Islands entity bought stock of a foreign bank, either Deutsche Bank or UBS, with funds borrowed on a nonrecourse basis from the same bank, in the amount of the artificial loss to be generated. A few weeks later, the same bank redeemed all the stock, and the Cayman Islands entity repaid the bank with the redemption proceeds. . . .

> Taxpayer as a part of the package purchased a modest amount of UBS stock, say 1,000 shares . . . .

---

[14] Sections 302 and 318 are both discussed in Chapter 5. *See* §§ 5.02, 5.03.

> Just as Cayman was redeemed out of UBS, the American purchasers bought an option, under the package, to buy the same number of UBS shares, . . . that Cayman was redeemed out of. Because optioned stock is considered to be constructively owned, without regard to whether exercise of the option was a realistic prospect or not, and because Cayman owned everything Taxpayer owned, Cayman was not completely redeemed out under section 302. Indeed, Cayman had no reduction of its ownership of UBS once constructive ownership was considered.

Id. at 434–35. Because the Cayman Islands entity did not reduce its ownership of UBS shares at all once section 318 was applied, the redemption apparently fails to qualify for exchange treatment under section 302.[15] *See* I.R.C. § 302(b), (d). Because the redemption is treated as a distribution, the Cayman Islands entity's stock basis is not used. Of course, the Cayman Islands entity is not subject to federal income tax, so it has no need to use that basis. However, its failure to do so is the key to the basis-shifting tax shelter. *Id.* at 436.

The shelter applies Treasury Regulation 1.302-2(c), which states that "[i]n any case in which an amount received in redemption of stock is treated as a distribution of a dividend, proper adjustment of the basis of the remaining stock will be made with respect to the stock redeemed." The regulation also provides an example in which Husband and Wife are the sole shareholders of a corporation and all of husband's shares are redeemed in a transaction constituting a dividend. The example provides that Wife holds the remaining stock of the corporation with a *basis that includes what used to be Husband's basis in the stock.* Treas. Reg. § 1.302-2(c) Ex. 2.

Professor Glenn Coven has commented:

> Because in this example there is no other stock outstanding, the statement that W holds the remaining stock is an undeniably true statement of fact. However, the example contains no guidance regarding the principle that might be applied to determine the identity of the remaining stock in a more complex case. The reader is left to speculate on the importance of the family relationship, the transfer of the stock from Husband to Wife, the recency of that transfer, or the fact that after the shifting of basis Wife still had a gain in her stock! Nevertheless, the example does make clear that under some circumstances, when all of the stock of a shareholder is redeemed, the basis of that stock will shift to another taxpayer.

Glenn E. Coven, *Basis Shifting—A Radical Approach to an Intractable Problem*, 105 TAX NOTES 1541, 1542 (2004).

The basis-shifting tax shelter interprets the text of the regulations and the example to provide for allocation of the Cayman Islands' entity's unused basis to the shares held by the U.S. taxpayer (1,000 shares in Professor

---

[15] The tax treatment under section 302 of corporate redemptions of stock is discussed in § 5.03.

Johnson's example). Johnson, *supra*, at 435. The relationship between the U.S. taxpayer and the Cayman Islands entity was created by having the U.S. taxpayer purchase options to buy most of the stock of that entity. *Id.* at 434. The basis shift provides the U.S. taxpayer with a basis in its stock that far exceeds the value of that stock. It can then sell the shares for a large tax loss. If, for example, $100 million of unused basis transfers to the few shares of stock owned by the U.S. taxpayer, they can be sold for nearly a $100 million tax "loss," worth $20 million dollars after tax at the 20 percent capital gains rates applicable to individuals in 1998. *Id.* at 435.

The crux of the problem is that a basis increase was obtained without a corresponding payment of tax. *See* Coven, *supra*, at 1544. In effect, what the shelter strives for is a form of "tax cost basis" without the tax cost. The IRS responded to this type of shelter with Notice 2001-45, stating:

> It is the position of the Service and the Treasury that such [a basis] adjustment is not proper in every case in which the redeemed shareholder retains no stock in the redeeming corporation. The example in the regulations is premised on the concept that an adjustment is appropriate where the redeemed spouse is required to include the full redemption proceeds as a dividend in gross income that is subject to U.S. tax and such spouse retains no stock to which the basis of the redeemed stock could attach.

Notice 2001-45, 2001-2 C.B. 129, 129. The Treasury Department also responded, proposing regulations under which, in any redemption treated as a section 301 distribution, the taxpayer's unrecovered basis in the redeemed stock would be treated as a loss to that taxpayer on the disposition of the stock, but a loss that generally would not be taken into account at a later date. *See* Prop. Treas. Reg. § 1.302-5. The proposed regulations would therefore eliminate the shifting of basis in any redemption taxed as a distribution.[16]

Professor Johnson has argued that the basis-shifting tax shelter fails as a technical matter because, he argues, the redemption actually qualifies as an exchange, so that the Cayman Islands entity was entitled to use its own basis,[17] and even if that is not the case, it is not a proper adjustment for the basis to shift to the U.S. taxpayer. Johnson, *supra*, at 437–38. He further argued that no *bona fide* loss was sustained by the U.S. taxpayer on the sale of its shares, *id.* at 438–39; there was no reasonable expectation

---

[16] Proposed Treasury Regulation 1.302-5 is discussed further in § 5.03[C][2] of Chapter 5.

[17] Professor Johnson's argument in this regard is that the redemption of the Cayman Island entity's UBS shares was a real loss of interest except to the extent of its continued ownership of UBS. He argues that because the Cayman Island entity's constructive ownership of UBS after the redemption was only .2 percent, the Cayman Island entity only retained a .2 percent interest in the shares of UBS that it had previously owned, yielding a substantial (99.8 percent) reduction in the ownership of those shares. *See* Calvin H. Johnson, *Tales from the KPMG Skunk Works: The Basis-Shift or Defective-Redemption Shelter*, 108 TAX NOTES 431, 437 (2005) ("Even with constructive ownership under section 318, Cayman recaptured only that 0.2 percent of the UBS stock it gave up."). For a critique of this argument, see John F. Prusiecki, *Anti-FLIP/ DuPont Theories Don't Withstand Scrutiny*, 108 TAX NOTES 1475 (2005).

of making a pre-tax profit, *id.* at 439; the tax loss claimed did not clearly reflect income under section 446(b), *id.* at 339–40; and that the transaction collapses under the step-transaction doctrine so that "there is no borrowing, no purchase of stock, and no redemption and repayment, only the $100 million staying in the UBS vaults." *Id.* at 440.

In a 2002 Revenue Procedure, the IRS also announced a global settlement initiative of basis-shifting shelters "the same as or substantially similar to those described in Notice 2001-45." Rev. Proc. 2002-97, 2002-43 I.R.B. 757. The settlement initiative offered the opportunity for eligible taxpayers to settle by conceding 80 percent of the basis shift and all of the transaction costs, other than 20 percent of certain deemed transaction costs. *Id.* at 757. The Revenue Procedure further provided procedures with respect to the imposition of accuracy-related penalties. *Tax Notes* reported that "[o]n March 27, 2003, [then-IRS Chief Counsel B. John] Williams said the IRS was successful in inducing 92 percent of the 488 taxpayers involved in basis-shifting transactions to accept the settlement terms" and that "[b]y early June 2003, David Robison, head of IRS Appeals, said the basis-shifting transaction case participation rate was more than 80 percent." Stratton, *supra*, at 1249. As of July 2005, "there were still no reported cases on the FLIP/OPIS tax issues." Johnson, *supra*, at 433.

§ 16.04   Weapons in the War on Tax Shelters

As indicated above, corporate tax shelters proliferated for a variety of reasons including their complexity, *see* Canellos, *supra*, at 65, and confidentiality agreements that helped keep them secret, Korb, *supra*. Another part of the climate was "the perceived weakness of the IRS in discovering these new forms of tax shelters." *Id.* In the past several years, the government has been using various means in addition to audits, litigating individual cases, and global settlements to combat tax shelters.[18] Tax professionals now face indictment. *See* Stratton, Indictments, *supra*, at 1086 (reporting on indictment of nine tax professionals—eight from KPMG and R.J. Ruble from Brown & Wood); Carrie Johnson, *Shelter Probe Yields First Charges, Plea*, WASHINGTON POST (Aug. 12, 2005) (discussing guilty plea of banker involved in "BLIPS" deals).

Congress also may respond to a particular shelter by amending the Code in an attempt to prevent the tax result sought by the shelter. Section 358(h), mentioned above, is an example of that phenomenon. Of course, such legislation is after-the-fact, *ad hoc*, and may have unintended consequences, including possibly burdening non-abusive transactions. *See* Glenn Coven, *What Corporate Tax Shelters Can Teach Us About the Structure of Subchapter C*, 105 TAX NOTES 831, 836 (2004) ("Code section 358(h) is a major offender. Because the section was focused on preventing an immediate, duplicate loss, it produces results that are arbitrary, unfair, and irrational,"

---

[18] *See* Announcement 2005-80, 2005-46 I.R.B. 1, for an IRS settlement initiative with respect to a long list of types of transactions.

in part because the amount by which the basis of the property subject to the liability is reduced is affected by contributions of unrelated property).

[A] Disclosure Requirements and Penalties Applicable to Material Advisors

In addition to legislation targeting specific shelters, Congress has required increased record keeping and disclosure by tax shelter organizers and promoters; enacted penalties for violation of these requirements; and increased and strengthened the penalties applicable to tax shelter organizers, promoters and investors.[19] With respect to tax shelter organizers and promoters, section 6111 requires a "material advisor" to a "reportable transaction" to file a return disclosing information about the transaction. I.R.C. § 6111(a). The term "reportable transaction" includes "listed transactions" and transactions that must be disclosed under section 6011, which is discussed below.

"Listed transactions" are transactions that the IRS has identified as abusive and designated as such in published guidance, typically Notices. For example, Notice 2001-17, discussed above in connection with contingent liability shelters, states that "[t]ransactions that are the same as or substantially similar to those described in this Notice . . . (including transactions utilizing partnerships) are identified as 'listed transactions' . . . ." Notice 2001-17, 2001-1 C.B. 730, 731. Similarly, Notice 2001-45, discussed above in connection with basis-shifting shelters, designated transactions "the same as, or substantially similar to, those described in this Notice . . . as 'listed transactions' . . . ." Notice 2001-45, 2001-2 C.B. 129, 129. *See also* Notice 2004-67, 2004-41 I.R.B. 600 (providing a list of 30 listed transactions). As discussed below, listed transactions are separately mentioned in a number of provisions aimed at tax shelters.

A "material advisor" within the meaning of section 6111 is a person

> (i) who provides any material aid, assistance, or advice with respect to organizing, managing, promoting, selling, implementing, insuring, or carrying out any reportable transaction, and (ii) who directly or indirectly derives gross income *in excess of the threshold amount* (or such other amount as may be prescribed by the Secretary) for such advice or assistance.

I.R.C. § 6111(b)(1)(A) (emphasis added). The "threshold amount" is "$50,000 in the case of a reportable transaction substantially all of the tax benefits from which are provided to natural persons, and . . . $250,000 in any other case." I.R.C. § 6111(b)(1)(B). Each violation of the disclosure requirement of section 6111 generally is subject to a penalty of $50,000. I.R.C. § 6707(b)(1). For listed transactions, that penalty is increased to the greater of $200,000

---

[19] One penalty applicable to promoters of abusive tax shelters is in section 6700. A detailed discussion of penalties is beyond the scope of this book; for further reading on civil tax penalties, *see* Chapters 16 and 17 of LEANDRA LEDERMAN & ANN MURPHY, FEDERAL TAX PRACTICE AND PROCEDURE (2003).

or "50 percent of the gross income derived by such person with respect to aid, assistance, or advice which is provided with respect to the listed transaction before the date the return is filed under section 6111." I.R.C. § 6707(b)(2). That percentage is increased to 75 percent for intentional noncompliance. *Id.*

Congress has also required material advisors to maintain "list[s] . . . identifying each person with respect to whom such advisor acted as a material advisor with respect to such transaction . . . ." I.R.C. § 6112(a)(1). Upon written request from the IRS, a material advisor must make the list available to the IRS. I.R.C. § 6112(b)(1)(A). Failure to provide such a list within 20 business days of a request from the IRS is subject to a penalty of $10,000 per day after the twentieth day for each day the failure persists, unless there is reasonable cause for the failure. I.R.C. § 6708(a).

[B] Disclosure Requirements and Certain Penalties Applicable to Taxpayers Participating in Reportable Transactions

The Treasury Department is also participating in the war on tax shelters. Treasury regulations require each taxpayer who participates in a reportable transaction and is required to file a return to disclose that transaction in a statement attached to the return. Treas. Reg. § 1.6011-4(a). That requirement is enforced by a penalty of "$10,000 in the case of a natural person" (increased to $100,000 for a listed transaction) and $50,000 otherwise (increased to $200,000 for a listed transaction). I.R.C. § 6707A(b)(1). The Code now disallows a deduction for interest on understatements attributable to an undisclosed reportable transaction. I.R.C. § 163(m).

A number of penalties may apply to items a taxpayer reports incorrectly or fails to report, most of which are beyond the scope of this book. Most relevant here, a Code section enacted in 2004 provides a 20-percent penalty for an understatement of tax attributable to a reportable transaction. I.R.C. § 6662A(a). That percentage increases to 30 percent for undisclosed reportable transactions. Section 6664 precludes an undisclosed reportable transaction from qualifying for its reasonable cause exception. I.R.C. § 6664(d)(2)(A). In addition, the substantial understatement penalty of section 6662 now excludes tax shelter items from the exception to the penalty for items for which there is substantial authority or are disclosed on the taxpayer's return and have a reasonable basis. I.R.C. § 6662(d)(2)(C).[20]

[C] Opinion Practice Under Circular 230

Another piece of the tax shelter picture the Treasury Department has addressed is the legal opinions that typically accompany tax shelter (and other) transactions and that are often thought to provide protection from

---

[20] Sections 6662 and 6662A are coordinated so that they will not both apply to the same portion of an understatement of tax. *See* I.R.C. § 6662A(e)(1)(B).

penalties should the contemplated tax treatment not be upheld. The Treasury Department has addressed "covered opinions" in recently finalized regulations in Circular 230, which governs practice before the IRS. *See* T.D. 9165; T.D. 9201.

Under Circular 230, subject to a few exceptions, "[a] covered opinion is written advice (including electronic communications) by a practitioner concerning one or more Federal tax issues arising from":

- a listed transaction or transaction substantially similar to a listed transaction;

- "[a]ny partnership or other entity, any investment plan or arrangement, or any other plan or arrangement, the *principal purpose* of which is the avoidance or evasion of any tax imposed by the Internal Revenue Code," 31 C.F.R. § 10.35(b)(2)(i)(B) (emphasis added).; or

- "[a]ny partnership or other entity, any investment plan or arrangement, or any other plan or arrangement, a *significant purpose* of which is the avoidance or evasion of any tax imposed by the Internal Revenue Code if the written advice—

  (1) Is a reliance opinion;

  (2) Is a marketed opinion;

  (3) Is subject to conditions of confidentiality; or

  (4) Is subject to contractual protection." 31 C.F.R. § 10.35(b)(2)(i)(C) (emphasis added).

A "reliance opinion" is an opinion that "concludes at a confidence level of at least more likely than not (a greater than 50 percent likelihood) that one or more significant Federal tax issues would be resolved in the taxpayer's favor." 31 C.F.R. § 10.35(b)(4)(i). Written advice generally constitutes a "marketed opinion" "if the practitioner knows or has reason to know that the written advice will be used or referred to by a person other than the practitioner (or a person who is a member of, associated with, or employed by the practitioner's firm) in promoting, marketing or recommending a partnership or other entity, investment plan or arrangement to one or more taxpayer(s)." 31 C.F.R. § 10.35(b)(5)(i). However, if the opinion contains certain prominent disclosures, including a statement that "[t]he advice was not intended or written by the practitioner to be used, and that it cannot be used by any taxpayer, for the purpose of avoiding penalties that may be imposed on the taxpayer" and that the taxpayer should consult an independent tax advisor, the advice will not constitute a marketed opinion. 31 C.F.R. § 10.35(b)(5)(ii).

In general, the principal requirements for covered opinions are as follows:

- "The practitioner must use reasonable efforts to identify and ascertain the facts, which may relate to future events if a transaction is prospective or proposed, and to determine which facts are relevant. The opinion must identify and consider all facts that the practitioner determines to be relevant." 31 C.F.R. § 10.35(c)(1)(i).

- "The practitioner must not base the opinion on any unreasonable factual assumptions (including assumptions as to future events). An unreasonable factual assumption includes a factual assumption that the practitioner knows or should know is incorrect or incomplete. . . ." 31 C.F.R. § 10.35(c)(1)(ii).

- "The practitioner must not base the opinion on any unreasonable factual representations, statements or findings of the taxpayer or any other person. . . ." 31 C.F.R. § 10.35(c)(1)(iii).

- "The opinion must relate the applicable law (including potentially applicable judicial doctrines) to the relevant facts." 31 C.F.R. § 10.35(c)(2)(i).

- "The practitioner must not assume the favorable resolution of any significant Federal tax issue [subject to certain limited exceptions] . . . or otherwise base an opinion on any unreasonable legal assumptions, representations, or conclusions." 31 C.F.R. § 10.35(c)(2)(ii).

- "The opinion must not contain internally inconsistent legal analyses or conclusions." 31 C.F.R. § 10.35(c)(2)(iii).

Circular 230 also contains various mandatory disclosure requirements for covered opinions. See 31 C.F.R. § 10.35(e). Written advice that does not constitute a covered opinion is also regulated, but is subject to more limited requirements. See 31 C.F.R. § 10.37. The regulations further provide that "[a]ny practitioner who has (or practitioners who have or share) principal authority and responsibility for overseeing a firm's practice of providing advice concerning Federal tax issues must take reasonable steps to ensure that the firm has adequate procedures in effect for all members, associates, and employees for purposes of complying with § 10.35." 31 C.F.R. § 10.36(a).

The regulations also provide a list of four "best practices" for tax advisors: (1) "Communicating clearly with the client regarding the terms of the engagement. . .;" (2) "Establishing the facts, determining which facts are relevant, [and] evaluating the reasonableness of any assumptions or representations;" (3) "Advising the client regarding the import of the conclusions reached;" and (4) "Acting fairly and with integrity in practice before the Internal Revenue Service." 31 C.F.R. § 10.33(a).

> Tax advisors with responsibility for overseeing a firm's practice of providing advice concerning Federal tax issues or of preparing or assisting in the preparation of submissions to the Internal Revenue Service should take reasonable steps to ensure that the firm's procedures for all members, associates, and employees are consistent with the best practices set forth in paragraph (a) of this section.

31 C.F.R. § 10.33(b).

TABLE OF CASES

[References are to page numbers and footnotes]

A

Abdalla v. Commissioner 194
Achiro v. Commissioner 390
ACM Partnership v. Commissioner . . 16;
    17; 414; 417
ACM Partnership v. Commissioner, T.C.
    Memo. 1997-115 417
Adoption of (see name of party)
Alderman v. Commissioner 45
Alleged Contempt of (see name of party)
American Bantam Car Co. v. Commissioner
    . . . . 32; 71
Appeal of (see name of party)
Appeal of Estate of (see name of party)
Application of (see name of applicant)
Arctic Ice Machine Co. v. Commissioner . .
    295
Arnes v. Commissioner 150; 151n16
Arnes v. United States 150
ASA Investerings Partnerhip v. Commis-
    sioner 422n7
Associated Wholesale Grocers, Inc. v. United
    States 198
A.W. Chesterton Co. v. Chesterton . . 219

B

B. Forman Company, Inc. v. Commissioner
    390
B. Forman Company, Inc., Achiro v. Commis-
    sioner 392
Bardahl Mfg. Co. v. Commissioner, T.C.
    Memo. 1965-200, the Tax Court . . 375
Basic, Inc. v. United States 113
Bausch & Lomb Optical Co. v. Commissioner
    296
Bazley v. Commissioner 340
Bennet v. United States 334
Bercy Industries, Inc. v. Commissioner . . .
    344n6; 349
Black and Decker Corp. v. United States
    . . . . 48; 424; 425n12
Blatt v. Commissioner 150
Boca Investerings Partnership v. United
    States 422
Bollinger v. Commissioner, T.C. Memo. 1984-
    560. The Court of Appeals for 12
Bollinger; Commissioner v. 11
Brown v. Commissioner 55

C

Chamberlin v. Commissioner 173
Chapman v. Commissioner 290
Chapter 5. Berry Petroleum v. Commissioner
    361
Chicago, B. & Q. R.R.; United States v. . .
    66
Christian, Estate of v. Commissioner, T.C.
    Memo. 1989-413. 260
City v. (see name of defendant)
City and County of (see name of city and
    county)
Clark; Commissioner v. 265; 329
Coffey v. Commissioner 114
Coltec Indus. v. United States . . . 425n12
Commission v. (see name of opposing party)
Commissioner v. (see name of opposing party)
Commissioner of Internal Revenue (see name
    of defendant)
Commonwealth v. (see name of defendant)
Commonwealth ex rel. (see name of relator)
Conservatorship of (see name of party)
Consider Pinellas Ice and Cold Storage Co. v.
    Commissioner 253
Corp. and W Corp. v. Corp. 157
Cortland Specialty Co. v. Commissioner . . .
    251; 253
County v. (see name of defendant)
County of (see name of county)
Court Holding Co.; Commissioner v. . . . .
    146; 188; 326n12
Craven v. United States 151
Cumberland Pub. Serv. Co.; United States v.
    87
Cumberland Public Service Co.; United
    States v. 188
Custody of (see name of party)

D

Davis; United States v. 136n7; 266
Detroit Edison Co. v. Commissioner . . 66
DHL Corp. v. Commissioner 393
Donruss Co.; United States v. 372
Duberstein; Commissioner v. 46

E

Easson v. Commissioner 44n17
Eisner v. Macomber 64n34; 163; 165
Esmark, Inc. v. Commissioner 87

[References are to page numbers and footnotes]

Est. of (see name of party)
Estate of (see name of party)
Ex parte (see name of applicant)
Ex rel. (see name of relator)
Exacto Spring Corp. v. Commissioner . . . 13

F

Farley Realty Corp. v. Commissioner . . 81
Fink; Commissioner v. 64
Fireoved v. United States 182
First, in Groman v. Commissioner . . 277
First Nat'l Bank of Altoona; Commissioner v.
. . . . 295

G

Garber Indus., Inc. v. Commissioner 352n9
General Utilities & Operating Co. v. Commissioner 86
General Utilities & Operating Co. v. Helvering 86; 139n9; 185n2; 188n7
Generes; United States v. 74
Gitlitz v. Commissioner 228
Golsen v. Commissioner 150
Gordon; Commissioner v. 312
Granite Trust Co. v. United States . . 198; 199
Green v. United States 118
Gregory v. Helvering . . . 16; 17, n21; 250; 313; 315; 417n2
Grove v. Commissioner 146
Guardianship of (see name of party)

H

Hayes v. Commissioner 150
Helvering v. Alabama Asphaltic Limestone Co. 306
Helvering v. Bashford 278
Helvering v. Minnesota Tea Co. 254
Helvering v. Minnesota Tea Co., John A. Nelson Co., and Paulsen 256
Helvering v. Southwest Consol. Corp. . . . 289
Helvering v. Southwest Consolidated Corp.
. . . . 335
Hempt Bros. v. United States 26; 55
Hendler; United States v. 41
Hillsboro National Bank v. Commissioner
. . . . 201
Himmel v. Commissioner 137
Hurst v. Commissioner 129

I

In re (see name of party)
Intermountain Lumber Co. v. Commissioner
. . . . 32
Ivan Allen Co. v. United States 375

J

J.E. Seagram Corp. v. Commissioner 249; 259; 280; 285
John A. Nelson Co. v. Helvering 71; 255; 256
John B. White, Inc. v. Commissioner . . 67

K

Kamborian, Estate of v. Commissioner . . . 31
Kass v. Commissioner 258
Ken Brewer, Peracchi v. Lessinger . . . 45
Kenyatta Corp. v. Commissioner . . . 380
Kimbell-Diamond Milling Co. v. Commissioner 185; 203
King Enterprises, Inc. v. United States . . 33; 274; 280; 285
Kintner; United States v. 6
Kirby Lumber Co.; United States v. 73n7; 339
Kirchman v. Commissioner 16
Koshland v. Helvering 164

L

Lane, Fin Hay Realty Co., and In re v. United States 80
Lane, In re 79; 224n11
Larson v. Commissioner 7
Leavitt, Estate of v. Commissioner . . 224
Lessinger v. Commissioner . . . 4; 44, n18; 65
Libson Shops, Inc. v. Koehler . . 344; 347; 350
License of (see name of party)
Litton Industries, Inc. v. Commissioner . . 115
Lockwood, Estate of v. Commissioner 321
Long Term Capital Holdings v. United States
. . . . 17; 413
Lucas v. Earl 55

M

Marr v. United States 237
Marriage of (see name of party)
Mary Archer W. Morris Trust; Commissioner v. 276n8; 323

[References are to page numbers and footnotes]

Matter of (see name of party)

McDonald's Restaurants of Illinois, Inc. v. Commissioner 260

McLaulin v. Commissioner 322

Mixon, Estate of v. United States 77

Moline Properties Corp. v. Commissioner 11

Morrissey v. Commissioner 7

Myron's Enterprises v. United States 375

N

National Carbide Corp. v. Commissioner . . 11

National Tea Co. v. Commissioner . . 344

Nonetheless, in Bazley v. Commissioner . . 337

O

Old Colony Trust Co. v. Commissioner . . . 224

O'Sullivan Rubber Co. v. Commissioner . . 379

Otto Candies, LLC v. United States . . 374

P

Paulsen v. Commissioner 255

Penrod v. Commissioner 260

People v. (see name of defendant)

People ex (see name of defendant)

People ex rel. (see name of defendant)

Peracchi v. Commissioner 44n17; 45

Petition of (see name of party)

Phellis; United States v. 237

Philadelphia Park Amusement Co. v. United States 23

Pinellas Ice and Cold Storage Co. v. Commissioner 254

Q

R

Rafferty v. Commissioner 320

Read v. Commissioner 151

Refining Corp. v. Commissioner . . 306n24

Rice's Toyota World v. Commissioner . . 16

Richmond, Fredericksburg & Potomac R.R. Co. v. Commissioner 81

Robson v. Commissioner, T.C. Memo. 2000-201, the Tax Court 193

S

S. Tulsa Pathology Lab., Inc. v. Commissioner 317

Saba Partnership v. Commissioner . . 415; 422n7

Sammons v. United States 118

Schneider, Estate of v. Commissioner . . . 145

Selfe v. United States 223

Smith v. Commissioner 44; 149

Smothers v. United States 302

State v. (see name of defendant)

State ex (see name of state)

State ex rel. (see name of state)

State of (see name of state)

Sullivan v. United States 149

T

Telephone Answering Serv. Co. v. Commissioner 203

Trust Estate of (see name of party)

TSN Liquidating Corp., Inc. v. United States 115

U

United Parcel Service of America Inc. v. Commissioner 414

United States v. (see name of defendant)

V

Vogel Fertilizer; United States v. 388

W

Waterman Steamship Corp. v. Commissioner 112

Winn-Dixie Stores, Inc. v. Commissioner . . 16

Wolf Envelope Co. v. Commissioner . . 337

X

Y

Yoc Heating v. Commissioner 258

Yoc Heating Corp. v. Commissioner . . 257

Z

Zenz v. Quinlivan 147

Zenz v. Quinlivan and Revenue Ruling 75-447, 1975- 148

TABLE OF STATUTES

[References are to page numbers and footnotes]

Internal Revenue Code

Section

	Page
1(h)(1)	2; 15
1(h)(1)(B)	3; 399
1(h)(1)(C)	3; 231
1(h)(3)(B)	2n5; 3; 13; 89; 102; 316; 371; 372; 378; 399
1(h)(4)	2
1(h)(4)(i)	231
1(h)(9)	231
1(h)(10)	231
1(h)(11)	2n5; 3; 13; 89; 102; 316; 371; 372; 378; 399
1(h)(11)(B)(i)	103; 399
1(h)(11)(B)(ii)	399
1(h)(11)(B)(iii)(I)	103
1(h)(11)(B)(iii)(II)	103; 399
1(h)(11)(D)	400
1(h)(11)(D)(i)	103
1(h)(11)(D)(ii)	103n10
1(ii)	103
1.1361-1(l)(4)	215
11(b)	1
11(b)(1)	15n19
53	383, n12
55(a)	382; 383
55(b)(1)(B)	383, n11; 384
55(b)(1)(B)(i)	383
55(b)(2)	384
55(b)(2)(B)	384
55(d)(2)	383
55(d)(3)(A)	384
55(e)(1)(A)	383
55(e)(1)(B)	383
55(e)(1)(C)	383
56(a)	384
56(d)	384
56(g)(1)	384
56(g)(2)	384
56(g)(4)(A)	385n13
57(a)	384
58(a)	384
58(b)	384
61	13
61(a)(1)	26
61(a)(3)	2
61(a)(7)	2; 3; 89
61(a)(12)	73n7; 94; 201
62(a)	382n9
63(a)	382n9
83	26
108	73n7
108(a)(1)	340
108(a)(1)(B)	228
108(a)(3)	228
108(b)	94; 228
108(d)(7)(A)	228
108(e)(8)	339; 340
118(a)	65
118(b)	65
118(c)(3)(A)	65
163(a)	13
163(e)	73
163(f)	73
163(j)–(m)	73
163(m)	431
166(a)	73
166(d)(1)	73
172(b)(2)	347
172(d)(2)	73
199	1
199(a)	2
199(b)	2
199(c)(4)(i)	1n3
199(c)(4)(ii)	1n3
199(c)(4)(iii)	1n3
199(c)(5)(A)	1n3
199(c)(5)(B)	1n3
243	3; 13n18; 113n17; 399n5; 400
243(a)	318
243(a)(2)	104n12
243(c)	318
246A	110
246A(a)	106
246A(c)(2)	106
246A(e)	106
246(c)	110
246(c)(3)(B)	103n9; 107
263(a)	64
267(a)(1)	54
267(b)(2)	54; 189
267(b)(3)	189
267(f)	190
267(f)(1)	189n8
269	347
269(a)	368
269(a)(2)	368, n21
269(b)	368
269(c)	368
301	153
301(b)	90
301(b)(2)	90

[References are to page numbers and footnotes]

301(c) 175
301(c)(1) 41; 89; 90; 180
301(c)(2) 89; 90; 91n4; 401
301(c)(3) 89; 90; 91n4; 401
301(c)(3)(B) 89n3
301(e) 92; 102
301(e)(2)(B) 102
302 153
302(a) 14; 126
302(b) 126; 427
302(b)(1) 136
302(b)(2) 134
302(b)(2)(B) 132
302(b)(2)(C) 132
302(b)(2)(D) 135
302(b)(4) 122n2; 186
302(b)(5) 131; 136
302(c) 126
302(c)(2)(A) 128; 131
302(c)(2)(A)(i) 128
302(c)(2)(A)(ii) 128; 131
302(c)(2)(A)(iii) 128
302(c)(2)(B)(i) 130
302(c)(2)(B)(ii) 130
302(c)(2)(C)(i) 132
302(c)(2)(C)(ii)(II) 132
302(d) 14; 127; 140; 427
302(e)(1) 139
302(e)(2)(A) 139
302(e)(2)(B) 139
302(e)(3) 139
302(e)(4) 139
302(e)(5) 153
303(a) 153
304(a)(1) 155; 159
304(a)(2) 155; 157
304(a)(2)(A) 159
304(a)(2)(B) 159
304(b)(1) 157; 158
304(b)(2) 157
304(b)(3)(A) 161
304(b)(3)(B)(i) 161
304(b)(3)(B)(ii) 161
304(b)(3)(B)(iii) 161
304(c)(1) 155; 160; 303
304(c)(2) 155
304(c)(3) 160
304(c)(3)(B)(ii)(II) 156; 303
305(b) 166
305(b)(1) 172
305(b)(2) 172
305(b)(3) 172
305(b)(4) 172
305(b)(5) 172
305(c) 171

305(d)(1) 165
306(a)(1) 173
306(a)(1)(B) 180
306(a)(1)(D) 173; 180
306(b)(1)(A) 182
306(b)(1)(A)(ii) 182
306(b)(1)(B) 182
306(b)(2) 181
306(b)(4)(A) 182
306(b)(4)(B) 182
306(c)(1)(A) 174
306(c)(1)(B) 244; 339; 342
306(c)(1)(B)(ii) 175; 176
306(c)(1)(C) 178
306(c)(2) 175
306(c)(3) 177
306(c)(3)(A) 177
306(c)(3)(B) 178
306(e) 178
307(a) 165
307(b)(1) 165
311 192
311(a) 212
311(a)(2) 85
311(b) 85; 116
311(b)(1) 86; 87
312(a) 94
312(a)(2) 93
312(a)(3) 94
312(b) 94
312(c) 95
312(d)(1)(B) 165
312(n)(7) 144
316 . . . . 41; 90; 95; 180
316(a) 12n17
316(a)(2) 91; 94; 95
317(a) 26n5; 166
317(b) 121
318(a)(1)(A) 123
318(a)(1)(B) 123
318(a)(2)(A) 123
318(a)(2)(B)(i) 124
318(a)(2)(B)(ii) 124
318(a)(2)(C) 124
318(a)(3)(A) 125
318(a)(3)(B)(i) 125
318(a)(3)(B)(ii) 125
318(a)(3)(C) 125
318(a)(5)(A) 125
318(a)(5)(B) 126
318(a)(5)(C) 126
318(a)(5)(D) 126
318(a)(5)(E) 122; 123; 125; 126; 230
331 201
332 201

[References are to page numbers and footnotes]

332(b)(1) 195; 196
334(a) 195; 200; 201
334(b) 201
336 201
336(a) 187; 212
336(b) 88
336(d)(1)(A) 190
336(d)(1)(B) 190
336(d)(2)(A) 191
336(d)(2)(C) 191
337 . . . . 87; 201
337(a) 201
337(b) 201
337(c) 202
338(a)(1) 206
338(b)(1) 206
338(b)(4) 207
338(b)(5) 208
338(d)(3) 204
338(e) 205
338(f) 205
338(g)(1) 205
338(g)(3) 205
338(h)(1) 204
338(h)(2) 205
338(h)(3) 204
338(h)(4) 205
346(a) 186
351 . . . . 26; 62; 63
351(a) 25; 72
351(b) 72
351(b)(1) 38
351(b)(2) 38
351(e) 25
351(e)(1) 62n33
351(g) 72n5; 75
351(g)(2)(A) 38
354 271
354(a)(1) 264; 337; 339
354(a)(2) 341; 342
354(a)(2)(A) 264
354(a)(2)(C) 337n2
354(b)(1)(A) 302
355(a)(1) 327
355(a)(1)(A) 308
355(a)(1)(B) 317
355(a)(1)(D) 312
355(a)(1)(D)(ii) 311
355(a)(3)(A) 329
355(a)(3)(B) 329
355(a)(3)(C) 329
355(a)(3)(D) 311; 329
355(a)(4) 327
355(b)(1)(A) 323
355(b)(1)(B) 323n10

355(b)(2)(B) 320
355(b)(2)(C) 322
355(b)(2)(D)(i) 322
355(b)(2)(D)(ii) 322
355(c)(1) 330
355(c)(2) 330
355(c)(2)(A) 331
355(c)(2)(B) 331
355(c)(2)(C) 331
355(d)(1) 330; 333
355(e)(1) 333
355(e)(2)(D) 326
356 271
356(a) 277; 328; 341
356(a)(1) 328; 338
356(a)(2) 328; 338
356(b) 265n26; 327
356(c) 264; 327
356(d)(2) 341
356(d)(2)(A) 264
356(d)(2)(B) 264; 342
356(d)(2)(C) 329
356(e) 75
357 271
357(a) 270
357(b) 42; 43; 62; 270
357(b)(1) 17
357(c) 42; 62
357(c)(1) 43
357(c)(1)(B) 270; 304n23; 332n17
357(c)(2)(A) 43
357(c)(2)(B) 306
357(c)(3) 48; 52
357(d)(1) 41n14; 306
357(d)(1)(A) 42
357(d)(1)(B) 42
357(d)(2) 42; 61; 306
358 . . . . 63; 339; 342
358(a) 49; 50; 57; 276; 423
358(a)(1) 267; 298; 304; 338
358(a)(2) 267; 268
358(d) 51
358(d)(1) 424
358(d)(2) 424
358(h)(2)(A) 52
361 271
361(b) 276; 304
361(b)(1) 298
361(b)(3) 333
361(c)(1) 333
361(c)(2) 333
361(c)(2)(A) 333
361(c)(2)(B) 333
361(c)(2)(C) 333
362 63

[References are to page numbers and footnotes]

362(a) 45n19; 56; 67
362(a)(2)(A)(i) 57n29
362(b) 271; 281; 286; 291
362(c)(1) 67
362(c)(2) 67
362(e)(1)(A) 67
362(e)(2) 63
362(e)(2)(A) 57
362(e)(2)(A)(1) 57n28
362(e)(2)(A)(i) 67
362(e)(2)(B) 57
362(e)(2)(C) 58
368(a)(1)(B) 240; 287
368(a)(1)(C) 241; 293
368(a)(1)(D) 270
368(a)(1)(G) 305; 334
368(a)(2) 294
368(a)(2)(A) 247
368(a)(2)(C) 300
368(a)(2)(D) 273
368(a)(2)(D)(i) 279; 280
368(a)(2)(D)(ii) 279; 280
368(a)(2)(E) 273
368(a)(2)(G) 241; 270
368(a)(2)(H) 301; 303
368(a)(2)(H)(i) 332
368(a)(2)(H)(ii) 332
368(a)(3)(A) 305; 334
368(a)(3)(B) 306
368(a)(3)(C) 248
368(a)(3)(E) 306
368(b) 248
368(c) 26; 62; 248; 332
381(a) 195; 271; 347
381(c) 195; 272; 347
381(c)(10) 348
381(c)(11) 348
381(c)(16) 348
381(c)(18) 348
381(c)(19) 348
381(c)(23) 348
382(a) 351; 357
382(b)(1) 351; 357
382(b)(1)(B) 351
382(b)(2) 360
382(c) 351
382(c)(1) 358
382(c)(2) 358
382(d)(1) 351
382(e)(1) 357
382(f) 351; 358
382(g) 351; 355; 356
382(g)(2) 355
382(g)(3)(A) 355
382(g)(3)(B) 355

382(h) 357
382(h)(1)(A) 359
382(h)(1)(A)(ii) 359
382(h)(1)(B) 351
382(h)(1)(C) 360
382(h)(2)(A) 359
382(h)(3)(A) 351n6; 359; 367
382(h)(3)(B) 359; 366
382(h)(7)(A) 359
382(i)(1) 354; 356
382(i)(2) 357
382(i)(3) 357
382(j) 354n10
382(j)(1) 357
382(j)(2) 357
382(k)(1) 354
382(k)(3) 363n18
382(k)(5) 354
382(k)(6) 352
382(k)(6)(C) 354
382(l)(1)(B) 360
382(l)(3) 352
382(l)(3)(A) 353
382(l)(3)(A)(i) 352
382(l)(3)(A)(ii) 353
382(l)(3)(A)(iii) 353
382(l)(3)(A)(iv) 353
382(l)(3)(A)(v) 353
382(l)(3)(B) 353
382(l)(3)(C) 356
382(l)(4) 361
382(l)(4)(B)(ii) 360
382(l)(4)(C) 361
382(l)(4)(D) 361
382(l)(5)(A) 350n4
382(l)(7) 352
383(a) 363
383(b) 363
383(c) 363
383(e) 363
384(a) 366
384(a)(1) 366
384(b)(1) 366
384(b)(2) 366
384(c)(1) 366
384(c)(1)(C) 367
384(c)(2) 366
384(c)(3) 366
384(c)(4) 366
384(c)(5) 366
384(c)(8) 366; 367
384(e)(1) 367
385(a) 75; 76; 81
385(b) 76
385(c)(1) 76

[References are to page numbers and footnotes]

385(c)(2) 76	1014 389
444(c) 211n2	1014(a)(1) 179
453(k)(2)(A) 420	1014(f) 4n10; 179
482 390	1031(d) 190
531 . . . . 5; 372	1032 . . . . . 23; 25; 62; 63; 271; 299; 305
532(a) 372	1032(a) 280; 286
532(b) 371	1036 337
532(c) 372	1036(b) 337
533(b) 372	1059 . . . . 110; 116
534(a)(1) 373	1059(a)(2) 144
534(a)(2) 373	1059(c)(4) 109n16
534(b) 373	1059(d)(1) 109
535(a) 372; 376	1059(d)(6) 108
535(b)(1) 376	1059(e) 160
535(b)(2) 376	1059(e)(1) 108
535(b)(3) 376	1059(e)(1)(A) 144
535(b)(4) 376	1059(e)(1)(A)(ii) 144
535(c)(1) 377	1059(e)(2) 108
535(c)(2) 377	1059(e)(3) 108
537(a) 373	1059(e)(3)(A)(ii) 108
541 . . . . 234; 378; 380	1059(e)(3)(C)(i) 108
542(a) 378	1201 . . . . 15n19
542(a)(2) 378	1202(a)(1) 2
542(c) 379	1211(a) 15n20; 93
543 380	1211(b) 15n20
543(a)(7) 380	1212(a) 347
543(b) 378	1221(a) 14
543(b)(1) 378	1222 . . . . 14; 15
543(b)(2) 378	1223(1) 53; 63; 270; 338; 339; 342
543(b)(2)(A) 379	1223(2) 61; 63; 271
543(b)(2)(A)(i) 378	1223(4) 165
543(b)(2)(B) 379	1239(a) 54
543(b)(2)(C) 379	1239(b)(1) 40; 54
543(b)(2)(D) 379	1239(c)(1)(A) 40; 54
543(b)(3)(D) 379	1361(a)(1) 3; 211
544 378	1361(a)(2) 3; 211
545(a) 381, n7	1361(b) 9
545(b) 381	1361(b)(1) 213; 217
547(a) 381	1361(b)(1)(A) 9; 213
547(c) 381	1361(b)(1)(B) 9; 214
547(d)(1) 381; 382	1361(b)(1)(C) 9; 214
547(e) 382	1361(b)(1)(D) 9; 71
561 376	1361(c)(1)(A)(i) 9; 213
561(a) 381	1361(c)(1)(A)(ii) 9; 213
563(a) 376	1361(c)(1)(B)(i) 213
565 376	1361(c)(1)(B)(ii) 213n5
565(a) 376	1361(c)(2) 214
565(b)(2) 376	1361(c)(2)(B)(iv) 214
565(f)(1) 376	1361(c)(4) 9; 71; 215
641(c)(2)(A) 215	1361(c)(5) 9
704(b) 212	1361(c)(5)(B) 76; 216
704(d) 212	1361(c)(6) 215
722 212	1361(d)(1)(A) 214
1001 . . . . 62; 264	1361(d)(3) 214
1001(a) 14	1361(e) 214

[References are to page numbers and footnotes]

1361(e)(1)(A)(i) 215	1374(d)(4) 233n17
1361(e)(1)(A)(ii) 215	1375 . . . . 378n5; 382
1362(a)(1) 213; 217	1375(a) 234
1362(a)(2) 217	1375(b)(1)(A) 235
1362(b)(1) 217	1375(b)(1)(B) 235
1362(b)(2) 217	1375(b)(2) 235
1362(b)(5) 217	1375(b)(4) 235
1362(d) 218; 220	1375(c) 234
1362(d)(1) 218	1375(d) 235
1362(d)(1)(B) 9	1377(a)(2) 222
1362(d)(1)(C)(i) 218	1378(b) 211
1362(d)(1)(C)(ii) 218	1501–1504 371
1362(d)(1)(D) 218	1504(a)(2) 195
1362(d)(2) 9; 219	1551(a) 385n15
1362(d)(3)(A)(i) 219; 378n5; 382	1561(a) 385
1362(d)(3)(A)(ii) 219	1563(a)(1) 386
1362(d)(3)(C) 235	1563(a)(2) 189n9; 386; 388
1362(d)(3)(C)(i) 219	1563(a)(3) 190n10
1362(d)(3)(C)(ii) 219	1563(c)(1)(A) 386
1362(d)(3)(C)(iii) 220	1563(c)(1)(B) 386
1362(f) 219	1563(c)(1)(C) 386
1362(f)(1) 220	1563(c)(2)(A) 386
1362(iii) 219; 378n5; 382	1563(c)(2)(B) 386
1363(a) 211; 371; 378n5; 382	1563(d)(2) 386
1363(b) 104; 221	1563(e) 386
1363(b)(1)–(4) 221	1563(f)(3) 386
1363(e)(3) 227	1563(f)(5) 387
1366(a)(1) 221	6111(a) 430
1366(a)(1)(A) 228	6111(b)(1)(A) 430
1366(b) 221	6111(b)(1)(B) 430
1366(d)(1) 212; 222	6112(a)(1) 431
1366(d)(2) 223	6112(b)(1)(A) 431
1366(f)(2) 234	6662A(a) 431
1366(f)(3) 234	6662A(e)(1)(B) 431n20
1367 . . . . 9; 10	6662(a) 394
1367(a)(1) 228	6662(b)(3) 394
1367(a)(2)(A) 229	6662(d)(2)(C) 431
1367(a)(2)(B)–(E) 229	6662(e)(1)(B) 394
1367(b)(2)(A) 225	6662(e)(2) 394
1367(b)(3) 221	6662(e)(3)(A) 394
1368(b)(1) 225	6662(e)(3)(D) 394
1368(b)(2) 225	6662(h) 394
1368(c) 225; 226	6664(d)(2)(A) 431
1368(c)(1) 225; 227	6707A(b)(1) 431
1368(c)(2) 226; 227	6707(b)(1) 430
1368(c)(3) 226; 227	6707(b)(2) 431
1368(e)(1)(A) 226	6708(a) 431
1368(e)(1)(B) 226	6901 194
1372 230	7701(a)(2) 6
1374(a) 233	7701(a)(3) 6
1374(b) 233	7701(a)(14) 1n1
1374(c)(2) 233; 234n18	7701(a)(42) 49n23
1374(d)(1) 233	7701(a)(43) 49n23
1374(d)(2) 233	7701(a)(44) 49n23
1374(d)(3) 233n16	7704 . . . . 4n9

[References are to page numbers and footnotes]

7872(b)(1) 117n20
7872(c)(1)(C) 117n20
7872(f)(1) 117n20

Private Letter Ruling
Priv. Ltr. Rul.

Page
9102028 201
9733002 220
9828018 348

Proposed Treasury Regulations
Prop. Treas. Reg.

Page
1.302-5 428
1.302-5(a) 142
1.302-5(b)(3) 142
1.302-5(b)(3)–(4) 142
1.302-5(b)(4) 142
1.302-5(c) 142
1.302-5(c)(1) 142
1.302-5(f) 143
1.302-5(g) 143
1.304-2(a)(3) 160n19
1.304-2(c) 160n19
1.351-1(a)(1)(iii) 25n4
1.351-1(a)(1)(iv) 25n4
1.358-2(a)(2)(i) 269
1.358-2(a)(2)(iii) 269
1.358-2(c) 269
1.368-2(k) 300n17
1.368-2(m) 343
1.368-2(m)(4) 343n5

Revenue Procedures
Rev. Proc.

Page
77-37 . . . . 256n14; 279; 294; 302
84-42 . . . . 256n14
1977-2 C.B. 568 . . . 256n14; 279; 294; 302
1984-1 C.B. 521 . . . . 256n14
2002-43 . . . . 426; 429
2002-67 426
2002-97 429
2006-2 394
2006-9 394

Revenue Rulings
Rev. Rul.

Page
X 295

51 343
55-440 289
56-184 288
57-276 343
57-518 295
59-98 339
59-228 194
59-259 . . . . 27; 249
60-331 37
61-156 203
64–73 300
66-142 44
66-224 . . . . 256; 326
66-365 288
67-274 . . . . 248; 288
68-23 329
68-55 . . . . 39; 59; 329
68-285 289
68-629 45
69-608 149
69-630 390
70-106 197
70-108 289
72-327 271
72-530 324
73-54 289
73-257 . . . . 281; 301
74-164 96
74-296 139
74-515 262
75-33 289
75-161 247
75-247 182
75-321 313
75-447 148
75-469 313
75-502 . . . . 137; 138
75-512 138
75-521 . . . . 197; 198
75-561 345
76-188 248
76-364 138
76-385 138
77-11 55
77-226 148
77-293 130
77-377 315
77-455 183
78-375 . . . . 166; 167
78-401 137
79-67 130
79-274 248
79-289 248
80-198 . . . . 48; 55; 424
80-239 . . . . 41; 119

[References are to page numbers and footnotes]

80-284 248
80-285 248
81-91 175
81-289 138
82-191 176
83-119 . . . . 171, n4
84-71 . . . . 55; 248; 272
85-14 . . . . 135; 136
85-164 . . . . 53; 270
87-132 153
88-48 . . . . 295; 296
88-76 7
89-64 143
90-95 . . . . 205; 285n15
93-16 66
93-38 . . . . 7; 8
93-62 328
94-43 214
95-74 . . . . 48; 52; 424
96-29 343
98-27 326
99-58 262
107 248
111 315
116 249
436 275
1955-2 C.B. 226 289
1956-1 C.B. 190 288
1957-1 C.B. 126 343
1957-2 C.B. 253 295
1959-1 C.B. 76 339
1959-2 C.B. 59 194
1959-2 C.B. 115 . . . . 27; 249
1960-2 C.B. 189 37
1961-2 C.B. 62 203
1964-1 C.B. 142 300
1966-1 C.B. 66 44
1966-2 C.B. 114 . . . . 256; 326
1966-2 C.B. 116 288
1967-2 C.B. 141 . . . . 248; 288
1968-1 329
1968-1 C.B. 140 . . . . 39; 59; 329
1968-1 C.B. 247 289
1968-2 C.B. 154 45
1969-2 C.B. 43 149
1969-2 C.B. 112 390
1970-1 C.B. 70 197
1970-1 C.B. 78 289
1972-2 C.B. 148 324
1972-2 C.B. 197 271
1973-1 C.B. 187 289
1973-1 C.B. 189 . . . . 281; 301
1974-1 C.B. 80 139
1974-2 C.B. 118 262
1975-1 C.B. 104 182
1975-1 C.B. 114 247
1975-1 C.B. 115 289
1975-2 C.B. 111 137
1975-2 C.B. 112 138
1975-2 C.B. 113 148
1975-2 C.B. 120 197
1975-2 C.B. 123 313
1975-2 C.B. 126 313
1975-2 C.B. 129 345
1976-1 C.B. 99 248
1976-2 C.B. 91 138
1976-2 C.B. 92 138
1977-1 C.B. 93 55
1977-2 C.B. 90 148
1977-2 C.B. 91 130
1977-2 C.B. 93 183
1977-2 C.B. 111 315
1978-2 C.B. 127 137
1978-2 C.B. 130 . . . . 166; 167
1979-1 C.B. 128 130
1979-2 C.B. 131 248
1979-2 C.B. 145 248
1980-2 C.B. 103 . . . . 41; 119
1980-2 C.B. 113 . . . . 48; 55; 424
1981-1 C.B. 123 175
1981-2 C.B. 82 138
1982-2 C.B. 78 176
1983-2 C.B. 57 171
1984-1 C.B. 106 . . . . 55; 248; 272
1985-1 C.B. 93 135
1985-2 C.B. 117 . . . . 53; 270
1987-2 C.B. 82 153
1988-1 296
1988-1 C.B. 117 295
1988-2 C.B. 360 7
1989-1 C.B. 91 143
1990-2 C.B. 67 . . . . 205; 285n15
1993-1 C.B. 26 66
1993-2 C.B. 118 328
1993 C.B. 38 7
1994-2 C.B. 198 214
1995-2 C.B. 36 . . . . 48; 52; 424
1996-1 C.B. 50 343
1998-1 C.B. 1159 326
1999-2 C.B. 701 262
2000-1 C.B. 436 . . . . 240; 275
2000-5 . . . . 240; 275
2001-23 285
2001-26 . . . . 285, n15
2001-42 205
2001-46 205
2002-2 C.B. 288 322
2002-2 C.B. 986 300
2002-49 322
2002-85 300

[References are to page numbers and footnotes]

2003-7 . . . . 322; 343
2003-17 322
2003-18 322
2003-19 343
2003-38 322
2003-48 343
2004-32 205
2004-83 205
2005-45 358
2005-71 358

Technical Advice Memorandum

Technical Advice Memorandum

T.A.M.

Page

9748003 160

Treasury Regulations

Treasury Regulations

Treas. Reg.

Page

1.1(h)-1(a) 231, n15
1.1(h)-1(b) 231
1.1(h)-1(b)(2)(ii) 231
1.1(h)-1(f) 232
1.1(h)-1(c) 231
1.118-1 . . . . 64; 66
1.118-2 65
1.162-15(b) 65
1.166-1(c) 79
1.269-3(a) 368
1.269-3(b)(1) 369
1.269-3(b)(2) 369
1.269-3(b)(3) 369
1.269-3(c)(1) 369
1.269-3(c)(2) 369
1.269-7 369
1.301-1(j) 117
1.301-1(j)(1) 118
1.301-1(j)(2) 118
1.301-1(k) 117
1.301-1(l) 341; 342
1.301-1(m) 201
1.302-2(a) 137
1.302-2(c) 141; 148; 427
1.302-5 . . . . 428n16
1.305-1(b) 166; 167
1.305-3(b)(2) 168
1.305-3(b)(3) 168
1.305-3(b)(4) 168
1.305-3(c) 167
1.305-3(e) 170, n3

1.305-5 167
1.305-6(a)(2) 170
1.305-7 171
1.305-7(c) 338
1.305-7(c)(1) 338
1.306-1(b)(2) 180
1.306-2(b)(3) 182
1.306-3(d) 175; 339
1.306-3(e) 178
1.307-1(a) 165
1.312-1(d) 166
1.312-3 95
1.312-10(a) 333
1.312-10(b) 331
1.316-2(a) 95
1.316-2(b) 96
1.316-2(b), (c) 96
1.331-1(e) 194
1.332-2(b) 196n16; 197; 201
1.338(h)(10)-1(d)(2) 209
1.338(h)(10)-1(d)(4) 209
1.338-3(d)(1), (5) 258
1.338-3(d)(2) 257
1.338-3(d)(5) 258
1.338-5(d)(3) 207
1.338-5(d)(3)(i)(B) 208
1.338-5(d)(3)(ii) 208
1.338-5(e) 207n22
1.338-6 208
1.338-6(b)(2) 208
1.338-8(a)(2) 205
1.351-1(a)(1) 25; 29
1.351-1(a)(1)(ii) 30
1.351-1(a)(3)(i) 36n8
1.351-1(a)(3)(ii) 36n8
1.351-2(d) 41
1.354-1(d) 341
1.354-1(e) 256n13
1.355-1(c), 1.356-3(b) 311
1.355-2(b)(1) 315
1.355-2(b)(2) 313; 314
1.355-2(b)(5) 314; 315
1.355-2(c)(1) 326
1.355-2(c)(2) 326
1.355-2(d)(1) 315; 316
1.355-2(d)(2) 315
1.355-2(d)(2)(iii) 317
1.355-2(d)(2)(iii)(A) 317
1.355-2(d)(2)(iii)(B) 316
1.355-2(d)(2)(iv)(B) 317
1.355-2(d)(2)(iv)(C) 318
1.355-2(d)(2), (3) 315
1.355-2(d)(3) 316
1.355-2(d)(3)(ii) 318
1.355-2(d)(3)(iii) 318

[References are to page numbers and footnotes]

1.355-2(d)(3)(iv) 318
1.355-2(d)(4) 316
1.355-2(d)(5)(i) 319
1.355-2(d)(5)(ii) 319
1.355-2(d)(5)(iii) 319
1.355-2(d)(5)(iv) 319
1.355-2(e)(2) 313
1.355-3(a)(i) 319
1.355-3(a)(ii) 320
1.355-3(b)(2)(ii) 320
1.355-3(b)(2)(iii) 320
1.355-3(b)(2)(iv) 320
1.355-3(b)(3)(ii) 321
1.355-3(c) 321; 322; 323
1.355-7(b)(1) 325
1.355-7(b)(2) 325
1.355-7(b)(3), (4) 325
1.356-6(a)(1) 311; 329
1.356-6(a)(2) 311; 329
1.357-2(a) 306
1.358-1(a)(1) 268
1.358-2 268
1.358-2(a)(1) 268
1.358-2(a)(2) 268
1.358-2(a)(2), (3) 330
1.358-2(a)(4) 330
1.358-2(a)(5) 268n29
1.358-5T(a) 52n25
1.358-6 . . . . 271; 281; 286
1.358-6(b)(2)(ii) 299
1.358-6(b)(iv) 292
1.358-6(c) 286
1.358-6(c)(1) 280; 281; 282; 300
1.358-6(c)(1)(ii) 282
1.358-6(c)(2)(A) 286
1.358-6(c)(2)(B) 286
1.358-6(c)(3) 292
1.358-6(c)(4) 282; 287
1.362-2(a) 67
1.362-2(b) 67
1.362-2(b)(1)–(4) 67
1.368-1(b) . . . 244n6; 245n7; 251; 253; 256;
          257n16; 263n22, n23; 274n4; 291;
                                      337
1.368-1(c) 16; 251
1.368-1(d) 251; 252; 358
1.368-1(d)(1) 252
1.368-1(d)(2) 252
1.368-1(d)(2)(ii) 252
1.368-1(d)(5) 251
1.368-1(e) 261
1.368-1(e)(1)(i) 261
1.368-1(e)(2)(v) 258; 259; 326
1.368-1(e)(7) 262; 289
1.368-2(b)(1) 274

1.368-2(b)(1)(ii) 239n2
1.368-2(b)(1)(ii), (iii) 240; 275
1.368-2(b)(1)(iii) 276
1.368-2(b)(1)(v) 239n2
1.368-2(b)(2) 279; 280; 281, n12
1.368-2(c) 288; 290; 292
1.368-2(d)(1) 293; 300
1.368-2(d)(3) 294
1.368-2(d)(4)(i) 297
1.368-2(d)(4)(ii) 298
1.368-2(e)(1) 336; 339
1.368-2(e)(2) 336
1.368-2(e)(3) 336
1.368-2(e)(4) 336
1.368-2(j)(2) 247
1.368-2(j)(3)(iii) 284, n14
1.368-2(j)(6) 285
1.368-2(k)(2) 300
1.368-3(a) 249
1.382(a)(3)(i) 354
1.382-2T(a)(2)(i)(B) 355
1.382-2T(d)(3)(B)(ii) 357
1.382-2T(f)(13), (j)(1)(ii) 354
1.382-2T(f)(18)(ii) 352
1.382-2T(j)(1)(iii) 354
1.382-2T(j)(1)(vi) 355
1.382-2T(k)(2) 354
1.382-2(a)(1)(A) 351
1.382-2(a)(1)(C) 351
1.382-2(a)(3)(i) 352
1.383-1(b) 363
1.383-1(c)(1) 363
1.383-1(c)(6) 364
1.383-1(c)(6)(ii) 364
1.383-1(d)(2) 364
1.383-1(d)(3)(i) 364
1.383-1(e)(1) 365
1.383-1(e)(2) 365
1.383-1(f) 365
1.482-1 390
1.482-1(a)(1) 390
1.482-2 390
1.482-2(a) 391
1.482-2(b) 391
1.482-4 391
1.535-1(b) 376n3
1.535-2 . . . . 376n3
1.537-1(a) 373
1.537-1(b)(1) 373
1.537-2(a) 373
1.537-2(b) 374
1.537-2(c) 375
1.565-6(a) 376
1.704-1(b)(2) 6; 212
1.1001-1(a) 24n3

[References are to page numbers and footnotes]

1.1001-3 341

1.1032-1(a) 23; 25; 62

1.1032-1(d) 61

1.1032-3 . . . . 271n33

1.1036-1(a) 337

1.1041-1T 149; 150

1.1041-2 151

1.1041-2(a)(1) 151

1.1041-2(a)(2) 151

1.1041-2(c) 152

1.1041-2(d) 151

1.1041-2(e) 152

1.1239-1(c)(3)(ii) 40

1.1361-1(l)(1) 215

1.1361-1(l)(2)(iii)(A) 219

1.1361-1(l)(4)(ii) 215

1.1361-1(l)(4)(B) 216

1.1367-1(e), (g) 225n12

1.1367-1(f) 225

1.1368-2(a)(1) 226

1.1368-2(a)(3)(D)(iii) 226

1.1378-1(a) 211n2

1.1502-34 202

1.1561-2(c) 385n16

1.1563-1(a)(3) 388

1.6011-4(a) 431

1.7701-2(a)(1) 7

301.7701-2(a) 8

301.7701-2(b) 8

301.7701-2(b)(1) 1

301.7701-3 8

INDEX

[References are to pages.]

A

ACCUMULATED EARNINGS TAX (See ANTI-ABUSE MEASURES)

ACQUISITIVE REORGANIZATIONS
Generally . . . 273
"A" reorganizations (See subhead: Statutory mergers ("A" reorganizations))
Bankruptcy reorganizations ("G" reorganizations) . . . 245; 305
Basis rules
    Statutory mergers ("A" reorganizations) . . . 276
    Stock-for-assets acquisitions ("C" reorganizations) . . . 298
    Stock-for-stock acquisitions ("B" reorganizations) . . . 291
    Transfer of assets to controlled corporation (acquisitive "D" reorganizations) . . . 304
    Triangular mergers . . . 286
"B" reorganizations (See subhead: Stock-for-stock acquisitions ("B" reorganizations))
"C" reorganizations (See subhead: Stock-for-assets acquisitions ("C" reorganizations))
"D" reorganizations (See subhead: Transfer of assets to controlled corporation (acquisitive "D" reorganizations))
Drop-downs . . . 300
Forward triangular mergers
    Generally . . . 279
    Formalities . . . 279
    Liabilities, effect on triangular mergers of . . . 281
    Tax consequences . . . 280
"G" reorganizations (Bankruptcy reorganizations) . . . 245; 305
Mergers involving two or three corporations
    Generally . . . 273
    Forward triangular mergers (See subhead: Forward triangular mergers)
    Statutory mergers ("A" reorganizations) (See subhead: Statutory mergers ("A" reorganizations))
    Triangular mergers (See subhead: Triangular mergers)
Reverse triangular mergers . . . 247; 283
Statutory mergers ("A" reorganizations)
    Generally . . . 274
    "Divisive" mergers and mergers with disregarded entities . . . 275
    Tax consequences and basis rules . . . 276

ACQUISITIVE REORGANIZATIONS—Cont.
Stock-for-assets acquisitions ("C" reorganizations)
    Generally . . . 292
    Application of step-transaction doctrine: "Creeping C" reorganizations . . . 296
    "Solely for voting stock" requirement
        Generally . . . 293
        "Boot relaxation rule" . . . 294
        Effect of liabilities . . . 293
    "Substantially all of properties" requirement . . . 294
    Tax consequences and basis rules . . . 298
    Triangular C reorganizations . . . 299
Stock-for-stock acquisitions ("B" reorganizations)
    Generally . . . 287
    Application of step-transaction doctrine: "solely" in creeping B reorganizations . . . 290
    "Control" requirement . . . 290
    "Solely for voting stock" requirement
        Generally . . . 288
        Definition of "voting stock" . . . 289
        "Solely" requirement . . . 288
    Tax consequences and basis rules . . . 291
    Triangular B reorganizations . . . 292
Transfer of assets to controlled corporation (acquisitive "D" reorganizations)
    Generally . . . 301
    "Control" requirement . . . 303
    Distribution requirement . . . 303
    Overlap with "C" reorganizations . . . 304
    "Substantially all of assets" requirement . . . 302
    Tax consequences and basis rules . . . 304
Triangular mergers
    Generally . . . 277
    Background . . . 277
    Forward triangular mergers (See subhead: Forward triangular mergers)
    Reverse triangular mergers . . . 247; 283
    Tax consequences and basis rules . . . 286

[References are to pages.]

ALTERNATIVE MINIMUM TAX
Generally . . . 382
Mechanics . . . 383

ANTI-ABUSE MEASURES
Generally . . . 371
Accumulated earnings tax
    Generally . . . 371
    Mechanics . . . 376
    Reasonable needs of business . . 373
    Tax-avoidance purpose . . . 372
Alternative minimum tax
    Generally . . . 382
    Mechanics . . . 383
Carryover of tax attributes, limitations on
  (See CARRYOVER OF TAX ATTRIBUTES)
"Controlled group" restrictions
    Generally . . . 385
    Brother-sister controlled groups . . . .
    386
    Combined groups . . . 388
    Definition of "controlled group" . . . .
    386
    Parent-subsidiary controlled groups
    . . . 386
Income splitting
    Generally . . . 388
    Income splitting between corporation
    and shareholder . . . 389
    Income splitting between corporations
        Generally . . . 389
        Reallocation of income and deduc-
        tions under section 482 (See sub-
        head: Reallocation of income and
        deductions under section 482)
Personal holding company tax
    Generally . . . 377
    Avoiding personal holding company tax
    . . . 382
    Definition of "personal holding company"
    . . . 378
    Mechanics of . . . 380
    Types of personal holding company in-
    come . . . 379
Reallocation of income and deductions under
  section 482
    Generally . . . 390
    Advance pricing agreements . . . 394
    Application of substantial valuation mis-
    statement penalty . . . 394
    Selected case law on arm's-length stan-
    dards . . . 391

B

BANKRUPTCY
"G" reorganizations (Bankruptcy reorganizations) . . . 245; 305

BUSINESS PURPOSE DOCTRINE
Generally . . . 16
Corporate divisions, Section 355 and . . . .
  313; 318
Reorganizations . . . 250; 337
Transfer of property to controlled corporation,
  nonrecognition treatment and basis rules
  upon . . . 37

C

**CAPITAL STRUCTURE OF CORPORA-
TION**
Generally . . . 82
Characterization: distinguishing debt from
  equity
    Generally . . . 75
    Case-law factors . . . 76
    Section 385 . . . 75
    Treatment of investment as in part debt
    and in part equity . . . 81
Debt and equity, tax consequences of
    Generally . . . 69; 72
    Characterization of (See subhead: Char-
    acterization: distinguishing debt from
    equity)
    Current distributions . . . 72
    Investment . . . 72
    Return of investment . . . 73
    Worthlessness . . . 73
Debt and equity, types of . . . 71

CARRYOVER OF TAX ATTRIBUTES
Generally . . . 347
Change-of-ownership limitations on net oper-
  ating and other losses: section 382
    Generally . . . 350
    Definitions
        "Five-percent shareholder" . . . .
        353
        "Ownership change" . . . 355
        "Stock" . . . 352
        "Testing period" . . . 356
    Losses subject to section 382 . . . 351
    Mechanics of section 382 limitation
        Anti-stuffing rule . . . 360
        Built-in gains, effect on section 382
        limitation of . . . 359
        Continuity of business enterprise
        . . . 358
        Excess nonbusiness assets, special
        rule for valuing corporations with
        . . . 360
        General rules . . . 357
        Long-term tax-exempt rate . . . .
        358

[References are to pages.]

CARRYOVER OF TAX ATTRIBUTES—
Cont.

Change-of-ownership limitations on net oper-
ating and other losses: section 382—Cont.
   Mechanics of section 382 limitation—
   Cont.
      Redemptions and other corporate
      contractions, effect of . . . 361
      Reductions and increases in section
      382 limitation . . . 358
      Unused section 382 limitation, ef-
      fect of . . . 360
      Valuation issues . . . 360
Limitations in section 381 . . . 348
Limitations on carryovers
   Generally . . . 349
   Acquisitions with tax-avoidance motive:
   section 269
      Generally . . . 368
      Mechanics . . . 368
   Change-of-ownership limitations on net
   operating and other losses: section 382
   (See subhead: Change-of-ownership
   limitations on net operating and other
   losses: section 382)
   Change-of-ownership limitations on
   other tax attributes: section 383
      Generally . . . 363
      Mechanics of section 383 credit lim-
      itation . . . 363
   History . . . 350
   Limitation on use of pre-acquisition
   losses to offset built-in gains: section
   384
      Generally . . . 365
      Mechanics . . . 366
Reorganizations . . . 271
Tax attributes subject to carryover . . 347
Transactions eligible for carryover . . 347

CONTROLLED CORPORATIONS
Transfer of property to (See TRANSFER OF
   PROPERTY TO CONTROLLED CORPO-
   RATION)

CORPORATE DIVISIONS
Generally . . . 307
Divisive "D" reorganizations
   Generally . . . 332
   Qualification under section 355 . . . .
   332
   Tax consequences, basis, and earnings
   and profits rules . . . 333
Divisive "G" reorganizations . . . 334
Section 355
   Generally . . . 307
   Active trade or business requirements
      Generally . . . 319

CORPORATE DIVISIONS—Cont.
Section 355—Cont.
   Active trade or business requirements—
   Cont.
      Acquired business . . . 322
      Five-year history . . . 320
      "Immediately after" distribution
      . . . 323
      Same or different business . . . .
      321
   "Business purpose" requirement . . . .
   313
   Continuity of proprietary interest . . .
   326
   "Control" and "distribution" require-
   ments . . . 311
   "Device" prohibition
      Generally . . . 315
      Corporate business purpose . . .
      318
      "Device" factors . . . 316
      Distribution to domestic corpora-
      tions . . . 318
      Nonbusiness or "secondary busi-
      ness" assets, presence of . . . .
      317
      "Non-device" factors . . . 318
      "Non-device" transactions . . 318
      Pro rata distribution . . . 316
      Publicly traded, widely held distrib-
      uting corporation . . . 318
      Subsequent sale or exchange of
      stock distributed . . . 316
   Spin-offs . . . 308
   Split-offs . . . 309
   Split-ups . . . 310
   "Stock or securities" . . . 311
   Tax consequences and basis rules (See
   subhead: Tax consequences and basis
   rules)
   Types of section 355 transactions . . .
   308
Tax consequences and basis rules
   Generally . . . 327
   Allocation of earnings and profits . . .
   331
   Distributing corporation . . . 330
   Divisive "D" reorganizations . . . 333
   Shareholders
      General tax consequences . . 327
      Shareholder basis . . . 330

CORPORATE LIQUIDATIONS
Generally . . . 185
Liquidation-reincorporation transactions
   . . . 202

[References are to pages.]

CORPORATE LIQUIDATIONS—Cont.
Non-taxable liquidation of controlled subsidiary
  Generally . . . 195
  Basis rules . . . 200
  Controlling parent corporation
    Generally . . . 196
    Avoiding application of section 332 . . . 198
  Earnings and profits . . . 200
  Effects of indebtedness . . . 201
  Minority shareholders . . . 200
  Mirror transactions . . . 202
  Subsidiary corporation . . . 195
Partial liquidations . . . 186
"Tainted stock" (Section 306 stock) dividends . . . 181
Taxable acquisitions (See TAXABLE ACQUISITIONS)
Taxable liquidations
  Generally . . . 186
  Basis rules . . . 194
  Corporate-level tax consequences
    Built-in losses, distributions of property with . . . 191
    Distributions of loss property . . 189; 191
    General rule . . . 187
    Historical importance of substance-over-form doctrine in liquidations . . . 188
    Related persons, distributions to . . . 189
  Earnings and profits . . . 195
  Shareholders . . . 193
Tax consequences of complete liquidations, generally . . . 186

CORPORATE TAX SHELTERS
Generally . . . 413
Disclosure requirements and certain penalties applicable to taxpayers participating in reportable transactions . . . 431
Disclosure requirements and enforcement penalties applicable to material advisors . . . 430
Opinion practice under circular 230 431
Paradigmatic corporate tax shelter: *ACM Partnership v. Commissioner* . . . 417
Subchapter C shelters
  Generally . . . 422
  Basis-shifting shelters . . . 426
  Contingent liability shelters . . . 423
Weapons in war on tax shelters . . . 429

D

DIVIDENDS
Non-liquidating distributions of property to shareholders (See NON-LIQUIDATING DISTRIBUTIONS OF PROPERTY TO SHAREHOLDERS (DIVIDENDS))
Stock dividends (See STOCK DIVIDENDS)

DOUBLE TAXATION
Generally . . . 1; 20
Avoiding double taxation
  Generally . . . 5
  Avoiding corporate form . . . 5
  Avoiding Subchapter C
    Corporation as agent . . . 11
    Subchapter S . . . 8
  Disguised dividends
    Generally . . . 12
    Debt versus equity . . . 13
    Salary, dividends disguised as . . . 13
  Integration of corporate and shareholder-level taxes . . . 14
  Limited liability companies (LLC) (See LIMITED LIABILITY COMPANIES (LLC))
  Partnerships
    Formation of . . . 5
    Overview of partnership tax regime . . . 6
Limited liability companies (LLC) (See LIMITED LIABILITY COMPANIES (LLC))
Partnerships
  Formation of . . . 5
  Overview of partnership tax regime . . . 6

E

ECONOMIC SUBSTANCE DOCTRINE
Judicial doctrines backstopping corporate tax system . . . 17

I

INCOME SPLITTING (See ANTI-ABUSE MEASURES)

INTEGRATION OF CORPORATE-LEVEL AND SHAREHOLDER-LEVEL TAXES
Generally . . . 14; 397
Additional corporate integration possibilities
  Dividends-paid deduction system . . . 411
  Split rate systems . . . 412

[References are to pages.]

INTEGRATION OF CORPORATE-LEVEL AND SHAREHOLDER-LEVEL TAXES—Cont.
Current system of partial integration . . . 399
Major integration proposals
    Generally . . . 401
    American Law Institute's shareholder credit proposal . . . 409
    Dividend exclusion methods
        Generally . . . 402
        President Bush's 2003 proposal . . . 403
        Treasury's dividend exclusion prototype . . . 402
    Treasury's comprehensive business income tax system . . . 405
    Treasury's imputation credit prototype . . . 407
    Treasury's shareholder allocation prototype . . . 405

L

LIMITED LIABILITY COMPANIES (LLC)
Generally . . . 6
"Check-the-box" rules . . . 7
History of taxation of unincorporated entities . . . 6

LIQUIDATION (See CORPORATE LIQUIDATIONS)

M

MERGERS (See ACQUISITIVE REORGANIZATIONS; REORGANIZATIONS)

N

NON-LIQUIDATING DISTRIBUTIONS OF PROPERTY TO SHAREHOLDERS (DIVIDENDS)
Generally . . . 85
"Bootstrap acquisitions" . . . 110
Constructive dividends . . . 117
Corporate shareholders and the dividends received deduction
    Generally . . . 103
    Dividends received deduction, in general . . . 104
    Exceptions and special rules
        Generally . . . 105
        Debt-financed portfolio stock . . . 105
        Extraordinary dividends . . . 107
        Holding period . . . 106

NON-LIQUIDATING DISTRIBUTIONS OF PROPERTY TO SHAREHOLDERS (DIVIDENDS)—Cont.
Distributing corporation, tax consequences to
    Generally . . . 85
    Appreciated property . . . 86
    Treatment of liabilities . . . 88
Earnings and profits
    Generally . . . 91
    Calculating earnings and profits
        Discharge of indebtedness, effect on earnings and profits of . . . 94
        Distributions, effect on earnings and profits of . . . 94
        General rules . . . 92
    Current versus accumulated earnings and profits . . . 91
    Using earnings and profits to calculate dividends (See subhead: Using earnings and profits to calculate dividends)
Shareholders, tax treatment of
    Amount of distribution . . . 90
    Calculating dividend amount . . . 90
    Corporate shareholders and the dividends received deduction (See subhead: Corporate shareholders and the dividends received deduction)
    Earnings and profits (See subhead: Earnings and profits)
    General rules under section 301 . . . 89
    Tax treatment of individuals' qualified dividends . . . 102
    Using earnings and profits to calculate dividends (See subhead: Using earnings and profits to calculate dividends)
Using earnings and profits to calculate dividends
    Generally . . . 95
    Multiple distributions, multiple shareholders . . . 100
    Multiple distributions, sole shareholder . . . 99
    Single distribution, multiple shareholders . . . 97
    Single distribution, sole shareholder . . . 96
    Special rule for calculating dividend of corporate 20-percent shareholder . . . 102

P

PARTNERSHIPS
Formation of . . . 5
Overview of partnership tax regime . . . 6

[References are to pages.]

PARTNERSHIPS—Cont.

Pass-through regime of Subchapter S, partnership pass-through regime of Subchapter K compared with . . . 212

PASS-THROUGH REGIME OF SUBCHAPTER S

Generally . . . 211

Corporate-level taxes imposed on S Corporations

    Built-in gains . . . 233

    Excess net passive investment income . . . 233

Election of s status . . . 217

Eligibility for S Corporation status

    Generally . . . 213

    Ineligible corporations . . . 217

    "One class of stock" rule . . . 215

    Restriction on number of shareholders . . . 213

    Types of permitted shareholders . . . 214

Partnership pass-through regime of Subchapter K, comparison with . . . 212

Revocation of S status . . . 218

S Corporation shareholders, tax treatment of

    Application of Subchapter C rules to S Corporations . . . 229

    Basis adjustments

      Generally . . . 227

      Decreases in basis . . . 229

      Increases in basis . . . 228

    Calculation of taxable income . . 221

    Pass-through of items

      Election to terminate taxable year . . . 222

      General rules . . . 221

      Limitation on deductions . . 222

    Sale of S Corporation shares . . . 231

    Treatment of distributions

      S corporations with earnings and profits . . . 225

      S corporations with no earnings and profits . . . 225

Termination of S status

    Excess passive investment income, termination based on . . . 219

    Inadvertent terminations . . . 220

    Revocation, termination by . . . 218

    Small business corporation, termination by ceasing to qualify as . . . 219

PERSONAL HOLDING COMPANY TAX

(See ANTI-ABUSE MEASURES)

R

REDEMPTIONS OF STOCK

Generally . . . 121

Combined redemptions and sales . . . 147

Competing analogies . . . 121

Complete termination of interest

    Generally . . . 127

    Family-owned shares (See subhead: Family-owned shares)

Constructive ownership of stock

    Generally . . . 122

    Attribution from entities to investors . . . 123

    Attribution to entities from investors . . . 124

    Family attribution . . . 123

    Operating rules . . . 125

    Options . . . 125

Death taxes, redemptions to pay . . . 152

Distributions, redemptions treated as

    Generally . . . 140

    Basis-shifting redemptions . . . 141

    Seagram/Dupont transaction . . . 143

Divorce, redemptions incident to . . . 149

Earnings and profits, effect on . . . 144

Exchange treatment, redemptions qualifying for

    Complete termination of interest (See subhead: Complete termination of interest)

    Family-owned shares (See subhead: Family-owned shares)

    Partial liquidations . . . 139

    Redemptions "not essentially equivalent to dividend"

      Generally . . . 136

      Majority shareholder's redemption . . . 137

      Minority shareholder's redemption . . . 138

    Substantially disproportionate redemptions

      Generally . . . 132

      Series of redemptions . . . 135

Family-owned shares

    Attribution of, generally . . . 127

    Waiver of attribution of family-owned shares

      Generally . . . 128

      No acquisitions within succeeding ten years . . . 131

      No interest in corporation except as creditor . . . 129

      No related-party transfers within previous ten years . . . 129

[References are to pages.]

REDEMPTIONS OF STOCK—Cont.
Family-owned shares—Cont.
  Waiver of attribution of family-owned
  shares—Cont.
    Pre-redemption receipt of shares
    from related person . . . 130
    Pre-redemption transfer of shares
    to related person . . . 130
  Waiver of family attribution by entities
  . . . 131
Form versus substance
  Charitable gift or redemption . . 146
  Sale or redemption . . . 145
Related corporations, redemptions through
  Generally . . . 153
  Control requirement
    Generally . . . 155
    Constructive stock ownership rules,
    application of . . . 155
  Overlap of section 304 with section 351
  . . . 161
  Section 302, application of
    Generally . . . 158
    Taxing redemptions treated as section 301 distributions . . . 159
    Variations on constructive stock ownership rules . . . 158
  Types of section 304 transactions . . . 156
Section 302, overview of . . . 126

REORGANIZATIONS
Generally . . . 237
Acquiring corporation . . . 271
Acquiring corporation's shareholders 271
Acquisitive reorganizations (See ACQUISITIVE REORGANIZATIONS)
"Business purpose" requirement . . . 250
Carryover of tax attributes, introduction to . . . 271
Changes in form ("F" reorganizations)
  Generally . . . 343
  Carryback of tax attributes . . . 344
  Definition of "reorganization" includes change in form . . . 245
Continuity of business enterprise requirement
  Generally . . . 251
  Acquisition of target's historic business or historic business assets . . . 251
  Continuation of target's historic business or use of target's historic business assets . . . 252
Continuity of proprietary interest requirement
  Generally . . . 253

REORGANIZATIONS—Cont.
Continuity of proprietary interest requirement—Cont.
  Requisite continuity: application of step-transaction doctrine . . . 259
  Requisite proprietary interest
    Generally . . . 254
    Qualitative aspects . . . 254
    Quantitative aspects . . . 256
Definition of "reorganization"
  Generally . . . 239
  Acquisitive and divisive "D" reorganizations . . . 242
  "A" reorganizations: statutory mergers . . . 239
  "B" reorganizations: stock-for-stock swaps . . . 240
  "C" reorganizations: "de facto mergers" . . . 241
  "E" reorganizations: recapitalizations . . . 244
  "F" reorganizations: changes in form . . . 245
  "G" reorganizations: bankruptcy reorganizations . . . 245
  Ordering rules . . . 247
  Section 368(a)(2)(d) reorganizations: forward triangular mergers . . . 246
  Section 368(a)(2)(e) reorganizations: reverse triangular mergers . . . 247
  Triangular B and C reorganizations . . . 245
Historical background . . . 237
Intersection of section 351 and section 368 . . . 272
One corporation, reorganizations involving only
  Generally . . . 335
  Changes in form ("F" reorganizations) (See subhead: Changes in form ("F" reorganizations))
  Recapitalizations ("E" reorganizations) (See subhead: Recapitalizations ("E" reorganizations))
"Plan of reorganization" requirement . . . 249
Rationales for nonrecognition in corporate reorganizations . . . 237
Recapitalizations ("E" reorganizations)
  Generally . . . 335
  Business purpose requirement . . 337
  Defined . . . 244
  Types of recapitalizations
    Generally . . . 337
    Corporate debt securities for investors' debt securities . . . 341

[References are to pages.]

REORGANIZATIONS—Cont.
Recapitalizations ("E" reorganizations)—Cont.
  Types of recapitalizations—Cont.
    Corporate debt securities for investors' stock . . . 340
    Corporate stock for investors' debt securities . . . 339
    Corporate stock for investors' stock . . . 337
Section 368, overview of
  Generally . . . 238
  "Control" . . . 248
  Definition of "reorganization" (See subhead: Definition of "reorganization")
  Party to reorganization . . . 248
Statutory and common law requirements of valid reorganizations . . . 238
Target corporation . . . 270
Target shareholders
  Generally . . . 263
  Basis
    Generally . . . 267
    Securities or multiple classes of stock, basis with respect to . . 268
  Calculating gain recognized . . . 264
  Character of recognized gain . . . 265
  Holding period . . . 269

S

SALE OR EXCHANGE TREATMENT
Relevance to corporate taxation . . . 14

SHAM TRANSACTION DOCTRINE
Judicial doctrines backstopping corporate tax system . . . 16

STEP-TRANSACTION DOCTRINE
Generally . . . 18
Acquisitive reorganizations . . . 290; 296
Reorganizations and continuity of proprietary interest requirement, application of step-transaction doctrine to . . . 259
Three tests for "step transaction"
  Binding commitment test . . . 19
  End result test . . . 20
  Mutual interdependence test . . . 19
Transfer of property to controlled corporation . . . 32

STOCK DIVIDENDS
Generally . . . 163
Disguised dividends and double taxation
  Generally . . . 12
  Debt versus equity . . . 13
  Salary, dividends disguised as . . . 13

STOCK DIVIDENDS—Cont.
Excludible stock dividends
  Basis in new stock and in old stock; holding period . . . 165
  Section 305(a) . . . 165
Non-liquidating distributions of property to shareholders (See NON-LIQUIDATING DISTRIBUTIONS OF PROPERTY TO SHAREHOLDERS (DIVIDENDS))
Redemptions of stock (See REDEMPTIONS OF STOCK)
"Tainted stock" (section 306 stock)
  Generally . . . 173
  Definition
    Certain preferred stock received in section 351 transaction . . 177
    Preferred stock received tax-free in reorganization . . . 175
    Preferred stock received tax-free under section 305(a) . . . 174
    Stock with basis obtained from section 306 stock . . . 178
  Disposition of section 306 stock by gift or bequest . . . 179
  Exceptions to general tax treatment
    Generally . . . 181
    Complete liquidation of corporation . . . 181
    Complete termination of shareholder interest in corporation . . . 182
    Transactions not for tax avoidance . . . 182
  General tax consequences on redemption of section 306 stock . . . 181
  General tax consequences on sale of section 306 stock
    Generally . . . 179
    Computing amount of "taint" . . 179
    Tax treatment of additional sales proceeds . . . 180
  History of "preferred stock bailout" . . . 173
Taxable stock dividends
  Basis and holding period . . . 172
  Deemed distributions of stock . . 170
  Section 305(b): exceptions to section 305(a)
    Generally . . . 166
    Choice of stock or property 166
    Disproportionate distributions . . . 167
    Distributions of common and preferred stock to common stockholders . . . 168

[References are to pages.]

STOCK DIVIDENDS—Cont.
Taxable stock dividends—Cont.
    Section 305(b): exceptions to section 305(a)—Cont.
        Distributions of convertible preferred stock . . . 170
        Distributions to preferred stockholders . . . 169

STOCK REDEMPTIONS (See REDEMPTIONS OF STOCK)

SUBCHAPTER S CORPORATIONS
Double taxation, avoidance of . . . 8
Pass-through regime of (See PASS-THROUGH REGIME OF SUBCHAPTER S)

SUBSTANCE OVER FORM DOCTRINE
Judicial doctrines backstopping corporate tax system . . . 15

T

TAXABLE ACQUISITIONS
Generally . . . 185; 203
Calculation and allocation of target corporation's new asset basis . . . 206
History and background . . . 203
Section 338 elections
    Generally . . . 204
    Consistency provisions . . . 205
    "Qualified stock purchase" . . . 204
Section 338(h)(10) election . . . 208
Tax consequences to target of section 338 election . . . 206

TRANSFER OF PROPERTY TO CONTROLLED CORPORATION
Generally . . . 23
Acquisitive reorganizations (See ACQUISITIVE REORGANIZATIONS)
Basis rules
    Corporation, tax consequences to (See subhead: Corporation, tax consequences to)
    Shareholders, tax consequences to (See subhead: Nonrecognition treatment and basis rules)
Contributions to capital
    Generally . . . 63
    Corporation, tax consequences to
        Generally . . . 65
        Corporation's basis . . . 66
        Transfers by non-shareholders . . . 66
    Non-shareholder contributors, tax consequences to . . . 65
    Shareholder contributors, tax consequences to . . . 64

TRANSFER OF PROPERTY TO CONTROLLED CORPORATION—Cont.
Corporation, tax consequences to
    Basis rules
        Generally . . . 56
        Absence of boot . . . 56
        Corporate basis if section 351 applies . . . 56
        Corporate basis if section 351 does not apply . . . 61
        Corporate basis in contributions to capital . . . 66
        Liabilities, effect on corporate basis of . . . 60
        Presence of boot . . . 59
    Contributions to capital (See subhead: Contributions to capital)
    Holding period . . . 61
    Nonrecognition on issuance of stock . . . 55
Liabilities, treatment of
    Exceptions to section 357(a)
        Generally . . . 42
        Excluded and contingent liabilities . . . 47
        Liabilities in excess of basis: section 357(c) . . . 43
        Shareholder promissory note, effect of . . . 44
        Tax-avoidance motive: section 357(b) . . . 42
    General nonrecognition rule of section 357(a) . . . 41
Nonrecognition treatment and basis rules
    Generally . . . 25
    "Accommodation transferor" problem . . . 29
    Basis rules
        Generally . . . 49
        Effect of liabilities on basis . . . 51
        Transferor basis in absence of boot . . . 49
        Transferor basis in presence of boot . . . 49
    Business purpose . . . 37
    "Control" . . . 27
    Holding period . . . 53
    "Immediately after" requirement . . . 32
    Liabilities, treatment of (See subhead: Liabilities, treatment of)
    "Property" . . . 26
    Receipt of "boot" (See subhead: Shareholder boot)
    Section 351, general nonrecognition treatment under . . . 26

[References are to pages.]

TRANSFER OF PROPERTY TO CON-TROLLED CORPORATION—Cont.

Nonrecognition treatment and basis rules—Cont.

    Step-transaction doctrine, application of . . . 32

    "Transferor group" . . . 29

Shareholder boot

    Character of gain recognized

        Generally . . . 38

        Allocation of boot . . . 39

        Special characterization issues . . . 40

    Dividend treatment . . . 41

TRANSFER OF PROPERTY TO CON-TROLLED CORPORATION—Cont.

Shareholder boot—Cont.

    General recognition rules . . . 37

Shareholders, tax consequences to

    Boot (See subhead: Shareholder boot)

    Capital contributions . . . 64

    Nonrecognition treatment and basis rules (See subhead: Nonrecognition treatment and basis rules)

    Provisions that override section 351 . . . 54

    Taxable incorporations . . . 53